Lecture Notes in Computer Science 6744

Commenced Publication in 1973
Founding and Former Series Editors:
Gerhard Goos, Juris Hartmanis, and Jan van Leeuwen

Sergei O. Kuznetsov Deba P. Mandal
Malay K. Kundu Sankar K. Pal (Eds.)

Pattern Recognition and Machine Intelligence

4th International Conference, PReMI 2011
Moscow, Russia, June 27 – July 1, 2011
Proceedings

Springer

Volume Editors

Sergei O. Kuznetsov
National Research University Higher School of Economics
School for Applied Mathematics and Information Science
11 Pokrovski Boulevard, 109028 Moscow, Russia
E-mail: skuznetsov@hse.ru

Deba P. Mandal
Malay K. Kundu
Sankar K. Pal
Indian Statistical Institute, Machine Intelligence Unit
203, B.T. Road, Kolkata 700108, India
E-mail: {dpmandal, malay, sankar}@isical.ac.in

ISSN 0302-9743   e-ISSN 1611-3349
ISBN 978-3-642-21785-2   e-ISBN 978-3-642-21786-9
DOI 10.1007/978-3-642-21786-9
Springer Heidelberg Dordrecht London New York

Library of Congress Control Number: 2011929642

CR Subject Classification (1998): I.4, F.1, I.2, I.5, J.3, H.3-4, K.4.4, C.1.3

LNCS Sublibrary: SL 6 – Image Processing, Computer Vision, Pattern Recognition, and Graphics

Typesetting: Camera-ready by author, data conversion by Scientific Publishing Services, Chennai, India

Printed on acid-free paper

Springer is part of Springer Science+Business Media (www.springer.com)

Preface

This volume contains the proceedings of the 4th International Conference on Pattern Recognition and Machine Intelligence (PReMI-2011) which was held at the National Research University Higher School of Economics (HSE), Moscow, Russia, during June 27 - July 1, 2011. This was the fourth conference in the series. The first three conferences were held in December at the Indian Statistical Institute, Kolkata, India, in 2005 and 2007 and at the Indian Institute of Technology, New Delhi, India, in 2009.

PReMI has become a premier international conference presenting the state-of-art research findings in the areas of machine intelligence and pattern recognition. The conference is also successful in encouraging academic and industrial interaction, and in promoting collaborative research and developmental activities in pattern recognition, machine intelligence and other allied fields, involving scientists, engineers, professionals, researchers and students from India and abroad. The conference is scheduled to be held every alternate year making it an ideal platform for sharing views, new results and experiences in these fields in a regular manner.

PReMI-2011 attracted 140 submissions from 21 different countries across the world. Each paper was subjected to at least two reviews; the majority had three reviews. The review process was handled by the PC members with the help of additional reviewers. These reviews were analyzed by the PC Co-chairs. Finally, on the basis of reviews, it was decided to accept 65 papers for oral and poster sessions. We are grateful to the PC members and reviewers for providing critical reviews. This volume contains the final version of these 65 papers after incorporating reviewers' suggestions. These papers have been organized under nine thematic sections.

For PReMI-2011, we had a distinguished panel of keynote and plenary speakers. We are grateful to Rakesh Agrawal for agreeing to deliver the keynote talk. We are also grateful to John Oommen, Mikhail Roytberg, Boris Mirkin, Santanu Chaudhury, and Alexei Chervonenkis for delivering the plenary talks. Our Tutorial Co-chairs arranged an excellent set of pre-conference tutorials. We are thankful to all the tutorial speakers.

We would like to take this as an opportunity to thank the host institute, National Research University Higher School of Economics, Moscow, for providing all facilities to organize this conference. We are grateful to the co-organizer Laboratoire Poncelet (UMI 2615 du CNRS, Moscow). We are also grateful to Springer, Heidelberg, for publishing the volume and the National Centre for Soft Computing Research, ISI, Kolkata, for providing the necessary support. The success of the conference is also due to the funding received from different agencies and industrial partners, among them ABBYY, the Russian Foundation for Basic Research, Yandex, and Russian Association for Artificial Intelligence (RAAI). We are thankful to all of them for their active support. We are grateful to the Organizing Committee for their endeavor in making this conference a success. The volume editors would like to especially thank our Organizing Chair Dmitry Ignatov for his enormous contributions toward the organization of the conference and publication of these proceedings. Our special thanks are also due to Dominik Ślęzak for his kind co-operation, co-ordination and help, and for being involved in one form or other with PReMI since its first edition in 2005. And last, but not least, we thank the members of our Advisory Committee who provided the required guidance and sponsors. PReMI-2005, PReMI-2007 and PReMI-2009 were successful conferences. We believe that you will find the proceedings of PReMI-2011 to be a valuable source of reference for your ongoing and future research activities.

April 2011   Sergei O. Kuznetsov
                                                                 Deba P. Mandal
                                                                 Malay K. Kundu
                                                                 Sankar K. Pal

Pushpak Bhattacharyya   Indian Institute of Technology Bombay,
                                 Mumbai, India
Kanad Biswas   Indian Institute of Technology Delhi,
                                 New Delhi, India
Prabir Kumar Biswas   Indian Institute of Technology Kharagpur,
                                 Kharagpur, India
Sambhunath Biswas   Indian Statistical Institute, Kolkata, India
Smarajit Bose   Indian statistical Institute, Kolkata, India
Lorenzo Bruzzone   University of Trento, Italy
Roberto Cesar   University of São Paulo, São Carlos, Brazil
Partha P. Chakrabarti   Indian Institute of Technology Kharagpur,
                                 Kharagpur, India
Mihir Chakraborty   Indian Statistical Institute, Kolkata, India
Bhabatosh Chanda   Indian Statistical Institute, Kolkata, India
Subhasis Chaudhuri   Indian Institute of Technology Bombay,
                                 Mumbai, India
Santanu Chaudhury   Indian Institute of Technology Delhi,
                                 New Delhi, India
Sung-Bae Cho   Yonsei University, Seoul, Korea
Sudeb Das   Indian Statistical Institute, Kolkata, India
Sukhendu Das   Indian Institute of Technology Madras,
                                 Chennai, India
B.S. Dayasagar   Indian Statistical Institute, Bangalore, India
Rajat K. De   Indian Statistical Institute, Kolkata, India
Kalyanmoy Deb   Indian Institute of Technology Kanpur,
                                 Kanpur, India
Lipika Dey   Tata Consultancy Services Ltd., New Delhi,
                                 India
Sumantra Dutta Roy   Indian Institute of Technology Delhi,
                                 New Delhi, India
Utpal Garain   Indian Statistical Institute, Kolkata, India
Ashish Ghosh   Indian Statistical Institute, Kolkata, India
Hiranmay Ghosh   Tata Consultancy Services Ltd., New Delhi,
                                 India
Kuntal Ghosh   Indian Statistical Institute, Kolkata, India
Sujata Ghosh   University of Groningen, Netherlands
Susmita Ghosh   Jadavpur University, Kolkata, India
Phalguni Gupta   Indian Institute of Technology Kanpur,
                                 Kanpur, India
C.V. Jawahar   IIIT, Hyderabad, India
Grigori Kabatianski   Institute for Information Transmission
                                 Problems of Russian Academy of Sciences,
                                 Moscow, Russia
Vladimir F. Khoroshevsky   Computing Centre of Russian Academy of
                                 Sciences, Moscow, Russia

Organization

General Chair	Sankar K. Pal, ISI Kolkata, India
Conference Chair	Sergei O. Kuznetsov, Higher School of Economics, Russia
Program Co-chairs	Malay K. Kundu, ISI, Kolkata, India
	Deba P. Mandal, ISI, Kolkata, India
Organizing Chair	Dmitry I. Ignatov, Higher School of Economics, Russia
Tutorial Co-chairs	Chris Cornelis, Ghent University, Belgium
	Sanghamitra Bandyopadhyay, ISI, Kolkata, India
Publicity Co-chairs	Goutam Chakraborty, Iwate Prefectural University, Japan
	Joydeep Ghosh, University of Texas, USA
Coordination Chair	Simon C. K. Shiu, HK Polytechnical University, Hong Kong

Advisory Committee

Lotfi Zadeh, USA
Michael Brady, UK
Anil Jain, USA
Josef Kittler, UK
Rama Chellappa, USA
Gennady S. Osipov, Russia
Witold Pedrycz, Canada
Andrzej Skowron, Poland

Brian C. Lovell, Australia
Dwijesh Dutta Majumdar, India
Arun Majumder, India
Konstantin V. Rudakov, Russia
Konstantin Anisimovich, Russia
Gabriella Sanniti di Baja, Italy
B. Yegnanarayana, India
B.L. Deekshatulu, India

Program Committee

Tinku Acharya	Intelectual Ventures, Kolkata, India
Aditya Bagchi	Indian Statistical Institute, Kolkata, India
Sanghamitra Bandyopadhyay	Indian Statistical Institute,Kolkata, India
Roberto Baragona	Sapienza University of Rome, Rome, Italy
Andrzej Bargiela	University of Nottingham, Selangor Darul Ehsan, Malaysia
Jayanta Basak	IBM Research, Bangalore, India
Tanmay Basu	Indian Statistical Institute, Kolkata, India
Dinabandhu Bhandari	Indian Statistical Institute, Kolkata, India
Bhargab B. Bhattacharya	Indian Statistical Institute, Kolkata, India

Ravi Kothari	IBM Research, New Delhi, India
Malay K. Kundu	Indian Statistical Institute, Kolkata, India
Sergei O. Kuznetsov	Higher School of Economics, Moscow, Russia
Yan Li	The Hong Kong Polytechnic University, Hong Kong, China
Lucia Maddalena	National Research Council, Naples, Italy
Pradipta Maji	Indian Statistical Institute, Kolkata, India
Deba P. Mandal	Indian Statistical Institute, Kolkata, India
Anton Masalovitch	ABBYY, Moscow, Russia
Francesco Masulli	Universita' di Genova, Genova, Italy
Pabitra Mitra	Indian Institute of Technology Kharagpur, Kharagpur, India
Suman Mitra	DAIICT, Gandhinagar, India
Sushmita Mitra	Indian Statistical Institute, Kolkata, India
Dipti P. Mukherjee	Indian Statistical Institute, Kolkata, India
Jayanta Mukherjee	Indian Institute of Technology Kharagpur, Kharagpur, India
C.A. Murthy	Indian Statistical Institute, Kolkata, India
Narasimha Murty Musti	Indian Institute of Science, Bangalore, India
Sarif Naik	Philips India, Bangalore, India
Tomaharu Nakashima	University of Osaka Prefecture, Osaka, Japan
B.L. Narayana	Yahoo India, Bangalore, India
Ben Niu	The Hong Kong Polytechnic University, Hong Kong, China
Sergei Obiedkov	Higher School of Economics, Moscow, Russia
Nikhil R. Pal	Indian Statistical Institute, Kolkata, India
Pinakpani Pal	Indian Statistical Institute, Kolkata, India
Sankar K. Pal	Indian Statistical Institute, Kolkata, India
Swapan K. Parui	Indian Statistical Institute, Kolkata, India
Gabriella Pasi	Universita' di Milano Bicocca, Milano, Italy
Leif Peterson	The Methodist Hospital Research Institute, Houston, USA
Alfredo Petrosino	University of Naples, Italy
Arun K. Pujari	LNM IIT, Jaipur, India
Ganesh Ramakrishnan	Indian Institute of Technology Bombay, Mumbai, India
Shubhra S. Ray	Indian Statistical Institute, Kolkata, India
Siddheswar Roy	Monash University, Melbourne, Australia
Suman Saha	Indian Statistical Institute, Kolkata, India
P.S. Sastry	Indian Institute of Science, Bangalore, India
Debashis Sen	Indian Statistical Institute, Kolkata, India
Srinivasan Sengamedu	Yahoo! Labs, Bangalore, India
Rudy Setiono	National University of Singapore, Singapore
B. Uma Shankar	Indian Statistical Institute, Kolkata, India
Roberto Tagliaferri	Universita' di Salerno, Italy

Tieniu Tan	Chinese Academy of Sciences, Beijing, China
Yuan Y. Tang	Hong Kong Baptist University, Hongkong, China
Dmitri V. Vinorgadov	All-Russian Institute for Scientific and Technical Information of Russian Academy of Sciences, Moscow, Russia
Yury Vizliter	State Research Institute of Aviation Systems, Moscow, Russia
Konstantin V. Vorontsov	Computing Centre of Russian Academy of Sciences, Moscow, Russia
Guoyin Wang	Chongqing University of Posts and Telecommunications, China
Jason Wang	New Jersey Institute of Technology, USA
Narahari Yadati	Indian Institute of Science, Bangalore, India
Ning Zhong	Maebashi Institute of Technology, Japan

Additional Reviewers

Bhadra, Tapas
Dhara, Bibhas
Gupta, Lalit
Halder, Anindya
Jayaraman, Umarani
Khan, Aquil
Kumar, Rajesh
M., Arunkumar
Makkapati, Vishnu

Marrara, Stefania
Nigam, Aditya
Prakash, Surya
Saha, Sanjoy Kumar
Samanta, Syamal
Sen, Jayanta
Sengupta, Debarka
Vajinepalli, Pallavi

Message from the General Chair

Machine intelligence conveys a core concept for integrating various advanced technologies with the basic task of pattern recognition and learning. Intelligent autonomous systems (IAS) is the physical embodiment of machine intelligence. The basic philosophy of IAS research is to explore and understand the nature of intelligence involved in problems of perception, reasoning, learning, optimization and control in order to develop and implement the theory into engineered realization. Advanced technologies concerning machine intelligence research include fuzzy logic, artificial neural networks, evolutionary computation, rough sets, their different hybridizations, approximate reasoning, probabilistic reasoning and case-based reasoning. These technologies are required for the designing of IAS. While the role of these individual tools is apparent in designing pattern recognition and intelligent systems, making judicious integration of these tools has drawn considerable attention from researchers for more than a decade under the term soft computing, whose aim is to exploit the tolerance for imprecision, uncertainty, approximate reasoning and partial truth to achieve tractability, robustness, low-cost solutions, and close resemblance with human-like decision making.

One may note that there are several conferences being held over the globe on pattern recognition and machine intelligence separately, but hardly any that combines them, although both communities share many of the concepts and tasks under different names. Based on this realization, The first International Conference on Pattern Recognition and Machine Intelligence, called PReMI-05, was initiated by the Machine Intelligence Unit (MIU) of the Indian Statistical Institute (ISI) at its headquarters in Kolkata in December 2005. One of the objectives is to provide a common platform to both communities to share thoughts for the advancement of the subjects. This conference is a biannual event. The next version PReMI-2007 was also held at ISI, Kolkata, in December 2007.

During PReMI-2005 and PReMI-2007, we received several requests to let this conference be held outside ISI, Kolkata, and even abroad to increase its visibility and provide more benefits to researchers elsewhere. Accordingly, PReMI-2009 was held at IIT-Delhi, India, in December 2009. I am extremely happy to mention that Sergei Kuznetsov volunteered to organize the fourth event (PReMI-2011) in the series at the National Research University Higher School of Economics, Moscow, Russia, during June 26–30, 2011 in collaboration with the Machine Intelligence Unit, ISI, Kolkata.

Like the previous edition, PReMI-2011 was planned to be held in conjunction with RSFDGrC-2011, an international event on rough sets, fuzzy sets and granular computing. RSFDGrC deals mainly with the development of theoretical and applied aspects of the concerned topics. On the other hand, PReMI has a wider scope and focuses broadly on the development and application of those topics along with other classic and modern computing paradigms, including pattern recognition, machine learning, mining and related disciplines with various real-life problems as in bioinformatics, Web mining, biometrics, document processing, data security, video information retrieval, social network mining and remote sensing, among others. All these make the joint event an ideal platform to both theoretical and applied researchers as well as practitioners for collaborative research.

I take this opportunity to thank the National Research University, Higher School of Economics, Moscow, for holding the meeting, Dominik Ślęzak for his initiative and co-ordination, and the members of the Organizing, Program and other Committees for their sincere effort in making it a reality. Thanks are also due to all the financial and academic sponsors for their support of this endeavor, and Springer for publishing the PReMI proceedings in their prestigious LNCS series.

Sankar K. Pal

Table of Contents

Image Analysis

Image and Video Information Retrieval

Natural Language Processing and Text and Data Mining

Watermarking, Steganography and Biometrics

Soft Computing and Applications

Clustering and Network Analysis

Bio and Chemo Informatics

Document Image Processing

Enriching Education through Data Mining

Rakesh Agrawal, Sreenivas Gollapudi,
Anitha Kannan, and Krishnaram Kenthapadi

Search Labs, Microsoft Research
Mountain View, CA, USA
{rakesha,sreenig,ankannan,krisken}@microsoft.com

Education is acknowledged to be the primary vehicle for improving the economic well-being of people [1,6]. Textbooks have a direct bearing on the quality of education imparted to the students as they are the primary conduits for delivering content knowledge [9]. They are also indispensable for fostering teacher learning and constitute a key component of the ongoing professional development of the teachers [5,8].

Many textbooks, particularly from emerging countries, lack clear and adequate coverage of important concepts [7]. In this talk, we present our early explorations into developing a data mining based approach for enhancing the quality of textbooks. We discuss techniques for algorithmically augmenting different sections of a book with links to selective content mined from the Web. For finding authoritative articles, we first identify the set of key concept phrases contained in a section. Using these phrases, we find web (Wikipedia) articles that represent the central concepts presented in the section and augment the section with links to them [4]. We also describe a framework for finding images that are most relevant to a section of the textbook, while respecting global relevancy to the entire chapter to which the section belongs. We pose this problem of matching images to sections in a textbook chapter as an optimization problem and present an efficient algorithm for solving it [2].

We also present a diagnostic tool for identifying those sections of a book that are not well-written and hence should be candidates for enrichment. We propose a probabilistic decision model for this purpose, which is based on syntactic complexity of the writing and the newly introduced notion of the dispersion of key concepts mentioned in the section. The model is learned using a tune set which is automatically generated in a novel way. This procedure maps sampled text book sections to the closest versions of Wikipedia articles having similar content and uses the maturity of those versions to assign need-for-enrichment labels. The maturity of a version is computed by considering the revision history of the corresponding Wikipedia article and convolving the changes in size with a smoothing filter [3].

We also provide the results of applying the proposed techniques to a corpus of widely-used, high school textbooks published by the National Council of

S.O. Kuznetsov et al. (Eds.): PReMI 2011, LNCS 6744, pp. 1–2, 2011.

Educational Research and Training (NCERT), India. We consider books from grades IX–XII, covering four broad subject areas, namely, Sciences, Social Sciences, Commerce, and Mathematics. The preliminary results are encouraging and indicate that developing technological approaches to enhancing the quality of textbooks could be a promising direction for research for our field.

References

1. Knowledge for Development: World Development Report 1998/99. World Bank (1998)
2. Agrawal, R., Gollapudi, S., Kannan, A., Kenthapadi, K.: Enriching textbooks with web images (working paper, 2011)
3. Agrawal, R., Gollapudi, S., Kannan, A., Kenthapadi, K.: Identifying enrichment candidates in textbooks. In: WWW (2011)
4. Agrawal, R., Gollapudi, S., Kenthapadi, K., Srivastava, N., Velu, R.: Enriching textbooks through data mining. In: First Annual ACM Symposium on Computing for Development, ACM DEV (2010)
5. Gillies, J., Quijada, J.: Opportunity to learn: A high impact strategy for improving educational outcomes in developing countries. In: USAID Educational Quality Improvement Program (EQUIP2) (2008)
6. Hanushek, E.A., Woessmann, L.: The role of education quality for economic growth. Policy Research Department Working Paper 4122, World Bank (2007)
7. Mohammad, R., Kumari, R.: Effective use of textbooks: A neglected aspect of education in Pakistan. Journal of Education for International Development 3(1) (2007)
8. Oakes, J., Saunders, M.: Education's most basic tools: Access to textbooks and instructional materials in California's public schools. Teachers College Record 106(10) (2004)
9. Stein, M., Stuen, C., Carnine, D., Long, R.M.: Textbook evaluation and adoption. Reading & Writing Quarterly 17(1) (2001)

How to Visualize a Crisp or Fuzzy Topic Set over a Taxonomy

Boris Mirkin[1,2], Susana Nascimento[3], Trevor Fenner[2], and Rui Felizardo[3]

[1] Division of Applied Mathematics and Informatics, National Research University -
Higher School of Economics, Moscow, Russian Federation
[2] Department of Computer Science, Birkbeck University of London
London WC1E 7HX, UK
[3] Department of Computer Science and Centre for Artificial Intelligence (CENTRIA)
Faculdade de Ciências e Tecnologia, Universidade Nova de Lisboa
2829-516 Caparica, Portugal

Abstract. A novel method for visualization of a fuzzy or crisp topic set is developed. The method maps the set's topics to higher ranks of the taxonomy tree of the field. The method involves a penalty function summing penalties for the chosen "head subjects" together with penalties for emerging "gaps" and "offshoots". The method finds a mapping minimizing the penalty function in recursive steps involving two different scenarios, that of 'gaining a head subject' and that of 'not gaining a head subject'. We illustrate the method by applying it to illustrative and real-world data.

1 Background and Motivation

The concept of ontology as a computationally feasible environment for knowledge representation and maintenance has sprung out rather recently. The term refers, first of all, to a set of concepts and relations between them. These pertain to the knowledge of the domain under consideration. At the inception, the relations typically have been meant to be rule-based and fact-based. However, with the concept of "ontology" expanding into real-world applied domains such as in biomedicine, it would be fair to say that the core knowledge in ontology currently is represented by a taxonomic relation that usually can be interpreted as "is part of". Such are the taxonomy of living organisms in biology, ACM Classification of Computing Subjects (ACM-CCS) [1], and more recently a set of taxonomies comprising the SNOMED CT, the 'Systematized Nomenclature of Medicine Clinical Terms' [15]. Most research efforts on computationally handling ontologies may be considered as falling in one of the three areas: (a) developing platforms and languages for ontology representation such as OWL language (e.g. [14]), (b) integrating ontologies (e.g. [17,7,4,8]) and (c) using them for various purposes. Most efforts in (c) are devoted to building rules for ontological reasoning and querying utilizing the inheritance relation supplied by the ontologys

S.O. Kuznetsov et al. (Eds.): PReMI 2011, LNCS 6744, pp. 3–12, 2011.

taxonomy in the presence of different data models (e.g. [5,3,16]). These do not attempt at approximate representations but just utilize additional possibilities supplied by the ontology relations. Another type of ontology usage is in using its taxonomy nodes for interpretation of data mining results such as association rules [10,9] and clusters [6]. Our approach naturally falls within this category. We assume a domain taxonomy has been built. What we want to do is to use the taxonomy for representation and visualization of a query set comprised of a set of topics corresponding to leaves of the taxonomy by related nodes of the taxonomy's higher ranks. The representation should approximate a query topic set in a "natuaral" way, at a cost of some "small" discrepancies between the query set and the taxonomy structure. This sets our work apart from other work on queries to ontologies that rely on purely logical approaches [5,3,16].

Computational treatises such as [11] mainly rely on the definition of visualization presented in the Merriam-Webster dictionary regarding the transitive verb "visualize" as follows: "to make visible, to see or form a mental image of" (see http://www.merriam-webster.com/dictionary/visualize). Here we assume a somewhat more restrictive view that computational visualization necessarily involves the presence of a ground image the structure of which should be well known to the viewer. This can be a Cartesian plane, a geography map, or a genealogy tree, or a scheme of London's Tube . Then visualization of a data set is such a mapping of the data on the ground image that translates important features of the data into visible relations over the ground image. Say, objects can be presented by points on a Cartesian plane so that the more similar are the objects the nearer to each other the corresponding points. Or geographic objects can be highlighted by a bright colour on a map.

Such is the visualization for a company delivering electricity to homes in a town zone. Figure 1, taken from [2], represents the energy network over a map of the corresponding district on which the topography and the network data are integrated in such a way that gives the company "an unprecedented ability to control the flow of energy by following all the maintenance and repair issues on-line in a real time framework.

There are three major ingredients that allow for a successful representation of the energy network:

(1) map of the district (the ground image),
(2) the energy network units (entities to be visualized), and
(3) mapping (2) at (1).

The mapping here needs not be overly complicated because the units are located at the very same ground image in real. Moreover, one could imagine an extension of this mapping to other infrastructure items, such as the water supply, sewage type, and transports, so that the map could be used for more long-term city planning tasks such as development of leisure or residential areas and the like.

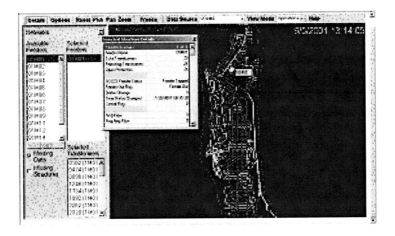

Fig. 1. Energy network of Con Edison Company on Manhattan New-York USA visualized by Advanced Visual Systems [2]

Is a similar mapping possible for a long-term analysis of an organization whose activity is much less tangible? For a research department, the following analogues to the elements of the mapping in Fig. 1 can be considered:

(1') a tree of the ACM-CCS taxonomy of Computer Science, the ground image,
(2') the set of CS research subjects being developed by members of the department, and
(3') representation of the research on the taxonomy tree.

Potentially, this can be used for:

- Positioning of the organization within the ACM-CCS taxonomy;
- Analyzing and planning the structure of research being done in the organization,
- Finding nodes of excellence, nodes of failure and nodes needing improvement for the organization;
- Discovering research elements that poorly match the structure of AMS-CCS taxonomy;
- Planning of research and investment
- Integrating data of different organizations in a region, or on the national level, for the purposes of regional planning and management.

2 Lifting Model and Method

2.1 Statement of the Problem

We assume that there are a number of concepts in an area of research or practice that are structured according to the relation "a is part of b" into a taxonomy, that is a rooted hierarchy T. We denote the set of its leaves by I. Each interior node $t \in T$ corresponds to a concept that generalizes the concepts corresponding to the subset of leaves $I(t)$ descending from t, viz. the leaves of the subtree $T(t)$ rooted at t, which will be referred to as the leaf-cluster of t.

A fuzzy set on I is a mapping u of I to the non-negative real numbers assigning a membership value $u(i) \geq 0$ to each $i \in I$. We refer to the set $S_u \subset I$, where $S_u = \{i : u(i) > 0\}$, as the support of u.

Given a taxonomy T and a fuzzy set u on I, one can think that u is a, possibly noisy, projection of a high rank concept to the leaves I. Under this assumption, there should exist a "head subject" h among the interior nodes of the tree T that more or less comprehensively (up to small errors) covers S_u. Two types of possible errors are gaps and offshoots as illustrated in Figure 2.

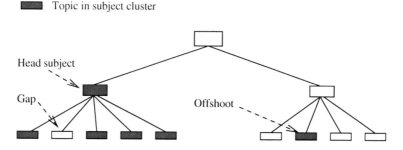

Fig. 2. Three types of features in lifting a topic set within taxonomy

A gap is a maximal node g in the subtree $T(h)$ rooted at h such that $I(g)$ is disjoint from S_u. The maximality of g means that $I(parent(g))$, the leaf-cluster of g's parent, does overlap S_u. A gap under the head subject h can be interpreted as a loss of the concept h by the topic set u. In contrast, establishing a node h as a head concept can be technically referred to as a gain.

An offshoot is a leaf $i \in S_u$ which is not covered by h, i.e., $i \notin I(h)$,

Since no taxonomy perfectly reflects all of the real-world phenomena, some topic sets u may refer to general concepts that are not captured in T. In this case, two or more, rather than just one, head subjects are needed to cover them. This motivates the following definition.

The pair (T, u) will be referred to as an interpretation query. Consider a set H of nodes of T that covers the support S_u; that is, each $i \in S_u$ either belongs to H or is a descendant of a node in H, viz. $S_u \subseteq \cup_{h \in H} I(h)$. This set H is a possible result of the query (T, u). Nodes in H will be referred to as head subjects if they are interior nodes of T or offshoots if they are leaves. A node $g \in T$ is a gap for H if it is a gap for some $h \in H$. Of all the possible results H, those bearing the minimum penalty are of interest only. A minimum penalty result sometimes is referred to as a parsimonious one.

Any penalty value $p(H)$ associated with a set of head subjects H should penalize the head subjects, offshoots and gaps commensurate with the weighting of nodes in H determined from the membership values in the topic set u. We assign the head penalty to be *head*, offshoot penalty, *off*, and the gap penalty, *gap*.

To take into account the u membership values, we need to aggregate them to nodes of higher rank in T. In order to define appropriate membership values for interior nodes of tree T, we assume one of the following normalization conditions:

(P) Probabilistic condition

$$\sum_{i \in I} u(i) = 1$$

(Q) Quadratic condition

$$\sum_{i \in I} u^2(i) = 1$$

(N) No condition

$$0 \le u(i) \le 1$$

We observe that a crisp set $S \subseteq I$ can be considered as a fuzzy set with the non-zero membership values defined according to the normalization principle.

The three normalization conditions correspond to three possible ways of aggregating a set of individual membership values. For each interior node $t \in T$, its membership weight is defined as follows:

(P) $u(t) = \sum_{i \in I(t)} u(i)$

(Q) $u(t) = \sqrt{\sum_{i \in I(t)} u(i)^2}$ (1)

(N) $u(t) = \max_{i \in I(t)} u(i)$

Under each of the definitions, the weight of a gap is zero. The membership weight of the root is 1 with each of the three normalizations. In the case of a crisp set S with no condition (N), the weight of node $t \in T$ is equal to zero if $I(t)$ is disjoint from S, and it is unity, otherwise.

We now define the notion of pruned tree. Pruning the tree T at t results in the tree remaining after deleting all descendants of t. The definitions in (1) are consistent in that the weights of the remaining nodes are unchanged by any sequence of successive prunings. Note, however, that the sum of the weights assigned to the leaves in a pruned tree with normalizations (Q) and (N) is typically less than that in the original tree. With the normalization (P), it unchanges. One can notice, as well, that the decrease of the summary weight at the repeated pruning of the tree is steeper with no normalization (N).

We consider that weight $u(t)$ of node t influences not only its own contribution, but also contributions of those gaps that are children of t. Therefore, the contribution to the penalty value of each of the gaps g of a head subject $h \in T$ is weighted according to the membership weight of its parent, as defined by $\gamma(g) = u(parent(g))$. Let us denote by $\Gamma(h)$ the set of all gaps below h. The gap contribution of h is defined as $\gamma(h) = \sum_{g \in \Gamma(h)} \gamma(g)$. For a crisp query set S with no condition, (N), this is just the number of gaps in $\Gamma(h)$.

To distinguish between proper head subjects and offshoots in H we denote the set of leaves and interior nodes in H as H^- and H^+, respectively.

Then our penalty function $p(H)$ for the tree T is defined by:

$$p(H) = head \times \sum_{h \in H^+} u(h) + gap \times \sum_{h \in H^+} \gamma(h) + off \times \sum_{h \in H^-} u(h).$$

The problem is to find such a set H that minimizes the penalty - this will be the result of the query (T, u).

2.2   Lifting Method

A preliminary step is to prune the tree T of irrelevant nodes. We then annotate all interior nodes $t \in T$ by extending the leaf membership values as in (1). Those nodes in the pruned tree that have a zero weight are gaps; they are assigned with a γ-value which is the u-weight of its parent. This can be accomplished as follows:

(a) Label with 0 all nodes t whose clusters $I(t)$ do not overlap S_u. Then remove from T all nodes that are children of 0-labeled nodes since they cannot be gaps. We note that all the elements of S_u are in the leaf set of the pruned tree, and all the other leaves of the pruned tree are labelled 0.

(b) The membership vector u is extended to all nodes of the pruned tree according to the rules in (1).

(c) Recall that $\Gamma(t)$ is the set of gaps, that is, the 0-labeled nodes of the pruned tree, and $\gamma(t) = \sum_{g \in \Gamma(t)} u(parent(g))$. We compute $\gamma(t)$ by recursively assigning $\Gamma(t)$ as the union of the Γ-sets of its children and $\gamma(t)$ as the sum of the γ-values of its children. For leaf nodes, $\Gamma(t) = \oslash$ and $\gamma(t) = 0$ if $t \in S_u$. Otherwise, i.e. if t is a gap node (or, equivalently, if t is labelled 0), $\Gamma(t) = t$ and $\gamma(t) = u(parent(t))$.

The algorithm proceeds recursively from the leaves to the root. For each node t, we compute two sets, $H(t)$ and $L(t)$, containing those nodes at which gains and losses of head subjects occur. The respective penalty is computed as $p(t)$.

I **Initialisation**

At each leaf $i \in I$: If $u(i) > 0$, define $H(i) = i$, $L(i) = \oslash$ and $p(i) = off \times u(i)$.

If $u(i) = 0$, define $H(i) = \oslash$, $L(i) = \oslash$ and $p(i) = 0$.

II **Recursion**

Consider a node $t \in T$ having a set of children W, with each child $w \in W$ assigned a pair $H(w)$, $L(w)$ and associated penalty $p(w)$. One of the following two cases must be chosen:

(a) The head subject has been gained at t, so the sets $H(w)$ and $L(w)$ at its children $w \in W$ are not relevant. Then $H(t)$, $L(t)$ and $p(t)$ are defined by: $H(t) = t$;
$L(t) = \Gamma(t)$;
$p(t) = head \times u(t) + gap \times \gamma(t)$

(b) The head subject has not been gained at t, so at t we combine the H- and L-sets as follows:

$$H(t) = \bigcup_{w \in W} H(w), L(t) = \bigcup_{w \in W} L(w) \quad \text{and} \quad p(t) = \sum_{w \in W} p(w).$$

Choose whichever of (a) and (b) has the smaller value of $p(t)$.

III **Output**: Accept the values at the root:
$H(root)$ - the heads and offshoots, $L(root)$ - the gaps, $p(root)$ - the penalty.

It is not difficult to prove that the algorithm does produce a parsimonious result.

3 An Example of Application

Table 1 presents a fuzzy cluster obtained in our project (on the data from a survey conducted in CENTRIA of Faculdade de Ciencias e Tecnologia, Universidade Nova de Lisboa (DI-FCT-UNL) in 2009) by applying our Fuzzy Additive Spectral clustering (FADDIS) algoritm [13]. This cluster is visualized with the lifting method applied at penalty parameter values displayed in Figure 3. The description of the visualization is presented in Table 2.

Table 1. A cluster of research activities undertaken in a research centre

Membership value	Code	ACM-CCS Topic
0.69911	I.5.3	Clustering
0.3512	I.5.4	Applications in I.5 PATTERN RECOGNITION
0.27438	J.2	PHYSICAL SCIENCES AND ENGINEERING (Applications in)
0.1992	I.4.9	Applications in I.4 IMAGE PROCESSING AND COMPUTER VISION
0.1992	I.4.6	Segmentation
0.19721	H.5.1	Multimedia Information Systems
0.17478	H.5.2	User Interfaces
0.17478	H.5.3	Group and Organization Interfaces
0.16689	H.1.1	Systems and Information
0.16689	I.5.1	Models in I.5 PATTERN RECOGNITION
0.14453	I.5.2	Design Methodology (Classifiers)
0.13646	H.5.0	General in H.5 INFORMATION INTERFACES AND PRESENTATION
0.13646	H.0	GENERAL in H. Information Systems
0.16513	H.1.2	User/Machine Systems

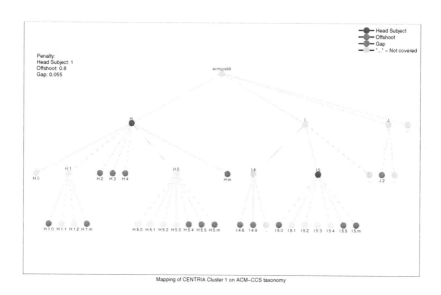

Fig. 3. Visualization of the optimal lift of the cluster in Table 1 in the ACM-CCS tree; most irrelevant leaves are not shown for the sake of simplicity

Table 2. Interpretation of the cluster with optimal lifting

	HEAD SUBJECTS
H.	Information Systems
I.5	PATTERN RECOGNITION
	OFFSHOTS
I.4.6	Segmentation
I.4.9	Applications
J.2	PHYSICAL SCIENCES AND ENGINEERING
	GAPS
H.2	DATABASE MANAGEMENT
H.3	INFORMATION STORAGE AND RETRIEVAL
H.4	INFORMATION SYSTEMS APPLICATIONS
H.5.4	Hypertext/Hypermedia
H.5.5	Sound and Music Computing
I.5.5	Implementation

4   Conclusion

The lifting method should be a useful addition to the methods for interpreting topic sets produced by various data analysis tools. Unlike the methods based on the analysis of frequencies within individual taxonomy nodes, the interpretation capabilities of this method come from an interplay between the topology of the taxonomy tree, the membership values and the penalty weights for the head subjects and associated gap and offshoot events.

On the other hand, the definition of the penalty weights remains of an issue in the method. One can think that potentially this issue can be overcome by using the maximum likelihood approach. This can happen if a taxonomy is used for visualization queries frequently – then probabilities of the gain and loss events can be assigned to each node of the tree. Using this annotation, under usual independence assumptions, the maximum likelihood criterion would inherit the additive structure of the minimum penalty criterion. Then the recursions of the lifting algorithm will remain valid, with respective changes in the criterion of course.

We can envisage, that such a development may put the issue of building the taxonomy tree onto a firm computational footing according to the structure of the flow of queries. An ideal taxonomy in an ideal world would be annotated with very contrast, one or zero probabilities, because most query topic sets would coincide with the leaf-clusters. On the contrary, the taxonomy at which the loss probabilities are similar to each other across the tree may be safely claimed unsuitable for the current query flow.

Acknowledgments

This work has been supported by the grant PTDC/EIA/69988/2006 from the Portuguese Foundation for Science & Technology. B.M. The partial financial support of the Laboratory of Choice and Analysis of Decisions at the State University – Higher School of Economics, Moscow RF, to BM is acknowledged.

References

1. ACM Computing Classification System (1998),
   http://www.acm.org/about/class/1998 (Cited September 9, 2008)
2. Advanced Visual Systems (AVS),
   http://www.avs.com/solutions/avs-powerviz/utility_distribution.html
   (Cited November 27 2010)
3. Beneventano, D., Dahlem, N., El Haoum, S., Hahn, A., Montanari, D., Reinelt, M.: Ontology-driven semantic mapping. In: Enterprise Interoperability III, Part IV, pp. 329–341. Springer, Heidelberg (2008)
4. Buche, P., Dibie-Barthelemy, J., Ibanescu, L.: Ontology mapping using fuzzy conceptual graphs and rules. In: ICCS Supplement, pp. 17–24 (2008)
5. Cali, A., Gottlob, G., Pieris, A.: Advanced processing for ontological queries. Proceedings of the VLDB Endowment 3(1), 554–565 (2010)

6. Dotan-Cohen, D., Kasif, S., Melkman, A.: Seeing the forest for the trees: using the gene ontology to restructure hierarchical clustering. Bioinformatics 25(14), 1789–1795 (2009)
7. Gahegan, M., Agrawal, R., Jaiswal, A., Luo, J., Soon, K.-H.: A platform for visualizing and experimenting with measures of semantic similarity in ontologies and concept maps. Transactions in GIS 12(6), 713–732 (2008)
8. Ghazvinian, A., Noy, N., Musen, M.: Creating mappings for ontologies in Biomedicine: simple methods work. In: AMIA 2009 Symposium Proceedings, pp. 198–202 (2009)
9. Mansingh, G., Osei-Bryson, K.-M., Reichgelt, H.: Using ontologies to facilitate post-processing of association rules by domain experts. Information Sciences 181(3), 419–434 (2011)
10. Marinica, C., Guillet, F.: Improving post-mining of association rules with ontologies. In: The XIII International Conference Applied Stochastic Models and Data Analysis (ASMDA), pp. 76–80 (2009), ISBN 978-9955-28-463-5
11. Mazza, R.: Introduction to Information Visualization. Springer, London (2009), ISBN: 978-1-84800-218-0
12. Mirkin, B., Nascimento, S., Pereira, L.M.: Cluster-lift method for mapping research activities over a concept tree. In: Koronacki, J., Raś, Z.W., Wierzchoń, S.T., Kacprzyk, J. (eds.) Advances in Machine Learning II. SCI, vol. 263, pp. 245–257. Springer, Heidelberg (2010)
13. Mirkin, B., Nascimento, S.: Analysis of Community Structure, Affinity Data and Research Activities using Additive Fuzzy Spectral Clustering, TR-BBKCS-09-07, p. 24 (2009)
14. OWL 2 Web Ontology Language Overview (2009),
   http://www.w3.org/TR/2009/RECowl2overview20091027/
   (Cited November 27, 2010)
15. SNOMED CT (2011),
   http://www.connectingforhealth.nhs.uk/systemsandservices/data/uktc/snomed
   (Cited March 2011)
16. Sosnovsky, S., Mitrovic, A., Lee, D., Prusilovsky, P., Yudelson, M., Brusilovsky, V., Sharma, D.: Towards integration of adaptive educational systems: mapping domain models to ontologies. In: Dicheva, D., Harrer, A., Mizoguchi, R. (eds.) Procs. of 6th International Workshop on Ontologies and Semantic Web for ELearning (SWEL 2008) at ITS 2008 (2008),
   http://compsci.wssu.edu/iis/swel/SWEL08/Papers/Sosnovsky.pdf
17. Thomas, H., O'Sullivan, D., Brennan, R.: Evaluation of ontology mapping representation. In: Proceedings of the Workshop on Matching and Meaning, pp. 64–68 (2009)

On Merging the Fields of Neural Networks and Adaptive Data Structures to Yield New Pattern Recognition Methodologies

B. John Oommen

School of Computer Science, Carleton University, Ottawa, Canada[*]

Abstract. The aim of this talk is to explain a pioneering *exploratory* research endeavour that attempts to merge two completely different fields in Computer Science so as to yield very fascinating results. These are the well-established fields of Neural Networks (NNs) and Adaptive Data Structures (ADS) respectively. The field of NNs deals with the training and learning capabilities of a large number of neurons, each possessing minimal computational properties. On the other hand, the field of ADS concerns designing, implementing and analyzing data structures which adaptively change with time so as to optimize some access criteria. In this talk, we shall demonstrate how these fields can be merged, so that the neural elements are themselves linked together using a data structure. This structure can be a singly-linked or doubly-linked list, or even a Binary Search Tree (BST). While the results themselves are quite generic, in particular, we shall, as a *prima facie* case, present the results in which a Self-Organizing Map (SOM) with an underlying BST structure can be adaptively re-structured using conditional rotations. These rotations on the nodes of the tree are local and are performed in constant time, guaranteeing a decrease in the Weighted Path Length of the entire tree. As a result, the algorithm, referred to as the Tree-based Topology-Oriented SOM with Conditional Rotations (TTO-CONROT), converges in such a manner that the neurons are ultimately placed in the input space so as to represent its stochastic distribution. Besides, the neighborhood properties of the neurons suit the best BST that represents the data.

Summary of the Research Contributions

Consider a set $A = \{A_1, A_2, \ldots, A_N\}$ of records, where each record A_i is identified by a unique key, k_i. The records are accessed with respective probabilities $S = [s_1, s_2, \ldots, s_N]$, which are assumed unknown. In the field of Adaptive Data Structures (ADS), we try to maintain A in a data structure which is constantly changing so as to optimize the average or amortized access times.

[*] *Chancellor's Professor*; *Fellow : IEEE* and *Fellow : IAPR*. The Author also holds an *Adjunct Professorship* with the Dept. of ICT, University of Agder, Norway. The author is grateful for the partial support provided by NSERC, the Natural Sciences and Engineering Research Council of Canada. Although the research associated with this paper was done together with my students including Rob Cheetham, David Ng and Cesar Astudillo, the future research proposed is truly of an *exploratory* nature, and in one sense, could be "wishful thinking".

S.O. Kuznetsov et al. (Eds.): PReMI 2011, LNCS 6744, pp. 13–16, 2011.
© Springer-Verlag Berlin Heidelberg 2011

If the data is maintained in a list, adaptation is obtained by invoking a Self-Organizing List (SLL), which is a linear list that rearranges itself each time an element is accessed. The goal is that the elements are eventually reorganized in terms of the descending order of the access probabilities. Many memoryless update rules have been developed to achieve this reorganization, [5,8,13,15,16,17]. Foremost among these are the well-studied Move-To-Front (MTF), Transposition, the POS(k) and the Move-k-Ahead rules. Schemes involving the use of extra memory have also been developed [16,17]. The most obvious of these, uses counters to achieve the estimation of the access probabilities. Another is a stochastic Move-to-$Rear$ rule due to Oommen and Hansen [15], which moves the accessed element to the rear with a probability which decreases each time the element is accessed. Stochastic MTF [15] and various stochastic and deterministic Move-to-$Rear$ schemes [16,17] due to Oommen $et.$ al have also been reported. All of these rules can also be used for Doubly-Linked Lists (DLLs), where accesses can be made from either end of the list.

A Binary Search Tree (BST) may also be used to store the records where the keys are members of an $ordered$ set, A. Each record A_i is identified by a unique key, and the records are stored in such a way that a symmetric-order traversal of the tree (with respect to the identifying key) will yield the records in an ascending order. The problem of constructing an optimal BST given A and S requires $O(N^2)$ time and space [11]. Generally speaking, all the BST heuristics use the primitive **Rotation** operation [1] to restructure the tree. Memoryless BST schemes also employ the Move-To-Root [4] and Simple Exchange [4] rules which are analogous to the MTF and transposition rules for SLLs. Sleator and Tarjan [18] introduced a scheme, which moves the accessed record up to the root of the tree using the $splaying$ operation – a multi-level generalization of rotation. Schemes requiring extra memory such as the Monotonic Tree scheme and Melhorn's D-Tree etc. have also been proposed [14]. In spite of the fact that SLLs and BSTs could have conflicting reorganization criteria, there is a close mapping between $certain$ SLL heuristics and the corresponding BST heuristics as reported by Lai and Wood [13]. With regard to $Adaptive$ BSTs, the most effective solution is due to Cheetham et $al.$ which uses the concept of $Conditional$ Rotations [6]. The latter paper proposed a solution where an accessed element is rotated towards the root if and only if the overall Weighted Path Length of the resulting BST decreases.

The field of NNs [7,9] deals with the training and learning capabilities of a large number of computing elements (i.e., the neurons), each possessing minimal computational properties. There are scores of families of NNs described in the literature, including the Backpropagation, the Hopfield network, the Neocognitron, the SOM etc. [12]. However, unlike the traditional concepts useful in developing families of NNs, we propose to "link" the neurons together using a data structure which can be a SLL, a DLL or even a BST. As far as we know, such an attempt to merge the fields of NNs and ADS is both novel and pioneering.

The advantage of using an ADS is that during the training phase, we can modify the configuration of the data structure by moving a neuron closer to its head (root), and thus explicitly recording the relevant role of the particular node with respect to its nearby neurons. This leads us to the concept of **Neural Promotion**, which is the process by which a neuron is relocated in a more privileged position[1] in the network with respect to the other neurons in the neural network. Thus, while "all neurons are born equal", their importance in the society of neurons is determined by what they represent. This is achieved, by an explicit advancement of its rank or position.

While the results themselves are quite generic and can potentially lead to many new avenues for further research, in particular, we shall, as a *prima facie* case, present the results [2,3] in which the NN is the Self-Organizing Map (SOM) [12]. Even though numerous researchers have focused on deriving variants of the original SOM strategy, few of the reported results possess the ability of modifying the underlying topology, leading to a dynamic modification of the structure of the network by adding and/or deleting nodes and their inter-connections. Moreover, only a small set of strategies use a tree as their underlying data structure. From our perspective, we believe that it is also possible to gain a better understanding of the unknown data distribution by performing *structural* tree-based modifications on the tree, by rotating the nodes within the BST that holds the whole structure of neurons. Thus, we attempt to use rotations, tree-based neighbors *and* the feature space as an effort to enhance the capabilities of the SOM by representing the underlying data distribution and its structure more accurately. Furthermore, as a long term ambition, this might be useful for the design of faster methods for locating the SOM's Best Matching Unit.

The *prima facie* strategy for which we have obtained encouraging results is the Tree-based Topology-Oriented SOM with Conditional Rotations (TTO-CONROT). TTO-CONROT has a set of neurons, which, like all SOM-based methods, represents the data space in a condensed manner. Secondly, it possesses a connection between the neurons, where the neighbors are based on a learned tree-based nearness measure. Similar to the reported families of SOMs, a subset of neurons closest to the BMU are moved towards the sample point using a vector quantization rule. But, unlike many of the reported SOM families, the identity of the neurons moved is based on the tree-based proximity (and not on the feature-space proximity). CONROT-BST achieves neural promotion by performing a *local* movement of the node, where only its direct parent and children are aware of the neuron promotion. Finally, the TTO-CONROT incorporates tree-based mutations, namely the above-mentioned conditional rotations.

Our proposed strategy is adaptive, with regard to the migration of the points *and* with regard to the identity of the neurons moved. Additionally, the distribution of the neurons in the feature space mimics the distribution of the sample points. Lastly, by virtue of the conditional rotations, it turns out that the entire tree of neurons is optimized with regard to the overall accesses, which is a unique phenomenon – when compared to the reported family of SOMs.

The potential to extend these results for other NN families and ADSs is open.

---

[1] As far as we know, we are not aware of any research which deals with the issue of Neural Promotion. Thus, we believe that this concept, itself, is pioneering.

References

1. Adel'son-Velski'i, G.M., Landis, E.M.: An algorithm for the organization of information. Sov. Math. Dokl. 3, 1259–1262 (1962)
2. Astudillo, C.A., Oommen, J.B.: A novel self organizing map which utilizes imposed tree-based topologies. In: Kurzynski, M., Wozniak, M. (eds.) Computer Recognition Systems 3. Computer Recognition, vol. 57, pp. 169–178. Springer, Heidelberg (2009)
3. Astudillo, C.A., Oommen, B.J.: On using adaptive binary search trees to enhance self organizing maps. In: Nicholson, A., Li, X. (eds.) AI 2009. LNCS, vol. 5866, pp. 199–209. Springer, Heidelberg (2009)
4. Allen, B., Munro, I.: Self-organizing binary search trees. Journal of the ACM 25, 526–535 (1978)
5. Arnow, D.M., Tenenbaum, A.M.: An investigation of the move-ahead-k rules. In: Proceedings of Congressus Numerantium, Proceedings of the Thirteenth Southeastern Conference on Combinatorics, Graph Theory and Computing, Florida, pp. 47–65 (1982)
6. Cheetham, R.P., Oommen, B.J., Ng, D.T.H.: Adaptive structuring of binary search trees using conditional rotations. IEEE Transactions on Knowledge and Data Engineering 5, 695–704 (1993)
7. Duda, R., Hart, P.E., Stork, D.G.: Pattern Classification, 2nd edn. Wiley Interscience, Hoboken (2000)
8. Gonnet, G.H., Munro, J.I., Suwanda, H.: Exegesis of self-organizing linear search. SIAM Journal of Comput. 10, 613–637 (1981)
9. Haykin, S.: Neural Networks and Learning Machines, 3rd edn. Prentice-Hall, Englewood Cliffs (2008)
10. Hester, H.J., Herberger, D.S.: Self-organizing linear search. In: ACM Computing Surveys, pp. 295–311 (1976)
11. Knuth, D.E.: The Art of Computer Programming, vol. 3. Addison-Wesley, Reading (1973)
12. Kohonen, T.: Self-Organizing Maps. Springer-Verlag New York, Inc., Secaucus, NJ, USA (1995)
13. Lai, T.W., Wood, D.: A relationship between self organizing lists and binary search trees. In: Proceedings of the 1991 Int. Conf. Computing and Information, May 1991, pp. 111–116 (1991)
14. Mehlhorn, K.: Data Structures and Algorithms 1: Sorting and Searching. Springer, Berlin (1984)
15. Oommen, B.J., Hansen, E.R.: List organizing strategies using stochastic move-to-front and stochastic move-to-rear operations. SIAM Journal of Computing 16, 705–716 (1987)
16. Oommen, B.J., Hansen, E.R., Munro, J.I.: Deterministic optimal and expedient move-to-rear list organizing strategies. Theoretical Computer Science 74, 183–197 (1990)
17. Oommen, B.J., Ng, D.T.H.: An optimal absorbing list organization strategy with constant memory requirements. Theoretical Computer Science 119, 355–361 (1993)
18. Sleator, D.D., Tarjan, R.E.: Self-adjusting binary search trees. Journal of the ACM 32, 652–686 (1985)
19. Walker, W.A., Gotlieb, C.C.: A top-down algorithm for constructing nearly optimal lexicographical trees. In: Graph Theory and Computing (1972)

Quality of Algorithms for Sequence Comparison

Mikhail Roytberg[1,2]

[1] Institute of Mathematical Problems in Biology RAS, Institutskaya, 4, Pushchino,
Moscow Region, 142290, Russia
[2] National Research University Higher School of Economics, Myasnitskaya, 20,
Moscow, 101000, Russia
mroytberg@lpm.org.ru

Abstract. Pair-wise sequence alignment is the basic method of comparative analysis of proteins and nucleic acids. Studying the results of the alignment one has to consider two questions: (1) did the program find all the interesting similarities ("sensitivity") and (2) are all the found similarities interesting ("selectivity"). Definitely, one has to specify, what alignments are considered as the interesting ones. Analogous questions can be addressed to each of the obtained alignments: (3) which part of the aligned positions are aligned correctly ("confidence") and (4) does alignment contain all pairs of the corresponding positions of compared sequences ("accuracy"). Naturally, the answer on the questions depends on the definition of the correct alignment. The presentation addresses the above two pairs of questions that are extremely important in interpreting of the results of sequence comparison.

Keywords: alignment, seed, sequence comparison, sensitivity, selectivity, accuracy, confidence.

1   Seeds, Sensitivity and Selectivity

Many programs of sequence similarity search (e.g. BLAST, FASTA) are based on the filtration paradigm; they firstly mark the regions of putative similarity and then restrict the search with the regions only. To perform the first step the seeding scheme is usually implemented: one searches only for the similarities containing the strong similarity of special form, e.g. the similarities containing k consecutive matches. This seeding scheme leads to the drastic speed up compared to the more rigorous dynamic programming based methods at the price of possible loss of some interesting similarities.

In the framework of similarity search in biological sequences, a *seed* specifies a class of short sequence motifs which, if shared by two sequences, are assumed to witness a potential similarity. We say that a seed *matches* a similarity (or a similarity is recognized by a seed) if it contains a sub-similarity corresponding to a seed. To define what is sensitivity and selectivity of a seed we have to make some preliminary definitions. First, we have to describe the set of considered possible sequence alignments and the subset of interesting similarities ("target similarities"). For example, we may consider all ungapped similarities

S.O. Kuznetsov et al. (Eds.): PReMI 2011, LNCS 6744, pp. 17–20, 2011.
© Springer-Verlag Berlin Heidelberg 2011

(alignments) of a given length and the set of target similarities consisting of all ungapped alignments having identity level higher than a given cut-off. Second, we have to consider the two probability distributions on alignments: the *background* distribution, corresponding to the random alignments and the *foreground* distribution that corresponds to the target alignments. E.g. one can consider both distributions as Bernoulli distributions in two-letter alphabet (match-mismatch) and define the probability of match as 0.25 for the background distribution and as (say) 0.7 for the foreground distribution.

Given the set of target alignments and the distributions, the *sensitivity* of a seed is the probability that a random similarity is recognized by a seed according to a foreground distribution and the *selectivity* of a seed is the probability that a random similarity is recognized by a seed according to a background distribution. For the Bernoulli distribution the selectivity is often defined as a probability that a seeding similarity can be found for two random independent sequences of a length equal to the seeds length.

The seed implemented in BLASTN program [1] describes a class of k consecutive matches (default $k = 11$). The selectivity of the default seed is $0.25^k = 0.25^{11} \sim 10^{-6}$. The sensitivity of the seed for ungapped nucleotide similarities of length 64 with 70% identity is ~ 0.3. Several years ago Ma, Tromp and Li [2] have proposed to use k nonconsecutive letters as a seed. This change surprisingly led to a significant improvement of sensitivity without loss of selectivity that depends only on the desired number of matches k and on the background match probability. E.g. the seed 110100110010101111 (1 stands for the match positions and 0 stands for "spaces") has the sensitivity 0.46 with the same number of matches $k = 11$. The seminal work of Ma, Tromp and Li (2002) have caused the investigation of various seed models both for nucleic and amino acid sequences, e.g. vector seeds, subset seeds, multyseeds, etc [3]-[12].

We will consider advantages and disadvantages of the models and will present the unifying framework to compute the seed sensitivity.

2   Alignments, Accuracy and Confidence

For many applications it is important to evaluate the quality of algorithmically obtained alignments, i.e. how close the algorithmic alignment is to the evolutionarily true one. Here the evolutionarily true alignment is an alignment superimposing the positions originating from the same position of the common predecessor [13].

Moreover, it is important not only to know the quantitative measure of the average similarity of alignments but also to understand the typical differences between the algorithmic and the evolutionary true alignments. However, the evolutionarily true alignment of given sequences is usually unknown, and thus an approximation is needed.

There are two possible ways to obtain such an approximation: (1) to use artificial sequences pairs obtained according to a proper evolutionary model [14,15] and (2) to use alignments based on the superposition of the protein 3D-structures (that is possible only for the comparison of amino acid sequences) [13,16].

Accuracy and confidence of global and local alignments were studied in several papers [13,14], [16]-[19]. The data show that the main difference between the algorithmic and true alignments is the number of gaps while the average length of a gap is approximately the same. Surprisingly, the 3D-structure based protein alignments contain significant number of ungapped fragments of negative score that can not be restored in algorithmic alignments.

The significant gain both in accuracy and in confidence of protein alignments can be achieved using the information on the secondary structure (experimentally obtained or predicted) [20,21].

Acknowledgments

The work was supported by grant RFBR 09-04-01053-a.

References

1. Altschul, S.F., Gish, W., Miller, W., et al.: Basic local alignment search tool. J. Mol. Biol. 215, 403–410 (1990)
2. Ma, B., Tromp, J., Li, M.: PatternHunter: Fasterand more sensitive homology search. Bioinformatics 18(3), 440–445 (2002)
3. Brejová, B., Brown, D.G., Vinař, T.: Optimal Spaced Seeds for Hidden Markov Models, with Application to Homologous Coding Regions. In: Baeza-Yates, R., Chávez, E., Crochemore, M. (eds.) CPM 2003. LNCS, vol. 2676, pp. 42–54. Springer, Heidelberg (2003)
4. Brejová, B., Brown, D.G., Vinař, T.: Vector seeds: An extension to spaced seeds allows substantial improvements in sensitivity and specificity. In: Benson, G., Page, R.D.M. (eds.) WABI 2003. LNCS (LNBI), vol. 2812, pp. 39–54. Springer, Heidelberg (2003)
5. Brejova, B., Brown, D., Vinar, T.: Optimal spaced seeds for homologous coding regions. Journal of Bioinformatics and Computational Biology 1(4), 595–610 (2004)
6. Brown, D.: Optimizing multiple seeds for protein homology search. IEEE Transactions on Computational Biology and Bioinformatics 2(1), 29–38 (2005)
7. Buhler, J., Keich, U., Sun, Y.: Designing seeds for similarity search in genomic DNA. In: Proceedings of the 7th Annual International Conference on Computational Molecular Biology (RECOMB 2003), Berlin, Germany, April 2003, pp. 67–75. ACM Press, New York (2003)
8. Kucherov, G., Noé, L., Roytberg, M.: Multiseed lossless filtration. IEEE Transactions on Computational Biology and Bioinformatics 2(1), 51–61 (2005)
9. Li, M., Ma, B., Kisman, D., Tromp, J.: Pattern Hunter II: Highly sensitive and fast homology search. Journal of Bioinformatics and Computational Biology (2004), Earlier version in GIW 2003 (International Conference on Genome Informatics)
10. Kucherov, G., Noé, L., Roytberg, M.: A unifying framework for seed sensitivity and its application to subset seeds. Journal of Bioinformatics and Computational Biology 4(2), 553–569 (2006)
11. Xu, J., Brown, D.G., Li, M., Ma, B.: Optimizing Multiple Spaced Seeds for Homology Search. In: Sahinalp, S.C., Muthukrishnan, S.M., Dogrusoz, U. (eds.) CPM 2004. LNCS, vol. 3109, pp. 47–58. Springer, Heidelberg (2004)

12. Yang, I., Wang, S., Chen, Y., Huang, P., Ye, L., Huang, X., Chao, K.: Efficient methods for generating optimal single and multiple spaced seeds. In: Proceedings of the IEEE 4th Symposium on Bioinformatics and Bioengineering(BIBE 2004), Taichung, Taiwan, May 19-21, 2004, pp. 411–416. IEEE Computer Society Press, Los Alamitos (2004)

13. Sunyaev, Bogopolsky, G.A., Oleynikova, N.V., Vlasov, P.K., Finkelstein, A.V., Roytberg, M.A.: From Analysis of Protein Structural Alignments Toward a Novel Approach to Align Protein Sequences. PROTEINS: Structure, Function, and Bioinformatics 54(3), 569–582 (2004)

14. Stoye, J., Evers, D., Meyer, F.: Rose: generating sequence families. Bioinformatics 14, 157–163 (1998)

15. Polyanovsky, V., Roytberg, M., Tumanyan, V.: Reconstruction of Genuine Pair-Wise Sequence Alignment. J. Comput. Biol. (April 24, 2008) (Epub ahead of print)

16. Vogt, G., Etzold, T., Argos, P.: An assessment of amino acid exchange matrices in aligning protein sequences: the twilight zone revisited. J. Mol. Biol. 249, 816–831 (1995)

17. Domingues, F.S., Lackner, P., Andreeva, A., et al.: Structure-based evaluation of sequence comparison and fold recognition alignment accuracy. J. Mol. Biol. 297, 1003–1013 (2000)

18. Mevissen, H.T., Vingron, M.: Quantifying the local reliability of a sequence alignment. Prot. Eng. 9, 127–132 (1996)

19. Vingron, M., Argos, P.: Determination of reliable regions in protein sequence alignments. Prot. Eng. 3, 565–569 (1990)

20. Litvinov, I.I., Lobanov, Yu, M., Mironov, A.A., et al.: Information on the Secondary Structure Improves the Quality of Protein Sequence Alignment. Mol. Biol. 40, 474–480 (2006)

21. Wallqvist, A., Fukunishi, Y., Murphy, L.R., et al.: Iterative sequence/secondary structure search for protein homologs: Comparison with amino acid sequence alignments and application to fold recognition in genome databases. Bioinformatics 16, 988–1002 (2000)

Problems of Machine Learning

Alexei Ya. Chervonenkis

Institute of Control Sciences, Moscow, Russia
chervnks@ipu.ru

The problem of reconstructing dependencies from empirical data became very important in a very large range of applications. Procedures used to solve this problem are known as "Methods of Machine Learning" [1,3]. These procedures include methods of regression reconstruction, inverse problems of mathematical physics and statistics, machine learning in pattern recognition (for visual and abstract patterns represented by sets of features) and many others. Many web network control problems also belong to this field. The task is to reconstruct the dependency between input and output data as precisely as possible using empirical data obtained from experiments or statistical observations.

Input data are composed of descriptions (curves, pictures, graphs, texts, messages) of input objects (we denote an input by x) and may be presented by vectors in Euclidian space or vectors of discrete values. In the latter case they may be sets of discrete features or even textual descriptions. An output value y may be given by a real value, vector or a discrete value. In the case of pattern recognition problem, output values may be names of classes (patterns), to which the input object belongs.

A training set is given by a sequence of pairs $(x_1, y_1), (x_2, y_2), \ldots, (x_l, y_l)$. One needs to find a dependency $y = F(x)$ such that forecast output values $y^* = F(x)$ for new input objects are most close to actual output values y, corresponding to the inputs x. Several schemes of training sequence generation are possible. From the theoretical point of view, it is most convenient to consider that the pairs are generated independently by some constant (but unknown) probability distribution $P(x, y)$, and the same distribution is used to generate new pairs. However, in practice the assumption of independency fails. Sometimes the distribution changes in time. In this case adaptive schemes of learning should be used, where the reconstructed function also changes in time. In some tasks there is no assumption about existing of any probability distribution on the set of pairs. Then the solution is to construct a function that properly approximates real dependency over its domain. If dependency between input and output variables is linear (or the best linear approximation is looked for), then well known Least Square Method is used to estimate the dependency coefficients. Still, if the training set is small (not large enough) in comparison with the number of arguments, then LSM does not work or works inefficiently. In this case some kinds of regularization are used. If dependency is sought in the class of polynomials of finite degree, then the problem may be reduced to the previous one by adding degrees of initial arguments. In the case of many arguments it is necessary to

S.O. Kuznetsov et al. (Eds.): PReMI 2011, LNCS 6744, pp. 21–23, 2011.
© Springer-Verlag Berlin Heidelberg 2011

include degree products of initial arguments. In this case, of course, the number of unknown coefficients grows rapidly and the problem becomes intractable. Besides algebraic polynomials, trigonometric ones can be used, or, in general, expansions over preselected system of basis functions. If the dependency is sought in the form of piece-wise linear or piece-wise continuous function, then the standard least square method cannot be applied and other tools should be used, such as artificial neural networks. If the number of basis function necessary for proper approximation is too large, then kernel technique may be applied, which allows one to estimate the function value at a given point or at a set of given points. The so-called inverse problems of mathematical physics and statistics are also of this type.

Machine learning in pattern recognition is a particular case of dependency reconstruction. Here the output value is the name of a class. This class of problems covers a very large range of applications from image recognition to recognition of certain type of DNA sites, message classification, or recognition of unauthorized access attempts. In all cases of dependency reconstruction, one chooses a priori a certain class of models and then selects from it a model that in a sense is the best for describing dependency between input and output.

Three general questions arise in relation to any learning approach:

1. Is there a good model in the class that we have chosen?
2. May we hope that if the model behaves well on the training set, will it also behave well on new data?
3. Is there an efficient algorithm for selecting a proper model from a given class of models?

The smaller is the set of models, the closer is the point delivering minimum to empirical risk to the point delivering minimum to the true risk (within the class). On the other hand, the chance to find a good model within a small class is less than that for a large class. A solution may be as follows: Consider a set of expanding classes and choose the optimal size of a class, depending on the size of the training sample. For example, it is possible to increase (or decrease) the degree of approximating polynomial, or increase the number of terms in trigonometric expansion (or expansion over any other system of basic functions). In the case of linear function it is possible to define an order on the arguments and then sequentially increase the number of input variables in this order. One also can look over all combinations of arguments, increasing their number. In the case of piece-wise linear approximation one may change the number of pieces or number of neurons of the artificial neural network.

How one can find the best size of the class? The simplest way is to reserve a part of data set given for learning (validation set), using the rest part for finding the best model within expanding classes and then testing the result using the validation set, and at last selecting the model with the best score on the validation test. However, usually training data are lacking and it is costly to reserve some part of it. In this case one can use a means of control that does not need reservation, e.g. cross-validation. Another way is to estimate analytically the difference between empirical and real risk values depending on training data and the size of a class from which we select the best model. The reason is that the empirical risk always deceases (not increases) with the class size, while the true risk passing its minimum starts increasing with the class size. Analytically it is possible to determine a corresponding correction. Other methods for choosing optimal complexity of a decision are possible. Note that the model complexity does not always directly correlates with the size of a class of models. For example, some very complicated procedures of feature preprocessing may be proposed, and the best decision rule is sought for a narrow class described in terms of secondary features resulting from preprocessing.

Let us consider in more detail some principles of choosing optimal model complexity within analytical approach. It is well known that maximum likelihood principle gives good results if the number of model parameters is rather low in comparison with the size of training data. On the other hand, Bayesian approach [2] gives the optimal result in the case where the number of parameters is very large or even infinite, but it requires a priori distribution over the set of their possible values. This approach results in a form of regularization, and it gives optimal degree of the selected model complexity. But how one can find this a priori distribution? Bayesian approach does not give any answer to this question. However, in many cases the a priori distribution depends on few parameters. Hence, it is promising to hybridize maximum likelihood and Bayesian approaches [4]: constructing likelihood function for the parameters of the a priori distribution, finding their optimal value and using them in Bayesian method. In some cases this approach gives very efficient algorithms.

Another idea is to use analytical estimates of the uniform closeness of empirical risk to the true risk (in absolute or relative form) and to use them as the estimates of the difference between empirical and real risk values. Then it is possible to use the estimates for choosing the best model complexity as it is mentioned above.

References

1. Vapnik, V.N., Chervonenkis, A.Y.: Theory of Pattern Recognition (in Russian). Moscow, Nauka (1974)
2. MacKay, J.D.C.: Bayesian interpolation. Neural Computation 4(3), 415–447 (1992)
3. Vapnik, V.N.: The Nature of Statistical Learning Theory. Springer, Heidelberg (2000)
4. Chervonenkis, A.Y.: A combined Bayes - Maximum Likelihood method for regression. In: Riccia, G.D., Lenz, H.-J., Kruse, R. (eds.) Data Fusion and Perception, Springer, Wien, New-York (2001)

Bayesian Approach to the Pattern Recognition Problem in Nonstationary Environment

O.V. Krasotkina[1], V.V. Mottl[2], and P.A. Turkov[1]

[1] Tula State University, Tula, Russia
krasotkina@tsu.tula.ru
[2] Computing Centre of RAS

Abstract. The classical learning problem of the pattern recognition in a finite-dimensional linear space of real-valued features is studied under the conditions of a non-stationary universe. The training criterion of non-stationary pattern recognition is formulated as a generalization of the classical Support Vector Machine. The respective numerical algorithm has the computation complexity proportional to the length of the training time series.

The majority of modern methods for pattern recognition works under the assumption that properties of the environment and consequently required decision rule doesn't change in a process of data collection as well as during the exam. However, recently there have appeared many applications, in which samples of training set are entering the system over a long period of time, when the properties of the analyzed phenomenon may undergo considerable changes. The example of such problem is task of filtering irrelevant or publicity hyperlinks as a result of retrieval request. The behavior of internet advertising distributors constantly turns and it causes changes of publicity hyperlinks features that should result in the adequate correction of search mechanism. Often in this kind of tasks both the nature of changes in the environment and the fact of changes itself are hidden from direct observation and this makes learning even more difficult. In literature this problem is called *concept drift* [1].

At present there are three approaches to the construction of algorithms taking into account non-stationary character of decision rule: algorithms based on selecting instances, algorithms based on weighted instances and algorithms based on classifier selection and mergers. The goal of algorithms using selection of instances is the choice of prototypes which are relevant for decision rule at the present moment. As a rule, it is realized with the help of running window technology when decision rule at the present moment is made only on the basis of the instances obtained from previous time points. The examples of such algorithms can be FLORA family of algorithms [1] and TMF [2].

Algorithms based on weighting of instances [3] obtained from different time points use the ability of some learning algorithms such as Support Vector Machines (SVMs) method to assign weights to different instances. As a rule, weights are assigned to the instances according to their "age" (e.g. period of time from their obtaining).

S.O. Kuznetsov et al. (Eds.): PReMI 2011, LNCS 6744, pp. 24–29, 2011.

By ensemble-based approach [5] for pattern recognition in non-stationary environment, required decision rule is made as voting or weighted voting of classifiers obtained for different conditions. For example, in the paper [4] it is proposed to cluster training samples and to construct its own classifier for each cluster.

In general, we can mark that all existing algorithms are more or less heuristic and a certain set of heuristics is determined by a specificity of the current task. In this paper we propose stochastic concept of the non-stationary environment based on Bayesian approach to the pattern recognition problem. The main instantaneous property of the non-stationary environment is understood as time-dependent separating hyperplane that in the best way describes the differences between feature vectors of samples of two classes. The proposed concept brings about the learning algorithm that is a generalization of the classical SVM for the case when the parameters of the separating hyperplane change with time.

1   Bayesian Definition of the Pattern Recognition Problem in Non-stationary Environment

Let every instance of the environment $\omega \in \Omega$ is presented by a point in the linear feature space $\mathbf{x}(\omega) = \left(x^1(\omega), \ldots, x^n(\omega)\right) \in \mathbb{R}^n$, and its hidden membership in one of two classes is determined by an index value of the class $y(\omega) \in \{1, -1\}$. The paper [6] proposed a stochastic model of the universe. The main model assumption is a priori parametric distribution of the instances

$$\phi\left(\mathbf{x}|\mathbf{a}, b, y; c\right) = \begin{cases} \text{const}, & yz\left(\mathbf{a}, \mathbf{x}\right) \geq 1, \\ e^{-c(1-yz(\mathbf{a},x))}, & yz\left(\mathbf{a}, \mathbf{x}\right) < 1, \end{cases} \tag{1}$$

And this distribution is defined by the objectively existing hyperplane $z(\mathbf{x}, \mathbf{a}) = \mathbf{a}^T \mathbf{x} + b = 0$ with an unknown directing vector of features $\mathbf{a} = (a_1, a_2, \ldots, a_n)$, having a priori distribution $\Psi(\mathbf{a}, b|\sigma^2) \propto \exp\left(-\frac{1}{2\sigma^2}\mathbf{a}^T\mathbf{a}\right)$. Using the maximum a posteriori probability principle for the directing vector parameters estimation $(\mathbf{a}, b)$ leads us to the widely-known support vector criterion

$$\begin{cases} J(\mathbf{a}, b, \delta_1, \ldots, \delta_N|c) = \mathbf{a}^T\mathbf{a} + c\sum_{j=1}^{N}\delta_j \to \min, \\ y_j\left(\mathbf{a}^T\mathbf{a} + b\right) \geq 1 - \delta_j, \ \delta_j \geq 0, j = 1, \ldots, N, \end{cases} \tag{2}$$

that was proposed by V. N. Vapnik from a strictly deterministic point of view. Of course, the concept of time is completely absent here.

The principal distinction of the concept of non-stationary environment given in this paper consists in taking into consideration time factor t. We suppose that the main property of non-stationary environment is expressed by time-dependent separating hyperplane that characterizes primary difference of the feature vectors of instances of two classes. This separating hyperplane, in turn, is completely defined by its own direction vector and location parameter, which should be considered as time functions $\mathbf{a}_t$ b_t: $f_t\left(\mathbf{x}(\omega)\right) = \mathbf{a}_t^T\mathbf{x} + b_t$. In the terms of the improper probability distributions of two classes in the feature space such idea is formulated in the form of hypothesis that parameters of this pair of distributions are time varying:

$$\phi\left(\mathbf{x}|\mathbf{a}_t, b_t, y; c\right) = \begin{cases} \text{const}, & yz(\mathbf{a}_t, \mathbf{x}) \geq 1, \\ e^{-c(1-yz(\mathbf{a}_t, \mathbf{x}))}, & yz(\mathbf{a}_t, \mathbf{x}) < 1, \end{cases} \tag{3}$$

where $z(\mathbf{x}, \mathbf{a}_t) = \mathbf{a}_t^T \mathbf{x} + b = 0$.

We will suppose that at the zero time moment a priori distribution of the separating hyperplane is improper and has the appearance: $\psi_0(\mathbf{a}_0, b_0) \propto \psi_0(\mathbf{a}_0) = N(\mathbf{a}_0|\mathbf{0}, \mathbf{I})$. In turn we will regard directing vector $\mathbf{a}_j$ as a stochastic stationary process: $\mathbf{a}_t = q\mathbf{a}_{t-1} + \boldsymbol{\xi}_t, M(\boldsymbol{\xi}_t) = \mathbf{0}, M(\boldsymbol{\xi}_t\boldsymbol{\xi}_t^T) = d\mathbf{I}, 0 \leq q < 1$.

2   Dynamic Support Vector Machine Criterion

Now every instance $\omega \in \Omega$ is considered only together with the indication of time point when this instance was presented (ω, t). As a result the training set represents as the set of triplet $\{(\mathbf{X}_t \in \mathbb{R}^n, \mathbf{Y}_t, t)\}_{t=1}^T$, $(\mathbf{X}_t, \mathbf{Y}_t) = \{(\mathbf{x}_{k,t}, y_{k,t})\}_{k=1}^{N_t}$ - a subset of instances, entered in time point t.

We obtain the sought-for sequence $(\mathbf{a}_t, b_t)_{t=1}^T$ as maximum point of joint a priori distribution of separating hyperplane's parameters and training sample. The maximum a posteriori probability principle lets to the criterion

$$J(\mathbf{a}_t, b_t, \delta_{t,j}, t = 0, ..., T) = \mathbf{a}_0^T \mathbf{a}_0 + \frac{1}{d} \sum_{t=1}^T (\mathbf{a}_t - q\mathbf{a}_{t-1})^T (\mathbf{a}_t - q\mathbf{a}_{t-1}) +$$
$$+ \frac{1}{d'} \sum_{t=1}^T (b_t - b_{t-1})^2 + \sum_{t=1}^T \sum_{j=1}^{N_t} \delta_{j,t} \to \min_{[\mathbf{a}_t, b_t]_{t=1}^T} \tag{4}$$
$$y_{j,t}(\mathbf{a}_t^T \mathbf{x}_{j,t} + b_t) \geq 1 - \delta_{j,t}, \delta_{j,t} \geq 0, j = 1, \ldots, N_t, t = 1, ..., T$$

The criterion (4) realizes the conception of the rather smooth sequence of optimal separating hyperplanes as opposed to the conception of the single optimal hyperplane in (2).

As the classic learning problem, the dynamical problem (4) is a quadratic programming problem but contains $T(n + 1) + N$ variables in contrast to $(n + 1)+N$ variables in (2). It is known that a computational complexity of the general quadratic programming problem is proportional to the cube of the number of variables, i.e. a dynamic problem ex facte is more complex than the classical problem.

But the objective function in a dynamic problem (4) is pair-wise separable, i.e. representing a sum of private functions every of which depends on the variables connected with one or two time points in their increasing order. The algorithm of the pair-wise separable criterion optimization suggested in this paper consists in an approximate implementation of the dynamic programming procedure and permits to solve the problem mentioned above within the number of iterations proportional to the length of the training sequence.

3 Quickly Optimization Procedure for a Dynamic SVM Criterion

The algorithm for the optimization of the obtained pair-wise separable criterion proposed in this paper is based on the using a general principle of the dynamic programming. Let us to introduce the following notation $\mathbf{z}_t = \begin{bmatrix} \mathbf{z'}_t^T & z''_t \end{bmatrix}^T$, $\mathbf{z'}_t = \begin{bmatrix} \mathbf{a}_t^T & b_t \end{bmatrix}^T$, $\mathbf{z''}_t = [\delta_j]_{j=1}^{N_t}$:

$$\zeta_t(\mathbf{z'}_t) = (\mathbf{z'}_t - \mathbf{z}_t^0)^T \mathbf{Q}_t^0(\mathbf{z'}_t - \mathbf{z}_t^0), \chi_t(\mathbf{z''}_t) = C\mathbf{e}_t^T \mathbf{z''}_t, \mathbf{e}_t = [1]_1^{N_t}, t = 1, ..., T,$$
$$\gamma_t(\mathbf{z'}_{t-1}, \mathbf{z'}_t) = (\mathbf{z'}_t - \mathbf{A}_j \mathbf{z'}_{t-1})^T \mathbf{U}_j(\mathbf{z'}_t - \mathbf{A}_j \mathbf{z'}_{t-1})$$

and rewrite the criterion (4) in a more convenient form

$$J(\mathbf{z}_0, ..., \mathbf{z}_T) = \sum_{t=0}^{T} \zeta_t(\mathbf{z'}_t) + \sum_{t=0}^{T} \chi(\mathbf{z''}_t) + \sum_{t=1}^{T} \gamma_t(\mathbf{z'}_{t-1}, \mathbf{z'}_t) \to \min, \mathbf{z}_t \in Z_t$$

where the areas of acceptable values for variables are determined by the conditions

$$\{\mathbf{z} \in R^{n+2} : \mathbf{g}_j^T \cdot \mathbf{z'}_t + z''_j - 1 \geq 0 , j = (N_{t-1} + 1), ..., N_t, t = 0, ..., T, z''_t \geq 0\}$$

The central idea of the dynamical programming method uses the concept of a sequence of Bellman functions $\tilde{J}_t(\mathbf{z}_t) = \min_{\mathbf{z}_0, ..., \mathbf{z}_{t-1}} J_t([\mathbf{z}_s]_{s=1}^t), [\mathbf{z}_s \in Z_s]_{s=0}^{t-1}$, connected with partial criteria $J_t(\mathbf{z}_0, ..., \mathbf{z}_t) = \sum_{s=0}^{t} \zeta_s(\mathbf{z'}_s) + \sum_{s=0}^{t} \chi(\mathbf{z}_s) + \sum_{s=1}^{t} \gamma_s(\mathbf{z'}_{s-1}, \mathbf{z}_s')$ having the same structure as the full objective function but defined on the set of variables $Z_t = (\mathbf{z}_s, s = 0, ..., t)$. In order to obtain the filtering estimations of the separating hyperplane's parameters we will use the fundamental property of Bellman function

$$\tilde{J}_t(\mathbf{z}_t) = \zeta_t(\mathbf{z'}_t) + \chi(\mathbf{z''}_t) + \min_{\mathbf{z'}_{t-1}, \mathbf{z''}_{t-1}} \left[\gamma_t(\mathbf{z'}_{t-1}, \mathbf{z'}_t) + \tilde{J}_{t-1}(\mathbf{z}_{t-1}) \right], \quad (5)$$

which is called the direct recurrence relation. The procedure begins with the first Bellman function $\tilde{J}_0(\mathbf{z}_0) = \zeta_0(\mathbf{z}_0') + \chi(\mathbf{z''}_0)$. Then Bellman functions are recurrently evaluated for the following observation. And the minimum of Bellman function on every step determines the filtering value of the parameters of the optimal separating hyperplane

$$\hat{\mathbf{z}}_t = \arg \min_{\mathbf{z}_t} \tilde{J}_t(\mathbf{z}_t), \mathbf{z}_t \in Z_t. \quad (6)$$

The optimization procedure is based on the hypothesis that there exists an appropriate compact form for Bellman functions representation, allowed to store this functions in the memory. But in the case then inequality constraints are imposed upon the sought-for variables and the Bellman functions are piecewise quadratic and consequently the dynamic programming procedure cannot be applied immediately. In order to save the computation advantages of the dynamic programming procedure we use here the following trick.

We heuristically replace the non quadratic functions $F_t(\mathbf{z}'_t) = \min_{\mathbf{z}_{t-1} \in \mathbf{Z}_{t-1}} \left[\gamma_t(\mathbf{z}'_{t-1}, \mathbf{z}'_t) + \tilde{J}_{t-1}(\mathbf{z}_{t-1}) \right]$ by the some appropriate quadratic approximation $\hat{F}_t(\mathbf{z}'_t) = \hat{c}_t + (\mathbf{z}'_t - \hat{\mathbf{z}}_t)^T \hat{\mathbf{Q}}_t(\mathbf{z}'_t - \hat{\mathbf{z}}_t)$. Then the following approximations of Bellman functions will be quadratic too and a numerical implementation of the dynamic programming procedure will be possible. Thus, the quadratic approximation of the Bellman function comes to the selection of appropriate values of the parameters $(\hat{c}_t, \hat{\mathbf{z}}_t, \hat{\mathbf{Q}}_t)$ of the quadratic function $\hat{F}_t(\mathbf{z}'_t)$, which would ensure invariance conservation of the main features of, generally speaking, non-quadratic function and consequently the initial Bellman function. Such features are the minimum point position $\hat{\mathbf{z}}_t = \arg\min F_t(\mathbf{z}'_t)$, minimum point value $\hat{c}_t = \min F_t(\mathbf{z}'_t)$, and also the matrix of the second derivatives at the minimum point $\hat{\mathbf{Q}}_t = \nabla^2 F_t(\mathbf{z}'_t)\big|_{\arg\min F_t(\mathbf{z}'_t)}$.

4   Case Study: Spam-Filtering Problem

The object of the experimental study in this paper is the problem of filtering spam-addresses in a result of retrieval request. The behavior of distributors of network advertising constantly improves and as a result a classifier of advertising links used by a search engine should adapt to the behavior of spammers. Consequently we come to problem of construction the time-dependent decision rule.

As the training data we took an anonymous set of hyperlinks URL Reputation Data Set from the repository UCI, first described in the paper [7]. This set consists of the addresses of Web resources for 121 days grouped according to the observation days and contains both advertising and relevant hyperlinks. Every instance in the data base is characterized by 3.2 million features which may be divided into two groups: lexical (hostname, primary domain, TLD and etc.) and host-based (WHOIS info, IP prefix, geographic and etc.). The values of features are normalized from 0 to 1, and the features themselves are anonymous. For carrying out the experiments from this data base in different ways there have been randomly selected 10 instances for each of 11 days taken from the 1st to the 110th day with the step of 10 days. The testing set was comprised by accidentally selected 4000 instances of the 120th day. We deleted the features with the values that are equal on all instances of the training set out of feature descriptions of the instances participating in the experiment, the number of the rest was 326. The experiment was repeated for different sets of training instances. Two algorithms were compared in the course of the experiment: normal support vector machine with the hyperplane, constructed on all instances of the training set and the algorithm of successive refinement of the decision rule, suggested in the paper. In the proposed algorithm of dynamic pattern recognition the parameters of the required decision rule d and d' were chosen by cross-validation procedure, on each iteration of which non-stationary decision rule was constructed without taking into account the instances entered over one of the days. The general per cent of erroneously classified links ε was calculated for each algorithm: the per cent of malicious URLs erroneously classified as benign ones, ε^- and the per cent of benign URLs, erroneously classified as malicious ones ε^+. As the results given in the table show, the incremental learning algorithm of the pattern recognition allows to improve significantly the quality of recognition that indirectly confirms non-stationary character of the data used for the experiments.

Algorithm	ε^-, %	ε^+, %	ε, %
SVM	32.32	5.94	16.0
Incremental Algorithm	14.96	4.49	8.49

5   Conclusions

In the paper the adaptation of the general definition of the pattern recognition learning problem with two classes of instances in the finite-dimensional space of real features is made under the conditions of non-stationary environment. The non-stationary property of environment is considered as time-changing decision rule. Under this assumption the learning criterion appeared a dynamic modification of SVM criterion. Also we have suggested optimization algorithm for Dynamic SVM having the linear computational complexity relative to the length of the training time series. Our algorithm was applied to the problem of filtering irrelevant or publicity hyperlinks as a result of retrieval request and its application achieved a good enough result as compared with classical SVM.

References

1. Widmer, G., Kubat, M.: Learning in the presence of concept drift and hidden contexts. Machine Learning 23(1), 69–101 (1996)
2. Salganicoff, M.: Tolerating concept and sampling shift in lazy learning using prediction error context switching. AI Review, Special Issue on Lazzy Learning 11(1-5), 133–155 (1997)
3. Klinkenberg, R.: Learning drifting concepts example selection vs. example weighting. Intelligent data analysis, Special Issue on Incremental Learning Systems Capable of Dealing with Concept Drift 8(3) (2004)
4. Harries, M., Sammut, C., Horn, K.: Extracting hidden context. Machine Learning 32(2), 101–126 (1998)
5. Muhlbaier, M.D., Polikar, R.: An Ensemble Approach for Incremental Learning in Nonstationary Environments. In: Haindl, M., Kittler, J., Roli, F. (eds.) MCS 2007. LNCS, vol. 4472, pp. 490–500. Springer, Heidelberg (2007)
6. Tatarchuk, A.I., Sulimova, V.V., Mottl, V.V., Windridge, D.: Method of relevant potential functions for selective combination of diverse information in the pattern recognition learning based on Bayesian approach. In: MMRO-14: Conf. Proc., Suzdal, pp. 188–191 (2009)
7. Ma, J., Saul, K.L., Savage, S., Voelker, G.: Identifying Suspicious URLs: An Application of Large-Scale Online Learning. In: Proceedings of the International Conference on Machine Learning (ICML), Montreal, Quebec, June 2009, pp. 681–688 (2009)

The Classification of Noisy Sequences Generated by Similar HMMs

A.A. Popov and T.A. Gultyaeva

Department of Software and Database Engineering,
Novosibirsk State Technical University, Russia
alex@fpm.ami.nstu.ru, gult_work@mail.ru

Abstract. The method for classification performance improvement using hidden Markov models (HMM) is proposed. The k-nearest neighbors (kNN) classifier is used in the feature space produced by these HMM. Only the similar models with the noisy original sequences assumption are discussed. The research results on simulated data for two-class classification problem are presented.

Keywords: Hidden Markov Model, Derivation, k Nearest Neighbors.

1 Introduction

HMM are a powerful tool for modeling of various processes and pattern recognition. By their nature, Markov models allow to deal with spatial-temporal sequence characteristics directly and therefore they became widely-used [1], [2], [3]. However, despite a wide circulation of models of this kind, HMM possess low enough classification abilities. Though these models are widespread HMM possess of sufficiently low classification properties. At the same time it is well known that the HMM have a fairly low classification ability.We understand the classification problem by the following. We have an object set discriminated on classes by expert (training with teacher). This object set is named the training set. We want to create an algorithm that will be able to classify a test object from origin set. The two-class classification problem using the matrix of distances between the objects is discussed in this article. In this case, the each object is being described by distances to all other objects from training set. The method of the nearest neighbors, the Parzen windows method and the method of potential functions work with input data of such type. The set of Gaussian time sequences generated by two HMMs with similar parameters are taken as classification objects. In order to approximate real-world examples all observed time sequences being distorted. The task was to compare the capabilities of traditional methods of classification with a simple nearest neighbor classifier [4] in the space of first derivatives of the likelihood function for the HMM parameters.

The remainder of this article is organized as follows. Section 2 introduces the method of solution of assigned task. Section 3 provides some results of computational experiments. Section 4 summarizes our findings.

S.O. Kuznetsov et al. (Eds.): PReMI 2011, LNCS 6744, pp. 30–35, 2011.

2   The Method of Sequences Classification

An HMM is completely described by the following parameters:

1. The initial state distribution $\Pi = \{\pi_i\}, i = \overline{1, N}$, where $\pi_i = P\{q_1 = i\}$ and N – is the number of hidden states in the model.
2. The matrix of state transition probabilities $A = \{a_{ij}\}$, where $a_{ij} = P\{q_t = j | q_{t-1} = i\}, i, j = \overline{1, N}, t = \overline{1, T}$, where T – is the length of observable sequence.
3. The matrix of observation symbols probabilities $B = \{b_{ij}\}, i = \overline{1, N}, j = \overline{1, M}$, where $b_i(j) = P\{o_t = v_j | q_t = i\}, o_t$ – is the symbol observed at the moment of time $t = \overline{1, T}, M$ – is the number of observation states in the model. In this work the case when function observable symbol probabilitie distribution is described by a mix of normal distributions is considered in such a manner that the one hidden state is associated with one observable state: $b_i(t) = (\sqrt{2\pi}\sigma_i)e^{-(o_t - \mu_i)^2/2\sigma_i^2}, i = \overline{1, N}, t = \overline{1, T}$.

Thus, HMM is completely described by the matrix of state transition probabilities, the probabilities of observation symbols and the initial state distribution: $\lambda = (A, B, \pi)$.

A classifier based on log-likelihood function is traditionally used. The sequence O is considered as being generated by model λ_1 if (1) is satisfied:

$$lnL(O|\lambda_1) > lnL(O|\lambda_2). \tag{1}$$

Otherwise, it is considered that the sequence is generated by model λ_2.

Some authors (e.g. [5],[6]) propose to use the spaces of the so-called secondary features as a feature space in which the sequences are being classified. For example, forward-probabilities and backward-probabilities, which are used for computation of probability that the sequence is generated by model λ, can be used as a secondary features. The first derivatives of space of likelihood function logarithm are also used. These derivatives are being taken with respect to different model parameters. The authors [5] offer to include the original sequence into the feature vector also. In this work the performance of two-class classification in the space of the first derivatives of the likelihood function is discussed.

The classification problem states as follows. There are two groups of training sequences: the first group consists of sequences generated by λ_1, and the second group – by λ_2. Usually, in order to determine which class the test sequence O^{test} is belongs to the rule (1) is used. Because the model parameters λ_1 and λ_2 are unknown, at first one needs to estimate them (for example, the algorithm of Baum-Welch is used for it), and then calculate them according to rule (1).

If the competing models have similar parameters, and the observed sequences are not purely Gaussian sequence, the traditional classification technique using (1) does not always give acceptable results.

The following schema that increases discriminating features of HMM.

Step 1. For each training sequence $O_l^{learn_i}, i = \overline{1, K_l}, l = \overline{1, 2}$ where K_l – the count of training sequences for class with number l, the characteristic vector which can consist of all or a part of the features is being formed. The likelihood function is being calculated as for true class model to which training vectors are belong to as for model of other class. As a result the characteristic vector for the training sequence $O_l^{learn_i}$ generated by model λ_1 consists of two subvectors: $V_l^{learn_i} = (\, Z(O_l^{learn_i}, \lambda_1), \qquad Z(O_l^{learn_i}, \lambda_2)\,)^T$, where the first subvector consists of features, initiated by the model λ_1, and the second – by the model λ_2.

Step 2. Similarly, the characteristic vector is calculated for the test sequence O^{test}.

Step 3. Using a metric based classifier (e.g. kNN) it is become clear to which class O^{test} belongs to.

3   Computing Experiments

Investigations were performed under following assumptions. The models λ_1 and λ_2 are defined on the hidden Markov chains with identical and they have differences in the matrix of transition probabilities only. For the first model λ_1 and for the second model λ_2 the difference was in transitive probabilities only:

$$\mathbf{A}_{\lambda_1} = \begin{pmatrix} 0.1 & 0.7 & 0.2 \\ 0.2 & 0.2 & 0.6 \\ 0.8 & 0.1 & 0.1 \end{pmatrix}, \; \mathbf{A}_{\lambda_2} = \begin{pmatrix} 0.2 & 0.6 & 0.2 \\ 0.2 & 0.3 & 0.5 \\ 0.7 & 0.1 & 0.2 \end{pmatrix}.$$

The Gaussian distribution parameters for the models λ_1 and λ_2 are chosen identical: $\mu_1 = 0$, $\mu_2 = 5$, $\mu_3 = 10$, $\sigma_1^2 = \sigma_2^2 = \sigma_3^2 = 1$. The probabilities of initial states are coincide also: $\pi = (1, 0, 0)$. Thus, models have turned out very close to each other, and, hence, sequences differ among themselves very weakly.

The training and testing sequences have been simulated by the Monte-Carlo method. It has been generated 5 training sets of 100 sequences for each of the classes to perform investigations. For each training set 500 test signals were generated for each class. The results of classification have been averaged. The length of the each sequence has been set to 100.

3.1   The Additive Noise

The first variant of distortion of a true sequence assumed additive superposition of the noise component distributed under some distribution law. We denoted the sequence simulated on model λ through u. Then at superposition of noise e on this sequence according to the following formula we received noisy sequence with an additive noise: $y = (1 - \omega)u + \omega e$, where ω shows the influence of sequence distortion.

The space of the first derivatives of likelihood function with respect to elements of transition probabilities matrix has been chosen as the feature space for the kNN classifier. Further in Tables 1–3 following designations are used: APD – the average percent of difference between the results of the kNN classifier and

Table 1. The comparison of classification's results at the additive noise

ω	$e \succ N(0, 25)$		$e \succ C(0, 0.01)$	
	APD	AP	APD	AP
0.1	-1.5	89.12	11.18	88.56
0.2	-1.48	88.98	7.86	84.86
0.3	-2.14	85.82	22.62	84.26
0.4	-1.64	80.58	2.4	74.14
0.5	-0.52	72.28	-1.88	72.44
0.6	-4.28	58.98	-3.44	68.08
0.7	-2.66	53.18	-3.08	67.18
0.8	-2.82	49.26	-0.12	49.76
0.9	-1.44	49.88	0.92	50.52

the results of traditional classification; AP – the average percent of correctly classified sequences using the kNN classifier.

The classification results with the normal noise distribution are shown in Table 1 in the 2nd and the 3rd columns. As follows from this experiment, the kNN classifier using the space of the first derivatives of likelihood function gives worse results than traditional classifier. It is explained by the fact that the noises and sequences have identical normal distribution, and the algorithm of Baum-Welch being used for parameters estimation is exactly tuned for parameters estimation of probability distribution function of observed sequences in the conditions when this function is the normal distribution function. The results of classification comparison at the noise distributed on the Cauchy distribution law are in Table 1 in the 4th and the 5th columns. In this case there is opposite situation: the kNN classifier gives better results at the noise level $\omega \leq 0.4$.

3.2   Probability Substitution of a Sequence by Noise

The second variant of distortion of a true sequence assumed partial substitution of a sequence by noise under the probability scheme, i.e. with some probability p instead of the true sequence associated with some hidden state, the noise sequence was appearing. At this time the parameters of noisy sequence were varying in the different experiments.

The results of classification comparison at the noise distributed on the normal distribution law are in Table 2 from the 2nd to the 5rd columns. In the 2nd and the 3rd columns as a result of superposition of such noise there was a displacement of the estimated parameters of expectation, but the traditional classifier showed better results than the proposed one. In the next two columns there is stable classification results improvement when the probability of noise appearance $p \leq 0.6$. It is explained by the fact that the parameters of distribution of noise generator are very big values unlike the previous case. The results of classification comparison when the noise has a Cauchy distribution are shown in

Table 2. The comparison of classification's results at the probability substitution of a sequence by noise that hasn't dependence on the hidden state

	$e \succ N(-5, 1)$		$e \succ N(30, 100)$		$e \succ C(0, 0.1)$	
p	APD	AP	APD	AP	APD	AP
0.1	-2.44	81.88	21.36	78.28	12.32	82.1
0.2	-2.96	78.38	3.96	52.88	17.4	76.76
0.3	-4.6	71.04	3.74	51.99	21.4	73.68
0.4	-2.62	69.84	6.46	52.61	6.42	61.32
0.5	-2.48	65.32	1.32	51.62	3.42	54.2
0.6	-2.45	59.81	2.84	52.72	2.58	52.22
0.7	-0.8	55.54	-1.3	50.85	0.71	50.49
0.8	-2.54	52.46	1.76	50.14	1.66	51.64
0.9	-0.1	50.1	0.04	50.24	1.09	50.83

Table 2 in the 6th and the 7th columns. In this case there is stable advantage of the kNN classifier based classifier.

Table 3. The comparison of classification's results at the probability substitution of a sequence by noise that has dependence from the hidden state

	$e \succ N$		$e \succ C$	
ω	APD	AP	APD	AP
0.1	-0.58	79.1	11.46	84.06
0.2	2.78	70.54	17.08	80.42
0.3	4.3	65.52	13.66	63.04
0.4	3.78	57.2	3.17	53.95
0.5	3.8	56.94	1.74	52.2
0.6	2.96	57.08	0.81	51.11
0.7	0.12	60.94	0.14	50.18
0.8	-0.6	70.04	0.85	51.53
0.9	-2.27	77.35	1.36	50.98

Classification results with the normal noise distribution: $e_1 \succ N(10, 1)$, $e_2 \succ N(0, 1)$, $e_3 \succ N(5, 1)$ (where e_i, $i = \overline{1, 3}$ – it is the noise appearing when the HMM is in the ith hidden state) are shown in Table 3 in the 2nd and the 3rd columns. The observed sequences have the double-mode distribution instead of single-mode distribution expected at $p \in [0.2; 0.7]$. The traditional classifier is slightly worse than the proposed kNN classifier in this situation. The results of classification comparison at the noise distributed on the Cauchy distribution law: $e_1 \succ C(0, 1)$, $e_2 \succ C(5, 1)$, $e_3 \succ C(10, 1)$, are in Table 3 in the 4th and the 5th columns. In this case the noise substituting the original sequences is differed from the last by using distribution law of random variables only. In this experiment it is observed the constant advantage of the offered method that used the kNN classifier. Similar results were obtained in the noise parameters distributed by Cauchy distribution law: $e_1 \succ C(0, 1)$, $e_2 \succ C(0, 0.5)$, $e_3 \succ C(0, 0.1)$, i.e. with the absence of noise displacement but with different scale of distribution.

4   Conclusion

In this article it was shown that the feature space generated by the HMM can be used for the classification of sequences generated by the similar models. The first derivatives of likelihood function logarithm with respect to the parameters of HMM were used as the features. The kNN classifier was used in this feature space. Studies have shown that with similar models and signals with the distortion the proposed method can improve the quality of classification.

References

1. Rabiner, L.R.: A Tutorial on Hidden Markov Models and Selected Applications in Speech Recognition. Proc. IEEE 77(2), 257–285 (1989)
2. Cappé, O.: Ten years of HMMs. CNRS, LTCI & ENST, Dpt. TSI,
   http://perso.telecom-paristech.fr/~cappe/docs/hmmbib.html
3. Mottl, V.V., Muchnik, I.B.: Hidden Markov Models in Structural Signal Analysis Moscow, Russia (1999) (in Russian)
4. Zagorujko, N.G.: Applied methods of analysis of data and knowledge. Novosibirsk, Russia (1999) (in Russian)
5. Chen, L., Man, H.: Combination of Fisher Scores and Appearance Based by Features For Face. In: Proc. of the 2003 ACM SIGMM Workshop on Biometrics Methods and Applications, Berkeley, California, USA, pp. 74–81 (2003)
6. Aran, O., Akarun, L.: Recognizing Two Handed Gestures with Generative, Discriminative and Ensemble Methods Via Fisher Kernels. In: Gunsel, B., Jain, A.K., Tekalp, A.M., Sankur, B. (eds.) MRCS 2006. LNCS, vol. 4105, pp. 159–166. Springer, Heidelberg (2006)

$NDoT$: Nearest Neighbor Distance Based Outlier Detection Technique

Neminath Hubballi[1], Bidyut Kr. Patra[2], and Sukumar Nandi[1]

[1] Department of Computer Science & Engineering, Indian Institute of Technology Guwahati,
Assam 781039, India
[2] Department of Computer Science & Engineering, Tezpur University, Tezpur
Assam-784 028, India
{neminath,bidyut,sukumar}@iitg.ernet.in

Abstract. In this paper, we propose a nearest neighbor based outlier detection algorithm, $NDoT$. We introduce a parameter termed as *Nearest Neighbor Factor* (NNF) to measure the degree of outlierness of a point with respect to its neighborhood. Unlike the previous outlier detection methods $NDoT$ works by a voting mechanism. Voting mechanism binarizes the decision compared to the top-N style of algorithms. We evaluate our method experimentally and compare results of $NDoT$ with a classical outlier detection method LOF and a recently proposed method $LDOF$. Experimental results demonstrate that $NDoT$ outperforms $LDOF$ and is comparable with LOF.

1 Introduction

Finding outliers in a collection of patterns is a very well known problem in the data mining field. An outlier is a pattern which is dissimilar with respect to the rest of the patterns in the dataset. Depending upon the application domain, outliers are of particular interest. In some cases presence of outliers adversely affect the conclusions drawn out of the analysis and hence need to be eliminated beforehand. In other cases outliers are the centre of interest as in the case of intrusion detection system, credit card fraud detection. There are varied reasons for outlier generation in the first place. For example outliers may be generated due to measurement impairments, rare normal events exhibiting entirely different characteristics, deliberate actions etc. Detecting outliers may lead to the discovery of truly unexpected behaviour and help avoid wrong conclusions etc. Thus irrespective of the underlying causes for outlier generation and insight inferred, these points need to be identified from a collection of patterns. There are number of methods proposed in the literature for detecting outliers [1] and are mainly of three types as distance based, density based and nearest neighbor based.

Distance based: These techniques count the number of patterns falling within a selected threshold distance R from a point x in the dataset. If the count is more than a preset number of patterns then x is considered as normal and otherwise outlier. Knorr. et. al. [2] define outlier as "an object o in a dataset D is a $DB(p, T)$-outlier if at least fraction p of the objects in D lies greater than distance T from o". DOLPHIN [3] is a recent work based on this definition of outlier given by Knorr.

S.O. Kuznetsov et al. (Eds.): PReMI 2011, LNCS 6744, pp. 36–42, 2011.

Density based: These techniques measure density of a point x within a small region by counting number of points within a neighborhood region. Breunig et al. [4] introduced a concept of local outliers which are detected based on the local density of points. Local density of a point x depends on its k nearest neighbors points. A score known as *Local Outlier Factor* is assigned to every point based on this local density. All data points are sorted in decreasing order of LOF value. Points with high scores are detected as outliers. Tang et al. [5] proposed an improved version of LOF known as *Connectivity Outlier Factor* for sparse dataset. LOF is shown to be not effective in detecting outliers if the dataset is sparse [5,6].

Nearest neighbor based: These outlier detection techniques compare the distance of the point x with its k nearest neighbors. If x has a short distance to its k neighbors it is considered as normal otherwise it is considered as outlier. The distance measure used is largely domain and attribute dependent. Ramaswamy et al. [7] measure the distances of all the points to their k^{th} nearest neighbors and sort the points according to the distance values. Top N number of points are declared as outliers.

Zhang et al. [6] showed that LOF can generate high scores for cluster points if value of k is more than the cluster size and subsequently misses genuine outlier points. To overcome this problem, they proposed a distance based outlier factor called $LDOF$. $LDOF$ is the ratio of k nearest neighbors average distance to k nearest neighbors inner distance. Inner distance is the average pair-wise distance of the k nearest neighbor set of a point x. A point x is declared as genuine outlier if the ratio is more than 1 else it is considered as normal. However, if an outlier point (say, O) is located between two dense clusters (Fig. 1) it fails to detect O as outlier. The $LDOF$ of O is less than 1 as k nearest neighbors of O contain points from both the clusters. This observation can also be found in sparse data.

In this paper, we propose an outlier detection algorithm, $NDoT$ (<u>N</u>earest Neighbor <u>D</u>istance Based <u>o</u>utlier Detection <u>T</u>echnique). We introduce a parameter termed as *Nearest Neighbor Factor* (NNF) to measure the degree of outlierness of a point. *Nearest Neighbor Factor* (NNF) of a point with respect to one of its neighbors is the ratio of distance between the point and the neighbor, and average knn distance of the neighbor. $NDoT$ measures NNF of a point with respect to all its neighbors individually. If NNF of the point w.r.t majority of its neighbors is more than a pre-defined threshold,

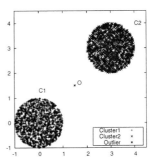

Fig. 1. Uniform Dataset

then the point is declared as a potential outlier. We perform experiments on both synthetic and real world datasets to evaluate our outlier detection method.

The rest of the paper is organized as follows. Section 2 describes proposed method. Experimental results and conclusion are discussed in section 3 and section 3.2, respectively.

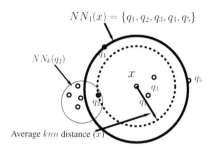

Fig. 2. The k nearest neighbor of x with $k = 4$

2   Proposed Outlier Detection Technique : $NDoT$

In this section, we develop a formal definition for $Nearest\ Neighbor\ Factor\ (NNF)$ and describe the proposed outlier detection algorithm, $NDoT$.

Definition 1 (*$k\ Nearest\ Neighbor\ (knn)Set$*). *Let $\mathcal{D}$ be a dataset and x be a point in $\mathcal{D}$. For a natural number k and a distance function d, a set $NN_k(x) = \{q \in \mathcal{D}|d(x,q) \leq d(x,q'), q' \in \mathcal{D}\}$ is called knn of x if the following two conditions hold.*

1. *$|NN_k| > k$ if q' is not unique in $\mathcal{D}$ or $|NN_k| = k$, otherwise.*
2. *$|NN_k \setminus N^{q'}| = k - 1$, where $N^{q'}$ is the set of all q' point(s).*

Definition 2 (*Average knn distance*). *Let NN_k be the knn of a point $x \in \mathcal{D}$. Average knn distance of x is the average of distances between x and $q \in NN_k.i.e.$*

$$Average\ knn\ distance\ (x) = \sum_q d(x,q|\quad q \in NN_k)/|NN_k|$$

Average knn distance of a point x is the average of distances between x and its knn. If *Average knn distance* of x is less compared to other point y, it indicates that x's neighborhood region is more densed compared to the region where y resides.

Definition 3 (*Nearest Neighbor Factor (NNF)*). *Let x be a point in $\mathcal{D}$ and $NN_k(x)$ be the knn of x. The NNF of x with respect to $q \in NN_k(x)$ is the ratio of $d(x,q)$ and Average knn distance of q.*

$$NNF(x,q) = d(x,q)/Average\ knn\ distance(q) \tag{1}$$

The NNF of x with respect to one of its nearest neighbors is the ratio of distance between x and the neighbor, and *Average knn distance* of that neighbor. The proposed method $NDoT$ calculates NNF of each point with respect to all of its knn and uses a voting mechanism to decide whether a point is outlier or not.

Algorithm 1 describes steps involved in $NDoT$. Given a dataset $\mathcal{D}$, it calculates knn and *Average knn distance* for all points in $\mathcal{D}$. In the next step, it computes *Nearest Neighbor Factor* for all points in the dataset using the previously calculated knn and *Average knn distance*. $NDoT$ decides whether x is an outlier or not based on a voting mechanism. Votes are counted based on the generated NNF values with respect to

---

Algorithm 1. $NDoT(\mathcal{D}, k)$

---

for each $x \in \mathcal{D}$ **do**
   Calculate knn Set $NN_k(x)$ of x.
   Calculate $Average\ knn\ distance$ of x.
end for
for each $x \in \mathcal{D}$ **do**
   $V_{count} = 0$ /*V_{count} counts number of votes for x being an outlier */
   for each $q \in NN_k(x)$ **do**
      if $NNF(x, q) \geq \delta$ **then**
         $V_{count} = V_{count} + 1$
      end if
   end for
   if $V_{count} \geq \frac{2}{3} \times |NN_k(x)|$ **then**
      Output x as an outlier in $\mathcal{D}$.
   end if
end for

---

all of its k nearest neighbors. If $NNF(x, q \mid q \in NN_k(x))$ is more than a threshold δ (in experiments $\delta = 1.5$ is considered), x is considered as outlier with respect to q. Subsequently, a vote is counted for x being an outlier point. If the number of votes are at least $2/3$ of the number of nearest neighbors then x is declared as an outlier, otherwise x is a normal point.

Complexity Time and space requirements of *NDoT* are as follows.

1. Finding knn set and *Average knn distance* of all points takes time of $O(n^2)$, where n is the size of the dataset. The space requirement of the step is $O(n)$.
2. Deciding a point x to be outlier or not takes time $O(|NN_k(x)|) = O(k)$. For whole dataset the step takes time of $O(nk) = O(n)$, as k is a small constant.

Thus the overall time and space requirements are $O(n^2)$ and $O(n)$, respectively.

3 Experimental Evaluations

In this section, we describe experimental results on different datasets. We used two synthetic and two real world datsets in our experiments. We also compared our results with classical LOF algorithm and also with one of its recent enhancement $LDOF$. Results demonstrate that $NDoT$ outperforms both LOF and $LDOF$ on synthetic datasets. We measure the *Recall* given by Equation 2 as an evaluation metric. *Recall* measures how many genuine outliers are there among the outliers detected by the algorithm. Both $LDOF$ and LOF are of top N style algorithms. For a chosen value of N, $LDOF$ and LOF consider N highest scored points as outliers. However, $NDoT$ makes a binary decision about a point as either an outlier or normal. In order to compare our algorithm with $LDOF$ and LOF we used different values of N.

$$Recall = TP/(TP + FN) \tag{2}$$

where TP is number of true positive cases and FN is the number of false negative cases. It is to be noted that top N style algorithms select highest scored N points as outliers. Therefore, remaining N-TP are false positive (FP) cases. As FP can be inferred based on the values of N and TP we do not explicitly report them for $LDOF$ and LOF.

3.1   Synthetic Datasets

There are two synthetic datasets designed to evaluate the detection ability (*Recall*) of algorithms. These two experiments are briefed subsequently.

Uniform dataset. Uniform distribution dataset is a two dimensional synthetic dataset of size 3139. .It has two circular shaped clusters filled with highly densed points. There is a single outlier (say O) placed exactly in the middle of the two densed clusters as shown in the Figure 1. We ran our algorithm along with LOF and $LDOF$ on this dataset and measured the *Recall* for all the three algorithms. Obtained results for different values of k are tabulated in Table 1. This table

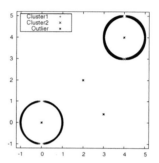

Fig. 3. Circular dataset

shows that, $NDoT$ and LOF could detect the single outlier consistently while $LDOF$ failed to detect it. In case of $LDOF$ the point O has knn set from both the clusters, thus the average inner distance is much higher than the average knn distance. This results in a $LDOF$ value less than 1. However, NNF value of O is more than 1.5 with respect to all its neighbors $q \in C_1$ or C_2. Because, q's average knn distance is much smaller than the distance between O and q.

Table 1 shows the *Recall* for all the three algorithms and also the false positives for $NDoT$ (while the number of false positives for $LDOF$ and LOF are implicit). It can be noted that, for any dataset of this nature $NDoT$ outperforms the other two algorithms in terms of number of false positive cases detected.

Circular dataset. This dataset has two hollow circular shaped clusters with 1000 points in each of the clusters. Four outliers are placed as shown in Figure 3. There are two outliers exactly at the centers of two circles and other two are outside.

The results on this dataset for the three algorithms are shown in the Table 2. Again we notice both $NDoT$ and LOF consistently detect all the four outliers for all the k values while $LDOF$ fails to detect them. Similar reasons raised for the previous experiments can be attributed to the poor performance of $LDOF$.

Table 1. *Recall* comparison for uniform dataset

k Value	*NDoT*		*LDOF*			*LOF*		
	Recall	FP	Top 25	Top 50	Top 100	Top 25	Top 50	Top 100
5	100.00%	47	00.00%	00.00%	00.00%	100.00%	100.00%	100.00%
9	100.00%	21	00.00%	00.00%	00.00%	100.00%	100.00%	100.00%
21	100.00%	2	00.00%	00.00%	00.00%	100.00%	100.00%	100.00%
29	100.00%	0	00.00%	00.00%	00.00%	100.00%	100.00%	100.00%
35	100.00%	0	00.00%	00.00%	00.00%	100.00%	100.00%	100.00%
51	100.00%	0	00.00%	00.00%	00.00%	100.00%	100.00%	100.00%
65	100.00%	0	00.00%	00.00%	00.00%	100.00%	100.00%	100.00%

Table 2. *Recall* comparison for circular dataset with 4 outliers

k Value	*NDoT*		*LDOF*			*LOF*		
	Recall	FP	Top 25	Top 50	Top 100	Top 25	Top 50	Top 100
5	100.00%	0	50.00%	100.00%	100.00%	100.00%	100.00%	100.00%
9	100.00%	0	25.00%	75.00%	100.00%	100.00%	100.00%	100.00%
15	100.00%	10	25.00%	75.00%	100.00%	100.00%	100.00%	100.00%
21	100.00%	10	25.00%	50.00%	100.00%	100.00%	100.00%	100.00%
29	100.00%	10	25.00%	50.00%	100.00%	100.00%	100.00%	100.00%

3.2 Real World Datasets

In this section, we describe experiments on two realworld datasets taken from UCI machine learning repository. Experimental results are elaborated subsequently.

Shuttle dataset. This dataset has 9 real valued attributes with 58000 instances distributed across 7 classes. In our experiments, we picked the test dataset and used class label 2 which has only 13 instances as outliers and remaining all instances as normal. In this experiment, we performed three-fold cross validation by injecting 5 out of 13 instances as outliers into randomly selected 1000 instances of the normal dataset. Results obtained by the three algorithms are shown in Table 3. It can be observed that *NDoT*'s performance is consistently better than *LDOF* and is comparable to *LOF*.

Table 3. *Recall* Comparison for Shuttle Dataset

k Value	*NDoT*	*LDOF*			*LOF*		
		Top 25	Top 50	Top 100	Top 25	Top 50	Top 100
5	80.00%	20.00%	20.00%	26.66%	26.66%	53.33%	66.66%
9	93.33%	26.66%	33.33%	33.33%	06.66%	26.66%	93.33%
15	100.00%	20.00%	33.33%	53.33%	00.00%	26.66%	100.00%
21	100.00%	20.00%	33.33%	66.66%	00.00%	26.66%	80.00%
35	100.00%	40.00%	73.33%	73.33%	00.00%	20.00%	53.33%

Forest covertype dataset. This dataset is developed at the university of Colarado to help natural resource managers predict inventory information. This dataset has 54 attributes having a total of 581012 instances distributed across 7 cover types (classes). In our experiential, we selected the class label 6 (Douglas-fir) with 17367 instances and randomly picked 5 instances from the class 4 (Cottonwood/Willow) as outliers. Results obtained are shown in Table 4. We can notice that, $NDoT$ outperforms both $LDOF$ and LOF on this dataset.

Table 4. *Recall* Comparison for CoverType Dataset

k Value	$NDoT$	$LDOF$			LOF		
		Top 25	Top 50	Top 100	Top 25	Top 50	Top 100
35	60.00%	40.00%	40.00%	40.00%	00.00%	10.00%	10.00%
51	80.00%	40.00%	40.00%	40.00%	00.00%	10.00%	10.00%

Conclusion

$NDoT$ is a nearest neighbor based outlier detection algorithm, which works on a voting mechanism by measuring $Nearest\ Neighbor\ Factor(NNF)$. The NNF of a point w.r. t one of its neighbor measures the degree of outlierness of the point. Experimental results demonstrated effectiveness of the $NDoT$ on both synthetic and real world datasets.

References

1. Chandola, V., Banerjee, A., Kumar, V.: Outlier detection: A survey. ACM Computing Survey, 1–58 (2007)
2. Knorr, E.M., Ng, R.T.: Algorithms for mining distance-based outliers in large datasets. In: VLDB 1998: Proceedings of 24th International Conference on Very Large Databases, pp. 392–403 (1998)
3. Angiulli, F., Fassetti, F.: Dolphin: An efficient algorithm for mining distance-based outliers in very large datasets. ACM Transactions and Knowledge Discovery Data 3, 4:1–4:57 (2009)
4. Breunig, M., Kriegel, H.P., Ng, R.T., Sander, J.: Lof: identifying density-based local outliers. In: SIGMOD 2000:Proceedings of the 19th ACM SIGMOD international conference on Management of data, pp. 93–104. ACM Press, New York (2000)
5. Tang, J., Chen, Z., Fu, A.W.-c., Cheung, D.W.: Enhancing Effectiveness of Outlier Detections for Low Density Patterns. In: Chen, M.-S., Yu, P.S., Liu, B. (eds.) PAKDD 2002. LNCS (LNAI), vol. 2336, pp. 535–548. Springer, Heidelberg (2002)
6. Zhang, K., Hutter, M., Jin, H.: A new local distance-based outlier detection approach for scattered real-world data. In: Theeramunkong, T., Kijsirikul, B., Cercone, N., Ho, T.-B. (eds.) PAKDD 2009. LNCS, vol. 5476, pp. 813–822. Springer, Heidelberg (2009)
7. Ramaswamy, S., Rastogi, R., Shim, K.: Efficient algorithms for mining outliers from large data sets. SIGMOD Record 29, 427–438 (2000)

Some Remarks on the Relation between Annotated Ordered Sets and Pattern Structures

Tim B. Kaiser[1] and Stefan E. Schmidt[2]

[1] SAP AG, Walldorf
[2] Institut für Algebra, Technische Universität Dresden

Abstract. We exhibit an intimate connection between the concept of an *annotated ordered set* and that of a *pattern structure*. This enables an exchange of ideas and techniques between both domains.

1   Introduction

Pattern structures were introduced in [KG01] to model information. The usefulness of annotated ordered sets for similar purposes was studied in [KSJ08]. Here, we compare and relate the two approaches. To keep the article rationably self-contained we recapitulate both concepts. We see how theorems can be moved between both domains and fix a theorem from [KG01].

In the first section we will introduce annotated ordered sets. In the second section we will outline pattern structures. In the third section we will argue that pattern structures can be understood as a certain sub-class of annotated ordered sets and review basic constructions and theorems. In the fourth section we will correct a theorem about pattern structures and their projections.

The reader is assumed to be knowledgeable about the basics of order theory and formal concept analysis as can be found in [DP90] and [GW99].

2   Annotated Ordered Sets

Annotated ordered sets were introduced to model taxonomies, e.g. appearing in the realm of the Gene Ontology.

Definition 1 ((elementary) annotated ordered set). *Let* $\mathcal{P} := (P, \leq_{\mathcal{P}})$ *be a finite ordered set (poset), let* X *be a finite set of* labels, *and let* $F : X \to 2^P$ *be an* annotation function. *Then we call* $\mathbb{O} := (\mathcal{P}, X, F)$ *an* annotated ordered set *and refer to* (X, F) *as an* annotation *of* $\mathcal{P}$. *In case* $\mathcal{P}$ *is a (complete) lattice we call* $\mathbb{O}$ *an* annotated (complete) lattice *denoted* $\mathbb{L}$. *If* $|F(x)| = 1$ *for all* $x \in X$, *for convenience, we regard* F *as a map from* X *to* P *and say that* $\mathbb{O}$ *is* elementary.

It is interesting to note that an annotated ordered set $(\mathcal{P}, X, F)$ can be regarded as a formal context with ordered attributes $(X, \mathcal{P}, F_R)$ since every mapping $T : A \to 2^B$ can be interpreted as a relation $T_R \subseteq A \times B$ where xT_Ry if and only if $y \in T(x)$. But the concept lattice of this formal context would not yield the

S.O. Kuznetsov et al. (Eds.): PReMI 2011, LNCS 6744, pp. 43–48, 2011.

intended concept lattice representation of the annotated ordered set, since it does not express the semantics of annotation in a taxonomy, that is, if we annotate an example to a class in a taxonomy we implicitly mean that it belongs to all the super-classes of the class it was annotated to. Additionally, modelling the annotated taxonomy as formal context would be rather counter-intuitive.

We describe how an appropriate formal context can be derived from an annotated ordered set to produce its *concept lattice representation*. For an ordered set $\mathcal{P} := (P, \leq_{\mathcal{P}})$ and node $q \in P$ we denote by $\uparrow q := \{p \in P \mid q \leq_{\mathcal{P}} p\}$ the principal filter of q and dually by $\downarrow q$ the principal ideal. Also, for later use, for $N \subseteq P$ let $\downarrow_N q := \{n \in N \mid n \leq_{\mathcal{P}} q\}$ and dually $\uparrow_N q := \{n \in N \mid q \leq_{\mathcal{P}} n\}$. Given an annotated ordered set $\mathbb{O} := (\mathcal{P}, X, F)$ we can construct a formal context $\mathbb{K}_{\mathbb{O}} := (X, P, I)$ where we define the relation $I \subseteq X \times P$ by $xIp :\Longleftrightarrow \downarrow p \cap F(x) \neq \emptyset$.

This means that I equals $F_R \circ \leq_{\mathcal{P}}$. Note that in the case of an elementary annotated ordered set the definition of I can be written as $xIp :\Longleftrightarrow F(x) \leq p$ since F is regarded as mapping to P (instead of 2^P).

The concept lattice of $\mathbb{K}_{\mathbb{O}}$ will be denoted by $\underline{\mathfrak{B}}_{\mathbb{O}} := (\mathfrak{B}_{\mathbb{O}}, \leq_{\underline{\mathfrak{B}}_{\mathbb{O}}})$, where $\mathfrak{B}_{\mathbb{O}} := \mathfrak{B}(\mathbb{K}_{\mathbb{O}})$ is the set of formal concepts of the formal context $\mathbb{K}_{\mathbb{O}}$ [GW99]. $\underline{\mathfrak{B}}_{\mathbb{O}}$ is called the *concept lattice representation* of the annotated ordered set $\mathbb{O}$.

In case $\mathbb{O}$ forms an annotated complete lattice and $(A, B) \in \mathfrak{B}_{\mathbb{O}}$ is a formal concept in $\mathfrak{B}_{\mathbb{O}}$, we observe that $A = B^I$ is the set of all $x \in X$ such that $\bigwedge B$ is an upper bound of $F(x)$. Also, for convenience, for a node $p \in P$ denote $p^I := \{p\}^I \subseteq X$.

3   Pattern Structures

In [KG01] *pattern structures* are introduced to model information in the realm of pharmaceutical research. How pattern structures serve to analyze many-valued data contexts is described in [Ku09].

Definition 2 (pattern structure). *Let G be a set, let $\mathcal{D} := (D, \sqcap)$ be a meet-semilattice, and let $\delta : G \to D$. Then $\mathbb{P} := (G, \mathcal{D}, \delta)$ is called* pattern structure *if $\delta(G)$ generates a complete subsemilattice $(D_\delta, \sqcap)$ of $\mathcal{D}$. The elements of G are called* objects *and the elements of D are called* descriptions *or* patterns*. The operation $\sqcap$ models a* similarity *operation on the descriptions.*

Pattern structures can be represented by the concept lattices of so called *representation contexts*. In the following we sketch the construction of representation contexts as given in [KG01]. First it is important to note that $(D_\delta, \sqcap)$ is complete and therefore, there exists a (unique) operation $\sqcup$ to make $(D_\delta, \sqcap, \sqcup)$ into a complete lattice. This operation (on D) is given by $\bigsqcup X := \bigsqcap \{c \in D_\delta \mid \forall x \in X : x \sqsubseteq c\}$. Furthermore, a subset M of D is called $\sqcup$-*dense* for $(D_\delta, \sqcap)$ if any element $d \in D_\delta$ can be recaptured as join of elements $N \subseteq M$, that is $d = \bigsqcup N$. Now (G, M, I) is a *representation context* for $(G, \mathcal{D}, \delta)$ if M is $\sqcup$-dense for $(D_\delta, \sqcap)$ and $I \subseteq G \times M$ is defined as $gIm :\Longleftrightarrow \delta(g) \sqsupseteq m$.

4   Basic Connections

On the one hand, given an elementary annotated ordered set $\mathbb{O} := (\mathcal{P}, X, F)$ we get a pattern structure $\mathbb{O} := (X, \mathcal{P}_\sqcap, F)$ if $\mathcal{P}$ allows for (finite) meets and $F(X)$ generates a complete subsemilattice of $\mathcal{P}_\sqcap$. On the other hand, given a pattern structure $\mathbb{P} := (G, \mathcal{D}, \delta)$ we always get an elementary annotated ordered set $(\mathcal{D}_\sqsubseteq, G, \delta)$ when considering the meet-semilattice as ordered set via the usual definition $c \sqsubseteq d :\Leftrightarrow c \sqcap d = c$. Therefore, we see that pattern structures are special cases of annotated ordered sets and we can immediately transfer all results on annotated ordered sets to pattern structures. When we consider the other direction we must be more careful. But let us first compare the constructions of formal contexts for representation in both cases.

For the time being, let us consider a pattern structure $\mathbb{P} := (G, \mathcal{D}, \delta)$ as elementary annotated ordered set and let us build its associated context via the annotated ordered sets method. We get $\mathbb{K}_\mathbb{P} := (G, D, I)$ where $I \subseteq G \times D$ is given by $gId :\Leftrightarrow \delta(g) \sqsubseteq d$. It is obvious that D is $\sqcup$-dense for D_δ. If we had dualized the order $\sqsubseteq$ upfront the above construction would have yielded a representation context for $\mathbb{P}$. Therefore, we can conclude that the method for representation context construction for pattern structures generalizes the method for concept lattice representation for annotated ordered sets in this case. It is important to note that Theorem 1 in [KG01] implies that the concept lattices of (different) representation contexts for a given pattern structure are isomorphic.

In [KG01], it follows directly from Theorem 1 that $(D_\delta, \sqsubseteq)$ and the concept lattice of a representation context of the underlying pattern structure are anti-isomorphic. In the following, we exhibit a connection between the concept lattice of a representation context and $\mathcal{D}$, the ordered set of *all* patterns. For elementary annotated complete lattices, Theorem 1 in [KSJ08] makes obvious that their concept lattice representations are tied to the underlying complete lattices via adjunctions. We need to generalize this result to pattern structures, since $(D, \sqsubseteq)$ is not necessarily a complete lattice.

Theorem 1. *Let $\mathbb{P} := (G, \mathcal{D}, \delta)$ be a pattern structure, let $\mathbb{K} := (G, M, I)$ be a representation context, let $\varphi : \mathfrak{B}(\mathbb{K}) \longrightarrow D, (A, B) \mapsto \sqcup B$ be a mapping, and let $\mu : D \longrightarrow \mathfrak{B}(\mathbb{K}), d \mapsto (d^I, d^{II})$ be a mapping. Then (φ, μ) forms a dual adjunction (or Galois connection) between the ordered set of patterns $\mathcal{D}$ and the concept lattice $(\mathfrak{B}(\mathbb{K}), \leq)$ of (G, M, I). In particular, φ is injective and μ is surjective.*

Proof. We show that φ is injective (the surjectivity of μ follows from the injectivity of φ). Assume we have two concepts (A, B) and (C, D) which are mapped to the same element, that is, $\sqcup B = \sqcup D$. We will show that $(\sqcup B)^I = A$ from which it follows that $(A, B) = (C, D)$. We have that $g \in (\sqcup B)^I$ if and only if $\delta(g) \sqsupseteq \sqcup B$ if and only if $\delta(g) \sqsupseteq b$ for all $b \in B$ if and only if $g \in B^I$.

The pair (φ, μ) forms a Galois connection since $\varphi(A, B) \sqsubseteq d \Longleftrightarrow \sqcup B \sqsubseteq d \Longleftrightarrow (\sqcup B)^I \sqsupseteq d^I \Longleftrightarrow (A, B) \geq (d^I, d^{II}) = \mu(d)$ $\qquad \square$

From the above theorem it follows that the concept lattice of a representation context is embedded as a closure system into $\mathcal{D}$.

In [KSJ08], it is investigated what can happen if we fix an ordered set and then vary the annotations. It turns out that the annotations are in one-to-one correspondence with the closure systems in the filter lattice of the ordered set. Clearly, this implies that in the case of pattern structures if a set of patterns or descriptions together with a similarity operation is given and we vary the annotation function δ freely, we can only get a one-to-one correspondence between (elementary) annotations and a certain subset of the closure systems in the ideal lattice (the dual of the filter lattice of the ordered set). In the following we will single out this subset.

Theorem 2. *Let G be a set of objects, and let $\mathcal{D} := (D, \sqcap)$ be a semi-lattice. The elementary annotations are, up to annotational equivalence, in one-to-one correspondence to the principally generated closure systems in the ideal lattice of $\mathcal{D}$.*

Proof. Given an elementary annotation $\delta : G \to D$ every $x^{\delta \circ \sqsupseteq}$ is a principal ideal in $\mathcal{D}_{\sqsubseteq}$ *and* an object intent of a formal concept of $(G, D, \delta \circ \sqsupseteq)$. Since, in general, the intents of all concepts of a formal context are exactly the meets of the object intents the annotation induces a principally generated closure system in the ideal lattice of $\mathcal{D}$.

Given a closure system $\mathcal{X} \subseteq 2^D$ in the ideal lattice of $\mathcal{D}_{\sqsubseteq}$ generated by the principal ideals $\mathcal{I} \subseteq 2^D$ we can define a corresponding elementary annotation $\delta_{\mathcal{I}} : \mathcal{I} \to D$ where $\downarrow i \mapsto i$.   □

5   Projections

For pattern structures so called *projections* where introduced in [KG01] to model the process of simplification of the underlying subsumption order. Projections are defined as kernel operators[1] on the ordered set of patterns or descriptions. The existence of projections can be characterized by the existence of certain representation contexts. We quote Theorem 2 from [KG01]:

> For pattern structures $\mathbb{P}_1 := (G, \mathcal{D}, \delta_1)$ and $\mathbb{P}_2 := (G, \mathcal{D}, \delta_2)$ the following two conditions are equivalent.
> (1) There exists a projection π with $\delta_2 = \delta_1 \circ \pi$.
> (2) There exist representation contexts (G, M, I) of $\mathbb{P}_1$ and $(G, N, I \cap (G \times N))$ of $\mathbb{P}_2$ with $N \subseteq M$.

In the proof of the theorem it is claimed that $\pi(d) := \bigsqcup \{n \in N \mid n \sqsubseteq d\}$ is a kernel operator on D if (G, N, I) is a representation context of $(G, \mathcal{D}, \delta)$. Examples 1 shows that condition (2) in Theorem 2 needs to be boosted [2] and Example 2 shows that the above operator used in the proof is not a kernel operator as claimed.

---

[1] Kernel operators on ordered sets are isotone, idempotent, and dually extensive self-maps.

[2] Thanks to Jan Frebel for valuable input.

Example 1. Let $\mathcal{D}$ be given by the structure depicted in Figure 1 and let $G_i :=$ $\{g\}$ and $\delta_i(g) := a_i$ and $M_i := \{0, c\}$ (visualized by the dotted compartment in Figure 1) for $i = 1, 2$. Note that the carrier set D_δ of the complete sub-semilattice generated by $\delta(G)$ is given by $\{a_i, 1\}$ for $i = 1, 2$. It is immediate that M_i is $\sqcup$-dense regarding δ_i for $i = 1, 2$ and that $M_2 \subseteq M_1$, but obviously there exists no projection π with $\delta_2 = \delta_1 \circ \pi$.

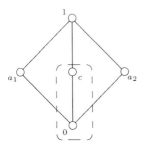
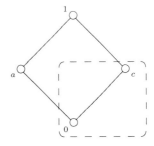

Fig. 1. (2) implies (1) does not hold in Theorem 2

Fig. 2. Operator from the proof is not a kernel operator

Example 2. Let $\mathcal{D}$ be given by the structure depicted in Figure 2 and let $G := \{g\}$ and $\delta(g) := a$ and $M := \{0, c\}$ (visualized by the dotted compartment in Figure 2). Note that the carrier set D_δ of the complete sub-semilattice generated by $\delta(G)$ is given by $\{a, 1\}$. It is immediate that M is $\sqcup$-dense regarding δ, but $\pi : D \to D : d \mapsto \sqcup\{m \in M \mid m \sqsubseteq d\}$ is not contractive since $\pi(c) = 1$, thus π is not a kernel operator.

To repair Theorem 2 we additionally require that δ_2 is point-wise contained in δ_1 in condition (2) and to repair the proof we make the above operator into a kernel operator.

Theorem 3. *For pattern structures* $\mathbb{P}_1 := (G, \mathcal{D}, \delta_1)$ *and* $\mathbb{P}_2 := (G, \mathcal{D}, \delta_2)$ *the following two conditions are equivalent.*

(1) *There exists a projection* π *with* $\delta_2 = \delta_1 \circ \pi$.
(2) *We have* $\delta_2 \sqsubseteq \delta_1$ *and there exist representation contexts* (G, M, I) *of* $\mathbb{P}_1$ *and* $(G, N, I \cap (G \times N))$ *of* $\mathbb{P}_2$ *with* $N \subseteq M$.

Proof. "(1) $\Rightarrow$ (2)": Since there exists a projection π with $\delta_2 = \delta_1 \circ \pi$ we have for $d \in D$ that $\delta_2(d) = \delta_1 \circ \pi(d) = \pi(\delta_1(d))$ which implies $\delta_2(d) \sqsubseteq \delta_1(d)$ since π is contractive. We construct the two representation contexts. Let $M := D$ and let $N := \pi(D)$. Obviously, we have $N \subseteq M$. Since $\delta_2 = \delta_1 \circ \pi$ we get $\delta_2(G) \subseteq \pi(D)$. It remains to show that arbitrary meets of elements from $\delta_2(G)$ can be recovered from N. Assume $F \subseteq \delta_2(G)$ and let $f := \bigsqcap F$. Since $\delta_2(G) \subseteq \pi(D)$ and π is idempotent we have $F = \pi(F)$ which yields $f = \bigsqcap \pi(F)$. Since kernel operators are (completely) meet-preserving we get $f = \bigsqcap \pi(F) = \pi(\bigsqcap F) \in \pi(D)$. That means $D_{\delta_2} \subseteq \pi(D)$ which shows that $\pi(D)$ is $\sqcup$-dense regarding D_{δ_2}. The relation I of the first representation context is given by $gId :\Leftrightarrow \delta_1(g) \sqsupseteq d$. If we look at the relation J of the second representation we see that for $d \in \pi(D)$ we have $gJd :\Leftrightarrow \delta_2(g) \sqsupseteq d$. But since π is a kernel operator for $d \in \pi(D)$ it follows that $\delta_2(g) \sqsupseteq d \iff \pi(\delta_2(g)) \sqsupseteq \pi(d) \iff \pi(\delta_2(g)) \sqsupseteq d \iff \delta_1(g) \sqsupseteq d$ which yields $J = I \cap (G \times \pi(D))$.

"(2) $\Rightarrow$ (1)": We define a self-map on D by $\pi(d) := d \sqcap \bigsqcup\{n \in N \mid n \sqsubseteq d\} = d \sqcap \bigsqcup \downarrow_N d$. Note that, in general, $\sqcup$ is not the supremum operation for D. Therefore, we must be extra-cautious while showing that π is a kernel operator. It is easy to see that π acts on D_{δ_2} as the identity since N is $\sqcup$-dense regarding D_{δ_2}. Also, by definition of $\bigsqcup$, the image of π equals $D \cap D_{\delta_2}$. For showing that π is monotone, we assume that $d \leq d'$. We have $\downarrow_N d \subseteq \downarrow_N d'$ which implies that $\{c \in D_\delta \mid \forall x \in \downarrow_N d' : x \sqsubseteq c\}$ is a subset of $\{c \in D_\delta \mid \forall x \in \downarrow_N d : x \sqsubseteq c\}$ and therefore $\bigsqcup \downarrow_N d = \bigsqcap\{c \in D_\delta \mid \forall x \in \downarrow_N d : x \sqsubseteq c\}$ is less or equal than $\sqsubseteq \bigsqcap\{c \in D_\delta \mid \forall x \in \downarrow_N d' : x \sqsubseteq c\} = \bigsqcup \downarrow_N d'$. This implies $\pi(d) = d \sqcap \bigsqcup \downarrow_N d \sqsubseteq d \sqcap \bigsqcup \downarrow_N d' = \pi(d')$ as required. Contractivity of π is immediate. It remains to show idempotency. It suffices to make sure that $\downarrow_N \pi(d) = \downarrow_N d$. Since π is contractive we have $\downarrow_N \pi(d) \subseteq \downarrow_N d$. Let $n \in N$ with $n \sqsubseteq d$. Obviously $n \sqsubseteq d \sqcap \bigsqcup \downarrow_N d = \pi(d)$. We get $\downarrow_N \pi(d) \supseteq \downarrow_N d$ which gives $\downarrow_N \pi(d) = \downarrow_N d$. We have shown that π is a kernel operator on D. It remains to show that $\delta_2 = \delta_1 \circ \pi$ holds. Let $g \in G$ and $n \in N$. From condition (2) it follows that $n \sqsubseteq \delta_1(g) \Leftrightarrow gIn \Leftrightarrow g(I \cap (G \times N))n \Leftrightarrow n \sqsubseteq \delta_2(g)$. We deduce $\sqcap \bigsqcup \downarrow_N \delta_1(g) = \sqcap \bigsqcup \downarrow_N \delta_2(g)$. Expanding the definitions and using the above equations we get $\pi(\delta_1(g)) = \delta_1(g) \sqcap \bigsqcup \downarrow_N \delta_1(g) = \delta_1(g) \sqcap \bigsqcup \downarrow_N \delta_2(g) = \delta_1(g) \sqcap \delta_2(g)$. Since we assume $\delta_1 \sqsubseteq \delta_2$ we have $\delta_1(g) \sqcap \delta_2(g) = \delta_2(g)$ and deduce $(\delta_1 \circ \pi)(g) = \delta_2(g)$ to complete our proof. $\qquad \square$

References

[DP90]   Davey, B.A., Priestly, H.A.: Introduction to Lattices and Order. Cambridge University Press, Cambridge (1990)

[GW99]   Ganter, B., Wille, R.: Formal Concept Analysis. Mathematical Foundations. Springer, Berlin Heidelberg New York (1999)

[KSJ08] Kaiser, T.B., Schmidt, S.E., Joslyn, C.A.: Adjusting Annotated Taxonomies. International Journal of Foundations of Computer Science (IJFCS): Special Issue: Concept Lattices and Their Applications 18(2), 345–358 (2008)

[KG01]   Ganter, B., Kuznetsov, S.O.: Pattern Structures and Their Projections. In: Delugach, H.S., Stumme, G. (eds.) ICCS 2001. LNCS (LNAI), vol. 2120, pp. 129–142. Springer, Heidelberg (2001)

[Ku09]   Kuznetsov, S.O.: Pattern Structures for Analyzing Complex Data. In: Sakai, H., Chakraborty, M.K., Hassanien, A.E., Ślęzak, D., Zhu, W. (eds.) RSFD-GrC 2009. LNCS, vol. 5908, pp. 33–44. Springer, Heidelberg (2009)

Solving the Structure-Property Problem Using k-NN Classification

Aleksandr Perevoznikov, Alexey Shestov,
Evgenii Permiakov, and Mikhail Kumskov

Lomonosov Moscow State University, Faculty of Mechanics and Mathematics,
Department of Computational Mathematics
GSP-1, Leninskie Gory, Moscow, 119991, Russian Federation
qsar_msu@mail.ru,sperev@yahoo.com
http://www.math.msu.su/department/vychmath/index.html

Abstract. The solution of the "structure-property" based on the molecular graphs descriptors selection with k-NN classifier is proposed. The results of comparing the construction of predictive models using the search and without it are given. The stability of the classifier function construction quality is tested using the test sample.

Keywords: Pattern Recognition, QSAR, QSPR, k-NN.

1 Introduction

The task of the "structure-property" problem is to estimate the relationship between the structure of chemical compounds and their properties. Solution of this problem can be divided into two stages: choosing the description of molecular graphs and the construction of the classifying function. structural descriptors (features) [1] - pairs and triples of singular points [2,3] defined on a triangulated molecular surface of the compound were selected for description and singular points, defined on molecular graphs.The structural character spectrum of the molecular graph represents the number of the molecular fragments repetitions in a molecular graph by complete enumeration of all pairs, triples, quadruples of the singular points [1,4,5]. As a result, the number of descriptors obtained is very large (about 1000 - 10000) and we must choose how to use them. There are several approaches: the use of descriptors, principal component analysis [8], the selection of features. Then the classifying function on the base of the k-NN is constructed.

2 Problem Statement

The task is to develop a method of descriptors selection of based on the k-NN classifier and compare it with two other approaches, as well as the construction of the classifier function, we denote it by F. $\phi(F)$ - the quality functional, it allows us to determine which function is the best. In our calculations we used 2

S.O. Kuznetsov et al. (Eds.): PReMI 2011, LNCS 6744, pp. 49–53, 2011.

types of the $\phi(F)$ - the percentage of correctly classified objects for the molecular sets which have discrete activity and the following formula

$$\phi(F) = 1 - \frac{\sum_{i=1}^{n}(F(M_i) - A_i)^2}{\sum_{i=1}^{n} A_i^2}. \tag{1}$$

where $F(M_i)$ is the value of the classifying function on the i-th molecule, A_i is activity of the i-th molecule (numeric expression of the property), N is a number of molecules, for molecular sets which have a numeric activity value.

3   Building of a Classifying Function Based on k-NN

Let each molecule is compared a point in Euclidean space R^M (coordinates are the descriptors values) and the activity value, such as class number, boiling point. Then there are two possible cases:

1. The activity is discrete. Assume for simplicity that should classify molecules into two classes (C_1, C_2), and we have a training set C. In order to determine a class of a new molecule x we need to find the k nearest points to it from C (denote this set as C_x). Let m_1 be a number of points from $C_x \cap C_1$, and m_2 be a number of points from $C_x \cap C_2$. If $m_1 > m_2$, then the new molecule belongs to the first class, if $m_2 > m_1$ the new molecule belongs to the second class.

2. Activity is indiscrete. Suppose we have a training set C. In order to estimate the activity of a new molecule x we must find the k nearest points to it from C and take the average of their activities.

More about k-NN method can be found in [7,8].

Our classification method is based on the assumption that closely related molecules have a similar value of the activity, so distant molecules should not be allowed to affect the result. Given this, we found it necessary to use the limited radius(not to take into account molecules which are located outside the circle of some radius). To determine it we construct a minimal spanning tree for the molecules of the set represented as points in R^M and take an average of its edges length.

4   Algorithm of Descriptors Selection of Based on the k-NN

The input is a matrix of descriptors. Denote it A. The output is a set of descriptors, where $\phi(F)$ has its greatest value. The algorithm consists of four steps:

1. Using the k-NN method we classify molecules on the base of each descriptor of the matrix A. The best n descriptors are selected by the $\phi(F)$ value.

2. For each set of descriptors obtained in the previous step, in turn, we add another column of the matrix A, classify molecules on the base of this new set, and the best n^2 sets of descriptors are selected.

3. Values of ϕ, obtained at the second step, compared with the values on the first. For those sets that do not improve the quality of the forecast, we assume that $\phi = 0$. We select the N best sets.

4. If $\phi = 0$ for all sets or the number of descriptors in the set corresponds to the maximum m, then we end the calculation, otherwise proceed to the second step.

This algorithm can handle a matrix with a huge number of descriptors M. We cant use exhaustive search algorithm due to the the large computational complexity 2^M. When using the algorithm described above leading term in the evaluation of the complexity is nmN^2M, where N is the number of molecules.

5   Results

5.1   The Results on a Set of Amber Odorants

Comparison of the quality of the k-NN classification using the algorithm of selection of descriptors (method 1) , based on all features (method 2) and based on factors (method 3) was conducted on a set of amber odorants (low molecular weight compounds with amber scent), consisting of 129 molecules [2].

8 descriptors matrixes were used. The comparison of the classification quality is given in the table below.

Table 1. The comparison of the methods quality

	Method 1	Method 2	Method 3
1	75.9689	59.6899	59.6899
2	74.4186	59.6899	60.4651
3	75.1937	59.6899	63.5658
4	76.7441	59.6899	59.6899
5	75.9689	60.1562	61.2403
6	77.5193	59.6899	60.4651
7	76.7441	59.6899	61.2403
8	76.7441	59.6899	61.2403

It can be seen from the table that the quality of the algorithm of descriptors selection is better then the quality of the algorithm on all features and all factors. The difference is about 15 percents. But the quality of the algorithm based on all factors is better then the quality of the algorithm based on all features. So the selection of principal components can improve the quality of the forecast, but some pre-selection of descriptors must be done.

5.2   The Results on a Set of Toxic Compounds

First, let us say a few words about the set. Chemical toxicity can cause a lot of biologically hazardous effects such as damage to genes, or even result in death of man or animals. About 120000 chemical compounds are to be tested in the next 10 years. This will require up to 45 million laboratory animals. An alternative is to provide toxicity prediction based on models built on the previously tested compounds. We studied a set which is divided into two parts. A training set consists of 644 molecules and is used for building models and test set(449 compounds) - for their review. In total there are 5 different feature spaces. On this set the quality of classification was checked, both of them will predict new (not involved in constructing the model) of the molecules. Below is a table with the results.

Table 2. Comparison of the classification quality on the training and the test sets

	Training set	Test set
1	0,6114	0,6180
2	0,7441	0,6873
3	0,7297	0,6886
4	0,7809	0,8090
5	0,7852	0,7582

The table shows that in almost all the feature spaces results on the training set is better than on the test. This is due to the fact that the features used for construction of models are not universal. But, nevertheless, the result did not deteriorated greatly, and so the model can be used for prediction.

6   Conclusion

An algorithm of molecular graphs descriptors selection based on the k-NN classifier solving the structure-property problem was developed and implemented. Computational experiments have shown that the application of this algorithm can significantly improve the quality of classification, and the decreasing of the quality on the learning set is not significant. In the future, we plan to improve the quality of the prediction through the implementation of connection with the construction of descriptors. The algorithm of molecular graphs descriptors selection based on the k-NN classifier is fixed, and we vary the parameters of the construction of the alphabet descriptors. Structural descriptors are taken, and the initial parameters (denoted by T_0) are set. The quality functional $\phi(T_0)$ is computed. Then consider the set $M = T || T - T_0 | < \varepsilon$. $max_{T \in M} \phi(F(T))$ is found. T, where the maximum value is reached, is denoted T_m and the process is repeated until $T_m \neq T_0$. So we can find the best description of molecular graphs for the algorithm.

References

1. Kohov, V.A.: The Method of Quantifying the Similarity of Graphs Based on Structural Spectrs. Izvestiya RAN, Technical Cybernetics 5, 143–159 (1994)
2. Svitanko, I.V., Devetyarov, D.A., Tcheboukov, D.E., Dolmat, M.S., Zakharov, A.M., Grigoryeva, S.S., Chichua, V.T., Ponomareva, L.A., Kumskov, M.I.: QSAR Modeling on the Basis of 3D Descriptors Representing the Electrostatic Molecular Surface (Ambergris Fragrances). Mendeleev Communications 17(2), 90–91 (2007)
3. Svitanko, I.V., Kumskov, M.I., Tcheboukov, D.E., Dolmat, M.S., Zakharov, A.M., Ponomareva, L.A., Grigoryeva, S.S., Chichua, V.T.: QSAR Modeling on the Base of Electrostatic Molecular Surface (Amber Fragrances). In: 16th European Symposium on Quantum Structure-Activity Relationships and Molecular Modelling, EuroQSAR, Italy (2007)
4. Kumskov, M.I., Smolenskiy, E.A., Ponomareva, L.A., Mitushev, D.F., Zefirov, N.S.: System of structural descriptors for solving structure-property problem. Reports of the Academy of Sciences 336(1), 64–66 (1994)
5. Hurst, T., Heritage, T.: HQSAR - A Highly Predictive QSAR Technique Based on Molecular Holograms. In: 213th ACS National Meeting, San Francisco, CA, CINF 019 (1997)
6. Hoffman, B., Cho, S.J., Zheng, W., Wyrick, S., Nicols, D.E., Mailman, R.B., Tropsha, A.: Quantitative structure-activity relationship modelling of dopamine D[1] antagonists using comparative molecular field analysis, generic algorithms-partial least-squares, and K nearest neighbour methods. J. Med. Chem. 42, 3217–3226 (1999)
7. Zheng, W., Tropsha, A.: Novel variable selection quantitative structure-property relationship approach based on the k-nearest-neighbour principle. J. Chem. Inf. Comput. Sci. 40, 185–194 (2000)
8. Clark, M., Cramer III, R.D., Jones, D.M., Patterson, D.E., Simeroth, P.E.: Comparative Molecular Field Analysis(CoMFA) Toward Its Use with 3DStructural Databases. Tetrahedron Comput. Methodol. 3, 47–59 (1990)

Stable Feature Extraction with the Help of Stochastic Information Measure

Alexander Lepskiy

Higher School of Economics, Moscow, Russia

Abstract. This article discusses the problem of extraction of such set of pattern features that is informative and stable with respect of stochastic noise. This is done through the stochastic information measure.

1 Introduction

In describing of non deterministic system we must take into account the nature of its uncertainty. In pattern recognition uncertainty could have both probabilistic nature, that defined by some additive measure, and more "imprecise" nature, which can be described, for example, by using monotonous nonadditive measures. The feature extraction is the important task of pattern recognition in general and image analyses in particular. This task consists to extraction of some minimal set of features or combinations of them from a set of features with given informativeness, which would have sufficient integral informativeness in solution of given problem of recognition. The are traditional approaches to solving this problem, such as correlation analysis (principal components analysis, etc.), discriminant analysis [2].

In this article we concretized the general problem of informative features extraction as follows. Suppose that pattern X is defined by ordered set $X = \{x_0, ..., x_{n-1}\}$. We call every subset $A \in 2^X$ a representation of pattern X. The problem is to find such representation A that it will be minimal on the one hand and it will be near to X on the other hand. Elements in the X may have different priorities, in other words, they may have different informativeness. Therefore, we will establish correspondence between the element $x \in X$ and the nonnegative number – a feature $\omega(x)$, that characterize the importance of the element x for the representation of pattern X. We will determine the degree of representativeness of the set $A \in 2^X$ for pattern X using the set function $\mu(A)$ and require from the set function μ to satisfy all the axioms of monotonous measure: 1) $\mu(\emptyset) = 0$, $\mu(X) = 1$ (normalization); 2) $\mu(A) \leq \mu(B)$ if $A \subseteq B$, $A, B \in 2^X$ (monotonicity). In addition the measure μ meets the certain additional conditions related to the specific task of pattern recognition. We will call such measures monotonous information measures. In [1] information measures were used to set and solve the task of finding the most minimal informative polygonal representation of the curve.

In certain tasks of pattern recognition, in particular, in image processing, image analysis and image recognition random nature of image features can be

S.O. Kuznetsov et al. (Eds.): PReMI 2011, LNCS 6744, pp. 54–59, 2011.

caused by some noisy effects. For example, if the pattern is a discrete plane curve that extracted on the image and features are some characteristics of curve points (eg, feature is a estimation of curvature in given point of discrete curve [3]), then a random character of features (eg, curvature) is caused by the noise of image. In this case the expectation $\mathbf{E}[M(A)]$ characterize the level of informativeness of represenation $A \in 2^X$ and the variance $\sigma^2[M(A)]$ characterize the level of stability of representation to noise pattern. Then there is the problem of finding the most stable and informative representation $A \in 2^X$ of the pattern X. The complexity of solutions of this problem will be determined by the degree of dependence of random features of each other. Stochastic measure of informativeness M will be additive measure if the features are independent random variables. Otherwise, the measure would be nonadditive measure. In this article mentioned task will be discussed and resolved in the case of probabilistic independence of random features. The case of random dependency of features is investigated in [4].

2   The Average Set Function of Information of Pattern

In general case the feature may be depend from all or some elements from the representation A on which it calculated i.e. $w(x) = w(x, A)$. For example, let $X = \Gamma$ be a discrete plane close curve: $\Gamma = (\mathbf{g}_k)_{k=0}^{n-1}$, $\mathbf{g}_k = x_k\mathbf{i} + y_k\mathbf{j}$, and $w(\mathbf{g}, A) = \|\mathbf{g} - \mathbf{g}_+(A)\|$, where $\mathbf{g}_+(A)$ is a point that follows from the point $\mathbf{g}$ in ordered representation A or $w(\mathbf{g}, A) = k_\varepsilon[A](\mathbf{g})$ is a some estimation of curvature of plane discrete curve that is calculated in $\varepsilon-$ neighbourhood of point $\mathbf{g}$ [3].

The degree of completeness of representation $A \in 2^X$ in describing the pattern X with respect to feature $w(x) = w(x, A)$ may be assigned with the follow set function

$$\mu(A) = \sum_{x \in A} w(x, A) \bigg/ \sum_{x \in X} w(x, X), A \in 2^X, \tag{1}$$

which we call averaged set function of information of pattern X (with respect to feature w). We put $\mu(A) = 0$ if the value $w(x, A)$ is not defined for set A (in particular $\mu(\emptyset) = 0$).

Example 1. Let $X = \Gamma$ be a discrete plane close curve: $\Gamma = (\mathbf{g}_k)_{k=0}^{n-1}$, $\mathbf{g}_k = x_k\mathbf{i} + y_k\mathbf{j}$ and $B = \{\mathbf{g}_{i_1}, ..., \mathbf{g}_{i_l}\} \subseteq \Gamma$. Also we introduce the set functions $\mu_L(B) = L(B)/L(\Gamma)$ and $\mu_S(B) = S(B)/S(\Gamma)$, where $L(B)$ and $S(B)$ are perimeter and square correspondingly of figure, that is limited by polygon with vertex in points of ordered set B. Then μ_L and μ_S are averaged set functions of information of curve Γ, where $w(\mathbf{g}, A) = \|\mathbf{g} - \mathbf{g}_+(A)\|$ for set function μ_L and $w(\mathbf{g}, A) = 0.5 |\rho_O(\mathbf{g}) \times \rho_O(\mathbf{g}_+(A))|$ for set function μ_S, $\rho_O(\mathbf{g})$ is a radius vector of point $\mathbf{g} \in A$ with respect to arbitrary point O. Note that μ_L is a monotonous measure, and μ_S is a monotonous measure too if the domain bounded by polygons with vertexes in the points of discrete curve Γ is convex.

There is a question when the averaged set functions of information will be monotonous measure? It can be easily shown that follow proposition is true.

Proposition 1. *Averaged set functions of information μ on 2^X of form (1) are a monotonous measure iff μ obeys the following condition*

$$\sum_{x \in A} (\omega(x, A) - \omega(x, A \cup \{y\})) \leq \omega(y, A \cup \{y\})$$

for any set $A \in 2^X$ and $y \in X \backslash A$.

Corollary 1. *If $\omega(x, A) = \omega(x, X)$ for all $x \in A$ and $A \in 2^X$ then set function μ of form (1) is an additive measure on 2^X.*

Let $A = \{x_{i_1}, ..., x_{i_s}, x, \ x_{i_{s+1}}, ..., x_{i_l}\} \subseteq X$ be a some representation of pattern X. We denote $A_{k,m}(x) = \{x_{i_{s-k+1}}, ..., x_{i_s}, x, \ x_{i_{s+1}}, ..., x_{i_{s+m}}\} \subseteq X$, $k + m \leq l$.

Corollary 2. *Let $\omega(x, A) = \omega(x, A_{k,m}(x))$ for all $x \in A$ and $A \in 2^X$, $|A| > k + m$, then set function μ of form (1) is a monotonous measure iff*

$$\sum_{r=0}^{k-1} (\omega(x_{i_{s-r}}, A) - \omega(x_{i_{s-r}}, A \cup \{y\})) + \sum_{r=1}^{m} (\omega(x_{i_{s+r}}, A) - \omega(x_{i_{s+r}}, A \cup \{y\}))$$

$$\leq \omega(y, A \cup \{y\})$$

for all $A \in 2^X$ and $y \in X \backslash A$. In particular, let $\omega(x, A) = \omega(x, A_{0,1}(x))$ for all $x \in A$ and $A \in 2^X$, $|A| > 1$, then set function μ of form (1) is a monotonous measure iff $\omega(x_+(A), A) \leq \omega(x_+(A), A \cup \{y\}) + \omega(y, A \cup \{y\})$ for all $A \in 2^X$ and $y \in X \backslash A$, where $x_+(A)$ is a point that follows from the point x in ordered representation A.

3 The Stochastic Additive Average Information Measure

Let μ be a averaged information measure on 2^X of form (1) and $\omega(x, A) = \omega(x, X) = \omega(x)$ for all $x \in A$ and $A \in 2^X$. In other words the feature value at point x does not depend from considered representation. The estimation of curvature $\omega(\mathbf{g}, A) = k_\varepsilon[\Gamma](\mathbf{g})$ in ε- neighbourhood of point $\mathbf{g}$ for discrete plane curve $\Gamma = (\mathbf{g}_k)_{k=0}^{n-1}$ is an example of this feature. Then (see corollary 1) the measure $\mu(A) = \sum_{x \in A} \omega(x)/\sum_{x \in X} \omega(x)$, $A \in 2^X$, is an additive measure. We suppose that feature characteristics will be independence random variables $\Omega(x)$, $x \in X$. In this case the value of information measure $M(A) = \sum_{x \in A} \Omega(x)/\sum_{x \in X} \Omega(x)$ for fixed set $A \in 2^X$ will be random variable too. The set function $M(A)$ will be an additive measure for any random event. We considered the example of this situation. Suppose that discrete plane curve $\Gamma = (\mathbf{g}_k)_{k=0}^{n-1}$, $\mathbf{g}_k = x_k \mathbf{i} + y_k \mathbf{j}$ was subjected to additive stochastic noncorrelated noise. In result we get a random curve $\tilde{\Gamma} = (\mathbf{G}_k)_{k=0}^{p-1}$, $\mathbf{G}_k = X_k \mathbf{i} + Y_k \mathbf{j}$, where $X_k = x_k + \eta_k$, $Y_k = y_k + \xi_k$, η_k, ξ_k are random noncorrelated variables and $\mathbf{E}[\eta_k] = \mathbf{E}[\xi_k] = 0$, $\sigma^2[\eta_k] = \sigma^2_{x,k}$,

$\sigma^2[\xi_k] = \sigma_{y,k}^2$. Suppose that there is such basic set $B \subseteq \Gamma$ for which random variables $\Omega(\mathbf{g})$, $\mathbf{g} \in B$, are independent. In this case the feature characteristics $\omega(\mathbf{G}) = \Omega(\mathbf{g})$ will be random variables just as the value of measure $M(A)$, $A \in 2^B$, is.

Let $\mathbf{E}[\Omega(x)] = m_x$, $\sigma^2[\Omega(x)] = \sigma_x^2$. We will investigate numerical characteristics of random additive measure $M(A)$, $A \in 2^X$.

3.1   The Numerical Characteristics of Stochastic Additive Average Information Measure

Let us find the mathematical expectation of random variable $M(A)$ with a fixed $A \in 2^X$. Random variable $M(A)$ is equal to a quotient two random variables $\xi = \sum_{x \in A} \Omega(x)$ and $\eta = \sum_{x \in X} \Omega(x)$.

Lemma 1. *Let ξ and η be random variables that taking values in the intervals l_ξ, l_η respectively on positive semiaxis and $l_\eta \subseteq ((1 - \delta)\mathbf{E}[\eta], (1 + \delta)\mathbf{E}[\eta])$, $l_\xi \subseteq (\mathbf{E}[\xi] - \delta\mathbf{E}[\eta], \mathbf{E}[\xi] + \delta\mathbf{E}[\eta])$. Then it is valid the following formulas for mean and variance of distribution of $\frac{\xi}{\eta}$ respectively*

$$\mathbf{E}\left[\frac{\xi}{\eta}\right] = \frac{\mathbf{E}[\xi]}{\mathbf{E}[\eta]} + \frac{\mathbf{E}[\xi]}{\mathbf{E}^3[\eta]}\sigma^2[\eta] - \frac{1}{\mathbf{E}^2[\eta]}\mathbf{K}[\xi, \eta] + r_1, \tag{2}$$

$$\sigma^2\left[\frac{\xi}{\eta}\right] = \frac{1}{\mathbf{E}^2[\eta]}\sigma^2[\xi] + \frac{\mathbf{E}^2[\xi]}{\mathbf{E}^4[\eta]}\sigma^2[\eta] - \frac{2\mathbf{E}[\xi]}{\mathbf{E}^3[\eta]}\mathbf{K}[\xi, \eta] + r_2, \tag{3}$$

*where $\mathbf{K}[\xi, \eta]$ is a covariation of random variables ξ and η, could meet the certain additional conditions re i.e. $\mathbf{K}[\xi, \eta] = \mathbf{E}[(\xi - \mathbf{E}[\xi])(\eta - \mathbf{E}[\eta])]$; r_1, r_2 are the residuals that depend on numerical characteristics of ξ and η and $|r_1| \leq \frac{\delta}{1-\delta}$.
$\frac{\mathbf{E}[\xi]+\mathbf{E}[\eta]}{\mathbf{E}^3[\eta]}\sigma^2[\eta] \leq \frac{\mathbf{E}[\xi]+\mathbf{E}[\eta]}{(1-\delta)\mathbf{E}[\eta]}\delta^3$, $|r_2| \leq C\delta^3$.*

Let $\xi = \sum_{x \in A} \Omega(x)$ and $\eta = \sum_{x \in X} \Omega(x)$. Then $\mathbf{K}[\xi, \eta] = \mathbf{K}\left[\sum_{x \in A}\Omega(x), \sum_{y \in X}\Omega(y)\right] = \sum_{x \in A}\mathbf{K}[\Omega(x), \Omega(x)] + \sum_{x \in A, y \in X | x \neq y}\mathbf{K}[\Omega(x), \Omega(y)]$. Because random variables $\Omega(x)$, $x \in X$, are independent, $\mathbf{K}[\Omega(x), \Omega(y)] = 0$ for $x \neq y$, and $\mathbf{K}[\Omega(x), \Omega(x)] = \sigma_x^2$ by definition. Hence, $\mathbf{K}[\xi, \eta] = \sum_{x \in A}\sigma_x^2$. Using the notation $S(A) = \sum_{x \in A} m_x$, $D(A) = \sum_{x \in A}\sigma_x^2$, we can rewrite formulas (2), (3) for our case as follows

$$\mathbf{E}[M(A)] = \frac{S(A)}{S(X)} + \frac{S(A)}{S^3(X)}D(X) - \frac{1}{S^2(X)}D(A) + r_1, \tag{4}$$

$$\sigma^2[M(A)] = \frac{S(X) - 2S(A)}{S^3(X)}D(A) + \frac{S^2(A)}{S^4(X)}D(X) + r_2. \tag{5}$$

Notice that, $\sigma^2[M(X \backslash A)] = \sigma^2[1 - M(A)] = \sigma^2[M(A)]$ for $A \in 2^X$. We will use formulas (4) and (5) without their residuals. Respective values $\tilde{\mathbf{E}}[M(A)] = \mathbf{E}[M(A)] - r_1$, $\tilde{\sigma}^2[M(A)] = \sigma^2[M(A)] - r_2$ we will call estimations of numerical characteristics. The class of random variables $\{M(A) : A \in 2^X\}$ satisfies all the requirements for a finitely additive stochastic measure [5]: 1) $\mathbf{E}[M^2(A)] < \infty$ for all $A \in 2^X$; 2) $M(A)$ is an almost probably finitely additive measure.

Note that mathematical expectation $\mathbf{E}\left[M(A)\right]$ define the set function on 2^X and $\mathbf{E}\left[M(\emptyset)\right] = 0$, $\mathbf{E}\left[M(X)\right] = 1$. Since $S(A)$ and $D(A)$ are additive set function then measure $\tilde{\mathbf{E}}\left[M(A)\right]$ will be additive too.

3.2 Finding of Optimal Stable Pattern Representation

We set a problem of finding such representation B of pattern X, which cardinality is less or equal to the given number $k \geq 3$ for which the summarized variance $\sum_{A \subseteq B} \tilde{\sigma}^2\left[M(A)\right]$ will be minimal but the sum of squares of mathematical expectations of all representations $\sum_{A \subseteq B} \tilde{\mathbf{E}}^2\left[M(A)\right]$ will be maximal. The value of summarized variance characterizes the stability of representation and all its subset to noise level of pattern and it depends also from number of elements in representation. The more elements in the presentation we have, then the summarized value of variance is greater. We will use mathematical expectations of nonnormalized information measures $S(A)$, $A \subseteq X$, instead of $\mathbf{E}\left[M(A)\right]$, $A \subseteq X$, for simplification of computations. We introduce follow criteria: $f(X) = \sum_{A \subseteq X} \tilde{\sigma}^2\left[M(A)\right] \Big/ \sum_{A \subseteq X} S^2(A)$, $|X| \leq k$.

Then it is necessary to find such set B, $3 \leq |B| \leq k$, for which $f(B) \to \min$. We simplify function $f(B)$. Let $S_2(B) = \sum_{x \in B} m_x^2$, $SD(B) = \sum_{x \in B} \sigma_x^2 m_x$.

Proposition 2. *If feature characteristics of pattern X are independent random variables then following equality is true for every $B \in 2^X$:*

$$f(B) = \tfrac{1}{S^4(B)}\left\{D(B) - \tfrac{2S(B)}{S_2(B)+S^2(B)} SD(B)\right\}.$$

Corollary 3. *If $\sigma_x^2 = \sigma^2 = const$ for all $x \in B$ then*

$$f(B) = \tfrac{1}{S^4(B)}\left\{|B| - \tfrac{2S^2(B)}{S_2(B)+S^2(B)}\right\}\sigma^2.$$

As $S^2(B)/|B| \leq S_2(B) \leq S^2(B)$ then following corollary is true.

Corollary 4. *If $\sigma_x^2 = \sigma^2 = const$ for all $x \in B$ then*

$$\tfrac{|B|^2-|B|}{(|B|+1)S^4(B)}\sigma^2 \leq f(B) \leq \tfrac{|B|-1}{S^4(B)}\sigma^2.$$

We will use the "inclusion-exclusion" procedure for finding of optimal representation which minimize the function $f(B)$. We estimate the variation of function $f(B)$ to the exclusion of element x from B and inclusion of element $y \in X \backslash B$.

Theorem 1. *If feature characteristics of pattern X are independent random variables then following asymptotic equality*

$$f\left((B\backslash\{x\}) \cup \{y\}\right) - f(B) = \tfrac{1}{S^4(B)}\left(Q_1(B)(m_y - m_x) + \sigma_y^2 - \sigma_x^2\right) + o(\tau),$$

is true for every $x \in B$ and $y \in X \backslash B$, where $Q_1(B) = \dfrac{2\left(3S_2(B)+5S^2(B)\right)}{(S_2(B)+S^2(B))^2} SD(B) -$
$\tfrac{4}{S(B)}D(B)$, $\tau = \sqrt{\tfrac{1}{S^2(B)}\left(m_y^2 + m_y^2\right) + \tfrac{1}{D^2(B)}\left(\sigma_x^4 + \sigma_y^4\right)}$.

Corollary 5. *If* $\sigma_x^2 = \sigma^2 = const$ *for all* $x \in X$, *then for any* $x \in B$ *and* $y \in X\backslash B$ *we have* $f\left((B\backslash\{x\}) \cup \{y\}\right) - f(B) = Q_2(B)\sigma^2\left(m_y - m_x\right) + o(\tau)$, *where* $Q_2(B) = \frac{2}{S^3(B)}\left(\frac{3S_2(B) + 5S^2(B)}{(S_2(B) + S^2(B))^2} - \frac{2|B|}{S^2(B)}\right)$, $Q_2(B) < 0$ *for all* $B \subseteq X : |B| \geq 3$ *and* $\tau = \sqrt{\frac{1}{S^2(B)}\left(m_y^2 + m_y^2\right) + \frac{1}{D^2(B)}\left(\sigma_x^4 + \sigma_y^4\right)}$.

Formulas from theorem 1 and corollary 5 may be use for construction of algorithmic procedures for finding of representation B, which minimize the function f. Let $K_B(x, y) = Q_1(B)(m_y - m_x) + \sigma_y^2 - \sigma_x^2$. The algorithm for finding of representation B of cardinality k which minimize the function f (if random variables $\Omega(x)$, $x \in X$, are independent), consist of following steps:

1) we select the set B_0 consisting of k elements of pattern X with maximal values of informativeness $\mathbf{E}\left[\Omega(x)\right] = m_x$, $x \in X$, as a initial representation;

2) we compute the value $Q_1(B_0)$ from Theorem 1 and we find $(\tilde{x}, \tilde{y}) = \arg\min\{K_{B_0}(x, y) : x \in B, y \in X\backslash B, K_{B_0}(x, y) < 0\}$, if this pair is exist. Then $B_1 = (B_0\backslash\{\tilde{x}\}) \cup \{\tilde{y}\}$ is a new representation for which $f(B_1) \leq f(B_0)$ accurate within to small values of second order. This step will be repeating so long as will be pairs (x, y): $K_B(x, y) < 0$.

If $\sigma_x^2 = \sigma^2 = const$ for all $x \in X$, then following conclusion follows from the corollary 5, if we disregard small values: the optimal representation B with cardinality is less or equal k, which minimize the function f will be consist of elements with the greatest values $\mathbf{E}\left[\Omega(x)\right] = m_x$ (on the assumption of random variables $\Omega(x)$, $x \in X$, are independent).

Acknowledgement. This work was supported by the grants 10-07-00135, 10-07-00478, 11-07-00591 of RFBR (Russian Foundation for Basic Research).

References

[1] Bronevich, A., Lepskiy, A.: Geometrical Fuzzy Measures in Image Processing and Pattern Recognition. In: Proc. of the 10th IFSA World Congress, Istanbul, Turkey, pp. 151–154 (2003)

[2] Duda, R.O., Hart, P.E., Stork, D.G.: Pattern Classification and Scene Analysis: Part I Pattern Classification. John Wiley and Sons, Chichester (1998)

[3] Lepskii, A.E.: On Stability of the Center of Masses of the Vector Representation in One Probabilistic Model of Noiseness of an Image Contour. Automation and Remote Control 68, 75–84 (2007)

[4] Lepskiy, A.E.: Application of Stochastic Information Measure in Problem of Finding of Optimal Polygonal Curve Representation. In: Proc. of Intern. Conf. Pattern Recognition and Image Analysis, Nizhni Novgorod, vol. 1, pp. 397–400 (2008)

[5] Shiryaev, A.N.: Probability (Graduate Texts in Mathematics). Springer, Heidelberg (1995)

Wavelet-Based Clustering of Social-Network Users Using Temporal and Activity Profiles

Lipika Dey and Bhakti Gaonkar

Innovation Labs, Tata Consultancy Services, Delhi, India
(lipika.dey,bhakti.g)@tcs.com

Abstract. Encouraged by the success of social networking platforms, more and more enterprises are exploring the use of crowd-sourcing as a method for intra-organization knowledge management. There is not much information about their effectiveness though. While there has been some emphasis on studying friend networks, not much emphasis has been given towards understanding other kinds of user behavior like regularity of access or activity. In this paper we present a wavelet-based clustering method to cluster social-network users into different groups based on their temporal behavior and activity profiles. Cluster characterization reveals the underlying user-group characteristics. User data from web and enterprise social-network platforms have been analyzed.

Keywords: Social Network Analysis, Wavelet transformation, Hierarchical K-means clustering.

1 Introduction

Social networking sites like Twitter and Facebook are figuring in an increasingly important way to market researchers due to their astronomically rising user base over a very short time. Efforts are on to tap the content that is generated in these sites to get valuable business insights. There is also an attempt to replicate these platforms within the secure environments of enterprises and motivate employees to engage in similar social interactions. It is expected that these platforms can motivate knowledge and expertise sharing in a more pro-active and effective way. However, these initiatives can only succeed if user participation is considerably steady and continuous, which is not necessarily true. Studies show that though popular social network sites like Twitter have an increasing user base, but there is also a huge attrition rate. Characterization of users based on their temporal behavior and activity profiles can not only help in identifying valuable and active user groups, but also help in improving the effectiveness of such platforms by identifying rare or infrequent users and motivating them to participate more through various incentives. Identifying anomalous behavior can be yet another important application of this.

In this paper, we present an efficient way of clustering users into different groups based on their temporal behavior in social network forums. While there has been a lot of focus on studying user-groups based on content generated by them, not much work exist on analyzing their temporal behavior. We show that wavelet-based analysis can

S.O. Kuznetsov et al. (Eds.): PReMI 2011, LNCS 6744, pp. 60–65, 2011.

effectively identify different categories of users, whose behaviors can be easily characterized. The rest of the paper is organized as follows. Section 2 surveys related works. Section 3 presents the background of wavelet analysis. The details of our wavelet based clustering algorithm are discussed in Section 4. Section 5 describes the experiments conducted and the results obtained.

2   Survey of Related Work

Wavelet transform being spatial-temporal in nature can capture temporal as well as frequency-based behavior of signals. In [1], a technique based on Discrete Wavelet Transform was proposed to cluster ECG signals. Though wavelet based analytical techniques are very powerful, they have not seen much use in the field of social-network analysis. There have been several earlier attempts to cluster web-site users into different groups based on their access patterns. In [2] a novel approach was presented to cluster user profiles based on mass distribution using Dempster-Shafer's theory. Profile similarity was used to make recommendations, personalize Web sites, and create targeted advertisements.   In [3], a trace analysis was conducted to characterize user access to videos over web (VOW). Their analysis revealed interesting discoveries like requests for same video spanned over short span of time and that small number of machines accounted for large number of overall requests. In [4], a very recent work, it has been shown how content popularity grows and fades over time in Twitter. In order to uncover the temporal dynamics of online content this has been formulated as time series clustering problem using a similarity metric that is invariant to scaling and shifting. K-Spectral Centroid (K-SC) clustering algorithm is proposed, that can effectively find cluster centroids with their similarity measure applied on wavelet coefficients of the time series.

3   Brief Overview of Wavelet Analysis and Wavelet Transformation

Wavelets are mathematical functions that are very useful in representing data due to various properties like compact support, vanishing moments, dilating relations etc. [5, 6, 7]. Compact support guarantees the localization of wavelets, while vanishing moment guarantees that wavelet processing can distinguish the essential information from non-essential information. These features including facilities for hierarchical representation and manipulation make wavelets a very powerful tool. Wavelet transforms are spatial-temporal in nature. They capture the time as well as the frequency of the signals. In wavelet analysis, the scale that is used to look at data plays a special role.

The Discrete Wavelet Transform can be described as a series of filtering and sub sampling. In each level in this series, a set of $2j$ 1 coefficients are calculated, where j < J is the *scale* and $N = 2^J$ is the number of samples in the input signal. The coefficients are calculated by applying a high-pass *wavelet filter* to the signal and down-sampling the result by a factor of 2. At the same level, a low-pass *scale filtering* is also performed (followed by down-sampling) to produce the signal for the next level. Each set of scale-coefficient corresponds to a "smoothing" of the signal and the removal of details, whereas the wavelet-coefficients correspond to the "differences" between the scales.

Given a signal f_0 having dimension D_f, low frequency filter L and a high frequency filter H, the Fast wavelet transformation of the signal is computed as follows:

1. Apply H to f, returning a new signal f_H, with a domain half the size of D_f,
2. Similarly, apply L to f, returning another new signal f_L, with a domain half the size of D_f,
3. If size of D_f is 2, then return $[f_H, f_L]$
4. Apply Wavelet transform (recursively) on f_L,
5. Return f_H concatenated with the result.

The resultant transformed signal f_0 is $(Lf_k, Hf_{k-1}, Hf_{k-2}, ..., Hf_0)$ where Lf_k is the wavelet coefficient of signal f_0 at the kth (coarsest) level. It contains the approximated information about original signal. Hf_j are the wavelet coefficients of the signal at j^{th} level containing the detailed information of the signal at that level.

The simplest wavelet transformation function is Haar transform which has a single vanishing moment. Haar transform performs an average and difference on a pair of value. We have used Daubechies2 wavelet transforms having two vanishing moments. The corresponding low-level and high-level filters are given by (0.12940952, 0.22414386,-0.8365163, 0.4829629) and (0.4829629, 0.8365163, 0.22414386, -0.12940952) respectively.

4 Wavelet-Based Clustering of User Interaction Data

We assume that user interaction data is represented as a time-series, which records the activity of the user at regular time-intervals. Measure of activity in a given time interval is the number of times the user repeats the activity in that period. Activity definition depends on the type of social network and may include actions like asking a question or answering one, sending messages or tweets, or simply updating status.

Grouping users based on their behavior is performed in two phases. In phase I, Fast Daubechies Transform is applied to the time series data. This transformation yields a set of values that are linear combinations of the original elements of the time series. As mentioned earlier, the coarsest level coefficients obtained with the transformation can provide approximate information about the users, while at each higher level more detailed information about the behavior can be captured. In phase II, we exploit this property of wavelet coefficients to refine the process of clustering repeatedly and obtain more refined and homogeneous groups.

The hierarchical clustering algorithm has been designed based on *k-means*. Initially, the coefficients obtained at the coarsest level are segregated into k clusters. Phases II is repeated for each new cluster, till the most detailed coefficients are taken into account. The clustering process is summarized below

Wavelet based Hierarchical Clustering Algorithm

Let n denote the number of users and m denote the
number of time-intervals considered

Input: Set   of   signals $\bar{U}_n$,where $u_n = <f_i(t_j)>$, i =
1,2 ... n and j = 1,2 ....m. Since m should be a power of 2,
let m = 2^s. Extra fields in the signal, if needed,
are padded with zeroes.

- Parameters k_1, k_2,...,k_s, where k_t is the number of
  clusters to be created during the tth iteration.

- Output: p clusters, where p = $k1*k_2*...*k_m$

1. Apply   Fast   Daubechies   Transform (FDT) on   each
   element u_n of $\bar{U}_n$. The data set is transformed to $\bar{W}_n$,
   where $W_i(t_j) = ,$ $W\left(f_i(t_j)\right) = W_i(t_j)$

2. Assign $C_{s+1}^1 = W_i(t_j)$

3. For $t = s, s - 1, ...,$

   For c=1,2,...,$k_1*k_2*...*k_{s-1-t}$

   a. Apply   K-means   clustering   on   set   of   elements
      belonging   to C_{t+1}^c considering   only t^{th} level
      coefficients   of   the   elements w_n belonging   to
      C_{t+1}^c,dividing each cluster into k_t clusters.

   b. As a result of step a. $k_1*k_2*...*k_t$ are formed.

5 Experiments and Results

Several experiments were conducted to study users of different types of social
networks. The first and second dataset comprise of Twitter users for a period of one
month in 2009 and fifteen days in 2010 respectively. The third and fourth datasets
comprise data from an Enterprise Social Network Portal (ESNP) where users ask
questions or answer questions posted by other users. It consists of employees and
their monthly behavior over 25 months from April 2008 to April 2010. The Twitter
data time-series contain the number of tweets sent by each user on the different days.
The Enterprise data contains number or questions or answers posted by users in a
given month. Table 1 presents details of the datasets as well as the results obtained.
   It can be observed from Table 1 that the distributions are identical with one large
cluster receiving majority of the data points. It is found that the major cluster always
contains infrequent users with low activity profiles. This cluster emerges at the end of
first level itself, and remains unchanged through the next iterations. Figure 1 shows
the clusters formed for the different datasets after the first level of clustering, i.e. at
the coarsest level of approximation. These plots have been generated using total
activity during the period. The last column of Table 1 shows that the percentage of
users exhibiting significant volumes of activity and continuous presence is very low.

Table 1. Details of Datasets and Clustering results

Dataset	Number of users	Time Period	Clusters (#)	% users in largest cluster	% users with high-activity
Twitter I	200000	31 days	48	54	0.16
Twitter II	44895	16 days	16	63	0.27
ESNP Answers	21420	25 months	32	93	0.47
ESNP Question	19810	25 months	32	78	0.35

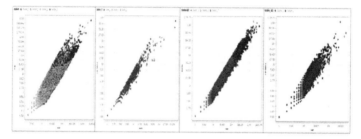

Fig. 1. [a] Twitter data I   [b] Twitter data II   [c] ESNP Answers [d] ESNP Questions

Figures 2[a] and 2[b] show activity profiles of sample users from the major cluster (red dots) and one minor cluster (blue dots) from second Twitter and ESNP answers data sets respectively. In figure 2[a], red dots depict low-profile users with an average activity of 2 tweets and an average presence of 1.6 days over the period of 16 days. Blue dots in the figure depict highly active users with an average activity of 4.5 tweets and an average presence of 12 days. Similarly in figure 2[b], red dots depict low-profile users with an average activity of 2.7 answers and an average presence of 3 months, over the period of twenty five months. Blue dots in the figure present high-profile users with an average activity of 30.7 answers and an average presence of 11.2 months. Figure 2c analyses the content of ESNP high activity users and will be discussed later.

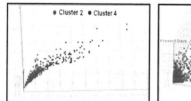
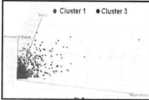
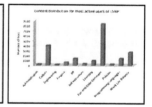

Fig. 2. Inactive and most active users [a] Second Twitter dataset [b] ESNP answers [c] Category distribution of content posted by most active ESNP users

It is obvious that majority of social network users are not regular and maintain a low profile. Analysis of Twitter user profiles further reveal that users with highest levels of activity are almost always news groups. In both the datasets, the most active group consisted of IDs of global news agencies like *breaking news* and *TOInews*, while the second most active set of users included regional news agencies like *AtlantaNews, TOIMumbai, TOIDelhi* etc. It is interesting to observe that the patterns of users and usage have remained same over the years, in spite of growing number of users. Further, analysis of ESNP data showed that around 57% of users who logged into the network on any given month, did not do so the very next month. Since very few users take an active role on a continuous basis, the purpose of such networks may not be fulfilled.

The ESNP data used for this experiment had user-given category tags Technology, Programming Languages, HR, Finance, Fun and Entertainment etc. associated to the content. Figure 2c shows that bulk of content contributed by the most active users belong to the Fun and Entertainment category. The other popular categories are culture and Work Life balance. Thus it can be concluded that social networks are positively contributing towards employee bonding. But more can be done to make social networks a platform for enterprise knowledge sharing effectively.

6 Conclusions

In this paper we have explored the temporal behavior of users in social network. We have proposed an effective way of clustering users into different groups and characterized them. It is found that majority of users in any social network are low-profile and irregular. Within enterprise, active interaction is mostly restricted to non-technical content. Schemes to engage users effectively are also essential. Introduction of proper incentives are needed to make social network a viable platform for knowledge sharing. Further work is being carried on to analyze the content and its effectiveness for enterprise.

References

1. Ramakrishnan, A.G., Saha, S.: ECG coding by wavelet-based linear prediction. IEEE Trans. on Biomedical Engineering 44, 1253–1261 (1997)
2. Acharya, S., Smith, B., Parnes, P.: Characterizing User Access to videos on the World Wide Web. In: Proceedings of MMCN (2000)
3. Xie, Y., Phoha, V.V.: Web user clustering from access log using belief function. In: Proceedings of the First International Conference on Knowledge Capture (K-CAP 2001), pp. 202–208. ACM Press, New York (2001)
4. Yang, J., Leskovec, J.: Patterns of Temporal variation in Online Media
5. Graps, A.: An introduction to Wavelets. IEEE, Los Alamitos (1995)
6. Li, T., Li, Q., Zhu, S., Ogihara, M.: A Survey on wavelet Application in Data Mining. ACM SIGKDD Exploration Newsletter 4(2) (2002)
7. Daubechies, I.: Ten lectures on Wavelets. SIAM, Philadelphia (1991)

Tight Combinatorial Generalization Bounds for Threshold Conjunction Rules*

Konstantin Vorontsov and Andrey Ivahnenko

Dorodnycin Computing Center RAS, Moscow, Russia
Moscow Institute of Physics and Technology, Moscow, Russia
voron@forecsys.ru, ivahnenko@forecsys.ru

Abstract. We propose a combinatorial technique for obtaining tight data dependent generalization bounds based on a splitting and connectivity graph (SC-graph) of the set of classifiers. We apply this approach to a parametric set of conjunctive rules and propose an algorithm for effective SC-bound computation. Experiments on 6 data sets from the UCI ML Repository show that SC-bound helps to learn more reliable rule-based classifiers as compositions of less overfitted rules.

Keywords: computational learning theory, generalization bounds, permutational probability, splitting-connectivity bounds, rule induction.

1 Introduction

Obtaining exact generalization bounds remains an open problem in Computational Learning Theory [1]. Experiments [8,9] have shown that two fine effects should be taken into account simultaneously to obtain exact bounds: the *splitting* of the set into error levels and the similarity of classifiers. Many practically used sets contain a lot of similar classifiers that differ on one object, they are called *connected*. In this work we develop a combinatorial approach that deals with splitting and connectivity together and gives tight or even exact bounds on probability of overfitting. We apply a new SC (splitting and connectivity) combinatorial bound to the set of conjunctive rules and propose the overfitting reduction method compatible with most usual rule induction engines.

2 Definitions and Notation

Let $\mathbb{X} = \{x_1, \ldots, x_L\}$ be a set of objects and A be a set of classifiers. A binary loss function $I \colon A \times X \to \{0, 1\}$ exists such that $I(a, x) = 1$ if a classifier a produces an error on an object x. A binary vector $(a_i) \equiv \big(I(a, x_i)\big)_{i=1}^{L}$ of size L is called an *error vector* of the classifier a. Assume that all classifiers from A have pairwise different error vectors.

* Supported by Russian Foundation for Basic Research grant 11-07-00480 and the program "Algebraical and combinatorial methods of cybernetics and new generation information systems" of Russian Academy of Sciences, Branch of Mathematics.

S.O. Kuznetsov et al. (Eds.): PReMI 2011, LNCS 6744, pp. 66–73, 2011.

The number of errors of a classifier a on a sample $X \subseteq \mathbb{X}$ is defined as $n(a, X) = \sum_{x \in X} I(a, X)$. For shorter notation denote $n(a) = n(a, \mathbb{X})$.

The error rate is defined as $\nu(a, X) = \frac{1}{|X|} n(a, X)$.

The *learning algorithm* is a mapping $\mu \colon 2^{\mathbb{X}} \to A$ that takes a training sample $X \subseteq \mathbb{X}$ and gives a classifier $\mu X \in A$.

Transductive (permutational) probability. Denote $[\mathbb{X}]^{\ell}$ the set of all $\binom{L}{\ell} = \frac{L!}{\ell!(L-\ell)!}$ samples $X \subset \mathbb{X}$ of size ℓ. Assume that all partitions of the general set $\mathbb{X}$ into an observed training sample X of size ℓ and a hidden test sample $\bar{X} = \mathbb{X} \setminus X$ of size $k = L - \ell$ can occur with equal probability The classifier $a = \mu X$ is said to be *overfitted* if the *discrepancy* $\delta(a, X) = \nu(a, \bar{X}) - \nu(a, X)$ is greater than a given nonnegative threshold ε. Define the *probability of overfitting* as

$$Q_{\varepsilon}(\mu, \mathbb{X}) = \mathsf{P}\big[\delta(\mu X, X) \geq \varepsilon\big] = \frac{1}{\binom{L}{\ell}} \sum_{X \in [\mathbb{X}]^{\ell}} \big[\delta(\mu, X) \geq \varepsilon\big].$$

where brackets transform a logical value into numerical one: $[true] = 1$, $[false] = 0$. The *inversion* of a bound $Q_{\varepsilon} \leq \eta(\varepsilon)$ is an inequality $\nu(\mu X, \bar{X}) \leq \nu(\mu X, X) + \varepsilon(\eta)$, which holds with probability at least $1 - \eta$, where $\varepsilon(\eta)$ is the inverse for $\eta(\varepsilon)$.

Empirical risk minimization (ERM) is a classical and perhaps most natural example of the learning algorithm:

$$\mu X = \arg \min_{a \in A} n(a, X).$$

Hypergeometric distribution. For a classifier a such that $m = n(a, \mathbb{X})$ the probability to make s errors on a sample X is given by a hypergeometric function: $\mathsf{P}\big[n(a, X) = s\big] = h_L^{\ell, m}(s)$, where $h_L^{\ell, m}(s) = \binom{m}{s}\binom{L-m}{\ell-s}/\binom{L}{\ell}$, argument s runs from $s_0 = \max\{0, m - k\}$ to $s_1 = \min\{m, \ell\}$, parameter m takes values $0, \ldots, L$. It is assumed that $\binom{m}{s} = h_L^{\ell, m}(s) = 0$ for all other integers m, s. Define the cumulative distribution function (left tail) of the hypergeometric distribution

$$H_L^{\ell, m}(z) = \sum_{s=s_0}^{\lfloor z \rfloor} h_L^{\ell, m}(s).$$

Consider a set $A = \{a\}$ containing one *fixed classifier*, so that $\mu X = a$ for any X. Then the probability of overfitting Q_{ε} transforms into the probability of large deviation between error rates in two samples $X, \bar{X}$.

Theorem 1 (FC-bound). *For a fixed classifier a such that $m = n(a)$, for any set $\mathbb{X}$ and any $\varepsilon \in [0, 1]$ the probability of overfitting is given by the left tail of hypergeometric distribution:*

$$Q_{\varepsilon}(a, \mathbb{X}) = H_L^{\ell, m}\left(\tfrac{\ell}{L}(m - \varepsilon k)\right). \tag{1}$$

The exact FC-bound plays a role of the Law of Large Numbers in permutational probabilistic framework because it predicts the error rate on the hidden sample from the observed one, whereas the "probability of error" is undefined here. The hypergeometric distribution is fundamental for all further bounds.

Theorem 2 (VC-bound). *For any set* $\mathbb{X}$, *any learning algorithm* μ, *and any* $\varepsilon \in [0, 1]$ *the probability of overfitting is bounded by the sum of FC-bounds over A:*

$$Q_\varepsilon(\mu, \mathbb{X}) \leq \sum_{a \in A} H_L^{\ell,\, m}\left(\tfrac{\ell}{L}(m - \varepsilon k)\right), \quad m = n(a). \tag{2}$$

Further weakening this bound gives a well known form of the VC-bound: $Q_\varepsilon(\mu, \mathbb{X}) \leq |A| \max\limits_m H_L^{\ell,\, m}\left(\tfrac{\ell}{L}(m - \varepsilon k)\right) \leq |A| \cdot \tfrac{3}{2} e^{-\varepsilon^2 \ell}$ for a case $\ell = k$.

VC-bound is highly overestimated because all classifiers make approximately equal contributions to the VC-bound. However, the set of classifiers is usually split into error rates in quite nonuniform manner. Most classifiers are unsuitable, have vanishing probability to be obtained as a result of learning and make a negligible contribution to the probability of overfitting. On the other hand, similar classifiers share their contribution, thus each of them contributes poorly again. VC theory totally ignores both advantageous effects.

3   Splitting and Connectivity Bounds

Define the order relation on classifiers $a \leq b$ as a natural order on their error vectors: $a_i \leq b_i$ for all $i = 1, \ldots, L$. Introduce Hamming distance between error vectors: $\rho(a, b) = \sum_{i=1}^{L} |a_i - b_i|$. Classifiers a and b are called *connected* if $\rho(a, b) = 1$. Define the precedence relation on classifiers $a \prec b$ as $(a \leq b) \wedge (\rho(a, b) = 1)$.

The set of classifiers A can be represented by a multipartite directed graph that we call the *splitting and connectivity graph* (SC-graph) in which vertices are classifiers, and edges (a, b) are pairs of classifiers such that $a \prec b$. Partite subsets $A_m = \{a \in A \colon n(a) = m\}$ are called *error layers*, $m = 0, \ldots, L$. Each edge of the SC-graph (a, b) can be uniquely labeled by an object $x_{ab} \in \mathbb{X}$ such that $I(a, x_{ab}) = 0$ and $I(b, x_{ab}) = 1$.

Upper connectivity $q(a) = \#\{x_{ab} \in \mathbb{X} \mid a \prec b\}$ of a classifier a is the number of edges leaving the vertex a.

Inferiority $r(a) = \#\{x_{bc} \in \mathbb{X} \mid b \prec c \leq a\}$ of a classifier a is the number of different objects assigned to edges below the vertex a in the SC-graph. If a correct classifier $a_0 \in A$ exists such that $n(a_0) = 0$ then inferiority is equal to the number of errors, $r(a) = n(a)$. In general case $r(a) \leq n(a)$.

Theorem 3 (SC-bound). *If* μ *is ERM then for any* $\varepsilon \in [0, 1]$ *the probability of overfitting is bounded by the weighted sum of FC-bounds over the set A:*

$$Q_\varepsilon(\mu, \mathbb{X}) \leq \sum_{a \in A} P_a H_{L-q-r}^{\ell-q,\, m-r}\left(\tfrac{\ell}{L}(m - \varepsilon k)\right), \tag{3}$$

where $q = q(a)$ *is upper connectivity,* $r = r(a)$ *is inferiority,* $m = n(a)$ *is the number of errors of classifier* a, $P_a = \binom{L-q-r}{\ell-q}/\binom{L}{\ell}$ *is an upper bound on the probability to learn the classifier* a, $\mathsf{P}[\mu X = a] \leq P_a$.

The weight P_a decreases exponentially as connectivity $q(a)$ and inferiority $r(a)$ increase. This fact has two important consequences.

First, connected sets of classifiers are less subjected to overfitting. Not only the fact of connectedness but better the number of connections is important.

Second, only lower layers contribute significantly to the probability of overfitting. This fact encourages effective procedures for SC-bound computation.

SC-bound (3) is much more tight than the VC-bound (2). It transforms to the VC-bound by substituting $q = r = 0$, i.e. by disregarding the SC-graph.

4   SC-Bound for Threshold Conjunctive Rules

Consider a classification problem with labels $y_i \in Y$, $i = 1, \ldots, L$ assigned to each object $x_i \in \mathbb{X}$ respectively. Consider a parametric set R of *conjunctive rules*

$$r(x; \theta) = \prod_{j \in J} \left[x^j \leq \theta^j \right],$$

where $x = (x^1, \ldots, x^n)$ is a vector of numerical features of object x, $J \subseteq \{1, \ldots, n\}$ is a subset of features, $\theta^j \in \mathbb{R}$ is a threshold parameter for j-th feature. An object x is said to be *covered* by the rule $r(x)$ if $r(x) = 1$.

A rule induction system learns a rule set R_y for each class $y \in Y$ from a training set X. Two criteria are optimized simultaneously to select useful rules — the number of positive and negative examples covered by r, respectively:

$$p(r, X) = \#\{x_i \in X \mid r(x_i) = 1, \ y_i = y\} \rightarrow \max;$$
$$n(r, X) = \#\{x_i \in X \mid r(x_i) = 1, \ y_i \neq y\} \rightarrow \min.$$

In practice the two-criteria optimization task is reduced to one-criterion task by means of heuristic function $H(p, n)$. Examples of H are Fisher's exact test [5], entropy, Gini index, χ^2- and ω^2-tests, and many others [4].

Rule based classifier. After learning the rule sets R_y for all $y \in Y$ the classifier can be buildup as a composition of rules, e.g. as a weighted voting:

$$a(x) = \arg\max_{y \in Y} \sum_{r \in R_y} w_r r(x),$$

where weights $w_r \geq 0$ are learned from the training set X. So, there are three things to learn: (1) thresholds θ^j, $j \in J$ for each subset J; (2) feature subset J for each rule r; (3) weight w_r for each rule r. Respectively, there are three reasons for overfitting. In this work we use SC-bound to estimate overfitting resulting from thresholds learning and build a criterion for feature subset selection, with motivation that a good classifier can be hardly build up from overfitted rules.

The idea of heuristic modification is to obtain the SC-bound on p and n for a fixed J; then to get inverted estimates that hold with probability at least $1 - \eta$:

$$\tfrac{1}{k} p(r, \bar{X}) \geq \tfrac{1}{\ell} p(r, X) - \varepsilon_p(\eta), \quad \tfrac{1}{k} n(r, \bar{X}) \leq \tfrac{1}{\ell} n(r, X) + \varepsilon_n(\eta),$$

and to use them instead of p, n in a heuristic $H'(p, n) = H\big(p - \ell\varepsilon_p(\eta), n + \ell\varepsilon_n(\eta)\big)$. The modified heuristic H' gives a more accurate features selection criterion that takes into account the overfitting resulting from thresholds learning.

Specialization of SC-bound for conjunctive rules. Define the binary loss function as $I(r, x_i) = \big[r(x_i) \neq [y_i = y]\big]$, $i = 1, \ldots, L$, for any rule r of class y. For the sake of simplicity suppose that all values x_i^j are pairwise different for each feature j, features take integers $1, \ldots, L$ and the thresholds take integers $0, \ldots, L$.

For any pair of vectors $u = (u^j)_{j \in J}$, $v = (v^j)_{j \in J}$ define an order relation $(u \leq v) \leftrightarrow \forall j \in J \ (u^j \leq v^j)$. Define $(u < v) \leftrightarrow (u \leq v \text{ and } u \neq v)$.

A *boundary point* of the subset $S \subseteq \mathbb{X}$ is a vector θ_S: $\theta_S^j = \max\limits_{x \in S} x^j$, $j \in J$. Note that $r(x, \theta_S) = 1$ for any $x \in S$.

A *boundary object* of the subset $S \subseteq \mathbb{X}$ is any object $x \in S$: $\exists j \in J$: $x^j = \theta_S^j$.

A *boundary subset* is a subset $S \subseteq \mathbb{X}$ such that all objects $x \in S$ are its boundary objects. Each boundary subset is unambiguously defined by its boundary point. Empty set is a boundary subset with boundary point $\theta_\varnothing^j = 0$, $j \in J$.

The following theorem states that the sum over all rules in SC-bound (3) can be calculated by running over all boundary subsets.

Theorem 4. *The set of rules $r(x; \theta_S)$ where S runs over all boundary subsets coincide with the set of all rules $r(x; \theta)$ having pairwise different error vectors.*

Then our idea is to iterate all rules (really, boundary subsets) from bottom to upper levels of SC-graph and use early stopping to bypass rules from higher levels that make no significant contribution to the SC-bound. To do this effectively we first consider an algorithm for the neighbor search of boundary subsets.

Searching the set of neighbor rules. Consider a rule $r(x; \theta)$ defined by a threshold vector $\theta = (\theta^j)_{j \in J}$. Its neighborhood V_θ is defined as a set of all rules $r(x, \theta')$ that differ from $r(x; \theta)$ on single object. Algorithm 4.1 iterates all neighbor rules $r(x, \theta')$ such that θ' is a boundary point of a boundary subset.

At first stage (steps 1–5) neighbor rules $r(x; \theta')$ are produced from θ by decreasing thresholds $\theta' \leq \theta$. For each boundary object thresholds θ decrease until another object becomes boundary.

At second stage (steps 6–11) neighbor rules $r(x; \theta')$ are produced from θ by increasing thresholds $\theta' \geq \theta$. This is a more involved case that requires a recursive procedure. The preliminary work at steps 6, 7 helps to reduce further search by determining the maximal boundary $\bar{\theta}$ that neighbor rules may fall in.

Each object $x \in \mathbb{X}$ can have one of three states: $x.\text{checked} \in \{\text{false}, \text{bad}, \text{good}\}$, what enables to avoid the repeated processing of objects at second stage.

Initially all objects are not checked. Then for each object $x \in \mathbb{X}$ covered by the rule $r(x; \bar{\theta})$ but not covered by the rule $r(x; \theta)$ the recursive procedure Check(x) is invoked. If the rule $r(x; \theta')$ covers only one object x in addition to objects covered by $r(x; \theta)$ then x is good. Otherwise the rule $r(x; \theta')$ covers two objects $x, \tilde{x}$ not covered by the rule $r(x; \theta)$; in such case x is bad and the procedure Check$(\tilde{x})$ is invoked recursively with the object $\tilde{x}$. Each good object x induces the neighbor rule $\theta' = \max\{\theta, x\}$, which is added to the set V_θ.

Algorithm 4.1 guarantee that all neighbor rules will be found. Besides it calculates all characteristics of the rule needed to calculate SC-bound: $q(\theta)$, $r(\theta)$,

---

Algorithm 4.1. Seek the neighborhood V_θ of the rule $r(x; \theta)$.

Require: features subset J, thresholds $\theta = (\theta^j)_{j \in J}$, class label $y \in Y$, general set $\mathbb{X}$.
Ensure: V_θ, X_θ, X'_θ, $q(\theta)$, $r(\theta)$, $n(\theta)$.

1: $V_\theta := \varnothing$;
2: **for all** $x \in \mathbb{X}$ such that $r(x; \theta) = 1$ and $\theta^j = x^j$ for some $j \in J$ **do**
3:      **for all** $j \in J$ such that $x^j = \theta^j$ **do**
4:          $\theta'^j := \max\{x_i^j \mid x_i \in \mathbb{X},\ x_i < \theta\}$;
5:          AddNeighbor(θ, θ', x);
6: **for all** $j \in J$ **do**
7:      $\bar{\theta}^j := \max\{L, x^j \mid x \in \mathbb{X},\ x^j > \theta^j,\ x^t \le \theta^t,\ t \ne j\}$;
8: **for all** $j \in J$ **do**
9:      **for all** x such that $\theta^j < x^j \le \bar{\theta}^j$ **do**
10:          **if** $x < \bar{\theta}$ and x.checked $=$ false **then**
11:              Check(x);

12: **Procedure** Check(x)
13: **for all** $j \in J$ such that $\theta^j < x^j$ **do**
14:      **for all** $\tilde{x}$ such that $\theta^j < \tilde{x}^j < x^j$ **do**
15:          **if** $\theta < \tilde{x} < x$ **then**
16:              x.checked $:=$ bad;
17:              **if** $\tilde{x}$.checked $=$ false **then** Check$(\tilde{x})$;
18:              **exit**;
19: x.checked $:=$ good;
20: $\theta'^j := \max\{\theta^j, x^j\}$, for all $j \in J$;
21: AddNeighbor(θ, θ', x);

22: **Procedure** AddNeighbor (θ, θ', x_i)
23: add the rule θ' into the set of neighbors V_θ;
24: **if** $r(x_i; \theta) = [y_i{=}y]$ **then**
25:      $X_\theta := X_\theta \cup \{x_i\}$; $q(\theta) := |X_\theta|$;
26: **else**
27:      $X'_\theta := X'_\theta \cup X'_{\theta'} \cup \{x_i\}$; $r(\theta) := |X'_\theta|$; $n(\theta) := n(\theta') + 1$;

---

and $n(\theta)$. To avoid the exhaustive search of all objects at steps 4, 7, 9, 14 the sorting index is to be built in advance for each coordinate $j \in J$.

Level-wise bottom-up calculation of SC-bound. Algorithm 4.2 starts from a lowest layer of classifiers. At each step it process a layer Θ consisting of all rules θ that makes $m = n(\theta)$ errors on general set. For each rule θ Algorithm 4.2 calculates its contribution to the SC-bound, builds its neighborhood, and forms the $(m{+}1)$-th layer Θ' joining upper parts of all neighborhoods. The steps are repeated until layer contribution becomes sufficiently small. Note that early stopping gives a lower estimate for (3), witch is upper bound on probability of overfitting.

Experiment. We used following state-of-the art algorithms as baseline rule learners: C4.5 [7], C5.0 [6], RIPPER [2], and SLIPPER [3]. Our rule learning engine was based on breadth-first search as feature selection strategy and Fisher's exact test (FET) as heuristic H. To build compositions of rules three algorithms

Algorithm 4.2. SC-bound calculation for the set of conjunction rules.

Require: features subset J, class label $y \in Y$, set of objects $\mathbb{X}$.

Ensure: Q_ε — SC-bound on probability of overfitting (3).

1: $\Theta := \operatorname*{Arg\,min}_\theta n(\theta); \quad Q_\varepsilon := 0;$
2: **repeat**
3: $\quad Q_{\varepsilon,m} := 0; \quad \Theta' := \varnothing;$
4: $\quad$ **for all** $\theta \in \Theta$ **do**
5: $\quad\quad$ **call** Algorithm 4.1 to build the neighborhood V_θ;
6: $\quad\quad Q_{\varepsilon,m} := Q_{\varepsilon,m} + \frac{1}{C_L^\ell} C_{L-q(\theta)-r(\theta)}^{\ell-q(\theta)} H_{L-q(\theta)-r(\theta)}^{\ell-q(\theta),\, n(\theta)-r(\theta)} \left(\frac{\ell}{L}(n(\theta) - \varepsilon k) \right);$
7: $\quad\quad \Theta' := \Theta' \cup \{\theta' \in V_\theta : n(\theta') = n(\theta) + 1\};$
8: $\quad Q_\varepsilon := Q_\varepsilon + Q_{\varepsilon,m}; \quad \Theta := \Theta';$
9: **until** the contribution of the m-th layer $Q_{\varepsilon,m}$ becomes small.

has been implemented. Logistic Regression (LR) is a linear classifier that aggregates rules learned independently. Weighted Voting (WV) is a boosting-like ensemble of rules similar to SLIPPER which learns each subsequent rule from reweighted training set. Decision List (DL) is a greedy algorithm which learns each subsequent rule from training objects not covered by all previous rules.

We implemented two modifications of heuristic $H'(p, n)$. The SC modification uses SC-bound on the probability of overfitting Q_ε as described above. The MC modification uses the Monte-Carlo estimation of Q_ε via 100 random partitions $\mathbb{X} = X \sqcup \bar{X}$. For both modifications we set $\ell = k$.

Table 1. Experimental results on 6 real data sets from UCI Machine Learning Repository. For each pair $\langle$task, algorithm$\rangle$ an average testing error obtained from 10-fold cross validation is given, in percents. For each task three best results are bold-emphasized. Algorithms 1–7 are baseline rule learners. Our algorithms: WV — Weighted Voting, DL — Decision List, SC — using heuristic modified by SC-bound, MC — using heuristic modified by Monte-Carlo estimation of the probability of overfitting.

	algorithms	tasks					
		australian	echo-card	heart dis.	hepatitis	labor	liver
1	RIPPER−opt	15.5	**2.9**	19.7	20.7	18.0	32.7
2	RIPPER+opt	15.2	5.5	20.1	23.2	18.0	**31.3**
3	C4.5 (Tree)	14.2	5.5	20.8	18.8	14.7	37.7
4	C4.5 (Rules)	15.5	6.8	20.0	18.8	14.7	37.5
5	C5.0	**14.0**	4.3	21.8	20.1	18.4	31.9
6	SLIPPER	15.7	4.3	**19.4**	**17.4**	**12.3**	32.2
7	LR	14.8	4.3	19.9	18.8	14.2	32.0
8	WV	14.9	4.3	20.1	19.0	14.0	32.3
9	DL	15.1	4.5	20.5	19.5	14.7	35.8
10	**WV+MC**	**13.9**	**3.0**	**19.5**	**18.3**	**13.2**	**30.7**
11	**DL+MC**	14.5	3.5	19.8	18.7	13.8	32.8
12	**WV+SC**	**14.1**	**3.2**	**19.3**	**18.1**	**13.4**	**30.2**
13	**DL+SC**	14.4	3.6	19.5	18.6	13.6	32.3

Results are presented in Table 1. Initial unmodified versions of our algorithms WV and DL with FET heuristic have a performance comparable to the baseline. WV outperforms DL, what corresponds to the results of other authors. Both SC and MC modifications of the FET heuristic reduce overfitting of rules and of classifier as a whole. Both modified classifiers outperform their respective initial versions for all 6 tasks. It must be emphasized that the only modification is the rule evaluation heuristic, all other things being equal. Thus, all difference in performance is due to generalization bound used in modified FET heuristic. The difference between SC and MC results is not significant, but MC estimation is much more time consuming. A moderate looseness of the SC-bound really takes place but does not reduce its practical usefulness as a rule selection criterion.

5   Conclusion

This work gives a new SC (splitting and connectivity) combinatorial bound on probability of overfitting. It takes into account a fine internal structure of the set of classifiers formalized in terms of the SC-graph. For a set of threshold conjunctive rules a level-wise bottom-up algorithm with early stopping is proposed for effective SC-bound computation. The inverted SC-bound is used to modify standard rule evaluation heuristic. This modification can be build in most known rule learners. It enables to take into account an amount of overfitting resulting from thresholds learning, and then to select features subset for each rule more accurately. Experiments on six real data sets show that the proposed modification reduces overfitting significantly.

References

1. Boucheron, S., Bousquet, O., Lugosi, G.: Theory of classification: A survey of some recent advances. ESAIM: Probability and Statistics (9), 323–375 (2005)
2. Cohen, W.W.: Fast effective rule induction. In: Proc. of the 12th International Conference on Machine Learning, Tahoe City, CA, pp. 115–123. Morgan Kaufmann, San Francisco (1995)
3. Cohen, W.W., Singer, Y.: A simple, fast and effective rule learner. In: Proc. of the 16 National Conference on Artificial Intelligence, pp. 335–342 (1999)
4. Fürnkranz, J., Flach, P.A.: Roc 'n' rule learning-towards a better understanding of covering algorithms. Machine Learning 58(1), 39–77 (2005)
5. Martin, J.K.: An exact probability metric for decision tree splitting and stopping. Machine Learning 28(2-3), 257–291 (1997)
6. Quinlan, J.R.: C4.5: Programs for machine learning. Morgan Kaufmann, San Francisco (1993)
7. Quinlan, J.R.: Bagging, boosting, and C4.5. AAAI/IAAI 1, 725–730 (1996)
8. Vorontsov, K.V.: Combinatorial probability and the tightness of generalization bounds. Pattern Recognition and Image Analysis 18(2), 243–259 (2008)
9. Vorontsov, K.V.: Splitting and similarity phenomena in the sets of classifiers and their effect on the probability of overfitting. Pattern Recognition and Image Analysis 19(3), 412–420 (2009)

An Improvement of Dissimilarity-Based Classifications Using SIFT Algorithm*

Evensen E. Masaki and Sang-Woon Kim

Dept. of Computer Science and Engineering,
Myongji University, Yongin, 449-728 South Korea
{evenalexjr,kimsw}@mju.ac.kr

Abstract. In dissimilarity-based classifications (DBCs), classifiers are not based on the feature measurements of individual objects, but rather on a suitable dissimilarity measure among the objects. In this paper, we study a new way of measuring the dissimilarity between two object images using a SIFT (Scale Invariant Feature Transformation) algorithm [5], which transforms image data into scale-invariant coordinates relative to local features based on the statistics of gray values in scale-space. With this method, we find an optimal or nearly optimal matching among differing images in scaling and rotation, which leads us to obtain dissimilarity representation after matching them. Our experimental results, obtained with well-known benchmark databases, demonstrate that the proposed mechanism works well and, compared with the previous approaches, achieves further improved results in terms of classification accuracy.

1 Introduction

Dissimilarity-based classifications (DBCs) [6] are a way of defining classifiers among classes; the process is not based on the feature measurements of individual objects, but rather on a suitable dissimilarity measure among them. The problem with this strategy is that we need to measure the inter-pattern dissimilarities for all the training samples to ensure there is no zero distance between objects of different classes. Several strategies can be employed to address this problem, which include the regional distance [1], the Euclidean distances of images [9], a dynamic programming technique [4], and classification of regions of interest (ROIs) [8]. In [9], Wang et al. propose a new Euclidean distance, called IMage Euclidean Distance (IMED). Unlike the traditional one, IMED takes into consideration the spatial relationships of pixels. From this point of view, the researchers claim to get a more reliable similarity measure.

In addition, in [4], Kim and Gao propose a way of measuring the dissimilarity distance between two images of an object when the images have different directions and sizes and there is no direct feature correspondence. In this method, a dynamic programming technique, such as dynamic time warping, is used to overcome the limitations of one-to-one mapping. Recently, in [8], Sorensen et al. proposed a method of directly measuring dissimilarities between images by using region of interests (ROIs) of the segments. When computing the dissimilarity between two images, x_1 and x_2, they consider

---

* This work was supported by the National Research Foundation of Korea funded by the Korean Government (NRF-2011-0002517).

S.O. Kuznetsov et al. (Eds.): PReMI 2011, LNCS 6744, pp. 74–79, 2011.

an associated weight, $\triangle(x_{1i}, x_{2j})$, that expresses the textural dissimilarity between the two corresponding ROIs, x_{1i} and x_{2j}. Here, to avoid a case in which all ROIs in x_1 are matched to all ROIs in x_2, they employ a way of matching every ROI in one image with the most similar ROI in the other image.

On the other hand, Lowe [5] proposed the scale invariant feature transformation (SIFT) algorithm for extracting distinctive invariant features from images that can be used to perform reliable matching between different views of an object. The features are invariant to image scale and rotation, and are shown to provide robust matching across a substantial range of affine distortion, addition of noise, and change in illumination. Thus, SIFT can be used to detect distinct features in an image and to transform image data into scale-invariant coordinates relative to local features. The algorithm consists of four main steps to generate the set of image features: scale-space peak detection, keypoint localization, orientation assignment, and keypoint descriptor.

The major task of this study is to deal with how dissimilarity measure can be effectively computed. However, when there are many kinds of variations based on such factors as pose (direction), scaling, and illumination [1], [3], it is difficult to improve the performance of DBCs in the dissimilarity space. To overcome this limitation and thereby improve the classification performance of DBCs, in this paper, we study a new way of enriching the representational capability of dissimilarity measures. In particular, this goal can be achieved by using a SIFT algorithm based on the statistics of gray values in scale-space. With regard to measuring the dissimilarity of the object images, we prefer not to directly measure the dissimilarity from the images; rather, we employ a particular way of using SIFT to *adjust* or *scale* the object images. This measure effectively serves as a new "feature" component in the dissimilarity space.

2   DBCs with SIFT Algorithm

Scale Invariant Feature Transformation (SIFT) [5]: SIFT is an algorithm for extracting distinctive invariant features from images that can be used to perform reliable matching between different views of an object. The features are invariant to image scale and rotation, and are shown to provide robust matching across a substantial range of affine distortion, changes in 3D viewpoint, addition of noise, and changes in illumination [5]. Four computational stages of SIFT are scale-space peak detection, keypoint localization, orientation assignment, and keypoint descriptor, respectively. The details of SIFT are omitted here in the interest of brevity, but can be found in the literature [5].

Dissimilarity-Based Classifications (DBCs) [6]: A dissimilarity representation of a set of samples, $T = \{x_i\}_{i=1}^n \in \mathbb{R}^d$, is based on pairwise comparisons and is expressed, for example, as an $n \times m$ dissimilarity matrix $D_{T,Y}[i, j]$, where $Y = \{y_j\}_{j=1}^m \in \mathbb{R}^d$, a prototype set, is extracted from T, and the subscripts of D represent the set of elements, on which the dissimilarities are evaluated. Thus, each entry, $D_{T,Y}[i, j]$, corresponds to the dissimilarity between the pairs of objects, x_i and y_j. Consequently, an object, x, is represented as a column vector, $\delta(x)$. In image classification, one of the most intractable problems is the distortion caused by the differences in illumination, scaling, and rotation. To overcome this problem, in this paper, we use the SIFT algorithm. The proposed approach, which is referred to as DBC-with-SIFT, is summarized as follows:

1. Select the whole training set, T, as the representation subset, Y.

2. For all the pairs of objects, x_i and y_j, where $x_i \in T$ and $y_j \in Y$, compute $D_{T,Y}[i,j]$ as follows: (1) After extracting the entire set of *keypoints* from x_i and y_j with SIFT, select the primary *keypoints* among them using heuristic methods [1]. (2) Compute $D_{T,Y}[i,j]$ in the following sub-steps: The first sub-step is to generate two queues, Q_x and Q_y, by inserting the selected primary keypoints and $d = 0$. The second sub-step is to compute the Euclidean distance, $d = d + \|x(i,j) - y(k,l)\|$, between two pixels (keypoints), $(i,j) \in Q_x$ and $(k,l) \in Q_y$, which have been deleted from the two queues, respectively. Then, the 8-nearest neighbors around the pixels are inserted into the queues. If Q_x and Q_y are empty, then exit; otherwise, go to the second sub-step.

3. For a testing sample, z, compute $\delta(z)$ by using the same measure used in Step 2.

4. Achieve the classification by invoking a classifier built in the dissimilarity space defined with $D_{T,Y}[\cdot,\cdot]$ and by operating the classifier on the dissimilarity vector, $\delta(z)$.

The time complexities (i.e., the increase in computational complexity) of the above algorithm are omitted here, but will be presented in the journal version.

Primary Keypoint Selections: In DBC-with-SIFT, to select the primary keypoints to compensate for the differences in direction or illumination, we consider two heuristic rules: *slope-based (SB)* rule and *number-based (NB)* rule. For each pair of keypoints, slope values, $\{\phi_i\}_{i=1}^M$, where ϕ_i is the angle between the ith slope and a base line and M the number of the keypoints, can be calculated by using their frames [2]. In the SB rule, after computing all the slope values of the keypoints, we select *primary* keypoints from the keypoints, which are within the range of $-\alpha \leq \phi_i \leq \alpha$, where $\{\alpha | \alpha = 0.2, 0.3, \cdots, 1.0\}$. In the NB rule, on the other hand, after sorting all the slope values, we select the β number of keypoints in an ascending order from the smallest values of $\{\phi_i\}_{i=1}^M$ as the primary keypoints, where $\{\beta | \beta = 1, 3, \cdots, 17\}$.

3   Experimental Results

Experimental Data: The proposed method has been tested and compared with conventional methods. This was done by performing experiments on three benchmark databases, namely, AT&T [3], CMU (CMU-Expression) [4], and Leaves [5]. Here, the numbers of samples, dimensions, and classes of these databases are, respectively, (400, 10304, 40), (200, 16384, 10), and (45, 530432, 3). Also, Leaves was employed as a benchmark database for object classification, while AT&T and CMU were utilized as examples of the non-background and background face recognition, respectively.

Experimental Method: First, data sets are split into training sets and test sets in the ratio of 75 : 25. The training and testing procedures are repeated 30 times and the results obtained are averaged. Next, in the conventional DBCs, which is referred to as

---

[1] This method will be presented in a later section.

[2] The SB rule is based on assumption that face images are well posed in vertical shift and size. If such positioning is not perfect, some special detectors of human face could be considered.

[3] http://www.cl.cam.ac.uk/Research/DTG/attarchive/facedatabase.html

[4] http://www.ri.cmu.edu/research_project_detail.html?project_id=418&menu_id=261

[5] http://www.vision.caltech.edu/html-files/archive.html

Fig. 1. Plots of the pairwise keypoints obtained with SIFT and the primary keypoints selected with the NB rule for two objects of AT&T: (a) left and (b) right; (a) is for the entire set of keypoints. (b) is for the primary keypoints selected from (a).

DBCs-without-SIFT (shortly SIFT-without), we computed the dissimilarity between two object images using their gray values. In DBC-with-SIFT (shortly SIFT-with), however, after extracting the primary keypoints from the two objects using SIFT and NB (or SB) rule, we computed the dissimilarity. For example, Fig. 1 shows plots of the pairwise keypoints and the selected primary keypoints for two objects of AT&T. Finally, to evaluate DBCs built in the SIFT-without and SIFT-with methods, different classifiers, such as k-nearest neighbor classifiers (referred to *nnc*) and support vector machines (named *svm*), are employed and implemented with PRTools [2].

Experimental Results: Fig. 2 shows a comparison of the estimated error rates of *two* classifiers designed with the SIFT-without (*nnc1* and *svm1* - dashed lines of ○ and ◁ markers, respectively) and SIFT-with (*nnc2* and *svm2* - solid lines of the same markers) methods for the databases.

First, the estimated error rates for AT&T are very small but for the rest of the databases (i.e., CMU and Leaves) are higher. This might be because when capturing photos, the former method is non-background. Next, from the pictures shown in Fig. 2, it should be observed that, in general, the dashed lines are higher than the solid lines. That is, for the three databases, the estimated error rates of *nnc1* and *svm1* are higher than those of *nnc2* and *svm2*, respectively. From this observation, the following conclusion is derived: measuring dissimilarities between images with SIFT-with method leads to lower error rates than measuring the distance with SIFT-without method.

The other observations obtained from the figures are the following:

- For AT&T (SB), the *svm*-lines of ◁ markers show that there is more improvement in classification error rate when using the SB rule than when using the NB rule. This indicates that we have achieved the goal that we desired to solve using the proposed methods (refer to Figs. 2(a) and (b) on top).

- For AT&T and Leaves, it should be observed that *svm* is the best classifier for the SB and NB rules in terms of classification accuracies. However, for CMU database, *svm* is the best classifier for SB rule, while for the case of NB rule, the best working classifier varies: For $1 \leq \beta \leq 5$ and $14 \leq \beta \leq 17$, *svm* works well. For $6 \leq \beta \leq 13$, however, *nnc* acts well (refer to Figs. 2(c) and (d) in middle).

- For the Leaves database, SB rule gives almost the same estimated error rates (flat), but for the case of NB rule, there is an increase and decrease of estimated error rates, which makes it difficult to find the optimal or nearly optimal slope values and the number of keypoints (refer to Figs. 2(e) and (f) at bottom).

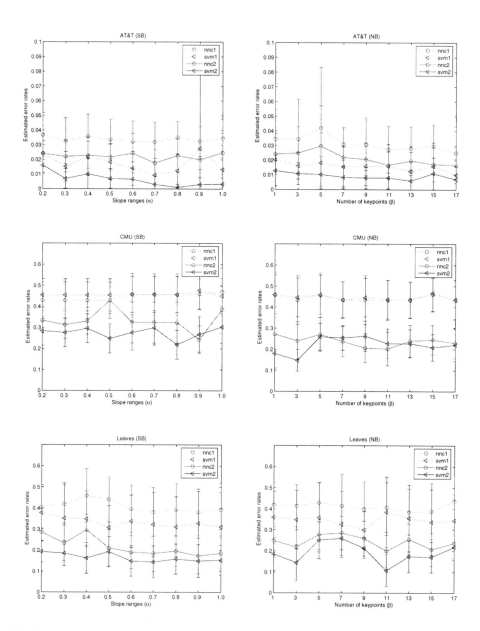

Fig. 2. A comparison of the estimated error rates of *two* classifiers designed with the SIFT-without (*nnc1* and *svm1* - dashed lines of ∘ and ◁ markers) and SIFT-with methods (*nnc2* and *svm2* - solid lines of the same markers) for the three databases: (a) top left, (b) top right, (c) middle left, (d) middle right, (e) bottom left, and (f) bottom right; (a) and (b) are for the two rules (i.e., SB and NB rules) for AT&T; (c) and (d) are for the two methods of CMU; (e) and (f) are for Leaves

4   Conclusions

In order to improve the classification performance of DBCs, in this paper we used the SIFT algorithm based on the local statistics of gray values in scale-space. With SIFT, we first obtained the entire set of keypoints from paired images and, in turn, selected a few primary keypoints using either the slope-based or the number-based rule, eliminating inappropriate keypoints. Using the selected primary keypoints, we generated a dissimilarity representation, in which DBCs have been performed. Our experimental results, obtained with three benchmark databases, demonstrate that the classification accuracy of DBCs was improved when the number of primary matched keypoints was appropriately chosen. Although we have shown that DBCs can be improved by employing SIFT, many tasks remain. One of them is to improve the classification efficiency by selecting an optimal or nearly optimal number of the primary keypoints from the entire set of keypoints obtained with SIFT for the paired object images. Also, it is not yet clear which kinds of significant data sets are more suitable for the scheme.

References

1. Adini, Y., Moses, Y., Ullman, S.: Face recognition: the problem of compensating for changes in illumination direction. IEEE Trans. Pattern Anal. and Machine Intell. 19(7), 721–732 (1997)
2. Duin, R.P.W., Juszczak, P., de Ridder, D., Paclik, P., Pekalska, E., Tax, D.M.J.: PRTools 4: a Matlab Toolbox for Pattern Recognition. Technical Report, Delft University of Technology, The Netherlands (2004), http://prtools.org/
3. Georghiades, A.S., Belhumeur, P.N., Kriegman, D.J.: From few to many: Illumination cone models for face recognition under variable lighting and pose. IEEE Trans. Pattern Anal. and Machine Intell. 23(6), 643–660 (2001)
4. Kim, S.-W., Gao, J.: A dynamic programming technique for optimizing dissimilarity-based classifiers. In: da Vitoria Lobo, N., Kasparis, T., Roli, F., Kwok, J.T., Georgiopoulos, M., Anagnostopoulos, G.C., Loog, M. (eds.) S+SSPR 2008. LNCS, vol. 5342, pp. 654–663. Springer, Heidelberg (2008)
5. Lowe, D.G.: Distinctive image features from scale-invariant keypoints. International Journal of Computer Vision 60(2), 91–110 (2004)
6. Pekalska, E., Duin, R.P.W.: The Dissimilarity Representation for Pattern Recognition: Foundations and Applications. World Scientific Publishing, Singapore (2005)
7. Sim, T., Baker, S., Bsat, M.: The CMU pose, illumination, and expression (PIE) database of human faces. Technical report CMU-RI-TR-01-02, Robotics Institute, Carnegie Mellon University, Pittsburgh, PA (2001)
8. Sørensen, L., Loog, M., Lo, P., Ashraf, H., Dirksen, A., Duin, R.P.W., de Bruijne, M.: Image dissimilarity-based quantification of lung disease from CT. In: Jiang, T., Navab, N., Pluim, J.P.W., Viergever, M.A. (eds.) MICCAI 2010. LNCS, vol. 6361, pp. 37–44. Springer, Heidelberg (2010)
9. Wang, L., Zhang, Y., Feng, J.: On the Euclidean distance of images. IEEE Trans. Pattern Anal. and Machine Intell. 27(8), 1334–1339 (2005)

Introduction, Elimination Rules for ¬ and ⊃: A Study from Graded Context

Soma Dutta

Indian Institute of Bio-Social Research and Development,
Prafulla Kanan, VIP Road, Kestopur, Kolkata - 700101
somadutta9@gmail.com

Abstract. This paper is aimed to study the algebraic background of some proof theoretic rules in a set up where distinct levels of logic activity have been maintained carefully. In this regard, Introduction, Elimination rules for ¬, and ⊃ have been considered as specific cases whose necessary and sufficient conditions from the perspective of graded consequence will reveal a new analysis.

Keywords: Graded consequence, Object level algebra, Meta level algebra, Introduction and Elimination rules, Proof theory.

1 Introduction

Natural deduction system was introduced [5] to bring into notice the prototypes of human reasoning in the form of some rules of inference. Sentences (wffs) i.e. elements of F, the set of all wffs are object level entities; whereas, the notion of inference is a meta level concept. Rules of inference lie at meta meta level to talk about the interrelation between two or more than two inferences. This distinction between levels is generally missing in the existing approaches. Gentzen's own interpretation to ⊃-Introduction [5] is a clear evidence of mixing up meta level implication namely 'provability' with object level implication 'follows'. Later on, when Sequent calculus was introduced [5], a sequent viz., $A_1, A_2, \ldots A_n \vdash B_1, B_2 \ldots B_m$ is assumed to represent the truth of the object level sentence '$A_1 \wedge A_2 \wedge \ldots \wedge A_n \supset B_1 \vee B_2 \vee \ldots \vee B_m$'. In [7], it has been clearly mentioned that in LJ and LK (the sequent calculus presentations for Intuitionistic logic and Classical logic respectively) the presence of contraction left, weakening left, cut, &-left and &-right jointly claim the proposition '$\delta, \phi \vdash \psi$ if and only if $\delta \& \phi \vdash \psi$'. This indicates that usual practice in LJ and LK is to see meta level symbol ',' and object level conjunction '&' equivalently. Apart from LJ, LK, it has been a convenient practice in many other logical systems [6] also. In substructural logics [7] where some of the structural rules remain absent, the rules for & are modified in such a way that in absence of any one of the above mentioned structural rules '$\delta, \phi \vdash \psi$ if and only if $\delta \& \phi \vdash \psi$' remains unaltered. Thus in all these approaches a lack of clarity in distinction between levels of logic activity is envisaged.

Theory of graded consequence which was introduced by Chakraborty [1] in order to generalize two-valued notion of consequence relation in many-valued context, throws light on this issue. Suppose L is a set of truth values assigned

S.O. Kuznetsov et al. (Eds.): PReMI 2011, LNCS 6744, pp. 80–85, 2011.

to the sentences of F endowed with some operators, say, $\rightarrow_o$, $\neg_o$, $*_o$ in correspondence to each connective $\supset$, $\neg$, & of the object language. Now with respect to $\{T_i\}_{i \in I}$, a set of fuzzy subsets any formula α gets a truth value in L. Thus $\{T_i\}_{i \in I}$ determines the value of the meta-linguistic sentence 'X semantically entails α' or in symbol '$X \models \alpha$'. In two-valued context, '$X \models \alpha$' i.e. 'for all T_i, if $X \subseteq T_i$ then $\alpha \in T_i$', where each T_i is identified with the valuation under which all formulae of T_i get the value 1, involves a meta-level 'if-then' and quantifier 'for all'. So, a complete lattice along with an implication $\rightarrow_m$ is needed for meta level algebra.

Now, let us consider the following form of Deduction Theorem ($\supset$-Introduction).

$$\frac{X, \alpha \vdash \beta}{X \vdash \alpha \supset \beta}$$

where X is a set of formulas and α, β are single formulas. In algebraic term this can be restated as – 'truth value $(X, \alpha \vdash \beta) \leq$ truth value $(X \vdash \alpha \supset \beta)$. Or more formally abbreviating 'grade' by 'gr' one can write –

$$\mathrm{gr}(X \cup \{\alpha\} \vdash \beta) \leq \mathrm{gr}(X \vdash \alpha \supset \beta) \qquad \ldots (A)$$

So, to obtain Deduction Theorem (DT) as a rule of inference demands should be made to the operators $\rightarrow_m$ computing $\vdash$ and $\rightarrow_o$ computing $\supset$ in such a way that as a result (A) gets satisfied.

This clarifies that the algebras of different levels of logic give rise to different rules of inference. Having this as the main theme of the paper, in Section 2, the basic concept of the notion of graded consequence will be introduced and then as a specific case of study the necessary and sufficient conditions for graded Introduction, Elimination rules for $\supset$ and $\neg$ will be discussed. In Section 3 we will try to show that this study of proof theoretic results from the perspective of graded consequence gives a different analysis in comparison to the existing approaches.

2 In the Context of Graded Consequence

In graded context depending on a collection of fuzzy sets $\{T_i\}_{i \in I}$ over well-formed formulas the sentence 'α is a consequence of X' may get values other than the top (1) and least (0). That is, the notion of derivation of a formula from a set of formulae is in general a graded concept. Usually logics dealing with uncertainties do not feel the necessity to address many-valuedness in the concept of derivation. In this regard, an overlapping standpoint with ours can be found in [6] in the concept of degree of soundness of a rule. A graded consequence relation [3] is assumed to be a fuzzy relation $|\sim$ satisfying the following conditions.

(GC1) if $\alpha \in X$ then $\mathrm{gr}(X |\sim \alpha) = 1$ (Reflexivity),
(GC2) if $X \subseteq Y$ then $\mathrm{gr}(X |\sim \alpha) \leq \mathrm{gr}(Y |\sim \alpha)$ (Monotonicity),
(GC3) $inf_{\beta \in Y} \, \mathrm{gr}(X |\sim \beta) *_m \mathrm{gr}(X \cup Y |\sim \alpha) \leq \mathrm{gr}(X |\sim \alpha)$ (Cut)

Given a context i.e a collection $\{T_i\}_{i \in I}$ of fuzzy subsets over formulae and a meta-level algebra $(L, \rightarrow_m, *_m)$, consisting of operators for meta-level implication

and conjunction, a sentence 'α is a consequence of X' gets a truth value, denoted by $gr(X \mid\approx_{\{T_i\}_{i\in I}} \alpha)$ in L. In two-valued context, Shoesmith and Smiley [8], generalized the definition of semantic consequence with respect to a set of $\{0,1\}$-valued valuations $\{T_j\}_{j\in J}$. According to this definition $X \models \alpha$ basically means 'for all T in $\{T_j\}_{j\in J}$, if for all $x \in X$, $x \in T$ then $\alpha \in T$'. Generalizing this idea in graded context the value of $X \mid\approx_{\{T_i\}_{i\in I}} \alpha$ is calculated by the expression – $gr(X \mid\approx_{\{T_i\}_{i\in I}} \alpha)$
$= inf_i \{inf_{x\in X} T_i(x) \to_m T_i(\alpha)\}$

In [2], it had been proved that given a context $\{T_i\}_{i\in I}$ and a complete residuated lattice $(L, \to_m, *_m)$ for meta level algebra, $\mid\approx_{\{T_i\}_{i\in I}}$ is a graded consequence relation. On the other hand, it also had been proved [2] that given any graded consequence relation $\mid\sim$ there exists $\{T_i\}_{i\in I}$, a collection of fuzzy subsets over formulas, such that the fuzzy relation $\mid\approx_{\{T_i\}_{i\in I}}$ coincides with $\mid\sim$. These two results together constitutes the representation theorem.

Now let us come to the context of graded rule DT i.e. $gr(X \cup \{\alpha\} \mid\sim \beta) \leq gr(X \mid\sim \alpha \supset \beta)$

Theorem 1. A necessary and sufficient condition for graded DT (or $\supset$-introduction rule)
For any $\mid\sim$ defined over a complete residuated lattice L, a necessary and sufficient condition for $gr(X \cup \{\alpha\} \mid\sim \beta) \leq gr(X \mid\sim \alpha \supset \beta)$ is that for any $a,b \in L$, $a \to_m b \leq a \to_o b$.

Theorem 2. A necessary condition for graded MP (or $\supset$-Elimination)
For any $\mid\sim$, defined over a complete residuated lattice L, the necessary condition for $gr(X \mid\sim \alpha) *_m gr(Y \mid\sim \alpha \supset \beta) \leq gr(X \cup Y \mid\sim \beta)$ is that for any $a,b \in L$, $a \to_o b \leq a \to_m b$.

Theorem 3. A sufficient condition for graded MP (or $\supset$-Elimination)
Let $\mid\sim$, defined over a complete residuated lattice L, satisfy the conditions viz., (i) for any $a,b \in L$, $a \to_o b \leq a \to_m b$ and (ii) $(a \to_m b) *_m (a \to_m c) \leq a \to_m (b *_m c)$. Then $gr(X \mid\sim \alpha) *_m gr(Y \mid\sim \alpha \supset \beta) \leq gr(X \cup Y \mid\sim \beta)$ holds.

From this study on the necessary and sufficient condition of the graded rule DT and MP we can see that an interrelation between the two levels of implication is needed for the viability of the rules. In two valued context (both classical and intuitionistic) $\to_o$ and $\to_m$ are the same. Also for $*_m = \wedge$, $(a \to_m b) *_m (a \to_m c) \leq a \to_m (b *_m c)$ holds. So, both DT and MP are valid in classical as well as intuitionistic cases. As a non-trivial example, let us consider $[0,1]$ endowed with Gödel adjoint pair as the meta-level algebra for $\mid\sim$ and Lukasiweciz implication for computing $\supset$. Then these structures for object and meta level satisfy $a \to_m b \leq a \to_o b$ and hence DT holds in this case. On the other hand, with Gödel algebra as meta structure and computing $\supset$ by Gödel implication, one can find a model for graded rule MP.

Let us now consider the rule $\neg$-Introduction viz., $[\alpha]$

$$\vdots$$

$$\Lambda$$
$$\overline{\neg\alpha}.$$

This presentation is due to Gentzen [5]. In a language where Λ, the falsum constant is not present the above form is equivalent to $[\alpha]$

$$\vdots$$
$$\beta \quad \text{for all } \beta$$
$$\overline{\neg\alpha}$$

As in this present study we are considering sequents of the form $X \vdash \alpha$, the respective translation will be $\dfrac{X, \alpha \vdash \beta \quad \text{for all } \beta}{X \vdash \neg\alpha}$

Theorem 4. A necessary condition for graded $\neg$-Introduction
For any $|\sim$, defined over a complete residuated lattice L, the necessary condition for $\inf_\beta gr(X \cup \{\alpha\} \mid\sim \beta) \leq gr(X \mid\sim \neg\alpha)$ is that $a \to_m 0 \leq \neg_o a$ for any $a \in L$.

Theorem 5. A sufficient condition for graded $\neg$-Introduction
Let $|\sim$, defined over a complete residuated lattice L, satisfy the conditions viz.,

(i) there is an element $c(\neq 1) \in L$, such that $x \leq c$ or $x > c$ for any $x \in L$,
(ii) for any $a(\neq 1) \in L$, $a \to_m c \leq \neg_o a$ and (iii) $a > c$ implies $\neg_o a \leq c$.
Then $\inf_\beta gr(X \cup \{\alpha\} \mid\sim \beta) \leq gr(X \mid\sim \neg\alpha)$ holds.

Proof. As for any $|\sim$ there exists $\{T_i\}_{i \in I}$ such that $|\approx_{\{T_i\}_{i \in I}} = |\sim$ we have
$\inf_\beta gr(X \cup \{\alpha\} \mid\sim \beta) = \inf_\beta[\inf_i\{(\inf_{\gamma \in X} T_i(\gamma) \wedge T_i(\alpha)) \to_m T_i(\beta)\}]$
$\leq \inf_i\{(\inf_{\gamma \in X} T_i(\gamma) *_m T_i(\alpha)) \to_m \inf_\beta T_i(\beta)\}$
$= \inf_i\{(\inf_{\gamma \in X} T_i(\gamma) *_m T_i(\alpha)) \to_m \inf_\beta T_i(\beta) : T_i(\alpha) \neq 1\}$
$\qquad\qquad \wedge \inf_i\{(\inf_{\gamma \in X} T_i(\gamma) *_m T_i(\alpha)) \to_m \inf_\beta T_i(\beta) : T_i(\alpha) = 1\}$
$= \inf_i\{(\inf_{\gamma \in X} T_i(\gamma) *_m T_i(\alpha)) \to_m [\inf_\beta\{T_i(\beta) : T_i(\beta) \leq c\}] : T_i(\alpha) \neq 1\} \wedge$
$\qquad \wedge \inf_i\{\inf_{\gamma \in X} T_i(\gamma) \to_m \inf_\beta T_i(\beta) : T_i(\alpha) = 1\}$
[Using $\{T_i(\beta) : \beta \in F\} = \{T_i(\beta) : T_i(\beta) \leq c\} \cup \{T_i(\beta) : T_i(\beta) > c\}$ and (iii)]
$\leq \inf_i\{(\inf_{\gamma \in X} T_i(\gamma) *_m T_i(\alpha)) \to_m c : T_i(\alpha) \neq 1\} \wedge$
$\qquad\qquad \inf_i\{\inf_{\gamma \in X} T_i(\gamma) \to_m \inf_\beta T_i(\beta) : T_i(\alpha) = 1\}$
$= \inf_i\{\inf_{\gamma \in X} T_i(\gamma) \to_m (T_i(\alpha) \to_m c) : T_i(\alpha) \neq 1\} \wedge$
$\qquad\qquad \inf_i\{\inf_{\gamma \in X} T_i(\gamma) \to_m \inf_\beta T_i(\beta) : T_i(\alpha) = 1\}$
$\leq \inf_i\{\inf_{\gamma \in X} T_i(\gamma) \to_m \neg_o T_i(\alpha) : T_i(\alpha) \neq 1\} \wedge$
$\qquad\qquad \inf_i\{\inf_{\gamma \in X} T_i(\gamma) \to_m \neg_o T_i(\alpha) : T_i(\alpha) = 1\} \qquad$ [By (ii)]
$= gr(X \mid\sim \neg\alpha) \qquad\qquad\qquad\qquad\qquad\qquad\qquad\qquad\qquad\qquad \square$

$\neg$-Elimination presented in [5] is of the form $\dfrac{\alpha, \neg\alpha}{\beta}.$

In graded context $\neg$-Elimination is generalized as – 'There is some $k > 0$, such that $\inf_{\alpha,\beta} gr(\{\alpha, \neg\alpha\} \mid\sim \beta) = k$'. The necessary and sufficient conditions for graded $\neg$-Elimination are as follows.

Theorem 6. A necessary condition for graded $\neg$-Elimination
For any arbitrarily chosen complete residuated lattice L if graded $\neg$-Elimination holds for any $|\sim$, then for any non-zero $b \wedge \neg_o b$ of L, there exists some non-zero z in L such that $(b \wedge \neg_o b) * z = 0$.

Theorem 7. A sufficient condition for graded $\neg$-Elimination

Let $(L, *, \rightarrow_m, 0, 1)$ be a complete residuated lattice determining a graded conse-
quence relation $|\sim$ and $\neg_o$ be the operator for object language negation $\neg$ with
the conditions – (i) there is some $c(\neq 1)$, such that $b \wedge \neg_o b \leq c$ for any b in L
and (ii) if $c \neq 0$ then there exists $z(\neq 0)$ such that $c * z = 0$.
Then graded $\neg$-Elimination holds.

In two-valued context $a \wedge \neg a$ is always 0 and hence $\neg$-Elimination holds for k = 1. Also, the conditions suffice to have $\neg$-Introduction are true in two-valued context and hence we get $\neg$-Introduction in two-valued case. To have a non-trivial example let us consider $L = \{0, 1/2, 1\}$ with Lukasiewicz adjoint pair at meta level algebra. $\neg$ is defined by $\neg_o a = 0$ for $a = 1$ and 1 otherwise. Then for $c = 1/2$ one can verify the sufficient conditions for graded $\neg$-Introduction. The same structure also suffices to have graded $\neg$-Elimination; but in this case value of k will be 1. On the other hand, instead of the above definition of $\neg_o$ if we consider $\neg_o a = 1 - a$, then the value of k will be 1/2.

3 An Analysis of Proof Theoretic Rules of Inference: Existing Approaches versus the Theory of Graded Consequence

In the introduction, it has already been discussed that the existing approaches of looking at the notion of inference are so designed that the distinction between object level and meta level connectives gets mingled up. DT states $\alpha, \beta \vdash \gamma$ implies $\alpha \vdash \beta \supset \gamma$. But this turns out to be $\alpha \& \beta \vdash \gamma$ implies $\alpha \vdash \beta \supset \gamma$ due to the equivalent treatment given to ',' and '&'. On the other hand, $\supset$-left [7] along with reflexivity and cut gives rise to $\alpha \vdash \beta \supset \gamma$ implies $\alpha \& \beta \vdash \gamma$. The algebraic counterpart of $\alpha \& \beta \vdash \gamma$ if and only if $\alpha \vdash \beta \supset \gamma$ is given by $a *_o b \leq c$ iff $a \leq b \rightarrow_o c$ i.e. residuation in object level operators $*_o$ and $\rightarrow_o$. In this regard, the study of the background of DT from the perspective of graded consequence reveals a different analysis. In graded context, the summary of the semantic background of DT is – (i) the notion of consequence $|\sim$ depends on a meta-linguistic residuation pair $(*_m \rightarrow_m)$ and (ii) the object level $\rightarrow_o$ computing $\supset$ satisfies $a \rightarrow_m b \leq a \rightarrow_o b$.

This seems more close to the understanding of the rule viz., $[\alpha]$

$$\vdots$$
$$\frac{\beta}{\alpha \supset \beta}$$

as the rule asserts an object level implication viz., '$\alpha \supset \beta$' provided 'β is provable from α'.

In Section 2, we have discussed the necessary and sufficient condition for graded $\neg$-Introduction. The necessary condition for graded $\neg$-Introduction is $a \rightarrow_m o \leq \neg_o a$. On the other hand, the sufficient condition demands $a \rightarrow_m c \leq \neg_o a$ for some $c \neq 1$ which in two-valued scenario will reduce to $a \rightarrow_m o \leq \neg_o a$.

In algebraic term $\dfrac{\alpha \vdash \varLambda}{\vdash \neg\alpha}$, the special case of ¬-Introduction can be translated as

$a \rightarrow_m o \leq \neg_o a$ where algebraic interpretation of $\alpha, \varLambda, \vdash$ and the bold line between the upper and lower sequents are represented by a, 0, $\rightarrow_m$ and $\leq$ respectively. Then algebraic translation of $\alpha \vdash \varLambda$ would be $a \rightarrow_m 0$ and $\vdash \neg\alpha$ would be $1 \rightarrow_m \neg_o a$ (see definition of $|\approx_{\{T_i\}_{i \in I}}$ in page 3). This translation of ¬-Introduction becomes transparent due to the study of graded consequence.

4 Conclusion

Logic generally consists of three distinct levels viz, object, meta and meta-meta level. Each of these levels has a set of vocabulary which need not be the same. So, one can think of to have different algebraic structures for different levels of language, in general. Existing approaches have not paid much attention to this. As a result, the prevalent understanding for proof theoretic rules lacks a certain degree of clarity in maintaining the distinction of levels. In this paper we tried to provide an alternative analysis taking care of the distinction between levels. In this connection, exploring an alternative semantic background for classical and intuitionistic logic from the perspective of graded proof theoretic rules can be a new direction of study.

References

1. Chakraborty, M.K.: Use of fuzzy set theory in introducing graded consequence in multiple valued logic. In: Gupta, M.M., Yamakawa, T. (eds.) Fuzzy Logic in Knowledge-Based Systems, Decision and Control, pp. 247–257. Elsevier Science Publishers, B.V., North Holland (1988)
2. Chakraborty, M.K.: Graded Consequence: further studies. Journal of Applied Non-Classical Logics 5(2), 127–137 (1995)
3. Chakraborty, M.K., Basu, S.: Graded Consequence and some Metalogical Notions Generalized. Fundamenta Informaticae 32, 299–311 (1997)
4. Chakraborty, M.K., Dutta, S.: Graded Consequence Revisited. Fuzzy Sets and Systems 161(14), 1885–1905 (2010)
5. Gentzen, G.: Investigations into Logical Deductions. In: Gentzen, G., Szabo, M.E. (eds.) The collected papers, pp. 68–131. North Holland Publications, Amsterdam (1969)
6. Gottwald, S.: An approach to handle partially sound rules of inference. In: Bouchon-Meunier, B., Yager, R.R., Zadeh, L.A. (eds.) IPMU 1994. LNCS, vol. 945, pp. 380–388. Springer, Heidelberg (1995)
7. Ono, H.: Substructural Logics and Residuated Lattices - an Introduction. In: Hendricks, V.F., Malinowski, J. (eds.) Trends in Logic 20, pp. 177–212. Kluwer Academic Publishers, Netherlands (2003)
8. Shoesmith, D.J., Smiley, T.J.: Multiple Conclusion Logic. Cambridge University Press, Cambridge (1978)

Discrete Circular Mapping for Computation of Zernike Moments

Rajarshi Biswas and Sambhunath Biswas

Machine Intelligence Unit
Indian Statistical Institute
203, B T Road, Kolkata - 700108, India
rajarshi.biswas87@gmail.com, sambhu@isical.ac.in

Abstract. Zernike moments are found to have potentials in pattern recognition, image analysis, image processing and in computer vision, apart from its traditional field of optics. Their invariance and orthogonality are attractive in many applications. However, the study of its computational structure can lead to some efficient and fast algorithms. In this paper, we have examined the use of a discrete circular map to compute Zernike moments in polar coordinates. It should be noted that such a discrete circular map, to represent a garylevel image in polar coordinates, does not require any special kind of sampling. Hence, zernike moments in polar coordinates can be computed easily. Comparison shows the proposed method is also efficient in computation.

1 Introduction

Moments based on the theory of orthogonal polynomials can be used in a number of applications, namely in image analysis, image processing and pattern recognition. Teague [1] suggested to recover image from orthogonal moments using Zernike moments. An example of other orthogonal moments is based on Legendre polynomial. Teh et al. [2] made a study on the evaluation of various types of moments and their properties. Some other authors [3,4] examined Zernike moments and implemented that in the area of image analysis. Unfortunately, adequate attention has not been paid for the efficient computation of Zernike moments, though attempts are already made to speed up the calculation through geometric moments [6]-[11]. Mukundan and Ramakrishnan in [8] used a recursive algorithm to compute Zernike and Legendre moments. Their method takes a large number of computing operations [12]. J. Gu et al. [12] has used an iterative algorithm for the fast computation of Zernike moments. He used one dimensional FFT when the radius is a power of two and took help of Chan et al.'s algorithm [10] to compute a recursion. Yongqing Xin et al. [13] has revealed an interesting as well as very important fact about Zernike moments. They have shown that the polar Zernike moments outperform the Cartesian Zernike moments in terms of rotational invariance property. Wee et al. [14] has computed Zernike moments in polar coordinates through a traditional circle mapping technique.

S.O. Kuznetsov et al. (Eds.): PReMI 2011, LNCS 6744, pp. 86–91, 2011.

In this paper, we have proposed an algorithm to compute Zernike moments in a completely different way. To compute Zernike moments, we consider discrete circular mapping [5] to map a gray-level image onto a discrete circular disc. The mapping is different from that of Wee et al. [14]. The symmetry property of the discrete circle drastically reduces the computation for moments. Rotational invariance is also found to be in line with that in [13].

2   Zernike Polynomials and Zernike Moments

Zernike provided a set of complex polynomials, known as Zernike polynomials, that form a complete orthogonal set on the unit disc, i.e., over the interior of the unit circle $x^2 + y^2 = 1$ and are described by

$$V_{nm} = V_{nm}(\rho, \theta) = R_{nm}(\rho)e^{im\theta}, \tag{1}$$

where n is a non-negative integer and m is an integer, subject to the condition $n - |m|$ is even and $0 \leq |m| \leq n$, and ρ is a vector from the origin of the disc to a point on it. θ is the angle that the vector ρ makes with the positive direction of x-axis in the counter clockwise direction. $R_{nm}(\rho)$ are the Zernike radial polynomials in (ρ, θ) polar co-ordinates and are defined by

$$R_{nm}(\rho) = \sum_{s=0}^{(n-|m|)/2} (-1)^s \frac{(n-s)!}{s!(\frac{n+|m|}{2} - s)!(\frac{n-|m|}{2} - s)!} \rho^{n-2s}. \tag{2}$$

It is easy to note that $R_{nm}(\rho) = R_{n,-m}(\rho)$. Polynomials in equation(2) are orthogonal and therefore, we must have according to orthogonality condition

$$\int\int_{x^2+y^2\leq 1} V_{nm}^*(x,y)V_{pq}(x,y)dxdy = \frac{\pi}{n+1}\delta_{np}\delta_{mq}, \tag{3}$$

where $\delta_{np} = 1$ when $n = p$ and zero otherwise. δ_{np} is the Kronecker delta. Similarly. δ_{mq} is also the Kronecker delta.

With the Zernike polynomials described above, we are now in a position to define Zernike moments corresponding to some continuous function $f(x, y)$. Zernike moment for order n and repetition m is given by

$$A_{nm} = \frac{n+1}{\pi} \int\int_{x^2+y^2\leq 1} f(x,y)V_{nm}^*(\rho,\theta)dxdy. \tag{4}$$

Obviously, Zernike moment outside the unit disc is zero. If $f(x, y)$ is a digital image, we replace the integral by summation to get Zernike moments for the image. Then A_{nm} in this case reduces to

$$\begin{aligned} A_{nm} &= \tfrac{n+1}{\pi} \sum_x \sum_y f(x,y)V_{nm}^*(\rho,\theta), \\ &= \tfrac{n+1}{\pi} \sum_{\rho=0}^{1} \sum_{\theta=0}^{2\pi} f(\rho,\theta)R_{nm}(\rho)e^{-im\theta} \\ &= \tfrac{n+1}{\pi} \sum_{\rho=0}^{1} R_{nm}(\rho) \sum_{\theta=0}^{2\pi} f(\rho,\theta)e^{-im\theta} \end{aligned} \tag{5}$$

where, $\frac{1}{2} < x^2 + y^2 < \frac{3}{2}$. Note that we have taken a unit circle or a unit disc is as $\frac{1}{2} < x^2 + y^2 < \frac{3}{2}$ in the discrete plane [5] and not normally defined $x^2 + y^2 \leq 1$ in the continuous plane. $f(\rho, \theta)$ is the image pixel value on a unit discrete circle of radius vector ρ. When the image is mapped on a unit discrete disc, we get the image pixels mapped on different discrete circles that define the disc. We can take $\rho = \frac{r}{r_{max}}$ where $r = 0, 1, 2, 3 \cdots r_{max}$. Thus, $\rho = 0$ when $r = 0$ and $\rho = 1$ when $r = r_{max}$, r_{max} depends on the size of the image under test. For a $P \times P$ image, $r_{max} = \sqrt{2} \times \frac{P}{2}$. As r rotates from zero to 2π, there is as such no way to find uniquely the correspondence between $f(\rho, \theta)$, i.e., $f(r, \theta)$ and the image pixel. This problem also has not been addressed before. To solve this problem we have taken help of a mathematical definition of discrete circles, rings and discrete discs [5]. Below, we review, in brief, the definitions and their properties; error behavior and their generation algorithm, as they play a very significant role in the computation of Zernike moments. Thus, finally we get,

$$A_{nm} = \frac{n+1}{\pi} \sum_{r=0}^{r=r_{max}} R_{nm}(\rho) \sum_{\theta=0}^{2\pi} f(\rho, \theta) e^{-im\theta}, \tag{6}$$

where

$$R_{nm}(\rho) = \sum_{s=0}^{\frac{n-|m|}{2}} (-1)^s \frac{(n-s)!}{s!(\frac{n+|m|}{2} - s)!(\frac{n-|m|}{2} - s)!} (\rho)^{n-2s}, \tag{7}$$

where $\rho = \frac{r}{r_{max}}$ and $r = 0, 1, 2, \cdots r_{max}$. Since to compute the Zernike moments we need to map the graylevel image onto a discrete disc, we examine the definitions and properties of discrete circle, ring and disc in the following.

3   Discrete Circle, Ring, Disc and Their Properties

Discrete circle (dc):
A dc is a discrete space approximation to the circle defined in Euclidean geometry. In the present scheme of generation, a dc is defined as follows

Definition 1. A dc with radius r and center (α, β) is a set S_r of 8-connected pels so that each pel (x, y) satisfies the inequality

$$r - \frac{1}{2} < |\sqrt{(x-\alpha)^2 + (y-\beta)^2}| < r + \frac{1}{2} \tag{8}$$

Proposition 1. For concentric S_r and S_t

$$S_r \cap S_t = \phi , \qquad\qquad r \neq t \tag{9}$$

Proposition 2. There cannot exist any gap or hole between any two concentric dcs of radii r and r+1.

Rings and Discs

Definition 2. A discrete ring (dr) with integer radius r_1 and r_2, $r_2 > r_1$ and integer center (α, β) is given by

$$R(r_1, \ r_2, \ \alpha, \ \beta) = \bigcup_{r=r_1}^{r_2} S_r \qquad (10)$$

if $r_1 = 0$ a discrete disc (dd) is generated. Here S_0 is assumed to be the center pel itself.

For the complete generation of a discrete circle, ring and disc, one can see the article [5].

4 Proposed Algorithm for Computation of Zernike Moments

For a particular order n we propose to compute the radial polynomial $R_{nm}(\rho)$ (equation(2)) not term by term but in a batch. We propose two recursive relations which can be obtained in a straightforward way from the following considerations. We have,

$$T_s^{n,m} = \frac{(n-s)!}{s!(\frac{n+m}{2} - s)!(\frac{n-m}{2} - s)!}$$

and

$$T_s^{n,m+2} = \frac{(n-s)!}{s!(\frac{n+m+2}{2} - s)!(\frac{n-m-2}{2} - s)!},$$

where $T_s^{n,m}$ is the term within the summation in the radial polynomial, apart from two multiplicative factors, corresponding to the summation index s, running from $s = 0$ to $s = \frac{n-|m|}{2}$. We shall show later on how to handle these two multiplicative factors. After algebraic manipulation, one can get

$$T_s^{n,m} = \frac{\frac{n+m}{2} + 1 - s}{\frac{n-m}{2} - s} T_s^{n,m+2}. \qquad (11)$$

Similarly, it is easy to deduce

$$T_s^{n,m} = \frac{(\frac{n+m}{2} - s + 2)(\frac{n+m}{2} - s + 1)}{s(n - s + 1)} T_{s-1}^{n,m+2}, \qquad (12)$$

Now, for a particular value of s, say $s = 0$, we use equation(11) to compute all the T_0 terms for different values of n and m. Note that we always have, $T_0^{i,i} = 1$. We use equation(12) when we change the index in the term, say from T_0 to T_1. It is important to note in this context that the denominator of equation (11) is infinite when $s = \frac{n-m}{2}$ but we never encounter this situation because under such a condition, the term is computed either using the equation (12) or in terms of the previously computed value. Thus, when all the T_0 terms are known, we compute the first term in T_1 in the next step, starting with the maximum value of m, i.e., $m = n - 2$, the same value of m we started with to compute the first T_0 term using equation (11).

4.1   Computational Analysis

For a $P \times P$ image, total number of multiplications can be shown to be

$$N_{mult} \approx P/2(n^2/4 + n + 1) + 64P^2 + N_T + S_n + 14/8P^2 \tag{13}$$

and the total number of additions as,

$$N_{add} \approx r_{max} + 53P^2 + 5[S_{n/2} + 2(S_{n/2-1} + S_{n/2-3} + \cdots + S_1)] + 6S_n + 7/8P^2. \tag{14}$$

where,

$$N_T = 8S_{n/2} + 8(S_{n/2-1} + S_{n/2-3} + \cdots + S_1), \tag{15}$$

4.2   Comparison

Below we present a comparison computational analysis of three other different methods, on an image of size $P \times P$ and maximum order of Zernike moments M. Comparison shows that in the proposed method, number of multiplications drastically reduces and is minimum of all the cases. For additions, the number also reduces very significantly, except for the method described in [9] by Belkasim et al. Our method takes a slightly more number of additions than that of Belkasim et al. (approximately 1.38 times more) but it takes approximately 11.25 times less number of multiplications than their method. This shows the effectiveness of the proposed method. It is obvious the Zernike moments are scale invariant. As computations depend on the size (P) of the image it takes care the computation of scales.

Table 1. Comparison of multiplications and additions of different methods

References	Number of additions	Number of multiplications
[8]	$\approx P^2 M^2/2 + \frac{1}{8}PM^3$	$\approx 2M^2 + P^2M^2 + \frac{1}{4}PM^3$
P=64, M=40	4,054,477	8,122,321
[9]	$\approx M(P+2)(P-1)$	$\approx \frac{M^2 P^2}{2} + 2PM$
P=64, M=40	166,320	3,281,920
[12]	$\approx \frac{3}{8}M^2 P + 2P^2 M +$	$\approx \frac{1}{2}M^2 P + 2P^2 M$
P=64, M=40	$\frac{1}{12}M^3 P + \frac{1}{4}M^2 P^2$	
	2,562,198	397,358
Our method	Equation (14)	Equations (13), (15)
P=64, M=40	230,289	291,164

5   Conclusion

Recently Zernike moments are gaining popularity in applications of pattern recognition, image analysis and image processing but direct computation of factorials in them is time consuming and discouraging. A faster algorithm is therefore necessary and its need is already felt to various research communities. We have presented an efficient algorithm that computes the Zernike moments in a nice way. The comparison shows our algorithm is faster than the existing algorithms. Also the mapping of pixels through discrete circles, maintains the rotational invariance. The mapping is unique and leaves no holes or gaps on a disc.

References

1. Teague, M.R.: Image analysis via the general theory of moments. J. Opt. Soc. Am. 70(8), 920–930 (1980)
2. Teh, C., Chin, R.T.: On image analysis by the methods of moments. IEEE Trans. Pattern anal. Mach. Intell. 10(4), 496–513 (1988)
3. Khotanzad, A., Hong, Y.H.: Rotation invariant image recognition using features selected via a systematic method. Pattern Recognition 23(10), 1089–1101 (1990)
4. Liao, S.X., Pawlak, M.: On the accuracy of Zernike moments for image analysis. IEEE Trans. Pattern anal. Mach. Intell. 20, 1358–1364 (1998)
5. Bisaws, S.N., Chaudhuri, B.B.: On the generation of discrete circular objects and their properties. Comput. Vision, Graphics Image
6. Jiang, X.Y., Bunke, H.: Simple and fast computation of moments. Pattern Recognition 24(8), 801–806 (1991)
7. Li, B.C., Shen, J.: Fast computation of moment invariant. Pattern Recognition 24(8), 807–813 (1991)
8. Mukundan, R., Ramakrishnan, K.R.: Fast computation of Legendre and Zernike moments. Pattern Recognition 28(9), 1433–1442 (1995)
9. Belkasim, S.O., Ahmadi, M., Sridhar, M.: Efficient algorithm for fast computation of Zernike moments. J. Franklin Inst. Eng. Appl. Math. 333, 577–581 (1996)
10. Chan, F.H.Y., Lam, F.K.: An all adder systolic structure for fast computation of moments. J. VLSI Signal Process. 12, 159–175 (1996)
11. Shu, H.Z., Luo, L.M., Yu, W.X., Fu, Y.: A new fast method computing Legendre moments. Pattern Recognition 33(2), 341–348 (2000)
12. Gu, J., Su, H.Z., Toumoulin, C., Luo, L.M.: A novel algorithm for fast computation of Zernike moments. Pattern Recognition 35, 2905–2911 (2002)
13. Xin, Y., Pawlak, M., Liao, S.: Accurate computation of Zernike moments in polar coordinates. IEEE Trans. on Image Processing 16(2), 581–587 (2007)
14. Wee, C.Y., Raveendran, P.: On the computational aspects of Zernike moments. Image and Vision Computing 25(6), 967–980 (2007)

Unsupervised Image Segmentation with Adaptive Archive-Based Evolutionary Multiobjective Clustering

Chin Wei Bong[1] and Hong Yoong Lam[2]

[1] School of Computer Science, Universiti Sains Malaysia
[2] Department of Cardiothoracic Surgery, Hospital Pulau Pinang
Penang, Malaysia
bongwendy@gmail.com, drlamhy@yahoo.ca

Abstract. The aim of this paper is to propose and apply state-of-the-art multiobjective scatter search for solving image segmentation problem. The algorithm incorporates the concepts of Pareto dominance, external archiving, diversification and intensification of solutions. The multiobjective optimization method is Archive-based Hybrid Scatter Search (AbYSS) for image segmentation. It utilized fuzzy clustering method with optimization of two fitness functions, viz., the global fuzzy compactness of the clusters and the fuzzy separation. We have tested the methods on two types of grey scale images, namely SAR (synthetic aperture radar) image and CT scan (Computer Tomography) image. We then compared it with fuzzy c-means (FCM) and a popular evolutionary multiobjective evolutionary clustering named NSGA-II. The performance result for the proposed method is compatible with the existing methods.

Keywords: Multiobjective clustering, soft computing.

1 Introduction

Image segmentation process is defined as the extraction of the important objects from an input image [1]. It partitions the pixels in the image into homogeneous regions, each of which corresponds to some particular information. There are many approaches available for image segmentation including threshold methods [2], morphologic methods [3] and clustering algorithms. However, the segmentation results from these methods are still not satisfactory.

Majority of existing clustering algorithms are based on only one internal evaluation function, which is a single-objective function that measures intrinsic properties of a partitioning such as spatial separation between the clusters or the compactness of the clusters. However, it is sometimes difficult to reflect the quality of partitioning reliably with only one internal evaluation function which may be violated for certain datasets [7]. In this paper, we use multiobjective optimization (MOP) to overcome the defects of the single-objective clustering algorithms, such as FCM. Given that the objective functions (no less than two) for clustering are complementary, the simultaneous optimization of several of

S.O. Kuznetsov et al. (Eds.): PReMI 2011, LNCS 6744, pp. 92–97, 2011.
© Springer-Verlag Berlin Heidelberg 2011

those objectives may lead to high quality solutions and improve the robustness towards different data properties. MOCK proposed in [9] may be the first application of MOP in data clustering. However, only few applications have been reported in image segmentation [10]. Among those applications, NSGA-II [8] was found to be the most popular method being used so far. It is difficult to apply current MOP clustering technology to image segmentation, owing to an extremely large amount of data need to be handled and thus the handling of population in an evolutionary algorithm (EA) is tedious.

Scatter search [4] is an EA in the sense that it incorporates the concept of population. As compared to other EA, it usually avoids using many random components, and it is based on using a small population, known as the reference set, whose individuals are combined to construct new solutions which are generated systematically. The reference set is initialized from an initial population composed of diverse solutions, and it is updated with the solutions resulting from the local search improvement. Scatter search has been found to be successful in a wide variety of optimization problems [6], and until recently it had been extended to deal with MOPs. Scatter search can act as a powerful local search engine for tasks such as generating missing parts of a Pareto front because of its flexibility and ease of use [11]. Therefore, this paper first proposes and applies the state-of-the-art multiobjective scatter search for image segmentation using Archive-based Hybrid Scatter Search (AbYSS). The framework incorporates the concepts of Pareto dominance, external archiving, diversification and intensification of solution.

In the rest of this paper, we first present our proposal, followed by the experimental conducted to compare the proposed method with other standard image segmentation methods. Finally, we conclude the paper in the last section.

2   Multiobjective Clustering with AbYSS

The image segmentation problem is posed as clustering the pixels of the images in the intensity space. Here, a fuzzy clustering algorithm produces a membership matrix $U(X) = [\mu_{kj}], k = 1, ..., K$ and $j = 1, ..., n$, where μ_{kj} denotes the membership degree of pattern x_j to cluster C_k. Here the individual are made up of real numbers which represent the coordinates of the cluster centers. If individual encodes the centers of K_i clusters in p dimensional space then its length l_i will be $p \times K_i$. In the initial population, each string i encodes the centers of a some K_i number of clusters, such that $K_i = (rand()\%K^*) + 2$, where $rand()$ is a function returning a random integer, and K^* is a soft estimate of the upper bound of the number of clusters [6]. Therefore, the number of clusters will vary from 2 to $K^* + 1$. The K_i centers encoded in an individual of the initial population are randomly selected distinct points from the input data set.

Two fitness functions, viz., the global fuzzy compactness J of the clusters and the fuzzy separation S are optimized simultaneously[5]. For computing the objective functions, first the centers, $V = \{v_1, v_2, ...v_k\}$ encoded in a given individual are extracted. The fuzzy membership values $\mu_{kj}, i = 1, ..., K, k = 1, 2, ..., n$

are computed using $\mu_{ik} = \sum_{j=1}^{K} \frac{D(v_i,x_k)}{D(v_j,x_k)}^{-2/(m-1)}, 1 \le i \le K; 1 \le k \le n$, where $D(v_i, x_k)$ denotes the distance between ith cluster center and kth data point and $m \in [1, \infty]$ is the fuzzy exponent. Each cluster center $v_j = 1, 2, ..., K$, is updated using $v_i = \frac{\sum_{k=1}^{n} \mu_{ik}^m x_k}{\sum_{k=1}^{n} \mu_{ik}^m}$. The membership values are then recomputed. The variation σ_i and fuzzy cardinality n_i of the ith cluster, $i = 1, 2, ..., K$ are calculated as $\sigma_i = \sum_{k=1}^{n} \mu_{ik}^m D(v_i, x_k), 1 \le i \le K$ and $n_i = \sum_{k=1}^{n} \mu_{ik}, 1 \le i \le K$. The global compactness of the solution represented by the chromosome is then computed as $J = \sum_{i=1}^{K} \frac{\sigma_i}{n_i} = \sum_{i=1}^{K} \frac{\sum_{k=1}^{n} \mu_{ik}^m D(z_i, x_k)}{\sum_{k=1}^{n} \mu_{ik}}$.

The other fitness function fuzzy separation S is computed as follows: the center v_i of the ith cluster, is assumed to be the center of a fuzzy set . Hence the membership degree of each v_j to $v_i, j \ne i$, is computed as

$$\mu_{ij} = \sum_{l=1, l \ne j}^{K} \frac{D(v_i, v_j)}{D(v_j, v_l)}^{-2/(m-1)}, i \ne j.$$

Subsequently, the fuzzy separation is defined as $S = \sum_{i=1}^{K} \sum_{i=1, j \ne i}^{K} \mu_{ij}^m D(v_i, v_j)$. In order to obtain compact clusters, the measure J should be minimized. On the contrary, to get well separated clusters, the fuzzy separation S should be maximized. As in this article the multiobjective problem is posed as minimization of both the objectives, hence the objective is to minimize J and $\frac{1}{S}$ simultaneously.

AbYSS is based on the scatter search template adopted from [4]. The template defines six methods, as depicted in Figure 1, are described below:

1) Diversification Generation Procedure: The procedure is the same as that proposed in [4]. The goal is to generate an initial set P of diverse solutions. This is a simple method based on dividing the range of each variable into a number of subranges of equal size; then, the value for each variable of every solution is generated.

2) Improvement procedure: This procedure is to use a local search algorithm (a simplex method) to improve new solutions obtained from the diversification generation and solution combination methods. The improvement method takes an individual as a parameter, which is repeatedly mutated with the aim of obtaining a better individual. The term "better" is defined here in a similar way to the constrained-dominance approach used in NSGA-II [8].

3) Reference Set Update procedure: The reference set is a collection of both high-quality and diverse solutions that are used to generate new individuals. The set itself is composed of two subsets, $RefSet1$ and $RefSet2$, of size p and q, respectively. The first subset contains the best quality solutions in P, while the second subset should be filled with solutions promoting diversity.

4) Subset Generation procedure: This procedure generates subsets of individuals, which will be used to create new solutions with the solution combination method. The strategy used considers all pairwise combinations of solutions in the reference set [7]. Furthermore, this method should avoid producing repeated subsets of individuals, i.e., subsets previously generated.

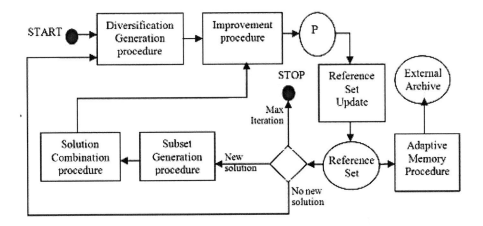

Fig. 1. Template for the six methods in the proposed framework

5) Solution Combination procedure: This procedure is to find linear combinations of reference solutions. The use of a simulated binary crossover operator (SBX) makes AbYSS more robust [6].

6) Adaptive Memory Procedure: The aim of External Archive is to store a record of the non-dominated individuals found during the search in order to keep those individuals producing a well distributed Pareto front. This archive is empty at the beginning of the method. We will continuously update it whenever a new individual or solution is not dominated by the $RefSet1$. Besides, we use the following rules to reduce the computational requirements: (a) New solution y obtained from x should be used to update External Archive only if it is not dominated by x. (b) New potentially Pareto-optimal solutions could be added to External Archive only if they differ enough from all solutions already contained in this set. We propose to use a threshold defining the minimum Euclidean distance in the space of normalized objectives between solutions in External Archive. A new potentially Pareto optimal solution is neglected if it is closer to at least one solution in External Archive than the threshold. We have observed experimentally that the solutions added to External Archive in early iterations have a good chance to be removed from this set in further iterations. In other words the time spent on updating External Archive in early iterations is likely to be lost. Thus, it is possible to neglect updating External Archive in a number of starting iterations.

Initially, the diversification generation method is invoked to generate initial solutions, and each one is passed to the improvement method and the result is the initial set P. Then, a fix number of iterations are performed. At each iteration, the reference set is built, the subset generation method is invoked, and the main loop of the scatter search algorithm is executed until the subset generation method stops producing new subsets of solutions. Then, there is a restart phase, which consists of three steps. First, the individuals $RefSet1$ in are inserted into

P; second, the best individuals n from the external archive, according to the crowding distance, are also moved to P; and, third, the diversification generation and improvement methods are used to produce new solutions for filling up the set P. The idea of moving n individuals from the archive to the initial set is to promote the intensification capabilities of the search towards the Pareto front already found. The intensification degree can vary depending on the number of chosen individuals. The best single solution is then selected based on the method introduced by MetaClustering algorithm (MCLA)[5].

3   Experimental Study

We have compared our algorithm with standard FCM and a popular evolutionary multobjective clustering, NSGA-II. For NSGA-II, we executed 100 generations with fixed population size 50. The crossover and mutation probabilities are fixed as 0.8 and 0.01, respectively. FCM is executed for a maximum of 100 iterations, with m, the fuzzy exponent, equal to 2.0. First, the experiment was done for a 3-class SAR images obtained from http://www.sandia.gov/radar/imageryku.html. The image is a Ku-band SAR image with one meter spatial resolution in the area of Rio Grande River near Albuquerque, New Mexico, USA. This image consists of three types of land cover, namely, the river, the vegetation and the crop. Then, the experiment was extended to real CT scan image for Lung obtained from Penang Hospital, Malaysia. The results of the algorithms are compared with two cluster validity functions: partition coefficient, $V_{pc}(U) = \frac{\sum_{j=1}^{n} \sum_{i=1}^{c} \mu_{ij}^2}{n}$ and partition entropy value, $V_{pe}(U) = \frac{1}{n} \sum_{j=1}^{n} \sum_{i=1}^{c} \mu_{ij} \log \mu_{ij}$ [7]. The clustering result is better with a higher $V_{pc}(U)$ value and a lower $V_{pe}(U)$ value. Table 1 shows the performance comparison of FCM, NSGA-II and the proposed method in terms of cluster validity functions with both index. The values of $V_{pc}(U)$ are higher in the proposed method than the FCM and NSGA-II methods. Meanwhile, the values of $V_{pe}(U)$ are lower in the proposed method than the FCM and NSGA-II methods. This result indicates that the proposed method is outperformed than other two methods. Fig. 2 shows the example of images and their segmented results. For SAR image, FCM and the proposed method are better than NSGA-II in terms of the regional consistency of the water and the buildings region. However, all the three algorithms cannot achieve the visually correct segmentation in the right top region, i.e. FCM, and the proposed method misclassifies a big area of land region as the water. Comparatively, the proposed method performs best in this area where the misclassification is not so serious as FCM and NSGA-II.

Table 1. Result of partition coefficient and partition entropy for the two types of images with different methods

Methods	Index	FCM	NSGA-II	Proposed	Index	FCM	NSGA-II	Proposed
SAR IMAGE	V_{pe}	0.14230	0.14025	0.11227	V_{pc}	0.91031	0.91106	0.92180
CT Scan IMAGE	V_{pe}	0.06910	0.05150	0.0403	V_{pc}	0.93113	0.94170	0.95943

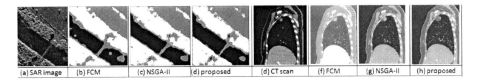

Fig. 2. Two 3-Class SAR images and their segmentation results

4 Conclusion

Most real-world image segmentation problems involve simultaneously optimizing multiple criteria where considerations of trade-offs is important. This paper has presented the concepts of Pareto dominance, external archiving, diversification and intensification of solutions. The performance of the proposed method was encouraging and future work will focus on enhancing the performance speed of the algorithm. More in-depth research will be conducted in analysing the variables used in the algorithm. Besides, we are also interested to include a few more criteria into our existing bi-criteria optimization.

References

[1] Gonzalez, R.C., Woods, R.E.: Digital Image processing. Prentice-Hall, Englewood Cliffs (2007)

[2] Zaart, A.E., Ziou, D., Wang, S., Jiang, Q.: Segmentation of SAR images using mixture of gamma distribution. Pattern Recognition 35(3), 713–724 (2002)

[3] Lemarechal, C., Fjortoft, R., Marthon, P., Cubero-castan, E., Lopes, A.: SAR image segmentation by morphological methods. In: Proc. SPIE, vol. 3497, pp. 111–121 (1998)

[4] Glover, F., Laguna, M., Martí, R.: Scatter search. In: Ghosh, A., Tsutsui, S. (eds.) Advances in Evolutionary Computing: Theory and Applications, pp. 519–537. Springer, Heidelberg (2003)

[5] Mukhopadhyaya, A., Maulik, U.: A multiobjective approach to MR brain image segmentation. Applied Soft Computing 11, 872–880 (2011)

[6] Nebro, A.J., Luna, F., Alba, E., Dorronsoro, B., Durillo, J.J., Beham, A.: AbYSS: Adapting Scatter Search to Multiobjective Optimization. IEEE Transactions on Evo. Comp. 12(4) (2008)

[7] Bezdek, J.C.: Cluster validity with fuzzy sets. Cybernetics and Systems, 58–73 (1974)

[8] Deb, K., Pratap, A., Agarwal, S., Meyarivan, T.: A fast and elitist multiobjective genetic algorithm: NSGA-II. IEEE Trans. on Evolutionary Computation 6(2), 182–197 (2002)

[9] Handl, J., Knowles, J.: An evolutionary approach to multiobjective clustering. IEEE Trans. on Evolutionary Computing 11(1), 56–76 (2007)

[10] Saha, S., Bandyopadhyay, S.: Unsupervised pixel classification in satellite imagery using a new multiobjective symmetry based clustering approach. In: TENCON IEEE Region 10 Conference (2008)

[11] Coello, C.A.C.: Evolutionary multi-objective optimization: some current research trends and topics that remain to be explored. Frontiers of Computer Science in China 3(1), 18–30 (2009)

Modified Self-Organizing Feature Map Neural Network with Semi-supervision for Change Detection in Remotely Sensed Images

Susmita Ghosh and Moumita Roy

Department of Computer Science and Engineering, Jadavpur University,
Kolkata 700032, India

Abstract. Problem of change detection of remotely sensed images using insufficient labeled patterns is the main topic of present work. Here, semi-supervised learning is integrated with an unsupervised context-sensitive change detection technique based on modified self-organizing feature map (MSOFM) network. In this method, training of the MSOFM is performed iteratively using unlabeled patterns along with a few labeled patterns. A method has been suggested to select unlabeled patterns for training. To check the effectiveness of the proposed methodology, experiments are carried out on two multitemporal remotely sensed images. Results are found to be encouraging.

Keywords: Semi-supervised learning, change detection, fuzzy set, self-organizing feature map.

1 Introduction

Change detection, a process of finding out changes in a land cover over time by analyzing remotely sensed images of a geographical area captured at different times [9], can be viewed as an image segmentation problem, where two groups of pixels (changed and unchanged) are formed. Between the two traditional approaches (supervised and unsupervised), the applicability of supervised method [1] is less for insufficient ground truth information. Whereas, ground truth is not necessary for unsupervised methods [1,5]. Due to the depletion of labeled patterns, unsupervised techniques seem to be compulsory here. The three consecutive steps used for unsupervised technique are image preprocessing, image comparison and image analysis [9]. In preprocessing step, images are made compatible by operations like radiometric and geometric corrections, co-registration etc. Then, image comparison is done pixel by pixel to generate a difference image (DI). A situation may occur where the categorical information of a few labeled patterns can be collected easily by experts. If the number of these labeled patterns is less, then this information may not be sufficient for developing supervised methods. In such a scenario, knowledge of labeled patterns, though very poor, will be unutilized if unsupervised approach is taken. Under this circumstance, semi-supervised approach [2] could be opted instead of unsupervised or supervised one.

S.O. Kuznetsov et al. (Eds.): PReMI 2011, LNCS 6744, pp. 98–103, 2011.

In the present work, a neural network based semi-supervised change detection method is proposed. Here, the idea of semi-supervised learning [2] is incorporated into the existing unsupervised change detection technique based on the MSOFM network [6]. This work is inspired from a work on change detection using semi-supervised multilayer perceptron (MLP) [8]. The MSOFM network [4,6] has two layers: input and output. For each feature of the input pattern, there is a neuron in the input layer. The output layer is two dimensional and there is a representative neuron for each pixel position of DI. In the present work, change vector analysis (CVA) technique [1,9] is used for generating DI. The input pattern for a particular pixel position is generated using gray value of the said pixel as well as those of its neighborhood pixels for considering (spatial) contextual information from neighbors. In the present work 2nd order neighborhood is used. A mapping algorithm [4,6] is used to normalize the feature values of the input pattern in $[0,1]$. Each neuron in the output layer is connected to all the neurons in the input layer. The connection weights of the representative neuron of the labeled pixel position are initialized with the normalized feature values of the corresponding labeled pattern; whereas the weight vector for others is initialized randomly between $[0,1]$. Iterative learning of the MSOFM network is performed by the labeled patterns along with the selected unlabeled patterns until a given convergence criterion is satisfied.

2   Kohonen's Self-Organizing Feature Map

In the proposed algorithm, we have used the same MSOFM network as used in [4,6]. The MSOFM network is motivated from the Kohonen's self-organizing feature maps (SOFM) [7] and has similar network structure as that of the SOFM. SOFM is learned iteratively and generates topological map of input patterns gradually. The input pattern is represented by $\overrightarrow{X}$ and $\overrightarrow{W_j}$ denotes the synaptic weight vector of jth output neuron (where $j = 1, 2, ..., z$ and z be the number of neurons in the output layer). The winner neuron j in the output layer is selected as the best-matched neuron for the given input pattern where the similarity measure $(\overrightarrow{W_j} \cdot \overrightarrow{X})$ is maximum. Let, $h(itr)$ be the topological neighborhood function at iteration itr that shrinks after each iteration. The weight updating of winning neuron is done as,

$$\overrightarrow{W}(itr+1) = \overrightarrow{W}(itr) + h(itr)\eta(itr)(\overrightarrow{X} - \overrightarrow{W}(itr)), \tag{1}$$

where, $\eta(itr)$ denotes the learning rate in iteration itr and decreases with increase of itr.

3   The Proposed Algorithm

In the present technique, labeled patterns from both the classes are picked up randomly from the ground truth. Let, the y-dimensional input pattern of $(m,n)^{th}$ pixel position of DI is denoted by $\overrightarrow{X_{mn}} = [x_{mn,1}, x_{mn,2}, ..., x_{mn,y}]$. The

y-dimensional weight vector between $(m,n)^{th}$ neuron in the output layer and all the neurons of the input layer is represented by $\overrightarrow{W_{mn}} = [w_{mn,1}, w_{mn,2}, ..., w_{mn,y}]$. During training, input patterns $\overrightarrow{X_{mn}}$ are passed to the network one by one. Each time, the dot product $d(m,n)$ between $\overrightarrow{X_{mn}}$ and $\overrightarrow{W_{mn}}$ is calculated as,

$$d(m,n) = \overrightarrow{X_{mn}} \cdot \overrightarrow{W_{mn}} = \sum_{k=1}^{y} x_{mn,k} \cdot w_{mn,k}. \tag{2}$$

At the beginning of the training phase, the connection weights of the MSOFM network are updated in the following manner using the labeled patterns only. If the class label of the $(m,n)^{th}$ pixel position is known, then the weight vector $\overrightarrow{W_{ij}}$ for all neighboring neurons (defined by $h_{mn}(.)$) of $(m,n)^{th}$ output neuron is updated using equation (1), iff $(i,j)^{th}$ input pattern is unlabeled. For the labeled patterns, the weight vector is not updated during the entire learning process. Learning using labeled patterns is continued iteratively until convergence. To check convergence, $O(itr)$ is calculated at each iteration using,

$$O(itr) = \sum_{d(m,n) \geq t} d(m,n), \tag{3}$$

where, t is a predefined threshold value [6]. The weight updating is preformed until $(O(itr) - O(itr - 1)) < \delta$, where δ is a small positive quantity. The value of t varies within $[0,1]$. The components of the weight vector $\overrightarrow{W_{mn}}$ are normalized in a way so that the dot product $d(m,n)$ lies between $[0,1]$. After each epoch, the learning rate $\eta(itr)$ and the size of the topological neighborhood $h(itr)$ decrease.

After each training step, the soft class labels of unlabeled patterns are calculated by presenting them to the network. Let us consider that there exists two fuzzy sets: one for the changed class and the other for unchanged one. For each $(i,j)^{th}$ unlabeled pattern, $d(i,j)$ is computed by equation (2); if, $d(i,j) \geq t$, then $(i,j)^{th}$ pattern is more likely to belong to changed class than unchanged one; else in unchanged class. Let, $\mu(i,j) = [\mu_1(i,j), \mu_2(i,j)]$ be the membership value of $(i,j)^{th}$ unlabeled pattern, where $\mu_1(i,j)$ and $\mu_2(i,j)$ are the membership values in unchanged class and changed class, respectively. The values can be calculated as,

$$[\mu_1(i,j), \mu_2(i,j)] = \begin{cases} [\min(d(i,j), 1 - d(i,j)), \\ \max(d(i,j), 1 - d(i,j))] & \text{if } d(i,j) \geq t \\ \\ [\max(d(i,j), 1 - d(i,j)), \\ \min(d(i,j), 1 - d(i,j))] & \text{Otherwise.} \end{cases} \tag{4}$$

After that, the target value of the unlabeled pattern is updated by K-nearest neighbor technique as it was used in [8]. To search for K-nearest neighbors, instead of considering all the patterns, we consider only those which lie within a window around that unlabeled pattern. Let, M be the set of K-nearest neighbors of $(i,j)^{th}$ unlabeled pattern. Now, target value $t(i,j) = [t_1(i,j), t_2(i,j)]$ of $(i,j)^{th}$ unlabeled pattern is estimated as,

$$t(i,j) = \left[\frac{\sum\limits_{\overrightarrow{X_{sl}} \in M} \mu_1(s,l)}{K}, \frac{\sum\limits_{\overrightarrow{X_{sl}} \in M} \mu_2(s,l)}{K} \right]. \tag{5}$$

Then, the unlabeled patterns which are more likely to belong to the changed class, are selected for training the MSOFM network again. The process of training the MSOFM using labeled patterns and the selected unlabeled patterns continued until convergence. The training of network and re-estimation of soft class labels of unlabeled patterns using equations (4) and (5) are continued iteratively (for DI of size $p \times q$) by computing the sum of square error, $\xi(N)$, after each Nth training step as,

$$\xi(N) = \sum_{i=1}^{p} \sum_{j=1}^{q} \sum_{k=1}^{2} (\mu_k(i,j) - t_k(i,j))^2. \tag{6}$$

4   Results and Analysis

To evaluate the effectiveness of the proposed method, experiments are carried out on two multitemporal remotely sensed images corresponding to the geographical areas of Mexico and Sardinia island. Similar findings are obtained for both the data sets. For illustration, results of Mexico data sets are presented here. The performance of the proposed technique is compared with those of the existing unsupervised technique using MSOFM [6] and a supervised method using MLP. The performance indices are the number of missed alarms (changed class pixels identified as unchanged ones-MA), the number of false alarms (unchanged class pixels classified as changed ones-FA), the number of overall errors (OE) and Kappa measure (KM) [3]. The average (Avg.) and standard deviation (written in brackets in the table) values (over 10 simulations) of overall errors and Kappa measure are considered for comparison. The best results (denoted by 'Min' in table) and the worst results (denoted by 'Max' in table) for MA, FA and OE, considering all the simulations, are also given in the table.

The data set of Mexico is made of two multispectral images over an area of Mexico [6,8] taken on April 18, 2000 and May 20, 2002 (Fig. 1). The corresponding difference image and the reference map are shown in Figure 1. The change detection maps corresponding to minimum overall error (over 10 simulations) obtained using optimal threshold with the unsupervised technique and the proposed semi-supervised technique (using 0.1% patterns from the changed class and 0.1% from the unchanged class) are depicted in Figure 2.

Table 1 presents the comparative results obtained using the unsupervised method, the supervised method and the proposed semi-supervised method. From the table, it is noticed that the proposed method (considering all the cases of percentage of training patterns) outperforms the corresponding unsupervised version. It is also found that the standard deviations obtained for both overall error and Kappa measure using MLP based supervised technique are very high

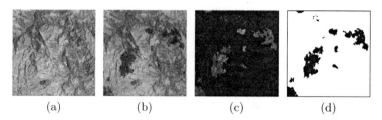

(a)   (b)   (c)   (d)

Fig. 1. Images of Mexico area. (a) Band 4 image acquired in April 2000, (b) band 4 image acquired in May 2002, (c) corresponding difference image, and (d) a reference map of the changed area.

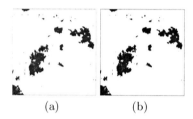

(a)   (b)

Fig. 2. Change detection maps obtained for Mexico data set: (a) using the unsupervised method based on optimal threshold, and (b) using the proposed semi-supervised technique based on optimal threshold (with 0.1% training pattern)

Table 1. Results and comparison

Techniques used	Threshold	Training patterns used	Max/ Min	MA	FA	OE	Avg.OE	Avg.KM
Unsupervised (based on MSOFM)	0.216 (optimal)	-	Min	1366	1618	2984	2991.70 (4.360046)	0.935532 (0.000089)
			Max	1366	1634	3000		
Supervised (based on MLP)	-	0.1%	Min	1345	1429	2774	3086.40 (186.277857)	0.927558 (0.004676)
			Max	2268	1139	3407		
		0.5%	Min	1269	1406	2675	2834.3 (95.736148)	0.915087 (0.001731)
			Max	875	2192	3067		
Proposed semi-supervised (based on MSOFM)	0.216 (optimal)	0.1%	Min	1512	1218	2730	2741.40 (6.666333)	0.940312 (0.000141)
			Max	1516	1239	2755		
		0.5%	Min	1470	1235	2705	2723.70 (8.331266)	0.940475 (0.000193)
			Max	1502	1232	2734		

as compared to the corresponding unsupervised and semi-supervised approaches. This may be due to the unavailability of sufficient number of training samples which reflect the real life scenario. By comparing the results of the supervised and the proposed semi-supervised methods, it is seen that the maximum overall error (denoted by 'Max') obtained by the semi-supervised approach is less than that of the corresponding supervised method. In short, the results show that the proposed semi-supervised version has an edge over the unsupervised as well as the supervised techniques when a few labeled patterns are available.

5 Conclusion

In this paper, an attempt has been made to improve the performance of change detection of remotely sensed images under the scarcity of sufficient number of labeled patterns by exploring the self-organizing capacity of Kohonen's network integrated with semi-supervision. From the results, it has been found that the proposed algorithm is better suited for change detection where a small amount of labeled patterns is available.

Acknowledgments. The authors like to thank the Department of Science and Technology (DST), Government of India and University of Trento, Italy, the sponsors of the ITPAR program and Prof. L. Bruzzone, the Italian collaborator of this project, for providing the data.

References

1. Canty, M.J.: Image Analysis, Classification and Change Detection in Remote Sensing. CRC Press, Taylor & Francis (2006)
2. Chapelle, O., Schölkopf, B., Zien, A.: Semi-supervised Learning. MIT Press, Cambridge (2006)
3. Congalton, R.G., Green, K.: Assessing the Accuracy of Remotely Sensed Data: Principles and Practices, 2nd edn. CRC Press, Taylor & Francis Group (2009)
4. Ghosh, A., Pal, S.K.: Neural network, self-organization and object extraction. Pattern Recognition Letters 13, 387–397 (1992)
5. Ghosh, A., Mishra, N.S., Ghosh, S.: Fuzzy clustering algorithms for unsupervised change detection in remote sensing images. Information Sciences 181(4), 699–715 (2011)
6. Ghosh, S., Patra, S., Ghosh, A.: An unsupervised context-sensitive change detection technique based on modified self-organizing feature map neural network. International Journal of Approximate Reasoning 50(1), 37–50 (2009)
7. Kohonen, T.: Self-Organizing Maps, 2nd edn. Springer, Berlin (1997)
8. Patra, S., Ghosh, S., Ghosh, A.: Change detection of remote sensing images with semi-supervised multilayer perceptron. Fundamenta Informaticae 84, 429–442 (2008)
9. Singh, A.: Digital change detection techniques using remotely sensed data. International Journal of Remote Sensing 10(6), 989–1003 (1989)

Image Retargeting through Constrained Growth of Important Rectangular Partitions

Rajarshi Pal[1], Jayanta Mukhopadhyay[2], and Pabitra Mitra[2]

[1] Center for Soft Computing Research, Indian Statistical Institute, Kolkata, India
[2] Department of Computer Science and Engineering, Indian Institute of Technology,
Kharagpur, India

Abstract. The challenge of displaying an image in a much smaller target area is to maintain recognizability of its contents. A novel rectangular partitioning based retargeting scheme is proposed in this paper to address this issue. Constrained growth of rectangular partitions containing important objects is major characteristic of this scheme. Subjective evaluation by a group of volunteers establishes usefulness of this scheme.

Keywords: Image retargeting.

1 Introduction

Resizing an image, even of moderate size, to display it on a small gadget (such as, cell-phones) reduces recognizability of its contents. Content-aware processing addresses this issue by differentiating image contents on the basis of their importance. Image cropping [1,2,3] and fisheye-view warping [4] are effective for images with single important object. But they are not that much effective when important contents are sparsely distributed within the image. Unimportant contents still occupy a major portion of the display in such case. Rapid Serial Visual Presentation (RSVP) [5] displays important portions of the image one-by-one.

On the other hand, seam carving (originally proposed by [6]) and optimized scale-and-stretch warping [7] are effective irrespective of spatial distribution of important contents within the image. Seam carving fits an image to the target space by iteratively removing seams that pass through less important contents of the image. Removing excessive number of seams to fit the image in small target space often induces distortion. Later on, controlled seam carving [8,9] strategies have been proposed to check such distortion. Optimized scale-and-stretch warping [7] iteratively computes local scaling factors for each local region.

This paper introduces another novel scheme that also can operate irrespective of spatial distribution of important contents. Relative enlargement of important contents is estimated here by considering their size and spatial positioning only. A simplistic rectangular partitioning of image space based on the importance of each individual content and similar partitioning of the target space add novelty to the proposed scheme. Unlike some previous literature on image retargeting, this paper does not focus on deriving importance of individual image content. Rather it focuses only on how important contents can be enlarged.

S.O. Kuznetsov et al. (Eds.): PReMI 2011, LNCS 6744, pp. 104–109, 2011.

The organization of the paper is as follows: A brief discussion on extracting rectangular regions of importance is presented in section 2. In section 3, the retargeting scheme is described where important rectangles are disproportionately enlarged. Section 4 discusses about subjective control over the relative size change to obtain distortion free result. Results along with subjective evaluation are presented in section 5. Finally, conclusions are drawn in section 6.

2   Region of Importance Extraction

Visual attention models which compute saliency based on low-level image features are commonly used in deriving importance of image contents. The saliency model in [10] is used here for our experiments as recent experiments have established its superiority as compared to others (for e.g., the model in [11]). Face detectors [12,13] can also be combined with saliency models to incorporate some semantic knowledge in importance computation. Though face detection module is not considered in our current study.

Once the importance map is obtained, important objects are extracted as follows. A line parallel to X-axis passing through the center point of the importance map partitions it in two portions: L and R. Again, a line parallel to Y-axis passing through this center point partitions the importance map in two portions: U and B. Let M_L, M_R, M_U and M_B be the maximum importance values in L, R, U and B, respectively. A threshold T_s is fixed at $p\%$ of the lowest of these four importance values.

$$T_s = p/100 * min\,(M_L, M_R, M_U, M_B) \tag{1}$$

Then the importance map is binarized using the threshold T_s to get pixels with high importance. Each set of connected important pixels form one important object. For ease of computation, we do away with the irregular shapes of important objects using a minimum rectangle r_i for each important object i. The saliency map along with important rectangles identified for an image is shown in Figure 1.

Fig. 1. A sample input image (left) and important rectangles superimposed on the importance map of the image (right)

3   Proposed Retargeting Scheme

The retargeting scheme, proposed in this section, uses the important rectangles identified in previous section to generate the retargeted image.

3.1   Initial Position of Important Rectangles in Target Space

Edges of the important rectangles are parallel to the horizontal and vertical axis. Such a rectangle r_i can be specified by its top-left and bottom-right corner points. Let, (c_i, d_i) and (f_i, g_i) are these points for r_i in the original image. Scaled down versions of the important rectangles are positioned in the target space (i.e., smaller display). Their positions in the target space are indicated by end points of main diagonal (c_t, d_t) and (f_t, g_t). These points are estimated as follows:

$$(c_t, d_t) = \left(\left\lceil \frac{c_i\, h_t}{h_i} \right\rceil, \left\lceil \frac{d_i\, w_t}{w_i} \right\rceil \right) \tag{2}$$

$$(f_t, g_t) = \left(\left\lceil \frac{f_i\, h_t}{h_i} \right\rceil, \left\lceil \frac{g_i\, w_t}{w_i} \right\rceil \right) \tag{3}$$

where h_i and w_i are height and width of the original image, respectively. h_t and w_t denote height and width of the target space, respectively. $\lceil \cdot \rceil$ returns the smallest integer greater than or equal to its input argument.

3.2   Growing Important Rectangles in Target Space

Important rectangles are allowed to grow within the target space. But few basic constraints are also maintained to prevent arbitrary growth of these rectangles. These constraints are:

1. Aspect ratio of each important rectangle is preserved.
2. All important rectangles are enlarged equally.
3. Rectangles do not cross the boundary of target space while being grown.
4. Relative ordering in position of the horizontal and vertical edges of these rectangles is preserved.

To ensure condition 1, height and width of a rectangle are multiplied with equal resizing gain factor λ. Condition 2 is preserved by enlarging all the rectangles with equal value for λ. It is also checked whether boundary of a rectangle crosses the boundary of the target space (condition 3). If it crosses the target space boundary, it is translated back into target space. Across any direction (vertical or horizontal), relative ordering of horizontal and vertical edges of these rectangles is maintained (condition 4). To maintain relative ordering of horizontal edges, rank correlation coefficient of x coordinates of the corner points before and after enlargement is checked. If there is no change in ordering, the value of the coefficient will be 1. Similar checking with y coordinates preserves relative ordering of vertical edges. Condition 4 also ensures that there is no overlapping between two rectangles. The maximum possible value for the resizing gain factor (λ_{max}) that satisfies all these constraints is estimated using an iterative procedure. At first iteration, its value is assigned to 1. In subsequent iterations, it is increased by a small value $\Delta\lambda$ (0.01 in our implementation) and is checked whether the constraints are satisfied. Remaining computation is performed using the maximum possible value of the resizing gain factor that satisfies the afore mentioned constraints.

3.3   Partitioning into Rectangles and Mapping

After locating the important rectangles in both the original image and the target space, the remaining areas (outside these important rectangles) are partitioned into small rectangular pieces through following steps:

Step 1: All the four sides of each important rectangle r_i (or its resized version in the target space) are drawn (in the raster space) with black in a white background which is of same size as original image (or target space). This produces a binary image. The upper horizontal edge of a rectangle r_i is the line segment between points (c_i, d_i) and (c_i, g_i) (or between points (c_t, d_t) and (c_t, g_t) in the target area). The lower horizontal edge of a rectangle r_i is the line segment between points (f_i, d_i) and (f_i, g_i) (or between points (f_t, d_t) and (f_t, g_t) in the target area).

Step 2: Each horizontal edge (upper and lower sides of the important rectangles) is elongated in both direction until it touches either a vertical line, a collinear horizontal line or area boundary. Whenever the elongating line encounters a black point, it is understood that it has touched either a vertical line or a collinear horizontal line.

Number of important rectangles and their edge orderings are same in both the original image and target space. Therefore, this partitioning scheme produces equal number of partitions in these spaces unless two parallel line segments become collinear or overlap with each other. But the constraint 4 mentioned in the previous section prevents two noncollinear lines to become collinear or overlap with each other. Here, the image boundaries are also considered as line segments.

One-to-one mapping between partitions in original image and target space is established. After that, content of each partition in the original image is fitted into the corresponding partition in the target area. Thus the retargeted image is obtained.

4   Obtaining a Distortion-Free Image

The target area being fixed, the relative enlargement of important rectangles reduces unimportant rectangles. In some cases, this may introduce various types of distortion in the retargeted image if the resizing gain factor λ is large. As of the current stage of research, automatic identification of appropriate value of λ is not possible considering all the artifacts. Moreover, some artifacts introduced due to relative size change of important and unimportant objects may be of subjective nature. Therefore, a possible implementation of the proposed scheme is as follows: It presents the viewer with a retargeted image with $\lambda = \lambda_{max}$. If the viewer is not satisfied with the quality of the result, she is allowed to gradually decrease the value of λ until the desired quality is obtained.

5   Results and Discussions

The proposed scheme is tested using 100 images. Results for these were generated using a λ value that suits the subjective quality according to our observation. These results are compared against those from cropping [1] and controlled seam carving [8]. The results obtained for some of the images are shown in Figure 2. To test the effectiveness of various retargeting strategies, it is necessary to prepare the outcomes of the comparing schemes using the same importance map. Therefore, the saliency [10] based importance map is used for all three concerned methods. The results of these retargeting schemes are presented in Figure 2. It can be observed from Figure 2 that enlargement of the important objects is much in the proposed scheme as compared to other schemes at the presence of multiple important objects. Performance of the proposed scheme is also comparable to other schemes for images with single important object.

Fig. 2. Columns from left to right: down sampled version of the original image, output of the proposed scheme, image cropping [1] and seam curving base method [8], respectively

Evaluation of retargeting is essentially of subjective nature. Hence, it is resorted to manual judgments for evaluation. All the results were presented to forty-one volunteers. They were asked to evaluate each result of each scheme as either good (score 2), average (score 1) or poor (score 0). For each scheme, scores of 100 images are summed up to find a score for that scheme. Mean score is computed for each scheme over scores given by all volunteers. Average score per image (and per volunteer) of the proposed rectangle partitioning based scheme is 1.39, whereas those for the cropping and the controlled seam curving based scheme are 0.99 and 1.09, respectively. Therefore, subjective evaluation demonstrates the usefulness of the proposed scheme over cropping and seam carving.

6   Conclusion

Enlarging important contents of the image through a rectangular partition based scheme restores their recognizability. All important objects are enhanced uniformly and their aspect ratios are kept unchanged. Relative ordering of their placement in the target area is also kept same as that in the original image. Ability to perform in the presence of multiple sparsely distributed important objects is another notable point for the proposed scheme.

References

1. Suh, B., Ling, H., Bederson, B.B., Jacobs, D.W.: Automatic thumbnail cropping and its effectiveness. In: Proc. of 16th Annual Symposium on User Interface Software and Technology, November 2003, pp. 95–104 (2003)
2. Luo, J.: Subject content-based intelligent cropping for digital photos. In: Proc. of IEEE International Conference on Multimedia and Expo, July 2007, pp. 2218–2221 (2007)
3. Ciocca, G., Cusano, C., Gasparini, F., Schettini, R.: Self-adaptive image cropping for small displays. IEEE Transactions on Consumer Electronics 53, 1622–1627 (2007)
4. Liu, F., Gleicher, M.: Automatic image retargeting with fisheye-view warping. In: Proc. of 18th Annual ACM Symposium on User Interface Software and Technology, October 2005, pp. 153–162 (2005)
5. Fan, X., Xie, X., Ma, W.Y., Zhang, H.J., Zhou, H.Q.: Visual attention based image browsing on mobile devices. In: Proc. of International Conference on Multimedia and Expo (July 2003)
6. Avidan, S., Shamir, A.: Seam carving for content-aware image resizing. ACM Transactions on Graphics 26 (July 2007)
7. Wang, Y.S., Tai, C.L., Sorkine, O., Lee, T.Y.: Optimized scale-and-stretch for image resizing. ACM Transactions on Graphics 27 (December 2008)
8. Hwang, D.S., Chien, S.Y.: Content-aware image resizing using perceptual seam carving with human attention model. In: Proc. of IEEE International Conference on Multimedia and Expo, June 2008, pp. 1029–1032 (2008)
9. Utsugi, K., Shibahara, T., Koike, T., Naemura, T.: Proportional constraint for seam carving. In: Proc. of International Conference on Computer Graphics and Interactive Techniques (August 2009)
10. Pal, R., Mukherjee, A., Mitra, P., Mukherjee, J.: Modelling visual saliency using degree centrality. IET Computer Vision 4(3), 218–229 (2010)
11. Itti, L., Koch, C., Niebur, E.: A model of saliency-based visual attention for rapid scene analysis. IEEE Transactions on Pattern Analysis and Machine Intelligence 20(11), 1254–1259 (1998)
12. Li, S., Zhu, L., Zhang, Z., Blake, A., Zhang, H., Shum, H.: Statistical learning of multi-view face detection. In: Proc. of European Conference on Computer Vision, pp. 67–81 (2002)
13. Viola, P., Zones, M.J.: Robust real-time face detection. International Journal of Computer Vision 57(2), 137–154 (2004)

SATCLUS: An Effective Clustering Technique for Remotely Sensed Images

Sauravjyoti Sarmah and Dhruba K. Bhattacharyya

Dept. of CS & Engg., Tezpur University, India
{sjs,dkb}@tezu.ernet.in

Abstract. This paper presents a grid density based clustering technique (SATCLUS) to identify clusters present in a multi spectral satellite image. Experimental results are reported to establish that SATCLUS can identify clusters of any shape in any satellite data effectively and dynamically.

1 Introduction

A multi-spectral satellite image is a remotely sensed image of the earth's surface which is a collection of huge amount of information in terms of number of pixel data. In such an image, each pixel represents an area on the earth's surface. Segmentation or clustering a multi-spectral satellite image is a process of discovering finite number of non-overlapping as well as overlapping regions or clusters in an image data space which has been a complex problem for a long time. Region-growing [1] is a local optimization procedure, while pixel clustering is a global analysis of color space. The segmentation technique based on pixel clustering is an important approach. Segmentation using clustering involves the search for points that are similar enough to be grouped together in the color space. Many clustering algorithms have been developed in the past few years to detect clusters from satellite images. K-means [2] and ISODATA [3] are two popular algorithms widely used for detecting clusters in satellite images. Other approaches to segmentation of remotely sensed satellite images include fuzzy thresholding techniques reported in [4], combining SOM and FCM as in [5], using mean-shift algorithms as in [6], Genetic algorithm as a classifier ([7]), combination of region-growing algorithm with mean shift clustering technique [8]. High resolution multi-spectral satellite images cause problems for clustering methods due to clusters of different sizes, shapes and densities as they contain huge amount of data. Due to this reason, most algorithms for clustering satellite data sacrifice the correctness of their results for fast processing time. The processing time may be greatly influenced by the use of grids. In this paper, we propose a grid density based clustering technique, SATCLUS, for multi-spectral satellite images. We have used a combination of density based and grid based clustering due to the fact that density based clustering gives clusters of good quality of different shapes and sizes ([2], [9], [10]); and grid based clustering has the added advantage of fast processing time([2]). SATCLUS can handle the

S.O. Kuznetsov et al. (Eds.): PReMI 2011, LNCS 6744, pp. 110–115, 2011.

detection of irregular shaped clusters by pixel level processing of the cluster borders. Most region growing algorithms are executed in a left to right, top-down manner, whereas SATCLUS initiates the cluster expansion process starting with the maximum hue value. Due to the use of grid-based technique, SATCLUS is scalable even for large datasets. SATCLUS does not require the initial of cluster centers; neither does the number of clusters play any role in the clustering process. SATCLUS was tested on a large number of multi-spectral satellite imagery and the cluster results are found very satisfactory.

2   The Proposed Technique

The aim of our clustering algorithm is to discover clusters over multi spectral high resolution satellite images. Following definitions [11] provide the basis of SATCLUS.

Definition 1. *Difference value of a pixel w.r.t. the seed pixel is the distance (dist) between the HSI values of that pixel and the seed. If dist $\leq \theta$, then the difference value of that pixel is considered as 1 otherwise 0, where dist, is any proximity measure (here we have used Mahalanobis distance).*

Definition 2. *Population-object ratio is the ratio of the population count (number of ones in each grid cell) and cell density (number of pixels within a particular grid cell) of a grid cell, i.e., population_count/ cell_density*

Definition 3. *If the difference of the population-object ratio of the current cell and one of its neighbors is greater than or equal to some threshold α then α is the confidence between them. For two cells p and q to be merged into the same cluster the following condition should be satisfied:*
$$\alpha \leq \mid P_o(p) - P_o(q) \mid, \text{ and } \alpha = \theta \times P_o(seed)$$
where P_o represents the population-object ratio of that particular cell and seed is the cell which initiates the expansion of a cluster.

Definition 4. *Cell reachability: A cell p is reachable from a cell q if p is a neighbor cell of q and cell p satisfies the confidence condition w.r.t. cell q.*

Definition 5. *Rough cluster: A rough cluster is defined to be the set of points belonging to the set of reachable cells. A rough cluster C w.r.t. α is a non-empty subset satisfying the following condition,*
$\forall p, q$: if $p \in C$ and q is reachable from p w.r.t. α, then $q \in C$, where p and q are cells.

Definition 6. *Border cell: A cell p is a border cell if it is part of a rough cluster C_i and at least one of its neighbors is part of another rough cluster C_j.*

Definition 7. *Noise: Noise is simply the set of points belonging to the cells not belonging to any of its clusters. Let $C_1, C_2, \cdots C_k$ be the clusters w.r.t. α, then Noise $= \{no\_p \mid p \in n \times n, \forall i : no\_p \notin C_i\}$, where no_p is the set of points in cell p and C_i (i $= 1, \cdots, k$).*

2.1   Procedure of SATCLUS

The algorithm starts with dividing the image space into $n \times n$ non-overlapping square grid cells, where n is a user input, and maps the image pixels to each cell. It then calculates the density of each cell. Next, it converts the RGB values of each pixel to its corresponding HSI values. The algorithm uses the cell information (density) of the grid structure and clusters the data points according to their surrounding cells. The clustering process is divided into two steps. In the first step a rough clustering of the image space is obtained and the second step deals with cluster smoothening for quality cluster identification. The execution of the rough clustering algorithm (Step I) includes the following steps:

Input: The Image dataset

1. Create the grid structure.
2. Compute the density of each cell.
3. Convert the RGB values of each pixel into their HSI values.
4. Identify the maximum hue value as the seed.
5. Calculate each pixels difference value w.r.t. the seed.
6. The population count of each grid cell is computed and the corresponding population-object ratio calculated.
7. Traverse the neighbor cells starting from the grid-cell having the highest population-object ratio value.
8. Merge the cells and assign cluster_id.
9. Repeat steps 5 through 9 till all cells are classified.

The value of θ mostly depends on the values of the h, s, i (i.e., hue, saturation and intensity) and the resolution of the image. However, based on our exhaustive experimentation over various multi-spectral and pan-chromatic satellite images, it has been observed that an effective range of θ for multi-spectral images is $15 \leq \theta \leq 30$ and for pan-chromatic images, the range is found to be $0.5 \leq \theta \leq 4.0$. The rough clusters obtained in Step I are grainy in nature which is a drawback of a grid based algorithm. To obtain clusters with smooth and accurate borders, the border cells are detected and re-clustered using a partitioning based approach as given in Step II. The algorithm for the cluster smoothening is given below:

Input: q border cells; k seeds corresponding to the k rough clusters obtained from Step I

1. Start with an arbitrary border pixel x
2. Find the distance of x to each of the k seeds
3. Assign x to the cluster to which it has minimum distance w.r.t. the seed
4. Repeat steps 1 to 3 till all border pixels have been reassigned

The partitioning of the dataset into $n \times n$ non-overlapping cells results in a complexity of $O(n \times n)$. The complexity of rough clustering in step I is $O(k \times p)$, where p is the number of cells in a cluster so formed and $p \ll n \times n$ in the average case and k is the number of clusters obtained. Similarly in step II, for identification of the q border cells require $O(q)$ times where $q \ll n \times n$ and assignment of r pixels to k clusters requires $O(k \times r)$ times, where r is the total number of pixels in q cells. However, $O(k \times r)$ dominates the overall time complexity since n, p, $q \ll r$.

3   Performance Evaluation

To evaluate SATCLUS in terms of quality of clustering, we used several synthetic and real datasets. SATCLUS was implemented using Java in Windows environment with Pentium-IV processor with 1 GHz speed and 4 GB RAM. We have tested SATCLUS on several synthetic and multi-spectral satellite image datasets and seven of them are reported in this paper. SATCLUS has been found capable of detecting arbitrary shaped clusters as can be seen from Figure 1 (a) and (b). SATCLUS was compared with several relevant algorithms using the image shown in Figure 1 (c) and the results have been found satisfactory, as can be seen from Figure 2. The clusters obtained from Landsat MSS image (4 spectral bands, 79m resolution) of Figure 3 (a) is shown in Figure 3(b). Figure 3(c) shows the plain built up area of Sonari in Sibsagar district of Assam (Cartosat-I image, 4 spectral bands, 2.5m resolution). SATCLUS automatically detects 5 clusters (Figure 3(d)) corresponding to Brahmaputra river, road, agricultural land, water bodies and human settlements. SATCLUS automatically detects four clusters for the IRS LISS II image of Kolkata, West Bengal (Figure 4(a)) as observed in Figure 4(b). From our ground knowledge, we can infer that these four clusters correspond to the classes: Water Bodies (black color), Habitation and City area (deep grey color), Open space (light grey color) and Vegetation (white color). Figure 4(c) and Figure 4(d) shows the IRS Kolkata image partitioned using the GA algorithm of [7] and FCM algorithm respectively. From the figure, it can be noted that the river Hoogly and the city area has not been correctly classified by FCM. In fact, those have been classified as belonging to the same

Fig. 1. (a) Example dataset (b) Output of SATCLUS (c) SPOT image of Canberra Australia

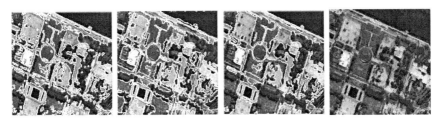

Fig. 2. Outputs of SPOT image of Canberra Australia using (a) Region-growing (b) Mean shift (c) Segmentation method of [8] (d) SATCLUS

Table 1. Homogeneity values for SATCLUS over some satellite images

Dataset	Homogeneity measure
Dataset I	0.9873
Dataset II	0.9915
Dataset III	0.9908
Dataset IV	0.9933
Dataset V	0.9887
Dataset VI	0.9917

Table 2. Comparison in terms of β value and CPU time for different clustering algorithms

Method	beta	CPU time (in hrs)
k-means	5.30	0.11
Astrahan's	7.02	0.71
Mitra's	9.88	0.75
SATCLUS	17.82	0.08

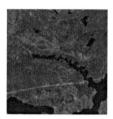 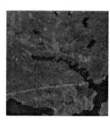 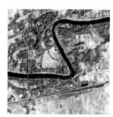 

Fig. 3. (a) Landsat-MSS   (b) Output of SATCLUS on Landsat-MSS (c) Cartosat-1 image of Sonari, Assam (d) Output of SATCLUS on Cartosat-1 image of Sonari

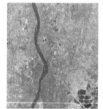 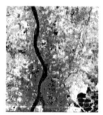 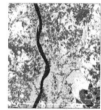 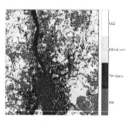

Fig. 4. (a) IRS Kolkata (4 spectral bands, 36.25m resolution) (b) Output of SATCLUS (c) Output of NSGA-II-based clustering technique [7] (d) Output of FCM clustering

  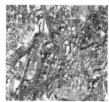 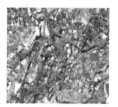

Fig. 5. (a) IRS image of Borapani (b) Output of SATCLUS on image of Borapani (c) Ikonos image of Shillong city (d) Output of SATCLUS on the image of Shillong city

class. Another misclassification is that the whole Salt Lake city has been put into one class. Although some portions have been correctly identified such as canals, the Dumdum airport runway, fisheries, etc. still there is a significant amount of confusion in the FCM clustering result. The characteristic regions of Dataset IRS P6 LISS IV image of Borapani, Meghalaya (Figure 5(a), 4 spectral bands, 5.8m resolution) are the Deep water (Deep Blue color), Wetlands (light blue color), Vegetation (Red and Pink colors) and Open spaces (White color). Executing SATCLUS on this image resulted in the detection of the above four classes as shown in Figure 5(b). The clustered image output obtained by SAT-CLUS on the IKONOS image of Shillong, Meghalaya (Figure 5(c), 4 spectral bands, resolution of 4m for multispectral and 1m for panchromatic imagery) is shown in Figure 5(d) which relate well with the ground information known to us (concrete structures, roads, open spaces, etc). The performance of SATCLUS in terms of homogeneity measure [2] for some satellite images is shown in Table 1. SATCLUS has also been evaluated quantitatively using an index β [4] and the results for Dataset II can be seen from Table 2. SATCLUS has the highest β value in comparison to the comparable algorithms.

4 Conclusions and Future Work

The proposed SATCLUS was experimentally tested and found capable in detecting the clusters qualitatively and efficiently in light of several real-life satellite images. Work is going on to extend the SATCLUS algorithm for handling hyperion (hyper spectral) data and also to extend the work using a fuzzy-rough set based approach. As a future direction of our work, we a plan to experiment the technique on microwave remote sensing data.

References

1. Baatz, M., Schape, A.: Multiresolution segmentation: an optimization approach for high quality multi-scale image segmentation. Journal of Photogrammetry and Remote Sensing 58(3-4), 12–23 (2000)
2. Han, J., Kamber, M.: Data Mining: Concepts and Techniques. Morgan Kaufmann Publishers, San Fransisco (2004)
3. Ball, G.H., Hall, D.J.: A clustering technique for summarizing multivariate data. Behavioural Science 12, 153–155 (1967)
4. Pal, S.K., Ghosh, A., Shankar, B.U.: Segmentation with remotely sensed images with fuzzy thresholding and quantitative evaluation. IJRS 21(11), 2269–2300 (2000)
5. Awad, M.M., Nasri, A.: Satellite image segmentation using self- organizing maps and fuzzy c-means. In: IEEE International Symposium on Signal Processing and Information Technology (ISSPIT), pp. 398–402 (2009)
6. Comaniciu, D., Meer, P.: Robust analysis of feature spaces: Color image segmentation. In: Proc. of the IEEE Conf. on Computer Vision and Pattern Recognition (CVPR), pp. 750–755 (1997)
7. Bandyopadhyay, S., Maulik, U., Mukhopadhyay, A.: Multiobjective genetic clustering for pixel classification in remote sensing imagery. TGRS 45(2), 1506–1511 (2007)
8. Bo, S., Ding, L., Jing, Y.: On combining region-growing with non-parametric clustering for color image segmentation. In: CISP, pp. 715–719 (2008)
9. Astrahan, M.M.: Speech analysis by clustering, or the hyper-phoneme method. Stanford A. I. Project Memo (1970)
10. Mitra, P., Murthy, C.A., Pal, S.K.: Density-based multiscale data condensation. IEEE TPAMI 24(6) (June 2002)
11. Sarmah, S., Das, R., Bhattacharyya, D.K.: A distributed algorithm for intrinsic cluster detection over large spatial data. IJCS 3(4), 246–256 (2008)

Blur Estimation for Barcode Recognition in Out-of-Focus Images

Duy Khuong Nguyen, The Duy Bui, and Thanh Ha Le

Human Machine Interaction Laboratory
University Engineering and Technology
Vietnam National University, Hanoi
{khuongnd,duybt,ltha}@vnu.edu.vn

Abstract. Recently, with the popularity of hand-held devices with camera, many applications requiring barcode identification in images have appeared. There are several problems with these applications because of the limitation of camera capability. Among them, heavily blur problems are the most significant and popular. In this paper, we propose a novel approach to estimate blur for recognising barcodes in heavily blurred images. With this approach, we are able to extract correctly the barcode from heavily blurred images, which existing methods cannot.

Keywords: Blur estimation, Barcode identification, pattern recognition, heavily blurred images.

1 Introduction

Recently, with the popularity of mobile phones aimed with integrated camera, there is a need for recognising barcodes from images captured from these devices. However, due to the limitation of controlling focus lens, the captured images are often heavily distorted by the out of focus blur. Therefore, it is very hard to extract the barcode from these heavily distorted images with existing methods proposed for conventional barcode reader. There are several approaches reported in literature for solving the blur problem in barcode recognition, e.g. edge detection-based approach [3,5,6], inverse-problem-based approach [2] and statistical machine learning techniques[7]. These techniques cannot work well for heavily distorted signals [7] because it is difficult to extract features such as edges and peaks of the bars and spaces from these signals.

In this paper, we propose a novel approach to estimate blur for recognising barcodes in heavily blurred images. We first estimate the ranges of blur parameters, and then search through these ranges with sampled values to find the parameters that allow us to extract correctly the most number of barcode values along the scan lines of the barcode image. For each scan line, we generate candidate signals by utilising the structure of the barcode, blur them with blur parameters in process, and compare with the distorted signal of the scan line to find the best matched candidate signal. The checksum of the barcode is used to

S.O. Kuznetsov et al. (Eds.): PReMI 2011, LNCS 6744, pp. 116–121, 2011.

verify the candidate. With this approach, we are able to extract correctly the barcode from heavily blurred images, which existing methods cannot.

The paper is organised as follows. In Section 2, barcode representation is described in details. The emphasis of the paper is in Section 3 which presents related works. Subsequently, our proposed algorithm in Section 4 is followed by experiments and results in Section 5.

2   Barcode Signal Reconstruction

From a 2D image of the barcode, a unique 1D signal can be extracted by scanning a horizontal line through the barcode image. Therefore, the barcode can be represented as a series of 1D patterns representing 0s and 1s (see Fig. 1):

$$S = \{u(x) \in L^2(R) : u(x) \in 0, 1\} \tag{1}$$

If the signal obtained from the image looks sharp and clear like in Fig. 1, the barcode can be recognised easily. However, as the captured barcode image is blurred and noised as in Fig. 2, the extracted 1D signal is heavily distorted (see Fig. 2). In this case, it is very hard to recognise the barcode precisely.

Fig. 1. Clear barcode image and orginal signals

Fig. 2. Blurred barcode image and blurred signals

The sharpness of the captured signal depends on the reader device and its distance between the reader and the surface of barcode. The longer the distance between them, the more blurred the original signal is. The blurred signal f(x) is often modelled as the noise added convolution of the original signal u(x) with a Gaussian kernel of unknown amplitude α and standard deviation σ [2]:

$$f(x) = \alpha * G_\sigma * u(x) + n(x) \tag{2}$$

where n(x) is a noise function, α is a strictly positive constant, and

$$G_\sigma = \frac{1}{\sigma\sqrt{2\pi}} * e^{-\frac{x^2}{2\sigma^2}} \tag{3}$$

3 Related Works

In the approach based on edge detection, traditional barcode decoding techniques such as peak locations [3], selective sampling [5] and EM algorithm [6] have been employed. These approaches cannot work well if the phone cameras are designed with low quality [7] or the images are heavily distorted. In fact, with handheld cameras, noises and focusing errors may appear frequently. In other words, it is really difficult to extract features such as edges and peaks of the bars and spaces from the heavily distorted images. In another approach, barcode is extracted after the process of signal restoration through solving an inverse problem [2]. There are two serious problems with this approach. Firstly, restored signals usually have errors because the degrading process is often unknown and complex. Secondly, the cost of computation is considerably high because of the process of signal restoration. Finally, this approach is only suitable with simulated images. For real images, barcode cannot be recognised correctly. Besides two above approaches, statistical machine learning techniques [7] are also used to identify barcode. Based on the nature of the contaminated barcode symbols, the trained classifiers are able to discriminate different code patterns by extracting their statistical features [7]. However, the cost for maintaining the system is considerably high because collecting training data is often an absolutely great task. In addition, each type of barcode or a change of capturing device needs a particular recognition system.

4 Our Proposed Approach

To recognise barcode patterns in heavily distorted images, we propose an effective algorithm in both of accuracy and performance, in which the prior structural knowledge of barcode is used thoroughly.

Despite that images may be distorted, barcodes can be located quite easily because of several reasons: they contains black and white vertical lines and every barcode have less than four consecutive 1s or 0s; they are often printed in separated area; and they often have the ratio of 3:4 between the height and width. After locating the barcode in the distorted image, we estimate the blur parameters. This is done by comparing the size of the barcode in the distorted image with the actual size of a barcode and locating the position of two border guard bars by optimising the error function. Blurred signals of digits are pre-computed with the estimated blur parameters. This pre-computation is conducted in order to speed up our algorithm. We then go through each scan line of the barcode image to find the barcode value that that best matches the signal of scan line. This is done by first re-locating the guard bars, calculating position of each digit

---

input : A heavily distorted image containing a barcode
output: The value encoded in the barcode

Locate the rectangle containing the barcode;
Estimate blur parameters via locating border guard bars;
Compute blurred signals of digits;
foreach *line of horizontal scan lines of the barcode image* **do**
    re-locate the guard bars of barcode;
    stretch signals of barcode with pixels per bit equal to
    Gaussian kernel size/2 + 1;
    foreach *position of surrounding positions of left border* **do**
        foreach *digit of left digits* **do**
            choose the digit having minimum function;
            move left_boder to the next position of the best pattern;
        end
    end
    determine the first digit based on the left digit code;
    do similarly for the right digits;
    reconstruct the whole of barcode;
    if *checksum of the found barcode value is true* **then**
        the barcode value is added as a vote
    end
end
if *the maximal number of vote for a barcode exceed a threshold* **then**
    return the barcode value is added as a vote;
end
else
    return that barcode cannot be recognised;
end

Algorithm 1. Pseudo-code for barcode recognition algorithm

in the barcode and comparing the signal of the scan line with blurred signals of digits. The first digit is implied by the patterns of six left digits. If the checksum of the detected value of the barcode is true, the barcode value is added as a vote. The barcode value with maximal number of vote is returned as result. The very detail of barcode recognition process is explained in Algorithm 1.

4.1 The Error Function

The error function that we use when finding the best matched candidate for each considered pattern is as follows:

$$E = ||f(x) - \alpha \bullet G_\sigma * u(x)|| \tag{4}$$

where $u(x)$ is the signal pattern of a generated candidate, $f(x)$ is the signal pattern of the scan line at the calculated position.

4.2 Estimating the Blur Parameters

Parameters of image degradation can be auto-extracted based on image processing techniques [1,2,4]. However, the high computation needed by these techniques is a burden to real-time application. To avoid this computation, we apply the following process. Firstly, the fixed Gaussian size needs to be set large enough for heavily distorted images. Secondly, we can α assign 1 to , by which the range of value of each pixel is from minimum to maximum value appearing in the image instead of 0 to 255, because this parameter is related to the light intensity radiating over the region of interest. Finally, parameter σ can be estimated by using the extracted position of border guard bars. By experiment, we found that the error function of border guard bar patterns has a convex parabolic curve when the parameter changes. Therefore, this parameter can be estimated approximately via a search technique.

4.3 Algorithm Complexity

The complexity of our algorithm is $O(size\ of\ image + K * R * 6 * (10 + 20) *$ $the\ number\ of\ pixels\ representing\ a\ bit)$ where $O(size\ of\ image)$ is the complexity of locating barcodes. K is the number of horizontal scan lines. R is the number surrounding of positions of left border. 6, 20 and 10 are related to the number of digits in barcodes and the number of candidates for each digit. The number of pixels representing a bit is depended on the Gaussian size. The required memory does not exceed $O(size\ of\ image)$.

5 Experiment and Result

We tested our algorithm on 50 blurred images with the various ranges of blur degree and the light intensity radiating over the region of barcode. The obtained results can be considerable and competitive. The correct identification rate is 46/50. For each barcode, it takes about 0.5 second to recognise in a Windows PC of the Pentium 4, 2.4 GHz, 1 GB RAM. Our algorithm can recognise correctly many barcodes in heavily blurred images, which it is difficult to recognise by previous algorithms [6] (see Fig. 3). However, there are still some distorted images with the appearance of geometric transform, so barcodes cannot be recognised (see Fig. 4). We have also carried the experiments by first deblurring the distorted signal using the extension of Lucy-Richardson maximum likelihood algorithm[2], and then decoding the barcode to compare with our approach. However, the deblurring did not improve the recognition on heavily distorted image.

Fig. 3. Barcodes are recognized correctly

Fig. 4. Barcodes are recognized incorrectly

6   Conclusion

In this paper, we have proposed an effective algorithm based on prior knowledge for barcode identification in heavily blurred images. The algorithm utilises prior knowledge of barcodes in order to first estimate the blur and then successfully decode the barcode in heavily blurred images. In addition, this approach can avoid expensive computation such as image restoration. We have performed experiments on real blurredly captured images to show the effectiveness of our algorithm.

Acknowledgement

This work is financially supported by the Research Grant from Vietnam National University, Hanoi No. QG.10.23.

References

1. Chan, T.F., Chiu-Kwong, W.: Total variation blind deconvolution. IEEE Transactions on Image Processing (1998)
2. Esedoglu, S.: Blind Deconvolution of Barcode Signals. Inverse Problems 20 (2004)
3. Joseph, E., Pavlidis, T.: Barcode waveform recognition using peak locations. IEEE Transactions on Pattern Analysis and Machine Intelligence (2002)
4. Likas, A.C., Galatsanos, N.P.: A variational Approach for Bayesian Blind Image Deconvolution. IEEE Transactions on Signal Processing (2004)
5. Shellhammer, S.J., Goren, D.P., Pavlidis, T.: Novel signal processing techniques in barcode scanning. IEEE Robotics and Automation Magazine, 57–65 (1999)
6. Turin, W., Boie, R.A.: Barcode recovery via the EM algorithm. Signal Processing, IEEE Transactions (2002)
7. Wang, K., Zou, Y., Wang, H.: Barcode reading from images captured by camera phones. ICMTAS 2005 (2005)

Entropy-Based Automatic Segmentation of Bones in Digital X-ray Images

Oishila Bandyopadhyay[1], Bhabatosh Chanda[2], and Bhargab B. Bhattacharya[2]

[1] Department of CSE, Camellia Institute of Technology, Kolkata -700129, India
[2] Center for Soft Computing Research, Indian Statistical Institute, Kolkata - 700 108, India

Abstract. Bone image segmentation is an integral component of orthopedic X-ray image analysis that aims at extracting the bone structure from the muscles and tissues. Automatic segmentation of the bone part in a digital X-ray image is a challenging problem because of its low contrast with the surrounding flesh, which itself needs to be discriminated against the background. The presence of noise and spurious edges further complicates the segmentation. In this paper, we propose an efficient entropy-based segmentation technique that integrates several simple steps, which are fully automated. Experiments on several X-ray images reveal encouraging results as evident from a segmentation entropy quantitative assessment (SEQA) metric [Hao, et al. 2009].

Keywords: Entropy, Digital X-ray, LOCO, Medical imaging, Segmentation.

1 Introduction

Segmentation of an anatomical object from an X-ray, MRI or a CT-scan image is a challenging task as the intensity values of the region-of-interest and the surrounding region are very close, and the contour clarity is often low. Many traditional image segmentation approaches are computationally intensive or need manual intervention [1, 2].

In last two decades, numerous segmentation models and algorithms for analyzing various classes of medical images have been reported. The selection of proper segmentation method is another important issue as this choice widely depends on specific application, image modality and several other factors [1, 2]. In this paper, we briefly discuss some notable segmentation algorithms used in medical imaging and then propose an integrated entropy-based technique suitable for bone segmentation in a digital X-ray image from the surrounding flesh region. The method is simple and fully automated and it uses a new thresholding parameter. The quality of segmentation is observed to outperform those obtained by several earlier methods [3, 13] as indicated by the segmentation entropy quantitative assessment (SEQA) [16].

2 Medical Image Segmentation: Prior Art

Image segmentation is defined as its partitioning into different parts, which are homogenous in nature with respect to some characteristics. The region-of-interest

S.O. Kuznetsov et al. (Eds.): PReMI 2011, LNCS 6744, pp. 122–129, 2011.
© Springer-Verlag Berlin Heidelberg 2011

(ROI) may be a complete object or a part of it [2, 5]. Medical image segmentation algorithms can be classified into categories like those based on analysis of edges, regions, pixel classification, graphs, or on deformable model, fuzzy logic, artificial neural network, statistical or morphological approaches. The segmentation algorithms based on region analysis or pixel classification, make use of the homogeneity in the image, whereas the edge detection and graph-based algorithms perform segmentation by detecting any abrupt change in the image within a small neighborhood [5]. The Canny edge detector uses two levels of thresholding. Šćepanović et al. adopted Canny's method for probabilistic bone edge detection [6].

The deformable model based approaches allow elastic decomposition of the objects by incorporating concepts of continuum mechanics. The active contour or snake model was proposed by Kass et al. [7]. In deformable models like *snake*, the user provides an initial guess of contour of ROI, which is then moved by the image-driven forces to the boundary of the desired object. However, the snake method with gradient vector flow (GVF) has slow convergence on irregular objects with high concavities like X-ray images of deformed bone structure.

The active shape model and active appearance model are also used in medical image segmentation. Unfortunately, both the methods require large training samples to build a point distribution in the high-dimensional eigen space. The statistical models like probability distribution map and Markov random field model have also been used widely for medical image segmentation. Liang et al. have used statistical and morphology based technique for fracture identification in an X-ray image [19]. Pal et al. [10] studied segmentation of MRI samples using fuzzy-based approaches.

Several semi-automatic image segmentation methods incorporate user interaction and allow the user to mark the ROI or background objects roughly on the image. Ning et al. proposed an interactive image segmentation algorithm based on maximal similarity based region merging [12].

Thresholding-based segmentation approaches are widely used in medical image analysis [8, 9]. Sen et al. proposed a method based on gradient histogram and applied it on a chest X-ray image among others [8].Yan et al. used an entropy-based thresholding approach for segmentation of bacteria images from a low intensity background [13]; however, this method requires a tuning parameter, which is chosen based on experience.

3 Proposed Approach for X-ray Image Segmentation

In an X-ray image, the bone parts appear along with the surrounding tissues or muscles (i.e. flesh) image. In many regions of an X-ray image, the intensity range of pixels belonging to the bone region and that of its surrounding flesh region may overlap, which makes the segmentation inaccurate. The bone region of an X-ray image is to be extracted out of two distinct background components, the image background and the overlapping flesh region. Thus, bone segmentation from the flesh region using pixel based thresholding or edge based approaches often do not produce accurate results.

In this paper, we have proposed a new entropy-based approach, which instead of direct entropy thresholding [13], first produces an intermediate image from the entropy matrix and then uses intensity-thresholding for segmenting the bone region in an X-ray image. Finally, for contour correction, multilevel LOCO (Linear combination of Open-Close and Close-Open) filtering methods [11] are used.

3.1 Integrated Segmentation Algorithm

In the proposed algorithm, the transition regions in an input image are identified using entropy analysis and a gray scale entropy image is generated. This entropy image is used to compute the threshold value required for segmentation.

A high entropy value represents the presence of maximum information, i.e., higher gray value pixels in the image. An image with a very low entropy value represents noise with no meaningful information. The overlapping flesh and bone regions in an X-ray image cause the presence of a large number of pixels with similar intensity values. Computation of local entropy values of each pixel in a window helps to group the pixels with similar intensity values with a marked transition region. As a bone region has higher intensity values than those in the flesh region in an X-ray image, the transition boundaries are accentuated in the entropy image. The steps of the proposed algorithm are summarized below, details of which are elaborated subsequently.

Step 1: Convert an input X-ray image to a gray scale image.

Step 2: Perform entropy computation of each image pixel around (9×9) neighbors. For pixels at the border of the image, symmetric padding is used where the padded pixels are obtained by mirror reflection of the border pixels of the image.

Step 3: Generate an entropy image by converting the entropy matrix to a gray scale image, where the maximum entropy value is mapped to 255 and the minimum entropy value is mapped to 0. Other entropy values are linearly scaled between 0 and 255.

Step 4: Apply median filter on the entropy image.

Step 5: Compute the intensity threshold value for binarization of the entropy image.

Step 6: Produce the segmented bone image.

Step 7: Apply multilevel LOCO filter to enhance the contour of the segment.

3.2 Entropy Computation and Constructing Entropy Image

The entropy value represents the measure of randomness associated with pixel values belonging to each gray level.

Following Shannon's definition of entropy and Pun's representation of image entropy, for an image with G gray levels, and probability of k-th gray level P_k, the image entropy can be represented as

$$E = \sum_{k=0}^{G-1} P_k log_2(1/P_k) = - \sum_{k=0}^{G-1} P_k log_2(P_k) \tag{1}$$

where $P_k = n_k/M{\times}N$, n_k is the number of pixels with grayscale k and $M{\times}N$ is the size of the image [5].

Local entropy represents the discrepancy between two probability distributions on the same event space [13]. It is related to the variance of grayscales in the neighborhood of a pixel. Local entropy divides the image into separate regions and then analyzes each region as a separate information source. If a small neighborhood window Ω_k of size $M_k \times N_k$ is defined within the image, then entropy of Ω_k can be represented as:

$$E(\Omega_k) = - \sum_{j=0}^{G-1} P_j log_2(P_j) \ where \ P_j = n_j / M_k \times N_k \qquad (2)$$

where, P_j denotes the probability of gray scale j in the neighborhood Ω_k, n_j is the number of pixels with gray scale j in Ω_k, and $E(\Omega_k)$, the local entropy of Ω_k.

Yan et al. had applied local entropy based thresholding for transition region extraction [13]. It was shown that the local entropy is larger for heterogeneous regions and smaller for homogeneous neighborhoods. So, a transition region will have larger local entropy values than those in the non-transition regions of the image. This boundary enhancement aids thresholding for segmentation of the transition region from the image. Kang et al. used local entropy values to identify transition regions on region extraction from coronary angiograms [14].

In the proposed algorithm, we calculate the local entropy values by taking a (9×9) neighborhood window for each pixel of the X-ray image. The pixels at the transition region enhance their entropy values compared to those of other pixels.

In an X-ray image of foot (Fig. 1a), the intensity variation of the transition region s1 ranges between 0 to 80, whereas, for the transition region s2, it varies from 150 to 190 (Fig. 1b). In Fig. 1c we show the variation in entropy values for the transition regions s1 and s2. It is observed that the entropy values at transition region show a high peak irrespective of the difference in the intensities at the transition regions. We have used this entropy behavior to construct an intermediate gray scale image (called *entropy image*) in which the bone boundaries appear at high entropy regions (i.e., transition regions). Next, an intensity thresholding approach is applied to segment the bone.

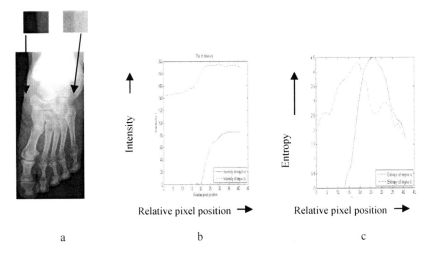

      a   b   c

Fig. 1. a: Gray scale image of foot X-ray with transition regions s1 and s2, b: Intensity variation in s1 and s2, c: Entropy variation in s1 and s2

3.3 Morphological Filter: Multilevel LOCO

Since X-ray image processing is often corrupted by noise and spurious edges, we use a morphology-based special filtering technique to improve the contour definition of the segmented bone parts. Morphological opening is defined as erosion followed by dilation and closing is dilation followed by erosion using some structuring element [5].

A LOCO filter (Linear combination of Open-Close (OC) and Close-Open (CO)) is designed by averaging the cascaded opening and closing operations within a generalized filter structure [11]. The LOCO filtering on an image I with a structuring element N can be represented as:

$$LOCO\ (I;N)=1/2((I_N)^N+(I^N)_N) \tag{3}$$

The segmented bone structure obtained using the proposed algorithm may suffer from having thin or disconnected boundaries. A LOCO filter with multiple structuring elements is applied to enhance the bone boundary and to improve the visual quality of the segmented bone image. We use three different (3×3, 5×5 and 7×7) diamond-shaped structuring elements [5] and generate enhanced contour image using each of them. Finally, the output image is produced by taking the average of these pixel values.

3.4 Thresholding

The OTSU method is a well known thresholding algorithm, which selects the threshold by minimizing within class the variance between two groups of pixels separated by thresholding operator [3]. However, this method may not work well if the two classes are very unequal and if the image has variable illumination. This is a very common problem in an X-ray image. So we have used global thresholding approach based on mean intensity value to determine the threshold for bone image segmentation. In this approach, the threshold value is determined by computing the maximum of the mean intensity value for each column of the image matrix and the mean intensity value for each row; this value can then be used for binarization of the gray scale X-ray image.

4 Experimental Results

We have run the proposed algorithm on 40 digital X-ray images of different portions of human body, collected from the literature and other sources. For lack of space, the output generated only for a few of them are shown in this section (Figs. 2, 3).

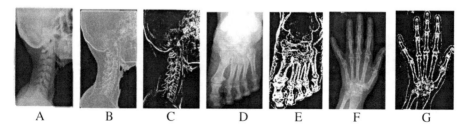

Fig. 2. A: Input X-ray image of throat, B: Gray image of A after entropy analysis, C: Segmented bone image by the proposed algorithm, D: Input X-ray image of foot, E: Segmented bone image, F: Input X-ray image of broken wrist, G: Segmented bone image of F using the proposed method

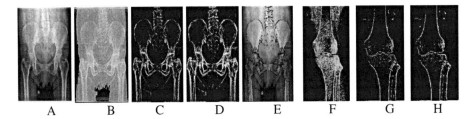

Fig. 3. A: Input X-ray image of pelvic bone, B: Gray image of A after entropy analysis, C: Segmented bone image after thresholding, D: Segmented bone image with bone boundary enhanced by applying multilevel LOCO, E: Segmented image superimposed on original image, F: Segmented knee image for α = 0.7, G: Segmented knee image for α = 0.8, H: Segmented knee image using the proposed algorithm

The proposed segmentation algorithm is compared with another entropy-based thresholding approach proposed by Yan et al. [13]. The idea of local entropy thresholding approach was applied on several bacteria images for segmenting them from the background. The thresholding value is computed as α times maximum entropy, where α is a coefficient between 0 and 1.

$$E_T = \alpha \, E(\Omega_k)_{max}, \tag{4}$$

where $E(\Omega_k)_{max}$ is the maximum entropy value for region Ω_k. In this approach α is empirically chosen between 0.6 to 1.0, which requires manual intervention. In the proposed X-ray segmentation approach, the entropy matrix of the input image is converted into a gray scale entropy image and thresholding is performed after binarization. Hence, this approach is fully automated and does not need any training samples.

Figs. 3F, 3G, 3H reveal that the segmentation of the bone boundary of knee image is more accurate for α = 0.8, whereas for a pelvic bone image α = 0.7 gives better results when the earlier algorithm [13] is applied. The proposed segmentation method yields an improved result automatically (Fig. 3H).

5 Quantitative Performance Evaluation

We have evaluated the performance of the proposed algorithm using a recent *segmentation entropy quantitative assessment* (SEQA) method, which is based on segmentation entropy to compute an evaluation metric [16]. Another evaluation method called *ultimate measurement accuracy* (UMA) [17], uses the area of segmented object as a powerful evaluation metric. However, in the case of a bone image, this is difficult to compute because of fragmentation of contours. Thus, we have used the SEQA method for our purpose. In this approach, if the segmentation process S divides an image I into n subregions and $E(r_i)$ represents the entropy of r_ith region, the segmentation entropy $E(S)$ is defined as:

$$E(S) = (\sum_{i=1}^{n}(ri) - E(I))/E(I) \tag{5}$$

where $E(I)$ represents the total entropy of the original image. The segmentation entropy $E(S)$ measures how much the image entropy changes during segmentation. Better segmented regions will be more homogeneous in nature and thus they will have lower region entropy. If the same image is segmented using two different segmentation algorithms A and B, and if $E(A)$ is smaller than $E(B)$, then according to Eqn (5), the performance of A is better than that of B [16]. We have compared the segmentation entropy E of the proposed method with those of OTSU thresholding [3] and entropy thresholding [13]. These values for different digital X-ray images as listed in Table 1 support the effectiveness of the algorithm.

Table 1. Computation of segmentation entropy for some digital X-ray images

Image file	$E(S)$ for OTSU	$E(S)$ for entropy thresholding; $\alpha = 0.7$	$E(S)$ for proposed method
Finger-Left.jpg (Fig. 2F)	3.52	2.63	2.05
Foot.jpg (Fig. 2D)	2.09	0.80	0.83
Leg.jpg (Fig. 3F)	2.48	1.92	1.48
Pelvic Bone.jpg (Fig. 3A)	1.77	0.82	0.77
Throat.jpg (Fig. 2A)	1.11	0.30	0.28

6 Discussion and Conclusion

We have developed an entropy-based X-ray image segmentation technique for bone part extraction. This is based on automatic thresholding of an entropy image defined by the entropy values in a neighborhood window of the given image. It has been observed that in many cases the bone boundary becomes fragmented after thresholding. To overcome this problem, we have applied a multilevel-averaging LOCO filter to enhance the bone contour of the segmented image. The method is fully automated and has superior performance over two earlier methods as evident by the SEQA metric. This algorithm will be useful for fracture detection in an X-ray image where, separation of bone from the surrounding flesh is needed for further analysis.

Acknowledgment. Some of the digital X-ray images were supplied by Dr. A. R. Sikdar and Sudarshan Polyclinic, Kolkata. We thankfully acknowledge their support.

References

1. Sezgin, M., Sankur, B.: Survey over image thresholding techniques and quantitative performance evolution. Journal of Electronic Imaging 13(1), 146–165 (2004)
2. Pham, D.L., Xu, C., Prince, J.L.: A survey of current methods in medical image segmentation. Annual Review of Biomedical Engineering 2, 315–337 (1998)
3. Otsu, N.: A threshold selection method from gray-level histograms. IEEE Transactions on Systems, Man and Cybernetics 9, 62–66 (1979)

4. Yang, J., Staib, L.H., Duncan, V.: Neighborhood-constrained segmentation with level based 3-D deformable models. IEEE Transactions on Medical Imaging 23(8), 940–948 (2004)
5. Gonzalez, R.C., Woods, R.E.: Digital Image Processing. Pearson, London (2008)
6. Šćepanović, D., Kirshtein, J., Jain, A.K., Taylor, R.H.: Fast algorithm for probabilistic bone edge detection (FAPBED). In: SPIE, vol. 5747, pp. 1753–1765 (2005)
7. Kass, M., Witkin, A., Terzopoulos, D.: Snakes: Active contour models. International Journal of Computer Vision 1(4), 321–331 (1988)
8. Sen, D., Pal, S.K.: Gradient histogram thresholding in a region of interest for edge detection. Image and Vision Computing 28, 677–695 (2010)
9. Kundu, M.K., Pal, S.K.: Thresholding for edge detection using human psycho-visual phenomena. Pattern Recognition Letters 4(6), 433–441 (1986)
10. Pal, S.K., King, R.A.: On edge detection of X-ray images using fuzzy set. IEEE Transactions on Pattern Analysis and Machine Intelligence 5, 69–77 (1983)
11. Schulze, M.A., Pearce, J.A.: Linear combinations of morphological operators: The midrange, pseudomedian, and LOCO filters. In: IEEE International Conference on Acoustics, Speech, and Signal Processing, pp. 57–60 (1993)
12. Ning, J.L., Zhang, J., Zhang, D., Wu, C.: Interactive image segmentation by maximal similarity based region merging. Pattern Recognition 43, 445–456 (2010)
13. Yan, C., Sang, N., Zhang, T.: Local entropy-based transition region extraction and thresholding. Pattern Recognition Letters 24, 2935–2941 (2003)
14. Kang, W., Wang, K., Wang, Q., An, D.: Segmentation method based on transition region extraction for coronary angiograms. In: IEEE International Conference on Mechatronics and Automation, pp. 905–909 (2009)
15. Pal, N.R., Pal, S.K.: A review on image segmentation techniques. Pattern Recognition 23(9), 1277–1294 (1993)
16. Hao, J., Shen, Y., Xu, H., Zou, J.: A region entropy based objective evaluation method for image segmentation. In: IEEE International Conference on Instrumentation and Measurement Technology, pp. 373–377 (2009)
17. Zhang, Y.: A survey on evaluation methods for image segmentation. Pattern Recognition 29(8), 1335–1346 (1996)
18. Ding, F.: Segmentation of bone structure in X-ray images. Thesis Proposal, School of Computing, National University of Singapore (2006)
19. Liang, J., Pan, B.-C., Fan, Y.-H.: Fracture identification of X-ray image. In: International Conference on Wavelet Analysis and Pattern Recognition, pp. 67–73 (2010)

Principle and Method of Image Recognition under Diffusive Distortions of Image

Jaser Doroshenko[1], Lev Dulkin[1], Viktor Salakhutdinov[2], and Yury Smetanin[3]

[1] Central Clinical Hospital of the Russian Academy of Sciences, Litovsky boul. 1a,
119333, Moscow, Russia
`retinaretina.ru`
[2] Research Institute of System Investigations of the Russian Academy of Sciences,
Nahimovsky av.36-1, 117218, Moscow, Russia
`vsalakhutdinovgmail.com`
[3] Computer Center of the Russian Academy of Sciences, Vavilov st. 40, 119333,
Moscow, Russia
`smetaninrfbr.ru`

Abstract. The results of investigation and development of software and hardware tools for processing images of ring objects under diffusive dissipation are presented. The proposed algorithm was demonstrated to be efficient in endoscopy for measuring the sizes of biological objects. A principal scheme of a hardware system for the implementation of the new method is presented. A plan of clinical testing of the new system is developed.

Keywords: evidence-based medicine, biomedical informatics, image recognition, endoscope, measurement algorithm.

1 Introduction

One of the most important topics in evidence-based medicine is the objective evaluation of the quality of clinical research. Practice demonstrates that many contemporary methods of measuring do not meet the requirements of evidence-based medicine. That is especially true for medical image processing and analysis.

The importance of endoscopic images in medicine is the consequence of the fact that now they are the main, and sometimes the only possible source of information for noninvasive visualization of internal anomalies and for the diagnostics of various diseases [1]. The implementation of the endoscopic imaging is based on small size TV systems that are inserted into the investigated region. If the size is large, mosaicking is necessary.

The most important deadlock is that modern endoscopic methods and systems do not measure the distance between the camera and the object, therefore, it is impossible to match visible sizes of the objects in the image to their real size. The error in the estimation of the distance inevitably causes a wrong estimation of the size of the pathology, and as a consequence, a wrong strategic selection of treatment. In practice, the error of measurement in traditional endoscopic

S.O. Kuznetsov et al. (Eds.): PReMI 2011, LNCS 6744, pp. 130–135, 2011.

methods in some cases (e.g., in urologic checkup) is up to 3 to 5 times higher than it is needed for the selection of the adequate strategy of treatment [4]. It reduces the efficiency of endoscopic monitoring and diagnostics in TV medicine.

Below, we consider an approach to solving this problem that is based on scaling using test images with a priori known sizes. A light spot is projected onto the image of the object. The size of the projection is used for the estimation of the scaling factor of the pathologies. The approach is well known and extensively used [5,6], but is precision is limited. In all practical implementations of the approach, difficulties appear that are related to great aberrations of the optical system of the endoscope [7]. Moreover, light dispersion occurs in a biological tissue which results in blurring and incorrect scaling.

A new system is proposed for imaging and processing. The system makes it possible to evaluate the real size of the pathologies using their endoscopic images. It is also possible to evaluate the errors caused by the light dispersion and to correct them.

2   Principle and Methods

The measuring system consists of a PC, TV endoscope whose brightening sub-system uses an inertia-free light-emitting diode, and light fibers. At one end, a laser light source is situated, at the other, micro collimator, which gives at the output a light beam whose section is equal along the whole length.

The light fiber is situated in the instrumental channel of the endoscope in such a way that it is possible to measure the direction of the laser beam by standard manipulators fixed at the distal end of the endoscope. This solution makes it possible to use optical systems with various angles between their optical axis and the axis of the instrumental channel (Fig. 1).

Microcollimator situated at the end of the light fiber transforms the divergent light beam into the beam with constant section. The PC controls the light-emitting diode used as the light source, the laser at the input of the light fiber, and the image processing for the TV endoscope.

The object whose size is measured is placed near the center of the image. After receiving the signal:

1. A current image of the object near the center is registered in the operating memory and displayed at the monitor as a static frame.

2. Along the foreground of the pulse of the frame synchronization for the TV endoscope, the light-diode source at the input of the light fiber is switched on.

3. The next frame, which consists of the image of the projection of the colli-mated laser beam light onto the measured object, is registered in the operating memory.

4. As the result of the image processing (step 3), the section of the laser beam is quantified (in pixels).

5. In the static image, a line is manually marked whose size is to be measured. The length of the line is defined as its size in pixels divided by the size in pixels

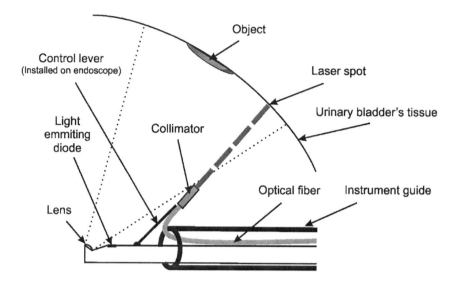

Fig. 1. The principal scheme of the distal end of the endoscope

Fig. 2. Various halos around the laser beam

of the section of the laser beam and multiplied by the section of the laser beam in millimeters; the latter is known a priori.

3   Calibration Using Circular Spots

The considered problem is not trivial because, depending on the characteristics of the tissue of the measured object, the laser beam can either penetrate or not penetrate into the object, and the penetration may be up to the considerable depth. It may result in a halo whose intensity is comparable to the intensity of the main beam (Fig. 2, the blue circle is the initial laser spot) and, as a consequence, considerable errors of measurements appear The results of clinical testing demonstrate that the error caused by the dispersion may reach 70 % in the processing of real images in medical endoscopy [8].

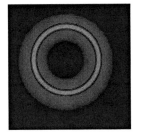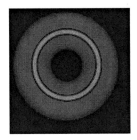

Fig. 3. Various halos around the laser beam that has the form of a circle

In order to enhance the precision, the laser beam at the output of the collimator has the form of the circle. In the process of measuring, the size of the projection of the laser beam onto the measured object (step 4), the measured value of the intensity in the center is used as the threshold. In Fig. 3, the dissipation of the circular laser beam is demonstrated.

Evidently, the diameter of the circle, which is clearly discernible at the images, is almost the same for all the values of the dispersion.

Clinical tests have demonstrated that eliminating the dispersion in the tissue reduces the error of measurements approximately by a factor of three, which is sufficient for practical medicine. The experiments with laboratory animals have demonstrated that the proposed system enhances the precision more than by an order of magnitude; that results in the substantially reduced fraction of incorrect diagnostic decisions.

The next step of image processing is the elimination of disturbances caused by the inhomogeneity of optical properties of biological tissue. The aim of this step is to obtain regular circles.

4   Thresholds for the Determination of Regular Circles

The proposed method is based on the model of optical coherence tomography of heterogeneous tissue [9] and the principles of the diffusion wave spectroscopy in inhomogeneous flows [10].

The transport equation is

$$\frac{1}{c}\frac{\partial I(r,s,t)}{\partial t} + \nabla I(r,s,t)s + \mu_t I(r,s,t) = \mu_s \int I(r,s,t)p(s,s')ds' + S(r,s,t),$$

where c is the velocity of light in the environment and $S(r,s,t)$ is the spatial and angular distribution of sources.

To cope with the complexity of this integro-differential equation, the expansion in series of spherical harmonics $Y_{l,m}$ is used, which results in a system of $(N+1)^2$ coupled partial differential equations. Thus we obtain

$$I(r,s,t) = \sum_{l=0}^{m} \sum_{m=-1}^{l} \psi_{l,m} Y_{i,m}(s)$$

$$S(r,s,t) = \sum_{l=0}^{m} \sum_{m=-1}^{l} q_{l,m} Y_{i,m}(s)$$

and in P_1 approximation,

$$I(r,s,t) = U(r,t) + \frac{3}{4\pi} F(r,t)s,$$

where

$$F(r,t) = \int_{4\pi} I(r,s,t)s ds.$$

In practice, it is sufficient to take the intensity in the center of the light spot multiplied by a const. > 1. The result is used as the threshold to deduct from the signal. The exact value of the const. is defined by the quality of the input image and the required reliability.

5   Conclusion

The presented data demonstrate that the proposed method of measuring and reconstructing gives images with high quality topological structure, which are convenient for the interpretation. The system is easy to implement since it does not demand any complex hardware. The system is convenient for users that have no experience in computer technologies. It does not demand any changes in the optical system; it is important in the considered domain, where stable spectral and temporal characteristics, small thermal effect, etc. are required. After solving the problems of safety, which are inevitable in medical devices, the new system may be used as a subsystem of hardware and software tools for noninvasive registration not demanding contrast agents, localization of objects and regions, and monitoring of zones of abnormal blood supply of fundus. A plan of clinical testing of the new system is developed.

Acknowledgments. The work was partly supported by Russian Foundation for Basic Research, grants no. 09-07-00309-a, 09-07-00444-a, and 09-08-00993-a.

References

1. Cotton, P.B., Williams, C.B.: Practical Gastrointestinal Endoscopy: The Fundamentals, vol. 1. Blackwell Science, Oxford (2003)
2. McPhee, S.J., Papadakis, M.A.: Current Medical Diagnosis and Treatment 2009, vol. 1. McGraw Hill, New York (2009)
3. Sokolov, B.A., et al.: Endoscopic tactics in concretions that are hard to remove (in Russian). In: 9th Moscow International Congress on Endoscopic Surgery, Moscow, April 6 - 8, 2005, pp. 353–355.

4. Dul'kin, L.M., Salakhutdinov, V.K., et al.: Method of longitudinal stereoscopy for 3D visualization of endoscopic images (in Russian). In: Proc. of Int. Symp. Topical Problems of Biophotonics-2007, pp. 1–30 (2007)
5. Horn, B.K.P.: Robot Vision, vol. 1. MIT Press, Cambridge (1986)
6. Kuriksha, Zhulina, Y.V.: Processing of corrupted optical images (in Russian). Radiotekhnika i elektronila 66(3), 23–40 (2000)
7. Born, M., Wolf, E.: Principles of Optics. Cambridge University Press, Cambridge (1999)
8. Dul'kin, L.M., et al.: Classification of complexity categories of diagnostical and clinical endoscopic retrograde pancreatocholangiography and the degree of risk of complications. In: 6th Moscow International Congress on Endoscopic Surgery, Moscow (2002)
9. Schmitt, J.M., Knutel, A.: Model of optical coherence tomography of heterogeneous tissue. J. Opt. Soc. Am. A. 14, 1231–1242 (1997)
10. Bicout, D., Maynard, R.: Diffusion wave spectroscopy in inhomogeneous flows. Physica A 199(3-4), 387–411 (1993)

Regression Models for Texture Image Analysis

Anatoliy Plastinin

Samara State Aerospace University,
Molodogvardeiskaya st 151, Samara, 443001 Russia
anatoliy.plastinin@gmail.com

Abstract. The article describes universal model for creating algorithms for calculating textural image features. The proposed models are used for images that are realizations of Markov Random Field. Experimental classification results are shown for different images sets.

Keywords: Textutre Image Analysis, Textutre Image Recognition, Regression models, Markov Random Fields.

1 Introduction

Many natural micro and macro images are combinations of textural primitives, e.g. aerial photographs of the earth surface, images of material nanostructures, biomedical images. That's why in many applied problems of the image processing (like, segmentation, coding, simulation, etc.) texture processing methods can be used.

Two main approaches to the texture analysis can be noted: structural and stochastic [1]. In structural approach textures are considered as a combination of repeating primitive elements, which relative position is defined by specific rules. In stochastic approach, the texture is defined as a realization of a 2D random process, and specified by a set of random statistics. In our research work we used statistical approach.

It should be noted, that common texture analysis methods, like co-occurrence matrix [2], spectral descriptors, Tamura features [3], etc., give common features for all types of images and ignore problem peculiarities. However, in practice it becomes necessary to calculate features for classification of limited texture sets. Also many methods deal with gray-scale images only i.e. these methods can't be applied to analysis of some classes of texture images. Methods based on Markov random field are successfully used in many applied problems. This methods proved to be efficient in image segmentation problems, image synthesis, etc. [4,5,6,7]. Thus, the goal of our investigation is to provide general framework for estimation of color-texture features based on domain specific information.

2 Problem of Texture Image Recognition

Let $\mathfrak{I}$ is a set of all possible images, that consists of K classes $C_1, \ldots, C_K$, i.e. $\bigcup_{k=0}^{K} C_k = \mathfrak{I}$ and $C_i \cap C_j = \varnothing, i \neq j$, here C_0 — set of objects that are not included in any class. Original class separation is unknown.

S.O. Kuznetsov et al. (Eds.): PReMI 2011, LNCS 6744, pp. 136–141, 2011.

Suppose we are given a finite set of images $\mathcal{I} = \{I_1, \ldots, I_N\} \subset \mathfrak{I}$, the class label is specified for each image from this set, i.e. following map is defined $u : \mathcal{I} \rightarrow \mathfrak{L}$, where $\mathfrak{L} = \{1, \ldots, K\}$ is a set of class labels. A training set is defined as a set of image-class pairs: $T = \mathcal{I} \times \mathfrak{L}$.

The goal is to design a method that allows to identify class label based on image I. To use pattern recognition theory [7,8], one should associate features vector $f \in \mathfrak{F} = \mathbb{R}^n$ with each image, thus following map should be defined: $F : \mathfrak{I} \rightarrow \mathfrak{F}$, where $\mathfrak{F}$ is a feature space. Hence, here exists an unknown dependence $\hat{u} : \mathfrak{F} \rightarrow \mathfrak{L}$, values are observed on finite training set $\hat{T} = \{(f_i, l_i)\}_{i=1}^N$. One should define a map $\tilde{u} : \mathfrak{F} \rightarrow \mathfrak{L}$, that is an approximation of unknown target dependency on both elements of training set and whole set $\mathfrak{F}$.

All existing feature calculation methods are defined for a wide range of problems, i.e. it doesn't fully utilize domain specific information from training set.

To exploit domain specific information we should define parametric feature calculation method F_a, where a is a set of method parameters. Thus, specific method parameters $a = P(\mathcal{I})$ are calculated based on training set $\mathcal{I}$ at a training step, and feature vector is estimated for each specific image using calculated parameters vector $f = F_a(I)$. The general classification scheme is shown in figure 1.

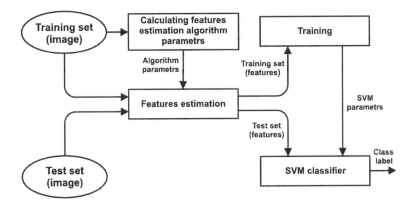

Fig. 1. Classification scheme

On first step the method's vector parameters $a = P(\mathcal{I})$ are calculated based on training set $\mathcal{I}$. Then resulted parameters used for estimation of features are used on next classifier training step.

3 Image Model

To design features estimation algorithm in case of texture images analysis, one can use Markov Random Field (MRF) model [7], it's effectively used in many texture analysis problems.

Let's define image as map:

$$I: L_x \times L_y \to G, \tag{1}$$

where $L_x = \{1, \ldots, K_x\}$ and $L_y = \{1, \ldots, K_y\}$ are spatial coordinates, and G is a set of colors; e.g. for gray-scale image $G = [0; 1]$, and for colored image (RGB color space) $G = [0; 1]^3$.

Let the image be a realization of any Markov random field [7]. Following notation will be used below:

- $\mathcal{N}_p$ — neighborhood of a pixel p;
- $\mathcal{N}_p^k$ — k-th neighborhood element;
- $I_{\mathcal{N}_p} = \left(I_{\mathcal{N}_p^1}, \ldots, I_{\mathcal{N}_p^K}\right)$ — vector of pixel values in the neighborhood of current pixel.

4   Features Design Method

Since the value of central pixel I_p depends on values of pixels in the neighborhood, we can consider approximation function — the function where the pixels from the neighborhood are arguments and the value of function is an estimate of central pixel value. This function can be defined as:

$$\hat{I}_p = f(I_{\mathcal{N}_p}) = \arg\max_x \mathsf{P}(x|I_{\mathcal{N}_p}), \tag{2}$$

or using regression equation:

$$\hat{I}_p = f(I_{\mathcal{N}_p}) = \mathsf{E}[x|I_{\mathcal{N}_p}]. \tag{3}$$

Let's consider solving regression problem. $D = \{(x_i, y_i)\} = \{(I_{\mathcal{N}_p}, I_p)|p \in L_x \times L_y\} \subset \mathbb{R}^K \times \mathbb{R}$ — training set of regression problem.

We use kernel ridge regression method [9]. According to representer theorem [8] we're going to find solution in form:

$$\hat{f}(x) = \sum_{i=1}^{l} \alpha_i k(x, x_i), \tag{4}$$

where k is positive defined kernel [8].

The cost function, which needs to be minimized for ridge regression is:

$$\sum_{i=1}^{l} (y_i - \alpha_i k(x, x_i))^2 + \lambda \sum_{i=1}^{l} \alpha_i^2. \tag{5}$$

The ridge model coefficients are given by: $\alpha = (K + \lambda I)^{-1} y$, where $K_{i,j} = k(x_i, x_j)$. We use Gaussian kernel in our study:

$$k(x, x') = \exp\left(-\gamma||x - x'||\right). \tag{6}$$

Hence, each image is associated with its own set of parameters α. Overall, the parameters are similar for images from the same class.

To build features separating several classes, we should use regression function based on all images from training set. But it leads to the next issue — increasing of regression problem training set size. To avoid increasing of the set size, only a subset of training set for image can be used, it's possible because a lot of vectors in the training set are similar. Hence, only linear independent (in RKHS for kernel k) vectors can be used from the training set.

5   Selecting of Linearly Independent Subset

Consider we need to select M linear independent vectors from set $\{x_i\}_{i=1}^N$. Let $\phi(x)$ be a fixed finite dimensional mapping from domain space to Reproducing Kernel Hilbert Space with kernel k, such that $k(x, y) = \langle \phi(x), \phi(y) \rangle$ [9].

Let's use following iterative procedure [10]. On each step t, subset of vectors $D_{t-1} = \{\tilde{x}_j\}_{i=1}^{m_{t-1}}$ have been collected, after $t-1$ vectors were observed, where $\{\phi(\tilde{x}_j)\}_{i=1}^{m_{t-1}}$ are approximately linearly independent vectors by construction. We test if $\phi(x_t)$ is approximately linearly dependent on subset D_{t-1}, if not we add it to D_{t-1}, i.e. $D_t = D_{t-1} \cup x_t$. Hence, all vectors $x_1, \ldots, x_t$ can be approximated as linear combination of vectors D_t. x_t is approximately linearly dependent on set D_{t-1}, it means that it satisfies following condition:

$$\min \left\| \sum_{j=1}^{m_{t-1}} a_j \phi(\tilde{x}_j) - \phi(x_t) \right\|^2 < \delta, \qquad (7)$$

where δ is accuracy parameter.

To sum it all up, the set of method parameters a for each particular problem is a set of linear independent neighborhood vectors, generated from all training set images. Thus, feature vector is regression coefficients of approximation function.

6   Experiments with Test Images

Classification experiments on 2 sets of test images were performed, each set of images consists of 2 classes (see Fig. 2 and 3). N indicates the number of linearly independent vectors used, and S indicates the radius of non-causal neigborhood (e. g. S1; N5 means that 3×3 non-causal neigborhood used and number of linearly independent vectors was 5).

Non-linear SVM classifier [8,11] is used for experiments. Each class of images is split into training set of 10 images and validation set of 100 images. Training set is used to estimate parameters of feature calculation algorithm, that are used to calculate features for images in test set. Then these features are used for training of the SVM classifier. Accuracy of classification was investigated for images distorted by additive and impulse noise, using the decision function obtained on previous step. The results are shown in Fig. 4 and 5.

Fig. 2. Sample images from 1st set

Fig. 3. Sample images from 2nd set

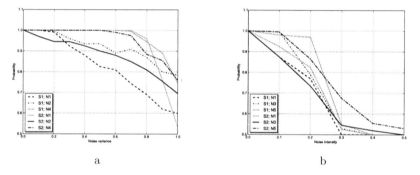

a   b

Fig. 4. Effect of white and impulse noise on 1st image set: a — white noise, b — impulse noise

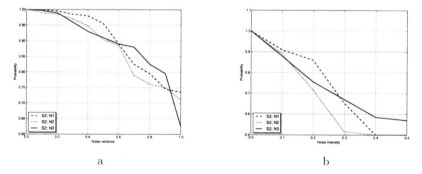

a   b

Fig. 5. Effect of white and impulse noise on 2nd image set: a — white noise, b — impulse noise

7   Conclusion

In our research work the general framework for estimating textural features, which utilizes domain specific information from training set, is described. Proposed method is used for formalization of features estimation algorithm based on approximation of pixels dependency function, for images with markov random field model.

The method has following advantages: domain specific features increase classification quality (in terms of correct classification probability); features are stable to additive and impulse noise.

References

1. Haralick, R.M.: Statistical and structural approaches to texture. Proceedings of the IEEE 67(5), 786–804 (1979)
2. Haralick, R.M., Shanmugam, K., Dinstein, I.: Textural Features for Image Classification. IEEE Transactions on Systems, Man, and Cybernetics SMC-3(6), 610–621 (1973)
3. Tamura, H., Mori, S., Yamawaki, T.: Textural Features Corresponding to Visual Perception. IEEE Transaction on Systems, Man, and Cybernetcs SMC-8(6), 460–472 (1978)
4. Winkler, G.: Image Analysis, Random Fields and Dynamic Monte Carlo Methods, p. 324. Springer, Heidelberg (1995)
5. Paget, R.: Nonparametric Markov Random Field Models for Natural Textures Images, Ph.D. thesis, University of Queensland, St Lucia, QLD Australia (December 1999)
6. Kaulgud, N., Desai, U.B.: Efficient color image restoration using Markov random field. In: TENCON 1998. 1998 IEEE Region 10 International Conference on Global Connectivity in Energy, Computer, Communication and Control, vol. 1, pp. 41–44 (1998)
7. Li, S.Z.: Markov Random Field Modeling in Image Analysis, 3rd edn. Springer, Heidelberg (2009)
8. Scholkopf, B., Smola, A.J.: Learning with Kernels Support Vector Machines, Regularization, Optimization, and Beyond. MIT Press, Cambridge (2001)
9. Hastie, T., Tibshirani, R., Friedman, J.: The Elements of Statistical Learning. Data Mining, Inference, and Prediction, 2nd edn. Springer, Heidelberg (2009)
10. Engel, Y., Mannor, S., Meir, R.: The Kernel Recursive Least-Squares Algorithm. IEEE Transactions on Signal Processing 52(8) (2004)
11. Vapnik, V.: Statistical Learning Theory. Wiley, Chichester (1998)

Shape Descriptor Based on the Volume of Transformed Image Boundary

Xavier Descombes[1] and Sergey Komech[2]

[1] EPI Ariana, INRIA SAM, Sophia Antipolis, FR
xavier.descombes@inria.fr
[2] Dobrushin Lab., IITP, Moscow, RU
komech@iitp.ru

Abstract. In this paper, we derive new shape descriptors based on a directional characterization. The main idea is to study the behavior of the shape neighborhood under family of transformations. We obtain a description invariant with respect to rotation, reflection, translation and scaling. We consider family of volume-preserving transformations. Our descriptor is based on the volume of the neighbourhood of transformed image. A well-defined metric is then proposed on the associated feature space. We show the continuity of this metric. Some results on shape retrieval are provided on Kimia 216 and part of MPEG-7 CE-Shape-1 databases to show the accuracy of the proposed shape metric.

1 Introduction

Shape characterization is becoming a crucial challenge in image analysis. The increasing resolution of new sensors, satellite images or scanners provides information on the object geometry which can be interpreted by shape analysis. The size of data basis also requires some efficient tools for analyzing shapes, for example in applications such as image retrieval. Reviews of proposed representations can be found in [4,5]. One class of methods consists in defining shapes descriptors based on shape signatures histogram signatures, shape invariant moments, contrast, matrices or spectral features. A shape representation is evaluated with respect to its robustness, w.r.t. noise and/or intra-class variability, compaction of the description, its invariance properties and its efficiency in terms of computation time. According to Zhang and Lu [5], the different approaches can be classified into contour-based and region-based methods, and within each class between structural and global approaches. In this paper we consider shapes as binary silhouette of objects and concentrate on global approaches. Simple global shape descriptors embed area, orientation, convexity, bending energy [6,7]. Usually, these descriptors are not sufficiently sensitive to details to provide good scores in image retrieval. Distances between shapes or surfaces have been proposed, such as the Hausdorf distance or some modification to reduce sensitivity to outlier [8,9]. In this setting, the invariance properties can be obtained by taking the minimum distance over the corresponding group of transformation. A key issue is to consider a metric for which the minimum is computed with a low computational complexity.

S.O. Kuznetsov et al. (Eds.): PReMI 2011, LNCS 6744, pp. 142–147, 2011.
© Springer-Verlag Berlin Heidelberg 2011

In this paper, we derive a 2D signature of shapes and propose a metric on the associated feature space. The first idea consists of a description of the boundary regularity by comparing the volume of the boundary neighborhood with the shape volume. The second idea is to study the behavior of this descriptor under shape transformations. We thus define a family of diffeomorphisms consisting in expanding the shape in one direction and contracting it in the orthogonal direction. In that way, for a given detail, there exists at least such a transformation enlarging its contribution to the descriptor and another one reducing it. We then derive a well defined metric on the feature space, and show its performance for shape discrimination on databases of various size.

We describe the proposed shape space and define a metric on it in Section 2. A discretization of the metric is described and evaluated on two different databases in Section 3. Finally, conclusion and perspectives are drawn in Section 4.

2   A Topological Description of Shapes

2.1   Shape Space

We consider shapes as 2D silhouettes of bounded objects in the image plane.

Definition 1. *The pre-shape space S is the set of subsets of $\mathbb{R}^2$ satisfying the following conditions:*

1. *$\forall a \in S$, a is compact and connected, with a strictly positive area,*
2. *$\forall a \in S$, $\mathbb{R}^2 \setminus a$ is connected (a has no hole).*

Let us consider a shape $a \in S$. Define the closed ε-neighborhood of the set a in the sense of the Euclidean metric as $O^\varepsilon(a) = \{x \in \mathbb{R}^2 : e(x, a) \le \varepsilon\}, \varepsilon \ge 0$, where $e(\cdot, \cdot)$ is the Euclidean distance.

On this pre-shape space, we consider the Hausdorff metric (which is well-defined, see, for example, [2]) for the sets in $\mathbb{R}^2$:

$$\rho(a, b) = \inf\{\delta > 0 : a \subset O^\delta(b), b \subset O^\delta(a)\},$$

where $a, b \subset S$.

A shape space should embed some invariance properties. Let G be the group of transformations of $\mathbb{R}^2$ generated by rotations, translations, reflections and scaling : $G = SL_2^\pm(\mathbb{R}) \times \mathbb{R}_+$. To define a shape space $\$$ isometry- and scale-invariant, we consider:

$$\$ = S/G . \tag{1}$$

For a given $A \in \$$, we note $r(A) = \{a \in S : vol(a) = 1, G(a) = A\}$, where $vol(\cdot)$ is the area of the set.

Therefore, on the shape space $\$$, the Hausdorff metric becomes:

$$d(A, B) = \inf\{\rho(a, b) \mid a \in r(A), b \in r(B)\}, \tag{2}$$

where $A, B \in \$$ (note that this metric can be compared with the Procrustes distance for sets consisting of finite number of points [3,1]). The proof of the following proposition is not very hard and we will omit it due to the space limit.

Proposition 1. $d(\cdot, \cdot)$ *is a well-defined metric on* S.

2.2   Volume Descriptor and Family of Transformations

The main idea of the proposed description is to characterize the behavior of shapes under some transformations. These transformations aim at enlighting small characteristic details. We first consider the volume behavior under some dilation. Intuitively, this volume will increase more for sinuous shape boundaries than for smooth shapes. Let us consider a shape $a \in S$. Idea of our shape descriptor is based on analyzing the fraction

$$P^\varepsilon(a) = \frac{vol(O^\varepsilon(a) \setminus a)}{vol(a)} \quad , \tag{3}$$

where $vol(\cdot)$ is the area of the set. This parameter is well-defined $(vol(a) \neq 0)$.

We consider a family $\{F_{(\theta,\beta)}\}$ of linear transformations of $\mathbb{R}^2$ in order to obtain more significant information about shapes. The goal of such transformations is to emphasize "features" of the shape in specific direction. These transformations are defined as follows:

$$F_{(\theta,\beta)} := \begin{pmatrix} \beta \cos^2\theta + \frac{1}{\beta}\sin^2\theta & (\beta - \frac{1}{\beta})\sin\theta\cos\theta \\ (\beta - \frac{1}{\beta})\sin\theta\cos\theta & \beta\sin^2\theta + \frac{1}{\beta}\cos^2\theta \end{pmatrix}, \tag{4}$$

where $\theta \in [-\frac{\pi}{2}, \frac{\pi}{2}], \beta \geq 1$. Every $F_{(\theta,\beta)}$ is β-times expanding in one direction (with angle θ) and β-times contracting in orthogonal, so it is a volume-preserving transformation.

For every set $a \subset \mathbb{R}^2$, we obtain the map

$$a \mapsto P^\varepsilon_{(\theta,\beta)}(a) := \frac{vol(O^\varepsilon(F_{(\theta,\beta)}a) \setminus F_{(\theta,\beta)}a)}{vol(a)}, \quad \theta \in [-\frac{\pi}{2}, \frac{\pi}{2}], \ \beta \geq 1, \ \varepsilon > 0 \ . \tag{5}$$

It is clear that $P^\varepsilon_{(\theta,\beta)}(a)$ is a continuous function of ε, θ and β and $P^\varepsilon_{(-\frac{\pi}{2},\beta)}(a) = P^\varepsilon_{(\frac{\pi}{2},\beta)}(a)$. Note, that this function is a constant, if a is a ball (ε, β are fixed).

Let R_γ be the rotation by an angle γ. We have the following property:

Property 1. $\forall \theta \in [-\frac{\pi}{2}, \frac{\pi}{2}], P^\varepsilon_{(\theta,\beta)}(R_\gamma a) = P^\varepsilon_{((\theta+\frac{\pi}{2}+\gamma)mod(\pi)-\frac{\pi}{2},\beta)}(a)$.

We consider R_x, the reflection with respect to x axis (horizontal line). We have the following property:

Property 2. $\forall \theta \in [-\frac{\pi}{2}, \frac{\pi}{2}], P^\varepsilon_{(\theta,\beta)}(R_x a) = P^\varepsilon_{(-\theta,\beta)}(a)$.

Let us denote R the group of transformations generated by Properties 1 and 2. The shape representation space $\mathcal{R}$ we consider for the fixed $\varepsilon > 0$ is then defined by the following mapping:

$$\Phi : S \to \mathcal{R} = C^0([-\frac{\pi}{2}, \frac{\pi}{2}] \times [1, \infty])/R,$$
$$A \mapsto P^\varepsilon_{(\theta,\beta)}(a)/R, \quad a \in r(A), A \in S. \tag{6}$$

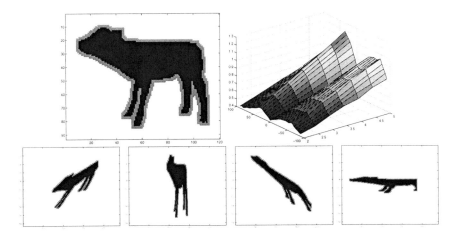

Fig. 1. Calf (top left) and the associated representation $P_n(F_{(\gamma,\beta)})$. The bottom line represents $F_{(\gamma,\beta)}$ for $\beta = 2$ and $\gamma = 45, 90, -45, 0$ (the shape is in black and the neighborhood in grey).

On Figure 1, we can remark that the function $P^n_{(\gamma,\beta)}(a)$ increases more in two directions, corresponding to an extention of both the calf body and its legs.

We consider situation with no information about foreshortening and all rotations are equally likely to occur. Finally, we consider the following metric on $\mathcal{R}$:

$$ l(\Phi(A), \Phi(B)) := \inf_{a,b} \left(\int_{[-\frac{\pi}{2}, \frac{\pi}{2}] \times [1, \infty]} (P^\varepsilon_{(\theta,\beta)}(a) - P^\varepsilon_{(\theta,\beta)}(b))^2 \, e^{-\kappa\beta} d\beta \, d\theta \right)^{1/2}, \quad (7) $$

where $\kappa > 0$ is a parameter, $a \in r(A)$, $b \in r(B)$. The integral on the right-hand side converges due to $P^\varepsilon_{(\theta,\beta)}(a)$ is almost linear function of β for β big enough.

We thus have defined a map between the shape space and the feature space. Two similar shapes should be associated to close points in the feature space. This property can be established by the continuity of mapping Φ with respect to the metrics defined in both spaces. The proof of the following theorem we will omit.

Theorem 1. $\Phi : (\$, d(,)) \to (\mathcal{R}, l(,))$ *is a continuous map.*

3 Implementation and Results

3.1 Discretization

In practice, to compute the distance between two shapes, we have to discretize equation (7). When analysing the surfaces representing the function $P^n(F_{(\theta,\beta)}a)$

on Figure 1 it is clear that the embeded information is redundant. Indeed, the surfaces are very smooth, so that we can employ a drastic discretization scheme, without loosing information. We consider $n = 5$ pixels neighbourhood.

Before computing the proposed feature, we normalize the shapes to $V = 4000$ pixels (area) in order to satisfy the scale invariance.

3.2 MPEG-7 CE Shape-1 Part-B Data Set

We first evaluate the proposed approach for the 7 classes of well-known MPEG-7 CE Shape-1 Part-B data set (70 classes, each class containing 20 similar objects). Although the classes are quite distinct, this data set contains important within-class variations (see [11]).

We consider four directions, $\theta \in \{-\frac{\pi}{4}, 0, \frac{\pi}{4}, \pi\}$, and two expanding coefficients $\beta \in \{3, 5\}$. The coefficient defined the metric is $\kappa = \frac{1}{5}$.

We consider the proposed metric between each pair of shapes (except itself of course, cause distance is 0) and report in Table 1 the percentage of correct n^{th} neighbors for each class. The total correct answers correspond to 98% for the first neighbors. If we consider the tenth neighbors, we still obtain a total score of 85% of good retrieval. This shows the robustness of the proposed metric.

Table 1. Retrieval scores on the 7 classes of MPEG-7 database

	1st	2nd	3rd	4th	5th	6th	7th	8th	9th	10th
Bonefull	95	70	85	85	90	85	85	85	70	75
Heart	100	100	100	100	100	100	95	95	95	100
Glas	100	100	100	100	100	100	100	90	100	95
Fountain	100	100	100	100	100	100	100	100	100	100
Key	100	100	95	100	95	95	90	90	95	95
Fork	95	90	65	70	65	75	65	75	70	60
Hammerfull	95	95	80	30	30	35	30	40	35	15

3.3 Kimia Database

We considered the extended database defined by Kimia. It consists of 216 shapes divided into 18 classes (see [11]). We consider $\theta \in \{90, 65, 45, 30, 0, -30, -45, -65\}$, and two expanding coefficients $\beta \in \{3, 5\}$. The global retrieval score is 91.2% for the first neighbour, 80.1% for the second neighbour, 74.5% for the third neighbour, 72.7% for the fourth neighbour and 63% for the fifth neighbour. It shows the robustness of the proposed metric in case of a rather big database.

Our results for the first neighbour 91.2% (as well as 98% for the first database) are comparable with 98% for SC-method and 100% stated recently in [10] for Kimia 216 database. We besides have good result 80.6% for Bullseye score. It shows good localization of different classes in feature space. Our descriptor is very clear and transparent in implementation. It takes about 0.23 sec in Mat-Lab(Pentium 4, 2Gb) to find the first neighbour for one image among 215 others.

4   Conclusion

We have proposed a new metric on a shape space based on the shape properties after applying family of diffeomorphisms. The proposed metric is well-defined and continuous. Retrieval results on two databases, one of them consisting of 216 shapes, divided in 18 classes, have proven the relevance of this metric. Our image descriptor is invariant with respect to rotation, reflection, translation and scaling. We are currently studying the surjectivity of the associated mapping. We conjecture that surjectivity holds, at least for star shapes. Further studies (in particular 3-D shape retrieval) also include the definition of a shape classification algorithm, based on this description.

References

1. Dryden, I.L., Mardia, K.V.: Statistical shape analysis. Wiley, New York (1998)
2. Serra, J.: Image Analysis and Mathematical Morphology. Academic Press, New York (1982)
3. Kendall, D.G.: Shape Manifolds, Procrustean Metrics, and Complex Projective Spaces. Bulletin of the London Mathematical Society 16, 81–121 (1984)
4. Loncaric, S.: A survey of shape analysis techniques, J. Pattern Recognition 31(8), 983–1001 (1998)
5. Zhang, D., Lu, G.: Reveiw of shape representation and description techniques. J. Pattern Recognition 37, 1–19 (2004)
6. Yong, I., Walker, J., Bowie, J.: An anlysis technique for biological shape. J. Comput. Graphics Image Process 25, 357–370 (1974)
7. Peura, M., Livirinen, J.: Efficiency of simple shape descriptors. In: Third International Workshop on Visual Form, Capri, Italy, May 1997, pp. 443–451 (1997)
8. Rucklidge, W.J.: Efficient locating objects using Hausdorff distance. Int. J. Comput. Vision 24(3), 251–270 (1997)
9. Belongie, S., Malik, J., Puzicha, J.: Matching shapes. In: IEEE Eighth Int. Conf. on Comput. Vision, Vancouver, Canada, July 2001, vol. I, pp. 454–461 (2001)
10. Bai, X., Latecki, L.J.: Path Similarity Skeleton Graph Matching. IEEE Trans Pattern Anal Mach Intell 30(7), 1282–1292 (2008)
11. Sebastian, T., Klein, P., Kimia, B.: Recognition of shapes by editing their shock graphs. IEEE Trans. Pattern Analysis and machine intelligence 25(5), 116–125 (2004)

Color Image Segmentation Using a Semi-wrapped Gaussian Mixture Model

Anandarup Roy[1], Swapan K. Parui[1], Debyani Nandi[2], and Utpal Roy[3]

[1] CVPR Unit, Indian Statistical Institute, Kolkata- 700108, India
roy.anandarup@gmail.com, swapan@isical.ac.in
[2] School of Education Tech., Jadavpur University, Kolkata- 700032, India
debyaninandi@gmail.com
[3] Dept. of Computer & System Sciences,
Visva-Bharati University, Santiniketan- 731235, India
roy.utpal@gmail.com

Abstract. This article deals with color image segmentation in the hue-saturation-value space. Hue, saturation and value components are samples on a cylinder. A model for such data is provided by the semi-wrapped Gaussian distribution. Further its mixture is used to approximate the hue-saturation-value distribution. The mixture parameters are estimated using the standard EM algorithm. The results are obtained on Berkeley segmentation dataset. Comparisons are made with vM-Gauss mixture model, GMM and Mean-Shift procedures. Experimental results reveal improvement in segmentation by our method.

1 Introduction

Color image segmentation is becoming important in many applications since color images are now easily available and can provide more information than gray level images. A popular way to represent a color image is the RGB system. However, due to its redundancy, many applications prefer the hue-saturation-value (HSV) color system. Consequently, segmentation in HSV space becomes crucial. In this article, we apply clustering based segmentation approach. The basic idea is to directly cluster the pixels in a certain color space by employing some clustering algorithms. Such algorithms include Mean-Shift and normalized-cut procedures [1] which are used widely. Segmenting an image into clusters involves determining which clusters generate the image pixels, which is the hidden information. Under this consideration, a mixture model based approach can be used. This approach assumes a mixture distribution approximating the distribution of image pixels. The mixture parameters can be estimated using expectation maximization algorithm. Such an earlier attempt was made by Carson et. al. [2] using Gaussian Mixture Model (GMM). Later, Bougulia et. al. [3] considered the aspect of skewness of color bands and applied a mixture of Dirichlet distributions for the joint distribution of RGB color spectrum.

The HSV system is a mixture of angular (hue) and linear (saturation, value) data. Mere linear mixture models may fail to model the hue distribution. Hue

S.O. Kuznetsov et al. (Eds.): PReMI 2011, LNCS 6744, pp. 148–153, 2011.

can be represented by a random variable $\Theta \in [0, 2\pi)$. A direct modeling of Θ can be avoided by transforming it into its linear representation $(\cos\theta, \sin\theta)$ and applying a linear mixture model. However the pair $(\cos\theta, \sin\theta)$ may be highly correlated, thus may pose the problem of singularity of the covariance matrix for some mixture components. Instead, we use the wrapped Gaussian distribution [4] for Θ. This distribution is a wrapping of linear Gaussian distribution around a circle. To cope with the circular-linear characteristics we need to wrap only one variable (corresponding to Θ) of a multivariate Gaussian distribution, whereas the other unwrapped variables represent linear portion. This distribution is termed as semi-wrapped Gaussian distribution [5]. Its mixture is used to approximate the HSV joint data distribution. An alternative model in hue-saturation (HS) space was suggested by Roy et. al. [6] using a mixture of vM-Gauss distribution. However, joint distribution in HSV space has not been proposed yet. An EM algorithm is designed to estimate the mixture parameters. The Berkeley segmentation Dataset [7] is used to test the performance of the methods. We compare our segmentation with vM-Gauss mixture model, GMM and Mean-Shift algorithms using probabilistic rand index.

2   Semi-wrapped Gaussian Distributions: Description and Mixture

Our aim is to devise a mixture of multivariate Gaussian distributions having both circular and linear variables. In this context, the wrapped Gaussian is a suitable choice. Otherwise, the von Mises distribution can replace wrapped Gaussian. However, forming a joint distribution using von Mises is difficult. Thus, in spite of the practical drawbacks in the parameter estimation, the wrapped Gaussian distribution, is chosen. The remaining part of this section presents a brief overview on semi-wrapped Gaussian distribution, and its mixture.

2.1   Wrapped Gaussian Distribution

In particular, for $\mathcal{N}_{\mu,\sigma}(x)$ being a univariate Gaussian distribution the wrapped univariate Gaussian distribution is defined as follows.

$$\mathcal{N}^{w}_{\mu^{c},\sigma^{c}}(\upsilon) = \sum_{w \in \mathbb{Z}} \mathcal{N}_{\mu,\sigma}(\upsilon + 2w\pi) \tag{1}$$

where $\upsilon \in [0, 2\pi)$. $\mathcal{N}^{w}_{\mu^{c},\sigma^{c}}(\upsilon)$ is unimodal and symmetric about μ^{c}. It can be shown that the circular mean and variance (μ^{c}, σ^{c}) are related to linear mean and variance (μ, σ) by the equations $\mu^{c} = \mu(\mathrm{mod}\ 2\pi)$ and $\sigma^{2} = -2\log(1 - \sigma^{c})$. In a similar way the multivariate Gaussian distribution can be wrapped onto a sphere to obtain the wrapped version.

2.2   Semi-wrapped Gaussian Distribution and Mixture

Let us consider an HSV image. Then, the hue component is angular, whereas saturation and value components are linear. For such situations, a suitable modeling should employ a distribution that is wrapped in the angular and non-wrapped in the linear dimensions. The semi-wrapped Gaussian distribution [5] serves this purpose well enough. For simplicity we assume only the first variable (Θ) is angular (this really is for our problem) and others ($\mathbf{x}$) linear. With these specifications the semi-wrapped Gaussian distribution can be formed by wrapping the first variable of a multivariate Gaussian distribution. Its density is given by:

$$\mathcal{N}^{sw}_{\boldsymbol{\mu}^c, \Sigma^c}(\theta, \mathbf{x}) = \sum_{w \in \mathbb{Z}} \mathcal{N}_{\boldsymbol{\mu}, \Sigma}(\theta + 2w\pi, \mathbf{x}), \tag{2}$$

with mean $\boldsymbol{\mu}^c$ and covariance matrix Σ^c.

Let us now define the mixture model of K semi-wrapped Gaussian distributions (SWGMM). The density of the mixture is given by:

$$f(\theta, \mathbf{x}|\boldsymbol{\Xi}) = \sum_{h=1}^{K} P(h)\mathcal{N}^{sw}_{\boldsymbol{\Xi}_h}(\theta, \mathbf{x}). \tag{3}$$

where $P(h)(0 \leq P(h) \leq 1$ and $\sum_{h=1}^{K} P(h) = 1)$ are the mixing proportions, $\mathcal{N}^{sw}_{\boldsymbol{\Xi}_h}(\theta, \mathbf{x})$ is the semi-wrapped Gaussian distribution representing the hth component of the mixture and $\boldsymbol{\Xi}_h$ is the set of parameters of the hth component. The symbol $\boldsymbol{\Xi} = (\boldsymbol{\Xi}_1, \ldots, \boldsymbol{\Xi}_K, P(1), \ldots, P(K))$ refers to the entire set of parameters to be estimated.

3   Maximum Likelihood Estimation

Let $\aleph = p_1, \ldots, p_N$ be a finite set of N samples drawn independently from the SWGMM. Here $p_i = (\theta_i, \mathbf{x}_i)$ is a circular-linear data. To maximize the likelihood function, the expectation maximization (EM) is widely used. The cluster information and wrapping are the hidden variables. The standard EM settings express the distribution of hidden variables by:

$$q(h, w|p_i) = \frac{P(h)\mathcal{N}_{\boldsymbol{\mu}_h, \Sigma_h}(p_i + 2w\pi)}{\sum_{l=1}^{K} P(l)\mathcal{N}^{sw}_{\boldsymbol{\Xi}_l}(p_i)}. \tag{4}$$

Here $p_i + 2w\pi$ indicates the tuple $(\theta + 2w\pi, \mathbf{x})$. The EM algorithm maximizes the log-likelihood modified by the inclusion of $q(h, w|p_i)$. To maximize the modified log-likelihood we may go independently for a priory probabilities $P(h)$ and the parameters $\boldsymbol{\Xi}_h$. The a priori probabilities can be found out with:

$$P(h) = \frac{1}{N} \sum_{i=1}^{N} \sum_{w \in \mathbb{Z}} q(h, w|p_i). \tag{5}$$

The expressions for $\boldsymbol{\mu}_h^c$ and Σ_h^c are quite similar to the linear Gaussian mixture and obtained using:

$$\boldsymbol{\mu}_h^c = \frac{\sum\limits_{i=1}^{N} \sum\limits_{w \in \mathbb{Z}} q(h, w|p_i)(p_i + 2w\pi)}{\sum\limits_{i=1}^{N} \sum\limits_{w \in \mathbb{Z}} q(h, w|p_i)} \tag{6}$$

$$\Sigma_h^c = \frac{\sum\limits_{i=1}^{N} \sum\limits_{w \in \mathbb{Z}} q(h, w|p_i)(p_i + 2w\pi - \boldsymbol{\mu}_h^c)(p_i + 2w\pi - \boldsymbol{\mu}_h^c)^T}{\sum\limits_{i=1}^{N} \sum\limits_{w \in \mathbb{Z}} q(h, w|p_i)}. \tag{7}$$

In practice w hold values $-1, 0$ and 1. We continue writing $w \in \mathbb{Z}$ for completeness.

4   Color Image Segmentation

Let us assume that the hue, saturation and value components of an HSV image arise from a SWGMM (Eq. 3). The EM method estimates mixture parameters by iterating expectation (Eq. 4) and maximization steps (Eqs. 5, 6 and 7). These steps iterate until the log-likelihood stabilizes. We apply K-Means algorithm on HSV image to obtain initial clustering. Initially, $\boldsymbol{\mu}_h^c$ and Σ_h^c are estimated as follows.

$$\boldsymbol{\mu}_h^c = \frac{\sum\limits_{i=1}^{N_h} \sum\limits_{w \in \mathbb{Z}} (p_i + 2w\pi)}{N_h} \quad \text{and} \quad \Sigma_h^c = \frac{\sum\limits_{i=1}^{N_h} \sum\limits_{w \in \mathbb{Z}} (p_i + 2w\pi - \boldsymbol{\mu}_h^c)(p_i + 2w\pi - \boldsymbol{\mu}_h^c)^T}{N_h}. \tag{8}$$

The a priori probabilities are set with $P(h) = \frac{N_h}{N}$ where N_h is the number of elements in h^{th} cluster. In order to detect the number of clusters automatically we use the Schwarz's *Bayesian Information Criterion (BIC)*. Optimum value of K is the first local minimum of *BIC*. Note, for the gray portions, the hue becomes undefined. We separate out the gray portions before employing EM. A separate clustering should be employed with the gray portions. Yet, here we encounter only a few gray pixels mostly in the background and thus leave them to minimize time complexity.

5   Evaluation of Segmentation

To evaluate the quality of segmentation algorithm we have to compare the resulting clusters with the ground-truth segmentations. A good survey on evaluation methodologies can be found in [8]. Recently, Unnikrishnan et. al. [9] proposed a Probabilistic Rand Index (PRI) which is a generalization of classical Rand Index. The PRI is further applied to evaluate a color segmentation procedure designed

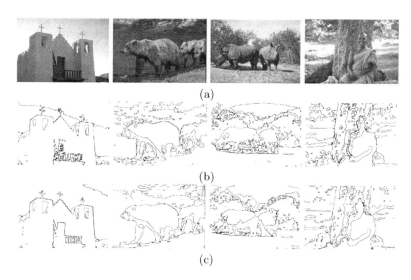

Fig. 1. (a) Example images of Berkeley segmentation dataset. Image Ids are (from top left to right) "24063", "100075", "112082" and "376020". (b)(c) Corresponding segmentations in HS and HSV space respectively.

by Ilea and Whelan [10]. The PRI allows comparison of a test segmentation with multiple ground-truth images by evaluating the pairwise relationships between pixels. It takes values in the range $[0, 1]$, where a higher PRI value indicates a better match between the segmented result and the ground-truth data. In this study we use PRI to evaluate the segmentation process.

6   Results and Discussions

The *Berkeley segmentation dataset* [7] contains several color images of natural scenes. The images contain at least one distinguishable and identifiable object embedded in a natural scene. The images we consider have ground-truth in the form of manual segmentation performed by several users independently. Let us now present some results after running the algorithm in HS (Fig. 1(b)) and HSV (Fig. 1(c)) space. Visually it is difficult to assess which segmentation is better. This can be done using the PRI. We compare SWGMM with the mixture model of vM-Gauss distribution (vMGMM), the GMM and the Mean-Shift procedures (last two in RGB). The comparison results are presented in Fig. 2. The Mean-Shift performs better for a few images. The GMM, on the other hand, outperforms Mean-Shift in most cases. The vMGMM assumes independence of hue and saturation. By noting that SWGMM outperforms vMGMM, we could conclude, the correlation present in hue, saturation and/or value should be crucial for segmentation. The SWGMM in HSV space can show better performance for some image than GMM and Mean-Shift. A detailed statistical study may reveal the significance of the results. We are in a process to design that.

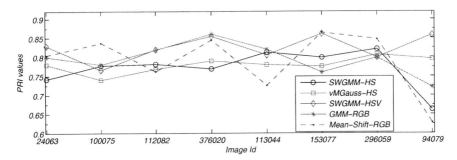

Fig. 2. Comparison of different segmentation algorithms with respect to PRI

7   Summery and Future Scope

We study the problem of color image segmentation in HSV space. A mixture of semi-wrapped Gaussian distributions is used to model hue, saturation and value data. Results and comparisons are on Berkeley segmentation dataset. Future work may include the study of different forms of joint distributions on circular-linear data.

References

1. Tao, W., Jin, H., Zhang, Y.: Color image segmentation based on mean shift and normalized cuts. IEEE Trans. on SMC(B) 37, 1382–1389 (2007)
2. Carson, C., Belongie, S., Greenspan, H., Malik, J.: Blobworld: Image segmentation using expectation-maximization and its application to image querying. IEEE Trans. on PAMI 24, 1026–1038 (2002)
3. Bougulia, N., Ziou, D., Vaillancourt, J.: Unsupervised learning of a finite mixture model based on the dirichlet distribution and its application. IEEE Trans. on Image Processing 13, 1533–1543 (2004)
4. Mardia, K.V., Jupp, P.: Directional Statistics. John Wiley and Sons Ltd., Chichester (2000)
5. Bahlmann, C.: Directional features in online handwriting recognition. Pattern Recognition 39, 115–125 (2006)
6. Roy, A., Parui, S.K., Roy, U.: A color based image segmentation and its application to text segmentation. In: Proc. of Indian Conf. on Computer Vision, Graphics and Image Processing, pp. 313–319 (2008)
7. Martin, D., Fowlkes, C., Tal, D., Malik, J.: A database of human segmented natural images and its application to evaluating segmentation algorithms and measuring ecological statistics. In: Proc. Int Conf. Computer Vision, pp. 416–423 (2001)
8. Chabrier, S., Laurent, H., Rosenburger, C., Marche, P.: A comparative study of supervised evaluation criteria for image segmentation. In: Proc. of the European Signal Processing Conference, pp. 1143–1146 (2004)
9. Unnikrishnan, R., Pantofaru, C., Hebert, M.: Toward objective evaluation of image segmentation algorithms. IEEE Trans. on PAMI 29, 929–944 (2007)
10. Ilea, D.E., Whelan, P.F.: Ctex—an adaptive unsupervised segmentation algorithm based on color-texture coherence. IEEE Trans. on Image Processing 17, 1926–1939 (2008)

Perception-Based Design for Tele-presence

Santanu Chaudhury[1], Shantanu Ghosh[1,2], Amrita Basu[3], Brejesh Lall[1],
Sumantra Dutta Roy[1], Lopamudra Choudhury[3], R. Prashanth[1],
Ashish Singh[1], and Amit Maniyar[1]

[1] Multimedia Lab, Department of Electrical Engineering, Indian Institute of
Technology Delhi, Hauz Khas, New Delhi - 110 016, India
`schaudhury@gmail.com,brejesh@ee.iitd.ac.in,`
`sumantra@ee.iitd.ac.in,prahanth.prbest@gmail.com,`
`ashish.iitd07@gmail.com,maniyar.amit@gmail.com`
[2] Behavioural & Cognitive Science Lab, Department of Humanities & Social Sciences,
Indian Institute of Technology Delhi, Hauz Khas, New Delhi - 110 016, India
`sghosh.neu@gmail.com`
[3] School of Cognitive Sciences, Jadavpur University, Kolkata - 700 032, India
`amrita8@gmail.com, choudhuryl@yahoo.com`

Abstract. We present a novel perception-driven approach to low-cost
tele-presence systems, to support immersive experience in continuity between projected video and conferencing room. We use geometry and spectral correction to impart for perceptual continuity to the whole scene.
The geometric correction comes from a learning-based approach to identifying horizontal and vertical surfaces. Our method redraws the projected video to match its vanishing point with that of the conference
room in which it is projected. We quantify intuitive concepts such as the
depth-of-field using a Gabor filter analysis of overall images of the conference room. We equalise spectral features across the projected video
and the conference room, for spectral continuity between the two.

Keywords: Tele-presence, Homography, Texture Transfer, Perceptual
Continuity, Spectral Correction.

1 Introduction

This paper presents a perception-driven approach to low-cost tele-presence systems. An immersive experience to a tele-presence system (so that the projected
video of another room appears to be 'continuous' with regard to the people in
the room, for instance) can come with 'normalisation' of two parameters: the
geometry, and the spectral characteristics, in the projected video. We present
an approach driven by perceptual cues and cognitive results, to enable the same
in a low-cost video conferencing system. To the best of our knowledge, such an
approach has not been reported before in the literature.

A teleconferencing system represents an elaborate set of projection systems
that allow rendering of 3-D objects from a real environment in specific 2-D
perspectives on a projective surface with a real environment depending on the

S.O. Kuznetsov et al. (Eds.): PReMI 2011, LNCS 6744, pp. 154–159, 2011.

projection angle of the camera. Such a technologically mediated communication involves certain degree of 'presence' or a 'feeling of being there' that allows the conferees to respond realistically to events and situations in the projected to real environment. Perception of such extensions may occur due to geometrical alignments, rendering of objects, and illumination patterns between real and projected environments. The present 'state of the art' teleconferencing systems utilize very high-end studios congruent in geometrical alignments and illumination patterns to enhance this 'same-room effect'. However, providing exactly similar environments for the virtual and the real counterparts is often difficult to achieve and may not provide a 'seamless' integration of the real and the virtual environments. There are obvious constraints associated with such a system, like small size and relative independence of location of the projection screen that drives the need for designing a cognitive cue-based geometrical and spectral correction algorithm for an 'immersive' experience during conferences. Hence we favour a scene recognition approach to the problem over the current reconstruction techniques and introduce an algorithm that leads to an enhanced visual continuity. This is achieved by extracting semantic category information and visual congruence.

In this paper, we present the results of a computational approach based on classification and organisation of tele-presence video conferencing frames into congruent and non-congruent domains with respect to projected-to-real symmetry-based continuity and depth perception of the two scenes. We utilise lower level information such as textures and perceptual feedback to build up a confidence contour of the context and compute the perceptual difference between the two contexts. Further, our method minimizes the perceptual difference by adjusting the intermediate level properties used for identification of contexts. The perceptual cue used is the continuity of vanishing lines from the projected images, matching the vanishing lines in an image of the conference room. Our method scores on three points: determination of the spectral match between real-to-projected environments, a continuous organisation between the real and the projected environments and determination of a geometric alignment match between the projected and real scenes.

2   Tele-presence and Video Conferencing

A scene may be described with reference to the observer who has a 'fixated point of view' in an image. Oliva and Torralba [5] propose to consider the absolute distance between the observer and the fixated zone as a principal property to define a 'scene'. A 'view on a scene' begins when there is actually a larger space between the observer and the fixated point, usually after 5 meters (typically it refers to a single image in image processing/computational vision). In a video conferencing situation however, an ambiguity in the perception of the fixated point is created by introducing a projected image (thereby creating at least a two scene system). Perception of a video conferencing scene may therefore be defined as a composite of two scenes where the fixation point is altered by an introduction of a projected scene. We seek to create a 'unified' scene in two different ways. First, we try to align the geometry of the two scenes in a computationally simple method (Section 3). Next, we seek to unify the spectral characteristics of the projected video, and a conference room, using low-level features which are descriptors of a higher level percept (Section 4). This creates a visual illusion of the same room in such a composite scene by describing feature composites to yield higher level features. The human visual system uses this for fast and efficient detection of scene congruence between the projected and real environments.

3   Geometric Correction: Novel View Generation

The first step in our approach is to correct for the geometry of the projected video scene, so that it appears to be perceptually 'continuous' with the geometry of the room in which the video is projected. There is a wealth of literature on novel view generation, given either a number of views, or a single one. (Representative references for the two are [2] and [1], respectively). For multiple views, for a slowly moving camera, one can establish correspondences between different views of the same scene (using any tracker, for instance). A typical approach first computes the projective structure, and using further constraints, updates it to affine, metric or Euclidean, depending on the nature of the constraints. For the single view method, again one needs specific constraints [1]. These methods are computationally complex, and often quite cumbersome.

We adopt a different methodology - one based on the ideas of Hoiem, Efros and Hebert [3]. This is a fully automatic method for creating a 3-D model from a single photograph. We use their basic idea of trying to statistically model geometric classes defined by their orientations, rather than trying to recover the precise geometry. In our case, we learn labels corresponding to coarse categories 'horizontal', 'vertical', and 'background' from representative images of video conferencing scenes. Based on the statistical learning of the labels, given a new video conferencing scene, the algorithm segments image regions, groups them together, and then uses the learnt information into the three categories, and then attempts to recreate the structure of the scene for the three categories. Given the estimated structure for the horizontal and vertical segments for instance, we specify sample camera parameters for the new viewpoint. The new viewpoint is estimated according to the orientation of the lines in an image of the video conferencing environment. We adopt a Hough transform-like approach, and vote on the different possible vanishing points (otherwise known as the FoE: 'focus of expansion') within the image of the video conferencing room in question. We assume that the one getting the highest vote is the required point, and we orient the camera parameters in order to project the above estimated structure on the projection screen in the video conferencing room, in order to equalise the two vanishing points. This is the essence of trying to 'equalise' the two viewing geometries. Fig. 1 shows two examples of using such an automatic correction for the projected frames. In the first one, the desired image has the

Fig. 1. Geometric Correction for two cases: each case shows the uncorrected, and the 'corrected' image, side-by-side. Details in Section 3.

principal vanishing point somewhere towards the centre of the image. This is slightly to the left, for the second example. The algorithm performs a texture mapping for each planar surface, and pastes this on the new projected orientation of the planar surface, using a homography between the planes in the two - the original image, and the projected image in the new orientation.

The above method - while being simple and easy to compute, suffers from obvious generalisation limitations. It works well for planar surfaces whose overall orientations are estimated well. For complex objects and non-planar ones such as human beings, the method fares poorly. For such cases, we use a simple heuristic. We can extract moving objects such as human beings using a simple but robust motion estimation algorithm, such as [4]. This algorithm segments out any number of foreground objects relatively quickly, against a slowly moving or static background, which is the case in any video conferencing application. The planar regions can be placed at their re-oriented locations, and the other objects pasted on top. The 'background' labelled regions are projected using a texture map homography.

The geometric alignment achieved in the previous section renders video frames, where the scene is conceived of as an 'image-within-an-image'. This alignment also allows us to 'equalise' the spectral parameters in the foreground and background of this composite scene, which completes the illusion of perceived continuity. This gives the entire scene a cognitively congruent interpretation.

4   Spectral Correction

We perform spectral correction between the given conference room, and the video that is projected in it. We take images of the conference room, and consider the projected video that has been subjected to the geometric correction of the previous section. We consider images in a 'perceptual colour space' such as the HSI (Hue-Saturation-Intensity) model. Initial results of our perceptual continuity experiments suggest that users get a better immersive experience with regard to the following three parameters. First, it is easy to have an overall hue of yellow in the conference room. We specify the histogram in the hue parameter in the projected video, to peak around yellow. Next, we perform a histogram equalisation on the saturation and intensity components.

We described the organisation of the projected-to-real tele-presence scenes along two semantic axes providing an ideal Spectral and Geometric Matching Template (SGMT) (i.e., from general indoor scenes to specific video conferencing scenes; from highly textured 'indoor'-scapes to no textures, from 'deep' rooms to 'shallow' rooms and from 'artificial' to 'natural' indoor scenes with respect to an alignment of vanishing lines). All images were pre-processed to reduce the effects of large shadows that may hide important parts of the scene and to minimize the impact of high contrasted objects which would disturb the power spectrum shape of the background image. First, we apply a logarithmic function to the intensity distribution. Then we attenuate the very low spatial frequencies by applying a high pass filter. Next, we apply an adjustment of the local standard deviation at each pixel of the image. This makes large regions of the image being equally bright.

To create the semantic axes, we choose two sets of prototypical scenes that determine the two extremities of the proposed semantic axes: 'shallow' – 'deep', and 'continuous' – 'discontinuous'. We extract spectral parameters (quantised PCA values from the output of a Gabor filter bank: details below) from the exemplar images, and use them to numerically quantify the extremities. A discriminant analysis computes the axes that both maximises the distance between the two prototypical groups and minimises the standard deviation of the images belonging to the same group.

The transfer function of each Gabor filter is tuned to spatial frequency f_r in the direction determined by the angle θ:

$$G(f_x, f_y) = K \exp(-2\pi^2(\sigma_x^2(f'_x - f_r)^2 + \sigma_y^2)f'^2_y) \qquad (1)$$

where f'_x and f'_y are obtained by rotation of the spatial frequencies $f'_x = f_x \cos\theta + f_y \sin\theta$ and $f'_y = -f_x \sin\theta + f_y \cos\theta$. σ_x and σ_y give the shape and frequency resolution of the Gabor filter. K is a constant. The full set of filters is obtained by rotation and scaling of this expression. This gives a high frequency resolution at low spatial frequencies and a low frequency resolution at high spatial frequencies. The values σ_x and σ_y are chosen in order to have coincidence in the contour section of the magnitude at -3 dB. Given an image, its semantic content is invariant with respect to a horizontal mirror transformation of the image. Therefore, we compute the symmetric energy outputs of the Gabor filters which are invariant with respect to a horizontal mirror transformation:

$$\Gamma_{f_r,\theta} = \int \int |I(f_x, f_y)|^2 [G_{f_r,\theta}^2(f_x, f_y) + G_{f_r,\pi-\theta}^2(f_x, f_y)] df_x df_y \qquad (2)$$

where $|I(f_x, f_y)|^2$ is the power spectrum of the image, $G_{f_r,\theta}$ and $G_{f_r,\pi-\theta}$ are two Gabor filters tuned to the spatial frequencies given by the radial frequency f_r and the directions θ and $\pi - \theta$. We then use normalised features:

$$\tilde{\Gamma}_{f_r,\theta} = (\Gamma_{f_r,\theta} - E(\Gamma_{f_r,\theta}))/std(\Gamma_{f_r,\theta}) \qquad (3)$$

where E and std are the mean and the standard deviation of the features $\Gamma_{f_{r,\theta}}$ computed over the entire image database. For each image, we have a feature vector defined by the collection of $\tilde{\Gamma}_{f_{r,\theta}}$ obtained at different frequencies and orientations. We reduce the dimensionality of this large feature output using PCA. In our experimentation, we take the first 10 coefficients as the required features - we have empirically found this value to be suitable for our experiments.

The above procedure establishes the two ends of the semantic axis, described above. Given a new image, we subject it to the same procedure - the first 10 coefficients of a PCA of the output of the Gabor filter bank, and plot the closest point (distance of least approach - the perpendicular from the point to the line in 10-dimensional space). The same image is rated on the above continuity and depth scales by human raters as well.

5   Conclusion

A projected video in a conference room - this paper envisages an immersive experience for participants in the room by 'equalising' geometric and spectral features in the projected video. This paper represents work in progress. We plan to experiment with various histogram features and modelling aspects in the colour space distributions, as inputs to perceptual experiments of visual continuity. We plan to extend our work to multiple displays with geometric correction induced by head movements of participants. Such rendering is possible using binaural cues needed for spatial discrimination [6]. We intend to make the system more robust by planning perception experiments, where the scene is visualised in noisy video environments.

References

1. Criminisi, A., Reid, I., Zisserman, A.: Single View Metrology. International Journal of Computer Vision 40(2), 123–148 (2000)
2. Faugeras, O.: Three-Dimensional Computer Vision. MIT Press, Cambridge (1993)
3. Hoiem, D., Efros, A.A., Hebert, M.: Automatic Photo Pop-up. In: ACM SIGGRAPH (2005)
4. Irani, M., Rousso, B., Peleg, S.: Computing Occluding and Transparent Motions. International Journal of Computer Vision 12(1), 5–16 (1994)
5. Oliva, A., Torralba, A.: Modeling the Shape of the scene: A Holistic Representation of the Spatial Envelope. International Journal of Computer Vision 42(3), 145–175 (2001)
6. Ralph Algazi, V., Duda, R.O.: Headphone-Based Spatial Sound. IEEE Signal Processing Magazine, 33–42 (2011)

Automatic Adductors Angle Measurement for Neurological Assessment of Post-neonatal Infants during Follow Up

Debi Prosad Dogra[1], Arun Kumar Majumdar[1], Shamik Sural[1],
Jayanta Mukherjee[1], Suchandra Mukherjee[2], and Arun Singh[2]

[1] IIT Kharagpur, India, 721302
{dpdogra,akmj,shamik,jay}@cse.iitgp.ernet.in
[2] IPGMER and SSKM Hospital, Kolkata, India, 700020
drsmukherjee71@gmail.com,drarunsingh61@yahoo.co.in

Abstract. In many medical examinations, image or video based automatic schemes are preferred over conventional approaches. Such schemes can greatly increase the efficacy and accuracy of various medical examinations. The work proposed in this article presents an image processing based method to automate adductors angle measurement which is carried out on infants as a part of Hammersmith Infant Neurological Examination (HINE). It is used for assessing neurological development of infants aged below two years. During HINE, postures and reactions of the infant under consideration are recorded. An overall score is estimated and used to quantify the neurological development index of the baby. In the conventional approach, for measuring adductors angle, doctors use rulers. The proposed method uses image segmentation and thinning techniques to measure the angle without involvement of rulers. Results show that the proposed scheme can be used as an aid to the doctors for conducting such examinations.

Keywords: Adductors Angle, Skeleton Generation, Image Segmentation, Neurological Assessment.

1 Introduction

Nowadays, computer vision based techniques are frequently used to improve various health-care services. Sophisticated instruments equipped with state-of-the-art video technologies are widely used in conducting medical examinations and tele-consultations. For example, video conferencing based tele-medicine applications, automatic analysis of X-ray, MRI, CT images and video EEG signals are popular in medical community. These technologically advanced tools can significantly improve the average turnaround time of examinations.

A widely used neurological examination which is conducted on infants of less than two years of age is the Hammersmith Infant Neurological Examination (HINE) [6]. The examination is carried out repetitively at the ages of 3, 6, 9, 12 months and onwards. An overall score is estimated to quantify the neurological development of the baby at the time of examination. The score is estimated using examination outcomes which are broadly classified into three groups namely,

S.O. Kuznetsov et al. (Eds.): PReMI 2011, LNCS 6744, pp. 160–166, 2011.

Neurological Items, Motor Milestones and Behavior. Among these three, the first group deals with the neurological development and it has five subgroups named as, cranial nerve function, postures, movements, tone, reflexes and reactions. According to HINE specification, all examinations under these subgroups are quantified by scores between zero to three. A score of three signifies that the development of the baby is normal and zero means abnormal. The remaining two groups deal with motor and behavioral development. There is no such standard scoring scheme available for motor development whereas behavioral development is a subjective evaluation [6].

Fig. 1. Sample image of conventional adductors angle measurement with reference templates and scores. The image was captured at the HINE clinic of the Neonatology department of IPGMER and SSKM Hospital, Kolkata, India.

In order to have accurate estimation of neurological parameters, video and image processing based algorithms can be developed to facilitate estimation of parameters like adductors, popliteal angle, ankle dorsiflexion, arm protection, pulled-to-sit, etc. Though, several applications in medical informatics domain adopt computer vision based approaches, none of them attempted to automate HINE. For example, Bhatt et al. [2] have proposed a video based scheme for recognizing gestures of baby to automatically detect accidental events. Similarly, the application developed by Singh et al. [15] is a tele-monitoring system for remote surveillance of infants. It was developed using safe, compact and non-invasive sensors to record the movements of a baby with a client / server based approach. Similar kinds of applications are also found in health-care domain which adopt computer vision based techniques. For example, a simulation based infant behavior analysis using a virtual environment is proposed in [14] where the authors have tried to avoid situations related to behavioral accidents. The authors of [4] have proposed an application that can be used to record the videos and patient details during HINE. However, there is no work reported in the literature that tries to automate the examinations of HINE through image or video processing based algorithms. Therefore, till date, doctors conduct and record the outcomes of HINE manually.

In the chart proposed by Dubowitz et al. [6], there are a few examinations which are related to angle measurement of various human body parts. We have selected one of those examinations for automation. The examination is called as adductors angle measurement. In Fig. 1, a sample image of the scene during adductors angle measurement is shown with reference templates and scores. It has been observed that during examinations involving measurement of various angles, especially adductors angle and popliteal angle, the examiner often finds it difficult to keep the baby in a stable state. Since the baby moves frequently, placing a ruler across body parts for angle measurements become difficult. In addition to that, often the baby starts showing sign of uneasiness during these examinations. This has motivated us to design image processing based algorithms to help the doctors during angle measurement examinations.

2   Proposed Angle Measurement Scheme

During adductors examination, the angle between the thighs of the infant at supine posture is measured and a score is assigned according to the reference templates (refer to Fig. 1). In the conventional approach, the examiner stretches the legs of the infant and rulers are used to measure the angle between the thighs as shown in the figure. An image based automatic scheme is proposed in this work. After surveying the HINE clinic of the Neonatology department of Institute of The Post-Graduate Medical Education & Research (IPGMER) and Seth Sukhlal Karnani Memorial (SSKM) Hospital, Kolkata, India, it was observed that a single camera is sufficient to capture the scene of the examination. The examination desk has been covered with soft mattress. This was done in accordance with the well established setup of the HINE clinic of the hospital. Normally, all clothings are removed from the baby before examination commences. Since the measurement of the adductors angle is recorded only when the expert feels first resistance from the infant while stretching the legs, we have captured one image per baby.

2.1   Segmentation and Binarization of Image

Estimation of adductors angle can be automated using the following image processing steps. First, a color based segmentation algorithm is used to distinguish between the background and foreground parts. Since the background is controlled, a color based separation is possible. We have tested with various popular image segmentation schemes that are commonly used for natural image segmentation [3], [8]–[11]. Performance of mean-shift based segmentation scheme proposed by Comaniciu et al. [3] for the images of the domain under consideration has been found to be satisfactory. Also, the authors of [5] and [12] have shown in their work that mean-shift outperforms other algorithms in terms of quality. After segmentation, small and insignificant regions are merged with surrounding regions of larger size and importance (see Fig. 2b). To separate the foreground object (infant at supine and hands of the examiner) from the background, region that is dominated by human skin color is selected. A binary image is produced where the black pixels represent foreground and white pixels represent background (see Fig. 2c).

2.2   Skeletonization of Binary Object

Next, a widely used thinning scheme based on safe point thinning algorithm (SPTA) [13] is applied on the foreground objects. SPTA iteratively removes the boundary points of the object from all directions and finally produces a thinned object. Some examples of thinned objects are shown in Fig. 2d. Since the thinning algorithm produces noisy outputs, measurement of angle between the legs of the infant using these outputs is difficult. Thus, for better estimation, a filtering process has been proposed which successfully removes insignificant edges and produces usable skeleton image of the baby.

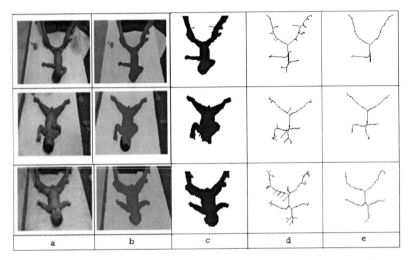

Fig. 2. a. Original images b. Segmented images using mean-shift [3] and region merging with spatial bandwidth $(h_s) = 7$ and range bandwidth $(h_r) = 12.5$ and minimum region area $= 400$ pixels c. Binarized outputs d. SPTA based thinning [13] e. Outputs after proposed filtering using $T = 0.1$.

2.3   Filtering

Let, the thinned object generated using the SPTA algorithm be represented by a graph $G(V, E)$ where the segments of the skeleton are considered as graph edges and joining or end points of the segments are denoted by nodes. An edge is marked as a hanging edge when one of its vertices is a leaf node. Set of hanging edges is denoted by H where $H \subseteq E$. Next, a greedy algorithm is adopted that iteratively removes the smallest edge out of all edges hanging from an interme-diate vertex (see **Algorithm 1**).   The algorithm is capable of removing small and insignificant hanging edges and produces a filtered output $G(V', E')$. The filtering steps are elaborated with a synthetic example shown in Fig. 4. Inter-mediate nodes and the leaf nodes are colored differently for better visualization. The proposed scheme produces filtered skeleton images as shown in Fig. 2e. Us-ing these filtered graphs, adductors angle can be measured. The threshold T as mentioned in the filtering algorithm is normally set to 10% of the largest edge of the entire graph.

Input: Skeleton produced by SPTA $\{ G(V, E)\}$
Output: Filtered output $\{G(V, E)\}$
1 **forall** $h \in H$ **do**
2   **if** $length(h) < T$ **then**
3          $H = H - h$;
4          $E = E - h$;
5 **forall** $h_1 \in H$ AND $h_2 \in H$ **do**
6   **if** h_1 AND h_2 are $connected$ to $same$ $intermediate$ $vertex$ **then**
7   **if** $length(h_1) > length(h_2)$ **then**
8              $E = E - h_1$;
9   **else**
10              $E = E - h_2$;
11   **if** No $change$ in the $graph$ in $successive$ $iterations$ **then**
12   Stop the algorithm and **return** $\{G(V, E)\}$;

Algorithm 1. Filtering after SPTA based skeletonization

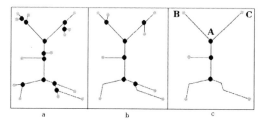

Fig. 3. Outputs at various intermediate steps of the filtering process a. Initial skeleton b. Intermediate skeleton c. Final skeleton.

2.4 Adductors Angle Measurement

The reduced graph generated by **Algorithm 1** is used for estimating adductors angle. In the graph, we search for the intermediate node A of $G(V', E')$ as shown in Fig. 3c. It is expected to be the joining point between two thighs since the baby is placed supine with an upside down view with respect to camera. Next, two straight lines are fitted along the edges representing the thighs of the baby using least square approximation method. Finally, the angle between the straight line segments denoted by AB and AC is estimated (refer to Fig. 3c).

3 Results and Discussions

We have recorded visuals of adductors angle measurement for 50 babies at the HINE clinic of SSKM hospital. Out of these 50 cases, the proposed filtering algorithm was capable of generating usable skeletons for 46 images. Comparative results using the proposed scheme with respect to ground truths are shown in Fig. 4. We have plotted the ground truths recorded by the experts and angle measured by the proposed scheme in the graph. In the graph, x-axis and y-axis denote sample number and angle in degree. It is evident from the graph that the results agree with ground truth measurements (angle measured by doctors) for majority of the samples. In the next part of the analysis, classification with respect to ground truth scores is presented (see Table 1).

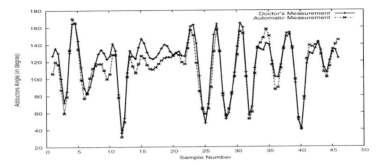

Fig. 4. Comparison of automatic measurement with respect to ground truths recorded during adductors angle measurement at SSKM hospital.

Since the scoring is done based on a range of angles, effect of errors in estimating the scores is less. Thus, high precision and recall is achieved. Fig. 5 shows some results of abductors angle measurement. For better visualization, we have drawn two thick straight lines (colored white) along the thighs of the baby and measured the angle between them.

Table 1. Classification of Results with respect to Recommended Scores of the HINE Chart

	$80^o < \theta < 150^o$ Score: 3			$150^o < \theta < 170^o$ Score: 2			$\theta < 80^o$ Score: 0		
GT(46)	33			6			7		
Outcomes	TP	FP	FN	TP	FP	FN	TP	FP	FN
	32	1	1	6	1	0	7	1	0
Precision	96.96%			85.71%			87.5%		
Recall	96.96%			100%			100%		
GT: Ground Truth, TP: True Positive, FP: False Positive, FN: False Negative									

Fig. 5. Results of abductors angle measurement on some of the sample images collected from IPGMER and SSKM Hospital

4   Conclusion and Future Directions

In this work, an image processing based algorithm has been proposed that can be used to measure the adductors angle of infants during HINE. This can be used to automate the neurological assessment process. Since rulers and other measuring instruments have to be used in a conventional approach, an automated scheme will reduce the workload of the examiner to a considerable extent. Though, in a few cases, our algorithm fails to measure the angle precisely, identifying range of angle instead of exact value is possible with high accuracy. Other examinations like measuring the popliteal angle, curvature in ventral suspension and ankle dorsiflexion can be automated using similar techniques.

Acknowledgement

The work has been funded by Ministry of Communication and Information Technology, Department of Information Technology, Govt. of India, under Approval No. 1(4)/2009-ME& TMD (28-08-2009).

References

1. Arbelaez, P., Maire, M., Fowlkes, C., Malik, J.: From Contours to Regions: An Empirical Evaluation. In: CVPR, pp. 2294–2301 (2009)
2. Bhatt, J., Bebis, G.: Automatic Recognition of a Baby Gesture. In: ICTAI, pp. 610–615 (2003)
3. Comaniciu, D., Meer, P.: Mean Shift: A Robust Approach Toward Feature Space Analysis. IEEE Transactions on Pattern Analysis and Machine Intelligence 24(5), 603–619 (2002)
4. Dogra, D., Nandam, K., Majumdar, A., Sural, S., Mukherjee, J., Mukherjee, S., Singh, A.: A User Friendly Implementation for Efficiently Conducting Hammersmith Infant Neurological Examination. In: Healthcom, pp. 374–378 (2010)
5. Dogra, D.P., Majumdar, A.K., Sural, S.: Evaluation of Segmentation Techniques Using Region Size and Boundary Information. In: Chaudhury, S., Mitra, S., Murthy, C.A., Sastry, P.S., Pal, S.K. (eds.) PReMI 2009. LNCS, vol. 5909, pp. 285–290. Springer, Heidelberg (2009)
6. Dubowitz, L., Dubowitz, V.: The Neurological Assessment of the Preterm and Full Term Infant. Clinics in Developmental Medicine 9 (1981)
7. Felzenszwalb, D.: Efficient Graph-based Image Segmentation. International Journal of Computer Vision 59(2), 167–181 (2004)
8. Kuan, Y., Kuo, C., Yang, N.: Color-Based Image Salient Region Segmentation Using Novel Region Merging Strategy. IEEE Transactions on Multimedia 10(5), 832–845 (2008)
9. Martin, D.: An Empirical Approach to Grouping and Segmentation. Ph.D. Dissertation, Univ. of California, Berkeley (2002)
10. Pal, N.R., Pal, S.K.: A Review on Image Segmentation Techniques. Journal of Pattern Recognition 26(9), 1277–1294 (1993)
11. Shi, J., Malik, J.: Normalized Cuts and Image Segmentation. IEEE Transactions on Pattern Analysis and Machine Intelligence 22(8), 888–905 (2000)
12. Unnikrishnan, R., Pantofaru, C., Hebert, M.: Toward Objective Evaluation of Image Segmentation Algorithms. IEEE Transactions on Pattern Analysis and Machine Intelligence 29(6), 929–944 (2007)
13. Naccache, N., Shinghal, R.: SPTA: A Proposed Algorithm for Thinning Binary Patterns. IEEE Transactions on Systems Man and Cybernatics 14(3), 409–418 (1984)
14. Nishida, Y., Motomura, Y.: Infant Behavior Simulation Based on an Environmental Model and a Developmental Behavior Model. ICSMC 2, 1555–1560 (2004)
15. Singh, S., Hsiao, H.: Infant Telemonitoring System. In: ICEMBS, pp. 1354–1357 (2003)

Interactive Image Retrieval with Wavelet Features

Malay K. Kundu[1], Manish Chowdhury[1], and Minakshi Banerjee[2]

[1] Machine Intelligence Unit, Indian Statistical Institute, Kolkata 700 108, India
[2] RCC Institute of Information Technology, Kolkata 700015, India
{malay,manish_t,minakshi_r}@isical.ac.in

Abstract. This paper presents an iterative Content Based Image Re-
trival(CBIR) system with Relevance Feedback (RF), in which M-band
wavelet features are used as representation of images. The pixels are
clustered using Fuzzy C-Means (FCM) clustering algorithm to obtain an
image signature and Earth Mover's Distance (EMD) is used as a distance
measure. Fuzzy entropy based feature evaluation mechanism is used for
automatic computation of revised feature importance and similarity distance at the end of each iteration. The performance of the algorithm is
tested on standard large multi-class image databases and compared with
MPEG-7 visual features.

Keywords: Relevance Feedback, Edge Histogram Descriptor, Color Structure Descriptor, Feature Evaluation Index.

1 Introduction

Content Based Image Retrieval (CBIR)[1] which aims at retrieving similar images from a large database by measuring visual similarities between the query
image and database images based on automatically derived features like color,
texture etc. has become a potential area of research. The performance of a CBIR
system strongly depends upon the availability of suitable features for proper representation of semantic aspects automatically and suitable similarity distance
measures.

The major problem in the conventional CBIR, is the semantic gap between
visual perception of a scene and feature based representation of the scene image.
To bridge this gap, user's feedback has come into picture in an interactive manner which is popularly known as Relevance Feedback (RF)[2]. Although several
solutions for suitable feature extraction and RF have been proposed, but results
achieved so far are not fully upto the user's expectation. Efficient feature extraction mechanism which keeps computation minimum and suitable RF mechanism
is still an important research issue.

Wavelet transform based low level features provide an unique multiresolution
analysis and highly suitable for characterizing textures of images[3]. Wang *et
al.*[4] have used a 2-step algorithm using subband variances of wavelet coefficients for image retrieval applications. Cheng *et al.*[5] have used M-band wavelet
transform based histogram for content based retrieval of aerial images.

S.O. Kuznetsov et al. (Eds.): PReMI 2011, LNCS 6744, pp. 167–172, 2011.

The relevance feedback which is a post-retrieval step for enhancing the retrieval results[1] mainly uses two approaches (a) "weighing approach" where higher weight is given to emphasize important features (b) "probability approach" where the information representing the query image is modified to make it more similar to the positive images than negative images, according to user feedback. Zin *et al.*[6] have proposed a feature re-weighting technique by using both the relevant and the irrelevant information, to obtain more effective results.

We propose a fuzzy entropy based RF method using EMD by considering both relevant and irrelevant images to adjust automatically the weights of the M-band wavelet features. The results are compared with MPEG-7 visual features which has become almost standard norms for the evaluation of newly proposed image features for CBIR system.

2   M-band Wavelet and Distance Measure

1. **M-band Wavelet:** An M-band wavelet system forms a tight frame for functions $f(x) \in L^2(\Re)$ with (M-1) unitary wavelet filters[7] is given by

$$f(x) = \sum_k c(k)\varphi_k(x) + \sum_{k=-\infty}^{\infty} \sum_{j=0}^{\infty} \sum_{i=1}^{M-1} M^{j/2} d_{i,j}(k)\psi(M^j x - k) \qquad (1)$$

where φ_k is the scaling function and ψ are the wavelet functions respectively and are associated with the analyzing (or synthesizing) filters. The wavelet coefficient is $c(k) = \int f(x)\varphi(x - k)dx$ and the expansion coefficient of coarser signal approximation is $d_{i,j}(k) = \int f(x)M^{j/2}\psi(M^j x - k)dx$. The scaling function and (M-1) wavelet function also define a Multiresolution Analysis(MRA)and the subspaces form an orthogonal decomposition of functional space for $L^2(\Re)$ defined by the space spanned by the translate of $\psi_i(x)$ for fixed j and $k\epsilon\mathbf{Z}$ as $W_{i,j} = Span\{\psi_{i,j,k}\}$.

2. **Earth Mover's Distance:** Earth Mover's Distance (EMD) by its definition extends to distance between sets or distributions of elements, thereby facilitating partial matches[8]. If p_i be the centroid of each cluster of a signature $P_i = \{(p_1, w_{p_1}), ..., (p_m, w_{p_m})\}$ with m clusters and w_{p_i} the weight of each cluster, similarly q_i be the centroid of each cluster of a signature $Q = \{(q_1, w_{q_1}), ..., (q_n, w_{q_n})\}$ with n clusters and $D = [d_{ij}]$ is the ground distance matrix, where $d_{ij} = d(p_i, q_j)$. Computing EMD thus becomes finding a flow between p_i and q_j which minimizes the overall cost. A flow between P and Q is any matrix $F = (f_{i\ j}) \epsilon R^{m \times n}$. Thus, EMD is defined as the work normalized by the total flow i.e. $EMD(P,Q) = \frac{\sum_{i=1}^{m}\sum_{j=1}^{n} d(p_i,q_j)f_{ij}}{\sum_{i=1}^{m}\sum_{j=1}^{n} f_{ij}}$ subject to the constraints (a) $f_{ij} \geq 0, 1 \leq i \leq m, 1 \leq j \leq n$, (b) $\sum_{j=1}^{n} f_{ij} \leq w_{p_i}, 1 \leq i \leq m$, (c) $\sum_{i=1}^{m} f_{ij} \leq w_{q_j}, 1 \leq j \leq n$, and (d) $\sum_{i=1}^{m}\sum_{j=1}^{n} f_{ij} = min(\sum_{i=1}^{m} w_{p_i}, \sum_{j=1}^{n} w_{q_j})$.

3   Proposed Technique

(1). 1D, 16 tap 4 band orthogonal filters with linear phase and perfect reconstruction for the MRA are used as a kernel for wavelet filter. (2). Before decomposing the image, RGB color plane of the image is converted into YCbCr color plane. (3). After color plane tranformation, each image plane is decomposed into M×M channels without downsampling and then energy feature at each pixel is computed. (4). FCM clustering algorithm is used in each pixel to obtain the signature. (5). EMD distance is computed between the query image and the stored image signature in the database and the images are displayed in the first pass. (6). Feature Evaluation Index (FEI) are calculated from the marked relevant and irrelevant set of images and recomputes the weighted EMD over each iteration.

3.1   Color-Texture Feature as Signature

Motivated from the idea that human visual system divides an image into several bands, than actually visualizing the complete image as a whole. M-band wavelet filters are used which are essentially frequency and direction oriented band pass filters. Wavelet transform is applied to Y, Cb and Cr planes where decomposition over the intensity plane characterizes texture and over chromaticity planes characterizes color. For each of 16 subbands, absolute Gaussian energy for each pixel is computed over a neighborhood and the size of which is determined using a spectral flatness measure(SFM) given by the ratio of arithmetic mean and the geometric mean of the Fourier coefficients of the image.

$$energy_{m_1,m_2}(i,j) = \sum_{a=1}^{N}\sum_{b=1}^{N}|Wf_{m_1,m_2}(a,b)|\,G(i-a,j-b), \qquad (2)$$

Here, N is the neighborhood size and $1 \le m_1 \le M, 1 \le m_2 \le M$ while Wf_{m_1,m_2} is the wavelet transform coefficient obtained by row-wise convolution using the filter H_{m_1} and column-wise convolution with the filter H_{m_2}. The nonlinear transform is succeeded by a Gaussian low-pass (smoothing) filter of the form $G(x,y) = \frac{1}{\sqrt{2\pi}\sigma}e^{-(1/2\sigma^2)(x^2+y^2)}$, where σ defines the spatial extent of the averaging filter. We use a neighborhood size of 11×11 for SFM between 1 and 0.65, 21×21 for SFM between 0.65 and 0.35 while 31×31 for 0 to 0.35.

3.2   Iterative Computation of Weighted Based on Feature Relevance

Perceptual importance as used in the JPEG 2000 is Y : Cb : Cr = 4 : 2 : 1. Here, the weights are chosen heuristically. However, an automatic scheme which chooses the weights depending on the color-texture complexity of the image will certainly boost the performance of the CBIR system.

Combining information of relevant and irrelevant images marked by the users, the fuzzy features evaluation index (FEI) is computed considering a pattern classification problem. If $C_1, C_2, ..., C_m$ are m pattern classes in N dimensional features space where class C_j contains, n_j number of samples. The features values along the qth co-ordinate along classes C_j are assigned as standard S-type membership function between 0 and 1[9]. Entropy(H) of C_j gives the measure of intraset ambiguity is given as $H(A) = (\frac{1}{n_j \ln 2})\sum_i S_n(\mu(f_{iqj}))$; $i = 1,2...n_j$, where $S_n(\mu(f_{iqj}))$=-$\mu(f_{iqj})\ln\mu(f_{iqj})$-$\{1$-$\mu(f_{iqj})\}\ln\{1$-$\mu(f_{iqj})\}$ is the Shannon's function (μ). $H_{min} = 0$ for μ=0 or 1, $H_{max} = 1$ for μ=0.5.

The FEI_q for the qth component is defined as $FEI_q = \frac{H_{qjk}}{H_{qj}+H_{qk}}$. H_{qk} is the entropy of class C_k along q^{th} dimension over n_k number of samples. H_{qjk}(interset ambiguity) is entropy along q^{th} dimension combining classes C_j and C_k with $(n_j + n_k)$ number of samples. Lower value of FEI_q, indicates better quality of importance of the qth feature because FEI_q should be decreasing after combining C_j and C_k as the goodness of the qth features in descriminating pattern classes C_j and C_k increases[9]. The weight w_q is a function of the evaluated (FEI_q) is $w_q = F_q(FEI_q)$.

H_{qj} is computed from the set of relevant images $I_r^{(q)} = \{I_{r1}^{(q)}, I_{r2}^{(q)}, I_{r3}^{(q)}, ..., I_{rk}^{(q)}\}$. Similarly, H_{qk} is computed from the set of irrelevant images where, $I_{ir}^{(q)} = \{I_{ir1}^{(q)}, I_{ir2}^{(q)}, I_{ir3}^{(q)}, ..., I_{irk}^{(q)}\}$. H_{qkj} is computed combining both the sets. Images are ranked according to EMD distance. The user marks the relevant and irrelevant set from 20 returned images, for automatic evaluation of FEI.

Presently an image I is represented as a signature $P = \{(p_1, w_{p_1}), (p_2, w_{p_2}), ..., (p_m, w_{p_m})\} = \{(p_i, w_{p_i})\}_{i=1}^m$ with m clusters. The cluster centroid p_i constitutes the wavelet features over 16 subbands of each Y, Cb and Cr plane and obtained with $p_i = [p_{iY}, p_{iC_b}, p_{iC_r}]$ which may be further represented as $[f_{1Y}, ..., f_{nY}, f_{1Cb}, ..., f_{nCb}, f_{1Cr}, ..., f_{nCb}]$. Here p_{iY}, p_{iC_b} and p_{iC_r} are the local energy values computed overall subbands of each Y, Cb and Cr planes respectively, for e.g $p_{iY} = [f_{1Y}, ..., f_{nY}]$ where $p_i \epsilon R^N$ and $N = 3n$ is the feature dimension. Here $n = 16$ and $w_i \geq 0$.

The features considered to compute the feature evaluation index along each component plane for e.g plane Y are $F_Y = \{f_{i_1Y}, ..., f_{i_qY}\}$, where $i = 1, 2, ..., m$ (m clusters) and $q = 1, 2, ..., n$ (n subband features). Similarly features are considered for Cb and Cr plane. The FEI_{qY} for the component feature q of Y plane are $FEI_{qY} = \frac{H_{qtotal}}{H_{qRel}+H_{qIrrel}}$. Here, H_{qRel}, H_{qIrrel} and H_{qtotal} are the entropies along the qth dimension of relevant, irrelevant and total returned images respectively. And the $(FEI)_{qCb}$ and $(FEI)_{qCr}$ of other two planes are computed similarly. The overall weight factor for the Y plane is given by $W_Y' = \sum_{i=1}^m \sum_{q=1}^n (FEI)_{qY}$, similarly W_{Cb}' and W_{Cr}' are computed and the weight for the Y plane is $W_Y = \frac{W_Y'}{W_Y'+W_{Cb}'+W_{Cr}'}$.

Similarly W_{Cb} and W_{Cr} are computed. Multiplying with the weight actually transforms the representative points p_i but leave its distribution fixed. The EMD is now computed between the transformed signature maps. $P' = \{g(p_i), w_{pi}\}_{i=1}^m$ and $Q' = \{g(q_j), w_{qj}\}_{i=1}^n$, where p_i and q_i are the centroids of the query and database images and g is the weight updating factor computed after each iteration. The $EMD_g(P, Q)$, where $g \epsilon (W_Y, W_{Cb}, W_{Cr})$ is computed from the work flow i.e. $WORK(F, P', Q') = \sum_{i=1}^m \sum f_{i,j} d(g(p_i), g(q_j))$.

The transformed p_i and q_j is represented as $p_i' = [W_Y p_{iY}, W_{Cb} p_{iC_b}, W_{Cr} p_{iC_r}]$ and $q_j' = [W_Y q_{jY}, W_{Cb} q_{jC_b}, W_{Cr} q_{jC_r}]$ respectively. The EMD is computed upto k^{th} iteration till it converges i.e $W(F^{(K+1)}, P_K'^{(K+1)}, Q_K'^{(K+1)}) \leq W(F^{(K)}, P_K'^{(K)}, Q_K'^{(K)})$. The signature maps for similar images are expected to be similar. After multiplying with weights, the ranks of the relevant images are not affected much.

(a)   (b)   (c)

Fig. 1. Database (A) (a) First Pass of the Retrieval Results using M-band Wavelet Features with the top left most image as a query image (b) First Iteration (c) Second Iteration

4   Experimental Results

Considering each image as a query, results are tested upon (A) SIMPLIcity images consisting of 1000 images from 10 different categories (B) Corel 10000 miscellaneous database which is labeled into 79 semantic categories. The results are also compared with ISO standard MPEG-7 visual features i.e. Edge Histogram Descriptor (EHD) and Color Structure Descriptor (CSD)[10].

The retrieval results using different features and distance norms can be best compared when tested upon same database. We grossly partition each image of the database into three meaningful clusters for computing EMD distance. For the query image of elephant as shown in Fig.1(a) on database (A), there are four irrelevant images. Such images are having quite similar color distribution but of different distribution weight. By suitable weighting of the feature planes the average precision ($Precision = \frac{No.\ of\ relevant\ images\ retrieved}{Total\ No.\ of\ images\ retrieved}$)is increased upto 100% after 2nd iteration which are shown in Fig. 1(b) and Fig.1(c). The results on database(B) are also satisfactory, one example is shown in Fig.2(a). Fig.2(b) shows results using M-band, EHD and CSD.

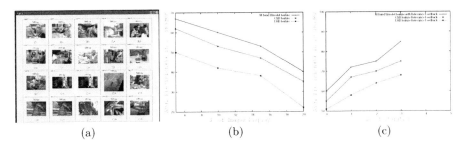

(a)   (b)   (c)

Fig. 2. (a) First Pass of the Retrieval Results using M-band Wavelet Features on Database (B) (b) Average Precision of CSD, EHD and M-band Wavelet Vs No. of Image on Database (A) without RF (c) Successive improvement(Average Precision) Vs No. of Iteration with RF

Fig. 2(c) shows an improvement in average precision (considering all database images) upto 30% (maximum) at 3rd iteration using our RF with EMD on M-band wavelet features. Our results are found better than CSD and EHD which show an improvement of about 10% to 15% after 3rd iteration, where FEI is used with Euclidean distance.

MPEG-7 CSD visual features and M-band wavelet features approximately take 1-2 secs whereas EHD takes 500 ms. The CPU-time taken for each iteration is approximately 50 ms for database (A) and 3 sec for database (B) using MATLAB R2008a on a Dell(T7400, 4GB, RAM) machine.

5   Conclusions

The proposed image retrieval system based on M-band wavelet features is able to improve the retrieval performance satisfactorily within 2 to 3 iterations of relevance feedback. We intend to incorporate partial query using EMD and relevance feedback in partial matching for videos in conjunction with motion information as future scope of research.

References

1. Heesch, D.: A survey of browsing models for content based image retrieval. Multimedia Tools Application 40, 1380–7501 (2008)
2. Chang, F.C., Hang, H.M.: A relevance feedback image retrieval scheme using multi-instance and pseudo image concepts. IEICE Transaction Information System E89-D, 1720–1731 (2006)
3. Acharyya, M., Kundu, M.K.: An adaptive approach to unsupervised texture segmentation using M-band wavelet tranform. Signal Processing 81, 1337–1356 (2001)
4. Wang, J.Z., Li, J., Wiederhold, G.: Simplicity: Semantics-sensitive integrated matching for picture libraries. IEEE Transactions on Pattern Analysis and Machine Intelligence 23, 947–963 (2001)
5. Cheng, Q., Yang, C., Chen, F., Shao, Z.: Application of M-band wavelet theory to texture analysis in content-based aerial image retrieval. International Geoscience and Remote Sensing Symposium 3, 2163–2165 (2004)
6. Jin, Z., King, I., Li, X.: Content-based image retrieval by relevance feedback. In: Laurini, R. (ed.) VISUAL 2000. LNCS, vol. 1929, pp. 521–529. Springer, Heidelberg (2000)
7. Burrus, C.S., Gopinath, A., Guo, H.: Introduction to Wavelets and Wavelet Transform: A Primer. Prentice Hall International Editions, Englewood Cliffs (1998)
8. Rubner, Y., Tomasi, C.: Perceptual Metrices for Image Database Navigation. Kluwer Academic Publishers, Boston (2001)
9. Pal, S.K., Majumder, D.D.: Fuzzy Mathematical Approach To Pattern Recognition. Willey Eastern Limited, New York (1985)
10. Manjunath, B.S., Salembier, P., Sikora, T.: Introduction to MPEG-7: Multimedia Content Description Interface. John Wiley and Sons Inc., USA (2002)

Moving Objects Detection from Video Sequences Using Fuzzy Edge Incorporated Markov Random Field Modeling and Local Histogram Matching

Badri Narayan Subudhi and Ashish Ghosh

Machine Intelligence Unit,
Indian Statistical Institute, Kolkata, India-700108
subudhi.badri@gmail.com, ash@isical.ac.in

Abstract. In this article, we put forward a novel region matching based motion estimation scheme to detect objects with accurate boundaries from video sequences. We have proposed a fuzzy edge incorporated Markov Random Field (MRF) model based spatial segmentation scheme that is able even to identify the blurred boundaries of objects in a scene. Expectation Maximization (EM) algorithm is used to estimate the MRF model parameters. To reduce the complexity of searching, a new scheme is proposed to get a rough knowledge of maximum possible shift of objects from one frame to another by finding the amount of shift in positions of the centroid. Moving objects in the scene are detected by the proposed χ^2-test based local histogram matching. It is noticed that the proposed scheme provides better results with less object background misclassification as compared to optical flow and label fusion based techniques.

1 Introduction

Detection of moving objects in a given video has becoming an important research area in both computer vision and pattern recognition community because of its wide application in video surveillance, driving assistance system, robotics etc. It is very difficult to detect a moving object from a video captured with moving camera. To solve such problems one can adhere to the approaches like optical flow or motion estimation scheme [7]. However this scheme is unable to give good results for objects with complex motions and dynamic background. A combination of spatial segmentation and motion prediction/estimation is proved to be a better approach towards this.

An early work for object detection by region growing scheme is suggested by Deng and Manjunath in [2], where the spatial segmentation of an image frame is obtained by color quantization followed by an edge preserving region growing scheme. For temporal segmentation, the regions corresponding to objects are matched in the temporal direction by computing the motion vectors of the object regions in the target frame. Gray level values of pixels in a video with high uncertainty and high ambiguity make it difficult to detect moving objects with affordable accuracy by non-statistical spatial segmentation schemes. Hence, it requires some kind of stochastic method to model the attributes of an image

S.O. Kuznetsov et al. (Eds.): PReMI 2011, LNCS 6744, pp. 173–179, 2011.

frame so that a better segmentation result can be obtained. Markov Random Field (MRF) model, in this context, proved to be a better framework. A robust work on MRF based object detection is demonstrated by Kuo et al. in [5], where a combination of temporal and spatial constraints of the image frames are used to obtain the moving object location from one frame to another of a video. Recently, Jodoin et al. [4] have proposed a robust moving object detection and tracking scheme for both fixed and moving camera captured video sequences, where MRF is used for label fields fusion. The label fields include two data: quickly estimated labels (i.e., a rough estimate of the location of object) and the spatial region map obtained by spatial segmentation with MRF model.

In this article, we propose a moving object detection scheme, that is able to detect moving objects with accurate object boundary from videos captured by moving camera. The technique uses a region based motion estimation scheme. Here we have proposed a new kind of MRF-MAP framework, where fuzzy edge strength at each pixel is incorporated in the MRF modeling. The scheme is able to preserve the object boundary. The spatial segmentation problem is solved using the Maximum a'posteriori probability (MAP) estimation principle. In region based motion estimation scheme, to reduce the complexity of searching, a rough knowledge of maximum possible shift in object from one frame to another is obtained by calculating the amount of shift in the centroid of the object from one frame to another. Moving objects in the target frame is detected by χ^2-test based local histogram matching. It is observed that the proposed scheme provide better results with less object background misclassification as compared to existing techniques.

2 Spatial Segmentation Using Proposed Fuzzy Edge Incorporated MRF Model

In this work it is assumed that the observed video sequence y is a 3-D volume consisting of spatio-temporal image frames. y_t represents a video image frame at time t and hence is a spatial entity of size $M \times N$. Each pixel in y_t is assumed as a site s denoted by y_{st}. Let us assume that X_t represents the MRF from which x_t is a realization. Here $X_t = X_t(i,j)$ is discrete valued and can take values from $Q = \{q_1, q_2, ..., q_m\}$. It is assumed here that due to the presence of noise (i.i.d) we are not able to observe X_t, and we observe a noisy version of X_t as Y_t.

In spatial domain, X_t represents the MRF model of x_t and using Hamersely Clifford's theorem the prior probability can be expressed as Gibb's distribution with $P(X_t) = \frac{1}{z} e^{\frac{-\bar{U}(x_t)}{T}}$, where z is the partition function expressed as $z = \sum_{x_t} e^{\frac{-\bar{U}(x_t)}{T}}$, $\bar{U}(x_t)$ is the energy function, a function of clique potentials $V_c(x_t)$. According to Pott's model the clique potential function $V_c(x_t) = -\alpha$ if all labels in possible set of cliques (C) are equal, otherwise $V_c(x_t) = +\alpha$. Equal penalization of all the boundary pixels results in a greater penalty to weak edge pixels and a lesser penalty to the strong edge pixels. This results in improper identification of boundary pixels in low resolution or blurred images. To reduce this effects one can adhere to the concept of incorporating local statistics based kernel function in MRF model as $\bar{U}(x_t) = \sum_{\eta_s} e^{-(x_t \otimes h)}$. This defines the energy function in MRF as a function of x_t convolved with some local statistic based edge sensitive kernel h.

Generally the change in gray level between the successive regions in an image frame is very common and edge detection techniques are found to be effective only for significant contrast. Hence the inclusion of a deterministic edge kernel in MRF modeling is not expected to yield a satisfactory solution. It justifies to apply the concept of fuzzy set based edge kernel [8] rather than a deterministic edge kernel. The operation of fuzzy edge kernel at a particular site (with a set of neighboring pixels) makes the energy function as $\bar{U}(x_{st}) = \sum_{\eta_s} e^{-\frac{(x_{st} \otimes h)}{F_c}}$, where $(x_{st} \otimes h) = \frac{1}{\left(1 + \frac{|x_{st} - \bar{x}_{rt}|}{F_d}\right)^{F_c}}$. Here F_e and F_d are two positive constants and are termed as the exponential and denominational fuzzifiers, respectively. The constant F_c is an MRF convergence parameter. There is no closed form solution for the estimation of parameters F_c, F_e and F_d and hence are fixed manually. Here $\hat{x}_{rt}$ represents $\max_{r \in \eta_s}\{x_{rt}\}$ or $\min_{r \in \eta_s}\{x_{rt}\}$. Hence we may write the prior probability $P(X_t)$ as $P(X_t) = e^{-\bar{U}(x_t)} = \frac{1}{z} \sum_{\eta_s} e^{-\frac{(x_t \otimes h)}{F_c}}$. The corresponding expression for MRF modeling with deterministic edge kernel can be obtained by replacing the fuzzy edge kernel with a deterministic edge kernel and termed as deterministic edge incorporated MRF modeling (DEMRF).

Here the segmentation problem is considered to be a process of determining a realization x_t that has given rise to the actual image frame y_t. One way to estimate $\hat{x}_t$ is based on the statistical MAP estimation by Bayes' theorem [6] as $\hat{x}_t = \arg \max_{x_t} P(Y_t = y_t | X_t = x_t)_\theta P(X_t = x_t)$, where θ is the parameter vector associated with estimation of x_t. The likelihood function $P(Y_t = y_t | X_t = x_t, \theta)$ can be expressed as a realization of Gaussian noise $N(x_t, \sigma)$. Hence including the prior probability and the likelihood function we can rewrite the a posterior probability of MRF as

$$\hat{x}_t = \arg \max_{x_t} \left\{ A - \left[\frac{\| y_t - x_t \|^2}{2\sigma^2} \right] - \left[\sum_{\eta_s} \frac{(x_t \otimes h)}{F_c} \right] \right\}, \tag{1}$$

where $A = -\frac{1}{2} \log((2\pi)^3 \sigma^6)$. $\hat{x}_t$ in eq (1) is the MAP estimate of x_t. We have considered a combination of both simulated annealing (SA) and iterated conditional mode (ICM) algorithm [9] for estimating the MAP of each incoming image frame and the parameter $\theta = \{\sigma^2\}$ is estimated recursively by EM algorithm [6].

3   Region Matching Based Motion Estimation

In the initial phase of the proposed object detection framework, the candidate frame (i.e., the frame in which object position is already known) and the target frame (i.e., the frame in which object is required to be detected) both are spatially segmented by the proposed fuzzy edge incorporated MRF modeling approach. The object detection task in different frames of the given video is accomplished by matching the gray level distributions of those regions corresponding to each moving object in the candidate frame to a region in the target frame by χ^2-test based histogram matching. To get an effective object detection, we propose an algorithm to find the rough estimation of maximum possible shift in object from one frame to another by calculating the amount of shift in the centroid of the object from one frame to another.

Calculation of Shift in Centroid and Local Histogram Matching: Let us consider two image frames at t^{th} and $(t+d)^{th}$ instant of times, where the tth frame is the candidate frame and $(t+d)^{th}$ frame is the target frame. Let us assume that there are d numbers of moving objects in the scene, and their positions in the candidate frame are known. From one frame to another as the object in the scene move, there will be a shift in the centroid of the object. Considering the relative camera movements in the scene as a multiplicative factor we can calculate the amount of shift of object in the scene as a function of distance. In the $(t+d)^{th}$ frame, the maximum possible shift of object in x-direction can be given as $shift_{(x,(t+d)b)} = const * max\{|Dist_{(t+d),b}(i) - Dist_{t,b}(i)|_{b=1,2...d}\}$. Similarly, in y-direction it can be given as $shift_{(y,(t+d)b)} = const * max\{|Dist_{(t+d),b}(j) - Dist_{t,b}(j)|_{b=1,2...d}\}$. The $Dist$ function represents distance of bth object centroid in the candidate frame to the target frame image centroid. The $const$ represents a $+ve$ constant that resolves the camera movements and scaling of the object in the scene.

For matching each region corresponding to a moving object in the candidate frame to a region within the search space in the target frame, a search is made up to $shift_{(x,(t+d)b)}$ in the $+ve$ and $-ve$ directions of the x-axis and $shift_{(y,(t+d)b)}$ in the $+ve$ and $-ve$ directions of the y-axis. Each time, we search a new region in the target frame, the histogram corresponding to the new region is matched with a region corresponding to the object in the candidate frame by χ^2-test [1]. By χ^2-test based measure, the distribution/histogram of two regions can be compared by the formula,

$$\chi^2((h^{(b_g,y_t)}),(h^{(g,y_{(t+d)})})) = \sum_{l=0}^{l=M-1} \frac{|(h^{(b_g,y_t)}) - (h^{(g,y_{(t+d)})})|}{(h^{(b_g,y_t)}) + (h^{(g,y_{(t+d)})})}.$$

The term $h^{(b_g,y_t)}$ represents the histogram corresponding to a region in b^{th} object of the candidate frame. The term $h^{(g,y_{(t+d)})}$ represents the histogram corresponding to a region within the search space (as obtained by centroid shifting scheme) in the target frame. Here g represents any region in the target frame within the obtained search space. M is the number of possible gray level bins in the histogram.

4   Results and Discussion

The proposed scheme is tested on several video sequences, however for page constraint we have provided the results on one test video sequence. The results obtained by the proposed fuzzy edge map incorporated MRF modeling for spatial segmentation is compared with those of the spatial segmentation by conventional MRF modeling [4] and MRF modeling with deterministic edge kernel (DEMRF). Similarly, the moving object detection results obtained by the proposed scheme are compared with those obtained by optical flow [7] and label fusion [4] schemes.

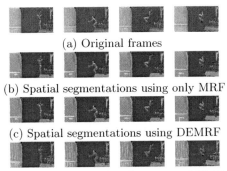

(a) Original frames

(b) Spatial segmentations using only MRF

(c) Spatial segmentations using DEMRF

(d) Spatial segmentations using the proposed FMRF scheme

Fig. 1. Spatial segmentation results for Diving video sequence

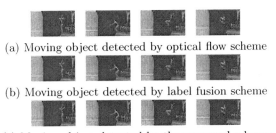

(a) Moving object detected by optical flow scheme

(b) Moving object detected by label fusion scheme

(c) Moving object detected by the proposed scheme

Fig. 2. Moving object detection for Diving video sequence

The video considered for our experiments is *Diving* video sequence having a single moving object, i.e. a gymnast. The considered frames of the sequence are shown in Fig. 1 (a). The spatial segmentation results obtained by the conventional MRF model and DEMRF are shown in Figs. 1 (b) and (c), respectively. It is observed from these results that the output obtained by these approaches are over-segmented. This is due to the fact that, the gray-level variation of one region to another of the image frames are very less. The boundary of the object in the scene are blurred and hence are indistinguishable. The results obtained by the proposed fuzzy edge incorporated MRF modeling (FMRF) scheme is shown in Fig. 1 (d). For evaluating the accuracy, we have used the pixel by pixel comparison of the manually constructed *ground-truth* images with the obtained spatial segmentation results. This measure is also called *number of misclassified pixels* (NMP). It is found that for the considered sequence, average NMP measure obtained for the conventional MRF scheme and the deterministic edge incorporated MRF are 2179.25 and 1777, respectively. The average NMP measure obtained for the proposed scheme is found to be 1114, much better than the existing methods. The time taken by the proposed scheme is 55 seconds.

The location of the moving object obtained for different frames of this sequence using optical flow based scheme are shown in Fig. 2 (a). It is found from these results that the diving gymnast was not properly identified. Similarly, the moving object location obtained by the label fusion scheme are shown in Fig. 2 (b). It is observed from these results that this technique is also not able to identify the different parts of the gymnast correctly. However the results obtained by the proposed scheme (as shown in Fig. 2 (c)) has correctly detected the gymnast in different frames of the considered sequence. To evaluate the performance of the detected moving object locations, we have considered the manually constructed ground-truth based performance evaluation scheme of Erdem *et al.* [3]. This scheme utilizes four different measures: *misclassification penalty* (Mi.P), *motion penalty* (M.P), *shape penalty* (S.P), and *combined penalty* (C.P) to evaluate the performance of the moving objects locations. It may be noted that all these measures should be low for better detection of moving objects. These measures obtained for optical flow scheme are $0.5, 0.4, 0.4$ and 0.45, respectively. Similarly these measure obtained for Label fusion scheme are $0.51, 0.38, 0.31$ and 0.39, respectively. The results obtained for the proposed scheme are $0.42, 0.22, 0.22$ and 0.29, respectively. Thus the proposed scheme is seen to provide better results as compared to the optical flow and label fusion schemes.

5   Conclusion

A new region based motion estimation scheme to detect moving objects from given video sequences has been formulated. We have proposed a spatial segmentation technique by incorporating the fuzzy edge strength of pixels in MRF modeling to preserve the object boundary. In this approach initially a rough estimate of object locations in the scene are obtained by finding the amount of shift in the centroid from one frame to another. The location of moving objects in a scene is obtained by χ^2-test based local histogram comparison. The proposed scheme is found to be better as compared to the existing moving object detection schemes. The proposed scheme does not yield good results, with oclussion/dis-occlusion condition. In our future work we will try to solve the above problem.

References

1. Ahonen, T., Hadid, A., Pietikäinen, M.: Face recognition with local binary patterns. In: Pajdla, T., Matas, J(G.) (eds.) ECCV 2004. LNCS, vol. 3021, pp. 469–481. Springer, Heidelberg (2004)
2. Deng, Y., Manjunath, B.S.: Unsupervised segmentation of color-texture regions in images and video. IEEE Transactions on Pattern Analysis And Machine Intelligence 23(8), 800–810 (2001)
3. Erdem, C.E., Sankur, B., Tekalp, A.M.: Performance measures for video object segmentation and tracking. IEEE Transactions on Image Processing 13(7), 937–951 (2004)
4. Jodoin, P.M., Mignotte, M., Rosenberger, C.: Segmentation framework based on label field fusion. IEEE Transactions on Image Processing 16(10), 2535–2550 (2007)

5. Kuo, C.M., Hsieh, C.H., Huang, Y.R.: Automatic extraction of moving objects for head-shoulder video sequence. Journal of Visual Communication and Image Representation 16(1), 68–92 (2005)
6. Li, S.Z.: Markov Random Field Modeling in Image Analysis. Springer, Japan (2001)
7. Lucas, B.D., Kanade, T.: An iterative image registration technique with an application to stereo vision. In: Proceedings of Imaging understanding workshop, pp. 121–130 (1981)
8. Pal, S.K., King, R.A.: On edge detection of x-ray images using fuzzy sets. IEEE Transactions on Pattern Analysis Machine Intelligence 5(1), 69–77 (1983)
9. Subudhi, B.N., Nanda, P.K., Ghosh, A.: Moving object detection using MRF model and entropy based adaptive thresholding. In: Proceedings of IEEE 2nd International Conference on Human Computer Interaction, vol. 1, pp. 155–161. Springer, Heidelberg (2010)

Combined Topological and Directional Relations Based Motion Event Predictions

Nadeem Salamat and El-hadi Zahzah

Université de La Rochelle
Laboratoire de Mathématiques, Images et Applications
Avenue M Crépeau La Rochelle 17042, France
{nsalam01,ezahzah}@univ-lr.fr, nadeemsalamat@hotmail.com

Abstract. Spatial changes plays a fundamental role in modeling the spatio-temporal relations and spatio-temporal or motion event predictions. These predictions can be made through the conceptual neighborhood graph using the common sense continuity. This paper investigates that the extension in the temporal interval can effect the whole spatio-temporal relation and motion events. Spatio-temporal predicates form a unit of a motion event. We use the point temporal logic to extend the spatial predicates into the spatio-temporal or motion event predicates.

Keywords: Spatio-temporal relations, Spatial predicates, Spatio-temporal predictions, motion events.

1 Introduction

Spatio-temporal predictions are useful to initiate the new processus and to understand a physical phenomenon, fundamentally the spatio-temporal predictions are based on the predictions in the topological and directional relations [5,6,4]. In these methods, topological relations are computed by 9-intersection model [7] or alternatively by Region Connected Calculus $RCC8$[3] and directional relations are studied through method described in [10]. To fit the model in spatio-temporal context, an interval temporal logic[2] or point logic [9] are used. An hybrid method for defining the spatio-temporal predicates is developed in [8], this method consider only topological changes and spatio-temporal predicates are developed for moving objects.

Spatio-temporal motion event prediction is a process closely related to the spatio-temporal reasoning. The difference is, existing spatio-temporal reasoning provide us information that a topological or directional relation exists at time t_1, what is the possible topological or directional relation at time t_2. In this paper we define that if a spatio-temporal relation holds during an interval T, then how it will change spatio-temporal relation if an interval is extended and next time point is added to the interval.

The change in spatial scene is captured by the difference in topological, directional and distance spatial relations between the snapshot taken at point t_1 and

S.O. Kuznetsov et al. (Eds.): PReMI 2011, LNCS 6744, pp. 180–185, 2011.

time point t_2. This change in relative position may result change in topological, metric or orientation structure of an image. This requirement needs analysis in topological, metric and orientation viewpoint at each step and comparison between two states, provided that both objects have a common lifetime.

Topological and directional relations are combined, method is argued in [13,14] and a complete Combined Topological and Directional relations (CTD) method is developed in [11]. Graph of CTD method represents all binary topological deformation in objects along with directional contents. In this graph, nodes represent the topological and directional position of object pair and edge represents the time. This neighborhood graph is used to predicate the spatio-temporal relations. Next section explains the CTD method and section 3 describes the spatio-temporal prediction some examples are considered in section 4 and section 5 concludes the paper.

2   CTD Method

1. **Oriented lines, segments and longitudinal sections** A and B be two spatial objects and $(v, \theta) \in \mathbb{R}$, $\Delta_\theta(v)$ is an oriented line at θ. $A \cap \Delta_\theta(v)$ is the intersection of object A and $\Delta_\theta(v)$, it is denoted by $A_\theta(v)$, called segment of object A and its length is x. Similarly length of $B_\theta(v)$ is z. y is the difference between minimum of $A \cap \Delta_\theta(v)$ and maximum of $B \cap \Delta_\theta(v)$. In case of polygonal object approximation (x, y, z) can be calculated from intersecting points of line and object's boundary, oriented lines are considered which pass through at least one vertex of two polygons. If there exist more than one segment, it is called longitudinal section as in case of $A_\theta(v)$ in figure 1(a).

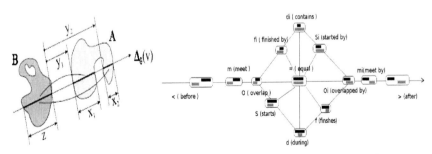

(a) Object pair and oriented line

(b) Neighborhood graph of Allen relations

Fig. 1. Black (dark grey) represents reference and light gray argument object

2. **Allen temporal relations in spatial domain and fuzziness** Allen[1] introduced 13 jointly exhaustive and pairwise disjoint (JEPD) interval relations. These relations are arranged as $\mathcal{A} = \{<, m, o, s, f, d, eq, d_i, f_i, s_i, o_i, m_i,>\}$ with meanings *before, meet, overlap, start, finish, during, equal, during_ by, finish_ by, start_ by, overlap_ by, meet_ by, and after*. Allen relations in space

are conceptually illustrated in figure (1(b)). These relations represent eight topological relations in one-dimensional spatial domain.

Fuzzy Allen relations represent fuzziness at relation's level. Trapezoidal membership function is used for fuzzification due to flexibility in shape change. Let $r(I, J)$ be an Allen relation between segments I(argument object) and J(reference object), r' is the distance between $r(I, J)$ and it's conceptional neighborhood. We consider a fuzzy membership function $\mu : r' \longrightarrow [0, 1]$ and relations are defined as $f_<(I, J) = \mu_{(-\infty, -\infty, -b-3a/2, -b-a)}(y)$, and $f_>(I, J) = \mu_{(0, a/2, \infty, \infty)}(y)$ where $a = min(x, z)$, $b = max(x, z)$ and x is length of(I), z is length of(J) and y is the difference between minimum value of $A_\theta(v)$ and maximum value of $B_\theta(v)$.

Most of relations are defined by one membership function but some of them are defined by conjunction of more than one membership functions like $d(during)$, $d_i(during\_by)$, f $(finish)$, f_i $(finished\_by)$, details are discussed in [12]. These relations have the properties: $f_<(\theta) = f_>(\theta+\pi)$, $f_m(\theta) = f_{mi}(\theta + \pi)$, $f_o(\theta) = f_{oi}(\theta + \pi)$, $f_s(\theta) = f_f(\theta + \pi), f_{si}(\theta) = f_{fi}(\theta + \pi), f_d(\theta) = f_d(\theta + \pi), f_{di}(\theta) = f_{di}(\theta + \pi)$, $f_=(\theta) = f_=(\theta + \pi)$. The whole two-dimensional space can be explored with one-dimensional Allen relations using oriented lines varying from $[0, \pi]$.

3. **CTD method and topological relations** We extend these Allen relations for the $2D$ objects through the logical implication, where a areal object is decomposed into parallel segments of a $1D$ lines in a given direction and Allen relations between each pair of line segments are computed. The process of object decomposition is repeated for each direction varying from 0 to π, then $2D$ topological relations are defined as it provides us the information that how the objects are relatively distributed.

These relations are not Jointly Exhaustive and Pairwise Disjoint (JEPD). To obtain JEPD set of topological and directional relations an algorithm for defuzzification of spatial relations was advocated in [11], it provides us the JEPD set of relations. Relations in this approach are called *Disjoint, Meet, Partial_overlap, Tangent Proper Part, Non Tangent Proper Part, Tangent Proper Part Inverse, Non Tangent Proper Part Inverse, Equal.* In the following figure, an example for computation of topological and directional relations information of areal objects is given.

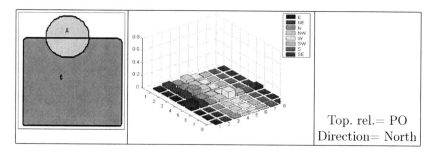

Top. rel.= PO
Direction= North

4. **Conceptual neighborhood graph in CTD method** A neighborhood graph for spatial relations in CTD method represents the possible transition in the topological and orientation perspective of spatial relations. Only one branch of translational-deformation is taken into account and possible transitions are presented into the graph.

In this figure 2, object can move to a circular path, *orientation neighborhood* and straightened path, a *topological neighborhood*, *diagonal path* a *topological and orientation neighborhood*. Neighborhood graph shows the allowable transitions among the relations, these transitions are possible when the objects move or change occurs in a spatial scene. In this figure 2, it is shown that every point of a neighborhood graph has eight possible direction nodes. Here relations are represented by a pair (α, β) where α represents topological and β represents the orientation relation.

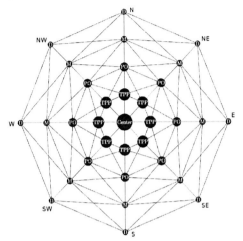

Fig. 2. Neighborhood graph in the system of combined topological and directional relations

3 Spatio-Temporal Predicates

The spatio-temporal predictions keep into account the history of spatio-temporal relation and they help us to estimate the spatio-temporal relations if the analysis interval is extended. For whole the clip, a relation exist if in each frame or at each partition, a separate relation exist in a particular sequence.

The relations depend upon topological changes, neighborhood graph depicts the physical transitions between spatial relations that can occur through the deformation of intervals. Spatio-temporal predictions about the moving objects are important and spatio-temporal change occurs when objects are continuously changing their position and temporal component is added to the interval and whole topological and directional relations change. At one end of the time space is closed and other end is an open end and different properties are used for example *holds, holds-at, occurs and occurs-at* and these properties are used to model the spatio-temporal predictions.

In this method, we combine the different information and a single method works in each situation and it provides us additional information. These spatio-temporal motion event predictions follow the mathematical relation. $STR_i = STR_{i-1} \cup SR_i$ or $STR_i = STR_{i-1} \cup SP_{i-1}, \forall\ i = 2, 3, ...$ where $STR(SR)$ stands for spatio-temporal relation (spatial relation), SP for spatial prediction which can predict only direction and topological relation and i denotes the time at which the relations are evaluated. These relations can be reformulated as $STP_i = STR_i \cup SP_i, \forall\ i = 2, 3, ...$ here $STP(SP)$ represents the spatio-temporal (spatial) prediction and spatio-temporal relation at i^{th} frame is the spatio-temporal prediction of $(i - 1)^{th}$ frame.

4   Examples

Motion is a continuous phenomenon, of course, it can be analyzed at a discontinuous time pints and between these two points it can be directly interpolated. These time points can be chosen at a predefined time intervals or a specific video frame called snapshot. In modeling the spatio-temporal relations and motion events we need at least two snapshots, or two basic intervals where a stable spatial temporal relations hold. We start from two snapshots, at initial point, both spatio-temporal and spatial predictions represents the same semantics and possible predicates are given in table 1.

Table 1. Spatio-temporal predictions for two frames

SR	SP	STR
(D,N)	(D,NE)	Changing direction, getting closer or going away from N to NE
(D,N)	(D,N)	getting closer or going away in N
(D,N)	(D,NW)	getting closer or going away N to NW
(D,N)	(M,NE)	Snap from NE
(D,N)	(M,N)	Snap from N
(D,N)	(M,NW)	Snap from NW

When the interval is extended, a new snapshot or a basic interval where the spatio-temporal relation is not changed is added to the interval.

Spatial relations are represented in the neighborhood graph, every point has the eight possible spatial predictions. we discuss here the possible spatial predictions from (M,NE) and the existing spatio-temporal relation at this point is *Snap from NE* then the spatio-temporal predicates are

Table 2. STR predictions for third frames

STR_{i-1}	SP_{i-1}	$STR_i or STP_{i-1}$
Snap from NE	D, E	Touching form NE
Snap from NE	M, E	Bypass
Snap from NE	PO, E	Graze, Enter, Into from E
Snap from NE	D, NE	Touch from NE
Snap from NE	PO, NE	Enter, Into from NE
Snap from NE	D, N	Touching from NE
Snap from NE	M, N	Bypass towards N
Snap from NE	PO, N	Graze, Enter, Into from N

depicted in table 2. These spatio-temporal predicates depend upon the current spatial predicates. Similarly, for other possibilities.

5 Conclusion

Spatio-temporal prediction is a closely related to the spatial reasoning methods. In this paper, it is discussed that if the interval for which a spatio-temporal relation is analyzed is extended then it can effect the whole spatio-temporal relation and motion events. In modeling the spatio-temporal predictions, spatial predictions for topological and directional relations and neighborhood graphs are also important. Temporal domain is handled through the interval or point temporal logic. We used the topological and orientation information at the same time and CTD method is used for binary topological and directional relations between the object pair.

References

1. Allen, J.F.: Maintaining Knowledge about Temporal Intervals. Communications of the ACM 26(11), 832–843 (1983)
2. Allen, J.F., Ferguson, G.: Actions and Events in Interval Temporal Logic. Journal of Logic and Computation 4, 531–579 (1994)
3. Cohn, A.G., Bennett, B., Gooday, J., Gotts, N.: RCC: a Calculus for Region-Based Qualitative Spatial Reasoning. GeoInformatica 1, 275–316 (1997)
4. Cohn, A.G., Hazarika, S.M.: Qualitative Spatial Representation and Reasoning: An Overview. Fundamenta Informaticae 46(1-2), 1–29 (2001)
5. Egenhofer, M., Mark, D.: Modeling Conceptual Neighborhoods of Topological Line-Region Relations. International Journal of Geographical Information Systems 9, 555–565 (1995)
6. Egenhofer, M.J., Al-Taha, K.K.: Reasoning about Gradual Changes of Topological Relationships. In: Proceedings of the International Conference On GIS - From Space to Territory, pp. 196–219. Springer, London (1992)
7. Egenhofer, M.J., Franzosa, R.D.: Point Set Topological Relations. International Journal of Geographical Information Systems 5(2), 161–174 (1991)
8. Erwig, M., Schneider, M., Hagen, F., Praktische Informatik Iv.: Spatio-Temporal Predicates. IEEE Transactions on Knowledge and Data Engineering 14, 881–901 (1999)
9. Galton, A.: A generalized topological view of motion in discrete space. Theor. Comput. Sci. 305(1-3), 111–134 (2003)
10. Goyal, R.K., Egenhofer, M.J.: Similarity of cardinal directions. In: Jensen, C.S., Schneider, M., Seeger, B., Tsotras, V.J. (eds.) SSTD 2001. LNCS, vol. 2121, pp. 36–58. Springer, Heidelberg (2001)
11. Salamat, N., Zahzah, E.h.: 2D Fuzzy Spatial Relations: New Way of Computing and Representation, http://hal.archives-ouvertes.fr/hal-00551281/en/
12. Salamat, N., Zahzah, E.h.: On the improvement of Combined topological and Directional Relations Information,
http://hal.archives-ouvertes.fr/hal-00551278/en/
13. Salamat, N., Zahzah, E.h.: Fusion of Fuzzy Spatial Relations. In: Proceedings of The 5th International Conference on Hybrid Artificial Intelligence Systems (HAIS (1)), pp. 294–301 (2010)
14. Salamat, N., Zahzah, E.h.: Fuzzy Spatial Relations For 2D Scene. In: Proceedings of The 2010 International Conference on Image Processing, Computer Vision, and Pattern Recognition (IPCV-2010), pp. 47–53 (2010)

Recognizing Hand Gestures of a Dancer

Divya Hariharan[1], Tinku Acharya[2], and Sushmita Mitra[1]

[1] Machine Intelligence Unit, Indian Statistical Institute, Kolkata 700 108, India
sushmita@isical.ac.in
[2] Videonetics Technology Private Limited, Kolkata, India
tinku.acharya@gmail.com

Abstract. A new and simple two-level decision making system has been designed for performing scale-, translation- and rotation-invariant recognition of various single-hand gestures of a dancer. The orientation filter is used at the first-level to generate a feature vector that is able to distinguish between several gestures. At the second-level the silhouette of the different gestures is extracted, followed by the generation of the corresponding skeleton and the evaluation of the gradients at its end points. These gradients constitute the second feature set, for recognizing those gestures which remain to be identified at the first-level. An application has been provided in the domain of single-hand gestures of Bharatanatyam, an Indian classical dance form.

Keywords: Gesture recognition, feature extraction, skeleton matching, orientation histogram.

1 Introduction

The term Indian Classical Dance comprises all the art forms of the Natyashastra written by the ancient musicologist Sage Bharata. The Natyashastra confers classical status to eight Indian dances, of which Bharatanatyam is one of the oldest. A popular interpretation of the name is
BHAva (expression) + RAga (musical mode) + TAla (rhythm) + NATYAM (dance) = BHARATANATYAM.

A distinctive feature of Bharatanatyam Dance is the use of expressive hand gestures as a way of communication. Hastas [3] refers to a variety of hand symbols that a dancer can use. Hastas can be broadly classified into two categories, *viz.*, Asamyukta Hastas (Single hand gestures) and Samyukta Hastas (Double hand gestures). There exist 28 Asamyukta Hastas and 24 Samyukta Hastas.

The objective of this research is to develop a suitable prototype for the recognition of the 28 Asamyukta Hastas of Bharatanatyam in a two dimensional space, using image processing techniques [1]. We aim to make the computer act as a teacher to correct the dance gestures, for the purpose of promoting e-learning of the nuances of Bharatanatyam across the world.

A major difficulty is associated with the rotation and scaling involved. For example, a gesture image rotated to any degree or scaled to any level should

S.O. Kuznetsov et al. (Eds.): PReMI 2011, LNCS 6744, pp. 186–192, 2011.

represent the same gesture. Orientation filters [2] have been used in various image processing and vision tasks, by applying filters of arbitrary orientation and phase. Typically a few filters, corresponding to a few angles, are employed and the intermediate responses are interpolated. With a correct filter set and interpolation rule, it becomes possible to evaluate a filter of any arbitrary orientation.

In this article we use the orientation filter at the first-level to generate a feature vector for distinguishing between different gestures. At the second-level the silhouette of the different gestures is extracted, followed by the generation of the corresponding skeleton and the evaluation of the gradients at its end points. This constitutes the second feature set, for recognizing those gestures which remain to be identified at the first-level. The rest of the paper is organized as follows. Section 2 describes the generation of the feature vector at the two levels, comprising computation of the orientation histogram and the gradients at the extremities of the hand. The experimental results are provided in detail in Section 3. Finally, Section 4 concludes the article.

2   Feature Extraction

The preprocessing of the hand gesture consists of detecting the skin color in the image, and cropping the hand region in order to avoid unnecessary details in the background. The images are then resized to 240×240 and converted to gray scale. The next step is the feature extraction procedure. A suitable feature vector which is invariant to translation, rotation, scaling and reflection needs to be chosen for the purpose of distinguishing between the different gestures.

2.1   Edge Orientation Histogram

Considering the aspects of translation and scaling invariance, the orientation histogram [2] was found to be a useful feature component. Here these constitute histograms of local orientation of the hand gesture. The orientation histograms are robust to illumination changes, and are simple and fast to compute.

Local orientation is obtained by the use of steerable filters, in which a filter of arbitrary orientation is synthesized as a linear combination of a set of "basis filters". A set of 36 one-dimensional Gaussian steerable filters and their first order derivatives have been used for extracting the local edge orientation properties of the hand gesture for every 10°, ranging from 0° to 350°. The gesture image I, filtered at an arbitrary orientation and convolved with the filters, can be synthesized for the oriented filter response

$$R_1^\theta = (G_1^{0^o} * I) \cos \theta + (G_1^{90^o} * I) \sin \theta, \tag{1}$$

where $*$ represents the convolution operator, and G_1^θ is considered at an arbitrary orientation θ.

In order to enhance the ability of the edge orientation histogram in recognizing the rotated gestures, the direction of maximum local orientation of every gesture is found. Accordingly the original gesture image is rotated in such a manner that

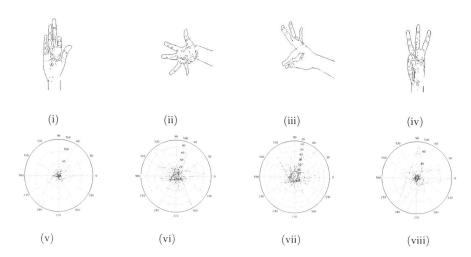

(i)   (ii)   (iii)   (iv)

(v)   (vi)   (vii)   (viii)

Fig. 1. Edges of sample single-hand Bharatanatyam gestures. (i) Aarala, (ii) Alapadma, (iii) Hamsaye, and (iv) Trishula. Polar plots of corresponding edge orientation histograms of gestures (v) Aarala, (vi) Alapadma, (vii) Hamsaye, and (viii) Trishula.

the maximum orientation is obtained at 180°. The edges of the hand gesture are extracted using the Laplacian of Gaussians (LOG) [1], and the image is multiplied with the filter response for every value of θ. Fig. 1 illustrates the polar plots of the edge orientation histogram corresponding to the edges from the gestures "Aarala", "Alapadma", "Hamsaye" and "Trishula".

2.2   Gradients at Corner Points of Skeleton

Those gestures that cannot be recognized at the first-level, by the use of edge orientation histograms, are processed further at a second-level. It is known that the end points of a skeleton correspond to a change of curvature. Refined categorization is next made, using the gradients at the extremities of the skeleton

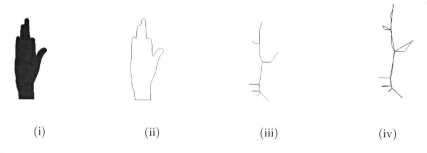

(i)   (ii)   (iii)   (iv)

Fig. 2. Sample gesture Aarala. (i) Silhouette, (ii) Boundary, (iii) Skeleton, and (iv) Connectivity graph.

as a new set of features. A given gray scale image is initially binarized in a uniform manner over hand gestures of different people. The boundary is extracted from the binary image, followed by the flood-fill operation to generate a uniform silhouette. This is depicted in Fig. 2(i) for a sample dance gesture "Aarala".

The skeleton [Fig. 2(iii)] is extracted by the morphological operation of thinning. Typically it consists of a number of branch points and end points, connected by curve segments. These points are considered to be the nodes of a graph, such that the skeletal curve segments form the edges. This graph [Fig. 2(iv)] is called the connectivity graph of the skeleton. It provides topological information about the hand gesture.

Matching of the connectivity graphs, based on their topologies and geometric features, provides a distance measure for determining the similarity (or dissimilarity) between the different shapes. The adjacency matrix of the connectivity graph is constructed. The degree of every node in the graph is computed and assigned as its weight. Subsequently, a depth-first traversal sequence is constructed for the connectivity graph starting from one end point (typically, the leftmost point). Preference is provided to a node with a lower weight during the traversal. Thereby, the number of backtracking sequences gets reduced.

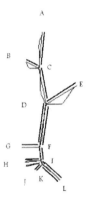

Fig. 3. Depth-first traversal in edge connectivity graph of Aarala

The thick black lines in Fig. 3 indicate the depth-first traversal sequence of the connectivity graph of Fig. 2(iv). The sequence obtained is expressed as

$$G \rightarrow F \rightarrow I \rightarrow H \rightarrow I \rightarrow K \rightarrow J \rightarrow K \rightarrow L \rightarrow K \rightarrow I \rightarrow F \rightarrow D \rightarrow E \rightarrow D \rightarrow$$
$$C \rightarrow B \rightarrow C \rightarrow A.$$

Repetitions of nodes correspond to the backtracking of edges during traversal of the graph.

For every end point in the skeleton, the nearest boundary point is obtained. Without loss of generality, it can be inferred that this nearest boundary point will be either a finger tip or a point in the hand gesture where the curvature change is large. Hence the gradient at these points will significantly vary over the different gestures. For the branch points, this value is assigned to be zero in order to avoid unnecessary weights due to backtracking sequences. The values of gradients are then substituted for the nodes, in the depth-first traversal sequence. This sequence of gradients and zeros forms the feature vector for the second-level of recognition.

3   Experimental Results

The gesture vocabulary was built by capturing ten images of each of the 28 single-hand gestures of Bharatanatyam from the hands of three different people, using a seven megapixel camera. These ten images were translated, rotated, scaled and reflected versions of a single gesture. Hence every image is unique. Out of the ten images, eight were randomly selected for training the system, while the remaining two were kept for testing. This amounted to a total of 224 training images. The test images were identified based on the closest match to the learned examples (prototypes) in terms of Euclidean distance. In the first-level, orientation histogram was used for feature extraction. In the second-level a shape-based skeleton matching was used, with the gradients at the corner points being used as a new set of features.

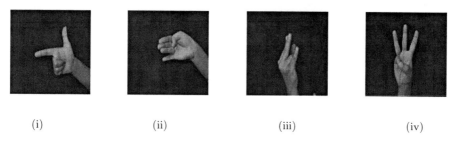

(i)   (ii)   (iii)   (iv)

Fig. 4. Distinctly identifiable gestures at the first-level. (i) Chandrakala, (ii) Chatura, (iii) Kangula, and (iv) Trishula.

Application of the edge orientation histogram resulted in the correct identification of four gestures, which were found to be distinctly unique from the others. These are Chandrakala, Chatura, Kangula and Trishula, as shown in Fig. 4. The remaining 24 gestures could be grouped into three classes, as indicated by the three rows of Fig. 5. These 24 images were used for subsequent processing at the second-level, as described below.

Shape-based skeleton matching was next used, with the set of gradients at the corner points in the skeleton serving as the new set of features for the remaining 192 (= 224 - 32) training images. The skeleton of the test image of a hand gesture was first obtained, and its connectivity graph generated. Then a depth-first traversal sequence with the gradient values was computed, for use as the feature vector. The left-most point of a skeleton image was generally considered as the starting point of the depth-first traversal for every gesture. Since all gestures are rotated to give a maximum orientation at 180°, therefore it is safe

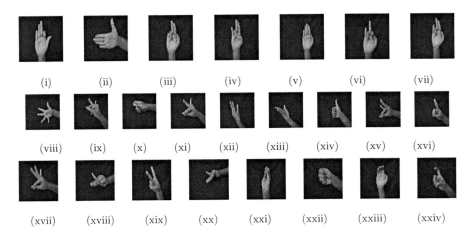

Fig. 5. Three groups of gestures at first-level. Class 1 with (i) Aarala, (ii) Ardhachandra, (iii) Ardhapataka, (iv) Mayura, (v) Pataka, (vi) Shukatunda, (vii) Tripataka. Class 2 with (viii) Alapadma, (ix) Bhramara, (x) Kapitta, (xi) Katakamukha, (xii) Padmakosha, (xiii) Sandamsha, (xiv) Shikara, (xv) Simhamukha, and (xvi) Suchi. Class 3 with (xvii) Hamsaye, (xviii) Hansapakshika, (xix) Kartarimukha, (xx) Mrigashirsa, (xxi) Mukula, (xxii) Mushti, (xxiii) Sarpashirsa, and (xxiv) Tamrachuda.

to assume that for the same gesture the starting point will be the same. The matching of two shapes now reduces to the problem of matching two feature sequences.

Let V and U be two such sequences of lengths n and m respectively. Using concepts from dynamic programming, a cost function $Cost(i, j)$ is defined as the cost of matching the ith element V_i of the first sequence with the jth element U_j of the second sequence. It is defined as $Cost(i, j) =$

$$\min\{Cost(i, j{-}1), Cost(i{-}1, j), Cost(i{-}1, j{-}1)\}+Weight(V_i)\times V_i-Weight(U_j)\times U_j.$$

(2)

In order to match the sequences V and U, one needs to compute the cost over their entire length. It is evident that the value of the cost function determines the similarity (or dissimilarity) between the shapes of different hand gestures. There are, however, possibilities of error due to the irregularities in the skeleton structure from the hands of different people with different textural properties.

After the second-level of processing only four of the gesture types remained incorrectly recognized. These images are presented in Fig. 6, with the upper row indicating the misclassified gesture and the lower depicting the corresponding category with which it has been mistaken. It can be easily observed that each of these image pairs, *viz.* those in lying in the same column of the figure, are highly similar to the human eye. Hence the performance of the designed system, on the whole, can be claimed to be reasonably good.

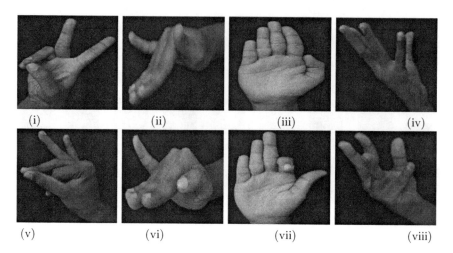

Fig. 6. Dance gestures still misclassified at the second-level. (i) Kartarimukha, (ii) Bhramara, (iii) Mrigashirsa, and (iv) Hansapakshika, were mistaken with (v) Pataka, (vi) Aarala, (vii) Sandamsha, and (viii) Padmakosha, respectively.

4   Conclusion

E-learning would be a very practical, simple and cost-effective mode of imparting training in the nuances of traditional dance across the globe, thereby assimilating the cultural divide between the Orient and the West. We aim to make the computer act as a teacher to correct the dance gestures for the purpose of promoting classical Indian dance across the world. A simple and new two-level decision making system has been designed for recognizing the gestures of Bharatanatyam, a well-known Indian classical dance form. It has been shown to be scale-, translation- and rotation-invariant while recognizing various single-hand gestures of a dancer.

Acknowledgement. This research was carried out while Ms. D. Hariharan was in ISI on an IASc-INSA-NASI summer fellowship.

References

1. Acharya, T., Ray, A.K.: Image Processing Principles and Applications. John Wiley, New Jersey (2005)
2. Freeman, W.T., Roth, M.: Orientation histograms for hand gesture recognition. In: Proceedings of IEEE International Workshop on Automatic Face and Gesture Recognition, pp. 296–301. IEEE, Los Alamitos (1994)
3. Verma, M.: Bharatanatyam: Origin, Styles and Techniques, chap, pp. 295–315. Abhishek Publishers, Hastas (2009)

Spatiotemporal Approach for Tracking Using Rough Entropy and Frame Subtraction

B. Uma Shankar and Debarati Chakraborty

Machine Intelligence Unit,
Indian Statistical Institute, Kolkata 700 108, India
uma@isical.ac.in, debarati.earth@gmail.com

Abstract. We present here an approach for video image segmentation where spatial segmentation is based on rough sets and granular computing and temporal segmentation is done by consecutive frame subtraction. Then the intersection of the temporal segmentation and spatial segmentation for the same frame is analyzed in RGB feature space. The estimated statistics of the intersecting regions is used for the object reconstruction and tracking.

Keywords: Segmentation, rough entropy, rough sets, video tracking.

1 Introduction

In computer vision, detection and tracking of moving object is very important task. The application of object tracking in video sequences has been studied over the years. In this task there are many types of uncertainties and ambiguities which is making this task a difficult problem. Over the years researchers have been trying to improve the accuracy and speed in detection and tracking [5,11,13]. Granular computing is a young, though rapidly expanding, and important area of research. Granular computing is the process of dealing with the information granules which is collection of some points similar in some respect and dealing with which proves to be effective for human cognition. In case of image and video processing, proper recognition of each part of the image from the available information is a well known problem where partitioning (segmentation or classification) of data set plays a very important role. Understanding of an image depends on efficient partitioning. So, granular computing can be useful for image processing. According to Butenkov [2] the most important problem regarding granulation of an image is different kind of input information. Here we propose to use Rough entropy as proposed by Pal *et al.* [7], incorporating some modification for video image segmentation and object detection for tracking in video image sequences.

In the present article we have proposed an approach for video image segmentation based on granular computing and rough sets. The contributions of the article are as follows : (i) We propose a method for detection of granule adaptively. Here we decompose the image into homogeneous granules using quadtree decomposition, which takes into account the spatially connectedness and gray level similarity, both. (ii) Then a general form of rough entropy function is defined, which can

S.O. Kuznetsov et al. (Eds.): PReMI 2011, LNCS 6744, pp. 193–199, 2011.

be computed with the estimated parameter (base of the logarithm) for the function for a given image. This function can be modified according to the choice of the user and the amount of noise present in the image. (iii) After having spatial segmented image frame, we have used a frame subtraction method to collect the temporal information of the frame [13]. Then we have considered the intersection of the spatial and temporal segmented regions in RGB feature space and calculated the mean and maximum deviation of the intersecting region (region/object statistics). Then we reconstruct the object in the current frame by using this statistics within a predefined tracker, thus tracked the required object. (iv) As here rough entropy based segmentation is applied on video sequence, we have the advantage of exploiting the threshold in the previous frame for the searching in the limited range over a window around the threshold in the previous frame, for detection of threshold in the current frame. Thus our proposed method is fast, efficient, accurate and different from the existing methods.

2   Rough Sets for Image Segmentation

In the process of image segmentation normally we have to take care of noise present in the image. Due to which there is always ambiguities in gray level as well as in spatial. These ambiguities lead to uncertainty in image segmentation. To demarcate the objects of interest in the image properly, we segment the image into some homogeneous regions. These regions put together normally provides the object of interest. Theory of Rough sets [8] has recently become a popular mathematical framework for granular computing. The focus of rough set theory is on the ambiguity caused by limited discernibility of objects in the domain of discourse [4,6]. Its key concepts are those of object 'indiscernibility' and 'set approximation'. The set approximation capability of rough sets is exploited in this investigation [7,12] to formulate an entropy measure, called rough entropy, quantifying the uncertainty in an object-background image. This has been done by defining an image as a collection of pixels and the equivalence relation induced partition as pixels lying within each non-overlapping (homogeneous in some respect) windows over the image. With this definition the roughness of various transforms (or partitions) of the image can be computed using image granules. Maximization of the said rough entropy measure minimizes the uncertainty arising from vagueness of the boundary region of the object and ambiguity caused by gray level. Therefore, for a given granulation the threshold for object-background classification can be obtained through its maximization. This has been successfully demonstrated in [3,7,12]. Here we propose a method of selecting the appropriate granules based on the local gray level distribution. The granules are obtained by quadtree decomposition of the image frame [3]. Therefore the granule sizes will not be same. We define the size of the ith granule as: $Size\_of\_granule_i = m_i \times n_i$. Incorporating these changes in the algorithm for computation of Rough entropy is presented below. The Rough entropy (as defined in [7,12]) has been modified to make it more general and presented in equation (1).

$$RE_T = -\frac{BASE}{2}\left[R_{O_T}\ log_{(BASE)}\left(R_{O_T}\right) + R_{B_T}log_{(BASE)}\left(R_{B_T}\right)\right] \qquad (1)$$

Here, we consider the R_{O_T} as the roughness of the object and R_{B_T} is the roughness of the background with respect to the threshold "T". Therefore the combined (object and background) entropy computed will be RE_T. In the present experiment we choose the $BASE$ as "10" which we found to be suitable for most of the images.

To detect the object, we describe the method of object enhancement/ extraction based on the principle of minimizing the roughness of both object and background regions, i.e., maximizing RE_T. One can compute for every T the RE_T of the image, representing the background and object regions $(0, \cdots, T)$ and $(T + 1, \cdots L - 1)$, respectively, and select the one for which RE_T is maximum. In other words, select $T^* = \arg \max_T RE_T$, as the optimum threshold to provide the object background segmentation.

We have taken the range of the data within a granule (or window) as the measure for the quadtree decomposition. This range should be less than a predefined threshold (say, $RT = half\ of\ the\ interquartile\ range$), which helps in finding the granules that are homogenous in gray level as well as spatially connected. Incorporating proposed changes in the algorithm for computation of the Rough entropy, assuming that the object is in the upper side of the histogram, is given below [3].

Algorithm for Threshold Selection: Following is the algorithm for efficient implementation of the aforesaid methodology for selecting T^* as defined above. Let max_gray and min_gray be the maximum and minimum gray level values of the image, respectively. Let the ith granule ($granule_i$) represent a window of $m_i \times n_i$ pixels. Let total number of granules be $total\_no\_granule$ and the size of the ith granule is $Size\_of\_granule_i = m_i \times n_i$.
Initialize: Four integer arrays namely $object\_lower$, $object\_upper$, $background\_lower$, $background\_upper$ each of size $(max\_gray$ - min_gray +1) to zero.

Step 1: for $i = 1$ to $total\_no\_granule$
    $max\_granule_i$ = maximum gray value of pixels in $granule_i$
    $min\_granule_i$ = minimum gray value of pixels in $granule_i$
    (a) for $max\_granule_i \leq j \leq max\_gray$
       $object\_lower(j) = object\_lower(j) + Size\_of\_granule_i$
    (b) for $min\_granule_i \leq j \leq max\_gray$
       $object\_upper(j) = object\_upper(j) + Size\_of\_granule_i$
    (c) for $min\_gray \leq j \leq min\_granule_i$
       $background\_lower(j) = background\_lower(j) + Size\_of\_granule_i$
    (d) for $min\_gray \leq j \leq max\_granule_i$
       $background\_upper(j) = background\_upper(j) + Size\_of\_granule_i$
Step 2: for $l = min\_gray$ to max_gray
    $object\_roughness(l) = 1$ - $[\ object\_lower(l)/object\_upper(l)]$
    $background\_roughness(l) = 1$-$[background\_lower(l)/background\_upper(l)]$
    IF $object\_roughness(l) \leq \frac{1}{(BASE)}$, then $object\_entropy(l) = 1$,
    ELSE $object\_entropy(l) = [object\_roughness(l)\ \log_{BASE}(object\_roughness(l))]$,
    AND
    IF $background\_roughness(l) \leq \frac{1}{(BASE)}$, then $background\_entropy(l) = 1$,

ELSE *background_entropy(l) =*
$$[background\_roughness(l) \, log_{BASE} \, (background\_roughness(l))]$$
$$Rough\_entropy(l) = - \left[\frac{BASE}{2}\right] \times [\, object\_entropy(l) + background\_entropy(l)].$$
Step 3: *Threshold*(optimal) $= \arg \max_{l} [rough\_entropy(l)].$ ◊

Remark: Given the *max_gray* and *min_gray* values, the computation of rough entropy (and hence the algorithm) requires only a single scan of pixels in the image, since max_granule$_i$ and min_granule$_i$ are computed exactly once for each granule. Therefore the computational complexity of the algorithm is same as that of histogram computation and scanning throughout all the gray level ranged from *min_gray* to *max_gray* is required only for the first incoming frame, after that we will scan only through those gray levels which are in the neighborhood of the optimum threshold value in the previous frame.

3   Detection and Tracking in Video Sequence

A video normally consists of a sequence of color images or gray level images. In the present work we have used both. We converted the color image to gray level image for spatial segmentation. Then perform the tracking by acquiring some temporal information and merging it with the spatial one. After that using the color information the object statistics is estimated in the RGB space. This object statistics helped in reconstruction of object in the RGB space, hence the detected and tracked properly and accurately.

The above proposed segmentation methods works with gray level images. Therefore, for implementing it on color images we convert the color image into a gray level image by using the relation $Y = 0.3R + 0.59G + 0.11B$ (see [10]), where R, G & B has its usual meaning and Y is the obtained gray level image. After conversion of color images into gray level the above proposed rough entropy for object segmentation is applied. After that we have performed a temporal segmentation approach to gather more information and reconstruct the object properly. This segmentation is done by estimating the change between two consecutive frames. Here we subtracted the current frame from the previous frame (i.e., if the object is in upper side of the histogram and the reverse one if the object is in the lower side). Then the noise in the difference image is eliminated by estimating a suitable threshold. The pixels greater than the threshold value will be treated as the part of the object in the temporal segmented image. After performing both the segmentations (i.e., spatial and temporal), we have combined the two results to reconstruct the object properly.

Target Localization and Tracking: At first reference model from the reference frame is marked. After having the two (spatial and temporal) segmented images of the current frame, we have taken the intersection of the two segments to get the object region which is common to both. The statistics of this common region is estimated in the RGB feature space. Here, we used the mean(mn) and maximum deviation (max_dev) of this intersecting region in the RGB feature space. Note, here the common region should have at least 5% of the object region, otherwise we can skip and take the next frame as the current frame. After having these information, we need to place a tracker on the current frame within which the pixels will be scanned. We have considered a rectangular tracker of size 1.25 times in both the direction (i.e., in width and length) of the size of the object in the previous frame, with location of center is the same as that was in the previous frame. That is we assume that after changing the location from the previous frame to the current frame, the whole object should be within the area considered by the tracker. Then we start to scan each pixel within the tracker, which belong to either spatial or temporal segmented region, and if the difference between a pixel and the mean (mn) in RGB feature space (i.e., all the three features) are less than the max_dev then that pixel will be considered as the part of the object otherwise as background.

Algorithm for Tracking: The object detection and tracking starts with selection of the tracker [5,11,13]. So we first decide the tracker. Here we have considered a rectangle tracker, which completely covers the object that will be tracked. Then the following are the steps to detect the object and tracking of the object. We first select the first (or reference frame), then we will segment it into regions and mark the object of interest.

Step 1: Convert the input color image (I) to gray level image (Y).

Step 2: If necessary, enhance the image for better contrast.

Step 3: Apply the Rough entropy based image segmentation. (Note: Here, the advantage of considering a window around the threshold in the previous frame is exploited for segmentation of video images in the current frame.)

Step 4: Do a temporal segmentation by subtraction between two consecutive frames and eliminate the noise from subtracted image by thresholding.

Step 5: The intersection of the two segmented images are considered in RGB feature space and the mean (mn) and maximum deviation(max_dev) of those points are calculated in the same feature space.

Step 6: Then design a rectangular tracker which is 1.25 times (in both directions) of the object size in the reference frame (i.e., in the previous frame) and place the center of the tracker at the location which is the center of the tracker in the previous frame.

Step 7: For every pixel (x, y) within the tracker, which belong to either spatial or temporal segmented region, do the following
IF $|f_R(x, y) - mn| < max\_dev_R$ and $|f_G(x, y) - mn| < max\_dev_G$ and $|f_B(x, y) - mn| < max\_dev_B$ then $F(x, y) = I(x, y)$ ELSE $F(x, y) = 0$ (here, F is the detected object image).

Step 8: Repeat the Steps 1 to 7, for all the frame in the video sequence for tracking of the moving object.

4   Results and Discussion

Here, we have considered two video sequences for demonstration of the proposed approach. These are *Baggage Detection Sequence* of *i-LIDS dataset* supplied to *AVSS-2007* [1] and *Surveillance Scenario Sequence* data used in PETS-2000 [9].

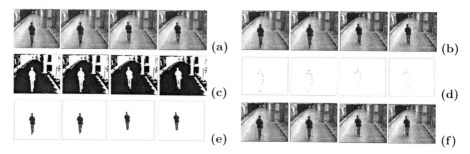

Fig. 1. The *Baggage Detection Sequence* from AVSS-2007, the results on frame nos. 1297, 1298, 1313 and 1314 are presented here: (a) Original images, (b) After converting to gray level, (c) Spatial Segmented regions, (d) Temporal Segmented regions, (e) Reconstructed object, and (f) Tracked object in the color images.

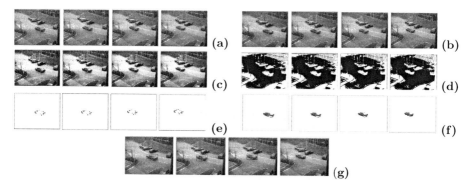

Fig. 2. The *Surveillance Scenario Sequence* from PETS-2000, the results on frame nos. 137, 141, 145 and 150 are presented here: (a) Original images, (b) After converting to gray level, (c) After enhancing by histogram equalization, (d) Spatial Segmented regions, (e) Temporal Segmented Regions, (f) Reconstructed Object, and (g) Tracked object in the color images.

The sample images for the two video sequences are shown in Figs. 1(a) and 2(a), respectively. After converting into gray level the two sets of sample images are presented in Figs. 1(b) and 2(b), respectively. The *Surveillance scenario Sequence* images are enhanced (histogram equalized) for better contrast, before segmentation, the sample images are presented in Fig. 2(c). And after spatial segmentation of the two sequences the results are presented in Figs. 1(c) and 2(d), respectively.

The proposed object detection and tracking is implemented and tested on various video sequences. For the demonstration of the results, we considered two sequences and four frames from each sequence and presented with the intermediate results obtained during various steps of processing. This provides the complete picture of the proposed methodology. The results obtained after temporal segmentation is shown in Fig. 1(d) and Fig. 2(e), respectively. The reconstructed object is shown in Fig. 1(e) and Fig. 2(f). These obtained color images along with the tracker are presented in the Figs. 1(f) and 2(g), respectively, for the two sequences. From the demonstrated results it can be seen that the moving objects are detected and tracked properly. The enhancement has helped in detection of object (car) accurately, in Fig. 2. However in the *Baggage Detection Sequence* the available contrast was sufficient to detect the moving person properly. We compared with another thresholding based method and found to be performing better, but results can not be presented here due to limitation on length of the paper.

5 Conclusions

Here we have proposed rough entropy and frame difference based spatiotemporal segmentation for object detection and tracking in a video sequence. We proposed a method of image granulation using quad-tree decomposition and a modification in the rough entropy function for object and background segmentation and then combined it with the results obtained after frame subtraction based temporal segmentation to reconstruct the moving object in the video sequence. The rough entropy based thresholding in window around the threshold detected in the previous frame makes it efficient. The proposed method has been tested on various video sequences, and the initial experimental results are very satisfying. The proposed method uses spatial as well as temporal information and gives an accurate and efficient algorithm.

References

1. AVSS-2007: Fourth IEEE Int. Conf. Adv. Video & Signal Based Surveillance (2007)
2. Butenkov, S.A.: Granular computing in image processing and understanding. In: Proc. IASTED Int. Conf. Artificial Intelligence and Applns, pp. 811–816 (2004)
3. Chakraborty, D., Shankar, B.U.: Rough entropy based object segmenatation and tracking in video images. Tech. Rep. MIU/TR/-02/10, MIU, ISI (2010)
4. Hassanien, A.E., et al.: Rough sets and near sets in medical imaging: A review. IEEE Trans. on Information Technology in Biomedicine 13(6), 955–968 (2008)
5. Maggio, E., Cavallaro, A.: Video Tracking - Theory and Practice. Wiley, Chichester (2010)
6. Pal, S.K., Peters, J.F. (eds.): Rough Fuzzy Image Analysis: Foundations and Methodologies. Chapman & Hall/CRC (2010)
7. Pal, S.K., Uma Shankar, B., Mitra, P.: Granular computing, rough entropy and object extraction. Pattern Recognition Letters 26(16), 2509–2517 (2005)
8. Pawlak, Z.: Rough Sets: Theoretical Aspects of Reasoning about Data. Kluwer Academic Publishers, Norwell (1992)
9. PETS-2000: IEEE Int. WS Perfor. Evaluation of Tracking and Surveillance (2000)
10. Pratt, W.K.: Digital Image Processing. John Wiley & Sons, New York (1991)
11. Tekalp, A.M.: Digital Video Processing. Prentice Hall, New Jersey (1995)
12. Shankar, B.U.: Novel classification and segmentation techniques with application to remotely sensed images. In: Peters, J.F., Skowron, A., Marek, V.W., Orłowska, E., Słowiński, R., Ziarko, W.P. (eds.) Transactions on Rough Sets VII. LNCS, vol. 4400, pp. 295–380. Springer, Heidelberg (2007)
13. Yilmaz, A., Javed, O., Shah, M.: Object tracking: A survey. ACM Computing Surveys 38(4), 1264–1291 (2006)

OSiMa: Human Pose Estimation from a Single Image

Nipun Pande and Prithwijit Guha

TCS Innovation Labs, New Delhi
{nipun.pande,prithwijit.guha}@tcs.com

Abstract. Human upper body pose estimation plays a key role in applications related to human-computer interactions. We propose to develop an avatar based video conferencing system where a user's avatar is animated following his/her gestures. Tracking gestures calls for human pose estimation through image based measurements. Our work is motivated by the pictorial structures approach and we use a 2D model as a collection of rectangular body parts. Stochastic search iterations are used to estimate the angles between these body parts through Orientation Similarity Maximization (OSiMa) along the outline of the body model. The proposed approach is validated on human upper body images with varying levels of background clutter and has shown (near) accurate pose estimation results in real time.

1 Introduction

Human pose estimation through visual sensing has potential applications in the fields of human computer interfaces and motion capture for realistic 3D animations, biomechanical analysis, robot control and visual surveillance (activity recognition). Our work is aimed at developing an avatar based video conferencing system where a user's avatar in a virtual meeting room is animated following his/her gestures. Here, we present a part of this work where we restrict ourselves to the pose estimation of *human upper body* only while assuming a single person in the view. Tracking human poses through image based measurements has two major sub-divisions – first, the (near) accurate estimation of the human pose from the very first image and second, re-estimation of the pose from the subsequent images using the previous instant's pose as a prior. Here, we focus on the necessary first step, i.e. human upper body pose estimation from a single image to initialize the gesture tracking procedure.

Existing literature on human body pose estimation is vast [1], most of which assume the existence of a background model to handle the scene clutter. However, we restrict our discussions to approaches aimed at retrieving human upper body pose from single images only (i.e. no temporal information). Ramanan describes an iterative parsing process to estimate the pose using region based body models e.g. color histogram to refine the body part positions [2]. An approach following this is [3]. Here an upper body detector is used with GrabCut to determine the foreground area followed by parsing to fit a pictorial structure

S.O. Kuznetsov et al. (Eds.): PReMI 2011, LNCS 6744, pp. 200–205, 2011.

model. An interesting work which takes into account natural shape and pose variations is Contour People [4]. Here segmentation of the scene into foreground and background regions is done and a shape deformation model is trained using 3D SCAPE model.[5] express a subset of model parameters as kernel regression estimates from a learned sparse set of exemplars. An exemplar based pose representation called "poselet" is used in [6]. To detect the presence of each poselet a classifier is trained for each poselet using standard linear SVM and the histogram of oriented gradients.

We have adopted a human body model consisting of rectangular body parts (head, torso and lower/upper arms) with circles at joints to render a smooth body contour in the image plane. A Haar feature based frontal face detector [7] is used to localize the head in the image. The dimensions of the different body parts are computed from the head (or face) width using available anthropometric ratio data [8]. Now, considering the head position as pivot, several body model outlines can be rendered by varying the angles between the body parts. This provides us with a set of straight lines on the image plane since the body model is a constructed as a collection of rectangles where each body part is a set of two parallel lines e.g. the two edges of the arm or the torso. The similarity between the image gradient directions and the line orientation along such an edge of some body part is defined as a measure for localizing the body part. An objective function is defined by combining these orientation similarity measures which is maximized through stochastic search iterations [9]. Existing approaches have employed color constancy assumptions, limb detectors along with body part connectivity constrained maximization for pose estimation [2,10,3]. Thus, these approaches are heavily dependent on clothing color constancy, hand skin exposure and are far from real time execution. On the other hand, we have used only the face detector and localized the body parts using image gradient measurements (and hence independent of color constancy assumptions) one by one thereby reducing the dimensionality of the domain of stochastic search leading to real time performance (Section 2). The proposed approach is experimentally validated on a number of human upper body images containing varying levels of background clutter (Section 3). Finally, we conclude in Section 4 and outline the future extensions.

2   Upper Body Pose Estimation

Figure 1 shows the $2D$ human body model (with body part dimensions and joint angles) used in our work. We assume the human body to be near vertical for our particular application domain and hence assume the joint angle between torso and the vertical axis of the head (θ_t) to lie in the interval $[-\frac{\pi}{12}, \frac{\pi}{12}]$. The joint angles made by the left (θ_{lua}) and right (θ_{rua}) upper arms with the torso axis are assumed to vary in the interval of $[0, \pi]$. However, considering the possibilities of roll in the upper arms, the angles between the lower and upper arms at left (θ_{le}) and right (θ_{re}) elbows are assumed to lie in the interval of $[\frac{\pi}{4}, \frac{7\pi}{4}]$. The image co-ordinates of the joints viz. J_{th} (between head and torso), J_{tl} (between torso and left upper arm), J_{tr} (between torso and right upper arm), J_{le} (left elbow) and J_{re} (right elbow) can be obtained in terms of the body part dimensions and the joint angles using forward kinematics computations [11].

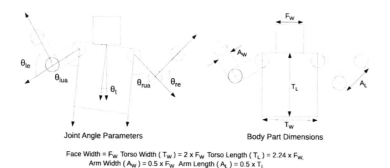

Joint Angle Parameters   Body Part Dimensions

Face Width = F_W Torso Width (T_W) = 2 x F_W Torso Length (T_L) = 2.24 x F_W,
Arm Width (A_W) = 0.5 x F_W Arm Length (A_L) = 0.5 x T_L

Fig. 1. The human upper body model – The face, torso and arms are modeled as rectangles with circular regions at the joints to generate the effect of smooth contour of the body. The relative length/width of the body parts are derived from anthropometric ratio data [8] in terms of the face width.

Consider the case of localizing a certain body part, e.g. the right upper arm. We first fix the joint co-ordinate (J_{tr}) of the base of the right upper arm. For different values of the joint angles (θ_{rua}), we compute the extent of alignment of the image edges with the outlines of the rectangle representing the right upper arm through an "orientation similarity measure". The final orientation of the right upper arm is obtained at the angle maximizing this measure (Figure 2(a)) and is described next.

Let $m(u, v)$ and $\theta(u, v)$ be the respective gradient magnitude and (unsigned[1]) direction computed from the image pixel position $I(u, v)$. Let the unsigned orientation of a body part outline at the position (x, y) is $\phi(x, y)$. We define the orientation similarity measure as $\gamma(u, v; x, y) = 1 - \frac{|\theta(u,v) - \phi(x,y)|}{\pi}$ ($\theta(u, v)$ and $\phi(x, y)$ being unsigned orientations $\gamma(u, v; x, y) \in [0, 1]$). However, computation of orientation similarity on a single pixel has two major disadvantages – first, the concerned image pixel (u, v) may have a week gradient magnitude indicating lesser importance of the gradient direction; and second, the computation might be susceptible to noise if computed only on a single pixel. Thus, we propose to use a magnitude and position weighted similarity measure ($osm(x, y, r)$) computed over a circular neighborhood $N(x, y, r)$ of radius r around the pixel position (x, y) defined as,

---

[1] In case of unsigned directions, a line at an angle of $-\alpha$ with the is considered to be equivalent to the line making an angle $\pi - \alpha$ with respect to the same reference axis. The unsigned orientations are thus considered to lie in the interval $[0, \pi)$.

$$osm(x, y, r) = \frac{\sum_{(u,v)\in N(x,y,r)} \gamma(u, v)d(u, v; x, y, r)m(u, v)}{\sum_{(u,v)\in N(x,y,r)} d(u, v; x, y, r)m(u, v)} \qquad (1)$$

$$d(u, v; x, y, r) = \begin{cases} 1 - \frac{(u-x)^2+(v-y)^2}{r^2}; & (u-x)^2 + (v-y)^2 \le r^2 \\ 0; & \text{Otherwise} \end{cases} \qquad (2)$$

where $d(u, v; x, y, r)$ is the position weighing function. Let $\mathcal{C}$ be the set of contour pixels of some body part (e.g. the edges of the arms or the torso). We define the net orientation similarity measure $OSM_r(\mathcal{C})$ over the contour $\mathcal{C}$ as $OSM_r(\mathcal{C}) = \frac{1}{|\mathcal{C}|} \sum_{(x,y)\in\mathcal{C}} osm(x, y, r)$ where $|\mathcal{C}|$ is the number of pixels in the contour $\mathcal{C}$. We next describe the process of maximizing OSM through stochastic search iterations.

The head region is located first using a Haar feature based frontal face detector [7]. This provides us with F_w from which the body part dimensions are computed using the anthropometric ratio data [8]. This also provides us with the image co-ordinates of the head-torso joint (J_{th}). We perform 3 stochastic search iterations with a population size of 5 angles to estimate the head-torso joint angle θ_t. Localizing the torso provides us with the joint co-ordinates J_{tl} and J_{tr}. To localize the left upper/lower arms, we execute 3 stochastic search iterations with a population size of 10 two-angle $(\theta_{lua}, \theta_{le})$ tuples. A Similar procedure is adopted for localzing the right upper/lower arm. Thus, we need a total of $15 + 30 + 30 = 75$ OSM computations per image at an average of 11.33 frames per second.

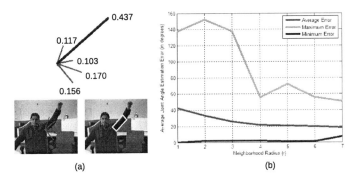

(a)   (b)

Fig. 2. Orientation Similarity Maximization. (a) The right upper arm modeled as rectangles are placed in different orientations and the direction (shown in blue) maximizes the orientation similarity measure. (b) The minimum/average/maximum joint angle estimation errors for varying sizes of the neighborhood radius. Note that there is not much change in error for values of r exceeding 5.

3   Results

We have performed our experiments on a set of (unrelated) single person (upper body) images downloaded from the web and an image sequence recorded in the laboratory settings with varying levels of background clutter. A set of 20 images from this data set are ground truthed through manual measurement of the joint angles. We note that the accuracy of pose estimation directly depends on the neighborhood radius r in the computation of OSM. For a certain value of r, we compute the average joint angle estimation error over 5 joint angles from 20 images. Figure 2(b) shows the maximum, average and minimum estimation errors for $1 \leq r \leq 7$. Significant changes in the error is not observed for $r > 5$. However, higher values of r lead to larger number of computations and hence we fix $r = 5$ for our experiments. The results of human upper body pose estimation on 12 images from the data set are shown in figure 3.

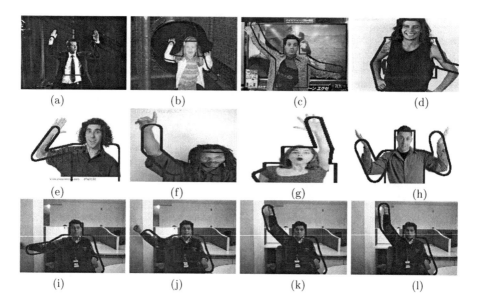

Fig. 3. Experimental results performed on a set of human upper body images with varying levels of background clutter. Although the joint angles are estimated accurately, the human body outline is not fitted tightly on some cases on account of person to person variations in anthropometric data and loose clothing. Failures in localizing in right lower arm is observed in (b) due to loose clothing and strong background clutter (red pipe); where as in (d) the reason is the deviation from the average anthropometric ratio data.

4   Conclusion

We have presented a methodology for human upper body pose estimation from a single image using a $2D$ model (motivated by pictorial structures approach). We have defined an orientation similarity measure to align the body parts (torso and arms) in images. A Haar feature based frontal face detection followed by stochastic search iterations are used to localize the body parts while maximizing the proposed orientation similarity measure computed along the outlines of the body parts. In contrast to the existing works in human pose estimation from single images, we have achieved high accuracy while performing in real time.

The current work has only focused on the pose estimation from a single image and is a necessary first step towards tracking the pose of the user. We identify the future extensions in two directions. First, the current work is to be extended to tracking where the stochastic search space is further reduced using temporal information. However, it is still not fully possible to estimate the accurate 3D pose from single view information. The second possible extension will be in the direction of combining the image based orientation similarity measurements with depth data obtained from range sensors to avail accurate 3D pose.

References

1. Moeslund, T., Hilton, A., Kruger, V.: A survey of advances in vision-based human motion capture and analysis. Computer Vision and Image Understanding 104, 90–126 (2006)
2. Ramanan, D.: Learning to parse images of articulated bodies. In: Neural Information Processing Systems (NIPS), pp. 1129–1136 (2006)
3. Ferrari, V., Marin-Jimenez, M., Zisserman, A.: Pose search: Retrieving people using their pose. In: IEEE Conference on Computer Vision and Pattern Recognition, pp. 1–8 (2009)
4. Freifeld, O., Weiss, A., Zuf, S., Black, M.J.: Contour people: A parameterized model of 2d articulated human shape. In: IEEE Conference Computer Vision and Pattern Recognition, pp. 639–646 (2010)
5. Sapp, B., Jordan, C., Taskar, B.: Adaptive pose priors for pictorial structures. In: IEEE Conference Computer Vision and Pattern Recognition, pp. 422–429 (2010)
6. Yang, W., Wang, Y., Mori, G.: Recognizing human actions from still images with latent poses. In: IEEE International Conference on Computer Vision and Pattern Recognition, pp. 2030–2037 (2010)
7. Viola, P., Jones, M.: Robust real-time face detection. International Journal on Computer Vision 57, 137–154 (2004)
8. NASA: Anthropometric Source Book, vol. 2. Springfield VA (1978)
9. Spall, J.C.: Introduction to Stochastic Search and Optimization: Estimation, Simulation and Control. Wiley-Interscience, Hoboken (2003)
10. Ferrari, V., Marin-Jimenez, M., Zisserman, A.: Progressive search space reduction for human pose estimation. In: IEEE Conference on Computer Vision and Pattern Recognition, pp. 1–8 (2008)
11. Craig, J.J.: Introduction to Robotics Mechanics and Control. Pearson Education Inc., London (2003)

Scene Categorization Using Topic Model Based Hierarchical Conditional Random Fields

Vikram Garg, Ehtesham Hassan, Santanu Chaudhury, and M. Gopal

Department of Electrical Engineering, IIT Delhi, India
gargvikram07@gmail.com, hassan.ehtesham@gmail.com,
santanuc@ee.iitd.ernet.in, mgopal@ee.iitd.ac.in

Abstract. We propose a novel hierarchical framework for scene categorization. The scene representation is defined by latent topics extracted by Latent Dirichlet Allocation. The interaction of these topics across scene categories is learned by probabilistic graphical modelling. We use Conditional Random Fields in a hierarchical setting for discovering the global context of these topics. The learned random fields are further used for categorization of a new scene. The experimental results of the proposed framework is presented on standard datasets and on image collection obtained from the internet.

Keywords: Scene categorization, Latent dirichlet allocation, Conditional random fields.

1 Introduction

In this paper we propose a novel hierarchical framework for scene categorization. The framework utilizes the latent concept information for scene categorization. The concept extraction is performed by latent topic modelling at the local patch level. For similar scenes, the organization of these topics represents similar graphical structure. We learn the graphical structure of these topics across various scene categories through a probabilistic graphical model. The framework recognizes a new scene based on the learned graphical structures.

The natural scene categorization is a widely researched problem in content based image retrieval. The fundamental problem here lies in identifying different objects and understanding their interaction for scene definition. However, the object extraction in a natural scene requires robust segmentation algorithm. Topic modelling based methods provide efficient solution to this problem. These methods represent the image through mixture of latent topics. The topic assignment effectively performs the semantic image segmentation in feature space. In the related works, Yamaguchi and Maruyama have used topic distribution based image representation for image classification [4]. The topic modelling is performed by Probabilistic Latent Semantic Analysis using the SIFT key points based bag-of-words model. In another work, Ergul and Arica perform the pLSA based topic analysis of the image at multiple scales [5]. The topic modelling by

S.O. Kuznetsov et al. (Eds.): PReMI 2011, LNCS 6744, pp. 206–212, 2011.

PLSA shows biased topic assignment towards training images. The LDA incorporates the document distribution for topic learning and provides robust topic modelling framework. [7] have learned a LDA based hierarchical model for image categorization while [11] have employed a generative hierarchical LDA model for unsupervised discovery of topic hierarchies in visual objects. The recent work Wang et al. have applied supervised LDA for discovering the latent topics [13]. The contextual relationship between the topics is important semantic information for scene categorization. [12] has used a generative Bayesian network to utilize the position and expected appearance of object parts while in the present work, we propose a novel scene categorization framework by exploiting the topic level contextual relationship in a natural image. The framework extracts the local patch level topics in scene using LDA. The probabilistic graphical models exhibit excellent capability to learn the sequential data. The recent works have extensively applied Conditional Random Fields (CRFs) based graphical model for Image classification [9][10][13]. However discovering the contextual relationship between the topics by CRFs is not yet explored. Our work presents a novel approach in this direction by applying hierarchical CRF to discover the topic based global context for scene recognition.

The organization of the paper is as follows: The section 2 presents scene representation patch level topic modelling of the image. The section 3 presents the proposed framework for scene categorization. The section 4 presents the experimental results. Finally we conclude and present perspective of our work.

2   Feature Based Image Representation Using LDA

The visual content representation forms important step for a scene understanding. The bag-of-words model has been the preferred approach for natural image representation. Using the model, image representation is defined as the distribution of local features properties. The SIFT based descriptor provide an efficient approach to extract the local image features [1]. The descriptor is computed as set of local orientation histograms centred at key-points obtained by multi-scale analysis of the image. The SIFT descriptor extracts dense points at the boundaries, and image segments having sharp changes. Whereas the smooth segments are represented by sparse key points. The bag-of-words model in this case represents the image by a biased representation leaving significant amount of visual information unutilized. For example, a landscape scene having sky tree and building will get biased distribution of key-points near tree and building. Therefore we follow grid based approach for extracting the local image features. The approach covers all the segment of the image and assigns uniform weight to all the segments. Using the image patches in the grid, bag-of-words model is generated. The bag-of-words representation is used to generate the image representation by discovering the latent topics in a scene. The topics here represent the semantic entity which defines the distribution of various image patches in the latent space. The Latent Dirichlet allocation is applied to extract the topic distribution over the scene image collection. The LDA is defined as a generative probabilistic model for collections of documents [2]. In the context of topic modelling, the documents could be a text corpus or image collection. The local image properties are defines as words of the image document. The documents are represented as as random mixtures over latent topics, where each topic is characterized by a distribution over words. The generative process for each document **w** in the collection D is defined as follows:

- Select $N = Poisson(\zeta)$
- Choose $\theta = Dirichlet(\alpha)$
- For each word w_n of the document **w**: select a topic $z_n = Multinomial(\theta)$, select w_n from multinomial probability $p(w_n|z_n; \beta)$

The inference step includes the computation of posterior distribution of the hidden variables for a given document.

$$p(\theta, \mathbf{z}|\mathbf{w}, \alpha, \beta) = \frac{p(\theta, \mathbf{z}, \mathbf{w}|\alpha, \beta)}{p(\mathbf{w}|\alpha, \beta)} \tag{1}$$

The intractable form of the above distribution is because of complex prior distributions. For the practical applications approximate inference based methods. The LDA assigns a topic distribution to each image patch (figure (1 shows topics on face image using color based bag-of-words model). The scene representation is defined as the vector of topic distributions which is subsequently used for categorization.

 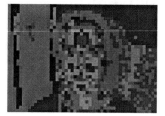

Fig. 1. Topic assignment over image patches

3   Hierarchical Framework for Scene Categorization Using CRFs

The figure (2) shows the proposed hierarchical framework for scene categorization. The initial step performs the topic analysis of the image at local patch level. The step performs robust topic assignment to all the image patches. The topic assignment essentially performs the coarse semantic segmentation of scene for the given number of topics [8]. The spatial context between these topics can be efficiently learned by a probabilistic graphical model. The CRFs are an efficient tool for such problems. However, the long range contextual dependencies in the semantic segmentation cannot be captured by a simple graphical model. Therefore, we introduce category specific graphical model (CRFs). We train category specific CRFs using the patch-ground-truth, and assign semantic labels over the latent topics. The exact notion of the category specific CRFs is the smoothening of latent topics by supervised learning. The top level CRFs learns the structure of the contextual graph belonging to each category of images.

The CRFs is a discriminative modelling tool for segmenting and labelling the sequential data [3]. The CRFs work under the maximum entropy principle and observe the features as sequence data. Consider X the random variable over data sequences to be labelled and Y the random variable for the corresponding label sequences. Using the fundamental theorem of random fields, joint distribution over the label sequence Y given X is defined as

$$p_\theta(y|x) \propto exp(\sum_{e \in E,k} \lambda_k f_k(e, y|_v, x) + \sum_{v \in V,k} \mu_k g_k(v, y|_e, x)) \qquad (2)$$

V and E represent the vertices and edges of graph G, such that label sequence Y is indexed by the vertices of G. Here x represents a data sequence, y represents a label sequence, and $y|_S$ is set of components of y associated with the vertices in sub-graph S. The function f_k defines the input dependent evidences and g_k g_k represents the pair-wise coupling labels of sequence data. The parameter estimation problem determines the parameters $\theta = (\lambda_1, \mu_1, \lambda_2, \mu_2, ...)$ by the maximization of log-likelihood objective as

$$O(\theta) = \sum_{i=1}^{N} log \ p_\theta(y^i|x^i) \propto \sum_{x,y} p(x,y) log \ p_\theta(y|x) \qquad (3)$$

For category specific CRFs, graph G is represented by function f_k as the likelihood of image patch having i^{th} topic and function g_k represents smoothness prior to encourage the neighbouring image patches to obtain same label. Function f_k has the form as $f_k(e, y|_v, x) = x_k \delta(y, l_k)$, δ is the Kronecker delta and k represents the indices of parameter set from θ and l_k is the label of the patch for kth parameter set. The smoothness prior g_k is defined as $\delta(y_1, l_k)\delta(y_2, l_k)$. It is clear that the smoothness prior is independent of patch features. The top level CRF learns the graphical structure of latent topics for image collection using the sequence of semantic labels assigned from first level CRFs.

A new image is categorized by topic assignment using patch level image features. The topic level representation of the image is supplied to the entire category specific CRFs. For N scene categories, the top level CRF receives N semantic graphs for the new image. For each semantic graph, the top level CRF assigns marginal probability distribution. The final category assignment for the new scene is done as the label corresponding to maximum marginal probability for all the semantic graphs.

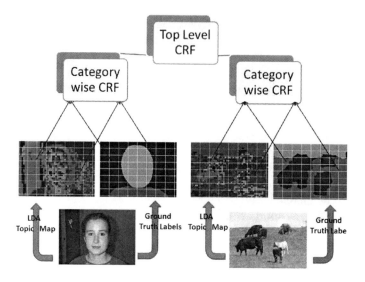

Fig. 2. Hierarchical framework for scene categorization

4 Experimental Results and Discussion

We have evaluated the proposed framework on standard MSRC dataset[1], Caltech 101 dataset[2] and image collection from internet. The MSRC dataset is applied for training our system as the dataset contains pixel level ground-truth. The pixel-level ground truth is converted to patch-level by majority voting. The training set consists of 30 randomly selected corresponding to 9 super categories {Bicycle, Building, Car, Cattle, Cow, Face, Sheep, Plane, and Tree}. The image set (270 images) have been normalized to 105X154. The images patches are detected by overlaying a grid of 15 × 22, therefore giving 330 patches of 7X7. The bag-of-words model is generated by clustering the image patches from 5 randomly selected training images corresponding to each category. The topic assignment over complete set of image patches is done by learning a LDA for 10 semantic concepts. We use topic modelling toolbox provided by Steyers and Griffiths [14] for topic modelling. The probabilistic graphical modelling is performed by CRF implementation provided by Sarawagi [15]. Initially the framework has been tested for the same set of training images. We have compared our results with the best case accuracy preseted in [8] in table 1. The second evaluation the proposed framework is performed using the Caltech 101 dataset images. The experiment evaluates the proposed framework for unseen images belonging to two categories. The experiment evaluates the robustness of the proposed framework as the dataset is primarily prepared for object recognition problem. The experiment is performed by randomly selecting 30 images corresponding to *Plane*

---

[1] http://research.microsoft.com/en-us/projects/objectclassrecognition/
[2] http://www.vision.caltech.edu/Image_Datasets/Caltech101/

Table 1. Recognition accuracy for training image set

Category	Bicycle	Building	Car	Cattle	Cow	Face	Sheep	Plane	Tree	Average
Presented Acc.	90	96	93	90	93	96	96	96	96	94
Best Average Acc. [8]	94	77	73	N.A.	86	99	N.A.	73	71	82

*categories with N.A. were not availabe in [8].

Table 2. Recognition accuracy for image set from Caltech dataset

Category	Plane	Face
Accuracy	67	45

Fig. 3. Evaluation Images and assigned category

and 30 images corresponding to *Face* category. The results are presented in the table 2. The third evaluation of the proposed framework is performed on image collection obtained from internet. The collection contains 30 images belonging to 6 training categories. The average accuracy of 60% is achieved. The image with their final category assignment are shown in the figure 3. The results (figure 3) establish the robustness of the proposed framework as testing images belong to variety of domains. The category assignment for these images can be easily verified by close observation. The results show that our framework efficiently utilizes semantic information of the scene for categorization.

5   Conclusion

A novel framework for scene categorization is presented. The patch level latent topics extracted by LDA have been used for scene representation. A novel application of hierarchical CRFs is demonstrated for scene recognition. The two-layer CRFs performs topic level smoothening at first layer and subsequently perform the scene recognition by learning the spatial context of different topics. The experimental evaluation on standard dataset and images obtained from the internet validate the efficiency and robustness of the proposed framework.

References

1. Lowe, D.G.: Object recognition from local scale-invariant features. In: Proceedings of the International Conference on Computer Vision, vol. 2, pp. 1150–1157 (2000)
2. Blei, D.M., Ng, A.Y., Jordan, M.I.: Latent Dirichlet allocation. Journal of Machine Learning Research, 993–1022 (2003)
3. Lafferty, J., McCallum, A., Pereira, F.: Conditional random fields: Probabilistic models for segmenting and labelling sequence data. In: Proceedings of the International Conference on Machine Learning, pp. 282–289. Morgan Kaufmann, San Francisco (2001)
4. Yamaguchi, T., Maruyama, M.: Image categorization by a classifier based on probabilistic topic model. Pattern Recognition (2008)
5. Ergul, E., Arica, N.: Scene Classification Using Spatial Pyramid of Latent Topics. In: International Conference on Pattern Recognition (2010)
6. Fei, L.F., Persona, P.: A Bayesian Hierarchical Model for Learning Natural Scene Categories. In: IEEE Conference on Computer Vision and Pattern Recognition (2005)
7. Wang, C., Blei, D., Fei, L.F.: Simultaneous Image Classification and Annotation. In: IEEE Conference on Computer Vision and Pattern Recognition (2009)
8. Passino, G., Patras, I., Izquierdo, E.: Latent Semantic Local Distribution for CRF-based Image Semantic Segmentation. In: British Machine Vision Conference (2009)
9. Zhong, P., Wang, R.: Learning Conditional Random Fields for Classification of Hyperspectral Images. In: IEEE Transactions on Image Processing (2010)
10. Wang, X., Liu, X., Shi, Z., Shi, Z., Sui, H.: Voting Conditional Random Fields for Multi-label Image Classification. In: International Congress on Image and Signal Processing (2010)
11. Sivic, J., Russell, B.C., Zisserman, A., Freeman, W.T., Efros, A.A.: Unsupervised discovery of visual object class hierarchies. In: Computer Vision and Pattern Recognition (2008)
12. Sudderth, E.B., Torralba, A., Freeman, W.T., Willsky, A.S.: Learning Hierarchical Models of Scenes, Objects, and Parts. In: IEEE International Conference on Computer Vision (2005)
13. Wang, Y., Gong, S.: Conditional Random Field for Natural Scene Categorization. In: British Machine Vision Conference (2007)
14. Steyvers, M., Griffiths, T.: Matlab Topic Modelling Toolbox Version 1.3.2
15. Sarawagi, S.: CRF package, http://crf.sourceforge.net/

Uncalibrated Camera Based Interactive 3DTV

M.S. Venkatesh, Santanu Chaudhury, and Brejesh Lall

Department of Electrical Engineering, IIT Delhi, India
msvenka@gmail.com, santanuc@ee.iitd.ac.in, brejesh@ee.iitd.ac.in

Abstract. In this paper we propose a novel architecture for an interactive 3DTV system based on multiple uncalibrated cameras placed at general positions. The signal representation scheme proposed is compatible with the standard multi view coding framework making it amenable to using existing coding and compression algorithms. The proposed scheme also fits naturally to the concept of *true* 3DTV viewing experience where the viewer can choose a novel viewpoint based on the contents of the scene.

Keywords: Interactive 3DTV, Uncalibrated cameras, Plane sweeping, Depth map.

1 Introduction

In this paper we propose a novel architecture for interactive 3DTV which enables a viewer to choose a 3D view of the scene based on scene content. We assume that the scene is captured by multiple uncalibrated cameras in general positions. We use a statistical learning method to automatically detect scene constraints that are then used to calibrate the cameras as well as provide orientation information to generate depth maps for each view. The advantage of our signal representation scheme is that it is compatible with the standard Multi View Coding framework of video plus depth[3,4]. This enables the direct application of the existing coding and compression algorithms. The scene orientation information can be easily embedded in the meta-data part of the signal. The novelty of our architecture is that the scene orientation information allows the user to select different viewpoints based on the scene content to interactively generate novel 3D views at the receiver's end. Typical applications of our methodology is in 3D viewing of outdoor scenes like monuments, urban buildings etc. The user can interactively specify which part of the monument he wants to view in 3D. The typical characteristics of such scenes like orthogonal planes assist in automatic detection of scene constraints and orientations.

3DTV is considered as the next step in enhancing the user viewing experience. A *true* 3DTV is supposed to give a 3D view of the scene as well allow the user to choose different viewpoints of the scene. Our approach fits naturally in this context. The video plus depth format [3] in which each video is accompanied by a per pixel depth data is considered most suitable for generation of high quality 3D views as well as intermediate view synthesis at the receiver. To generate

S.O. Kuznetsov et al. (Eds.): PReMI 2011, LNCS 6744, pp. 213–219, 2011.
© Springer-Verlag Berlin Heidelberg 2011

the depth map, camera calibration information is required. Camera calibration from scene constraints and generation of depth maps from stereo and multi view images are topics that have been extensively studied in computer vision [15]. In our methodology we automatically discover these scene constraints and exploit them for the calibration of the cameras. Plane sweeping algorithms like [5,6,7] outperform standard stereo matching algorithms for generation of depth map in presence of oblique structures in scenes. The directions along which the planes are swept are determined by analysis of a sparse or dense set of 3D points. In our approach, the scene classification step itself gives us the orientations used for plane sweeping. The dense depth map thus generated is then used to generate existing as well as interpolate novel stereo views of the scene without performing an explicit 3D reconstruction using a Depth Image Based Rendering technique [4]. These novel views are specified by new camera viewpoints with respect to the existing viewpoints.

Some work has been done regarding user interaction in 3DTV [12]. The authors in [13] allow for view switching, frozen moment and view sweeping at the receiver end. The novelty of our approach is that it allows the user to choose the viewpoint based on scene content to be able to view novel 3D views of parts of the scene as well as arbitrary novel views of the complete scene. Automatically extracting the scene constraints and orientations from the images to use them for camera calibration is also a novelty of our work. Another novelty of our method is that we obtain the direction of family of planes and the confidence measures from the scene classification [1] step itself.

In section 2, we present the basic outline of our system architecture. Section 3 outlines the novel view viewpoint selection and the DIBR technique used to synthesize novel views. In section 4 we present experimental results and discussions followed by the conclusion and future work.

2   System Architecture

We illustrate our proposed methodology with an example of a building as shown in the figure 1. Images are taken from multiple uncalibrated cameras placed at general positions. Then classifier of [1] is used to classify the image and identify the horizontal(green) and vertical (red) planes. This constraint is then used to calibrated the cameras. The orientations of scene (indicated by arrows) are also recovered along with their confidence measures. This is used to generate a depth map. The orientation information along with the video plus depth forms the signal representation. At the receiver end the user interactively chooses certain parts of the scene to view and then the orientation information in that part of the image is used to obtain the novel 3D views of the scene.

2.1   Scene Classification

The authors in [1] classify the outdoor scene into geometric classes that depend on the orientation of the particular object in the scene based on statistical

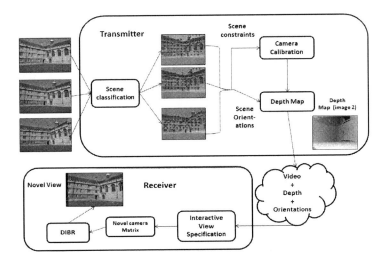

Fig. 1. Outline of the proposed architecture

learning. They classify an image into planar vertical regions (facing left, center, or right), ground (horizontal) regions, sky and non planar regions (porous and solid) without using any calibration information. A confidence measure is also associated with each class.

2.2   Camera Calibration

Many methods exist for calibrating the cameras using the scene constraints. Specifically, we use the orthogonality of the vertical and horizontal planes obtained from the scene classification step for calibration. We obtain automatic point correspondences from SIFT features [1] and filter mismatches by using epipolar constraint [2]. Using these point correspondences, we obtain a projective reconstruction and then impose the constraints of the absolute quadric as well as the scene constraints to upgrade it to a Euclidean one [15,2].

2.3   Obtaining the Dense Depth Map

We follow an approach closely related to [5]. Here every pixel is assigned a label which indicates which plane it belongs to and an energy function which penalizes abrupt changes in surface normals is minimized [8,9,10,11]. The confidence measures obtained in the scene classification step is incorporated into the cost function.

---

[1] http://www.vlfeat.org/
[2] http://www.csse.uwa.edu.au/~pk/research/matlabfns/

The normal to the planes (vertical planes and ground plane) are used to define "k" families of parallel planes Π_{ki} given by $n_k^T X + d_{ki} = 0$ where $d_{ki} \in [d_{min}, d_{max}]_k$ The range $[d_{min}, d_{max}]$ for each of the plane families are obtained empirically. For each of the planes we find the 3x3 homography induced between two images r and s [15].

This homography is used to warp the other images onto an image I_r for whom depth map is to be generated. Then for warped image I_w, we obtain a cost for every pixel (x, y) in the image I_r, for each of the planes Π_{ki} as

$$cost(x, y, \Pi_{ki}) = \sum_{(p,q)\in N} |I(x - p, y - q) - I_w(x - p, y - q)| - w * log(F(\Pi_{ki}))$$

where w is a weight factor determined by experiments and $F(\Pi_{ki})$ is the probability that the pixel belongs to the k^{ith} plane obtained from the confidence measures generated after the scene classification step. N is defined neighbourhood of the pixel taken to be 3x3.

We formulate an energy function similar to [5] and we find out the depth $Z(x, y)$ of each pixel (x, y) of image I_r. The depth map thus obtained is used in virtual view synthesis which is explained in the next section.

3   Virtual View Synthesis

A new virtual camera is defined by its camera parameters R_v, K_v, and C_v [15]. Given an image I_r whose camera parameters are R_r, K_r and C_r and its corresponding depth map Z_r, The image I_v is generated by [4]

The resulting virtual views have holes which are the results of either erroneous depth values or due to truncation of the pixel positions. To fill these holes, the homography corresponding to the nearest non zero plane label is computed and using it, the pixel value is transferred from the given image.

3.1   Interactively Choosing the Viewpoint

The user interactively selects a part of the scene through an interface like a mouse pointer or remote. For instance if a wall is selected, the virtual camera has to be placed such the wall is fronto parallel. The orientation of this part of the image obtained after scene classification gives the direction in which the camera has to be rotated. Once the direction is determined, the following steps are followed.

1. A rotation matrix R' is obtained by choosing an angle θ bounded by the angle between the normal to the plane (wall) and normal to the principal plane of the camera and a small translation t' is chosen such that the virtual camera undergoes a little translation so as to keep the view within the image bounds. This Euclidean transformation is used to get the destination camera centre C_v and rotation matrix R_v.

2. K_v is chosen to be the same as K_r. The destination camera matrix
   $P_v = K_v R_v [I \mid -C_v]$
3. The new camera matrices are chosen by interpolation between the camera
   P_r and P_v with interpolation parameter $\lambda \in [0..1]$ as
   $C_\lambda = (1 - \lambda)C_r + \lambda C_v$
   $R_\lambda = slerp(R_r, R_v, \lambda)$
   $P_\lambda = K_\lambda R_\lambda [I \mid -C_\lambda]$
   where $slerp$ refers to spherical linear interpolation.
4. To generate stereo pairs, the shift sensor algorithm [4] is used.

4   Results and Discussions

We illustrate the various steps of our proposed architecture on two standard data sets Wadham College and Merton College.[3] For Wadham College data set, we generate intermediate image sequences when the user wants to look at the left wall. For the Merton data set we generate sequences when the user wants to look at the right wall. Both of these sequences are generated from the image no 2 of each data set. As the rotation increases, the rendering quality decreases. This is because of erroneous depth values and also due to mis-classification.

The average 2D re projection errors (in pixel) from the camera calibration are shown below

Data Set	camera 1	camera 2	camera 3
Merton College	0.410790	0.343800	0.311718
Wadham College	0.405233	0.398542	0.295823

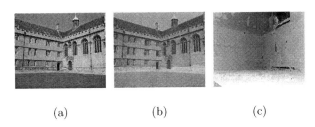

(a)   (b)   (c)

Fig. 2. Fig (a) shows image 2 of Wadham sequence. Fig (b) shows its scene classification and Fig (c) is the depth map extracted.

The stereo views were generated and were displayed on a samsung 3D LED TV. Subjective rendering quality measures were assigned based on a scale of 1 to 5 in increasing order of quality. The subjective scores are shown below. The sequences refer to the intermediate stereo views generated.

---

[3] http://www.robots.ox.ac.uk/~vgg/data2.html

Fig. 3. Some of the synthesized image sequences of Wadham when the user wants to "look" at the left wall

(a)   (b)   (c)

Fig. 4. Fig (a) shows image 2 of Merton sequence. Fig (b) shows its scene classification and Fig (c) is the depth map extracted.

Fig. 5. Some of the synthesized image sequence of Merton when the user wants to "look" at the right wall

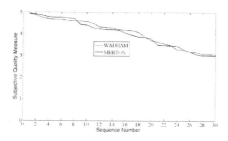

Fig. 6. Subjective Quality

5   Future Work and Conclusion

In this paper we have proposed a novel architecture for interactive rendering of outdoor scenes for 3DTV. The interactive selection of viewpoints based on scene content offers a different approach to novel view synthesis. We have worked with images. The extension to videos is straight forward. As part of the future work , we would also like to investigate the possibility of detecting objects in the scene and allow the user to view these objects interactively. Another extension would be in switching between groups of cameras and allowing the user to view objects captured by different groups.

Acknowledgement

This work was in part supported by the Department of Science and Technology, Govt. of India. (SR/S3/EECE/0006/2010). We would also like to thank Ayesha Chaudhary for valuable feedback.

References

1. Hoeim, D., Efros, A.A., Hebert, M.: Geometrical context from a single image. In: ICCV (2005)
2. Svoboda, T., Martinec, D., Pajdla, T.: A convenient multi-camera self-calibration for virtual environments. PRESENCE: Teleoperators and Virtual Environments 14(4), 407–422 (2005)
3. Muller, K.: View Synthesis for Advanced 3D Video Systems. EURASIP Journal on Image and Video Processing 2008, article ID 438148, 11 pages (2008), doi:10.1155/2008/438148
4. Fehn, C.: A 3D-TV Approach Using Depth-Image-Based Rendering (DIBR). In: Proceedings of 3rd IASTED Conference on Visualization, Imaging, and Image Processing, September 2003, pp. 482–487 (2003)
5. Gallup, D., Frahm, J.M., Mordohai, P., Yang, Q., Pollefeys, M.: Real-Time Plane-Sweeping Stereo with Multiple Sweeping Directions. In: CVPR (2007)
6. Micusik, B., Kosecka, J.: Multi-view Superpixel Stereo in Urban Environments. International Journal of Computer Vision 89(1) (2010)
7. Sinha, S.N., Steedly, D., Szeliski, R.: Piecewise Planar Stereo for Image-based Rendering. In: ICCV (2009)
8. Boykov, Y., Veksler, O., Zabih, R.: Efficient Approximate Energy Minimization via Graph Cuts. IEEE TPAMI 23(11) (November 2001)
9. Kolmogorov, V., Zabih, R.: What Energy Functions can be Minimized via Graph Cuts? IEEE TPAMI 26(2), 147–159 (2004)
10. Boykov, Y., Kolmogorov, V.: An Experimental Comparison of Min-Cut/Max-Flow Algorithms for Energy Minimization in Vision. IEEE TPAMI 26(9), 1124–1137 (2004)
11. Delong, A., Osokin, A., Isack, H.N., Boykov, Y.: Fast Approximate Energy Minimization with Label Costs. In: CVPR (2010)
12. Fehn, C., De La Barr, R., Pastoor, S.: Interactive 3-DTV.Concepts and Key Technologies. Proceedings of IEEE 94(3) (March 2006)
13. Lou, J., Cai, H., Li, J.: A RealTime Interactive MultiView Video System. In: MM 2005 Proceedings of the 13th ACM conference on Multimedia (2005)
14. Kubota, A., Smolic, A., Magnor, M., Tanimoto, M., Chen, T., Zhang, C.: Multiview Imaging and 3DTV. IEEE Signal Process. Mag. 24(6), 10–21 (2007)
15. Hartley, R., Zisserman, A.: Multiple view geometry in Computer Vision, March 2004. Cambridge University Press, Cambridge (2004)

Author Identification in Bengali Literary Works

Suprabhat Das and Pabitra Mitra

Department of Computer Science and Engineering
Indian Institute of Technology Kharagpur
West Bengal, Pin - 721302, India
{suprabhat,pabitra}@cse.iitkgp.ernet.in

Abstract. In this paper, we study the problem of authorship identification in Bengali literary works. We considered three authors namely Rabindranath Tagore, Bankim Chandra Chattopadhyay and Sukanta Bhattacharyay. It was observed that simple unigram and bi-gram features along with vocabulary richness were rich enough to discriminate amongst these authors. Although results degraded slightly when training set size was considerably small. For larger training set, a classification accuracy of above 90% for unigram feature and almost 100% for bi-gram feature was achieved. Results could be improved further by using more sophisticated features.

Keywords: Stylometry, authorship attribution, Bengali literary works, unigram, bi-gram.

1 Introduction

Stylometry is the study of the unique linguistic styles and writing behaviors of individuals. Author identification is one of the important problems in stylometrics and it can be seen as a single-label multi-class text categorization problem. It has many academic and literary applications, like author verification, plagiarism detection, genre classification etc. It has legal applications too, like forensic linguistics, detection of genuine confessions. In the last few years it has successfully been applied to broader areas, ranging from blogs, forums, wikis, email, chat and other forms of digital content to music and fine-art paintings.

Stylometry has been studied on English for long time. It was started by Mendenhall [1], in the 19th century, with his work on the plays of Shakespeare. He had reported few authorship attribution method by some characteristic curves, based on sentence length counts and word length counts. It was followed by some statistical studies by Zipf [2] and Yule [3] in the first half of 20th century. One of the most influential works in authorship attribution was done by Mosteller and Wallace [4] on the authorship of 'The Federalist Papers' (a series of articles published in 1787-88, written by John Jay, Alexander Hamilton and James Madison). They had employed Bayesian statistical analysis on a small set of function words such as prepositions, conjunctions and articles as discriminators. Burrows [5,6] first applied multivariate analysis (MVA) and principle

S.O. Kuznetsov et al. (Eds.): PReMI 2011, LNCS 6744, pp. 220–226, 2011.

components analysis (PCA) on some function words for attributing authorship, followed by Binongo & Smith [7], Holmes et al. [8] and also by Burrows [9,10] to resolve many authorship problems. Kjell et al. [11] used neural networks and k-nearest neighbors on character n-grams, whereas Baayen et al. [12] used only neural networks on the syntax of the sentence. Juola & Baayen [13] used cross entropy as classification method on function words. Zhao & Zobel [14] reported a different distance measure on function words and part-of-speech (POS) tags. Stamatatos [15] used support vector machines (SVM) on character n-grams to classify English and Arabic news corpus. Koppel et al. [16] reported approach of authorship attribution for thousands of candidate authors.

In Bengali no major work has been done. Mansur et al. [17] proposed an n-gram based text categorization algorithm and also analyzed its efficiency on few Bengali newspaper corpus. We make initial attempts on a collection of documents consisting of Rabindranath Tagore, Bankim Chandra Chattopadhyay and Sukanta Bhattacharyay. We found that using unigram and bi-gram words and vocabulary richness we could achieve a satisfactory result.

The rest of this paper is organized as follows: Section 2 gives a brief overview of stylometric features we have used for evaluation. In Section 3, we focus on the classifier algorithm. The details of the collection are given in Section 4. Section 5 describes the details of the experimental results. In Section 6, we have concluded about our evaluation result and also about some other features that can be included in future works for the betterment of our research work.

2   Stylometric Features

A wide variety of relevant features have been reported in many earlier works. Stamatatos [18] has surveyed on almost all stylometric features used till now and modern authorship attribution methods. There are different types of stylometric features to quantify the writing style. Character features are the simplest and basic stylometric feature, as this can be applied in any natural language without any prior knowledge about the language. Lexical features are most commonly used feature for authorship attribution problems whereas syntactic and semantic features are used for more advanced and complicated tasks like POS tagging, parsing. Application-specific features are used for some specialized applications, like lemmatizer or specialized dictionaries.

Feature selection and extraction is one of the biggest challenges in authorship attribution problems. Many types of features are often combined to select respective feature set. Some lexical features are used to build the feature set in our experiment. In first stage of the experiment, unigram words and vocabulary richness are taken as the feature set to quantify the authorship. A relevant tokenizer is used to segment text into tokens or unigram words. Punctuation marks, white space, mathematical notations and special characters are taken as separator to the consecutive tokens. Bi-gram words are nothing but combination of two consecutive unigram words. Bi-gram words and vocabulary richness are combined to use as feature set in the next stage of the experiment. For example, the test sentences "John is a good boy. He likes to play cricket" would be composed of following unigram and bi-gram words, tabulated in Table 1.

Table 1. Unigram and bi-gram words from the test sentence

Unigrams	John, is, a, good, boy, He, likes, to, play, cricket
Bi-grams	John is, is a, a good, good boy, boy He, He likes, likes to, to play, play cricket

Vocabulary richness is a measurement of diversity of the vocabulary of a text. It is defined by $\frac{V}{N}$, where V is number of unique tokens and N is the total number of tokens of the text. An example of calculating vocabulary richness from the test sentences "Tom always harasses Jerry. Jerry is intelligent. Mickey is friend of Jerry" is given in the Table 2.

Table 2. Frequencies of unigram words and corresponding vocabulary richness

Unigram words	Frequencies	Vocabulary richness
Tom	1	$\frac{1}{12}$
always	1	$\frac{1}{12}$
harasses	1	$\frac{1}{12}$
Jerry	3	$\frac{1}{4}$
is	2	$\frac{1}{6}$
intelligent	1	$\frac{1}{12}$
Mickey	1	$\frac{1}{12}$
friend	1	$\frac{1}{12}$
of	1	$\frac{1}{12}$

3   Classifier Algorithm

Classification is the next important step after feature selection. Test documents are attributed to a known author from the set of candidate authors. Starting from very basic statistical measures, like distance measure, Naive Bayes classifier, some advanced measures like neural networks, k-nearest neighbors are also used to quantify authorship. In our experiment, we have used a probabilistic classification method, which is variation of Naive Bayes classification method [19]. In our experiment, classification feature is measured by a simple probability metric

$$P_A = \frac{S_A}{F_A \times T} \tag{1}$$

where, P_A is probability of test document being written by Author A, S_A is total occurrence of test document tokens in training set of Author A, F_A is total frequency of tokens in training set of the corresponding author and T is total number of tokens in test document.

In the above formula, T, being a constant denominator, will have no effect on the probability P_A in a relative scale. The division by T will normalize the probability for documents of different size and it will be effective only when we would like to find out the more likely document for a candidate author from a set of test documents.

To calculate the probability metric of a test document for a candidate author, we need to find out correct tokens from test and training document first. In our experiment, initially unigram words are considered as the feature set for classification. In this step, all unigram words are taken as individual tokens to calculate the simple probability metric P_A mentioned earlier. In the next step, bi-gram words are considered as the feature set for classification and all the bi-gram words are taken as individual tokens to calculate the same.

The metric measures the probability of a test document being written by a candidate author. This classification metrics are calculated for all candidate authors to quantify the authorship of a test document. A test document is attributed to a candidate author, if the classification metric for that author is greater than that of other candidate authors.

Suppose there are N candidate authors $(A_1, A_2, \ldots, A_N)$ for a test corpus. A test document is attributed to a candidate author by using the following formula.

$$\text{If } (P_{Ai} > P_{Aj}) \text{ for } j = 1 \text{ to } N \text{ and } i \neq j$$
$$\text{Test document is attributed to author } A_i$$

The authorship attribution approaches are distinguished in mainly two ways according to the extraction of authors' style cumulatively or individually. In profile-based approach, all the training texts per author are concatenated in a file. On the other hand, each training text is individually represented in separate files for instance-based approach. We prefer instance-based approach for attributing authorship from the test collection.

4   Details of the Collection

We used test collection of Bengali documents consisting of Rabindranath Tagore and Bankim Chandra Chattopadhyay's novels and Sukanta Bhattacharyay's poems in our experiment. There are total 36 documents (13 novels by Rabindranath Tagore (RT), 14 novels by Bankim Chandra Chattopadhyay (BCC) and 9 poems by Sukanta Bhattacharyay (SB)) in the complete set of test collection. Detailed statistics of the test collection are given in the Table 3.

Table 3. Detailed statistic of the test collection

Author Name	Genre	No. of Docs	Total No. of Tokens	No. of Unique Tokens
Rabindranath Tagore (RT)	Novel	13	594757	40626
Bankim Chandra Chattopadhyay (BCC)	Novel	14	381119	36016
Sukanta Bhattacharyay (SB)	Poem	9	1093	691

There are several steps in our experiment. In each steps, we choose 30%, 50% and 70% documents respectively from the collection of each candidate authors as training data set. The selection of training data set was done randomly. The remaining documents are attributed on the basis of this training data set. Division of the whole corpus into training set and test set are tabulated in Table 4, when 30%, 50% and 70% of data from individual authors are used for training.

Table 4. Division of whole corpus into training set and test set when 30%, 50% and 70% data used for training

Author Name	No. of docs	30% data used for training		50% data used for training		70% data used for training	
		No. of docs in training set	No. of docs in test set	No. of docs in training set	No. of docs in test set	No. of docs in training set	No. of docs in test set
RT	13	4	9	7	6	9	4
BCC	14	4	10	7	7	10	4
SB	9	3	6	4	5	6	3
Total	36	11	25	18	18	25	11

5   Experimental Results

All the experiments have been done on the test corpus, mentioned earlier. In the first stage of our experiment, unigram words and vocabulary richness are taken as feature set. In this case at first 30% of documents from the collection of each candidate authors are selected randomly to train the classifier. So out of total 36 documents, 11 documents are selected for training set. Remaining 25 documents are classified on the basis of the training data set. In the next step, 50% and 70% data from each author are used for training and remaining documents are classified. Lastly each and every document is classified when all the remaining documents are used as training set. The percentages of correctly classified documents, taken unigram words as the feature set, are tabulated in the Table 5.

Table 5. Rate of correctly classified documents when unigram words are taken as feature set

No. of docs in training set	No. of docs to be classified	No. of correctly classified docs	Percentage of correct classification
11(30% from each candidate authors)	25	19	76.00%
18 (50% from each candidate authors)	18	14	77.78%
25 (70% from each candidate authors)	11	9	81.82%
35 (All the documents except the test case)	36	33	91.67%

From this observation, it is seen that the percentage of correct classification is improved with increasing size of training set.

In the next stage, same thing has been done except the selection of feature set. As feature set, bi-gram words and vocabulary richness are selected in this case. Similarly 30%, 50% and 70% data from individual authors is trained to classify remaining documents on the basis of new feature set. Then every document is classified separately when remaining documents are used as training data. In this case, there was a huge improvement in the percentage result. The percentages of correctly classified documents, taken bi-gram words as the feature set, are tabulated in the Table 6.

Table 6. Rate of correctly classified documents when bi-gram words are taken as feature set

No. of docs in training set	No. of docs to be classified	No. of correctly classified docs	Percentage of correct classification
11(30% from each candidate authors)	25	25	100.00%
18 (50% from each candidate authors)	18	18	100.00%
25 (70% from each candidate authors)	11	11	100.00%
35 (All the documents except the test case)	36	36	100.00%

From this observation, it is obvious that as a feature set, bi-gram words are good enough to classify authorship of the Bengali corpus. Even a small size of training data can quantify the authorship of test documents correctly.

6 Conclusion

It is evident from our experiment that the attribution results strongly depend on the size of test corpus as well as proper feature set selection. In our experiments, only some lexical features are taken into account. Using some advanced feature or combination of some features on Bengali test collection may result better. Many machine learning techniques like principle components analysis (PCA), support vector machines (SVM) can be used to quantify authorship of Bengali test documents in recent future. The application of the well-known tf-idf (term frequency*inverse document frequency) [20] principle for unigram and bi-gram features can also be useful. The main problem with the resource is the unavailability of Bengali literary works by different authors. The three candidate authors in our experiment (RT(1861-1941), BCC(1838-1894) and SB(1926-1947)) belong to distinct generation. So there are some differences in their vocabulary and style. The availability of many documents by different candidate authors from the same age and of similar style will validate the effectiveness of this method. In general, this result can be generalized to classify blog writers, detect plagiarism in Bengali also.

References

1. Mendenhall, T.C.: The characteristic curves of composition. Science ns-9, 237–246 (1887)
2. Zipf, G.K.: Selected Studies of the Principle of Relative Frequency in Language. Harvard University Press, Cambridge (1932)
3. Yule, G.U.: The Statistical Study of Literary Vocabulary. Cambridge University Press, Cambridge (1944)

4. Mosteller, F., Wallace, D.L.: Inference and Disputed Authorship: The Federalist. Addison-Wesley, Reading (1964)
5. Burrows, J.F.: Word patterns and story shapes: The statistical analysis of narrative style. Literary and Linguistic Computing 2, 61–70 (1987)
6. Burrows, J.F.: Not unles you ask nicely: The interpretative nexus between analysis and information. Literary and Linguistic Computing 7, 91–109 (1992)
7. Binongo, J.N.G., Smith, M.W.A.: The application of principal component analysis to stylometry. Literary and Linguistic Computing 14, 445–466 (1999)
8. Holmes, D.I., Robertson, M., Paez, R.: Stephen crane and the new-york tribune: A case study in traditional and non-traditional authorship attribution. Computers and the Humanities 35, 315–331 (2001)
9. Burrows, J.F.: Delta: a measure of stylistic difference and a guide to likely authorship. Literary and Linguistic Computing 17, 267–287 (2002)
10. Burrows, J.F.: The englishing of juvenal: Computational stylistics and translated texts. Style 36, 677–699 (2002)
11. Kjell, B., Woods, W.A., Frieder, O.: Information retrieval using letter tuples with neural network and nearest neighbor classifiers. In: IEEE International Conference on Systems, Man and Cybernetics, Vancouver, BC, vol. 2, pp. 1222–1225 (1995)
12. Baayen, H., Van Halteren, H., Tweedie, F.: Outside the cave of shadows: Using syntactic annotation to enhance authorship attribution. Literary and Linguistic Computing 11, 121–132 (1996)
13. Juola, P., Baayen, H.: A controlled-corpus experiment in authorship identification by cross-entropy. Literary and Linguistic Computing 20, 59–67 (2005)
14. Zhao, Y., Zobel, J.: Searching with style: Authorship attribution in classic literature. In: Proceedings of 30th Australasian Conference on Computer Science, vol. 62, pp. 59–68 (2007)
15. Stamatatos, E.: Author identification: Using text sampling to handle the class imbalance problem. Information Processing & Management 44, 790–799 (2008)
16. Koppel, M., Schler, J., Argamon, S., Messeri, E.: Authorship attribution with thousands of candidate authors. In: Proceedings of the 29th ACM SIGIR, pp. 659–660. ACM Press, New York (2006)
17. Mansur, M., UzZaman, N., Khan, M.: Analysis of n-gram based text categorization for bangla in a newspaper corpus. In: Proceedings of 9th International Conference on Computer and Information Technology, Dhaka, Bangladesh (2006)
18. Stamatatos, E.: A survey of modern authorship attribution methods. Journal of the American Society for Information Science and Technology 60, 538–556 (2009)
19. Mitchell, T.M.: Machine Learning. McGraw-Hill, New York (1997)
20. Manning, C., Raghavan, P., Schutze, H.: Introduction to Information Retrieval. Cambridge University Press, Cambridge (2008)

Finding Potential Seeds through Rank Aggregation of Web Searches

Rajendra Prasath* and Pinar Öztürk

Department of Computer and Information Science (IDI)
Norwegian University of Science and Technology (NTNU)
Sem Sælands Vei 7-9, NO - 7491, Trondheim, Norway
{rajendra,pinar}@idi.ntnu.no

Abstract. This paper presents a potential seed selection algorithm for web crawlers using a *gain - share scoring* approach. Initially we consider a set of arbitrarily chosen tourism queries. Each query is given to the selected N commercial Search Engines (SEs); top m search results for each SE are obtained, and each of these m results is manually evaluated and assigned a relevance score. For each of m results, a *gain - share* score is computed using their hyperlinks structure across N ranked lists. *Gain* score of each link present in each of m results and a portion of the gain score is propagated to the *share* score of each of m results. This updated *share* scores of each of m results determine the potential set of seed URLs for web crawling. Experimental results on tourism related web data illustrate the effectiveness of the proposed seed selection algorithm.

Keywords: Web Crawlers, Seed Selection, Link Data, Relevant Judgment.

1 Introduction

Online web documents, specifically in textual form, are massively growing and popular search engines process (SEs) these documents using the Information Retrieval (IR) components namely: *crawler*, *indexer* and *searcher* as shown in Figure 1. For a given set of Uniform Resource Locators(URL), the crawler fetches the content of the URLs, the indexer facilitates a comprehensive storage of the extracted content from each URL, through indexes, and the searcher estimates similarity between a user query and the indexed documents. Since searching the web upon each query would require processing millions of pages, a searcher makes the search on a smaller subset of documents collected through *seed URLs* and returns the top m results. The results of a particular search engine may not include the best possible web pages the user is interested in. Correspondingly, if a user queries for certain information, different search engines provide differently ranked top m search results. Two factors mainly determine the quality of search results: *similarity judgment* and *seed URLs*. The former is popularly known as "web ranking". The latter should be a good representative of the web in order to retrieve maximum number of relevant documents. However, it is often not, leading to inadequate relevant results.

---

* Currently at: Dept of CSE, Indian Institute of Technology, Kharagpur - 721 302, India; email:
rajendra@cse.iitkgp.ernet.in; drrprasath@gmail.com

S.O. Kuznetsov et al. (Eds.): PReMI 2011, LNCS 6744, pp. 227–234, 2011.

Rank aggregation can be seen as the problem of computing the "consensus" ranking of the alternatives, given the individual ranking preferences of several judges. Rank aggregation has been applied in the context of searching and retrieval of web content, such as meta-search, aggregating the ranking functions, spam reduction, word association techniques, airline reservation, ranking restaurants based on different criteria (cuisine, driving distance, ambiance, star or dollar rating, etc) and comparison of various search engines [5]. In this paper, we propose a rank-aggregation based seed selection algorithm for discovering a good representative subset of URLs as potential seeds.

The paper is organized as follows: Next section describes the notion of seed URL and a brief overview of the related research. Section 3 describes the proposed method for iteratively discovering seed URLs. Section 4 describes evaluation methodology and experimental results. Finally, section 5 concludes the paper.

2   Discovering Potential Seeds

Web crawlers download web pages by exploring the interconnected hyperlink structure of the World Wide Web. This process is known as *web crawling* or *spidering*. From these downloaded pages, search engines extract the content and adds to the index for searching. Since web pages are frequently changed, modified, added and / or deleted, it is necessary to perform the index update through periodic visits of the web content. General and specific purpose search engines apply modern search technologies. Still no single search engine has proven to satisfactorily meet the information needs of users due to the poor coverage and / or ranking of web contents [2,5].

To make the crawling more effective, it is essential to select proper seeds from which the crawler can start its discovery of web pages towards more "related" and less "noisy" web content [8,12]. More recently Zheng *et* al. [13] proposed a seed selection algorithm based on the analysis of the graph structure of the web. This method assumes that every crawled web page has been assigned a value. A higher value indicates higher quality or higher potential to discover new pages. In addition, the value can be negative if the page is undesirable, such as a spam page. It was shown that the addition of seeds representing "similar" web documents would improve the search results [11]. Hyperlink recommendations have also been used to increase the web coverage[6].

To crawl the specific type of web content, special crawlers like *focused crawlers* are being used[3]. These crawlers mainly focus on pages that are relevant to a predefined set of topics which shape the list of seed URLs. However focused crawlers heavily rely on the topical locality phenomenon in which web pages on a given topic are usually clustered together, with many links that connect one page to another. Once a good page is found, the crawler can analyze its cluster to retrieve pages on the same topic[7]. Bergmark *et* al. suggested a *tunneling* technique which allows the crawler to follow a limited number of bad pages in order to reach the good ones [1]. Recently Yahoo! invented a method to compare and choose seeds amongst potential sites[4]. Revisiting the same seed sites on a regular basis may not result in discovering enough new URLs.

3   Proposed Approach Using Rank Aggregation

In this section we present an algorithm that selects the seeds based on the link analysis of search results each obtained for a randomly selected query. Figure 1 shows the basic web crawler with the proposed modifications.

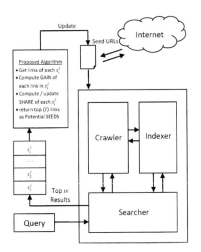 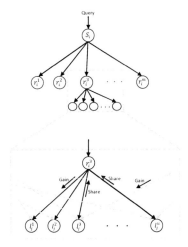

Fig. 1. The proposed algorithm and its role in a search engine

Fig. 2. The proposed *gain-share* strategy

The algorithm is based on a *gain and share* mechanism on the links present in the retrieved search results (see Figure 2). The *Gain* of a link is defined as the score contributed by the number of links pointed to it. Similarly, the *Share* of a search result is defined as the score that contributes to the seed score of qualified links. Initially, from the arbitrarily selected set of queries $\{q_1, q_2, \cdots, q_n\}$, each query is issued to N general purpose search engines. For each q_p, $1 \leq p \leq n$, we obtain N ranked sets of URLs: $S = \{S_1, S_2, \cdots, S_N\}$ where each S_i, $1 \leq i \leq N$ contains a ranked list of top m search results: $S_i = \{r_i^1, r_i^2, \cdots, r_i^m\}$. Each r_i^j, $1 \leq j \leq m$, is visited and its relevance as a seed is assigned manually. Then the links, present in each r_i^j, of all N ranked search results corresponding to the given query q_p, $1 \leq p \leq n$, are collected and gain - share score of each $r_i^j \in S$ is iteratively computed. For each link l_j^k, $1 \leq k \leq u$ (u = total number of links in r_i^j) present in r_i^j, a gain score is computed and a part of this score is propagated to r_i^j as a share score. This share score updates the seed score of r_i^j which, in turn, determines the subset of potential URLs for each query. Algorithm 1 presents the details of this mechanism.

It is to be noted that each of the search results, r_i^j, may contain links leading to relevant / related web pages (or may not in the worst case - in which it is a dead end page having no further links to span the web - this would not be a good seed URL and hence discarded directly). Now the crawler is used to get the content of each of the retrieved search results. This content is first segmented into blocks and the noisy blocks are eliminated using *link - to - text* ratio. Here *Link - to - text ratio* is defined as the ratio between the size of the text tagged with hyperlinks and the text without hyperlinks. This possibly eliminates noisy blocks from the web document using the structural properties of the underlying mark up language and presents the valid blocks. From these valid blocks, outgoing links are collected and used to estimate the gain - share scores.

Algorithm 1. Seed Selection Algorithm using Link Interrelatedness Based Scoring

---

Input: A query having d terms: $Q = \{t_1, t_2, \cdots, t_d\}$
        Top ranked n URLs of N SEs: $S_i = \{r_i^j \mid 1 \leq i \leq N \ \& \ 1 \leq j \leq n\}$;
        $threshold$ - The update limit for the share score at the parent link;

Procedure:
1: For each r_i^j, seed score(r_i^j) $\leftarrow \emptyset$;
2: **for** each search engine $\in N$ **do**
3:    For given q, retrieve top m URLs and assign $Share(r_i^j) := 0.0$;
4:    **for** each retrieved *URL* $r_i^j \in R$ **do**
5:       seed score(r_i^j) $\leftarrow$ manual relevance judgment in 0-1 scale & $UrlsInPage \leftarrow \emptyset$;
6:       Obtain valid blocks of r_i^j using *link-to-text* ratio ;
7:       Extract links l_j^k from valid blocks of r_i^j & $URLsInPage \leftarrow insert(l_j^k)$;
8:       $max = \#$(overlapping $l_j^k \in URLsInPage$);
9:       **for** each $l_j^k \in URLsInPage$ **do**
10:          $Gain(l_j^k) \leftarrow 0.0$ & Compute/update the gain of l_j^k using Equation. 1;
11:          **if** ($Gain(l_j^k) < threshold$) **then**
12:             Discard l_j^k from $URLsInPage$; $max = max - 1$;
13:          **else**
14:             Update $Share(r_i^j)$ using Equation 2;
15:          **end if**
16:       **end for**
17:       seed score(r_i^j) $\leftarrow Share(r_i^j)$
18:    **end for**
19: **end for**
20: **return** top l URLs, sorted by *seed score*(r_i^j), as SEEDS

Output: Top l SEED URLs sorted by their *seed score* in the decreasing order

---

For each search result, we obtain m URLs (delivered by one of the SEs) each of which is stored in $UrlsInPage_j$ where $1 \leq j \leq m$. Then we apply the rank aggregation process on each l_j^k, where $1 \leq k \leq n$ in each search result and obtain the gain scores.

$$Gain(l_j^k) = Gain(l_j^k) + \frac{\#OL(r_i^j)}{rank(r_i^j)} \times seed\ score(r_i^j) \tag{1}$$

where $r_i^j = P(l_j^k)$ - the parent of link l_j^k; $\#OL(r_i^j) = $ Total number of outgoing links from r_i^j; $rank(r_i^j) = \{v\} \ \forall v, 1 \leq v \leq n$. Initially, gain is assumed to be zero.

In the proposed algorithm, we have just used the outgoing links from the search engine results r_i^j, but in principle, one could use several levels of outgoing links from r_i^j. Thus the algorithm could be generalized where gain - share score is computed iteratively over a chain of links. Each of these links propagate a certain amount of share of their gain score to its parent (actual search results) to support it as a good seed. We term the final share score as the *seed score*.

$$Share(r_i^j) = Share(r_i^j) + (Gain(l_j^k)/max) \qquad (2)$$

where max - the number of overlapping outgoing links of search results across N search result sets for each corresponding query.

This score will be shared with the corresponding search result in the bottom up fashion and will support the search result for becoming a good candidate in seed selection. This is repeated for all links present in all subsets and then the top m search results of N search engines. Once we complete the gain - share computations for all top m search results which are then aggregated and based on their new seed score and top m links were selected as the potentially good seed URLs.

4   Evaluation and Discussions

We have selected 10 tourism queries (in English) from Cross Lingual Information Access (CLIA) Project - a major project for CLIA in Indian languages, funded by the Government of India, and being executed by a consortium of several academic institutions and industrial partners [1]. Each query is presented in three forms: title - the actual query, desc - the expanded query and narr - the narration of the query. Here we consider each query either with (title and / or desc). The structure of each query is shown in Figure 3 and selected list of queries are given in the Figure. 4.

4.1   Dataset and Evaluation Strategy

We have collected URLs of top $n = 30$ search results for each of the queries given in Figure 4 using four commercial search engines: *Google, Yahoo!, Bing* and *Cuil* during September 2010. Thus for each query, we have collected 120 (= 4 search engines each with top 30) search results which may be disjoint or may partly overlap across the search results of different search engines. We repeated this process for all 10 queries listed in the Figure 4 and collected 1200 web pages. Some of the links were obsolete, modified or removed. All these 1200 web pages were visited manually and relevance of each was judged in the scale of real numbers between 0 and 1 with 0.1 steps. The actual overlap among the search results of 4 search engines are listed in Table 1 and the rank of these overlapping URLs across 4 search results are different. We measure the goodness of seeds (in turn, the goodness of the crawl created by the ranked seed set) by *Precision* measure. Precision (P) is the fraction of retrieved documents that are relevant. We measure P@d ("Precision top d documents") with $d = 10$.

---

[1] http://www.clia.iitb.ac.in/clia-latest

QID	Query (title)
Q1	Amritsar and the Golden Temple
Q2	Rishikesh Water Rafting
Q3	Toy train Shimla
Q4	Mumbai Ganesh Festival
Q5	Sunderbans National Park and its tourist attractions
Q6	Cuisine of Tamil Nadu
Q7	Goa its beautiful beaches
Q8	Sun Temple at Konark
Q9	Meghalaya and its virgin beauty
Q10	Trekking in Darjeeling

Fig. 3. Query in XML format   **Fig. 4.** Selected 10 CLIA Queries

Table 1. Overlapping URLs among 300 [10 Queries × Top 30] Results

# Engines	Google	Yahoo!	Bing	Cuil
Google	0	90	108	38
Yahoo!	90	0	108	29
Bing	108	108	0	32
Cuil	38	29	32	0

4.2 Relevance Judgement

During the manual relevant judgement, we focus particularly on the search results leading to the "intent" of user's queries. Since the domain being tourism, it is natural to get lots of web content related to tour packages or planning trips (schedulers), or having forms for booking accommodation or transport. So we have given less importance to such contents and more to the focused content of the web documents. During manual evaluation, we have made some observations which mimic the characteristics of the commercial search engines. Some of the search results for the given query leads to video information and may be visually related to the given query. But it is not useful for the systems handling textual content or users having the intent in exploring the history behind the query. In a query related to "trekking", most of the pages contain schedules and plans about the trekking packages offered at various nearby hilly places. Forum discussions / answers describing the user experiences on a specific feature - may be event or place or hotel - are obtained for queries having proper name.

We eliminated the outdated or invalid results by marking it as -1. A few search results contained information about the subtopic of the given query than fetching the overall intent of the query. Such pages were proportionately marked with score deductions. The search results having site replications at different URLs were ranked in the list. For example, page having URL like "http://www.abc.com" and "http://abc.com" were considered as single entity and it is hardly possible to avoid this in the automated web crawling.

4.3 Discussions

Here we present the experimental results of the proposed method on selected tourism related queries. Out of total 1200 search results [= 10 Queries x top 30 results x 4 search engines], we have identified 320 links that are common across search results of different search engines. Hence 26% of same search results repeat on an average for top 10 queries. We have noticed similar amount of search results between Google and Yahoo! search engines. However the number of matching results between Google and Bing is high and Google and Cuil is low (please refer to Table 1). This forms a fair distribution among the search results across different search engines for different queries. During the preliminary analysis, we found that if more number of child link influence the gain - share score, then it is essential to modify the threshold so that more and more hyperlinked pages, even though they are irrelevant, would hardly dominate the score propagation.

First we selected top 40 urls for each query and crawled them to the depth 2. Now for each query, we have manually checked the precision @ top d (=10) documents score for selected queries(refer to Figure 6). The proposed method diverges in some cases for example, Q10 - "Trekking in Darjeeling", there are lots of pages with Nepal expeditions and Himalayan expeditions rather than focusing on Sandakphu and Kalimpong Treks. We have done this experiment with only 1200 relevant judged web documents and hence the diversity of the seed selection would be attempted with more data.

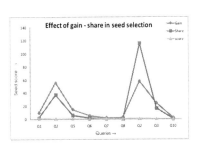

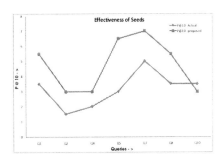

Fig. 5. Seed Score variations for the Selected Queries

Fig. 6. P@10 Scores

Figure 5 shows the preliminary results of our experiments towards seed selection among the selected queries. Here we have highlighted special cases in which manual judgment score is lower, but the gain - share score is considerably higher. This indicates that this seed could be a better candidate for selecting as the seed URL. Similarly the seed for the query $Q8$ which ranked 7 in the ranked list with partial relevance can be a better choice due to its link structures. These links carry forward to the relevance links in a few steps. In the sequel, we would like to experiment more in comparison with the recent web crawler seed selection algorithms.

5 Conclusion

In this paper, we proposed a seed selection algorithm for web crawlers using link data with gain - share based approach. The proposed method would capture the potential seeds from the ranked search results of commercial search engines in an indirect way. This approach could also be generalized to find better seeds by accounting the crawling to various depths. Analyzing the commercial search results can model the characteristics in finding good candidates towards computing the "interestingness" of a page(in turn, relevance to the user query). In our future work, attempts would be made to dynamically modify, update and / or remove the outdated URLs [9,10].

References

1. Bergman, M.K.: The deep web: Surfacing hidden value. Journal of Electronic Publishing 7(1) (August 2001)
2. Brin, S., Page, L.: The anatomy of a large-scale hypertextual web search engine. In: WWW7: Proceedings of the seventh international conference on World Wide Web 7, pp. 107–117. Elsevier Science Publishers B.V., Amsterdam (1998)
3. Chakrabarti, S., van den Berg, M., Dom, B.: Focused crawling: a new approach to topic-specific web resource discovery. Comput. Netw. 31(11-16), 1623–1640 (1999)
4. Dmitriev, P.: Host-based seed selection algorithm for web crawlers. US Patent (US20100114858A1) (May 2010)
5. Dwork, C., Kumar, R., Naor, M., Sivakumar, D.: Rank aggregation methods for the web. In: WWW 2001: Proceedings of the 10th international conference on World Wide Web, pp. 613–622. ACM, New York (2001)
6. Hawking, D., Craswell, N.: Which search engine is best at finding online services? In: Proceedings of WWW10, Hong Kong (2001)
7. Micarelli, A., Gasparetti, F.: Adaptive focused crawling. Springer, Heidelberg (2007)
8. Niu, C., Li, W., Ding, J., Srihari, R.K.: A bootstrapping approach to named entity classification using successive learners. In: ACL 2003: Proceedings of the 41st Annual Meeting on Association for Computational Linguistics, pp. 335–342. Association for Computational Linguistics, Morristown, USA (2003)
9. Pal, S.K., Talwar, V., Mitra, P.: Web mining in soft computing framework: relevance, state of the art and future directions. IEEE Transactions on Neural Networks 13(5), 1163–1177 (2002), http://dx.doi.org/10.1109/TNN.2002.1031947
10. Rumelhart, D.E., Hinton, G.E., Williams, R.J.: Learning internal representations by error propagation. MIT Press, Cambridge (1986)
11. Smucker, M.D., Allan, J.: Using similarity links as shortcuts to relevant web pages. In: SIGIR 2007: Proceedings of the 30th annual international ACM SIGIR conference on Research and development in information retrieval, pp. 863–864. ACM, New York (2007)
12. Yangarber, R.: Counter-training in discovery of semantic patterns. In: ACL 2003: Proceedings of the 41st Annual Meeting on Association for Computational Linguistics, pp. 343–350. Association for Computational Linguistics, Morristown, USA (2003)
13. Zheng, S., Dmitriev, P., Giles, C.L.: Graph based crawler seed selection. In: WWW 2009: Proceedings of the 18th international conference on World wide web, pp. 1089–1090. ACM, New York (2009)

Combining Evidence for Automatic Extraction of Terms

Boris Dobrov and Natalia Loukachevitch

Research Computing Center of Lomonosov Moscow State University,
Leninskie Gory, 4/1, Moscow, Russia
{dobroff,louk}@mail.cir.ru

Abstract. The paper describes the method of extraction of two-word domain terms combining their features. The features are computed from three sources: the occurrence statistics in a domain-specific text collection, the statistics of global search engines, and a domain-specific thesaurus. The evaluation of the approach is based on the terminology of manually created thesauri. We show that the use of multiple features considerably improves the automatic extraction of domain-specific terms. We compare the quality of the proposed method in two different domains.

Keywords: term acquisition, thesaurus, Internet search, machine learning.

1 Introduction

Technical terms represent domain-specific concepts in domain documents. It means that terms are key elements to understanding of the conceptual structure of the domain. Therefore automatic extraction of domain-specific terms from texts is a subject of constant interest in automatic processing of documents. The special difficulty is the automatic extraction of multiword terms [1].

When working with large subject areas and text collections, even the best methods for extracting terminological collocations show significant drop in term percentage from 90% in the first hundred of the list, down to 60% in the third thousand. Thus, an important problem is development of new methods to improve the quality of phrase ordering to increase the percentage of terms at the top.

For many years researchers tried to find the best statistical feature for term extraction. Now machine learning methods allow for the combination of many features. Thus, in [2] the combination of different statistical characteristics of phrases, based on the Czech text collection, is used to extract different types of collocations (such as phrasal verbs or idioms). The authors used over 80 features and obtained 20% improvement compared with the best individual feature. But the authors of this paper indicate that efficiency of different features is very variable and depends on a collection, types of expressions and so on.

In this paper we describe an experiment to extract two-word terms based on a combination of three types of features: features based on a domain-specific text

S.O. Kuznetsov et al. (Eds.): PReMI 2011, LNCS 6744, pp. 235–241, 2011.

collection, features obtained from an Internet search engine and features obtained from a domain-specific thesaurus. Working with a thesaurus we simulate the situation when a thesaurus partially exists. We want to study its potential to recognise new terms. The important point of our research is to study the stability of the term extraction model among different domains.

2   Description of Experiment: Data and Evaluation

We conduct our study in two domains. The first domain is the very broad domain of natural sciences and technologies. The second domain is domain of banking and bank regulation. For both domains we have Russian domain-specific thesauri developed manually, which we use as a basis for evaluation of term extraction methods. The current volume of Ontology on Natural Sciences is more than 140 thousand terms [3]. Banking thesaurus includes about 15 thousand terms.

Besides we have Russian domain-specific text collections used for development of these thesauri. From the text collections we have extracted single words and multiword expressions. Two-word expressions belong to two types of noun groups: Adjective+Noun and Noun+Noun_in_Genitive. The extracted expressions were ordered in descending order of their frequencies. Our experts worked with these term candidate lists paying more attention to expressions with high frequencies. However it was noted that the important terms could have medium or low frequencies because of the unbalance of the text collections. So the aim of our new term extraction method is to reorder the extracted expressions to provide the presence of more approved terms in the beginning of the candidate list. We experimented with five thousands of the most frequent two-word expressions from these candidate lists.

To evaluate the reordering quality of methods we use the measure of average precision adopted from information retrieval [4]. Average precision AvP in the task of extracting terminological expressions is calculated as follows. Suppose that in an ordered list of expressions there are k terms, and pos (i) - position of the i-th term from the beginning of the list. Then the precision on the level of the i-th terminological expression $PrecTerm_i$ in an ordered list is **PrecTerm(pos(i))**, that is the value of precision $PrecTerm_i$ is calculated at the time of inclusion to the list of i-th term and is equal to the percentage of terms in the list from 1 to pos (i) positions. Average precision for the given ordered list is equal to the average value of $PrecTerm_i$:

$$\mathbf{AvP} = \frac{1}{k} \sum_i \mathbf{PrecTerm_i}$$

Measure of average precision allows us to estimate the quality of term extraction with a single value because the more domain terms are located in the beginning of the list the more is the value of average precision.

3   Features for Term Candidate Reordering

For extracted phrases we compute features of three types. First, we use features calculated on the basis of the domain-specific text collection. In this experiment such features are **the frequency of the phrase**, **mutual information (MI)**, **MI3** (the same as MI but accounts the cube of the phrase frequency [5]) and **Insideness**. **Insideness** is calculated as the inverse ratio of the phrase frequency to maximal frequency of a three-word phrase comprising the given phrase.

We use not so many features from the domain-specific text collection because our main interest is to study other types of features based on Internet search and known terms desribed in a domain-specific thesaurus. We will consider these types of features in the following subsections.

3.1   Features Based on Internet Search

Internet-based features were obtained with xml-interface of Russian Search Engine Yandex on the basis of specially formulated queries. For our experiments we utilised so-called search snippets - short fragments of texts explaining search results. Example of one of Yandex snippets for phrase **internal debt** is as follows:

Internal debt is the part of a country's debts that is owed to creditors who are citizens of that country. It is a form of fiat creation of money, in which the government obtains cash not by printing it, but by borrowing it.

Use of Internet search for term extraction is important for the following reasons. First, the domain-specific text collection is always not sufficient because a lot of fairly significant terms of the domain may have relatively low frequencies in it. Involvement of the Internet helps us get additional information on such terms. Secondly, the use of information from the Internet allows us to find out if a given phrase is rigidly connected with the domain.

To calculate phrase features, 100 snippets from search results were utilised. Snippets from the same query were merged into one document and processed by the morphological processor. As a result, for each set of snippets lemmas (words in a dictionary form) were extracted and their frequencies of occurrence were calculated. For every query, we obtain a vector of lemmas with corresponding frequencies. Snippets are generated for the whole phrases and its constituent words. We denote S_{ab} - a vector of lemma frequencies derived from phrase snippets, S_a, S_b - vectors of lemmas from constituent word snippets. From such vectors, the following types of features were calculated.

The first group of features are scalar products of snippet vectors: $< S_{ab}, S_a >$ (**Scalar1**), $< S_{ab}, S_b >$ (**Scalar2**). Also we calculated scalar products of Boolean variants of snippet vectors (elements of vectors are from $\{0, 1\}$) : $< Sb_{ab}, Sb_a >$ (**Boolean1**), $< Sb_{ab}, Sb_b >$ (**Boolean2**). These features compare overall distinctions in lexical contexts of a phrase and its components.

The frequency of a phrase in its own snippets (FreqBySnip). We supposed that if the value of this feature is significantly greater than 100 (sometimes this feature reached 250-300 occurrences in 100 snippets), it means that there are many contexts, in which this phrase is explained in detail, is the theme of the fragment, and, most likely, this phrase denotes an important concept or a specific entity.

Features of semantically specific context ($SnipFreq_i$). Many domain-specific mulltiword terms have sense specificity, which can not be deduced from its components. This specificity of the term can be shown in additional relations to other terms not directly related to intial term components. To find such specificity we extract a single lemma that is very frequent in phrase snippets and absent (or rarely mentioned) in component snippets.

Let lemma L occur f_{ab} times in phrase snippets, f_a, f_b times occur in snippets of components. Then we calculate $SnipFreq_0$ feature as follows:

$$SnipFreq_0 = \max_L f_{ab-a-b} \log \frac{N - d_L col}{d_L col}$$

where

$f_{ab-a-b} = \max(f_{ab} - f_a - f_b, 0)$,

dlcol is a lemma frequency in documents of a contrastive collection, **N** - is the number of documents in the contrastive collection. Factor $\log \left(\frac{N - d_{L col}}{d_{L col}} \right)$ is so called **idf**-factor known from information retrieval research [4], it helps to diminish influence of frequent general words. The contrastive collection is the collection of documents of Belorussian Internet distributed in the framework of Russian seminar on information retrieval (www.romip.ru/ en/index.html).

$SnipFreq_1$ and $SnipFreq_2$ features are calculated in similar way excepting words in a window of 1 (2) words near every occurrence of ab phrase. These variants of SnipFreq feature are intended to remove partial fragments of longer terms from consideration.

Number of definitional words in snippets (NearDefWords). This feature calculates overall frequency of so called definitional words in phrase snippets. These words (as type, class, define etc.) are often used in dictionary definitions. Therefore their presence in snippets can mean that a snippet contains a definition of this phrase or the phrase is used in definition of other term. **NearDefWords** feature is equal to the number of these definitional words that appeared immediately adjacent (left or right) with the original phrase in snippets.

Number of marker words in snippets (Markers). This feature denotes number of five-ten the most important words of the domain in snippets of the expression. For the natural science domain these words were as follows: mathematics, mathematical, physics, physical, chemisry, chemical, geology, geological, biology, biological.

Number of Internet page titles (SnipTitle). We calculated number of Internet page titles coinciding with a given phrase, because we supposed that use of the expression in the title of an Internet page stresses significance of the phrase.

3.2   Features Based on Terms of Domain-Specific Thesaurus

In many domains there are well-known terms and even information-retrieval thesauri. The third type of our features is based on the assumption that the known terms can help to predict unknown terms. For the experiments in two domains, we used the relevant thesauri. If a phrase was a thesaurus term, then it was excluded from the terminological basis for feature generation. We considered the following features obtained from a domain-specific thesaurus.

Synonym to Thesaurus Term (SynTerm). Documents of the domain can contain a lot of variants of the same term [6]. Therefore we can suppose that a phrase similar to a thesaurus term is also a term. Let a and b be components of phrase ab. We consider phrase cd as a synonym of ab phrase if every component word of phrase cd is either equal to a component word of ab either is a synonym of a component word of ab. The order of components in a phrase is unimportant.

Synonym to Non-Term (SynNotTerm). We also fix a feature of similarity to a phrase not included to the thesaurus.

Completeness of Description (Completeness). It is possible that component words a and/or b of phrase ab have been already described in the domain thesaurus as domain terms. Completeness feature is a sum of thesaurus relations of component terms in the thesaurus.

4   Results of Experiments

We experimented in two domains: the banking domain and the domain of natural sciences. In all experiments, 5 thousand most frequent two-word expressions extracted from the corresponding text collections were used. For these expressions all above-mentioned features were calculated. To obtain the best combination of features generating the best reordering, we used machine learning methods implemented in programming package RapidMiner (www.rapidminer.com). The quality of reordering was evaluated with AvP measure. The training set was three-quarters of the phrase list, the testing set was a quarter. As basic minimal levels of AvP we used the alphabet order and the decreasing frequency order.

We tested various machine learning methods from RapidMiner package. Every time logistic regression achieved maximal level of AvP. Therefore we took this method as a basic method of machine learning for our experiments in term extraction. The table 1 shows values of AvP for single features and results of logistic regression method.

SynTerm and **SynNotTerm** features are Boolean and can not be evaluated with AvP. We concluded that **SynTerm** feature is highly informative: if **SynTerm** (ab) =1 then phrase ab is a domain term with probability of more than 80%.

We can see that in both cases the same set of features and use of machine learning methods lead to much higher values of average precision. However there are significant distinctions in ratios between AvP of features. For example, in the banking domain AvP of the frequency feature has the highest value, features with high average precision in the science domain have enough low values in the banking domain.

We explain this phenomenon with relative narrowness of the banking domain. Banking documents contain a lot of terminology from neighbour domains such as economy or politics. So among extracted expressions, there are many real terms having all specific qualities of "termhood" but not related to the banking activity. In the scientific text collection the share of terms from other domains is much lower.

Also we can see failure of $SnipFreq_i$ features in banking domain. The reason of this phenomenon, in our opinion, is as follows: the banking domain is subject to legal regulation, therefore documents of the domain contain a lot of citations from legal acts which leads to false large values of $SnipFreq_i$.

Table 1. Average Precision (AvP) for single features and logistic regression. Feature SnipTitle was not extracted for phrases in science domain.

Feature	AvP (Banking)%	AvP (Natural Sciences)%
Alphabet	40%	57%
Frequency	57%	66%
Mutual Information	43%	64%
MI_3	45%	67%
Inside	55%	75%
FreqBySnip	53%	69%
NearDefWords	49%	73%
$Scalar_1$	42%	61%
$Scalar_2$	45%	60%
$BinarScalar_1$	49%	64%
$BinarScalar_2$	48%	62%
$Snipfreq_0$	34%	66%
$Snipfreq_1$	38%	67%
$Snipfreq_2$	38%	67%
Markers	40%	65%
Completeness	52%	69%
SnipTitle	50%	-
Logistic Regression	79% (+38.6% from Freq)	83% (+25.8% from Freq)

5 Conclusion

In this paper we have proposed to use three types of features for extraction of two-word terms and have shown that all these types of features are useful for term extraction. The set of features includes new features such as features extracted from the existing domain-specific thesauri and features based on Internet search results.

We have shown that the combination of several types of features considerably enhances the quality of the term extraction procedure. The developed system of term extraction reorders terms in a list of candidates much better than the basic-line order with decreasing frequency.

We studied the set of features for term extraction in two different domains. We found that developing term extraction models in a specific domain, it is important to take into account such properties of the domain as broad scope or narrow scope (science vs. banking) and relatedness to the socio-political domain, which is regulated with legal acts. We suppose that it is possible to find the main types of domains for term extraction, to select the best feature sets and corresponding machine learning models for every type of domains.

References

1. Zhang, Z., Iria, J.: Brewster, Ch., Ciravegna, F.: A Comparative Evaluation of Term Recognition Algorithms. In: Sixth International Language Resources and Evaluation, LREC 2008 (2008)
2. Pecina, P., Schlesinger, P.: Combining association measures for collocation extraction. In: Annual Meeting of the Association for Computational Linguistics, ACL 2006, ACM Press, New York (2006)
3. Dobrov, B., Loukachevitch, N.: Development of Linguistic Ontology on Natural Sciences and Technology. In: Linguistic resources and Evaluation conference, LREC 2006 (2006)
4. Manning, C., Raghavan, P., Shutze, H.: Introduction to Information Retrieval. Cambridge University Press, Cambridge (2008)
5. Daille, B., Gaussier, E., Lang, J.M.: An evaluation of statistics scores for word association. In: Tbilisi Symposium on Logic, Language and Computation, pp. 177–188. CSLI Publications (1998)
6. Nenadic, G., Ananiadou, S., McNaught, J.: Enhancing automatic term recognition through recognition of variation. In: 20th International Conference on Computational Linguistics (COLING 2004), pp. 604–610 (2004)

A New Centrality Measure for Influence Maximization in Social Networks

Suman Kundu, C.A. Murthy, and S.K. Pal

Center for Soft Computing Research
Indian Statistical Institute
Kolkata, India - 700108
sumankundu_r@isical.ac.in, murthy@isical.ac.in, sankar@isical.ac.in

Abstract. The paper addresses the problem of finding top k influential nodes in large scale directed social networks. We propose a centrality measure for independent cascade model, which is based on diffusion probability (or propagation probability) and degree centrality. We use (i) centrality based heuristics with the proposed centrality measure to get k influential individuals. We have also found the same using (ii) high degree heuristics and (iii) degree discount heuristics. A Monte-Carlo simulation has been conducted with top k-nodes found through different methods. The result of simulation indicates, k nodes obtained through (i) significantly outperform those obtain by (ii) and (iii). We further verify the differences statistically using T-Test and found the minimum significance level (p-value) when $k > 5$ is 0.022 compare with (ii) and 0.015 when comparing with (iii) for twitter data.

1 Introduction

Large scale online social networks became popular in recent years. Twitter, Facebook, Orkut, LinkedIn is few examples. These social networks have millions of users. People around the globe are connected with the purpose of common interests. These applications are becoming a huge marketing platform of products and services, specially spreading the information to a large number of people in a short amount of time. However, the most important question arises "How to select the influential individual quickly, to target for marketing?"

Domingos et al. were the first to study the problem as an algorithmic problem and proposed probabilistic methods in [3, 10]. In [5] Kempe et al. formulated the problem as a discrete optimization problem and showed that the problem is NP hard. They also proposed a greedy hill climbing approach, which provides $(1 - 1/e - \epsilon)$ approximation of the optimal solution. Finally, they showed through experiments that their approach provides significant improvement over the classical degree, and centrality based heuristic. However, for large scale graphs, the greedy approach may be time consuming. Chen et al. recently proposed few improvements of the model in [1]. They provided NewGreedy and further modified it to MixedGreedy. Even after the improvement, this approach would take days

S.O. Kuznetsov et al. (Eds.): PReMI 2011, LNCS 6744, pp. 242–247, 2011.

to run on large scale social networks. So, Chen et al. in [1] provided the degree discount heuristic model which runs much faster than the greedy model. In [4], authors provided another approach to solve the problem in less time. They called it set covering greedy algorithm. This algorithm, however, needs more time compared to the centrality based heuristic models.

In this paper, we propose a centrality measure, *diffusion degree*, and then we use it to rank influential individuals of large sample of directed social networks. We simulate the information spread with top k nodes from different algorithms and compare it with the simulation results of the proposed algorithm. We found proposed algorithm provides statistically significant improvements.

The paper is organized as follows, in Section 2 we provide the information diffusion model. Section 3 describes some related works. In the Section 4, centrality measure *diffusion degree* is described. Section 5 shows experimental results.

2   Information Diffusion Model

Independent Cascade Model: Independent cascade model of information diffusion is proposed by Lopez-Pinatado [6]. It is the most common model for information diffusion. In this model, nodes can have two states, either active or inactive. Nodes are allowed to switch from inactive to active but not in the other. The diffusion model starts with an initial set of active nodes. In time t, an active node u will get chance to activate its inactive neighbor v. v will become active with a probability λ called diffusion probability or propagation probability. u will not get any further chance to activate v. The diffusion probability is a user-defined parameter of the model. The process of diffusion stops when no further activation is possible. This method is called independent because the activation of a node does not depend on the history of active nodes.

3   Related Works

High Degree Heuristic Model: The most classic approach to solve the influence maximization problem is *High Degree Heuristics*. Here the influence is calculated based on the degree of a node, i.e. if k nodes are required to select as seed then the top k high degree node will be selected.

Degree Discount Heuristic Model: General idea of the *degree discount* algorithm of Chen et al. is that if one node is considered as seed then the links connecting with the node will not be counted as a degree of the other nodes, i.e. when considering the next node, the links connecting with the nodes already in the seed set will be discounted.

4   Proposed Diffusion Degree and Heuristic Model

Several attempts are made to improve efficiency of the greedy algorithm. However, for a large scale network its efficiency is far from the speed of centrality based heuristics. Degree is commonly used for finding the seeds of the influence maximization problem. In [5], Kempe et al. showed through experimental results that high degree heuristics produces a large influence spread compared to other centrality based heuristics. In addition, some of the centrality measures like betweenness require huge computation load to calculate. In this section, we propose a centrality measure, *diffusion degree* based on the diffusion probability. The diffusion degree can be calculated quickly even for large scale networks. A heuristic model is then described for influence maximization problem.

Many of the available centrality measures considered only structural property of a node. However, when considering the diffusion process, diffusion probability plays a vital role in influence flow over the network. Additionally, the centrality based heuristic models did not consider the effect of neighborhood. Take an example of high degree heuristics, suppose a node (v_1) with the highest degree in the network is connected with some low degree nodes. Consider another node (v_2) with a less degree; and its neighbors are high degree nodes. Now, the obvious choice in the high degree model is v_1. In this case, the diffusion process propagate less level compared to v_2 because the neighborhood of v_2 can send the information to more nodes in the network than neighbors of v_1. Our contributed centrality measure considers the above mention properties of diffusion model and social networks.

The general degree centrality measure is proposed by Nieminen in [9]. The degree centrality of node v can be defined as

$$C_D(v) = \sum_{i=1}^{n} \sigma(u_i, v) \tag{1}$$

where function $\sigma(u_i, v)$ defined as,

$$\sigma(u_i, v) = 1 \ \textit{if and only if } u_i \textit{ and } v \textit{ are connected}$$
$$= 0 \ \textit{otherwise.}$$

In a diffusion process, a node v with propagation probability λ_v, can activate its neighbor u with probability λ_v. So, considerable contribution of node v in the diffusion process is

$$C'_{DD}(v) = \lambda_v * C_D(v). \tag{2}$$

When the diffusion process propagates to the next level, active neighbors of v will try to activate their inactive neighbors. Thus the cumulative contribution in the diffusion process by neighbors of v will be maximized when all of its neighbors will be activated in the previous step. In this scenario, the total contribution of neighbors of v is

$$C''_{DD}(v) = \sum_{i \in neighbors(v)} C'_{DD}(i). \tag{3}$$

The diffusion degree of a node is defined as the cumulative contribution score of the node itself and its neighbors. So, from the equations 2 and 3 we can define the diffusion degree C_{DD} of node v as

$$C_{DD}(v) = C'_{DD}(v) + C''_{DD}(v) \tag{4}$$

$$= \lambda_v * C_D(v) + \sum_{i \in neighbors(v)} C'_{DD}(i) \tag{5}$$

$$= \lambda_v * C_D(v) + \sum_{i \in neighbors(v)} \lambda_i * C_D(i). \tag{6}$$

The diffusion degree measure depends upon the diffusion probability. However, this measure is independent of the nodes already selected. Thus calculating the diffusion degree for every node of the network could be determined in $O(N + E)$ time where N is the number of nodes and E is the number of edges in the network. In defining the diffusion degree, we consider the effect of immediate neighbors to a node because for a small diffusion probability, the effect of neighbor's neighbor of a node may be ignored[1].

Our heuristics model works similar to other centrality based heuristics for finding top k influence maximization problem. The only difference is that we use the diffusion degree instead of classical centrality measures. The algorithm is as follows

1. Find diffusion degree (C_{DD}) for all nodes of the network
2. Select top k nodes for k-top influence maximization problem.

5   Experiment and Results

In our experiment, we use directed social networks e.g. twitter. In case of directed networks like twitter, one person (or node) can influence its followers. It is unlike that one can influence a person he/she following. So, the out degree of nodes is ignored in our experiments. We use Monte-Carlo simulations of the independent cascade model for a sufficiently large number of times to get an accurate approximation of final influence spread. Reader may refer to [7] for additional information about Monte-Carlo methods.

We compare our results with other centrality based heuristics. We avoid comparing results with the greedy approach because for a million node social networks and Monte-Carlo simulation, even the high end server takes days to compute results. Finally, we compare results statistically using T-Test. For more details about the T-Test and p-value readers may refer to [8].

5.1   Data Set

Our primary data set for experiment is twitter data used in [2]. It was obtained by a snowball sampling of the twitter site in late 2009. The data set contains over 400K nodes and more than 800K of relations. Unlike twitter, which is directly related to the problem domain, we use DBLP citation network [11] to verify our claim. The idea behind experimenting with a different data is to verify whether the improvements are only for a particular data set, or it has a similar impact on other real life data sets as well. The DBLP citation network contains over 447K nodes and over 2.3 million relations. Here also, we get better results compare to other centrality based model.

5.2   Results

Figure 1(a) clearly shows that our proposed algorithm outperforms high degree
heuristics and degree discount heuristics in case of twitter data set. It is also
clear that for directed network like twitter, the degree discount algorithm does
not provide any significant improvement over the high degree heuristic. Figure
1(b) shows the results for DBLP citation network. Significant improvement is
found in case of DBLP data set as well.

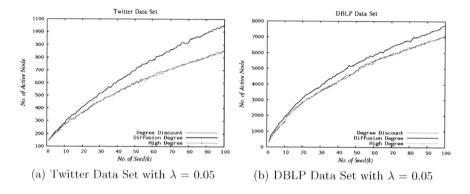

(a) Twitter Data Set with $\lambda = 0.05$ (b) DBLP Data Set with $\lambda = 0.05$

Fig. 1. Seed vs Influence Spread

In our experiment, we assumed that the diffusion probability for nodes is same
and we simulated the information spread for $\lambda \in \{0.01, 0.02, ..., 0.07\}$; we found
improvement when λ is more than or equal to 0.03. For smaller values of λ our
model shows comparable results and for higher values, we are getting further
improvements for both the data sets.

We have also performed experiments for different values of k. Specifically, we
simulated the information spread for $0 \leq k \leq 100$. Additionally, we verified
simulation results for each value of k using T-Test. In case of smaller value of
$k(k \leq 10)$ the differences among three algorithms are not significant. However,
as k increases, the results from T-Test show that the differences are significant.
For twitter data, the minimum observed significant level (p-value) of our method
compared to high degree heuristics is 0.022 when $k = 10$. For higher value of k,
we found increasing significant differences. We got the highest significant level
(p-value $1.46 * 10^{-138}$) when $k = 99$. Thus the results of the proposed method
are statistically found to be significantly different from the results of the existing
two methods.

6   Conclusion

In this paper, we proposed a centrality based heuristics model for influence
maximization problem in social networks. We showed through experiment and

statistical tests that it has a significant improvement over other existing central-ity based heuristics for directed networks. We believe our centrality measure, and the heuristic algorithm will provide comparable results for undirected social networks as well.

As a future work, we plan to test the algorithm with other samples of the twitter and to compare our results with a close optimal value produced by the greedy approach. In our model, we only considered the Independent Cascade Model. The work may be extended to see the outcomes in other cascade models as well.

References

[1] Chen, W., Wang, Y., Yang, S.: Efficient influence maximization in social networks. In: Proceedings of the 15th ACM SIGKDD international conference on Knowledge discovery and data mining, pp. 199–208. ACM Press, New York (2009)

[2] Choudhury, M.D., Sundaram, H., John, A., Seligmann, D.D., Kelliher, A.: "birds of a feather": Does user homophily impact information diffusion in social media? CoRR abs/1006.1702 (2010)

[3] Domingos, P., Richardson, M.: Mining the network value of customers. In: Proceedings of the seventh ACM SIGKDD international conference on Knowledge discovery and data mining, pp. 57–66. ACM Press, New York (2001)

[4] Estevez, P.a., Vera, P., Saito, K.: Selecting the Most Influential Nodes in Social Networks. In: International Joint Conference on Neural Networks, August 2007, pp. 2397–2402 (2007)

[5] Kempe, D., Kleinberg, J., Tardos, E.: Maximizing the spread of influence through a social network. In: Proceedings of the ninth ACM SIGKDD international conference on Knowledge discovery and data mining - KDD 2003, p. 137. ACM Press, New York (2003)

[6] López-Pintado, D.: Diffusion in complex social networks. Games and Economic Behavior 62(2), 573–590 (2008)

[7] MacKay, D.: Introduction to monte carlo methods. Learning in graphical models (1), 175–204 (1998)

[8] Montgomery, D., Runger, G.: Applied Statistics And Probability For Engineers. Wiley, India (2007)

[9] Nieminen, J.: On the Centrality in a Graph. Scandinavian Journal of Psychology 15, 332–336 (1974)

[10] Richardson, M., Domingos, P.: Mining knowledge-sharing sites for viral marketing. In: Proceedings of the eighth ACM SIGKDD international conference on Knowledge discovery and data mining - KDD 2002, p. 61 (2002)

[11] Tang, J., Yao, L., Zhang, D., Zhang, J.: A combination approach to web user profiling. ACM Transactions on Knowledge Discovery from Data V(March), 1–38 (2010)

Method of Cognitive Semantic Analysis of Russian Sentence

Alexander Bolkhovityanov and Andrey Chepovskiy

Higher School of Economics,
Moscow, Russia
alexander.bolkhovityanov@gmail.com,
achepovskiy@hse.ru

Abstract. In this paper, we propose two mathematical models intended for analyzing the Russian sentence to detect noun phrases and participial clauses. Considered algorithms designed on the basis of the proposed models can improve procedure of syntactic parsing. Algorithm for participial clause identification is based on the concept of syntactic relation between verb and dependent syntactic units in the Russian language.

1 Introduction

The main task of semantic analysis is creating representation of a text, allowing to correlate the information contained in the text with the knowledge system. The goal of cognitive semantic analysis [1] is formation of such intermediate representation. The creation of mathematical models which help to solve engineering problems of text processing requires to solve the problem of cognitive modeling of a text.

This problem well studied for languages with a simple syntactic structure, for example English. But it is a complicated task for languages which have more complex structure, for example Russian. There are a lot of syntactic relations in the Russian sentence.

The information about the syntactic structure of the analyzed text requires formation of the intermediate representation. The result of parsing is represented as a syntactic dependency tree [2], which can be obtained on the basis of syntactic relations among the constituent elements of the text. Thus, we are faced with the task of establishing syntactic relations among syntactic units of sentence.

In this paper we propose mathematical models and algorithms, which help us to solve the problem of identifying syntactic relationships among the elements of the text completely but in some acceptable approximation for the real systems of the text processing.

We describe mathematical models for noun phrase and participial clause identification. In Section 2 we propose mathematical models and algorithms for noun phrase and participial clause identification. We note that participial clause identification is based on the concept of syntactic relations between verb and dependent syntactic units, noun phrases for example.

S.O. Kuznetsov et al. (Eds.): PReMI 2011, LNCS 6744, pp. 248–253, 2011.

2 Mathematical Models

In this section, we provide mathematical models and algorithms for noun phrase and participial clause identification in the context of the Russian sentence.

Let us introduce some auxiliary sets which needed for formal definition of the following algorithms. These sets are:

1. Set of parts of speech in Russian $PoS = \{NOUN, ADJ, VERB, CNUM, PART\}$, where $NOUN$ — noun, ADJ — adjective, $VERB$ — verb, $CNUM$ — cardinal number, $PART$ — participle.
2. Set of grammar cases in Russian $GC = \{N, G, D, A, I, P\}$, where N — nominative case, G — genitive case, D — dative case, A — accusative case, I — instrumentative case, P — preposition case.
3. Set of genders in Russian $Genders = \{M, F, N\}$, where M – masculine gender, F — feminine gender, N — neuter gender.
4. Set of numbers in Russian $Numbers = \{SG, PL\}$, where SG – singular, PL – plural.

The word w may be represented as a list of the results of morphological analysis, grouped by parts of speech. $MA(w)$ function sets the correspondence between the set of words and results of morphological analysis mentioned above:

$$MA : w \rightarrow (G_1, \ldots, G_n) \tag{1}$$

where $G_i = (GI_1, \ldots, GI_k), GI_j = (pos, gc, gender, number), pos \in PoS, gc \in GC, gender \in Genders, number \in Numbers, \forall j \in [1, k-1] : pos_j = pos_{j+1}.$ GI_j is a particular result of morphological analysis of the word w. There are more groups of morphology analysis G_i because of the homonymy in the Russian language. Thus, the morphology analysis results may be represented in the unbundled form: $MA(w) = (GI_1, \ldots, GI_p)$. Further, we use the results of $MA(w)$ above mentioned.

2.1 Noun Phrase Identification

Let us introduce some auxiliary notations.

Subordinate syntactic relation is a pair where the first element of a pair w is a word and the second element $RL(w)$ is a list of subordinate words: $r_i \in R, r_i = (w, RL(w)), RL(w) = (w_1, \ldots, w_l)$.

R is a set of subordinate syntactic relations. At a preliminary step one may add subordinate syntactic relation with empty relations list: $\forall w : R = R \cup (w, ())$ where $()$ means empty list for each word w in the sentence.

The input of the algorithm is a sentence composed of words $Sent = w_1, \ldots, w_n$, where $w_i \in \Sigma^+$, and Σ is the Russian alphabet. The algorithm consists of three basic steps:

1. Setting subordinate syntactic relations in a pair (lw, rw), where lw is a left word, rw is a right word in a pair. For example, if we have an input sentence $Sent$ consisting of the sequence of the words $w_1, w_2, \ldots, w_n$, then we can consider the pair (w_1, w_2), where $lw = w_1, rw = w_2$.

2. Setting syntactic relations inside homogeneous parts of the sentence;
3. Identifying of the noun phrases.

Relations are set in the pair (lw, rw). Next, we propose conditions under which we add the corresponding relation to the relations set R.

Here are the basic steps of the algorithm.

Setting subordinate syntactic relations

1. If $\exists GI_i \in MA(lw) : pos_i = NOUN$ and $\exists GI_j \in MA(rw) : pos_j = NOUN$ and $gc_j = G$ then add relation for word lw: $RL(lw) = RL(lw) \cup (rw)$;
2. If $\exists GI_i \in MA(lw) : pos_i = ADJ$ and $\exists GI_j \in MA(rw) : pos_j = NOUN$ and $gc_i = gc_j, gen_i = gen_j$ and either $num_i = num_j$ or $num_i = SG$ then add relation for word rw: $RL(rw) = RL(rw) \cup (lw)$;
3. If $\exists GI_i \in MA(lw) : pos_i = CNUM$ and $\exists GI_j \in MA(rw) : pos_j = NOUN$ and $gc_j = G$ and either $gc_i = N$ or $gc_i = G$ then add relation for word lw: $RL(lw) = RL(lw) \cup (rw)$.

Setting syntactic relations inside homogeneous parts of the sentence. Let us introduce set of copulas C by which homogeneous parts of the sentence are separated. We form the list of homogeneous nouns $S = \{s_1, \ldots, s_m\}$ in accordance with following conditions:

1. Nouns are separated with copula $c_i \in C$;
2. $\forall s_i \in S, \exists s_j \in S : gc_i = gc_j$.

The algorithm is the sequential changing of subordinate syntactic relations for nouns from homogeneous parts of the sentence.

If two last nouns $s_{n-1}, s_n \in S$ are separated with "и" and $\exists s_l \in RL(s_n)$: $\exists GI_i \in MA(s_l) : pos_i = NOUN$ then if $\forall s_k \in RL(s_{n-1}), \neg\exists GI_i \in MA(s_k) :$ $pos_i = NOUN$ then $r_{n-1} = (s_{n-1}, RL(s_{n-1}) \cup s_l)$. If $\exists GI_i \in MA(s_k) : pos_i = NOUN$ then one should finish this part of the second step and perform next check.

If $\forall s_i \in S, \exists GI_j \in MA(s_i) : gc_j = G$ and if $\exists r_p \in R : s_1 \in RL(w_p)$ and $\exists GI_j \in MA(w_p) : pos_j = NOUN$ then $\forall r_q = (w_q, RL(w_q)$ if $s_1 \in RL(w_q)$ then $RL(w_q) = RL(w_q) \cup (s_2, \ldots, s_m)$

Noun phrase identification. We composite an undirected graph $G_R = (V, E), E =$ $E_q \cup E_u$ on the basis of relations from set R. The vertices in this graph are the sentence words, the edges are the subordinate syntactic relation. There are two types of edges: u-edges and q-edges. If $e_{q_l} = (v_i, v_j)$ then $\exists r_p \in R : v_j \in RL(v_i)$ and if $e_{u_l} = (v_i, v_j)$ then $\exists r_p \in R : v_j \in RL(v_i), pos_{v_j} = ADJ$. See Figure 1 for example.

Noun phrase can be identified by using graph G_R. The path $p = (v_1, \ldots, v_k)$ in the graph G_R corresponds to the noun phrase if met one of the following conditions:

1. if $k = 2$ then $e = (v_1, v_2), e \in E_q$;
2. if $k > 2$ then $\exists e_i \in E_u$ and $\exists e_j \in E_q$.

Identified noun phrases form the set $NPh = \{p_1, \ldots, p_f\}$

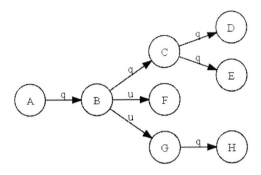

Fig. 1. Example of the relations graph

2.2   Participial Clause Identification

The algorithm for participial clauses identification works with the set of noun phrases NPh identified with the algorithm which was described in previous section. Grammatical information for noun phrase is determined by the main word of the noun phrase. The algorithm is based on the assumption that participle has the same model of relations with dependent syntactic units as verb from which it is formed. Let us introduce some definitions.

Definition 1. *Restriction is a tuple $r = (preposition, gc, type)$ where preposition defines preposition with which the verb is used in a sentence, gc defines grammar case of the dependence noun phrase, type defines the type of the dependence noun phrase, which may be free, connected or conditioned.*

Definition 2. *Relation between verb and dependent syntactic units is a map that assigns to each verb in the initial form a list of restrictions:*

$$VR : v \rightarrow (r_1, \ldots, r_n) \qquad (2)$$

The verb restrictions dictionary has been obtained from the dictionary [5] with some auxiliary modifications.

There are restrictions for some types of participles, for example the passive participles that supplement the list of restrictions obtained from the participle derived from the verb.

Thus, we can introduce the concept of the relation between participle and dependent syntactic units in the Russian sentence.

Definition 3. *Relation between participle and dependent syntactic units is a map that assigns to each participle a list of restrictions:*

$$PR : p \rightarrow (r_1, \ldots, r_k) \qquad (3)$$

The restrictions for the participle p are obtained from the verb v restrictions and the additional participle restrictions $r_1, \ldots, r_l$:

$$PR(p) = VR(v) \cup (r_1, \ldots, r_l) \qquad (4)$$

The participial clause is the participle p and dependent noun phrase $nph \in NPh$ which conforms one of the restrictions from the list $PR(p)$.

Thus, we may formulate the algorithm for participial clause identification: $\exists w_i : \exists GI_j \in MA(w_i) : pos_j = PART$ and $\exists r_p \in PR(w_i)$ and $\exists n_q \in NG : prep_p \in n_q, gc_p = gc_q$. Noun phrase n_q and participle w_i make the participial clause.

3   Evaluation and Example

For evaluation we use the texts from the news corpora on the political topics. The experiments show that the precision of the noun phrases identification is about 95%. In [3] is shown that for the Russian scientific texts precision is about 88%. Own system for noun phrase identification was developed in AOT project. In their paper [4] the authors describe the templates in the regular language. This formalism has some disadvantages. For example, it is impossible to describe the discontinuous noun phrases with the proposed regular language. We note, that our system is devoid of such shortcomings and it can analyze sentences any level of complexity.

The precision of the participial clause identification is about 98% and this is consistent with the results of our preliminary theoretical analysis.

Let us give an example of noun phrase identification algorithm. We have sentence: Оценки состояния и перспектив российской экономики. Denote words in sentence by letters: Оценки — A, состояния — B, перспектив — D, российской — X, экономики — C. In Figure 2 you can see syntactic relations graph between words in sentence.

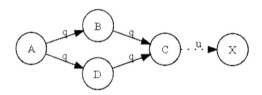

Fig. 2. Relations graph for sentence from example

As a result of the algorithm we found the following noun phrases (words is in the canonical form):

1. экономика российский;
2. перспектива экономика российский;
3. состояние экономика российский;
4. оценка перспектива;
5. оценка состояние;
6. оценка состояние экономика;

7. оценка перспектива экономика;
8. оценка состояние экономика российский;
9. оценка перспектива экономика российский.

4 Conclusion

In this paper we examined the mathematical models designed to solve a broad class of problems on cognitive analysis of text information. The algorithms, formulated in the terms of the proposed models can efficiently and with high accuracy detect dependent syntactical constructions that help us to realize the efficient algorithm of syntactical analysis of the Russian texts. This is achieved by reducing the large number of possible links in the graph arising after morphology analysis due to homonymy in the Russian language. This reduction is possible when we form chains from word combination, preposition and information about relations between verb or participle and dependent syntactic unit.

References

1. Croft, W., Cruse, D.A.: Cognitive linguistics (Cambridge Textbooks in Linguistics). Cambridge University Press, Cambridge (2004)
2. Jurafsky, D., Martin, J.H.: Speech and Language Processing: An Introduction to Natural Language Processing, Computational Linguistics, and Speech Recognition, 2nd edn. Prentice Hall, New Jersey (2008)
3. Belonogov, G.G., Kuznetsov, B.A.: Yazykovye sredstva avtomatizirovannyh informatsionnyh sistem (in russian). Nauka, Moscow (1983)
4. Pankratov, D.V., Gershenzon, L.M., Nozhov, I.M.: Opisanie fragmentacii i sintaksicheskogo analiza v sisteme Dialing. Tehnicheskaya documentacia (2000) (in russian), http://www.aot.ru/
5. Zolotova, G.A.: Sintaksicheskiy slovar: Repertuar elementarnykh edinits russkogo sintaksisa (in russian). Nauka, Moscow (1988)

Data Representation in Machine Learning-Based Sentiment Analysis of Customer Reviews

Ivan Shamshurin

National Research University – Higher School of Economics, School of Applied
Mathematics and Informatics,
20 Myasnitskaya Ulitsa, Moscow, 101000, Russia
ivanshamshurin@gmail.com

Abstract. In this paper, we consider the problem of extracting opinions
from natural language texts, which is one of the tasks of sentiment analysis. We provide an overview of existing approaches to sentiment analysis including supervised (Naive Bayes, maximum entropy, and SVM)
and unsupervised machine learning methods. We apply three supervised
learning methods–Naive Bayes, KNN, and a method based on the Jaccard index – to the dataset of Internet user reviews about cars and report
the results. When learning a user opinion on a specific feature of a car
such as speed or comfort, it turns out that training on full unprocessed reviews decreases the classification accuracy. We experiment with different
approaches to preprocessing reviews in order to obtain representations
that are relevant for the feature one wants to learn and show the effect
of each representation on the accuracy of classification.

Keywords: Supervised Learning, Unsupervised Learning, Sentiment
Analysis, K-nearest Neighbor, Naive Bayes method, Jaccard index.

1 Introduction

People need to collect a lot of information to make the right decision. For instance, when we choose an object O (car, pass to a health resort) we often ask
our friends about advantages and disadvantages of O. In this case we would
value opinions of those people, who used O in the past.

It should be noted that subjective estimations from our friends or O-object
customers are extremely important because potentially these estimations contain
more detailed, comprehensive information about positive and negative features
of the goods. It arises from the fact that information from official producers often
directs our attention to the advantages of the object O.

Generally, sentiment classification in Internet data is an essential modern
trend in the text mining [10]. As a result, a program for getting opinion-based
estimates of the car was developed.

There are two fundamental principles: supervised learning and unsupervised
learning. More detailed information will be given in the next sections of the
paper.

S.O. Kuznetsov et al. (Eds.): PReMI 2011, LNCS 6744, pp. 254–260, 2011.
© Springer-Verlag Berlin Heidelberg 2011

1.1   The Subject of Research and Problems of Sentiment Analysis

In [1] there is an overall survey of the sentiment analysis problems. Themes of tonality defining (a review or comment contains positive, negative or neutral evaluation of a car, film, etc.), objects features detection, summing up opinions, finding out dependent words are analyzed. First of all we are interested in topics related to the tonality defining.

In sentiment analysis a term "object" is used to represent what we attempt to evaluate. In the case of car evaluation the object is a car or its components and properties: saloon, economy of fuel, etc.

Let us consider the problems in sentiment analysis in the following fragment of review:

"(1) The dynamics is 140 h.p.; it is very good, people respect my car on the road. (2) The ergonomics is 5+. (3) The outside appearance left rivals trailing far behind. (4) The quality of sound insulation is insufficient. (5) In conclusion I have to say that this car is very nice".

First of all we have to decide what we want to understand from this review. In this text there are sentences with positive valuation (1, 2 and 3) and sentences with negative valuation (4). Also for every opinion there is a corresponding hypotactic object. For instance, in the sentence (5) the author says about the car as a whole, the sentences (1)–(4) are about the dynamics, ergonomics, outside appearance and the sound insulation correspondingly.

The problem of the implicit object description was investigated in [3]. In a car review we can find sentences like this one: "The fuel economy is great!". In this case we see the explicit cars feature as fuel economy valuation. At the same time there are sentences with implicit feature valuation: "All information can be seen". In this case it is more difficult to define that this positive valuation is about the speedometer.

In distinction from [3] in the current paper we took into account implicit valuations in certain experiments. After the analysis of examples of valuations we have an idea about problems, which appear in sentiment analysis. In the current study the following model will be considered: the object is a car; the tonality will be defined for every car feature: "outside appearance", "comfort", "safety", "reliability", "running characteristics".

2   Approaches to Sentiment Analysis

In the section 11 of [4] three supervised learning methods were compared on the Internet Movie Database (IMDb): Naive Bayes, Maximal Entropy and SVM methods. The classifiers chose a class (positive or negative) of a review and the accuracy was 81.5%, 81.0% and 82.9% correspondingly.

Contrary to [1], we do not define the tonality of the whole text about a car, but classify it positive or negative or neutral for every aspect of the car. In this sense we are much closer to [3].

In this research authors propose the unsupervised learning for tonality defining for every feature of the object. Contrary to [3] the speciality of the considering task is the fact that we know sentence valuations (i.e. tonality) in advance. This circumstance makes our task more difficult and will decrease the accuracy of the classification, because Internet users can write reviews contradictory to the estimates.

Thus our task is not to define the whole tonality of the car review, but to define the author's opinion about car features. It is important to note that reviews are not well structured, the style of narration is free. Some features may be not mentioned in the text. If the review is positive in general, it means that the author does not associate the missing feature with negative emotions and we can tag this feature as positive. That is why the task of defining the tonality of the whole text is a subproblem of our task.

3   Empirical Protocol

3.1   Data Collection and Preprocessing

The Supervised Learning needs the database of the opinions with known cars feature estimates. The comparative analysis of the car-related sites (in Russian) shows that:

- part of them contains opinions without estimates
- there are few sites with opinions with estimates

So, we decided to extract opinion database from the site `http://auto.ru`, because this site is well-known, has high reputation and popularity. Every opinion is placed on the individual page and consists of the title, text, feature's estimates, advantages and disadvantages.

For automatic opinion extraction the programming module was implemented on the Python. As a result, 5098 opinions about 33 car brands were collected.

Every review was transformed into the following structure: text, then the user's estimates.

The cross-validation technique [17] was used for obtaining the training and test sets: 5033 reviews were divided N times (N was approximately 100) into the training set by randomly selecting 90% of all the reviews and the test set (10% of all the reviews). The resulting error was considered to be the average of the errors in each partition.

3.2   Positive and Negative Examples

We should map scores to classes because the source scores are in the five-point scoring system, and we divide opinions into 2 (positive and negative) and 3 (positive, negative, neutral) classes.

$$\{scores\} \rightarrow \{classes\}$$

Mapping 1

Let us define the opinion as positive if it has the scores 4 or 5 and negative if it has the scores 1, 2 or 3.

$$\{1, 2, 3\} \rightarrow \{negative\} \quad \{4, 5\} \rightarrow \{positive\}$$

But as a rule the opinions with score 4 contain pros and cons, so it is preferable to use opinions with score 5 in supervised learning.

Mapping 2

The second type of mapping supposes classifying opinions into three classes:

$$\{4, 5\} \rightarrow \{positive\} \quad \{3\} \rightarrow \{neutral\} \quad \{1, 2\} \rightarrow \{negative\}$$

3.3 Data Representation

We need to transform the original text into 4 different types of text representation, with increasing level of linguistic processing. It was done with "pymorphy" - the Python library for morphological analysis of texts in Russian.

Text representation 1: Text of the opinion without digits, punctuation marks, words consisting of one or two letters, latin symbols.

Text representation 2: Text without pronouns, numerals, prepositions, disjunctive and coordinating conjunctions and parenthesises.

Text representation 3: Phrases of the following types: noun-adjective (with harmony of tenses, cases, gender).

Text representation 4: Normalized adjectives and adverbs.
   In all representations the "not" particle is concatenated to the following word.

Explanations to the text representation 3. After every phrase we wrote its concatenation, because some of the adjectives are both positive and negative: "a fast car" is a positive characteristic, "fast conked" is a negative one. So, we have 5 attributes for learning: "fast", "car", "conk", "fastcar", "fastconk".

4   Descriptions of the Methods

4.1 Naive Bayes Method

Naive Bayes Method is a classical machine learning method. We can find its implementation in [2]. Since the probability of a document is a small quantity, these measures were computed on a logarithmic scale.

4.2 The Method Based on the Jaccard Measure of Set Similarity

As a result of Naive Bayes learning for every word we have got the conditional probabilities of its appearance in every class. We propose the following method of Jaccard measure preprocessing: we can set the thresholds α_1 and α_2, so that three sets of words will be found: G, N and B.

$$G = \{word \mid P(category = \text{``good''} \mid word) \geq \alpha_1 P(category = \text{``neutral''} \mid word)$$

$$\& P(category = \text{``good''} \mid word) \geq \alpha_2 P(category = \text{``bad''} \mid word)\}$$

Likewise we find N and B. Then for every opinion we define T as the set of words of the opinion. The next stage is the Jaccard measure calculation [4] for pairs G and T, N and T, B and T:

$$M_1 = \frac{|T \cap G|}{|T \cup G|} \quad M_2 = \frac{|T \cap N|}{|T \cup N|} \quad M_3 = \frac{|T \cap B|}{|T \cup B|}$$

If the $M_1 = max\{M_1, M_2, M_3\}$ then we tag the opinion as the opinion with positive estimation of the feature (for example, comfort).

4.3   K-Nearest Neighbor

Every document in the analysis can be represented as the frequency vectors of the manually created terms with known tonality:

- positive
fantastic, safety, powerful, etc (83 words in Russian)
- negative
problem, bad, poor, etc (84 words in Russian)

For each opinion we assign the term frequency vector. We took words from the documents with scores 1 (extremely negative) or 5 (positive) with the weight 2.

When the classifier takes an opinion from the test data, we construct the term frequency vector and find k nearest neighbors from the train set. We used the Euclidean metric as the measure of vector similarity.

5   First Results

We know the true estimates from the data (each review contains user's estimate). The machine learning methods provide us with the experimental estimates. So we can compute the precision and recall [8]. It will be the criterium of the method's accuracy.

On the "positive"-"negative" classification (mapping 1) the most accurate results were achieved with the text representation 3 and 4: 63.3% for Bayes classifier and 56.6% for KNN and 68.1% for Jaccard method. In 3-class classification (mapping 2) the similar precisions were achieved.

The poor precision can be caused by the following noise factors:

- Not always users' estimates correspond to the text: there are some opinions with scores "1", but the text of the opinion is extremely positive
- Sometimes in spite of car feature disadvantages in the text, the score is "5"
- Sentences which are not related to the car features are encountered in opinions. People describe the prehistory of the car purchase, for example.

For these reasons the train set should contain only the sentences with the opinions about the cars features. It will decrease the noise influence and more accurate results may be achieved. For more details see section 6.

6 Learning with Advanced Data Representation

A list of terms-indicators was made. These 33 words include five cars features and contain other words which are similar to them: "bracket", "dynamics", "automatic gearbox", "body", "clearance", etc.

The most accurate result was achieved on nouns, adjectives, participles, verbs and adverbs from the sentences with the words from the list of terms-indicators.

The results of the sentences with terms-indicators learning, 3-class classification:

Bayes
Reliability
$Precision = 0.77$
$Recall = 0.77$
Comfort
$Precision = 0.66$
$Recall = 0.66$
Running Characteristics
$Precision = 0.72$
$Recall = 0.72$

KNN (k=5)
Running Characteristics
$Precision = 0.49$
$Recall = 0.36$

Jaccard
Reliability
$Precision = 0.68$
$Recall = 0.44$
Comfort
$Precision = 0.65$
$Recall = 0.32$
Running Characteristics
$Precision = 0.62$
$Recall = 0.3$

7 Conclusion and Future Work

The comparative analysis of the machine learning methods in sentiment analysis was performed. The database of the Internet users' opinions was extracted. Three methods for cars features estimates defining were tested on it. In general, we see a significant difference in classification accuracy depending on preprocessing reviews.

It stands to mention that the precision values are not very high (65%-70%), because of the noise in data, specific nature of the opinion texts: free style of narration, grammar mistakes.

In the future there is going to be more thorough linguistic processing for decreasing influence of the noise, in particular, tools for spelling correction, words relation defining and removing homonymy are going to be implemented.

References

1. Liu, B.: Web Data Mining: Exploring Hyperlinks, Contents, and Usage Data. Springer, Heidelberg (2006)
2. Segaran, T.: Programming Collective Intelligence: Building Smart Web 2.0 Applications. O'Reilly, Sebastopol (2007)

3. Hu, M., Liu, B.: Mining and summarizing customer reviews. In: ACM SIGKDD International Conference on Knowledge Discovery & Data Mining, Seattle, Washington, USA (2004)
4. Berry, M.W., Browne, M.: Lecture notes in data mining. World Scientific Publishing Co, Singapore (2007)
5. Giudici, P.: Applied Data Mining. Statistical Methods for Business and Industry. Wiley, Chichester (2003)
6. Hatzivassiloglou, V., McKeown, K.R.: Predicting the Semantic Orientation of Adjectives. In: Proceedings of the 35th Annual Meeting of the ACL and the 8th Conference of the European Chapter of the ACL, pp. 174–181. ACL, New Brunswick
7. Lutz, M.: Programming Python. O'Reilly, Sebastopol (2010)
8. van Rijsbergen, C.V.: Information Retrieval, 2nd edn. Butterworth, London; Boston (1979)
9. Bird, S., Klein, E., Loper, E.: Natural Language Processing with Python. O'Reilly, Sebastopol (2009)
10. Stavrianoui, A., Andritsos, P., Nicoloyannis, N.: Overview and Semantic Issues of Text Mining. SIGMOD Record 36(3), 23–34 (2007)
11. Poirier, D., Bothorel, C., Boulle, M.: Two possible approaches for opinion analysis in film reviews: statistic and linguistic. In: EMOT-2008: LREC 2008 Workshop on Sentiment Analysis: Emotion, Metaphor, Ontology (2008)
12. Williams, G.K., Anand, S.S.: Predicting the Polarity Strength of Adjectives Using WordNet. In: Third International AAAI Conference on Weblogs and Social Media (2009)
13. Turney, P.D.: Mining the Web for Synonyms: PMI-IR versus LSA on TOEFL. In: Flach, P.A., De Raedt, L. (eds.) ECML 2001. LNCS (LNAI), vol. 2167, pp. 491–502. Springer, Heidelberg (2001)
14. Budanitsky, A., Hirst, G.: Semantic distance in WordNet: An experimental, application-oriented evaluation of five measures. In: Workshop on WordNet and Other Lexical Resources, Second meeting of the North American Chapter of the Association for Computational Linguistics, Pittsburgh (2001)
15. Turney, P.D.: Thumbs up or thumbs down? semantic orientation applied to unsupervised classification of reviews. In: Proceedings of the 40th Annual Meeting of the Association for Computational Linguistics (ACL 2002), pp. 417–424 (2002)
16. Huang, A.: Similarity Measures for Text Document Clustering. In: Proceedings of the Sixth New Zealand Computer Science Research Student Conference NZCSRSC 2008, Christchurch, New Zealand, pp. 49–56 (2008)
17. Geisser, S.: Predictive Inference. Chapman and Hall, New York (1993)

Automatic Retrieval of Parallel Collocations

Valeriy I. Novitskiy

The Moscow Institute of Physics and Technology, Moscow, Russia
nov.valerij@gmail.com

Abstract. An approach to automatic retrieval of parallel (two-language) collocations is described. The method is based on comparison of syntactic trees of two parallel sentences. The key feature of the method is a sequence of filters for getting more precise results.

Keywords: NLP, parallel collocations, automatic information extraction, text mining.

1 Introduction

Most of natural languages consist of hundreds of thousands of words. The amount of two-word combinations is $\approx 10^{10}$, but only a few of them are real collocations.

In this work we study the problem of extracting parallel collocations. A parallel collocation is a combination of a collocation and its translation into another language. We are interested in non-trivial literal translations. Parallel collocations make a valuable linguistic resource. For example, they can be used as an auxiliary material by linguists or as a statistical data in different NLP tasks.

The key feature of the approach described in this work is a sequence of heuristic filters which help to extract the most valuable collocations. Extraction of every possible collocation is intractable, no precise algorithm for the solution of this problem is known. Hence, we have to use some simplifications coming to soft computing of collocations.

Suppose we are given a corpus of parallel texts[1]. These texts are aligned sentence-to-sentence, which means that we know the matchings between parallel units of texts (usually a text unit is one sentence). We use a syntactic analyzer to parse the texts and return respective syntactic trees.

The work described in this paper had several goals:

1. Designing an algorithm for automatic collocation retrieval (with some specific restrictions described below).
2. Collecting statistical data to improve the work of syntactic analyzer in use.
3. Improving two-language dictionary by adding new translations.
4. Creating a Translation Memory database of parallel collocations which can be used as a reference-book by linguists.

---

[1] Texts and its translations into different language.

S.O. Kuznetsov et al. (Eds.): PReMI 2011, LNCS 6744, pp. 261–267, 2011.

1.1 Environment

In our work we used several tools developed in ABBYY:

1. English-Russian dictionary
2. Syntactic analyzer
3. Word-to-Word matching algorithm used for sentence aligning.

The dictionary is based on semantic invariants (or *classes*). For every language there are several possible realizations of those classes (e.g., "competition", "gala" and "event" may be placed in one "competition" class). At the same time homonyms are placed in several classes simultaneously. The corporate dictionary is comprehensive enough and consists of more than 60 000 classes. Distinguishing between homonyms (disambiguation) is done during text analysis and is not discussed here.

The syntactic analyzer takes a single sentence and outputs the best syntactic tree[2] based on internal estimations of quality. The nodes of the tree are semantic classes and arcs are connections between words. It is possible to get wrong results (incorrect words sense selection). In this case we suppose that either wrong collocations will not be produced at all (due to differences of syntactic trees in different languages) or their frequency will be rather small to delete them by the following filtration procedures. The refinement of syntactic tree is attained by parallel analysis of sentences in both languages.

This work does not use such well-known criteria as Mutual Information [2], t-score measure or log-likelihood measure [3], because we choose more predictable selection algorithms. There are many purely statistical algorithms of collocation extraction based on words cooccurrence (e.g., see [4], [5]), but they do not use information about connections between words which we are interested in.

In contrast to other works where syntactic information from texts is used [6], we do not restrict our search to two-words collocations, but look for collocations of different length. In this case one encounters the problem of "partial" collocations: partial collocations are parts of some larger collocations. Here we introduce a new approach to discarding partial collocations.

2 Description of the Method

The algorithm for retrieving collocations can be divided into the following steps:

1. Word-to-word sentence aligning.
2. Single language collocations generation.
3. Matching collocations of different languages to compose parallel collocations.
4. Filtration of infrequent and occasional collocations.

Below we consider each step of the approach in detail.

---

[2] Different representation of sentence structure can be found in [1].

2.1 Word-to-Word Sentence Alignment

We use a dictionary based on semantic invariants, which means that all possible synonyms of a word-sense are placed in one *semantic class*. So the aligning process has to solve the following two main problems:

— Homonyms matching (due to possible incorrect semantic variant choice).
— Several synonyms in one sentence.

The first problem can be solved rather easily. We can take all possible semantic classes to which a word can belong and compare them with all possible classes of the opposite word (pic. 1). In the case they do not have empty intersection we can consider them as translations of each other.

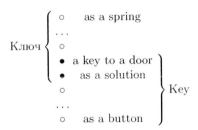

Fig. 1. Semantic classes intersection

The solution of the second problem is based on syntactic trees. We take into account dependencies between words in sentence. For example, we can match two words with better confidence if their parents in syntactic tree correspond to each other.

We compare all words between two sentences and estimate the "quality" of each pair (as a number). Impossible pairs are suppressed by setting prohibition penalty. Then we search for the best pairs (by their integral quality). Thus the problem is reduced to the well-known problem of searching for the best matching in a bipartite graph. This problem has a polynomial-time solution algorithm, e.g. a so-called "Hungarian algorithm" (see [7]).

2.2 One-Language Collocation Production

Let us impose the following constraints on collocations:

— The number of words in a collocation ranges from one to five.
— The result is a subtree of the syntactic tree.
— There are no pronouns in collocations.
— Syntactic word[3] can not be a root of collocation subtree.
— We allow only one "gap" of limited size in the linear realization of a collocation in a sentence.

---

[3] Like pronoun, preposition, auxiliary verb and so on.

2.3   Parallel Collocations Production

We use the results of two previous steps, namely the alignment of parallel sentences and the set of variants of one-language collocations from the same sentences. This information allows us to select one-language collocations and produce candidates for parallel collocations. We impose the following constrains:

- The length difference between a collocation and its translation is less or equal to one word.
- There are some word-to-word correspondences between collocations (the longer collocation the more correspondences there should be).
- It is possible to have no correspondences for short (1–2 words length) collocations. Instead, there should be correspondences between collocation roots and all of their children in the syntactic tree.
- There are no "outgoing" correspondences (that "go out" from a collocation but do not "come into" its translation).

During this step all possible collocations are produced. For example, in the corpus of $\approx 4, 2$ bln fragments there are more than 100 bln different collocations. But only 7 bln of them occur twice as frequent and more.

2.4   Filtration

At this step we select only valuable collocations from that variety we got during the previous step. The main idea is that stable collocations are rather frequent and (almost) always have the same translation. We will omit collocations that are infrequent and have different translations. Some other heuristics will be uncovered below.

There are several collocation filters:

1. Removal of rare collocations (preliminary filtration by frequency with lower threshold).
2. Removal of collocations with stop words.
3. Removal of inner collocations, i.e., those that are parts of another. For example, "Organization for Security" is an internal part of "Organization for Security and Co-operation in Europe".
4. Similarly we should remove "outer" collocations that can occasionally appear. For example, "in the United Nations" is the outer collocations to the just "United Nations".
5. Selection of one translation for each collocations (if it is not too ambiguous). We leave translation if it appears not less than in 70% cases.
6. Final removal of rare collocations.
7. Removal of well-known translations (found in the dictionary).

3 Discussion of Results

3.1 Explanation of Filters Order

Our experiments showed that the proposed sequence of filters results in the highest precision possible with these filters. The filters are applied step by step as they are listed above. Let us explain the reason for such ordering. The frequency filter discards rare collocations that are not interesting for further study. We consider that we cannot prove significance of a rare collocation by any of the following statistical examinations. The stop word filter discards a priori noninteresting variants, reducing the workload on the following steps. The important fact is these two filters remove more than 95% of collocations. Hence, other steps are performed faster and with more precision. Collocations are usually generated with their "sub" and "super" parts. The next filter aims at narrowing such a "range" of collocation (that have one-word difference with each other). Ideally it should leave only one collocation from this "range". Close collocations are compared to each other. Such comparison is sensitive to the "gaps" (absence of collocations with one changed word). That is why this filter is applied at the first steps.

Disambiguation of collocations translation (selection one main variant of translation) causes such "gaps". This is a reason why this filter is used after "sub-super" collocation filtration step. At the same time the previous two filters deal with single-language parts of collocations and disambiguation filter deals with both parts. It is significant to eliminate as many wrong rare variants as possible before this step. For example, if we have two variants of translation "старый дверной замок": "old door-lock" (right) and "door-lock"(partial, wrong) this filter would eliminate both of them (there are no dominant variant). But in fact wrong variant is removed on the previous step.

The second step of filtration by frequency removes those infrequent collocations that supported the performance of "inner-outer" and "disambiguation" filters. With the filter of word-to-word translations they remove collocations we are not interested in (rare or well-known translations). They can be run in any order with the same result.

3.2 Results of Filtration

Experiments were carried out on an English-Russian corpus which consists of about $4.2 \cdot 10^6$ parallel sentences.

There are $\approx 62 \cdot 10^6$ unique pairs of collocation and their translations after the step of "Parallel Collocations Generation". Most of them ($\approx 56 \cdot 10^6$) occur only once in corpus. Filtration results are shown in Fig. 2.

As a result we obtain about $42.5 \cdot 10^3$ of parallel collocations. The result may seem rather modest from the first glance, but it can be significantly improved by adjusting filters' thresholds (in particular, of the "Ambiguity translations" filter) and increasing the number of texts in the collection. Several examples are shown in Fig. 3.

Filter	Output
By frequency (preliminary)	2.5 bln.
By stop-word list	1.1 bln.
"Inner" and "outer" collocatios	≈ 568 000
Ambiguity translations	≈ 105 000
Translated by dictionary	≈ 66 500
By frequency (finally)	42 636

Fig. 2. Filtration process

English	Russian	Occurrences
job time	срок задания	12
galaxy space	космическое пространство	13
other foreign object	иной посторонний объект	5
air transport field	область воздушного транспорта	30
to be beyond the scope of book	выходить за рамки книги	29
to establish under article	учреждать в соответствии со статьёй	75

Fig. 3. Examples of extracted parallel collocations

There are two main measures of results quality: precision and recall. In this work the precision is much more important then the recall. The reason is that it is very difficult to inspect tens of thousand collocation to found ones with errors. The recall, as the amount of collocations generated, can be made larger with the growth of the text base. We prefer to omit rare collocations by analyzing matching errors, however statistical methods like Mutual Information can select them as rare and unexpected word combinations. The precision in our research computed by using collocations for analysis of test corpora. We compare results of analysis with and without collocations. Any found errors are analyzed and the general algorithm is updated to avoid them.

An open problem is how an efficient estimate of precision and recall. Manual markup of large text bases is almost unfeasible. We estimate precision by comparing results with opinions of a random subset of experts. Another problem is comparing with statistical algorithms. The comparison is connected with the difference in produced information (the existence of syntactic links between words in statistical collocations). However, the manual check of random collocations shows good quality in general. An example of such precision estimation is shown in Fig. 4. There are two categories of not good collocations that can be refined by either improving dictionary entities or by customizing the algorithm. An improvement of the algorithm may be attained by eliminating duplicates of text fragments (that can appear in manuals, government documents and so on). We can achieve precision of more than 80% on this sample by introducing this technique.

Quality	Percent
Good collocations	67
Improvable with dictionary	4
Improvable with algorithm	16
Others	12

Fig. 4. Result of manual checking of a random subset of 100 collocations

4   Conclusion

The main result of our work is a method which proved to be useful and is employed now in software for collocation search.

There are several possible way to improve the proposed method:

- Introducing a quality measure for collocations (for ranking them and selecting the best ones).
- Tuning filters thresholds.
- Improving corpora used in computations (by correcting spelling errors and removing occasional bad parallel fragments).

References

1. Bolshakov, I.A.: Computational Linguistics: Models, Resources, Applications. In: Bolshakov, I.A., Gelbukh, A.F. (eds.) IPN - UNAM - Fondo de Cultura Economica (2004)
2. Church, K.W.: Word association norms, mutual information, and lexicography. Computational Linguistics 16(1), 22–29 (1990)
3. Dunning, T.: Accurate methods for the statistics of surprise and coincidence. Computational Linguistics 19(1), 61–74 (1993)
4. Smadja, F.A.: Retrieving collocations from text: Xtract. Computational Linguistics 19(1), 143–177 (1993)
5. Bouma, G.: Collocation extraction beyond the independence assumption. In: Proceedings of the ACL 2010 Conference Short Papers. ACLShort 2010, pp. 109–114. Association for Computational Linguistics, Stroudsburg, PA, USA (2010)
6. Evert, S.: The Statistics of Word Cooccurences Word Pairs and Collocations. Ph.D. thesis / Universität Stuttgart. Institut für Maschinelle Sprachverarbeitung (IMS) (2004)
7. Burkard, R.: Assignment Problems. SIAM, Society for Industrial and Applied Mathematics, Philadelphia (2009)

Displacement Based Unsupervised Metric for Evaluating Rank Aggregation

Maunendra Sankar Desarkar, Rahul Joshi, and Sudeshna Sarkar

Department of Computer Science and Engineering,
Indian Institute of Technology Kharagpur,
Kharagpur, India - 721302
{maunendra,rahulrj,sudeshna}@cse.iitkgp.ernet.in

Abstract. *Rank Aggregation* is the problem of aggregating ranks given by various experts to a set of entities. In context of web, it has applications like *building metasearch engines, combining user preferences* etc. For many of these applications, it is difficult to get labeled data and the aggregation algorithms need to be evaluated against unsupervised evaluation metrics. We consider the Kendall-Tau unsupervised metric which is widely used for evaluating rank aggregation task. Kendall Tau distance between two permutations is defined as the number of pairwise inversions among the permutations. The original Kendall Tau distance treats each inversion equally, irrespective of the differences in rank positions of the inverted items. In this work, we propose a variant of Kendall-Tau distance that takes into consideration this difference in rank positions. We study, examine and compare various available *supervised* as well as *unsupervised* metrics with the proposed metric. We experimentally demonstrate that our modification in *Kendall Tau Distance* makes it potentially better than other available *unsupervised* metrics for evaluating aggregated ranking.

Keywords: Information Retrieval, Rank Aggregation, Distance Metrics, Kendall Tau Distance.

1 Introduction

Rank aggregation problem combines the ranking of entities obtained from multiple ranking functions in order to produce an aggregate ranked list. The input rankings are referred to as base rankers, or experts. There are various scenarios where it is difficult to obtain labeled data and the rankings from different sources need to be aggregated. In such cases, aggregate ranking needs to be evaluated with the help of unsupervised metrics. Generally, in such cases, the resultant aggregate ranking is evaluated by average distance with all available rankings given by different experts. Probably the most widely used distance metric used for this purpose is Kendall Tau Distance. The Kendall Tau distance is a metric that counts the number of pairwise disagreements between two ranked lists.

S.O. Kuznetsov et al. (Eds.): PReMI 2011, LNCS 6744, pp. 268–273, 2011.

However, inversion of a document pair having higher rank distance should be relatively more severe than that of a document pair having lower rank distance. Kendall Tau distance doesn't treat inversions based on their displacement distance. To get better distance between two ranked lists, we can consider displacement distance, displacement position and position weights while computing distance. In this paper, we propose a variant of Kendall Tau distance which treat document pair inversions based on their displacement distance.

There are several supervised and unsupervised metrics for judging the performance of ranking and rank aggregation algorithms. Supervised metrics such as Precision, Recall, NDCG use ground truth information about document relevance for determining the quality of the algorithm. Most of the unsupervised metrics for rank aggregation are based on distances between two ranked lists. Kendall Tau Distance, Spearman Footrule are two such distance measures widely discussed in literature.

Several researchers [10,2,8] have pointed out that it may not be suitable for evaluation of rank aggregation as it gives equal importance to all the pairs. [4] discusses of a modification to Spearman FootRule distance, called Canberra distance for ranked lists. Canberra distance considers element positions for computing the distance. Cost of inversions are high when the items are at the top in either of the lists. [5] extended both Spearman Footrule distance and Kendall Tau Distance and proposed new formulations of Kendall Tau distance and Spearman Footrule distance by taking into consideration element weights, position weights and pairwise distances between permutations. Each inverted pair (i, j), bears a penalty of $w_i w_j$ where w_i and w_j are determined by the positions of the items i and j in the two lists. Getting element weight and similarities between items are difficult. So we concentrate on the version where w_is are set according to position weights.

We propose a variant of Kendall Tau Distance where in we penalize a document pair inversion if it has higher rank distance. This way, the overall Kendall Tau distance will be more if the list has document inversions with higher rank distance and less with lower rank distance. We propose such a metric and name it KTDispSq. We compare this metric with existing unsupervised metrics, and experimentally demonstrate KTDispSq is potentially better than other metrics.

2   Some Existing Distance Measures

Let τ_1, τ_2 be two lists. Also assume that $\tau_1(i)$ denotes the rank of item i in τ_1. We now give the definitions of few distance measures that are used for evaluating rank aggregation outputs.

- **Kendall Tau Distance (KT):** KT distance between two ranked lists is defined as the number of inversions, i.e. item pairs (i, j) such that in one list i appears before j, and in the other list j appears before i. Formally, $KT(\tau_1, \tau_2) = \sum_{i<j} I_{ij}$. Value of I_{ij} is 1 if (i, j) is inverted and 0 otherwise.

- **Spearman Footrule (SF):** This metric can be expressed as: $\sum_i |\tau_1(i) - \tau_2(i)|$. SF is known to be a 2-approximation of KT.

- **Canberra:** Canberra distance [4] between two ranked lists τ_1 and τ_2 is defined as: $\sum_i \frac{|\tau_1(i) - \tau_2(i)|}{|\tau_1(i)| + |\tau_2(i)|}$. The denominator ensures that cost of inversions are high when the items are at the top in either of the lists.

- **Position weighted Kendall Tau:** We call this measure as PosWtD. It penalizes each inversion (i, j) by $w_i w_j$ where w_i and w_j are determined by the positions of the items i and j in the two lists. Mathematically, $PosWtD(\tau_1, \tau_2) = \sum_{i<j} w_i w_j I_{ij}$. Details on how the weights are set can be found in [5].

3   The Proposed Metric (KTDispSq)

The proposed metric KTDispSq penalizes an inverted pair by an increasing function of the rank distances d1 and d2 for the two lists. More formally, the cost of each inversion is defined as:

$$\bar{K}_{i,j}(\tau_1, \tau_2) = \frac{d_1^2 + d_2^2}{4n^2}$$

Here,

- d_1 = absolute rank distance between documents i and j in ranked list τ_1
- d_2 = absolute rank distance between documents i and j in ranked list τ_2
- n = total number of documents in ranked lists τ_1, τ_2

This way, an inverted docuemnt pair (i, j) with more rank distance in both lists gets penalized more and contributes more in computing distance. The distance between two ranked lists is computed as the sum of these penalties over all the inverted pairs.

Example: Consider two ranked lists as

$$\tau_1 = [1\ 4\ 3\ 2\ 5]\ and\ \tau_2 = [1\ 5\ 3\ 4\ 2].$$

Here we have four inverted pairs as (2,5) (3,4) (3,5) and (4,5). Inverted pair weights for KTDispSq can be computed as below:

- $(2,5) = \frac{(1^2 + 3^2)}{4*5^2} = 0.1$
- $(3,4) = \frac{(1^2 + 1^2)}{4*5^2} = 0.02$
- $(3,5) = \frac{(2^2 + 2^2)}{4*5^2} = 0.08$
- $(4,5) = \frac{(3^2 + 2^2)}{4*5^2} = 0.13$

Hence, the total distance KTDispSq between the two lists is: $(0.1 + 0.02 + 0.08 + 0.13) = .33$.

We later experimentally compare the performance of KTDispSq with that of some existing unsupervised measures such as KT, Canberra Distance [4], SF, and PosWtD [5].

4   Experiments and Results

In order to judge how good the proposed measure is, we propose two sets of experiments. Details of the experimental mechanisms, and the results are given in the following subsections.

We consider Borda[9], QuickSort[9], MC4[3], CombScore[1] as rank aggregation methods along with Precision, MAP, Kendall Tau (KT), KTDisp, KT-DispSq, Canberra [4], Spearman Footrule (SF) and PosWtD [5] as metrics. We worked on LETOR 4.0 MQ2007, MQ2008 and Yahoo LTRC datasets for all experiments. These datasets have querywise document scores for various features. We consider each feature as a ranker or an expert. Due to space constraints, we report results on MQ2007 dataset only.

4.1   Correlation with Other Metrics

In this experiment, we first try several unsupervised rank aggregation algorithms and evaluate them using the supervised evaluation metrics mentioned above. The unsupervised metrics compared in this paper are all distance metrics, and lower score indicates better quality of the aggregation result. On the other hand, for the supervised metric MAP, higher score indicates better performance. Hence, a good algorithm should get low score for the unsupervised metrics used in this paper, but high score for MAP. In other words, if we look at the scores given to the rank aggregation algorithm for different input rankings, then the scores given by the unsupervised metrics should be negatively correlated with the scores given by MAP. We can say that the more negative the correlation, the better the unsupervised distance metric.

We use this correlation analysis to compare the performances of the unsupervised evaluation measures. Results indicate that our modification makes Kendall Tau Distance more correlated with MAP. The results are shown in Table 1. KTDispSq is more negatively correlated for almost all rank aggregation methods we experimented. For two experiments KTDispSq is second to Canberra, but the differences are small in those cases. For the remaining experiments, KTDispSq outperforms others by large margins. This suggests that our variant makes Kendall Tau more closer to the supervised evaluation metric Mean Average Precision.

Table 1. Correlations with MAP for LETOR MQ2007 dataset. More negative is better.

	Borda	SumScore	MC4	QSort
KT	-0.015	-0.112	-0.129	-0.126
KTDispSq	**-0.058**	-0.123	-0.136	**-0.134**
SF	-0.020	-0.109	-0.124	-0.118
Canberra	-0.041	**-0.124**	**-0.137**	-0.127
PosWtD	0.031	0.240	0.041	0.049

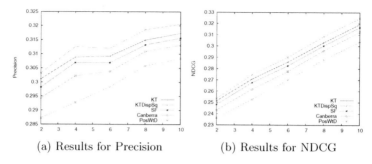

(a) Results for Precision   (b) Results for NDCG

Fig. 1. Improvement in Precision and NDCG by picking the best expert according to minimum average value of the measures. Higher values are better.

4.2   Pick the Best Expert

In the second set of experiments, we tried to see whether our modifications enable us to get better output for a rank aggregation task. For this, we took as experts some widely used features from the test datasets. For each query, we pick the expert which is closest to the remaining experts according to the metric value. Mathematically, if $R_1, R_2, \cdots, R_n$ are the input rankings, then we output as aggregate result R_i such that $i = \arg\min_i \frac{1}{n-1} \sum_{k=1}^{n} dist(R_i, R_k)$. Here $dist$ represents the distance metric used for selecting the best expert. Features 1, 11, 15, 16, 20, 21, 40, 41, 45 were used as experts for these experiments. The features correspond to scores of documents based on *tf, tf-idf*, BM25, Language Model scores. Such features are often used for evaluating rank aggregation results [7]. Details of the features can be seen from [6].

Figure 1 displays graphically the Precision and NDCG values for the experiments. We showed Precision values for rank positions $2, 4, 6, 8$ and 10. As the

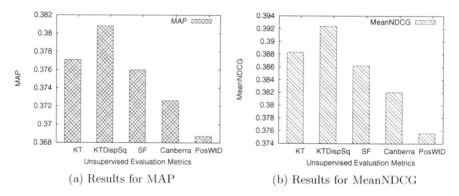

(a) Results for MAP   (b) Results for MeanNDCG

Fig. 2. Improvement in MAP and MeanNDCG by picking the best expert according to minimum average value of the measures. Higher values are better.

graph suggests, the average Precision and NDCG scores obtained by selecting the lists using our measure are higher than that obtained by using other methods.

We also compared the values of MAP and MeanNDCG for this experiment. Results are shown in Figure 2. For both the measures, higher values indicate better performance. Here also we see that the ranked lists selected by using our measure obtain better scores than others. The results seem to indicate the efficacy of the proposed measure.

5   Conclusions and Future Work

We proposed a displacement based variant of Kendall Tau Distance for evaluating aggregated ranking. We can say that displacement based modification in Kendall Tau Distance makes it closer to other supervised metrics such as Precision and NDCG. Using KTDispSq in rank aggregation approach gives better Precision and NDCG, we can conclude that use of KTDispSq in place of Kendall Tau Distance may improve Rank Aggregation results. We plan to take into consideration position of displacement/inversion of document pair. Displacement at upper ranks should get penalized more than that of lower ranks. We would like to devise an unsupervised rank aggregation algorithm which directly optimizes this metric to generate the aggregated ranking.

References

1. Belkin, N.J., Kantor, P., Fox, E.A., Shaw, J.A.: Combining the evidence of multiple query representations for information retrieval. In: TREC 1995, Elmsford, NY, USA, pp. 431–448. Pergamon Press, Inc., Oxford (1995)
2. Carterette, B.: On rank correlation and the distance between rankings. In: SIGIR 2009, pp. 436–443. ACM Press, New York (2009)
3. Dwork, C., Kumar, R., Naor, M., Sivakumar, D.: Rank aggregation methods for the web. In: WWW 2001, pp. 613–622 (2001)
4. Jurman, G., Riccadonna, S., Visintainer, R., Furlanello, C.: Canberra distance on ranked lists. In: Proceedings, Advances in Ranking NIPS 2009 Workshop, pp. 22–27 (2009)
5. Kumar, R., Vassilvitskii, S.: Generalized distances between rankings. In: WWW 2010, pp. 571–580 (2010)
6. T.-y. Liu, J., Xu, T., Qin, W., Xiong, H.: Li: Letor: Benchmark dataset for research on learning to rank for information retrieval. In: SIGIR 2007 Workshop on Learning to Rank for Information Retrieval (2007)
7. Liu, Y., Liu, T.-Y., Qin, T., Ma, Z., Li, H.: Supervised rank aggregation. In: WWW, pp. 481–490 (2007)
8. Sanderson, M., Soboroff, I.: Problems with kendall's tau. In: SIGIR 2007, pp. 839–840 (2007)
9. Schalekamp, F., van Zuylen, A.: Rank aggregation: Together we're strong. In: ALENEX, pp. 38–51 (2009)
10. Yilmaz, E., Aslam, J.A., Robertson, S.: A new rank correlation coefficient for information retrieval. In: SIGIR 2008, pp. 587–594 (2008)

Sentence Ranking for Document Indexing

Saptaditya Maiti[1], Deba P. Mandal[1], and Pabitra Mitra[2]

[1] Machine Intelligence Unit, Indian Statistical Institute, Kolkata, India
[2] Dept. of Computer Science and Engineering, Indian Institute of Technology,
Kharagpur, India
{saptaditya,dpmandal}@isical.ac.in,
pabitra@gmail.com

Abstract. This article discusses a new document indexing scheme for
information retrieval. For a structured (*e.g.*, scientific) document, Pasi *et
al.* proposed varying weights to different sections according to their importance in the document. This concept is extended here to unstructured
documents. Each sentence in a document is initially assigned weight
(significance in the document) with the help of a summarization technique. Accordingly, the term frequency of a term is decided as the sum
of weights of the sentences the term belongs. The method is verified on a
real life dataset using leading existing information retrieval models, and
its performance has been found to be superior to conventional indexing
schemes.

Keywords: information retrieval, document indexing, sentence ranking,
relative entropy.

1 Introduction

Information retrieval is finding content (usually documents) of an unstructured
nature (usually test) that satisfies an information need from within large collection [1]. Information retrieval System (IRS) is based on relevance of a document
to a query. Several methods have been proposed over years. The use of a strong
query and a good retrieval method do not ensure good performance. In fact, the
retrieval effectiveness is heavily affected by the model adopted for representing
documents, since the retrieval mechanism performs a comparison between the
user query and the representation of documents [2][3].

The conventional indexing schemes assume that the information is homoge-
neously distributed in documents. Pasi *et al.* [2][3] claimed that this assumption
does not hold for a structured (*e.g.*, scientific) document. The information content of a document varies from one section to another and hence, the terms in
the more important sections should contribute more in retrieval methods. We
argue that this is also true for unstructured documents. Usually, the flow of
information in a given document is not uniform, which means that some parts
are more important (informative) than others [4]. We know that summarization
techniques distinguish the more informative parts (*i.e.*, sentences) from the less
ones.

S.O. Kuznetsov et al. (Eds.): PReMI 2011, LNCS 6744, pp. 274–279, 2011.

In the present investigation, the weight/importance of a sentence in a document is initially measured with the help of a summarization technique, which is taken here as the relative entropy based method [5]. All of the terms in a sentence are assumed to have the same weight which is equal to the weight of the sentence. To obtain the term frequency (overall significance) of a term in a document, the weights for each of the occurrences of the term are aggregated. The effectiveness of the proposed indexing scheme is verified for a few leading retrieval models on FIRE dataset [6] and the results are found to be quite encouraging.

The rest of the paper is organized as follows. In section 2, we describe the proposed indexing scheme. The implementation and effectiveness of the scheme is demonstrated in section 3. Section 4 finds the conclusions.

2   Proposed Indexing Scheme

As mentioned earlier, the proposed document indexing scheme is an extension of the model proposed by Pasi *et al.* [2][3]. They suggested to provide different importance to different sections for indexing structured (*e.g.*, scientific) documents. For example, in a scientific document, the terms in the 'Title' carry more information than those in other sections (*e.g.*, 'abstract', 'introduction', etc.). In [2], different functions for different sections were proposed for providing varying weights/importance to the terms based on their belongingness in the document.

For the sake of extending the above model, we intend to impose structure to an unstructured document and then to allow varying weights to the terms based on their positions in the document. We find that extraction based text summarization methods analyze the importance/informativeness of different sentences in a document for selecting a few sentences as the summary of the document. Therefore, summarization techniques may be useful in finding the importance of the sentences in a document.

In the current investigation, each sentence in an unstructured document is visualized as to behave like a section of a structured document. With the help of a summarization technique, the informativeness of a sentence in a document is estimated, *i.e.*, a weight is obtained for the sentence signifying its importance in the document.

The proposed indexing scheme consists of two parts. In the first part, weights of the sentences in a document are obtained using a text summarization method. The second part is concerned with the calculation of the term frequency of each of the terms in the document.

A) Sentence ranking: A text summarization method is used for ranking the sentences of a document. In this report, we have considered the relative entropy based summarization technique proposed by Kumar *et al.* [5].

This technique initially estimates the probability of a word w in a sentence S as

$$P(w|S) = \frac{tf(w, S)}{|S|} \tag{1}$$

where $tf(w, S)$ is the frequency of w in S and $|S|$ is the number of words in S.

Similarly, the probability of w in a document D is estimated as

$$P(w|D) = \frac{tf(w,D)}{|D|} \tag{2}$$

where $tf(w,D)$ is the frequency of w in D and $|D|$ is the number of words in D.

A sentence S is provided a weight based on its comparison to the document D. Comparison is done with relative entropy, *i.e.*, KL-Divergence of S with D as

$$KL_S = \sum_w P(w|S) log \frac{P(w|S)}{P(w|D)}. \tag{3}$$

As explained in [5], the importance of a sentence, I_S, is inversely proportional to KL_S, *i.e.*,

$$I_S = \frac{1}{KL_S}. \tag{4}$$

We take I_S as the weights of the sentences.

B) Term frequency: The significance of a sentence in a document is obtained previously. We assume that the significance is same for all the terms in a sentence. Accordingly, we assign the sentence weight to all of its terms. It may be realized that a term belonging to two different sentences may not have the same information content and hence the term may have different scores. Aggregating the scores of a term for all of its occurrences in a document, the term frequency of a term t in D is calculated as

$$tf(t,D) = \sum_{S_i \ if \ t \epsilon S_i} I_{S_i} \tag{5}$$

The term frequency $tf(t,D)$ as in eqn.(5) reflects the importance of the term in document D based not only on the number of occurrences but also on the information content for each of its occurrences. For example, suppose a document has the same number of occurrences for two terms t_1 and t_2, but t_1 has appeared in more important sentences than t_2. It is easy to realize here that t_1 is more significant than t_2. In such a case, the proposed scheme will find tf value for t_1 higher than that of t_2 while the conventional indexing schemes will find the same tf value for both t_1 and t_2. Hence, the proposed scheme should be a better indexing scheme than the existing ones which are based on raw counts of terms.

3   Implementation and Results

A new indexing scheme is described in the previous section. The effectiveness of the scheme is verified on the FIRE dataset [6] using Terrier platform [7]. We have considered some of the leading retrieval models available in Terrier, namely, Okapi BM25 [8], DFRBM25, InexpB2, InexpC2, IFB2, InL2 and BB2 [9]. A brief description of these models is provided in Table 1. It is to be noted that all the models have some parameters which need to be tuned. The parameter values mentioned in Table 1 against each model are the ones which are set in the Terrier platform [7] as default and we have used those values in implementing the models. The results are evaluated here based on Mean Average Precision (MAP).

Table 1. Description of retrieval models considered

Model	Description	Parameter Values Considered
Okapi BM25	The original BM25 probabilistic model	k1=1.2, k2=0, k3=8, b=0.75
DFR_BM25	The DFR version of BM25	k1=1.2, k2=0, k3=1000, c=1
In_expB2	Inverse expected document frequency model for randomness, the ratio of two Bernoulli's processes for first normalisation, and Normalisation 2 for term frequency normalisation	c=1
In_expC2	Inverse expected document frequency model for randomness, the ratio of two Bernoulli's processes for first normalisation, and Normalisation 2 for term frequency normalisation with natural logarithm	c=1
IFB2	Inverse Term Frequency model for randomness, the ratio of two Bernoulli's processes for first normalisation, and Normalisation 2 for term frequency normalisation	c=1
InL2	Inverse document frequency model for randomness, Laplace succession for first normalisation, and Normalisation 2 for term frequency normalisation	c=1
BB2	Bose-Einstein model for randomness, the ratio of two Bernoulli's processes for first normalisation, and Normalisation 2 for term frequency normalisation	c=1

For, each of the models, we have experimented with both the conventional (based on raw counts) as well as proposed indexing schemes. In all the cases, the models with the proposed indexing scheme are found to perform better than that with the conventional indexing schemes. The MAP values of the said retrieval models with the conventional and the proposed indexing schemes are shown in Table 2. For more clarity, these results are shown graphically in Figure 1.

Table 2. MAP of different models with conventional and proposed indexing schemes on FIRE dataset

Indexing Scheme	BM25	DFRBM25	InExpB	InExpC	IFB2	InL2	BB2
Conventional	0.5298	0.5304	0.5347	0.5299	0.5339	0.5420	0.5280
Proposed	0.5732	0.5734	0.5798	0.5744	0.5803	0.5781	0.5747

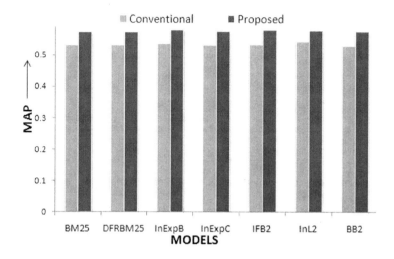

Fig. 1. MAP of different models with conventional and proposed indexing schemes

4   Conclusions

A new document indexing scheme is proposed in this article. Pasi *et al.* proposed different importance to terms in different sections of structured documents. We have extended this idea to unstructured documents. We assigned different scores to the sentences of a document using a summarization technique. It is to be mentioned here that we have taken relative entropy based summarization method for ranking the sentences, but one can take any other good summarization method. Instead of taking raw count for term frequency as in conventional indexing methods, we proposed the summation of scores of the sentences the term belongs to be the term frequency.

We have implemented this scheme in Terrier Platform and tested on FIRE dataset for a few leading information retrieval models. In all the cases considered, the performance of this scheme is found to be better than in the conventional term frequency. But, to make stronger claims the method is to be tested on more datasets.

References

1. Manning, C.D., Raghavan, P., Schütze, H.: An Introduction to Information Retrieval. Cambridge University Press, New York (2008)
2. Bordogna, G., Pasi, G.: Controlling retrieval through a user-adaptive representation of documents. International Journal of Approximate Reasoning 12, 317–339 (1995)
3. Pasi, G.: Fuzzy Sets in Information Retrieval: State of the Art and Research Trends. In: Bustince, H., Herrera, F., Montero, J. (eds.) Fuzzy Sets and Their Extensions: Representation, Aggregation and Models, pp. 517–535. Springer, Heidelberg (2008)
4. Das, D., Martins, A.: A Survey on Automatic Text Summarization. Literature Survey for the Language and Statistics II Course at CMU (2007)
5. Kumar, C., Pingali, P., Varma, V.: A light-weight summarizer based on language model with relative entropy. In: Proc. of the ACM symposium on Applied Computing (SAC 2009). ACM, New York (2009)
6. Forum for Information Retrieval Evaluation (FIRE),
   `http://www.isical.ac.in/~fire/`
7. Ounis, I., Lioma, C., Macdonald, C., Plachouras, V.: Research Directions in Terrier: a Search Engine for Advanced Retrieval on the Web. Novatica/UPGRADE, Special Issue on Next Generation Web Search 8(1), 49–56 (2007)
8. Robertson, S.E., Walker, S.: Some simple approximations to the 2-poisson model for probabilistic weighted retrieval. In: Proc. of 17th Annual Int. Conf. on Research and Development in Information Retrieval, Dublin, pp. 232–241 (1994)
9. Amati, G.: Probability models for information retrieval based on divergence from randomness. Phd thesis, University of Glasgow (2003)

Optimal Parameter Selection for Image Watermarking Using *MOGA*

Dinabandhu Bhandari, Lopamudra Kundu, and Sankar K. Pal

Center for Soft Computing Research, Indian Statistical Institute, Kolkata, India
dinabandhu.bhandari@gmail.com

Abstract. The notion of the proposed methodology is to optimize multidimensional nonlinear problem of conflicting nature that exists among imperceptibility and robustness in image watermarking. The methodology exploits the potentiality of Multi-Objective Genetic Algorithm (MOGA) in searching multiple non-dominated solutions lying on the Pareto front. The characteristics curve of the image are then analyzed and the most appropriate solution is selected using a merit function defined over evaluation measures. The efficacy of the suggested method is demonstrated by reporting the resultant watermarked images and restored watermarks extracted from their mean and median filtered versions.

Keywords: Image Characteristics Curve, Merit Function, Imperceptibility, Robustness, SSIM.

1 Introduction

Digital Watermarking, which is a digital adaptation of the traditional visible paper watermark, is an important sub-discipline of information hiding. Though visible digital watermarks are in use, most of the research works are centered on imperceptible digital watermarking that has wider applications [8]. It includes copyright protection, traitor tracking using fingerprinting, copy protection in digital multimedia distribution systems, image authentication and many more. Commonly used digital watermarking techniques for images include LSB (least significant bit) replacement, the patchwork algorithm by Bender et al.[12], predictive coding, discrete Fourier transform, discrete cosine transform, Mellin-Fourier transform [1], hierarchical watermark extraction process based on wavelet transformation by Xia et al.[14], spread spectrum technique [10], phase modulation, amplitude modulation etc. Progressive watermarking technique in DCT (Discrete cosine transform) domain was proposed by Huang et al. where genetic algorithm was used to search the optimal frequency band for embedding of watermark while improving simultaneously security, robustness and visual quality of the watermarked image[7].

Two major tasks are involved in fulfilling these requirements:

1. Selection of an appropriate modulation/mapping function (reversible) to embed the auxiliary image into the cover image for obtaining a desired output. Usually, a suitable nonlinear reversible mapping function is used.
2. Selection of objective functions to evaluate the embedded image.

S.O. Kuznetsov et al. (Eds.): PReMI 2011, LNCS 6744, pp. 280–285, 2011.

Given the images (cover and auxiliary), it is difficult to select a modulation function which will be best suited without prior knowledge of the image statistics [3]. Even if we are given the image statistics, it may be possible to estimate only approximately the function required for watermarking. Moreover, to make the evaluation process objective, it is necessary to define appropriate objective functions that will quantitatively measure the embedded image with respect to imperceptibility and robustness [2].

The effectiveness of multi-objective genetic algorithm (MOGA) is exploited to find a number of solutions in the Pareto-optimal front. Automatic selection of an optimum solution is made using the image characteristics curve (ICC) that follows the concept of operating characteristics curve (OCC). In this context, the merit of a solution is calculated taking into account the effect of evaluation measures and their importance [4]. The merit of a solution is derived keeping in mind the simultaneous optimization of multiple objectives and their characteristics.

2   Proposed Methodology

The proposed methodology consists of 3 major parts.

1. Selection of embedding region and modulation function.
2. Selection of evaluation measures and formulation of MOGA.
3. Automatic selection of suitable solution.

Embedding region and modulation function: The embedding region is determined based on the distribution of the gray values of the cover image. The region from the cover image can be selected from its histogram on the basis of higher frequency of occurrence in pixel values in either end or on the basis of the histogram of the difference matrix [9]. A mask, equal in size as that of the auxiliary image, is used to search dynamically for the proper window where the watermark can be embedded. Once the embedding region is chosen, proper modulation function is used to embed the watermark. Most commonly used modulation functions[9] are:

- Power-law function: $x'_{m+i,n+j} = A(a_{i,j} + \epsilon)^{\mu}$.
- Parabolic function: $x'_{m+i,n+j} = A(1 + \mu\sqrt{(a_{i,j} + \epsilon)})$.

Where A, ϵ and μ are parameters of modulation functions.

Estimation of parameters using MOGA and formulation of objective functions: To estimate the parameters of the modulation function, mentioned above, the non-dominated sorting algorithm (NSGAII) is adopted in implementing the proposed methodology [11]. Real coded genetic algorithm is used, where a string of 3 real numbers is considered as chromosome. Imperceptibility, robustness against mean and median filtering are the three objective functions considered in the implementation of the algorithm. They are defined as follows:
Imperceptibility (Imp):

$$\frac{\sum_{i=1}^{M} \sum_{j=1}^{N} |x'_{m+i,n+j} - x_{m+i,n+j}|}{M.N} \tag{1}$$

Robustness against mean filtering (R(mean):

$$\frac{\sum_{i=1}^{M} \sum_{j=1}^{N} |x'_{m+i,n+j}(mean) - a_{i,j}|}{M.N} \tag{2}$$

Robustness against mean filtering (R(median):

$$\frac{\sum_{i=1}^{M} \sum_{j=1}^{N} |x'_{m+i,n+j}(median) - a_{i,j}|}{M.N} \tag{3}$$

Where, $(M \times N)$ is dimension of the auxiliary image, $x_{i,j}$, $a_{i,j}$ and $x'_{i,j}$ respectively are gray values of (i,j)th pixel of the cover, auxiliary and embedded images. $x'_{i,j}(mean)$ and $x'_{i,j}(median)$ are respectively the mean and median of the (3×3) neighborhood of the (i,j)th pixel of the watermarked image. Watermark recovery process uses inverse transformation function that maps $x'_{m+i,n+j}$ into $x_{i,j}$ and thus the embedded image can be retrieved.

Automatic selection of suitable solution: The characteristics with respect to the objective functions of the non-dominated solutions contained in the archive are analyzed in selecting an appropriate and pragmatic solution. It is clear that a non-dominated solution optimizing one function does not optimize all others. Therefore, it is wise to select intuitively a solution that produces lower (near optimal) values for all the objective functions taken into account. To select such a suitable solution, a merit function can be defined taking into account the effect of all the objective functions with appropriate importance. In order to make a comparison between the decrease/ increase between the values of different functions, a better indicator is to divide these decrease/ increase by the range of the functions. This intuition helps to define a merit function (μ) for r objective functions as follows:

$$\mu(s) = \sum_{i=1}^{r} \frac{f_i(s) - f_{i,min}}{f_{i,max} - f_{i,min}}, \tag{4}$$

Where, $f_i(s)$ is the value of the ith objective function for string s, $f_{i,min}$ and $f_{i,max}$ respectively are the minimum and maximum values of the ith function among all strings present in the archive. The maximum and minimum values of the functions are taken with respect to the explored non-dominated strings belonging to the archive.

3   Implementation and Results

The proposed algorithm is implemented by embedding an auxiliary image into a cover image and extracting the watermark from mean and median filtered versions of watermarked image. Power law function is used as the modulation function. The domains of the parameters considered are $A \in [0, 10]$, $\epsilon \in [0, 0.1]$ and $\mu \in [0, 1]$. For both mean and median filtering, (3×3) window is used. The effectiveness of the methodology has been demonstrated here for two cover images :Bandon beach(Bandon) (size (610×403)) and Fontaine des Terreaux(Terreaux) (size (768×512)) and two auxiliary images (watermark): Intel logo (size (32×16)) and IAPR logo(size (44×18)), depicted in fig. 1 [5]. Imperceptibility and Robustness defined in (1)-(3) are taken as the objective functions. The genetic parameters used for MOGA based watermarking method are: Size of population and archive = 20, Number of generations = 500, Probability of cross-over = 0.8 and Probability of mutation = 0.1. The algorithm is executed several times (500 generations for each run)for a pair of cover and auxiliary image. In each run we get 20 different sets of parameter values.

(a)   (b)   (c)   (d)

Fig. 1. Cover Images - (a) Bandon and (b) Terreaux; Watermark Images - (c) Intel and (d) IAPR

Fig. 2(a) depicts image characteristics curve for 20 different set of solutions for a particular run when Bandon is the cover image and Intel is the embedded logo. The graph shows how the objective function values vary with different solutions. A closer look at ICC will clearly reveal that all the solutions from 12 to 15 produce low values for all the three objective functions and may therefore appear comparable. Further investigation shows that merit function value corresponding to solution number 14 is minimum. The watermarked image obtained using the solution 14, and extracted watermarks after mean and median filtering of the embedded image are shown in fig 2(b)-2(d). The resultant images show that the parameter values corresponding to minimum merit function value can produce high quality watermarked image in terms of imperceptibility and robustness. This proves indeed that merit function value can estimate properly the most suitable solution among the set of non-dominated solutions.

Similar results (not presented here for space scarcity) are obtained for other combinations of cover and watermark images mentioned before, viz., Bandon - IAPR, Terreaux - Intel and Terreaux - IAPR. Visual inspection of these 3 sets of ICC curves reveal similar scenario as explained before. Same set of watermark images are embedded in several other cover images available in [5] and found similar performance of the proposed methodology.

To validate the results obtained, we have calculated SSIM between a given pair of cover and watermarked images for different solutions to investigate the variation of SSIM index with merit function value. Greater is the SSIM index, better will be the imperceptibility of the watermarked image [13,6]. The SSIM measures for imperceptibility and robustness separately and the combined SSIM index for four sets of images are given in Table 1. The combined SSIM indices

(a)   (b)   (c)   (d)

Fig. 2. Watermarked image and extracted watermarks for Bandon and Intel together with ICC

Table 1. SSIM measures for different sets of cover and watermark images

Cover	Watermark	Soln.	SSIM(I)	SSIM(Rm)	SSIM(Rmd)	Combined
Bandon	Intel	14	0.9997	0.614	0.7576	2.3713
"	"	7	0.9998	0.1995	0.5911	1.7904
"	"	11	0.9993	0.623	0.7351	2.358
"	"	13	0.9997	0.3508	0.5988	1.9493
Bandon	IAPR	16	0.9996	0.4377	0.5308	1.9681
"	"	19	0.9995	0.0126	0.1909	1.203
"	"	15	0.9968	0.434	0.5336	1.9644
"	"	13	0.9993	0.0398	0.0246	1.0637
Terraux	Intel	15	0.9998	0.7007	0.7589	2.4594
"	"	16	0.9998	0.6853	0.766	2.4511
"	"	14	0.9998	0.6956	0.7595	2.4549
Terraux	IAPR	17	0.9998	0.4919	0.5686	2.0603
"	"	4	0.9998	0.497	0.5479	2.0447
"	"	16	0.9998	0.5006	0.5526	2.053
"	"	19	0.9998	0.5006	0.5526	2.053

corresponding to different solutions reveal that the individual SSIM indices for imperceptibility, robustness against mean and median filtering may not be maximum for the preferred solution, but the combined SSIM index is maximum for the solution corresponding to minimum merit function value. This indeed proves quantitatively that merit is a good measure in choosing the best optimum solution among the set of non-dominated solution which optimizes both imperceptibility and robustness and can produce high quality watermarked images. The distortion is introduced with the help of Stirmark benchmark software that is a generic tool used for introducing attacks on an image like JPEG compression, Gaussian noise, non-linear filtering, cropping, rotation etc.

4   Conclusions

The effectiveness of MOGA in the automatic selection of modulation operator is tested for various cover and watermark images. The algorithm determines number of optimum parameter sets rather than a single one in selecting an appropriate modulation function. Afterwards, The image characteristics curve and merit function are used to select automatically the best one among the optimal parameter sets. Further work may be carried out to extend the proposed concept involving different transformation and objective functions.

Acknowledgements

Authors sincerely acknowledge Prof. Malay K. Kundu of MIU, Indian Statistical Institute for constructive discussion and suggestion. Sankar K. Pal acknowledges the J. C. Bose National Fellowship of the Government of India.

References

1. Ruanaidh, J.J.K.Ó., Pun, T.: Rotation, translation and scale invariant digital image watermarking. In: Proceedings of the International Conference on Image Processing, Santa Barbara, California, October 1997, vol. 1, pp. 536–539 (1997)
2. Bhandari, D., Murthy, C.A., Pal, S.K.: Image enhancement using multi-objective genetic algorithms. In: Chaudhury, S., Mitra, S., Murthy, C.A., Sastry, P.S., Pal, S.K. (eds.) PReMI 2009. LNCS, vol. 5909, pp. 309–314. Springer, Heidelberg (2009)
3. Ekstrom, M.P.: Digital image processing techniques. Academic Press, New York (1984)
4. Hansen, M.P., Jaszkiewicz, A.: Evaluating the quality of approximations to the non-dominated set. Technical Report Technical Report IMM-REP-1998-7, Institute of Mathematical Modelling, Technical University of Denmark (1998)
5. http://www.cl.cam.ac.uk/fapp2/watermarking
6. http://www.ece.uwaterloo.ca/z70wang/research/ssim/
7. Huang, H.C., Pan, J.S., Huamg, Y.H., Huang, K.C.: Progressive watermarking techniques using genetic algorithms. Circuits, Systems and Signal Processing 8, 58–68 (2007)
8. Katzenbeisser, S., Petitcolas, F.A.P.: Information hiding techniques for steganography and digital watermarking. Artech House Publishers (2000)
9. Maity, S.P., Kundu, M.K.: Genetic algorithms for optimality of data hiding in digital images. Soft Computing 13(4), 361–373 (2009)
10. Schilling, D.L., Pickholtz, R.L., Millstein, L.B.: Theory of spread spectrum communications-a tutorial. IEEE Transactions on Communications 30(5), 855–884 (1982)
11. Srinivas, N., Deb, K.: Multiobjective function optimization using nondominated sorting genetic algorithms. Evolutionary Computation 2(3), 221–248 (1995)
12. Gruhl, D., Bender, W., Morimoto, N.: Techniques for data hiding. In: Proceedings of the SPIE 2420, Storage and Retrieval for Image and Video Databases III, pp. 164–173 (1995)
13. Wang, Z., Bovik, A.C., Sheikh, H.R., Simoncelli, E.P.: Image quality assessment: From error visibility to structural similarity. IEEE Transactions on image processing 13(4), 600–612 (2004)
14. Xia, X.G., Boncelet, C.G., Arce, G.R.: A robust digital image watermarking method using wavelet-based fusion. In: Wavelet Transform Based Watermark for Digital Images, vol. 3, pp. 497–511. Optics Express (1998)

Hybrid Contourlet-DCT Based Robust Image Watermarking Technique Applied to Medical Data Management

Sudeb Das and Malay Kumar Kundu

Machine Intelligence Unit, Indian Statistical Institute, Kolkata 700 108, India
to.sudeb@gmail.com, malay@isical.ac.in

Abstract. This paper describes a non-blind, imperceptible and highly robust hybrid Medical Image Watermarking (MIW) technique for a range of medical data management issues. The method simultaneously addresses medical information security, content authentication, safe archiving and controlled access retrieval. We propose the use of Contourlet Transform (CLT) followed by the Discrete Cosine Transform (DCT) to achieve higher robustness and imperceptibility. Experimental results and performance comparisons confirm the effectiveness and efficiency of the proposed scheme.

Keywords: Watermarking, Content Authentication, Data integrity, Contourlet Transform.

1   Introduction

The rapid and significant growth of the information and communication technologies has changed the medical data management systems immensely. The modern integrated health-care delivery systems (such as Hospital Management Systems (HISs), Picture Archiving and Communication Systems (PACS) etc.) provide easier access, effective manipulation and efficient distribution of medical data. On the other hand these advances have resulted in new risks of inappropriate use of medical information, due the ease with which digital data can be accessed and manipulated. Therefore, we need a system for effective storage, transmission, controlled manipulation and access of medical data keeping its authenticity, integrity and confidentiality intact [1].

Many MIW techniques have been proposed by various researchers. A spatial domain technique was proposed by Zain *et al.* [2] to improve the security of medical images by involving the ability to detect tamper and subsequently recover the images. A Region of Interest (ROI) lossless MIW technique with enhanced security and high payload embedding in the spatial domain was proposed by Kundu *et al.* in [3]. Chao *et al.* [4] proposed a DCT based data hiding scheme, capable of hiding EPR in the quantized DCT coefficients of an image. Wu *et al.* [5] proposed two schemes based on Modulo 256 and DCT, for tamper detection and recovery purpose. Recently few Discrete Wavelet Transform (DWT) based

S.O. Kuznetsov et al. (Eds.): PReMI 2011, LNCS 6744, pp. 286–292, 2011.

MIW methods have been proposed [6][7][8] by various researchers. Most of the previous researches have concentrated on preserving the resolution of the medical images after watermark embedding, regardless of testing the robustness of the schemes against different attacks. Moreover, most of the conventional watermarking schemes are semi-robust in nature. They can resist either the signal processing attacks destroying the high frequency (HF) components of the image, or the signal processing operations in which the low frequency (LF) components of the image is altered.

To overcome these problems, we propose a hybrid CLT-DCT based MIW technique to hide Electronic Patient Record (EPR), Doctor's Identification Code (DIC) and Indexing Keyword (INDX) in the medical image. The confidentiality of the EPR is improved by embedding the data in the image. DIC works as a source authenticator and INDX serves as a querying keyword for use in medical image databases for effective image retrieval. In addition to that, both the storage and transmission bandwidth requirements as well as the possibility of EPR detachment are reduced. In the proposed method, watermark's DCT coefficients are inserted into the DCT coefficients of the CLT transformed low pass version of the original image. Due to the special transform structure of Laplacian Pyramid (LP) [9], the DCT coefficients of the watermark are likely to be spread out into all subbands when we reconstruct the watermarked image. As a result the proposed technique is expected to be robust to various attacks resulting from both the signal processing operations which affect the HF or the LF components of the image.

The organization of the paper is as follows: in Section 2 we briefly describe the CLT. We outline in Section 3 the proposed watermark embedding and extraction algorithms. Experimental results and comparisons are presented in Section 4 and we draw conclusion in Section 5.

2   Contourlet Transform (CLT)

The major drawback of DWT in two dimensions is their limited ability in capturing directional information. In light of this, Do and Vetterli [9][10] developed the CLT based on an efficient two-dimensional multiscale and directional filter bank (DBF). CLT not only possess the main features of DWT, but also offer a high degree of directionality and anisotropy. It allows for different and flexible number of directions at each scale, while achieving nearly critical sampling. In addition, CLT uses iterated filter banks, which makes it computationally efficient ($O(N)$ operations for an N-pixels image).

CLT gives a multiresolution, local and directional expansion of image using Pyramidal Directional Filter Bank (PDFB). The PDFB combines LP which captures the point discontinuities, with a DFB which links these discontinuities into linear structures. LP is a multiscale decomposition of $L^2(R^2)$ into series of increasing resolution subspaces which are orthogonal complements of each other as follows:

$$L^2(R^2) = V_{j_0} \oplus (\bigoplus_{j=J_0}^{-\infty} W_j) \tag{1}$$

An l-level DFB generates a local directional basis for $l^2(Z^2)$ that is composed of the impulse response of the DFBs and their shifts. In CLT, the directional filter is applied to the detail subspace W_j. This results in a decomposition of W_j into 2^{l_j} subspaces at scale 2^j.

$$W_j = \bigoplus_{k=0}^{2^{l_j}-1} W_{j,k}^{l_j} \tag{2}$$

Fig. 1.(a) shows the flowchart of CLT for a 512×512 image. A DFB is designed to capture the high frequency content like smooth contours and directional edges. This DBF is implemented by using a k-level binary tree decomposition that leads to 2^k subbands with wedge shaped frequency partition as shown in Fig. 1.(b).

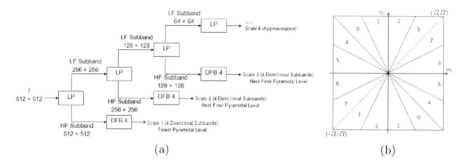

(a)   (b)

Fig. 1. (a) Flowchart of CLT for a 512×512 image. (b) Frequency partitioning ($k = 3, 2^k = 8$) wedge shaped frequency subbands.

3   Proposed Scheme

The watermark embedding and extraction algorithm is described here.

3.1   Watermark Embedding

The salient steps of the watermark embedding process are as follows:

1. Apply CLT on the original image I.
2. Divide the coefficients of the low pass subband (I_{LPS}) of the transformed I into 8×8 non-overlapping blocks.
3. Perform DCT to each block of I_{LPS} to get DCT_I_{LPS}.
4. Encrypt the EPR by Advanced Encryption Standard (AES) method using a secret key K_S to get EPR_{ENCRY}.

5. Concatenate DIC, $INDX$, EPR_{ENCRY} and represent the resultant string to its binary representation as WM_{BIN}.
6. Apply BCH error correcting code to WM_{BIN} to get WM_{BCH}.
7. Reshape WM_{BCH} as a 1D-binary string (WM_{BS}) and scatter its bits using the function given below:

$$f(x) = px \ mod \ n + 1 \tag{3}$$

where,
$n =$ size of the subband I_{LPS};
$p =$ secret prime number $\epsilon \ [1, n]$;
$x =$ bit position in WM_{BS} and $x \ \epsilon \ [1, length(WM_{BS})]$;
8. Reshape the resultant string in a matrix of equal size as I_{LPS} to get the final watermark payload WM_{FIN}.
9. Divide WM_{FIN} into 8×8 non-overlapping blocks, and perform DCT to each block to get DCT_{WM}.
10. Let, a coefficient of the matrix DCT_I_{LPS}, is represented by $Y(x, y)$, and $W(x, y)$ represents a coefficient of the matrix DCT_{WM}. Then, perform additive watermarking operation:

$$Y'(x, y) = Y(x, y) + \alpha W(x, y) \tag{4}$$

where,
$Y'(x, y) =$ coefficients of the reconstructed matrix DCT'_I_{LPS};
$\alpha =$ watermarking strength factor.
11. Perform Inverse DCT on DCT'_I_{LPS}, to get the modified I'_{LPS}.
12. To get the watermarked image I^*, apply Inverse CLT on the I'_{LPS}, along with other non-modified directional subbands.

3.2 Watermark Extraction

The proposed watermarking scheme is non-blind, which means we need the original image during the extraction process. The steps of the extraction process are as follows:

1. Apply CLT on I and I^* (possibly attacked) with the same decomposition configuration of the embedding process.
2. Divide the coefficients of the low pass subbands (I_{LPS} and I^*_{LPS} respectively) of the transformed I and I^* into 8×8 non-overlapping blocks.
3. Get DCT_I_{LPS} and $DCT\_I^*_{LPS}$ by performing DCT to each block of I_{LPS} and I^*_{LPS} respectively.
4. Let, a coefficient of the matrix DCT_I_{LPS}, is represented by $Y(x, y)$, and $Y^*(x, y)$ represents a coefficient of the matrix $DCT\_I^*_{LPS}$. Then, to get one coefficient $W'(x, y)$ of the reconstructed DCT watermark $DCT_{WM'}$ perform the following operation:

$$W'(x, y) = (Y^*(x, y) - Y(x, y))/\alpha \tag{5}$$

5. Perform the Inverse DCT on $DCT_{WM'}$, to get the reconstructed watermark WM'.
6. Reshape WM' as a binary string and rearrange the bits to their original positions using the equation 3 to get WM'_{BCH}.
7. Get WM'_{BIN} by applying BCH decoding procedure on WM'_{BCH}.
8. Transform WM'_{BIN} to its original format and separate DIC, $INDX$, and EPR_{ENCRY}.
9. Decrypt EPR_{ENCRY} using the same secret key K_S to get the original EPR.

4   Experimental Results and Comparisons

4 grayscale (8 bpp) medical images of different modalities (CT, MRI, USG), of size 512×512 were used in the experiments. The DIC and $INDX$ consist of 20 ($20 \times 7 = 140$ bits) and 14 ($14 \times 7 = 98$ bits) ASCII characters respectively. The size of the encrypted EPR was 1152 bits. After applying BCH(255,139,15) the size of the watermark was 2550 bits. After three level CLT [2,4,8] of the image with '9-7' pyramid filter and 'pkva' directional filter, the size of the low pass subband was 64×64. We used $p = 23$ in the equation 3. The value of α was set to 30 after lots of experiments.

We used Peak Signal-to-Noise Ration (PSNR) to measure the distortion produced after watermark embedding. Mean Structural SIMilarity index (MSSIM) was used to measure the similarity between the original image and the watermarked image. To prove the authenticity of the extracted watermark we used Normalized Correlation (NC) coefficient and Bit Error Rate (BER).

Table 1. shows the PSNR, MSSIM, NC and BER values in attack free case. The result shows that the watermark is retrieved successfully without any errors. Fig. 2. shows the effect of watermark embedding in the medical images. The results show that there is no visual difference between the original and the watermarked images.

The results (for abdomenCT image) in the Table 2. show that the propose method is robust against various image processing attacks. It also shows the visual and structural difference between the watermarked and the attacked image in terms of PSNR and MSSIM.

Comparisons with [7] and [8] reveals that, these methods are more imperceptible (in terms of PSNR), but less robust than our scheme. Specifically, these methods can only survive JPEG compression attack, even that also to a limited

Table 1. Results of Attack Free Case

Image	PSNR	MSSIM	NC	BER
abdomeCT	41.5895	0.8745	1.0000	0
cthead	41.5713	0.9567	1.0000	0
mriBrain	41.5157	0.9747	1.0000	0
usg	41.4776	0.9383	1.0000	0

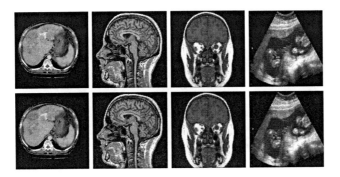

Fig. 2. Original images (above) and their corresponding watermarked images (below)

Table 2. Robustness Against Various Attacks

Attacks	Parameters	NC	BER	PSNR	MSSIM
Mean Filtering	Window size = 3 × 3	1.0000	0.0000	31.8707	0.9434
Median Filtering	Window size = 3 × 3	1.0000	0.0000	34.7341	0.9555
Salt & Pepper Noise	Noise density = 0.005	1.0000	0.0000	26.9014	0.8790
Cropping	315 × 27 pixels	1.0000	0.0000	20.6878	0.9588
Resize	256 × 256 pixels	1.0000	0.0000	33.2382	0.9525
Bit-Plane Removal	LSB-1	1.0000	0.0000	52.1812	0.9936
Sharpening	65	1.0000	0.0000	29.1512	0.9125
JPEG	Quality Factor = 25	1.0000	0.0000	34.5269	0.8819

quality factor (< 50). Whereas, our scheme can survive JPEG compression attack up to 25 quality factor. In [7] only the ROI of the image can be embedded, but no EPR or DIC or INDX. Comparison with [6] shows that, our method is more imperceptible (in terms of PSNR) and also more robust. Also the use of EPR encryption, scattering of bits in the embedding process makes our method much more secure than the methods mentioned above.

5   Conclusions

We have presented a non-blind, highly robust watermarking scheme applied to medical images with good imperceptibility and enhanced security. Our scheme can be used for different medical image modalities. The experimental results indicate that the proposed scheme is feasible and given its relative simplicity, it can be applied to the medical images at the time of acquisition to serve in many medical applications concerned with authenticity, integrity and confidentiality.

In future research, we will try to enhance our algorithm by making it blind, as well as, we will try to embed the watermark such that, it cause less visual degradation and better extraction accuracy.

References

1. Coatrieux, G., Maitre, H., Sankur, B., Rolland, Y., Collorec, R.: Relevance of watermarking in medical imaging, pp. 250–255 (2000)
2. Zain, J.M., Fauzi, A.R.M.: Medical image watermarking with tamper detection and recovery. In: Proc. 28th IEEE EMBS Annual International Conference, pp. 3270–3273 (2006)
3. Kundu, M.K., Das, S.: Lossless roi medical image watermarking technique with enhanced security and high payload embedding. In: Proc. IEEE International Conference on Patter Recognition (ICPR), pp. 1457–1460 (2010)
4. Chao, H., Hsu, C., Miaou, S.: A data-hiding technique with authentication, integration, and confidentiality for electronic patient records. IEEE Trans Inf. Technol. Biomed. 1, 46–53 (2002)
5. Wu, J.H.K., Chang, R.F., Chen, C.J., Wang, C.L., Kuo, T.H., Moon, W.K., Chen, D.R.: Tamper detection and recovery for medical images using near-lossless information hiding technique. Journal of Digital Imaging 21, 59–76 (2008)
6. Manasrah, T., Al-Haj, A.: Management of medical images using wavelets-based multi-watermarking algorithm. In: Proc. Int. Conf. Innovations in Information Technology, pp. 697–701 (2008)
7. Lee, H.K., Kim, H.J., Kwon, K.R., Lee, J.K.: Roi medical image watermarking using dwt and bit-plane. In: Proc. Asia-Pacific Conf. Communica, pp. 512–515 (2005)
8. Giakoumaki, A., Pavlopoulos, S., Koutsouris, D.: Multiple image watermarking applied to health information management. IEEE Trans. on Information Technology in Biomedicine 10, 722–732 (2006)
9. Do, M.N., Vetterli, M.: Contourlets. In: Welland, G.V. (ed.) Beyond Wavelets, Academic Press, New York (2003)
10. Do, M.N., Vetterli, M.: The contourlet transform: An efficient directional multiresolution image representation. IEEE Transactions on Image Processing 14, 2091–2106 (2005)

Accurate Localizations of Reference Points in a Fingerprint Image

Malay Kumar Kundu and Arpan Kumar Maiti

Center for soft computing Research, Indian Statistical Institute, Kolkata
malay@isical.ac.in, arpanmaiti@gmail.com

Abstract. Reference points play important role in the field of fingerprint recognition. It is mainly used for fingerprint classification and fingerprint matching. There are many methods proposed for fingerprint reference point detection like Poincare Index technique, Direction curvature technique etc. The purpose of this paper is to detect the reference points considering the uncertainty for imperfection of fingerprint reference point position.

1 Introduction

Biometric Application,Fingerprint, has taken part a major role to identify a particular person uniquely. We can analyze the fingerprint from global and local perspective.From local perspective we concentrate on minutiae like bifurcation point,trifurcation,ridge ending etc. At global level ,there are some unique landmarks of fingerprint,where the ridge curvature is higher than other areas and the orientation changes rapidly. They are commonly known as core and delta[4] which are shown in Fig1(a) and they are used as a reference point. Each fingerprint should have the local features and may or may not have the global feature. The number of core and delta point differs in different type of fingerprint. There are several techniques available for singular point detection. Most of the techniques developed on the basis of orientation field of the image. The poincare index method(PI) one of the commonly used method for reference point detection[1][7]. This method is efficient but very much sensitive to noise as the orientation deviation caused by image imperfection that effects the computation of PI. Another method is to detect the reference point by searching the curvature point from the orientation image[6][8][3].

The main problem of all such approaches is the uncertainty presents in the process of detection of the exact location of reference points. Though it is easy to detect the approximate region where reference point exists but it is difficult to get a unique point as a reference one. In this paper we have proposed a method where some template is to be used to detect the reference points using strength of similarity from which the exact (single) point may be detected from the approximate core and delta region using fuzzy reasoning.

Organization of the paper is as follows. The estimation of direction field and reference points are presented in section 2.1 and 2.2 The false reference Point

S.O. Kuznetsov et al. (Eds.): PReMI 2011, LNCS 6744, pp. 293–298, 2011.

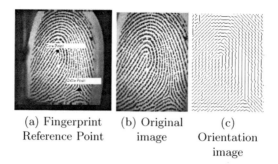

| (a) Fingerprint Reference Point | (b) Original image | (c) Orientation image |

Fig. 1. (a)Fingerprint Reference point (b)Original finger print image (c) field of Fingerprint image

removal technique is described in section 3. In section 4,A technique for identification of finer core point from core region is described. The experimental results and future works are given in section 5 and 6.

2   Proposed Method to Identify Reference Points

2.1   Formation of Orientation Image

Before going to minutiae extraction,an orientation field flow map is computed. The input image is subdivided into number of blocks of equal size and dominant ridge gradient direction is computed for each block. The average direction of all ridges represents the dominant direction of each block. Same algorithm is repeated for each block. So the image is scaled down by the size of factor w if We assume that the size of each block is $w \times w$. All possible directions should get converted only into eight discrete directions in the range of 90 degree to -67.5 degree[9][2]. The Direction angle $\theta(i,j)$ is representing the dominant direction of the block (i,j). Now the reduced image is represented as $D(i,j)$ and its position is represented by D_{ij} . The main steps to calculate the orientation of each block is as follows.

1)Divide the fingerprint image into non overlapping blocks of size $w \times w$.
2)Compute the gradient $\delta_x(i,j)$ and $\delta_y(i,j)$ of each pixel (i,j) corresponding to the Horizontal and vertical direction.The gradient operator used here is Sobel operator for simplicity.
3)Estimate the orientation of each block (i,j) by averaging the square gradients as follows.

$$V_y(i,j) = \sum_{u=i-w/2}^{i+w/2} \sum_{v=j-w/2}^{j+w/2} 2\delta_x(u,v)\delta_y(u,v) \qquad (1)$$

$$V_x(i,j) = \sum_{u=i-w/2}^{i+w/2} \sum_{v=j-w/2}^{j+w/2} (\delta_x^2(u,v) - \delta_y^2(u,v)) \qquad (2)$$

$$\theta(i,j) = (1/2)tan^{-1}(V_y(i,j)/V_x(i,j)) \tag{3}$$

The original Fingerprint image and its direction image is shown in Fig 1(a),(b).

2.2   Reference Point Detection

The Poincare index method and the modified Poincare Index Method are the most popular method to detect the singular points in the fingerprints. By using this method the core point,delta points and virtual core point for whorl type are extracted on the basis of gradient differences among the adjacent blocks[1][7]. But it has been shown that reference point detection is considerably difficult for low quality image and the image containing noise. This may cause the faulty detection of reference point.

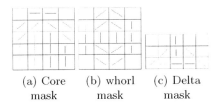

(a) Core   (b) whorl   (c) Delta
mask   mask   mask

Fig. 2. Different mask figure a)Core b)Whorl)delta

To overcome this problem,besides the gradient difference method proposed in PI method additionaly We have used block based matching technique where number of blocks are used which depicts the different kind of reference point pattern. This hugely improved the performance of fingerprint reference point detection methodology. The template masks, $CoreM(i,j),WhorlM(i,j)$ and $DeltaM(i,j)$ in fig2 are defined as a convolution mask for calculating similarity measurement strength of each pattern in the Direction image. Initially We consider three empty sets for the core,whorl and delta point ,let it say S_C,S_W,S_D.

Each point of direction image $D(i,j)$ is checked with all the template mask and correlation membership value or similarity measurement strength is calculated using the equation (4). As the convolution template are asymmetric the exact mid point or near mid point is chosen for calculating the correlation membership value,let say the point index as mid_i and mid_j.

$$\mu_C(D_{ij}) = \sum_{u=-1}^{M_H} \sum_{v=-1}^{M_W} 1 - \frac{|(D(i+u)(j+v) - CoreM(mid_i + u)(mid_j + v))|}{\delta_k} \tag{4}$$

$$\mu_C(D_{ij}) = \mu_C(D_{ij})/N_C \tag{5}$$

where M_H is the height of the Mask,M_W is Width of the Mask,δ_k is maximum possible phase angle difference,here 157.5(90 to -67.5) and N_C is No of considerable points in the Mask.

Using the above mentioned equation,correlation membership value is calculated using all the mask and say it $\mu_C(D_{ij})$,$\mu_W(D_{ij})$ and $\mu_D(D_{ij})$ for core,whorl type and delta. Now a cutoff value is decided to get the correct point into the set S_C,S_W, S_D using the equation (6).

$$S_C = \{D_{i,j} : \mu_C(D_{i,j}) > \mu_{CT}\} \quad S_W = \{D_{i,j} : \mu_W(D_{i,j}) > \mu_{WT}\}$$
$$S_D = \{D_{i,j} : \mu_D(D_{i,j}) > \mu_{DT}\} \tag{6}$$

where μ_{CT},μ_{WT} and μ_{DT} are the membership cut off value for core point,whorl type and Delta Point. The above mentioned approach is continued in reverse image to check any other reference point from the opposite direction using the same algorithm.

3   False Reference Point Detection and Removal

All the candidate points which has been detected in the set S_C,S_W and S_D are not the correct reference point. In this scenario it has been shown that if We take the help of poincare indexing method, it will remove the unnecessary core point and delta point from the set S_C and S_D.

From the experiment It has been shown that there may be some points in the set which are neighbor of each other. Multiple reference points can not be present within the neighborhood position so the points are to be removed from the set. In this scenario,Lower most Horizontal line of the Image has been taken as a base line and the candidate point having smallest distance from the base line considered as reference point.

The virtual core point(Whorl type) is a special type of point where two extreme curvature point exist above and below of the whorl pattern. As whorl point is being detected separately so at that particular case,these two extreme curvature points marked as a core point are removing from the set S_C using equation (7) and the new set is formed S_C^{New}. Finally We can draw a hypothetical line joining these two points and center of this line can be assumed as a virtual core point for whorl type which is shown in Fig 3(a).

$$S_C^{New} = S_C - \{x\} \tag{7}$$
$$If(x \in S_C \quad and \quad y \in x_8^n \quad and \quad y \in S_W \;), \quad Check \quad \forall x \in S_C$$

where x_8^n is the set of 8 neighbor points of x.

4   Identification of Finer Point from Core Region

Its a challenge to identify the exact core point position from the identified core region. It is found that the exact core point is the sharpest corner situated in the innermost ridge.To identify a corner point We have estimated some local shape parameters gradient,symmetry and straightness for this purpose. An ideal corner point should have high gradient value,high reflective symmetry and low level straightness in a local neighborhood of pixels[5].Cornerness is checked using the table in Fig3(b)for decision making. Each parameter value of the core region points are calculated and the range between the extreme low and extreme high value is equally subdivided into three range low,medium and high. An Example of finer core points (single pixel or cluster of very few pixels) detection using proposed method and core region detection using poincare method is shown in Fig4(e) and (d).

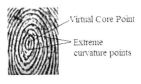

Gradient	Symmetry	Straightness	Cornerness
low	low	low	low
low	low	high	low
low	high	low	low
low	high	high	low
high	low	low	low
high	low	high	low
high	high	low	high
high	high	high	low

(a) Virtual core point   (b) Cornerness Decision making

Fig. 3.

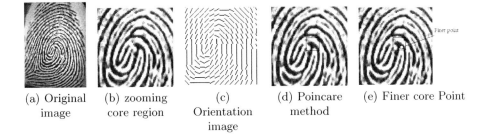

(a) Original image   (b) zooming core region   (c) Orientation image   (d) Poincare method   (e) Finer core Point

Fig. 4. Finer core point Identification

5 Experimental Results

To evaluate the performance of this algorithm, We have used the testing database FVC 2000 (http://bias.csr.unibo.it/fvc2000/databases.asp) for all type of fingerprint Image.The orientation image is formed using 8×8 block. The Similarity measurement strength cut off values are decided .8,.85 and .85 for μ_{CT},μ_{WT} and μ_{DT} respectively considering the effect for large number of images.Some Fingerprint Image and its reference points are shown in Fig 5.

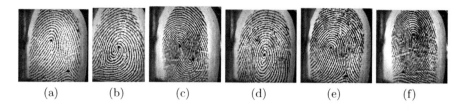

| (a) | (b) | (c) | (d) | (e) | (f) |

Fig. 5. Result Image with Core,Whorl and Delta Point

6   Conclusion

In this paper we have tried to overcome the uncertainty during the identification of exact reference point location using decision making rules. But We expect that any soft computing tool like fuzzy set theory can play important role for modeling such type of uncertainty and that is being persuaded currently.

References

1. Huang, T., Liu, C., Lin, J., Li, C., Kuo, T.: A novel scheme for fingerprint identification. In: The 2nd Canadian Conference on Computer and Robot Vision, Proceedings, pp. 392–396 (2005)
2. Jayadevan, R., Kulkarni, J.V., Mali, S.N., Abhyankar, H.K.: A new ridge orientation based method of computation for feature extraction from fingerprint images. Transactions on Engineering, Computing and Technology (2007)
3. Kekre, H.B., Bharadi, V.A.: Fingerprint's core point detection using orientation field. In: International Conference on Advances in Computing, Control, Telecommunication Technologies, ACT 2009, pp. 150–152 (2009)
4. Kekre, H.B., Bharadi, V.A.: Article: Fingerprint core point detection algorithm using orientation field based multiple features. International Journal of Computer Applications 1(15), 97–103 (2010)
5. Law, T., Yamada, K., Shibata, D., Nakamura, T., He, L., Itoh, H.: Edge extraction using fuzzy reasoning. In: Pal, S.K., et al. (eds.) Soft computing for image processing, vol. 42, pp. 44–78 (2000)
6. Mohammadi, S., Farajzadeh, A.: Fingerprint reference point detection using orientation field and curvature measurements. In: IEEE International Conference on Intelligent Computing and Intelligent Systems, ICIS 2009, vol. 4, pp. 25–29 (2009)
7. Ohtsuka, T., Watanabe, D., Tomizawa, D., Hasegawa, Y., Aoki, H.: Reliable detection of core and delta in fingerprints by using singular candidate method. In: IEEE Computer Society Conference on Computer Vision and Pattern Recognition Workshops, CVPRW 2008, pp. 1–6 (2008)
8. Yin, Y., Weng, D., Li, H., Ma, W.: A new robust method of singular point detection from fingerprint. In: International Symposium on Information Science and Engieering, vol. 2, pp. 330–334 (2008)
9. Zhang, W., Wang, Y.: Singular point detection in fingerprint image. In: The 5th Asian Conference on Computer Vision (2002)

Adaptive Pixel Swapping Based Steganography Reducing Embedding Noise

Arijit Sur[1], Piyush Goel[2], and Jayanta Mukhopadhyay[2]

[1] Department of Computer Science and Engineering,
Indian Institute of Technology, Guwahati-781039, India
[2] Department of Computer Science and Engineering,
Indian Institute of Technology, Kharagpur-721302, India
arijit@iitg.ernet.in, {piyush,jay}@cse.iitkgp.ernet.in

Abstract. In this paper[1], a block based steganographic algorithm is proposed where embedding is done by swapping two pixels within the block such that resulting additive noise can be adaptively controlled by using a prescribed threshold. The proposed algorithm is used to reduce the extra additive noise which is the main drawback of a existing PSSA algorithm [6]. Regarding the steganographic security, the proposed steganographic scheme inherently preserves first order image statistics such as image histogram and thus remains undetectable against any histogram based spatial domain steganalytic attacks. Experimental results show that the proposed adaptive scheme clearly outperforms the PSSA algorithm [6] against additive noise based blind attacks.

1 Introduction

Steganography is the art of hiding information in an innocent looking cover objects and thus visual and statistical undetectability is one of the major concerns in the steganographic security. In recent steganalytic literature, a major number of algorithms (e.g. [1][2]) are based on first order image statistics. The main problem of restoring image statistics is that an extra amount of additive noise is being added during restoration. This extra additive noise makes those algorithms more vulnerable against additive noise based blind attacks like WAM [3]. It is well known that the chance of detection is substantially reduced if embedding is done adaptively. In this paper, we have consider an existing pixel swapping based spatial domain embedding scheme [6] which can inherently restores image histogram and thus can resist histogram based targeted attacks. The main drawback of the PSSA algorithm [6] is that it essentially adds a substantial amount of extra additive noise due to the restoration process compared to that of LSB matching type of algorithms. In this paper, we have proposed a new *Adaptive Pixel Swapping based Steganographic Algorithm (APSSA)* algorithm by introducing a block based local adaptive threshold such that amount of noise added

---

[1] The first author gratefully acknowledge the support received from Infosys Technologies Ltd., Bangalore, under the Infosys Fellowship Award.

S.O. Kuznetsov et al. (Eds.): PReMI 2011, LNCS 6744, pp. 299–304, 2011.

(in a block) depends on certain local (within the block) image statistics. It is experimentally shown that proposed scheme has similar performance with PSSA against several recent targeted steganalysis attacks while the proposed adaptive modification made APSSA more secure than PSSA scheme [6] against additive noise based attacks like WAM [3]. The rest of the paper is organized as follows. The proposed encoding and decoding algorithm are described in Sec. 2. In Sec. 3, steganalytic security of the proposed scheme is discussed. The paper will be concluded in Sec. 4.

2   Proposed Scheme

In this paper, a block based pixel swapping algorithm is proposed which is an adaptive improvement over the pixel swapping scheme proposed in [6]. Firstly, the image is divided into non overlapping blocks with a fixed dimension. A single bit is embedded in a block. Let I be the gray scale cover image. Let $I_k(\alpha)$ be the intensity value of a fixed location α in the kth block of the image I. $I_k(\beta)$ and $I_k(\gamma)$ are another two block locations such that β and γ are defined as follows:

$$\beta = argmax_{m \in I_K} (I_K(m) < \mu_k) \tag{1}$$

$$\gamma = argmin_{m \in I_K} (I_K(m) > \mu_k) \tag{2}$$

where $I_K = I_k - I_k(\alpha)$. So $I_k(\beta)$ is a block element other than $I_k(\alpha)$ which is the maximum value just less than μ_k. Similarly $I_k(\gamma)$ is a block element other than $I_k(\alpha)$ having minimum value just greater than μ_k.

The embedding rule is constructed as follows:

$$bit\ embedded = \begin{cases} 1 & \text{if } I_k(\alpha) > \mu_k \\ 0 & \text{if } I_k(\alpha) < \mu_k \end{cases} \tag{3}$$

where μ_k = mean of the kth block. In other words, if $I_k(\alpha)$ is greater than the mean of kth block μ_k, the embedded bit is taken as 1; on the other hand if $I_k(\alpha)$ is less than μ_k, the embedded bit is taken as 0.

A bit is embedded in the kth block if following suitability condition is true for that block

$$|I_k(\alpha) - \mu_k| < \tau \tag{4}$$

where τ is the prescribed threshold.

For a suitable block (say b_k), the present secret bit ($S_{present}$) and $I_k(\alpha)$ are checked according to the embedding rule. If the embedding condition $[(S_{present} = 1)\ \&\ (I_k(\alpha) > \mu_k)]$ is satisfied, no operation is needed to embed the data bit, otherwise $I_k(\alpha)$ is swapped with $I_k(\beta)$ or $I_k(\gamma)$ according to $S_{present}$. A data bit is embedded if suitability condition is satisfied, otherwise no bit is embedded. In later case, swapping is needed to mark the corresponding block unsuitable for embedding.

This amounts to addition of extra noise. This particular situation happens when both the conditions $|I_k(\alpha) - \mu_k| < \tau$ and $|I_k(\beta) - \mu_k| > \tau$ [or, $|I_k(\alpha) - \mu_k| < \tau$ and $|I_k(\gamma) - \mu_k| > \tau$] are true. It is experimentally found that the probability of occurrences of these situations is very low. This is because $I_k(\beta)$ has the lowest intensity value greater than μ_k of the block and $I_k(\gamma)$ has the highest intensity value less than μ_k of that block. Again for a slightly higher value of τ the situation becomes more rare. Since the total noise added due to this extra swapping is almost negligible, it is not considered in the theoretical computation of noise. There is an obvious trade off between payload and embedding noise. For a relatively higher payload, embedding noise would be relatively high. However when the block size is greater than two, the choice of pixels used for swapping can be possible. This adaptiveness makes the $APSSA$ scheme more secure than $PSSA$ [6] scheme reducing the embedding noise. A step by step algorithm is given below:

2.1 Embedding Algorithm

Algorithm. *Adaptive Pixel Swapping based Steganographic Algorithm (APSSA)*
Input: *Cover Image I, Secret Bit Sequence S*, present secret bit is represented by $S_{present}$
Input Parameters: *Shared secret seed for generating pseudorandom sequence,* Threshold (τ)
Output: *Stego Image I_s*

1. The Cover image I is divided into non over lapping blocks of N pixels.
2. Blocks are arranged with a pseudorandom sequence using the shared secret seed.
3. For any block, (let k^{th} block is denoted as I_k), a fixed block location is determined. Let it be denoted by $I_k(\alpha)$. Another two block elements are defined as $I_k(\beta)$ and $I_k(\gamma)$ where $\beta = argmax_{m \in I_K}(I_K(m) < \mu_k)$ and $\gamma = argmin_{m \in I_K}(I_K(m) > \mu_k)$ where μ_k is the mean of the block I_k and $I_K = I_k - I_k(\alpha)$. Let the variable *done* act as a flag denoting, whether the block is used for embedding or not.
4. done $= 0$

> **if** $0 < |I_k(\alpha) - \mu_k| < \tau$
>   **if** ($S_{present} == 0$)
>   **if** $I_k(\alpha) > \mu_k$)
>   **swap** $(I_k(\alpha), I_k(\beta))$
>   **if** $|(I_k(\beta) - \mu_k)| > \tau$
>   done $= 0;$
>   **else**
>   done $= 1;$
>   **else**
>   done $= 1;$

    else
        if $I_k(\alpha) < \mu_k)$
            swap $(I_k(\alpha), I_k(\gamma))$
            if $|(I_k(\gamma) - \mu_k)| > \tau$
                done $= 0$;
            else
                done $= 1$;
        else
            done $= 1$;
    if $done == 1$
        $s_{present}$=next secret bit

5. Next block is taken and repeat steps 3 and 4 until either the secret sequence (S) is exhausted or all embedding blocks have been used.
6. Using above steps elements of S embedded into I to get stego image I_s.

End. *Adaptive Pixel Swapping based Steganographic Algorithm (APSSA)*

2.2 Extraction Algorithm

The extraction algorithm is quite simple. The pseudorandom sequence of blocks is regenerated at decoder with the help of the shared secret seed. A block (say I_k) is not considered for extraction if $|I_k(\alpha) - \mu_k| \geq \tau$ or $|I_k(\alpha) - \mu_k| = 0$. Otherwise, for any block if $I_k(\alpha) > \mu_k$, the corresponding secret bit is recovered as 1 and 0 if $I_k(\alpha) < \mu_k$. Bit stuffing is used to distinguish between secret sequence and terminator string.

3 Experimental Results

3.1 Reduction of Additive Noise

The main goal of the proposed APSSA scheme is to reduce the additive noise due to the embedding and restoration process of the embedding. In Figure 1, PSNR between cover and stego images are shown for both the PSSA [6] and the APSSA scheme. The experiments are done on 100 randomly chosen images from a never compressed image dataset UCID [4]. In Figure 1, it is observed that the PSNR between cover and stego images of the proposed APSSA scheme is relatively higher than that of PSSA [6] scheme which implies the reduction of additive noise due to adaptive modification.

3.2 Security against Blind Steganalysis

The main drawback of the *PSSA* [6] algorithm is that it added a substantial amount of extra additive noise during restoration process compared to the algorithms similar to the *LSBM*.

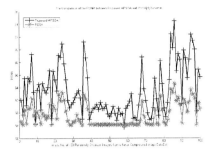

Fig. 1. Comparison of PSNR between Proposed APSSA and PSSA [6] Scheme

For testing the performance of the $APSSA$ algorithm, experiments are conducted on a data set of two thousand test images which were divided into two equal sets of one thousand cover images and one thousand stego images. 1000 never compressed images are taken from the UCID [4] as cover images and 1000 stego images are generated using the $APSSA$ algorithm. In these experiments, a block with four pixels is used. It is experimentally found that the payload for the bigger blocks are very less and is mostly undetectable. To evaluate the steganographic security using the proposed scheme, Area under the Receiver Operating Characteristic Curve $(AROC)$ and the Detection accuracy (P_{detect}) [5] which is computed using equations 5 and 6 have been used as the evaluation metrics.

$$P_{detect} = 1 - P_{error} \tag{5}$$

$$P_{error} = \frac{1}{2} \times P_{FP} + \frac{1}{2} \times P_{FN} \tag{6}$$

where P_{FP}, P_{FN} are the probabilities of false positive and false negative respectively. A value of $P_{detect} = 0.5$ shows that the classification is as good as random guessing and $P_{detect} = 1.0$ shows a classification with 100% accuracy.

For the evaluation of the proposed $APSSA$ scheme, Wavelet absolute moment (WAM) steganalyzer [3] is considered as steganalytic attack. In Figure 2,

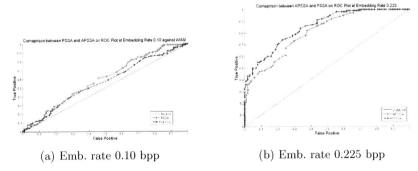

(a) Emb. rate 0.10 bpp   (b) Emb. rate 0.225 bpp

Fig. 2. ROC plot for comparing between $APSSA$ and $PSSA$ [6] against WAM

it is shown that proposed $APSSA$ scheme is relatively less detectable than the $PSSA$ scheme [6] against WAM at the same embedding rates using never compressed image dataset as cover image source. Since, the histogram of the image is kept intact during embedding, proposed adaptive improved scheme remains undetectable against any histogram based spatial domain steganalytic attacks similar to the $PSSA$ scheme [6].

4   Conclusion

In this paper, an adaptive improvement over $PSSA$ algorithm [6] is proposed by incorporating a block based local adaptive threshold such that the amount of additive noise can be controlled adaptively using block image statistics. We have experimentally shown that the enforced adaptiveness makes the scheme more secure than its non adaptive version (PSSA) against additive noise based steganalyzers while it maintains same performance as PSSA against targeted attacks since image histogram is kept intact during embedding.

References

1. Ker, A.D.: Steganalysis of LSB matching in grayscale images. IEEE Signal processing letters 12(6), 441–444 (2005)
2. Zhang, J., Cox, I.J., Doerr, G.: Steganalysis for LSB Matching in Images with High-frequency Noise. In: Proc. IEEE 9th Workshop on Multimedia Signal Processing MMSP 2007, pp. 385–388 (2007)
3. Goljan, M., Fridrich, J., Holotyak, T.: New blind steganalysis and its implications. In: Proceedings of SPIE for Security, Steganography, and Watermarking of Multimedia Contents VIII, vol. 6072, pp. 1–13 (2006)
4. Schaefer, G., Stich, M.: UCID - An Uncompressed Colour Image Database. In: Proc. SPIE, Storage and Retrieval Methods and Applications for Multimedia, vol. 5307, pp. 472–480 (2004)
5. Solanki, K., Sarkar, A., Manjunath, B.S.: YASS: Yet Another Steganographic Scheme That Resists Blind Steganalysis. In: Furon, T., Cayre, F., Doërr, G., Bas, P. (eds.) IH 2007. LNCS, vol. 4567, pp. 16–31. Springer, Heidelberg (2008)
6. Sur, A., Goel, P., Mukhopadhyay, J.: A Novel Steganographic Algorithm Resisting Targeted Steganalytic Attacks on LSB Matching. In: Kim, H.-J., Katzenbeisser, S., Ho, A.T.S. (eds.) IWDW 2008. LNCS, vol. 5450, pp. 199–208. Springer, Heidelberg (2009)

Classification and Quantification of Occlusion Using Hidden Markov Model

C.R. Sahoo[1], Shamik Sural[1], Gerhard Rigoll[2], and A. Sanchez[3]

[1] School of Information Technology, Indian Institute of Technology, Kharagpur, India
rawchitta@gmail.com, shamik.sural@gmail.com
[2] Technical University of Munich, Munich, Germany
rigoll@tum.de
[3] Universidad Rey Juan Carlos, Madrid, Spain
angel.sanchez@urjc.es

Abstract. Over the last few years, gait recognition has become an active area of research. However, one of the shortcomings is lack of a method for quantifying occlusion in scenes used for capturing gait of individuals. Occlusion can occur primarily because of two reasons. Firstly, movement of certain body parts of a human being occludes some other body parts of the same human, which is called self occlusion and secondly, occlusion of the body parts caused by some other human being. The objective of this paper is to quantify occlusion of different parts of the human body using Hidden Markov Model (HMM) and classify the scene of occlusion as one of the three cases of occlusion, namely, self occlusion (single individual moving), occlusion in a crowd moving in same direction and occlusion due to movement of human beings approaching from opposite direction. We train one HMM for each body part relevant for gait recognition. An HMM is a statistical representation of probability distribution of a large number of possible sequences and in the current context these are the sequences of frames extracted at regular interval from a given video. The steps involved in achieving the objective are feature extraction, HMM training and finally the classification or hidden state generation.

Keywords: Occlusion, Gait Recognition, Body Part, HMM.

1 Introduction

One of the most active research areas in computer vision, human gait recognition broadly deals with detecting, tracking and identifying people from a sequence of images. Gait recognition has attracted great interest due to its promising applications in visual surveillance, with the added advantage of not requiring any active participation of the subject whose gait is under consideration. Even low end cameras with very low resolution provide adequate accuracy in recognition. However, occlusion handling still remains an area of concern [8].

Other than human gait recognition, a number of algorithms have been proposed for tracking and motion detection [9, 4]. But none of them quantify occlusion. In this paper, we propose a method for quantifying occlusion by using

S.O. Kuznetsov et al. (Eds.): PReMI 2011, LNCS 6744, pp. 305–310, 2011.

HMM. HMM has been used successfully for speech recognition [5,6] and hand-written word recognition [3]. The availability of sequential information in frames extracted from a video makes HMM an obvious choice for classifying the video into any desired class. Here we use HMM for classification of a given video into three classes based on the degree of occlusion. These classes are (i) self occlusion, i.e., a single human walking, (ii) occlusion in a crowd moving in same direction and (iii) occlusion due to movement of human beings approaching from opposite direction.

The primary aim of most of the researches on occlusion has been to identify occlusion while dealing with detection and tracking algorithms [4,10,7,1]. Tracking methods can track individuals in image sequences, but real-world scenarios of crowded street scenes still pose a serious challenge for these methods because of occlusion during tracking. However, the focus on quantifying occlusion or to use occlusion as a tool has been negligible. We propose a method for quantifying occlusion and to use it for classification of the scene of occlusion. Until recently, the approximate reconstruction of scene of occlusion has been based on the knowledge of articulation. It is felt that knowledge of articulation along with the quantity of occlusion and scene of occlusion can result in a better approximation.

2   Elements of the Proposed HMM

States - A discrete HMM is characterized by a set of N hidden states, a set of M distinct observation symbols per state, state transition probability matrix $A = \{a_{ij}\}$, observation symbol generation probability matrix $B = \{b_j(\mathrm{k})\}$ and initial probability distibution matrix $\pi = \{\pi_i\}$ [5].

Although states are hidden in an HMM, there is some physical significance attached to them. Moreover, the number of states also affects the cost of computation of the solutions to the problems addressed by HMM. The number of states and the number of HMMs required to achieve the overall objective are closely linked. Therefore, after careful consideration, we propose six HMMs, one for each body part, namely, two hands, two legs, one torso and one head.

For states of each HMM, we divide each body part into four segments, i.e., a band of 25% coverage vertically and consider occlusion of combinations of each

(a) 1 band: state 1-4   (b) 2 bands: state 5-10   (c) 3 bands: state 11-14   (d) 4 bands: state 15

Fig. 1. Different HMM states corresponding to Left Leg of a human being

of these four bands as a state. Thus, at any given instant of time, the state can be occlusion of one of the four bands, or any combination of two bands out of four, or any combination of three bands out of four, or all the four bands or none of the four bands. Hence, the number of states (N) is 16. These states corresponding to occlusion of the left leg of a walking human being are explained with the help of images shown in Fig. 1. Similar state definitions are used for the other body parts.

For example let's consider the occlusion of left leg of a human being. We divide the leg into 4 segments and denote the occlusion of the lowest segment which includes foot, ankle and part of shinbone as state-1 and as we move up the leg, occlusion of the segments are numbered sequentially as state 2, 3 and 4. This is explained with the help of Fig. 1a where the segments are clearly marked, and state-1 is marked precisely. As explained above, Fig. 1a represents occlusion of one of the segments out of the four. We denote occlusion of combination of any 2 segments out of the 4 as states 5 to 10, i.e, occlusion of segment-1 + segment-2 = state-5, segment-1 + segment-3 = state-6 and so on. This is explained with the help of Fig. 1b where state-6 is marked precisely. Similarly, we denote occlusion of combination of any 3 segments as states 11 to 14 which is explained with the help of Fig. 1c where state-12 is marked precisely. We denote occlusion of combination of all the 4 segments as state-15 which is explained with the help of Fig. 1d and occlusion of none of the segments, i.e, when the entire leg is clearly visible as state-16.

Observation Symbol - For choosing observation symbol, color and shape information as proposed in [2] could be used. However, use of these observation symbols requires comparison with the original image, which may lead to false positives if the occluding object is of the same color or shape. We propose visibility of three reference points of different body parts as one observation vector for the HMM of that particular body part. These reference points are tabulated as follows -

Body Part	Reference Point	Body Part	Reference Point
Hand	Shoulder Joint Elbow Finger Tip	Torso	Neck Belly Lower Back
Leg	Hip Joint Knee Tip of Toe	Head	Top of Head Nose Neck Joint

Corresponding to each reference point in each part, an observation vector is prepared depending on the visibility of the reference point. A '1' corresponds to visibility of that part and a '0' corresponds to lack of visibility of that part. For example, if the visibilities for Shoulder Joint, Elbow and Finger Tip corresponding to a hand at any time t are respectively visible, not visible and visible, then the observation vector for that hand will be '101'. Different observation symbol vectors are explained with the help of images shown in Fig. 2.

(a) Observation Symbol Vector '001'   (b) Observation Symbol Vector '011'   (c) Observation Symbol Vector '100'

Fig. 2. Different Observation Symbol Vectors for the Left Leg

Parameters - For determining initial parameters of an HMM, the following quantities are computed:

$$a_{ij} = \frac{\text{No. of concurrent occurrences of state } S_i \text{ at time t and state } S_j \text{ at time t+1}}{\text{No. of occurrences of state } S_i \text{ for all time T}}$$

$$(1)$$

$$b_j(k) = \frac{\text{No. of concurrent occurrences of state } S_j \text{ and observation symbol } v_k}{\text{No. of occurrences of state } S_j}$$

$$(2)$$

Initially, we take all the states to be equiprobable and hence π is a vector having $1/16$ as all its elements. For reestimating these parameters we follow the EM algorithm explained in [5].

3   Experimental Setup

In order to evaluate the feasibility of the proposed method we use Matlab for extracting frames from a video at regular intervals of time, extract the feature vectors, and use Kevin Murphy's HMM tool box for training HMMs for different parts of the body under different scenes of occlusion.

Training - For training the scene of crowd, a group of two, three, four and five persons were made to walk in a group and the feature vectors for the body parts of the second and the third person away from the camera were taken for training. The feature vectors for the body parts of the first person of some of the sequences were used to train the HMM for a single person walking. This was done because there is no occlusion between the camera and the first person and, hence, he can be treated as one possibly with only self occlusion. As the first step, every fifth frame from the video was extracted for HMM training.

For building the observation vector, the input was taken sequentially for the reference points of every frame where a left click was symbolized as '1' and a right click was symbolized as '0'. If a reference point was not visible, an approximate point was clicked where the reference point was expected to be present. This was done to input the coordinates of the particular body part which influences the extent of body part occluded, and determine the corresponding hidden state for training the HMM. The coordinates were taken by clicking at the extremities of occlusion of the body parts and the states were determined by comparing the extent of occlusion from the coordinates. In certain frames, some portions of the body parts were out of the frame, and were assumed to be occluded. Input for them could not be provided automatically since they were out of frame and hence the states for these frames were input manually.

Re-estimation of the parameters was done using five iterations of EM algorithm. Log likelihood of the model using the parameters after the fifth iteration was calculated and the parameters along with the log likelihood were saved.

Classification - Observation vector for the given video was built and log likelihood (LL) was calculated for all the three classes using the corresponding learnt parameters. The video was identified as the class with the closest LL.

Sequence Generation - For sequence generation, parameters of the identified class are taken and Veterbi algorithm as explained in [5] is used to trace back the hidden states.

4   Experimental Results

We performed experiments on video sequences recorded by our group. The classification results of eighteen sequences comprising of six sequences for each of the three classes are represented in the following confusion matrix.

	Crowd	Opposite Direction	Single Individual
Crowd	6	-	-
Opposite Direction	2	3	1
Single Individual	1	2	3

The rows of the above matrix represent the actual sequences which were used as input and the columns represent the output of the trained HMM. From the above matrix it can be seen that the classification for all the six crowd sequences given as input were classified correctly while out of the six sequences of people crossing from opposite direction three were correctly classified and of the six sequences of single individual again three were correctly classified.

For sequence generation, we take 20 frames from each of the 18 sequences. Out of the 18 sequences, 12 sequences had an accuracy of 75% or more, i.e., these sequences had at least 15 frames depicting correct state of occlusion.

5   Conclusion

Tracking of people has been the focus of most researchers working with gait as a biometric tool and approximate reconstruction of scene of occlusion with prior knowledge of articulation. But knowledge of articulation along with the quantity of occlusion and scene of occlusion can help in better approximation.

In this paper we have presented a scheme for classification of the type of occlusion and quantifying occlusion using hidden Markov model. It takes into account the visible parts of the human body and the states based on occlusion of a band of certain percentage of the body part. The accuracy of the model can be increased by refining the states to smaller bands, i.e., 5% or 10% of the body part. But in that case, the number of states and hence computing cost will increase. The observation symbol can also be further refined to be six reference points instead of three per body part. However, the number of training samples required for that will also go up.

Acknowledgement

This work is partially supported by Alexander von Humboldt Fellowship for Experienced Researchers.

References

1. Apostoloff, N., Fitzgibbon, A.: Learning spatiotemporal t-junctions for occlusion detection. In: IEEE Computer Society Conference on Computer Vision and Pattern Recognition, June 2005, vol. 2, pp. 553–559 (2005)
2. Marchesotti, L., Piva, S., Regazzoni, C.S.: A dynamic model integrating colour and shape information for objects tracking in conditions of occlusion. In: IEEE International Conference on Multimedia and Expo, June 2004, vol. 3, pp. 1547–1550 (2004)
3. Mohamed, M.A., Gader, P.: Generalized hidden markov models. ii. application to handwritten word recognition. IEEE Transactions on Fuzzy Systems 8(1), 82–94 (2000)
4. Pan, J., Hu, B.: Robust occlusion handling in object tracking. In: IEEE Conference on Computer Vision and Pattern Recognition, June 2007, pp. 1–8 (2007)
5. Rabiner, L.R.: A tutorial on hidden markov models and selected applications in speech recognition. Proceedings of the IEEE 77(2), 257–286 (1989)
6. Veeravalli, A.G., Pan, W.D., Adhami, R., Cox, P.G.: A tutorial on using hidden markov models for phoneme recognition. In: Proceedings of the Thirty-Seventh Southeastern Symposium on System Theory, March 2005, pp. 154–157 (2005)
7. Velipasalar, S., Wolf, W.: Multiple object tracking and occlusion handling by information exchange between uncalibrated cameras. In: IEEE International Conference on Image Processing, September 2005, vol. 2, pp. II–418–II–421 (2005)
8. Wang, L., Hu, W., Tan, T.: Recent developments in human motion analysis. Pattern Recognition 36(3), 585–601 (2003)
9. Wang, Y., Liu, Z., Zhou, L.: Learning hierarchical non-parametric hidden markov model of human motion. In: Proceedings of International Conference on Machine Learning and Cybernetics, August 2005, vol. 6, pp. 3315–3320 (2005)
10. Yilmaz, A., Li, X., Shah, M.: Contour-based object tracking with occlusion handling in video acquired using mobile cameras. IEEE Transactions on Pattern Analysis and Machine Intelligence 26(11), 1531–1536 (2004)

IC-Topological Spaces and Applications in Soft Computing

Subrata Bhowmik

Department of Mathematics, Tripura University
Suryamaninagar, Tripura, India-799130
subrata_bhowmik_math@rediffmail.com

Abstract. The objective of this paper is to generalize the concept of topological space so that concepts of approximation spaces like Rough set, Pre-topological space, Approximation spaces generated by arbitrary relation etc. including topological space can be study by a single space. Here we considered a non-empty set X with two unary operators i and c on the power set $\wp(X)$ called respectively the interior and closure operators with some conditions on the operators. We will call the order triplet (X, i, c) an Interior-Closure Topological space or Simply IC-Topological space. In this paper we will discuss some applications of such spaces in real life problems.

Keywords: Topological Spaces, Incomplete information system.

1 IC-Topological Spaces

In the theory of different types of "Approximation spaces" like Rough set approximation space, Pre-topological space, Approximation by covering, Approximation spaces generated by a relation etc., the interior/lower approximation and closure/upper approximation of subsets may not be the interior and closure of the subsets with respect to a topology on the set. In this paper we will generalize the concept of topological space so that all these concepts can unified in a single space or its weaker space. This type of newly defined space can be useful in the study of "Approximation spaces" and also a useful tool in the the solution of real life problems like - diagnosis, data compression etc. by establishing soft computing techniques.

Definition 1. Let X be a non-empty set, we consider two unary operators i and c on $\wp(X)$, i.e. we consider two operators $i : \wp(X) \to \wp(X)$ and $c : \wp(X) \to \wp(X)$ satisfying the following conditions:

1. For any $A \subseteq X$, $i(A) \subseteq c(A)$ or simply $i \subseteq c$.
2. $i^2 = ii = i$ and $c^2 = cc = c$
3. i and c are monotone increasing, i.e. if $A \subseteq B \subseteq X$ then $i(A) \subseteq i(B)$ and $c(A) \subseteq c(B)$
4. $c(\varnothing) = \varnothing$, $i(X) = X$

S.O. Kuznetsov et al. (Eds.): PReMI 2011, LNCS 6744, pp. 311–317, 2011.

The unary operators i and c are respectively called a interior operator and a closure operator on X and the order triplet (X, i, c) is called a interior-closure topological space or simply IC-topological space.

For any A⊆X we will say i(A) is the lower approximation of A and c(A) is the upper approximation of A in the IC-topological space (X, i, c).

If we omit the condition (1), then the order triplet (X, i, c) is called quasi-IC-topological space or qIC-topological space; if we omit the condition (2) only, then the order triplet (X, i, c) is called pseudo IC-topological space or pIC-topological space and if we omit both the conditions (1) and (2), then the order triplet (X, i, c) is called quasi-pseudo-IC-topological space or qpIC-topological space,

For a IC-topological space (or qIC or pIC-topological space) (X, i, c) a subset U⊆X is called an open set if i(U)=U and a subset F⊆X is called a closed set if c(F)=F. It is easy to see that the whole set X is an open set and the empty set ∅ is a closed set.

Example 2. (i) Any topological approximation space $(\wp(X), \mathcal{O}(X), \mathcal{C}(X), l, u)$ induced from a topological space (X, $\mathcal{B}$) (see Cattaneo[1]), (X, l, u) is an IC-Topological space. We can also in similar way generate IC-topological space taking a supra topological space in the above approximation space.

(ii) If *int* and *cl* are interior and closure operator on a a non-empty set X (see Zhu [10]) then (X, *int*, *cl*) ia an IC-topological space.

(iii) Let R be relation on a non-empty set X, for each x∈X we define $R_x = \{y \in X : xRy\}$. We define unary operations i and c on the power set $\wp(X)$ as: for any subset A of X we define $i(A) = \{x \in X : R_x \subseteq A\}$ and $c(A) = \{x \in X : R_x \cap A \neq \emptyset\}$. It is very easy to see that (X, i, c) is a qpIC topological space.

(iv) For any rough set approximation space (X, R) generated by an equivalence relation R on X (see Pawlak[6]), if _ and ¯ be the lower and upper approximation operators respectively, then (X, _, ¯) is an IC-topological space.

(v) If $(\wp(X), \cap, \cup, \sim, \mathbf{L}, \mathbf{H})$ is a rough set algebra (see Yao[9]), then (X, $\mathbf{L}$, $\mathbf{H}$) is a qpIC-topological space.

(vi) For a pre-topological space (X, ε, κ) (see Pagliani and Chakraborty[5]), if I and C are corresponding κ-interior and ε-closure operator respectively then (X, I, C) is a IC-topological space.

Some properties of the IC-topological spaces are listed below, the proofs are easy forward, so proofs are omitted

Theorem 3. *For a IC-topological space (X, i, c), for any A, B⊆X, $i(A \cap B) \subseteq i(A) \cap i(B)$ and $c(A) \cup c(B) \subseteq c(A \cup B)$*

Theorem 4. *For a IC-topological space (X, i, c), for A∈X, i(A) contains every open set contained in A and c(A) is contained in every closed set containing A or in other word $\cup\{U : U \in \mathcal{O}O(X)$ and $U \subseteq A\} \subseteq i(A)$ and $c(A) \subseteq \cap\{F : F \in \mathcal{C}(X)$ and $A \subseteq F\}$.*

Theorem 5. *For a IC-topological space (X, i, c) for any $A \subseteq X$ the conditions $i(X - A) = X - c(A)$ and $c(X - A) = X - i(A)$ are equivalent.*

Definition 6. A IC-topological space (X, i, c) is said to be

(i) proper if for any $A \subseteq X$, $i(A) \subseteq A \subseteq c(A)$,
(ii) with duality if for any $A \subseteq X$, $i(X - A) = X - c(A)$.

Example 7. The IC-topological space generated by a rough set approximation is a proper IC-topological space with duality.

Theorem 8. *For a IC-topological space (X, i, c) with duality,*

(i) *for any $A \subseteq X$ the conditions (i) $i(A) \subseteq A$ and (ii) $A \subseteq c(A)$ are equivalent.*
(ii) *$U \subseteq X$ is open iff $X - U$ is closed.*

2 Application in Soft Computing When the Information from the Data Is Incomplete

IC-topological spaces can be use to apply in such problem like prediction, data compression etc which will be discussed in this section. Here the problems are associated with the decision with incomplete information. Before going to apply IC-topological spaces in these type of problems, let us first know the definition of incomplete information system. Following Shao[7], Cattanio[1], Kryszkiewicz[2] we define an incomplete information as:

Definition 9. An Incomplete information system (IIS) is a structure $\Re = (X, Att, Val, F)$ where

(i) X is a non-empty set called the sample space,
(ii) *Att* is a non-empty set called the set of attributes,
(iii) *Val* = {Y, N} called the set of values of attributes associated with the members of X (Y=Yes, N=No), and
(iv) $F = \{ f_a : a \in Att \}$ is a set of mappings called the attributive decision functions defined as: for each $a \in Att$ there exists a non-empty subset $X_a \subseteq X$ such that $f_a : X_a \to Val$.

If $X_a = X$ for each $a \in Att$ the information system $\Re = (X, Att, Val, F)$ is said to be complete(CIS).

Now let us assume that for each $a \in Att$ there exists $x \in X_a$ such that $f_a(x) = Y$ and for each $x \in X$, $\exists a \in Att$ such that $x \in X_a$ with $f_a(x) = Y$. us define two operators $s : Att \to \wp(X)$ and $m : Att \to \wp(X)$ as

$s(a) = \{x \in : f_a(x) = Y\}$, $m(a) = \{x \in : f_a(x) = Y\} \cup (X - X_a)$

We will say s(a) is the set having attribute "a" surely and m(a) is the set having attribute "a" possibly, but no one outside m(a) has the value of the attribute "a" "N".

Let us define attributes "1" and "0" and consider the information system $\Re = (X, Att', Val', F')$ where $Att' = Att \cup \{0, 1\}$ and $Val' = Val \cup \{f_0, f_1\}$ and $X_1 = X = X_0$, the attribute of possibly any one of the attribute that $f_1(x) = Y$

and $f_0(x)=N$ for each $a\in X$. So $s(1)=X=m(1)$ and $s(0)=\varnothing=m(0)$. We can say attribute "1" is characterized as: for each $x\in X$ "1" is the attribute having at least any one of the attribute from *Att* with "Y" and "0" is characterized as: for each $x\in X$ "0" is the attribute having all the attribute from *Att* with "N".

Again we define two operators $i : \wp(X) \to \wp(X)$ and $m : \wp(X) \to \wp(X)$ as

$i(A)=\cup\{s(a): a\in Att'$ and $s(a)\subseteq A\}$

$c(A)=\cap\{m(a) : a\in Att'$ and $A\subseteq m(a)\}$

It is easy to see that $i(A)\subseteq A\subseteq c(A)$.

Theorem 10. *(X, i, c) is a IC-topological space.*

Proof. 1. $i\subseteq c$ follows from the definition of i and c.

2. For $A\subseteq X$, $i(A)\subseteq A$, so $ii(A)\subseteq i(A)$. Let $x\in i(A)$, so $x\in s(a)\subseteq A$, so $x\in s(a)\subseteq i(A)$, i.e. $x\in ii(A)$, so $ii=i$.

For $A\subseteq X$, $A\subseteq c(A)$, so $c(A)\subseteq cc(A)$. Let $x\in cc(A)$, so $x\in m(a)$ for any $a\in Att'$ with $c(A)\subseteq m(a)$, now for any $a\in Att'$ with $A\subseteq m(a) \Rightarrow c(A)\subseteq m(a)$, but $x\in m(a)$, i.e. $x\in c(A)$, so $cc=c$.

3. i and c both are monotonic according to the definition of i and c.

4. $s(1)\subseteq X$ so $i(X)=X$, $\varnothing\subseteq m(0)$ so $c(\varnothing)=\varnothing$.

Hence (X, i, c) is a IC-topological space.

We define two operators $I : \wp(X) \to \wp(X)$ and $C : \wp(X) \to \wp(X)$ as

$I(A)=\cup\{s(a): a\in Att$ and $s(a)\cap A\neq \varnothing\}$

$C(A)=\cup\{m(a) : a\in Att$ and $m(a)\cap A\neq \varnothing\}$

It is very easy to see that:

Theorem 11. *(X, I, C) is a pIC-topological space.*

We again define two operators $\iota : \wp(X) \to \wp(X)$ and $\varepsilon : \wp(X) \to \wp(X)$ as

$\iota(A)=\cup\{s(a): a\in Att$ and $s(a)\subseteq A\}$

$\varepsilon(A)=\cup\{m(a) : a\in Att$ and $m(a)\cap A\neq \varnothing\}$

It is also very easy to see that:

Theorem 12. *(X, ι, ε) is a pIC-topological space.*

For any IIS we can generate different types of approximation spaces as IC-topological spaces as in Theorem10-12.

2.1 A Model of Decision Making When the Information from the Data Is Incomplete

Let S be a set or universes of elements with large numbers of objects and $\{a_1, a_2, ...,a_n; b_1, b_2, ...,b_m\}$, be n+m attributes. Let us say a_k's are symptom attributes and b_j's are decision attributes. The information is that all the members of S having at least one attribute with value "Y" and also the information is incomplete. Now the problem is: we are to decide if we pick up an object of S say "x" and observing the symptom attributes of "x" we are to decide which decision attribute is the concluding decision for "x". Another problem is if we select a subset W of S, then which decision attribute is corresponding to W.

For this let us take a subset X of S of suitable size and consider the IISs (X, $Att(A)$, Val, $F(A)$) and (X, $Att(B)$, Val, $F(B)$), where

$Att(A)=\{a_1, a_2, ...,a_n\}$
$Att(B)=\{b_1, b_2, ...,b_n\}$

We now construct the IC-topological spaces $(X, i_A, c_{A)})$ and $(X, i_B, c_{B)})$ according to Theorem10, qIC-topological spaces $(X, I_A, C_{A)})$ and $(X, I_B, C_{B)})$ according to Theorem11, $(X, \iota_A, \varepsilon_{A)})$ and $(X, \iota_B, \varepsilon_{B)})$ according to Theorem12.

2.1.1   Decision Model

For example let $\{a_1, a_2, ... ,a_k\}$ be a set of attributes corresponding to "x", now we are to decide whether "x" has the decision attribute b_j or not. For this we can apply the following method:

Let   (I) $s(a_1) \cap s(a_2) \cap \ .... \ \cap s(a_k) \subseteq s(b_j)$ and   (II) $m(a_1) \cup m(a_2) \cup \ ....$ $\cup m(a_k) \supseteq m(b_j)$, i.e. if some one having the attributes $a_1, a_2, ...\ , a_k$ surely is surely with the attribute b_j and if some one have the possibility of the decision b_j then it have the possible attributes $a_1, a_2, ...\ , a_k$, some or all but no need of more attributes for possibility of b_j.

Here we will conclude that "x" has the decision attribute B_j. If the collection $\{a_1, a_2,...... ,a_k\}$ is a smallest collection to hold the above conditions, we say that with the least symptom attributes $\{a_1, a_2,.... ,a_k\}$ an element has the decision attribute b_j . We will say $\{a_1, a_2, ...,a_k\}$ is a LSDAC (Least Symptom Decisional Attribute Class) for b_j.

2.1.2   Decision Model

Let W be any subset of S and we are to decide which decision attribute should be associate with W. For that we consider the following method:

Let $U=W \cap X$, if 1. $i_A(U) \supseteq s(b_j)$ and 2. $c_A(U) \subseteq m(b_j)$, i.e. 1. any one having the decision attribute b_j surely then it has at least one or more attributes surely, whose surety is (are) only seen in the class U is and 2. if any one have the possibility of the common symptom attributes that are possibly common to all the members in the class U, have the possibility of the decision attribute b_j. Here we will decide that b_j is a decision attribute corresponding to Y.

If we replace the space (X, i_A, c_A) by $(X, \iota_A, \varepsilon_A)$ then the conclusion obtained can be treated as stronger conclusion than the above and if replace by (X, I_A, C_A) then the conclusion can be treated as weaker conclusion than the above.

We can revert the role of symptom attribute and decision attributes in above, we can find the cause of a single symptom attribute in multiple decision attributes.

Example 13. Here we are going to see how the above model can be applied in Hospital Management. Here the example is only for example not on actual data or medical fact, this example is only to understand the application of above method.

Let in a hospital from some patients we have the following informa-
tion(recorder data):

Patient	Fever(a_1)	Headac.(a_2)	Indg.(a_3)	Cough(a_4)	Flue(b_1)	Stom.Inf.(b_2)
x_1	Y	Y	Y	Y	Y	Y
x_2	Y	Y	N	Y	Y	?
x_3	?	N	N	?	Y	N
x_4	N	N	N	Y	?	N
x_5	N	Y	?	?	N	?

Here the symptom attributes are $\{a_1, a_2, a_3, a_4\}$ and decision attributes are
b_1 and b_2. Now,

$X=\{x_1, x_2, x_3, x_4, x_5\}$
$s(a_1)=\{x_1, x_2\}$, $m(a_1)=\{x_1, x_2, x_3\}$
$s(a_2)=\{x_1, x_2, x_5\}$, $m(a_2)=\{x_1, x_2, x_5\}$
$s(a_3)=\{x_1\}$, $m(a_3)=\{x_1, x_5\}$
$s(a_4)=\{x_1, x_2, x_4\}$, $m(a_4)=X$
$s(b_1)=\{x_1, x_2, x_3\}$, $m(b_1)=\{x_1, x_2, x_3, x_4\}$,
$s(b_2)=\{x_1\}$, $s(b_2)=\{x_1, x_2, x_5\}$.

Obviously $s(0)=\varnothing$ and $m(1)=X$.
Now the collection $\{a_1, a_4\}$ is the LSDAC for the decision, since (I) $s(a_1)\cap s(a_4)$
$\subseteq s(b_1)$ and (II) $m(a_1)\cup m(a_4) \supseteq m(b_1)$.
Now we can decide that if a person coming to the hospital with symptoms
"Fever" and "Cough" then we will make a decision that the patient is with
"Flue". In this case the patient can say that he has the problem of "Headache"
or "Indigestion" or not. For example if a patient comes with the symptoms $\{a_1,$
$a_2, a_4\}$ then it is easy to see that the corresponding decision is also "Flue". Here
$\{a_1, a_4\}$ is a LSDAC for "Flue(b_1)".
Similarly $\{a_1, a_3\}$ is a LSDAC for "Stomach Infection(b_2)".
Again Let $U=\{x_1, x_2\}$ is the portion of a community say "T" of the region
(T is a specific subset of the population of the region of the hospital). Now,
$i(U)=s(a_1)\cup s(a_3)=\{x_1, x_2\}$ and $c(U)=m(a_1)\cap m(a_2)\cap m(a_4)=\{x_1, x_2\}$. We see
that $i(U)\supseteq s(b_2)$ and $c(U)\subseteq m(b_2)$.
Now we can make a decision that the disease b_2 is generally confined in
the community "T" and if a patient come from the community "T" and if he
suffering from the b_2 then we can suspect whether this infection comes from his
community or not and if he is not ill or we can expect the possibility of the
infection b_2 due to his community(in case of communicative disease).

2.2   Decision of Change of Set of Attributes

Let S be a population and $A=\{a_1, a_2,......,a_n\}$ and $B=\{b_1, b_2,......,b_m\}$ be two set
of attributers in two different stages, A is initial stage and B is the final stage.
The information is all the members of S having at least one attribute from the
two sets of attributes. Now the problem is: we are to decide whether the initial
attributes changed to the final attributes or not. Let X be a sample of suitable

size from the population, but the sample having with incomplete information regarding the attributes we construct the IC-topological space (X, i_A, c_B) with the set of attributes A and (X, i_B, c_B) with the set of attributes B.

2.2.1   Decision Model

If (1) U is open in (X, i_B, c_B) then U is open in (X, i_A, c_A) and (2) F is closed in (X, i_B, c_B) then F is closed in (X, i_A, c_A) holds, i.e. (1) if for any subset $\acute{B}$ of B $\exists$ a subset $\acute{A}$ of A such that if any element of X has one or more attributes form $\acute{B}$ surely in final stage $\Leftrightarrow$ it must had one or more attributes from $\acute{A}$ surely at initial stage and (2) for any subset $\grave{B}$ of B $\exists$ a subset $\grave{A}$ of A such that if any element of X has the possibility all the attributes from $\grave{B}$ finally $\Leftrightarrow$ it had the possibility of all the attributes from $\grave{A}$ initially.

In this case we will make a decision that the set A of attributes is changed to the set of attributes B.

2.2.2   Decision Model

We will say the set of attributes A and B are mutually dependent if $U \subseteq X$ is open(closed) in (X, i_A, c_A) iff U is open(closed) in (X, i_B, c_B).

Acknowledgements. I am thankful to the referees for their suggestions and valuable comments to revise the paper.

References

1. Cattaneo, G.: The Lattice Topological Approach to Roughness Theory by Approximation Spaces. In: Proceedings-Int. Conf. on Rough Sets, Fuzzy Sets and Soft Computing, November 5-7, 2009, pp. 9–74. Serial Pub., New Delhi (2011)
2. Kryszkiewicz, M.: Rough Set Approach to Incomplete Information Systems. Information Sciences 112, 39–49 (1998)
3. Mashhour, A.S., Allam, A.A., Mahmoud, F.S., Khedr, F.S.: On Supra Topological Spaces. Indian J. Pure and Appl. Math. 4(14), 502–510 (1983)
4. Pagliani, P.: Concrete and Formal Pre-Topological Systems and Their Approximate Operators. In: Proceedings-Int. Conf. on Rough Sets, Fuzzy Sets and Soft Computing, November 5-7, 2009, pp. 119–128. Serial Pub., New Delhi (2011)
5. Pagliani, P., Chakraborty, M.K.: A Geometry of Approximation, Rough Set Theory: Logic, Algebra and Topology of Conceptual Patterns, pp. 406–477. Springer, Heidelberg (2008)
6. Pawlak, Z.: Rough Sets. International Journal of Information and Computer Science 11(5), 341–356 (1982)
7. Shao, M.W.: A complete Method to Incomplete Information Systems. In: Yao, J., Lingras, P., Wu, W.-Z., Szczuka, M.S., Cercone, N.J., Ślęzak, D. (eds.) RSKT 2007. LNCS (LNAI), vol. 4481, pp. 50–59. Springer, Heidelberg (2007)
8. Willard, S.: General Topology. Addison Wesley Publishing Company, Reading (1970)
9. Yao, Y.: Constructive and Algebraic Method of the theory of Rough Sets. Information Sciences 109, 21–47 (1998)
10. Zhu, W.: Topological Approaches to Covering Rough Sets. Information Science 177, 1499–1508 (2007)

Neuro-Genetic Approach for Detecting Changes in Multitemporal Remotely Sensed Images

Aditi Mandal[1], Susmita Ghosh[2], and Ashish Ghosh[3]

[1] Ixia Technologies Pvt. Ltd., Sector V, Kolkata, India
maditi04@yahoo.co.in
[2] Department of Computer Science and Engineering, Jadavpur University, India
susmitaghoshju@gmail.com
[3] MIU and CSCR, Indian Statistical Institute, Kolkata, India
ash@isical.ac.in

Abstract. In the present work the searching capability of Genetic Algorithms (GAs) is exploited to evolve suitable Hopfield type neural network architectures for optimum change detection of multitemporal remotely sensed images. Experiments carried out on two remote sensing images confirm the effectiveness of the proposed technique.

Keywords: Change detection, Hopfield type neural network, Genetic Algorithm, Remote sensing, Multitemporal images.

1 Introduction

In remote sensing applications, change detection is the process of identifying differences in the state of an object or phenomenon by analyzing a pair of images acquired on the same geographical area at different times [1]. Two preprocessed images, radiometrically and geometrically [2] corrected, are compared pixel by pixel to generate a third image, called the difference image. Once image comparison is performed, the change detection process can be carried out by adopting either context-insensitive or context-sensitive procedure. Commonly used context-insensitive techniques are based on image or histogram thresholding which do not take into account the spatial correlation between neighboring pixels in the decision process. To overcome this limitation, a distribution free, context-sensitive and unsupervised change detection procedure based on Hopfield network is suggested in [3].

In the aforementioned neural network based change detection procedure [3], each spatial position (pixel) in the difference image is represented by a neuron in the Hopfield network and it is fully connected to its neighboring neurons. But sometimes full connectivity may result in misclassification of a pixel. It is, therefore, necessary to deal with variable connected networks for improving the quality of the change detection map. In this article the searching capability of GAs is exploited to evolve Hopfield type optimum neural network architectures for context-sensitive unsupervised change detection in multitemporal remotely sensed images.

S.O. Kuznetsov et al. (Eds.): PReMI 2011, LNCS 6744, pp. 318–323, 2011.

2   Hopfield's Model of Neural Networks

A Hopfield neural network consists of a set of neurons where output of each neuron is fed back to each of the other neurons in the network. There is no self feedback loop, and the synaptic weights are symmetric. Depending on the output values a neuron can take, there are two types of Hopfield models: discrete and continuous.

2.1   Discrete Model

In the discrete model, neurons are bipolar $i.e.$, the output V_i of neuron i is either $+1$ or -1. Hopfield defined the energy function of the network [4] as

$$E = -\sum_{i=1}^{z} \sum_{j=1,i\neq j}^{z} W_{ij}V_iV_j - \sum_{i=1}^{z} I_iV_j + \sum_{i=1}^{z} \theta_i V_i , \tag{1}$$

where the weight W_{ij} represents the synaptic interconnection strength from neuron j to neuron i, and z is the total number of neurons in the network; θ_i is the predefined threshold and I_i is the initial input bias applied externally to the neuron i. The change of energy ΔE due to a change of output state of a neuron i by ΔV is

$$\Delta E = -\left[\sum_{j=1,i\neq j}^{z} W_{ij}V_j + I_i - \theta_i\right]\Delta V_i = -\left[U_i - \theta_i\right]\Delta V_i. \tag{2}$$

Any change in V_i makes ΔE negative. At each iteration, the energy value decreases and the network reaches a stable state when its energy value reaches the minimum [4].

2.2   Continuous Model

In this model, the output of a neuron is continuous and V_i lies in the range $[-1, +1]$. The energy function E of the continuous model is given by

$$E = -\sum_{i=1}^{z} \sum_{j=1,i\neq j}^{z} W_{ij}V_iV_j - \sum_{i=1}^{z} I_iV_j + \sum_{i=1}^{z} \frac{1}{R_i}\int_0^{V_i} g^{-1}(V_i)dv. \tag{3}$$

The function E is a Liapunov function, and R_i is the total input impedance of the amplifier realizing a neuron i. The last term in (3) is the energy loss term, which becomes zero at the high gain region. Therefore, the only stable points of the very high-gain continuous deterministic Hopfield model correspond to the stable points of the discrete stochastic Hopfield model [4].

3   Change Detection Based on Modified Hopfield Neural Network Architecture

For change detection of two coregistered and radiometrically corrected multi-spectral images X_1 and X_2 of size $p \times q$, acquired over the same area at different times T_1 and T_2, at first the difference image $D = l_{mn}, 1 \leq m \leq p, 1 \leq n \leq q$ is obtained by applying the CVA technique [1,2], where l_{mn} is the gray value of the spatial position (m, n). A neuron is assigned to each $(m, n) \in D$ as introduced in [5]. The spatial correlation between neighboring pixels is modeled by defining the neighborhood systems N of order d, for a given position (m, n) as $N^d{}_{mn} = (m, n) + (u, v); (u, v) \in N^d$. The connection strength between the $(m, n)^{th}$ and $(u, v)^{th}$ neurons $W_{mn,uv} = 1$ if $(u, v) \in N^d{}_{mn}$; otherwise, $W_{mn,uv} = 0$. Each neuron in the network is initialized by external input bias I_{mn} which is computed considering the optimal initialization threshold t_0 and automatically derived initialization threshold t_1 [3]. The energy function of the network as defined in [5] is as follows

$$E = - \sum_{m=1}^{p} \sum_{n=1}^{q} \sum_{(u,v) \in N^d_{mn}} W_{mn,uv} V_{mn} V_{uv} - \sum_{m=1}^{p} \sum_{n=1}^{q} I_{mn} V_{mn}. \tag{4}$$

In terms of images, the first part of (4) can be seen as the impact of the gray values of the neighboring pixels, whereas the second part can be attributed to the gray value of the pixel under consideration [5]. The minimization of (4) results in a stable state of the network in which changed pixels (with output $+1$) are separated from unchanged ones (with output -1).

4   Architecture Evolution Using GAs for Change Detection

The connectivity of a neuron allows the neighborhood information to be used for deciding the class of the corresponding pixel as changed or unchanged. In case, some of the neighbors are not completely corrected (geometrically or radiometrically) in the preprocessing step or the pixel is in boundary region, then full connectivity (which considers maximum neighborhood information) may result in misclassification of the said pixel. It is, therefore, necessary to adopt variable connected networks for improving the performance of change detection. This will also enable us to have less connectivity (i.e., less expensive network) as compared to the fully connected one, besides the improved performance.

Here, each chromosome of a GA [6] represents a network architecture as it is viewed in [7]. For a $p \times q$ image, each pixel (neuron) being connected to at most k of its neighbors, the length of the chromosome is $p \times q \times k$. If a neuron is connected to any of its neighbors, the corresponding bit of the chromosome is set to 1, else 0. Each network is allowed to run for change detection as described in the previous section. The energy value obtained at the converged state of a network is taken as the index of fitness of the corresponding chromosome (minimum energy corresponds to maximum fitness) for its selection for the next generation. The best chromosome of the final population represents the Hopfield type optimum neural network architecture.

5 Results and Analysis

To assess the effectiveness of the proposed approach, we consider remote sensing data sets corresponding to geographical area of Mexico which is made up of two multispectral images acquired by the sensor of the Landsat-7 satellite in April 2000 and May 2002 (Figs. 1(a) and 1(b), respectively). Between the two afore-mentioned acquisition dates, a fire destroyed a large portion of the vegetation in the considered region. The corresponding difference image and the reference map are shown in Figs. 1(c) and 1(d), respectively.

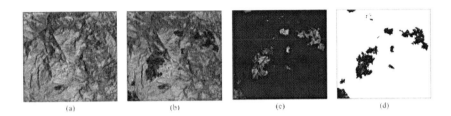

Fig. 1. Images of Mexico area. (a) Band 4 of the Landsat ETM+ image acquired in April 2000, (b) band 4 of the Landsat ETM+ image acquired in May 2002, (c) corresponding difference image generated by CVA technique, and (d) reference map of changed area.

After analyzing the histogram of the difference image (DI) generated by CVA technique, we observe that the highest peak is in the region of lower gray value. If we consider the properties of the DI, a reasonable assumption can be as follows: a pixel having lower gray value exhibits a high probability of being in unchanged class, whereas a pixel with higher gray value has a high probability of being in changed class. This implies that most of the pixels and their neighbors in the lower gray value region belong to the same area *i.e.*, unchanged area. Hence, for this region maximum neighborhood information can be used for deciding a pixel's class. On the contrary, as nature of the neighbors of rest of the pixels is unknown, use of maximum neighborhood information may lead to their misclas-sification. So we initialize the population of GA in such a way that if a pixel has lower gray value then the corresponding bits in the chromosome will be 1 with the probability 0.9; otherwise, it will be filled up with 0s and 1s with equal prob-ability. The population size is kept fixed to 50. The generational replacement technique and elitist model are adopted here along with linear normalization selection [6]. Multipoint crossover is implemented where number of cross-sites is set to 1000 and crossover probability, p_c, is set to 0.9. It is expected that in the final architecture we have more 1s than 0s because most of the pixels will be connected with more than half of their neighbors to use the contextual information. So we carry out the experiment with two different sets of mutation probabilities p_m and p_b to preserve 1s more than preserving 0s. We mutate the bit 0 with the probability p_m only, whereas bit 1 is mutated with probability $p_m \times p_b$. For second order connectivity, we have taken $p_m=0.01$, $p_b=0.01$. The mutation probability, p_m, is decreased to 0.001 in case of the first order connectivity as the the length of the chromosome is much less in the first order than in the second order. The network attains stable state around 350th and 200th generations for the first and the second order connectivity, respectively.

In order to establish the effectiveness of the proposed technique, a comparison is carried out between the change detection results produced by the proposed GA based method and those using the Hopfield-Type neural networks (HTNN) [3]. Results obtained using both the methods are put in Table 1. It shows that the proposed model always produces less overall error (and a network with less number of connections) as compared to the HTNN counterpart. Also, the second order connectivity is found to be more effective than the first order.

Table 1. Change detection results obtained by the HTNN and the proposed technique

Network Model used	Connectivity	Initialization Threshold		Technique used	No. of Missed alarms	No. of False alarms	Overall error	Number of Connections
		t_0	t_1					
Discrete	1st	34	-	HTNN	1252	1640	2892	1048576
		34	-	Proposed	1054	1749	**2803**	**1027330**
		-	33	HTNN	1102	1802	2904	1048576
		-	33	Proposed	915	1878	**2793**	**1035214**
	2nd	31	-	HTNN	1010	1740	2750	2097152
		31	-	Proposed	936	1711	**2647**	**2083341**
		-	27	HTNN	608	2404	3012	2097152
		-	27	Proposed	489	2309	**2798**	**2085111**
Continuous	1st	34	-	HTNN	1035	1554	2589	1048576
		34	-	Proposed	1120	1461	**2581**	**1037125**
		-	31	HTNN	660	2157	2817	1048576
		-	31	Proposed	767	1907	**2674**	**1035118**
	2nd	30	-	HTNN	733	2211	2944	2097152
		30	-	Proposed	766	2108	**2874**	**2077246**
		-	28	HTNN	558	2707	3265	2097152
		-	28	Proposed	718	2403	**3121**	**2060882**

Figs. 2(a) and 2(b) depict the change detection maps produced by the HTNN and the proposed technique, respectively for the first-order continuous model with $t_1=31$. Figs. 2(c) and 2(d), respectively, show the change detection maps obtained using the HTNN and the proposed technique for the second order discrete model with $t_1=27$. A visual comparison points out that the proposed approach, due to a proper exploitation of the contextual information, generates a more smooth change detection map compared to the fully connected one.

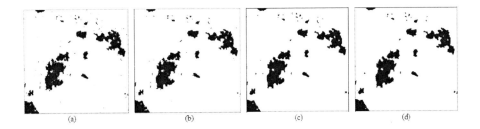

Fig. 2. Change detection maps obtained using (a) the HTNN technique, (b) the proposed technique for first-order continuous model with $t_1 = 31$ and (c) the HTNN technique, (d) the proposed technique for second-order discrete model with $t_1 = 27$

6   Conclusion

Experimental results obtained on multitemporal data sets confirm the effectiveness of the proposed GA based technique. The method always produces less overall change detection error compared to the one achieved using HTNN model. Additionally, the number of connections in the evolved network is always less compared to the corresponding fully connected version.

Acknowledgments. The authors like to thank the Department of Science and Technology (DST), Government of India and University of Trento, Italy, the sponsors of the ITPAR program and Prof. L. Bruzzone, the Italian collaborator of the project, for providing the data.

References

1. Singh, A.: Digital change detection techniques using remotely sensed data. International Journal of Remote Sensing 10(6), 989–1003 (1989)
2. Richards, J.A., Jia, X.: Remote Sensing Digital Image Analysis. Springer, Berlin (2006)
3. Ghosh, S., Bruzzone, L., Patra, S., Bovolo, F., Ghosh, A.: A context-sensitive technique for unsupervised change detection based on Hopfield type neural networks. IEEE Transactions on Geoscience and Remote Sensing 45(3), 778–789 (2007)
4. Hopfield, J.J.: Neural networks and physical systems with emergent collective computational abilities. Proceedings of the National Academy of Sciences, USA 79, 2554–2558 (1982)
5. Ghosh, A., Pal, N.R., Pal, S.K.: Object background classification using Hopfield type neural network. International Journal of Pattern Recognition and Artificial Intelligence 6(5), 989–1008 (1992)
6. Goldberg, D.E.: Genetic Algorithms in Search, Optimization, and Machine Learning. Pearson Education, London (2003)
7. Pal, S.K., De, S., Ghosh, A.: Designing Hopfield type networks using genetic algorithms and its comparison with simulated annealing. International Journal of Pattern Recognition and Artificial Intelligence 11(3), 447–461 (1997)

Synthesis and Characterization of Gold Nanoparticles – A Fuzzy Mathematical Approach

D. Dutta Majumder[1], Sankar Karan[2], and A. Goswami[3]

[1] ECSU, Indian Statistical Institute, 203, B.T. Road, Kolkata 700108, India
[2] Institute of Radiophysics and Electronics, C.U., 92, APC Road, Kolkata 700006, India
[3] Biological Science Division, ISI,203, B T Road, Kolkata 700108, India
duttamajumder.isi@gmail.com, sankar.karan@gmail.com,
agoswami@isical.ac.in

Abstract. This article presents the development of nanoparticles (NPs) with potentially useful size and shape dependent properties that have the advantage of ultra-fine size, high surface area and useful interfacial imperfections. When developing NPs as catalysts, their shape is very important. For a certain volume of material, nanoparticles make the best catalysts when they have a large surface area. It is a challenge to find the shape that has the largest surface area for its volume. The particle shape contours were measured by transmission electron microscope with high resolution. These TEM images are analyzed with image clustering techniques and generalized shape theory that results the computational indicators for shape, degree of atomic compactness and charge arrangement of NPs.

Keywords: Fuzzy C-Means Clustering, Generalized Shape Theory & Metric, Nanomaterial, Nanoimaging, Nano Synthesis.

1 Introduction

Nanometer sized(1×10^{-9} to 100×10^{-9})particles are of today's interests because of their shape and size-dependent[1] physical properties. The chemical and physical properties of such aggregates, comprising only a few hundred atoms are in a transition region between the bulk and individual atomic or molecular properties. By understanding size and shape related changes in these systems, it is hoped that advanced new materials can be developed together with a raft of new technologies. Nanotechnology[2] may be defined as the development at the atomic, molecular and micro-molecular levels in the length and scale of approximately 1-100 nanometer range, to provide a fundamental understanding of phenomena and materials at the nanoscale and to create and use structures, devices and systems that have novel properties and functions because of their size and shape related properties. NPs with potentially useful size and shape dependent properties have the advantage of ultra fine size, high surface area, useful interfacial defects and so are extensively utilized as key components in electronics and optical

S.O. Kuznetsov et al. (Eds.): PReMI 2011, LNCS 6744, pp. 324–332, 2011.

devices, pharmaceutics, paints, coatings, superconductors, semi conductors. In fact the reproducible preparation of shape controlled particles using the popular colloid–chemical approach is difficult. Using in-process measurement techniques and particle image analysis, our research characterizes the synthesis of gold NPs improve compactness and sphericalness. This type of characterization helps the researchers in shape and size-based spectral tuning, biological labeling, toxicity studies and suggest general protocols to address these problems.

Imaging beneath the surface of a sample has always been a challenge to microscopy as they cannot be seen in the traditional sense, but that should not prevent us from visualizing the nanoworld. The main goal of Nanotechnology is to analyze and understand the properties of matter at the atomic and molecular level. Non-destructive, nanoscale characterization techniques[3] are needed to understand both synthetic and biological materials. In this paper we propose a new nanoscale image-based characterization techniques to analyze and synthesis nanoscale images that requires algorithms to perform image analysis under extremely challenging conditions such as low signal-to-noise ratio and low resolution. To achieve this, we developed an imaging tools that are able to enhance images [4], detect objects and features [5] and analyze particle size and shape[6]. Here we present the algorithms, describe their representative methods, and conclude with several promising directions of future investigation. Nano scale photograph processing allows us to understand unique properties of matter at atomic and molecular level spanning a wide range of applications in areas such as nano-bio-medicine, nano-chip manufacturing, material sciences, nano-agri-biotechnologies and environmental toxicology[7-8].

2   Materials and Methods

Thiol, aspartic acid, Citrate protected gold nanoparticles of different size and shape were synthesized in the laboratory. Transmission Electron Microscopy(TEM) and spectroscopy study for Imaging and particle size distribution of Gold NPs were performed to observe the topology of the particles. These images are processed by fuzzy logic based clustering techniques. Mean diameter and compactness are measured automatically through algorithms by counting pixels belonging to every clusters. Surface(S) to Volume(V) ratio was measure considering the NPs are spherical in nature. Packing density is obtained by measuring the imperfections/defects from its segmented TEM images. Results are observed, compared with existing method and chemical measurement and manual counting.

2.1   Nano Scale Image Data Clustering Using Fuzzy C-Means(FCM)

TEM Image data of Gold NPs were (20nm) classified using fuzzy C-Means clustering [9-11] algorithm to separate the particle from its background, identify the defect and also the molecular arrangement inside the particle and developed an iterative optimization procedure for classification. Let $X = \{X_1, X_2, \dots, X_n\}$ be a set of samples to be clustered into c classes. Here we consider color as a feature for classification in RGB (red, green, blue) color space. The criterion function used for the clustering process is

$$J(V) = \sum_{k=1}^{n} \sum_{x_k \in C_1} |x_k - v_i|^2 \tag{1}$$

Where v_i, is the sample mean or the center of samples of cluster i, and $V = \{v_1, \dots, v_c\}$. To improve the similarity of the samples in each cluster, we can minimize this criterion function so that all samples are more compactly distributed around their cluster centers. Membership values (μ's) are assigned as per FCM algorithm.

In summary, the c-means clustering procedure consists of the following steps:

- S-1: Determine the number of clusters c.
- S-2: Partition the input samples into c clusters based on an approximation. If no rule of approximation exists, the Samples can be partitioned randomly.
- S-3: Compute the Cluster Centers
- S-4: Assign each input sample to the class of the closed cluster center.
- Repeat steps 3 and 4 until no change in J can be made and the algorithm converges.

For cluster validity[11-12], we consider three types of measures : partition coefficient, partition entropy and compactness and separation validity function.

2.2 Shape Based Image Registration of Gold NP's

The perception of shape has been used for pattern recognition, computer vision, shape analysis[13], and image registration. Here we proposed a generalized method of shape analysis and shape based similarity measures, shape distance and shape metric to measured the NPs shape. The shape of an object can be defined as a subset X in R^2 if (a) X is closed and bounded, (b) Interior of X is non-empty and connected and (c) Closure property holds on interior of X. This representation of shape remains invariant with respect to translation, rotation and scaling. Moreover another object Y in R^2 is of same shape to object $X \in R^2$ if it preserves translation, rotation and scaling invariance. In term of set these three transformations can be represented as

Translation : $Y = \{(x + a),(y + b): x, y \in X\}$ \hfill (2)

Rotation : $Y = \{P1(\alpha).P2(\beta)X\}$ where P1 & P2 are rotation around x and y axes. \hfill (3)

Scaling : $Y = \{(kx, ky): x, y \in X\}$ \hfill (4)

Distance d_1 between shape X and Y in F is defined as follows:
$d_1(X,Y)=m_2[(X-Y)\cup(Y-X)]$ \hfill (5)

where m_2 is Lebesgue measure in R^2 and d_1 satisfies following rules: (i) $d_1(X,Y) \geq 0$, (ii) $d_1(X,Y) = 0$ if and only if $X = Y$ (iii) $d_1(X,Y) = d_1(Y,X)$ and (iv) $d_1(X,Y) + d_1(Y,Z) \geq d_1(X,Z)$. We consider, two nano particles are of same shape if and only if one of the image is translation, Scaling and rotation of other.

• Shape extraction and similarity measure

To extract the feature of the boundary of the Region of Interest(ROI) it is helpful to represent the closed contour with a set of direction. The direction code may be taken among "n" selected points on the contour, which has same distance between any two consecutive points. The direction d makes an angle $45°$ with direction i, where real number $d \in 1$ to 8 and $i = (1,2,..8)$. Let $d_m = (d_{ij})$, $j = 1$ to n where m = A, B are the contour starting from each reference point A and B and are denoted by d_A and d_B respectively. If d_2 is a rotation of d_1 then $d_2 = d_1 + \gamma$ for any real number γ. For all j we can write $d_2 = d_1 + \gamma \ \forall \ j$ and the distance function D, in terms of the direction code between the contour of interest and the model is defined as:

$$D(d_1d_2) = \sum_{J=1}^{n} \min((d_{1j}d_{2j}),8 - (d_{1j}d_{2j})) \tag{6}$$

The normalized value of D is D/n and the shape similarity measure between the two shapes is given by $\mu = 1-D/n$, smaller value of D indicates higher degree of similarity [13].

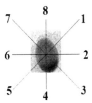

Fig. 1. Chain code representation

3   Experimental Procedure and Results

• Synthesis of thiol protected gold nanoparticle

Aqueous solution of $HAuCl_4$ is mixed with solution of ToABr in toluene. Vigorous stirring causes transfer of $HAuCl_4$ into the organic layer. Dodecanethiol is added to the organic phase followed by addition of aqueous solution of NaBH4 is slowly added with vigorous stirring. Aqueous solution of sodium borohydride is slowly added with vigorous stirring. A deep brown coloured solution appears at the interface. Excess ethanol is added to the separated brown coloured solution and kept overnight which causes precipitation of GNP. The ethanolic solution is filtered with nylon filter and the precipitate is re-dispersed in toluene

- Synthesis of aspartic acid protected gold nanoparticle

90 ml of 10^{-4}M aqueous solution of chloroauric acid is prepared. The solution is heated up to boiling condition. 10 ml of 10^{-2}M aspartic acid solution is added to the boiling solution. Aspartic acid acts as the reducing agent. The reduction process is continued under constant stirring. Heating is stopped. The reduction of the metal ions is evident with appearance of red color.

- Synthesis of Citrate capped gold nanoparticle

50 ml of 1mM aqueous solution of chloroauric acid is prepared. The solution is heated up to boiling under reflux condition. 5 ml of 1% tri sodium citrate dihydrate solution is added to the boiling solution. Sodium citrate here reduces the gold chloride. Stirring was continued until the color of the solution gradually changed from faint yellowish to clear to grey to purple to deep purple, and finally wine-red. Negatively charged citrate ions were absorbed onto the GNPs, introducing the surface charge that repels the particles and prevents them from aggregation.

Table 1. TEM imaging, absorbance study, shape tracing and size distribution of Gold nanoparticles

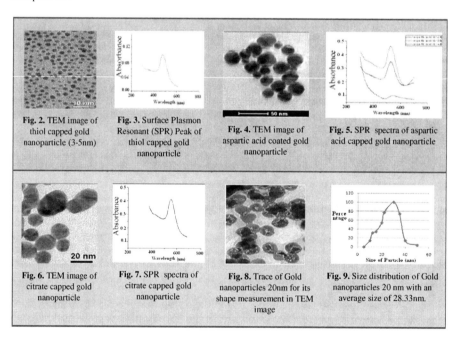

Fig. 2. TEM image of thiol capped gold nanoparticle (3-5nm)

Fig. 3. Surface Plasmon Resonant (SPR) Peak of thiol capped gold nanoparticle

Fig. 4. TEM image of aspartic acid coated gold nanoparticle

Fig. 5. SPR spectra of aspartic acid capped gold nanoparticle

Fig. 6. TEM image of citrate capped gold nanoparticle

Fig. 7. SPR spectra of citrate capped gold nanoparticle

Fig. 8. Trace of Gold nanoparticles 20nm for its shape measurement in TEM image

Fig. 9. Size distribution of Gold nanoparticles 20 nm with an average size of 28.33nm.

Table 2. Image Segmentation using Fuzzy C-Means

Coordinate		RGB Value			Initial Assignment			After 9th Iteration		
x	y	R	G	B	μ1	μ2	μ3	μ1	μ2	μ3
0	0	66	16	107	0.60	0.35	0.05	0.04	0.03	0.93
0	1	8	90	41	0.22	0.43	0.35	0.01	0.99	0.01
0	2	9	79	21	0.83	0.15	0.02	0.05	0.92	0.03
0	3	107	78	12	0.44	0.43	0.13	0.80	0.12	0.08
0	4	90	24	8	0.06	0.83	0.11	0.90	0.05	0.06
0	5	9	79	21	0.67	0.15	0.18	0.05	0.92	0.03
0	6	66	16	107	0.28	0.43	0.29	0.04	0.03	0.93
0	7	8	90	41	0.89	0.10	0.01	0.01	0.99	0.01
0	8	9	79	21	0.51	0.43	0.06	0.05	0.92	0.03
0	9	107	78	12	0.12	0.83	0.05	0.80	0.12	0.08
0	10	79	38	8	0.73	0.15	0.12	0.96	0.02	0.02
0	11	66	32	8	0.35	0.43	0.22	0.84	0.09	0.08
0	12	66	16	107	0.95	0.01	0.04	0.04	0.03	0.93
0	13	8	90	41	0.57	0.35	0.08	0.01	0.99	0.01
0	14	9	79	21	0.19	0.43	0.38	0.05	0.92	0.03
0	15	15	107	78	0.79	0.15	0.06	0.80	0.12	0.08

Cluster Centre for 3 classes			
RGB	V1	V2	V3
R	87.3	46.5	11.9
G	13.3	83.9	38.9
B	52.8	12.8	91.3

Fig. 10. Pixel value with Membership after clustering into 3 classes, with cluster centre V1,V2,V3

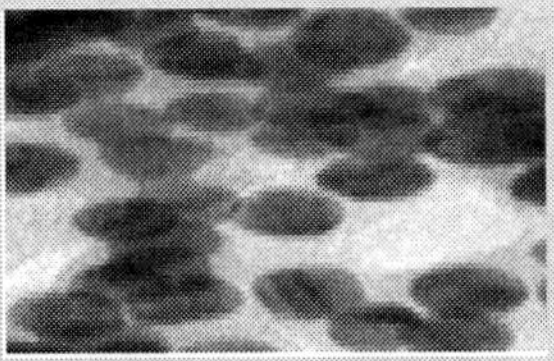

Fig. 11. Original TEM Image of Gold nanoparticles 20nm

Fig. 12. Segmented TEM Image of Gold nanoparticles 20 nm in 3 classes

4   Conclusion

A novel and simple method for measurement of the size, shape and other spectral response of gold NPs. These values may be used as the input of Artificial Neural Networks(ANN) to characterized the synthesis process of gold NPs as proposed in fig.15. The ANN offers a successful tool for NPs preparation analysis and modeling. Chemical routes for the Polymer based nanocomposites preparation offer the advantage of (a) a cluster or atomic level control, and (b) an efficient scale up for processing and production. Here the size and shape of the nanoparticles are measured using fuzzy based clustering and shape analysis and gives better results than automatic threshold generator. The high degree of particle size and shape measurement in the nm range suggest a successful application of this method to conclude the signature of quantum size effects occurring in the gold nano particles, realization of color filters, UV absorbers with particularly interesting performances. The flexibility offered by the choice of different polymeric agents as a future element of interest towards future advances in nano-optical and   nano-bio applications.

Table 3. Packing Density and S/V Measurement of Gold NP's (2nm)

NP ID	Origina l Image	Segmented Image (Cluster:2)	D	A	T	PD	S/V of Gold NPs	S/V of Normal Gold particle	S/V Increase Factor
GNP-1			489	439	928	0.325	0.537	0.175	3.07
GNP-2			794	840	1634	0.369	0.356	0.132	2.71
GNP-3			628	815	1443	0.424	0.330	0.140	2.36
GNP-4	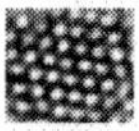		594	926	1520	0.476	0.287	0.136	2.10
GNP-5	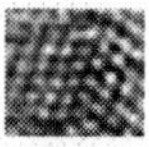		804	1002	1806	0.413	0.303	0.125	2.42
GNP-6			1054	1346	2400	0.420	0.258	0.109	2.38

GNP: Gold NP's , D: Defect Area , A: Actual Area, T: Total Area , PD: Packing Density

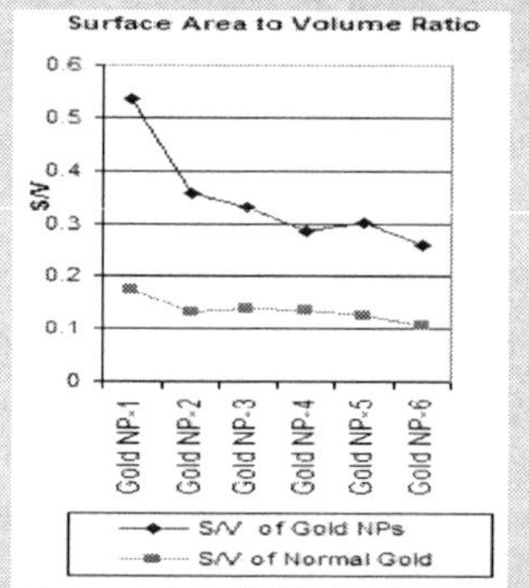

Fig. 13. Comparison of S/V of Gold NPs of 2nm range with its normal value.

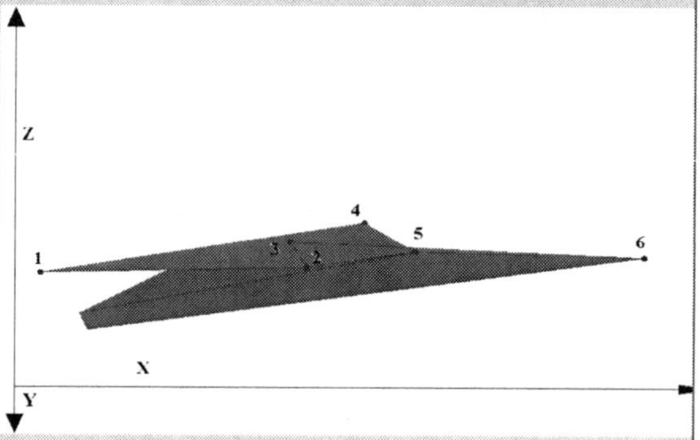

Fig. 14. Surface plot of Packing Density. X- Defect, Y- molecule occupied, Z- Packing Density

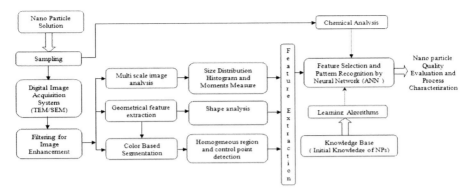

Fig. 15. Proposed architecture of NPs in process characterization

Acknowledgement(s)

We are thankful particularly to All engineers and Staff of Institute of Cybernetics Systems And Information Technology (ICSIT), all our colleagues at the Biological Science Division, Indian Statistical Institute, Kolkata and Department of Radiophysics and Electronics, Calcutta University, Kolkata.

References

1. Dutta Majumder, D., Karan, S., Goswami, A.: Characterization of Gold and Silver Nanoparticles using its Color Image Segmentation and Feature Extraction Using Fuzzy C-Means Clustering and Generalized Shape Theory. In: Proc. IEEE, International Conference on Communications and Signal Processing-2011, pp. 70–74 (2011)
2. Drexler, E.: Nano Systems: Molecular Machinery, Manufacturing, and Computation. MIT PhD thesis. Wiley, New York (1991)
3. Patra, P., Roy, I., Kumar, R., Gopal, M., Devakumar, C., Gogoi, R., Srivastava, C., Subramanium, B.S., Goswami, A.: Characterization of Nanocomposites in Flyash for Possible Pesticide Application. In: ICANN-2009, pp. 144–147. American Institute of Physics (2010)
4. González, R.C.: Richard Eugene Woods: Digital image processing. Prentice-Hall, Englewood Cliffs (2008)
5. Chanda, B., Dutta Majumder, D.: Digital Image Processing and analysis. PHI Learning Pvt. Ltd., New Delhi, India (2009)
6. Lindeberg, T.: Feature detection with automatic scale selection (abstract). International Journal of Computer Vision 30(2), 77–116 (1998)
7. Myllynen, P.: Nanotoxicology: Damaging DNA from a distance. Nature Nanotechnology 4, 795–796
8. Majumder, D., Banaerjee, R., Ulrichs, C., Mewis, I., Goswami, A.: Nano-Materials: Science of Bottom-Up and Top-Down, IETE Technical Review. Nanotechnology Education–a Paradigm Shift 24(1), 9–23 (2007)
9. Bezdek, J.C.: Pattern Recognition with Fuzzy Objective Function Algorithms. Plenum Press, New York and London

10. Bezdek, J.C., Ehrlich, R., Full, W.: FCM: The fuzzy c-means clustering algorithm. Computers & Geosciences 10(2-3), 191–203 (1984)
11. Bezdek, J.C., Hathaway, R.J., Sabin, M.J., Tucker, W.T.: Convergence theory for fuzzy C-means: counter examples and repairs. IEEE Trans. Syst. Man Cybern., 17873–17877 (1987)
12. Hathaway, R.J., Hu, Y.: Density-weighted fuzzy c-means clustering. IEEE Transactions on Fuzzy Systems 17(1), 243–252 (2009)
13. Parui, S., Sarma, E., Majumder, D.: How to discriminate shape using shape vector. Pattern Recognition Lett. 4, 201–204 (1986)
14. Dutta Majumder, D.: A Study on a Mathematical Theory of Shapes In Relation To Pattern Recognition And Computer Vision. India Journal of Theoretical Physics 43(4), 19–30 (1995)

A Rough Set Based Decision Tree Algorithm and Its Application in Intrusion Detection

Lin Zhou and Feng Jiang

College of Information Science and Technology, Qingdao University of Science and Technology, Qingdao 266061, P.R. China

Abstract. In this paper, we propose a novel rough set based algorithm to induce decision trees. To improve the computation efficiency of our algorithm, the rough set based attribute reduction technology is used to filter out the irrelevant attributes from the original set of attributes. And the notions of the significance of attribute and the uniformity of attribute in rough sets are adopted as the heuristic information for the selection of splitting attributes. Moreover, we apply the proposed algorithm to intrusion detection. The experimental results demonstrate that our algorithm can provide competitive solutions efficiently.

Keywords: Rough sets, decision trees, significance of attribute, uniformity of attribute, intrusion detection.

1   Introduction

Decision tree algorithms are used extensively in data mining [1-2]. Since most of the current algorithms use all attributes to construct decision trees, and do not concern the relevancy among attributes [1-2]. This may lead to extra overhead in terms of memory and computational efforts [5-6]. To solve that problem, rough set-based decision tree algorithms have been proposed within last few years [3-6].

Intrusion detection systems (IDS) have become an essential component of computer security. The concept of IDS was first introduced by Anderson in 1980 [7]. Due to the large volumes of security audit data as well as complex and dynamic properties of intrusion behaviors, to optimize the performance of IDS, many artificial intelligence techniques have been utilized, where decision tree technology plays an important role in IDS [8].

In this paper, we propose a novel rough set based decision tree algorithm RSDT and apply it to IDS. In our algorithm, the rough set based attribute reduction technology is used to filter out redundant information, which is crucial to IDS. Moreover, we introduce a new concept called the uniformity for each attribute in a given decision table. And we use the significance of attribute and the uniformity of attribute as the heuristic information for the selection of splitting attributes. Numerical experiments show that our algorithm is efficient for intrusion detection.

S.O. Kuznetsov et al. (Eds.): PReMI 2011, LNCS 6744, pp. 333–338, 2011.

2   Preliminaries

In rough sets, a *decision table* is a 5-ruple $DT = (U, C, D, V, f)$, where U is the set of objects; C is the set of condition attributes; D is the set of decision attributes; $V = \bigcup_{a \in C \cup D} V_a$ is the union of attribute domains; $f : U \times (C \cup D) \to V$ is a function such that for any $a \in C \cup D$ and $x \in U$, $f(x, a) \in V_a$ [4, 9].

Given a decision table $DT = (U, C, D, V, f)$, let $B \subseteq C \cup D$, we call equivalence relation $IND(B)$ an indiscernibility relation, which is defined as $IND(B) = \{(x, y) \in U \times U : \forall a \in B(f(x, a) = f(y, a))\}$. $IND(B)$ partitions U into disjoint equivalence classes, let $U/IND(B)$ denote the family of all equivalence classes of $IND(B)$. For simplicity, U/B will be written instead of $U/IND(B)$ [4, 9].

Definition 1 [Positive Region]. *Given a decision table $DT = (U, C, D, V, f)$, for any $B \subseteq C$, the positive region of D with respect to B is defined as [4, 9] :*

$$POS_B(D) = \bigcup_{E \in U/B \wedge \forall x, y \in E((x, y) \in IND(D))} E, \tag{1}$$

where E is an equivalence class in the partition U/B.

Definition 2 [Significance of Attribute]. *Given a decision table $DT = (U, C, D, V, f)$, let $B \subseteq C$, for any $a \in B$, the significance of attribute a with respect to B and D is defined as follows [4, 9] :*

$$SGF(a, B, D) = POS_B(D) - POS_{B-\{a\}}(D). \tag{2}$$

3   RSDT Algorithm and Its Application in IDS

Definition 3 [Uniformity of Attribute] *Given a decision table $DT = (U, C, D, V, f)$, for any $a \in C \cup D$, let $U/\{a\} = \{E_1, ..., E_k\}$ denote the partition induced by relation $IND(\{a\})$. The uniformity of attribute a is defined as:*

$$UN(a) = \frac{(|E_1| - Ave)^2 + ... + (|E_k| - Ave)^2}{k}, \tag{3}$$

where $Ave = \dfrac{|E_1| + ... + |E_k|}{k}$.

Algorithm 1. *RSDT.*

Input: decision table $T_1 = (U, C, D, V, f)$, i.e., the training set.
Output: set R of decision rules.

Function Main(T_1)
(1) *For each continuous attribute $c \in C$, discretize c by virtue of a discretization approach [9]. Let $T_2 = (U_2, C, D, V_2, f_2)$ denote the discretized dataset.*

(2) *Compute the reduct Red of C with respect to D in T_2, using a rough set based attribute reduction approach [9-11, 16].*
(3) *Reduce T_2 based on the reduct Red. Let $T_3 = (U_3, Red, D, V_3, f_3)$ denote the reduced dataset.*
(4) *Decision_Tree(T_3). //Call a function defined below to induce a decision tree.*
(5) *Generate a set R of rules by traversing all the paths from the root to the leaf node in the decision tree.*
(6) *Return R.*

Function Decision_Tree($T_{current}$)   *// $T_{current} = (U', C', D, V', f')$ is the decision table that is currently in use.*
(1) *For each attribute $a \in C'$, calculate the significance $SGF(a, C', D)$ of a with respect to C' and D in $T_{current}$.*
(2) *Select t from C' with the largest significance as the splitting attribute.*
(3) *If there exist more than one attributes with the largest significance, then calculate the uniformity for each of these attributes in $T_{current}$, and select attribute t with the largest uniformity (If there still exist more than one attributes with the largest uniformity, then arbitrarily select one from them).*
(4) *Create a node N, label N with attribute t, and let $C' = C' - \{t\}$.*
(5) *For each value v_j of attribute t*
    (5.1) Generate one branch of N, labeled with $t = v_j$;
    (5.2) Let $S_j = \{o \in U' : f'(o, t) = v_j\}$;
    (5.3) If $S_j = \emptyset$, then add one leaf node L labeled with the most common class in U';
    (5.4) If $S_j \neq \emptyset$, and all objects in S_j belong to the same class d, then add one leaf node L labeled with the class d;
    (5.5) If $S_j \neq \emptyset$, $C' = \emptyset$, and objects in S_j belong to different classes, then add a leaf node L labeled with the most common class in S_j.
    (5.6) If $S_j \neq \emptyset$, $C' \neq \emptyset$, and objects in S_j belong to different classes, then obtain a sub-table $T_{sub} = \{S_j, C', D, V_{sub}, f_{sub}\}$ of $T_{current}$, and call function Decision_Tree (T_{sub}) to construct a sub-tree.

In algorithm 1, before computing the partition U'/C', we first sort all objects of U' based on the counting sort [11], then we can calculate U'/C' in $O(m \times n)$ time, where $m = |C'|, n = |U'|$. Hence, we can calculate the significance $SGF(a, C', D)$ of a in $O(m \times n)$ time. Therefore, in the worst case, the time complexity of step (4) in function Main is $O(|Red|^3 \times |U_3|)$. And the overall time complexity of algorithm 1 is also determined by that of the discretization approach and that of the attribute reduction approach in Main [9-11, 16].

4   Experiment

To evaluate the performance of RSDT algorithm, we ran it on KDD-99 dataset [12]. Experiments were conducted on a 2.0GHz Pentium 4 machine with 2GB RAM. We compared algorithm RSDT with algorithms ID3 and C4.5 [1-2]. RSDT was implemented in Pascal. And ID3 and C4.5 are available in Weka [13].

Since the full KDD-99 training dataset is too large for our purposes, a concise subset of KDD-99, known as '10%KDD', will be discussed here. The 10%KDD dataset contains 22 different attack types and normal records. The 22 attack types fall into four main categories [12]: PROBE, DoS, U2R and R2L.

Although the 10%KDD dataset is a concise subset of the full KDD-99 training dataset, it contains 494021 records [12], which is still very large for our purposes. Here we follow the experimental technique of Chen et al. [14], which does *random sampling without replacement* from the 10%KDD dataset to form a smaller dataset called 'Final_Dataset'. The following table gives the numbers of instances that are selected for different attack types and normal records.

Table 1. The numbers of instances selected

Attack Type	Number of Instances	Number of Instances Selected	Attack Type	Number of Instances	Number of Instances Selected
back	2203	220	perl	3	3
buffer_overflow	30	30	phf	4	4
ftp_write	8	8	pod	264	264
guess_passwd	53	53	portsweep	1040	104
imap	12	12	rootkit	10	10
ipsweep	1247	125	satan	1589	160
land	21	21	smurf	280790	2808
loadmodule	9	9	spy	2	2
multihop	7	7	teardrop	979	100
neptune	107201	1072	warezclient	1020	102
nmap	231	231	warezmaster	20	20
normal	97278	9730	**Total**	494021	15095

There are four steps in our experiments:

(I) The first step is to prepare the dataset. As mentioned above, we do *random sampling without replacement* from the 10%KDD dataset to obtain a new dataset called Final_Dataset.

(II) Next is the discretization step. We use two simple discretization algorithms: Equal Width Binning (EW) and Equal Frequency Binning (EF), to respectively discretize the continuous attributes in Final_Dataset [9]. EW and EF algorithms are also available in Weka [13]. And for both of the two algorithms, the numbers of bins are set to 3. It should be noted that although Final_Dataset contains 34 continuous attributes, we only discretize the following 26 attributes of them: (1) Duration; (2) Src_bytes; (3) Dst_bytes; (4) Hot; (5) Num_compromised; (6) Num_root; (7) Num_file_creations; (8) Count; (9) Srv_count; (10) Serror_rate; (11) Srv_serror_rate; (12) Rerror_rate; (13) Srv_rerror _rate; (14) Same_srv_rate; (15) Diff_srv_rate; (16) Srv_diff_host_rate; (17) Dst_host _count; (18) Dst_host_srv_count; (19) Dst_host_ same_srv_rate; (20) Dst_host_diff_ srv_rate; (21) Dst_ host_same_src_port_ rate; (22) Dst_host_srv_diff_ host_rate; (23) Dst_host_ serror_ rate; (24) Dst_host_srv_serror_rate; (25) Dst_host_ rerror_ rate; (26) Dst_ host_srv_ rerror_rate.

Moreover, each discretized Final_Dataset is randomly divided into a training dataset (60% of the data) and a test dataset (40% of the data).

(III) The third step is constructing decision trees on training datasets using algorithms RSDT, ID3 and C4.5, respectively. Then different sets of rules can be generated from these trees. It should be noted that before applying RSDT to each training dataset, we first reduce the dataset by virtue of the attribute reduction algorithm proposed by Liu et al. [10].

(IV) The last step is applying the rules generated in (III) to classify the test dataset based on a given classifier. For ID3 and C4.5, the process is also implemented in Weka [13]. And for RSDT, we adopt the Standard Voting classifier available in Rosetta [15]. The corresponding options are: CLASSIFIER= StandardVoter; FALLBACK= True; FALLBACK.CLASS=DoS.

Tables 2 details the classification results of different decision tree algorithms on the dataset discretized by EW algorithm.

Table 2. The classification results on the dataset discretized by EW

Decision Tree Algorithm	Number of Attributes	Classification Accuracy(%)	Time Taken to Build Model(s)
RSDT	24	97.88	0.297
ID3	41	97.665	1.06
C4.5	41	97.582	1.63

From Table 2, we can see that for the dataset discretized by EW, RSDT algorithm perform better than ID3 and C4.5. Our algorithm generates a better rule learning scheme for IDS than the other two algorithms, since the detection rate (i.e., classification accuracy) of our algorithm is obviously higher than those of other algorithms, while the training time (i.e., time taken to build model) of our algorithm is much lower than those of other algorithms.

Moreover, the following table details the classification results of different decision tree algorithms on the dataset discretized by EF algorithm.

Table 3. The classification results on the dataset discretized by EF

Decision Tree Algorithm	Number of Attributes Used	Classification Accuracy(%)	Time Taken to Build Model(s)
RSDT	15	99.255	0.079
ID3	41	99.023	0.83
C4.5	41	98.924	0.74

From Table 3, it is easy to see that for the dataset discretized by EF, RSDT algorithm also has the best performance. Hence, this experiment also demonstrates the effectiveness of our decision tree algorithm for intrusion detection.

5   Conclusion

In this paper, a novel algorithm based on the significance of attribute and the uniformity of attribute in rough set theory was proposed for constructing decision trees. Differing from traditional algorithms, our algorithm employed a new kind of heuristic information for the selection of splitting attributes. And the positive region based attribute reduction technology was used to execute pre-pruning for decision trees, thus the attributes which are not correlated with the decision information are deleted and the total nodes of decision trees are limited. Hence, our algorithm is suitable to deal with the mass data in IDS. Experimental results on the KDD-99 dataset showed that our algorithm generated a better rule learning scheme for IDS than other algorithms.

Acknowledgements

This work is supported by the National Natural Science Foundation of China (grant nos. 60802042, 61035004), and the Natural Science Foundation of Shandong Province, China (grant nos. ZR2009GQ013, ZR2010FQ027).

References

1. Quinlan, R.: Induction of decision trees. Machine Learning 1(1), 81–106 (1986)
2. Quinlan, R.: C4.5: Programs for Machine Learning. Morgan Kaufmann, San Francisco (1993)
3. Pawlak, Z.: Rough Sets. Int. J. Comput. Informat. Sci. 11(5), 341–356 (1982)
4. Pawlak, Z.: Rough Sets: Theoretical Aspects of Reasoning about Data. Kluwer Academic Publishing, Dordrecht (1991)
5. Li, X.P., Dong, M.: An algorithm for constructing decision tree based on variable precision rough set model. In: Proc. of the 4th Int. Conf. on Natural Computation, pp. 280–283 (2008)
6. Jiang, Y., Li, Z.H., Zhang, Q., Liu, Y.: New method for constructing decision tree based on rough set theory. Computer Appliactions 24(8), 21–23 (2004)
7. Anderson, J.P.: Computer Security Threat Monitoring and Surveillance. James P. Anderson Co., Fort Washington (1980)
8. Li, X.Y., Ye, N.: Decision tree classifiers for computer intrusion detection. Journal of Parallel and Distributed Computing Practices 4(2), 179–190 (2001)
9. Wang, G.Y.: Rough set theory and knowledge acquisition. Xian Jiaotong University Press (2001)
10. Liu, S.H., Sheng, Q.J., Wu, B., Shi, Z.Z.: Research on efficient algorithms for rough set methods. Chinese Journal of Computers 26(5), 525–529 (2003)
11. Xu, Z.Y., Liu, Z.P., Yang, B.R., Song, W.: A Quick Attribute Reduction Algorithm with Complexity of $\max(O(|C||U|), O(|C|^2|U/C|))$. Chinese Journal of Computers 29(3), 391–399 (2006)
12. KDD Cup 99 Dataset (1999),
http://kdd.ics.uci.edu/databases/kddcup99/kddcup99.html
13. Witten, I.H., Frank, E.: Data Mining: Practical Machine Learning Tools and Techniques with Java Implementations. Morgan Kaufmann, San Francisco (2000)
14. Chen, S.T., Chen, G.L., Guo, W.Z., Liu, Y.H.: Feature Selection of the Intrusion Detection Data Based on Particle Swarm Optimization and Neighborhood Reduction. Journal of Computer Research and Development 47(7), 1261–1267 (2010)
15. Øhrn, A.: Rosetta Technical Reference Manual (1999),
http://www.idi.ntnu.no/_aleks/rosetta
16. Banerjee, M., Mitra, S., Banka, H.: Evolutionary-Rough feature selection in gene expression data. IEEE Transactions on Systems, Man, and Cybernetics, Part C: Applications and Reviews 37, 622–632 (2007)

Information Systems and Rough Set Approximations: An Algebraic Approach

Md. Aquil Khan[1] and Mohua Banerjee[2]

[1] The Institute of Mathematical Sciences,
C.I.T Campus, Chennai 600113, India
mdaquilkhan@gmail.com
[2] Department of Mathematics and Statistics,
Indian Institute of Technology, Kanpur 208016, India
mohua@iitk.ac.in

Abstract. The article proposes an algebraic formalism of (complete/ incomplete) information systems. Besides providing a complete description of information systems, the formalism captures the notion of rough set approximations that are induced by information systems.

1 Introduction

Rough set theory proposed by Pawlak involves two key notions: set approximations and information systems. It considers a situation where we only have partial information about a set U of objects, represented by an equivalence relation R on U. The pair (U, R) is called an *approximation space* [8] The relation R induces *lower* and *upper approximation operators* $\underline{R}$ and $\overline{R}$ on $\wp(U)$, the power set of U, as follows. Let $R(x)$ denote $\{y \in U : (x, y) \in R\}$.

$$\underline{R}(X) := \{x \in U : R(x) \subseteq U\}, \text{ and } \overline{R}(X) := \{x \in U : R(x) \cap X \neq \emptyset\}.$$

A practical realization of Pawlak's approximation spaces comes from the notion of *complete information systems* defined as follows.

Definition 1. *A complete information system (CIS)* $\mathcal{S} := (U, \mathcal{A}, \bigcup_{a \in \mathcal{A}} \mathcal{V}_a, f)$, *comprises a non-empty set U of objects, $\mathcal{A}$ of attributes, $\mathcal{V}_a$ of attribute values for each $a \in \mathcal{A}$, and $f : U \times \mathcal{A} \to \bigcup_{a \in \mathcal{A}} \mathcal{V}_a$ such that $f(x, a) \in \mathcal{V}_a$.*

Given a CIS $\mathcal{S} := (U, \mathcal{A}, \bigcup_{a \in \mathcal{A}} \mathcal{V}_a, f)$, and $B \subseteq \mathcal{A}$, we obtain an approximation space $(U, Ind_B^{\mathcal{S}})$, where

$$(x, y) \in Ind_B^{\mathcal{S}} \text{ if and only if } f(x, a) = f(y, a), \text{ for all } a \in B.$$

$Ind_B^{\mathcal{S}}$ is called the *indiscernibility relation* induced by B.

An algebraic approach to rough set theory was first presented by Iwiński in 1987 [6]. Since then, substantial work has been done on algebraic aspects of the theory. In one direction, different representations of rough sets have been considered, and endowed with algebraic structures. It is observed that the algebras induced from approximation spaces are instances of various known as well as new algebraic structures, such as quasi-Boolean algebra, double Stone algebra, Nelson algebra, Łukasiewicz algebra, topological quasi-Boolean algebra. A detailed

S.O. Kuznetsov et al. (Eds.): PReMI 2011, LNCS 6744, pp. 339–344, 2011.

survey can be found in [1]. In the other direction of research, approximation operators are viewed as abstract unary operators, which leads us to a class of Boolean algebra with operators (BAO). In fact, a CIS $\mathcal{S} := (U, \mathcal{A}, \bigcup_{a \in \mathcal{A}} \mathcal{V}_a, f)$ determines an algebra $(\wp(U), \cap, \sim, \emptyset, \{\underline{Ind}_B^\mathcal{S}\}_{B \subseteq \mathcal{A}})$, where $\emptyset$ denotes the empty set, $\sim$, complementation relative to U, and $\cap$, intersection. In [4], such an algebra is called a *knowledge approximation algebra of type $\mathcal{A}$ derived from CIS $\mathcal{S}$*. An abstract algebra for this class of algebras is proposed in [4], and a corresponding representation theorem obtained.

We note that the knowledge approximation algebra derived from a CIS $\mathcal{S}$ does not give a complete description of the CIS. In fact, attribute, attribute-value pairs, which are the main ingredients of a CIS, do not appear in this description. In this article, our aim is to propose an algebraic formalism of CISs which captures this aspect. Moreover, it also captures the notion of approximations defined on CISs. In Sect. 2, we shall consider an algebra induced by CISs. An abstract algebra is then proposed, of which such an induced algebra is an instance. Properties of the proposed abstract algebra are explored. Sect. 3 provides the corresponding representation theorem. Sect. 4 concludes the article.

2   Algebra for Complete Information Systems

Let us fix finite sets $\mathcal{A}$ of attributes and $\mathcal{V} := \bigcup_{a \in \mathcal{A}} \mathcal{V}_a$ of attribute values. Let $\mathcal{D}$ denote the set of all *descriptors* [9], viz. pairs (a, v), for each $a \in \mathcal{A}$, $v \in \mathcal{V}_a$. Observe that, given a complete information system $\mathcal{S} := (U, \mathcal{A}, \mathcal{V}, f)$, each descriptor (a, v) determines a nullary operation (constant) $c_{(a,v)}^\mathcal{S}$ on $\wp(U)$:

$$c_{(a,v)}^\mathcal{S} := \{x \in U : f(x, a) = v\}.$$

Thus we have the following definition. Let Ω be the tuple $(\mathcal{A}, \mathcal{V})$.

Definition 2. *Let $\mathcal{S} := (U, \mathcal{A}, \mathcal{V}, f)$ be a complete information system. A complete information system algebra (in brief, CIS-algebra) of type Ω generated by the complete information system $\mathcal{S}$ is the structure*

$$\mathcal{S}^* := (\wp(U), \cap, \sim, \emptyset, \{\underline{Ind}_B^\mathcal{S}\}_{B \subseteq \mathcal{A}}, \{c_\gamma^\mathcal{S}\}_{\gamma \in \mathcal{D}}).$$

Observe that a CIS-algebra generated by a CIS $\mathcal{S}$ is actually an extension of the knowledge approximation algebra derived from $\mathcal{S}$ with a collection of nullary operations.

One can show that a CIS-algebra satisfies the properties listed below.

Proposition 1. *1. $\bigcup_{v \in \mathcal{V}_a} c_{(a,v)}^\mathcal{S} = U$.*

2. $c_{(a,v)}^\mathcal{S} \cap c_{(a,u)}^\mathcal{S} = \emptyset$ when $v \neq u$.

3. $\underline{Ind}_C^\mathcal{S}(X) \subseteq \underline{Ind}_B^\mathcal{S}(X)$ for $C \subseteq B \subseteq \mathcal{A}$, and $X \subseteq U$.

4. $c_{(a,v)}^\mathcal{S} \subseteq \underline{Ind}_{\{a\}}^\mathcal{S}(c_{(a,v)}^\mathcal{S})$.

5. $c_{(b,v)}^\mathcal{S} \cap \underline{Ind}_{B \cup \{b\}}^\mathcal{S}(X) \subseteq \underline{Ind}_B^\mathcal{S}(\sim c_{(b,v)}^\mathcal{S} \cup X)$, $X \subseteq U$.

6. $\underline{Ind}_\emptyset^\mathcal{S}(X) \neq \emptyset$ implies $X = U$.

We shall see later that these properties are actually characterizing properties of CIS-algebras. Thus, we propose the following notion of an abstract CIS-algebra.

Definition 3. *An* abstract CIS-algebra of type Ω *is a tuple*
$$\mathfrak{A} := (U, \wedge, \neg, 0, \{L_B\}_{B \subseteq \mathcal{A}}, \{d_\gamma\}_{\gamma \in \mathcal{D}}),$$
where $(U, \wedge, \neg, 0)$ is a Boolean algebra and L_B and d_γ are respectively unary and nullary (constant) operations on U satisfying the following:

(C_1) $\bigvee_{v \in \mathcal{V}_a} d_{(a,v)} = 1$;
(C_2) $d_{(a,v)} \wedge d_{(a,u)} = 0$ *when* $v \neq u$;
(C_3) $L_C(x) \leq L_B(x)$ *for* $C \subseteq B \subseteq \mathcal{A}$;
(C_4) $d_{(a,v)} \leq L_{\{a\}}(d_{(a,v)})$;
(C_5) $d_{(b,v)} \wedge L_{B \cup \{b\}}(x) \leq L_B(\neg d_{(b,v)} \vee x)$;
(C_6) $L_\emptyset(x) \neq 0$ *implies* $x = 1$.

As a consequence of Proposition 1, the CIS-algebra $\mathcal{S}^*$ generated by a CIS $\mathcal{S}$ is an abstract CIS-algebra.

Let U_B be the dual of the operator L_B, that is, $U_B(x) := \neg L_B(\neg x)$. The following proposition presents a few properties of abstract CIS-algebras.

Proposition 2. *1. $U_B(0) = L_B(0) = 0$ and $U_B(1) = L_B(1) = 1$.*
2. $L_B(x) \leq x \leq U_B(x)$.
3. $U_B(x \wedge U_B y) = U_B(x) \wedge U_B(y)$ and $L_B(x \vee L_B y) = L_B(x) \vee L_B(y)$.
4. $x \neq 0$ implies $U_\emptyset x = 1$.
5. $U_B(U_B(x)) = U_B(x)$ and $L_B(L_B(x)) = L_B(x)$.
6. $U_B(x \vee y) = U_B(x) \vee U_B y$ and $L_B(x \wedge y) = L_B(x) \wedge L_B y$.

From Proposition 2, it is clear that U_B and L_B are respectively *closure* and *interior operators*. Moreover, the reduct $\mathfrak{A} := (U, \wedge, \neg, 0, \{L_B\}_{B \subseteq \mathcal{A}})$ is a *topological Boolean algebra* [1]. Furthermore, $(U, \wedge, \neg, 0, \{U_B\}_{B \subseteq \mathcal{A}})$ satisfies all the conditions of abstract knowledge approximation algebra [4] except the following. In the latter case, the reduct $(U, \wedge, \neg, 0)$ is taken to be a complete atomic Boolean algebra, while we do not have that requirement. An abstract knowledge approximation algebra also needs to satisfy $U_{B \cup C}(x) = U_B(x) \wedge U_C(x)$, x being an atom, and this, in general, may not hold in an abstract CIS-algebra.

Let us recall that a *cylindric algebra of dimension* $|\mathcal{A}|$ [5] is a structure $\mathfrak{A} := (U, \wedge, \neg, 0, \{A_a\}_{a \in \mathcal{A}}, \{\mu_{(a,b)}\}_{(a,b) \in \mathcal{A} \times \mathcal{A}})$, where $(U, \wedge, \neg, 0)$ is a Boolean algebra, and A_a, $\mu_{(a,b)}$ are respectively unary and nullary operations on U, such that

(L_1) $A_a(0) = 0$, (L_2) $x \leq A_a(x)$, (L_3) $A_a(x \wedge A_a y) = A_a(x) \wedge A_a(y)$,
(L_4) $A_a(A_b(x)) = A_b(A_a(x))$, (L_5) $\mu_{(a,a)} = 1$,
(L_6) If $a \neq b, c$, then $\mu_{(b,c)} = A_a(\mu_{(b,a)} \wedge \mu_{(a,c)})$,
(L_7) If $a \neq b$, then $A_a(\mu_{(a,b)} \wedge x) \wedge A_a(\mu_{(a,b)} \wedge \neg x) = 0$.

The difference between the signature of an abstract CIS-algebra of type $(\mathcal{A}, \mathcal{V})$, and that of a cylindric algebra of dimension $|\mathcal{A}|$ is now clear. The cylindric algebra has unary and nullary operations corresponding to each element of $\mathcal{A}$, and $\mathcal{A} \times \mathcal{A}$ respectively. Whereas, in the case of abstract CIS-algebra, unary and nullary operations are indexed respectively over the sets $\wp(\mathcal{A})$ and $\mathcal{A} \times \mathcal{V}$. Moreover, operators U_B of an abstract CIS-algebra satisfy (L_1)-(L_3), but may fail to satisfy (L_4). (L_5)-(L_7) do not make sense in the case of abstract CIS-algebras. However, the BAO $(U, \wedge, \neg, 0, U_B)$ obtained from an abstract CIS-algebra is a cylindric algebra of dimension 1.

3 Representation

In this section, we shall prove the representation theorem for abstract CIS-algebras. Here, we would like to mention that the proof of the representation theorem for abstract knowledge approximation algebras given in [4] makes use of the completeness and atomicity properties of the Boolean algebra reduct of the algebra. In fact, the embedding of an abstract knowledge approximation algebra $\mathfrak{A}$ is given in an extension of the power set algebra over the set $At(\mathfrak{A})$ of atoms of $\mathfrak{A}$. But in the case of abstract CIS-algebras, the Boolean algebra reduct may not be complete and atomic, and hence this technique will not work. We use *prime filters* [3] for our purpose.

Recall that a *filter* of a Boolean algebra $\mathfrak{A} := (U, \wedge, \sim, 0)$ is a subset F of U such that (i) $1 \in F$, (ii) if $a, b \in F$, then $a \wedge b \in F$, (iii) if $a \in F$ and $a \leq b$, then $b \in F$. A filter is *proper* if it does not contain the smallest element 0. A proper filter is *prime* if $a \vee b \in F$ implies that at least one of a and b belongs to F.

Let $PF(\mathfrak{A})$ denote the set of all prime filters of $\mathfrak{A}$.

Let us consider an abstract CIS-algebra $\mathfrak{A} := (U, \wedge, \neg, 0, \{L_B\}_{B \subseteq \mathcal{A}}, \{d_\alpha\}_{\alpha \in \mathcal{D}})$. $\mathfrak{A}$ determines a unique CIS $\mathfrak{A}_*$ as follows.

Consider the mapping $f_{\mathfrak{A}} : PF(\mathfrak{A}) \times \mathcal{A} \to \mathcal{V}$ such that

$$f_{\mathfrak{A}}(\Gamma, a) = v \text{ if and only if } d_{(a,v)} \in \Gamma.$$

Conditions (C_1) and (C_2) in Definition 3 guarantee that $f_{\mathfrak{A}}$ is a total function. Thus, we obtain the CIS $\mathfrak{A}_* := (PF(\mathfrak{A}), \mathcal{A}, \mathcal{V}, f_{\mathfrak{A}})$. $\mathfrak{A}_*$ determines the lower approximation operators $\underline{Ind_B^{\mathfrak{A}_*}}$, $B \subseteq \mathcal{A}$, on $\wp(PF(\mathfrak{A}))$.

We also recall that the reduct $(U, \wedge, \neg, 0, \{L_B\}_{B \subseteq \mathcal{A}})$ of an abstract CIS-algebra $\mathfrak{A} := (U, \wedge, \neg, 0, \{L_B\}_{B \subseteq \mathcal{A}}, \{d_\alpha\}_{\alpha \in \mathcal{D}})$ determines a *complex algebra* [3] as follows.

For each $B \subseteq \mathcal{A}$, let us consider the binary relation $Q_B^{\mathfrak{A}} \subseteq PF(\mathfrak{A}) \times PF(\mathfrak{A})$ defined as follows:

$$(\Gamma, \Delta) \in Q_B^{\mathfrak{A}} \text{ if and only if } L_B(x) \in \Gamma \text{ implies } x \in \Delta.$$

The relations $Q_B^{\mathfrak{A}}$ are used to define the operators $m_B^{\mathfrak{A}} : \wp(PF(\mathfrak{A})) \to \wp(PF(\mathfrak{A}))$:

$$m_B^{\mathfrak{A}}(X) := \{\Gamma \in PF(\mathfrak{A}) : \text{ for all } \Delta \text{ such that } (\Gamma, \Delta) \in Q_B^{\mathfrak{A}}, \ \Delta \in X\}.$$

The complex algebra corresponding to the reduct $(U, \wedge, \neg, 0, \{L_B\}_{B \subseteq \mathcal{A}})$ of the abstract CIS-algebra $\mathfrak{A}$ is given by extending the power set algebra over $PF(\mathfrak{A})$ with the operators $m_B^{\mathfrak{A}}$.

So, an abstract CIS-algebra $\mathfrak{A}$, on the one hand, determines the lower approximation operators $\underline{Ind_B^{\mathfrak{A}_*}}$. On the other hand, it gives rise to the complex algebra with operators $m_B^{\mathfrak{A}}$. Is there any relationship between the operators $m_B^{\mathfrak{A}}$, and the lower approximation operators $\underline{Ind_B^{\mathfrak{A}_*}}$? In fact, we shall now show that for each $B \subseteq \mathcal{A}$, the operators $m_B^{\mathfrak{A}}$ and $Ind_B^{\mathfrak{A}_*}$ are the same. This result will also lead us to the desired representation theorem. Let us begin with the following proposition listing a few properties of the relations $Q_B^{\mathfrak{A}}$.

Proposition 3. *1. $Q_B^{\mathfrak{A}} \subseteq Q_C^{\mathfrak{A}}$ for $C \subseteq B \subseteq \mathcal{A}$.*
2. $d_{(b,v)} \in \Gamma \cap \Delta$ for some $v \in \mathcal{V}_b$ if and only if $(\Gamma, \Delta) \in Q_{\{b\}}^{\mathfrak{A}}$.
3. If $(\Gamma, \Delta) \in Q_B^{\mathfrak{A}}$ and $d_{(b,v)} \in \Gamma \cap \Delta$ for some $v \in \mathcal{V}_b$, then $(\Gamma, \Delta) \in Q_{B \cup \{b\}}^{\mathfrak{A}}$.
4. $Q_{\emptyset}^{\mathfrak{A}} = PF(\mathfrak{A}) \times PF(\mathfrak{A})$.
5. $Q_B^{\mathfrak{A}} = \bigcap_{b \in B} Q_{\{b\}}^{\mathfrak{A}}$.

Proof. (1) is a direct consequence of (C_3). Let us prove (2). First suppose $d_{(b,v)} \in \Gamma \cap \Delta$ for some $v \in \mathcal{V}_b$, and let $L_{\{b\}}(x) \in \Gamma$. We need to show $x \in \Delta$. Using the properties of filters, we obtain $d_{(b,v)} \wedge L_{\{b\}}(x) \in \Gamma$ and hence by (C_5) with $B = \emptyset$, we obtain $L_{\emptyset}(\neg d_{(b,v)} \vee x) \in \Gamma$. This shows that $L_{\emptyset}(\neg d_{(b,v)} \vee x) \neq 0$ and hence by (C_6), we obtain $\neg d_{(b,v)} \vee x = 1$. Therefore, we have $\neg d_{(b,v)} \vee x \in \Delta$. Finally using the fact that $d_{(b,v)} \in \Delta$, we obtain $x \in \Delta$.

Conversely, suppose $(\Gamma, \Delta) \in Q_{\{b\}}^{\mathfrak{A}}$. By (C_1), there exists a $v \in \mathcal{V}_b$ such that $d_{(b,v)} \in \Gamma$. Therefore, using (C_4), we obtain $L_{\{b\}}(d_{(b,v)}) \in \Gamma$, and so $d_{(b,v)} \in \Delta$.

Let us now prove (3). Suppose $(\Gamma, \Delta) \in Q_B^{\mathfrak{A}}$ and $d_{(b,v)} \in \Gamma \cap \Delta$ for some $v \in \mathcal{V}_b$. Further suppose $L_{B \cup \{b\}}(x) \in \Gamma$. We need to show $x \in \Delta$. Due to the given conditions, we obtain $d_{(b,v)} \wedge L_{B \cup \{b\}}(x) \in \Gamma$, and hence by (C_5), $L_B(\neg d_{(b,v)} \vee x) \in \Gamma$. This gives $\neg d_{(b,v)} \vee x \in \Delta$, as $(\Gamma, \Delta) \in Q_B^{\mathfrak{A}}$. As $d_{(b,v)} \in \Delta$, $x \in \Delta$.

(4) is obvious due to (C_6). Let us now move to (5). From (1), we obtain $Q_B^{\mathfrak{A}} \subseteq \bigcap_{b \in B} Q_{\{b\}}^{\mathfrak{A}}$. It is also not difficult to see that the reverse inclusion holds when $|B| \leq 1$. To complete the proof, let us assume that the reverse inclusion holds for B, and prove it for $B \cup \{a\}$. Let $(\Gamma, \Delta) \in \bigcap_{b \in B \cup \{a\}} Q_{\{b\}}^{\mathfrak{A}}$. We need to show $(\Gamma, \Delta) \in Q_{B \cup \{a\}}^{\mathfrak{A}}$. Using (2) and the fact that $(\Gamma, \Delta) \in Q_{\{a\}}^{\mathfrak{A}}$, we obtain $d_{(a,v)} \in \Gamma \cap \Delta$ for some v. Now (3) gives $(\Gamma, \Delta) \in Q_{B \cup \{a\}}^{\mathfrak{A}}$. $\square$

As a consequence of Proposition 3, we obtain

Theorem 1. *Let $\mathfrak{A} := (U, \wedge, \neg, 0, \{L_B\}_{B \subseteq \mathcal{A}}, \{d_\gamma\}_{\gamma \in \mathcal{D}})$ be an abstract CIS-algebra. Then for each $B \subseteq \mathcal{A}$, $Ind_B^{\mathfrak{A}_*} = Q_B^{\mathfrak{A}}$ and $\overline{Ind_B^{\mathfrak{A}_*}} = m_B^{\mathfrak{A}}$.*

Theorem 2 (Representation theorem for abstract CIS-algebras).
Let $\mathfrak{A} := (U, \wedge, \neg, 0, \{L_B\}_{B \subseteq \mathcal{A}}, \{d_\gamma\}_{\gamma \in \mathcal{D}})$ be an abstract CIS-algebra. Then the mapping $\Psi : U \to \wp(PF(\mathfrak{A}))$ given by
$$\Psi(x) := \{\Gamma \in PF(\mathfrak{A}) : x \in \Gamma\}, \quad x \in U,$$
is an embedding of $\mathfrak{A}$ into $(\mathfrak{A}_*)^*$.

Proof. It is not difficult to see that $\Psi(d_\gamma) = c_\gamma^{\mathfrak{A}_*}$, $\gamma \in \mathcal{D}$. Due to Theorem 1, the rest follows in the lines of the proof of Jóhnson-Tarski theorem (cf. [3]). $\square$

Let us consider a language $\mathcal{L}$ consisting of a countable set $Var := \{p, q, r, \dots\}$ of variables, a binary operator $\wedge$, unary operators $\neg$, $\mathbf{L}_B$ and constants $\mathbf{0}$, $\mathbf{d}_{(a,v)}$, where $B \subseteq \mathcal{A}$, $(a, v) \in \mathcal{D}$. The *well-formed formulae* (wffs) of $\mathcal{L}$ are defined recursively: $\alpha := p \in Var \mid \mathbf{0} \mid \mathbf{d}_{(a,v)} \mid \neg\alpha \mid \alpha \wedge \beta \mid \mathbf{L}_B\alpha$.

Now consider an abstract CIS-algebra $\mathfrak{A} := (U, \wedge, \neg, 0, \{L_B\}_{B \subseteq \mathcal{A}}, \{d_\gamma\}_{\gamma \in \mathcal{D}})$. An *assignment* for $\mathfrak{A}$, is a map $V : Var \rightarrow U$. V can be extended to a mapping $\tilde{V}$ from the set of all $\mathcal{L}$-wffs to U in the obvious way: $\mathbf{0}, \mathbf{d}_{(a,v)}, \mathbf{L}_B$ correspond respectively to $0, d_{(a,v)}, L_B$. An *equation* $\alpha \approx \beta$ is said to hold in $\mathfrak{A}$, denoted as $\mathfrak{A} \models \alpha \approx \beta$, if $\tilde{V}(\alpha) = \tilde{V}(\beta)$ for all V.

The notion of equivalence defined above can be used to realize certain interesting laws related to CISs and approximations. For instance, one may easily verify that $(\neg(\mathbf{d}_{(b,v)} \wedge \mathbf{L}_{B \cup \{b\}}(x)) \vee (\mathbf{L}_B(\neg\mathbf{d}_{(b,v)} \vee x))) \approx \mathbf{1}$ holds in all abstract CIS-algebras. The representation theorem also leads to the complete axiomatization for the semantic notion of equivalence in CIS-algebras generated by CISs. More formally speaking, using Birkhoff's completeness theorem for equational logic [2], one can prove that if $\alpha \approx \beta$ holds in all CIS-algebras generated by CISs, then $\alpha \approx \beta$ is derivable from the equations (C_1)–(C_6). One can also show using the above representation theorem that abstract CIS-algebras form the algebraic counterpart of the logic LIS of complete information systems discussed in [7].

4   Conclusions

In this article we have proposed an algebraic formalism of complete information systems. This formalism can be extended to incomplete information systems in a natural way to capture approximations with respect to indiscernibility as well as similarity relations. It would be interesting to see if a similar approach could lead to algebras for non-deterministic information systems.

References

1. Banerjee, M., Chakraborty, M.K.: Algebras from rough sets. In: Pal, S.K., Polkowski, L., Skowron, A. (eds.) Rough-neuro Computing: Techniques for Computing with Words, pp. 157–184. Springer, Berlin (2004)
2. Birkhoff, G.: On the structure of abstract algebras. In: Proceedings of the Cambridge Philosophical Society, vol. 29, pp. 441–464 (1935)
3. Blackburn, P., de Rijke, M., Venema, Y.: Modal Logic. Cambridge University Press, Cambridge (2001)
4. Comer, S.: An algebraic approach to the approximation of information. Fundamenta Informaticae XIV, 492–502 (1991)
5. Henkin, L., Monk, J.D., Tarski, A.: Cylindric Algebras, Part I. North-Holland Pub. Co., Amsterdam (1971)
6. Iwiński, T.B.: Algebraic approach to rough sets. Bulletin of the Polish Academy of Sciences (Math) 35(9-10), 673–683 (1987)
7. Khan, M.A., Banerjee, M.: A logic for complete information systems. In: Sossai, C., Chemello, G. (eds.) ECSQARU 2009. LNCS, vol. 5590, pp. 829–840. Springer, Heidelberg (2009)
8. Pawlak, Z.: Rough sets. International Journal of Computer and Information Science 11(5), 341–356 (1982)
9. Pawlak, Z.: Rough Sets. Theoretical Aspects of Reasoning about Data. Kluwer Academic Publishers, Dordrecht (1991)

Approximation of a Coal Mass by an Ultrasonic Sensor Using Regression Rules

Marek Sikora[1,2], Marcin Michalak[1,3], and Beata Sikora[4]

[1] Silesian University of Technology, ul. Akademicka 16, 44-100 Gliwice, Poland
{Marek.Sikora,Marcin.Michalak}@polsl.pl
[2] Institute of Innovative Technologies EMAG, ul. Leopolda 31,
40-189 Katowice, Poland
[3] Central Mining Institute, Plac Gwarkow 1, 40-166 Katowice, Poland
Marcin.Michalak@gig.eu
[4] Silesian University of Technology, ul. Kaszubska 23, 44-100 Gliwice, Poland
Beata.Sikora@polsl.pl

Abstract. A method of approximation the mass of coal moving on a conveyor belt under the ultrasonic sensor that measures a height of coal pile is described in the paper. A process of defining a set of variables that affects the approximated coal mass is presented. A model of multiple regression and an algorithm of regression rules induction based on the M5 algorithm have been exploited to relate momentary values of the coal pile with the mass of moving coal.

Keywords: applications of data mining, regression rules, coal weight approximation.

1 Introduction

A problem of estimation the coal mass is the considerable problem in mining industry. Scales are usually installed at a few locations of the whole transportation system only. The transportation system is a web of joined conveyor belts. In majority of cases, belt scales are mostly installed at the and of transport routes due to high installation costs. However an information (at least approximate) about the mass of currently mined material is desired in many situations during production process. For example, such information is essential for the transportation system in which a sum of productivities of conveyors transporting output to the main conveyor belt is greater then a productivity of the main conveyor. Since a scale is usually installed at the end of the main conveyor, a situation in which the mining process is conducted so intensively that it causes overloading of the main conveyor and consequently its emergency stoppage may happen.

An attempt at substituting a sensor that measures the height of a coal pile shifting below for a scale is described in the paper. Since the correlation between the height of the coal pile and parameters of the conveyor and the shifting coal is unknown, it should be discovered experimentally. The model of multiple regression and the M5 regression rule induction algorithm [6] were applied for that purpose.

S.O. Kuznetsov et al. (Eds.): PReMI 2011, LNCS 6744, pp. 345–350, 2011.

The present paper is organized as follows: a problem of defining independent variables is presented in the second section, a problem of regression rules induction is presented concisely in the third section, next two sections contains the description of the conducted experiment and summary of the whole paper.

2   Determination of a Set of Independent Variables

Data coming from a system that consists of a scales, three conveyors and ultra-sonic sensor sampling the height of a shifting pile of material with the frequency 10 Hz were put to analysis. The scales frequency was equal to 1 Hz, thus the aggregation of data coming from the height sensor was made. An average value measured by the sensor was determined for each second.

The coal weight was measured at the beginning of a system of three coupled conveyors, whereas the sensor taking the height was placed about two kilometers farther. Therefore making data acquisition for next experiments, ink marking of the coal pile was resorted so as to gain the possibility of unequivocal comparing the weight and height taken by the sensor. Moreover, speed of the conveyor belt travel was known which even more facilitated weight reading at the required time. During the experiment the main conveyor was powered solely by the material from the conveyor on which the height sensor has been installed. After the brief look at the time series it occures that the distance between the series is about 1000 seconds. Normalized graphs of the coal pile mass and height after the 1000 seconds delay of the weight are presented in Fig. 1. It is visible that the real delay is about 80 seconds shorter. The final delay was calculated as the analysis of the difference between series and was equal to 922 seconds. As it was mentioned before, the research intention was to relate the weight of coal located on a conveyor with both the coal pile height and parameters characterizing a type of the given conveyor. The section area of coal shifted on the conveyor belt (Fig. 2) can be characterized by the following variables [1]:
λ – the angle between conveyor's surface and a side of the isosceles triangle (A2 – Fig. 2); β – the slope of the side edge of the conveyor's section to the horizon; l_s, l_b – widths of horizontal and slant belt of the conveyor; h – the height of coal section. Based on the parameters the following values can be determined:

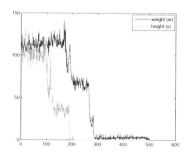
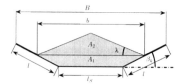

Fig. 1. A part of time series of the coal mass and the height of a coal pile.   **Fig. 2.** A section of coal transported on the conveyor belt

h_{li} – the value of height for which the coal section is a triangle while λ is fixed; h_1 – the height of the triangle part of the section (A2 – Fig. 2); h_2 – the height of the quadrangle part (A1 – Fig. 2); $h_{max} = h_1 + h_2$ – the height of coal pile which exceeded means that coal falls down from the conveyor.

Finally, the value of section area depending on the coal pile height can be expressed by the formula (1). For calculations concerning the analyzed data set purposes we assumed that $\lambda = 15°$ [5].

$$S = \begin{cases} h^2/tan\lambda & 0 \leq h \leq h_{li} \\ h^2/tan\lambda - 0.25\,(l_s(h - h_{li})/(h_{li}))^2\,\frac{tan\,\lambda\,tan\,\beta}{tan\,\lambda + tan\,\beta} & h_{li} < h \leq h_{max} \\ h_{max}^2/tan\lambda - 0.25(\frac{h_{max} - h_{li}}{h_{li}}\,l_s)^2\,\frac{tan\,\lambda\,tan\,\beta}{tan\,\lambda + tan\,\beta} & h > h_{maz} \end{cases} \quad (1)$$

Approximating the volume of a lump of coal which moved under the conveyor between two aggregated measurements of the height it has been assumed that the volume is the frustum's volume (2). The frustum has volumes of bases S_1 and S_2 which are sections of the coal pile at succeeding (equal) times $t - 1, t$.

$$V(t) = [S(t) + S(t - 1) + \sqrt{S(t)S(t - 1)}]/3 \quad (2)$$

In the manner presented above it can be generated a data set in which each row (describing the time t_i) contains the following values: areas of the section and the volume of coal lump under the conveyor at times t_{i-1}, t_i; the weight of coal pile which moved under the conveyor between times t_{i-1} and t_i.

3   Regression Rules Induction

An idea of the M5 algorithm was culled from so-called regression and classification trees (CART) [2] and from the C4.5 algorithm [7]. M5 analyzes the training set Tr and allows to create rules of the form (3).

$$\textbf{IF } w_1 \wedge w_2 \wedge \ldots \wedge w_k \textbf{ THEN } y = f(x) \quad (3)$$

where w_i is the so-called elementary condition which takes the form $a_i \in R_{a_i}$, $R_{a_i} \subset V_{a_i}$, (e.g. pressure small, average) for discrete-valued variables, and the form $a_i \in \langle v_1, v_2 \rangle$ (e.g. $gas\_concentration \in \langle 0.4, 1.3 \rangle$ or $gas\_concentration \geq 2$) for real-valued attributes. The function f is linear function of the form $s + s_{i1}a_{i1} + s_{i2}a_{i2} + \ldots + s_{it}a_{it}$, where $s, s_{i1}, s_{i2}, \ldots, s_{it}$ are real numbers (coefficients) and $\{a_{i1}, a_{i2}, \ldots, a_{it}\} \subseteq A$. Independent variables contained in a rule conclusion should be real-valued variables.

The M5 algorithm builds a tree which is next transformed into a rule set (nodes that are not leaves create rule premises, and the function f which is rule conclusion is contained in a leaf). The tree is built on the *divide-and-conquer* principle basis. On each stage of the tree construction (in each node that is not a leaf) a procedure checking which attribute $a \in A$ and limitary value $q \in V_a$ will partition an example set P connected with the given node into two subsets $P_{<q}$ and $P_{>q}$ so as to minimize the expected variance of dependent variable, i.e. to maximize the value of expression (4), is invoked.

$$\Delta V = V(P)[(|P_{<q}|/|P|)V(P_{<q}) + (|P_{>q}|/|P|)V(P_{>q})) \quad (4)$$

Additionally, the algorithm applies pruning and smoothing methods that usually lead to decrease of a prognosis error for testing data. Details concerning the algorithm operation can be found, inter alia, in [6] and [8].

4   The Experiment

While conducting the experiment, 252 tons of coal has been transported under the sensor. Results obtained by the multiple linear regression method, the interval multiple linear regression method and results get by the M5 algorithm are contained in Table 1.

A number of independent variables that are delivered to a learning algorithm is of great importance in regression tasks realized with the aid of machine learning methods. In the case described here only three independent variables were available: areas of a coal lump at times $t - 1, t$ (denoted by $s(1), s(2)$) and the lump's volume (denoted by $v(1)$). Applying merely the variables (together or separately) didn't lead to obtain good results neither by the regression methods (rows 4, 5 in Table 1) nor by the M5 algorithm. Therefore values of section's areas and volumes registered earlier were decided to be applied as independent variables, too. For example, the $s(4)$ designation denotes that the variable contains information about the section's area calculated at time $t - 4$. However our implementation of the M5 algorithm didn't bear the enlarged set of independent variables. The algorithm treats succeeding delays (e.g. $s(3), s(4), \ldots, s(max)$) of input variables as next independent variables automatically. The only parameter is the maximal delay which the algorithm can reach. The change can be found the useful modification of the M5 algorithm, because it significantly shortens time of data preparing and experiments conducting.

The smallest error, thus the difference between the approximated and real coal mass has been noticed for the M5 algorithm. Obtained rules are presented below. An experiment consisting in calculation the average value from average error and the total average deviation in the coal mass approximation in 10-fold cross validation mode has been also conducted for M5 and the interval regression. Regression rules obtained by the M5 algorithm:

If $v(t) \leq 90.36$, **then** $w(t) = 2.1 - 19.161v(3) + 11.918v(4) + 10.299s(3) - 8.682v(5) + 6.238s(4) - 5.57v(t) + 3.662s(t) + 3.322s(6) - 2.851s(5) + 1.32\ v(6)$

If $v(t) > 90.36$ **and** $v(3) \leq 284.9$, **then** $w(t) = 48.6 - 0.214s(3) + 0.152v(3) + 0.151v(t)$

If $v(t) \leq 425.09$ **and** $v(3) > 284.9$, **then** $w(t) = 87.7 - 1.665v(3) + 0.935s(4) + 0.853s(3) - 0.316v(t) + 0.191s(t)$

If $v(t) > 425.09$, **then** $w(t) = 113.8 + 0.152s(6) + 0.102v(3) - 0.1v(6) - 0.086v(4) - 0.061s(3) - 0.007v(5)$.

Results of the interval multiple regression model for the set of variables enlarged to 5th delay of input variables are presented in last row of the Table 1. One can noticed that the model is subtly worst than the model get by M5, whereas M5 matched a number of delays by itself. It can be observed while analyzing the form of get rules that the M5 algorithm built two regression models (two rules) depends on the volume of the shifting lump of coal. In a premise of the

Table 1. Values of regression error and differences between approximated and real values of coal mass

Method	Average error (%)	$R^2 \cdot 100\%$	Average difference/ Total average (kg)
Rule model – training set	0.11%	99.1	5.0/193
Rule model – cross validation	0.11%	99.0	5.2/194
Regression – volume, weight	7.8%	93.0	8.1/4869
Regression – section areas, weight	7.66%	91.0	8.0/6587
Interval regression – all variables beginning from 5th delay	0.12%	98.8	5.6/196
Interval regression – all variables from 5th delay – crossvalidation	0.13%	98.4	6.1/410

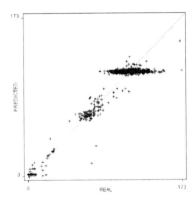

Fig. 3. The graph of estimated and real values for rule based model obtained in the cross validation mode

rules one variable $v(1)$ occurs. A complementation of the principal rules are two rules with additional condition $v(3) > (\leq)284.9$ in the premise. One may presume that the two rules describe situations in which big, not shattered coal lumps were transported on a conveyor belt between succeeding measurements of transported coal section's area, which perturbed the model realized by the principal rules. A graph of differences between estimated and real values of the coal mass is presented in Fig. 3.

5   Summary and Conclusions

The innovative method of measuring a mass of material (coal mass has been considered here) moving on a conveyor belt by an ultrasonic sensor has been presented in the paper. The correlation between height of a material pile and its mass has been determined by the M5 regression rules induction algorithm extended by automatic matching of variables reflecting succeeding delays of the time series. Efficiency of the method is high and it exceeds the obtained regression model. The innovative method of measuring a mass of material (coal mass has been considered here) moving on a conveyor belt by an ultrasonic sensor has been presented in the paper. The correlation between height of a material pile and its mass has been determined by the M5 regression rules induction algorithm extended by automatic matching of variables reflecting succeeding delays of the time series. Efficiency of the method is high and it exceeds the obtained regression model. The data analysis method itself seems to be sufficient for the considered task. Even higher accuracy can be surely get by fuzzy [9] or neuro-fuzzy methods [4]. For example, fuzzy reasoning was applied for approximate and on-line measurement of ash content in coal [3]. However, in conducted works, simplicity and potential of implementation in an electronic device converting measurement signals into mass values directly in mine tunnels should be an important feature of the obtained model. Calibration of such device would consist in transmitting from the mine head to the device values of the model parameters only. In the case of fuzzy or neuro-fuzzy systems, realization of such system is much more difficult in the case of fuzzy-neural networks than for rules of the form (3). Authors plan more measurement experiments, especially for other kinds of coal (a new dependent variable including the λ parameter values that change according to the mined coal kind will occur among measurement variables). Ultimately, the sensor and the method of relating the height of a coal pile with its weight will subject to the procedure for granting patents (for that reason Authors haven't named the sensor type and its specification).

Acknowledgments

Research described in the paper was supported by the Somar Sp. Ltd., Katowice, Poland. The second Author was supported by the European Community from the European Social Fund.

References

1. Antoniak, J.: Conveyor belts in underground and surface mining (in Polish). Silesian University of Technology Press, Gliwice, Poland (2007)
2. Breiman, L., Friedman, R.A., Olshen, R.S., Stone, C.: Classification and Regression Trees. Wadsworth, Belmont CA (1994)
3. Cierpisz, S., Heyduk, A.: A simulation study of coal blending control using a fuzzy logic ash monitor. Control Engineering Practice 10, 449–456 (2002)
4. Czogała, E., Łęski, J.: Fuzzy and Neuro-Fuzzy Systems. Studies in Fuzziness and Soft Computing, vol. 47. Physica-Verlag, Heidelberg NewYork (2000)
5. Gładysiewicz, L.: Conveyor belts. Theory and calculations. Wrocław (2003) (in Polish)
6. Quinlan, J.R.: Learning with continuous classes. In: Proc. of the International Conference on Artificial Intelligence (AI 1992), World Scientific, Singapore (1992)
7. Quinlan, J.R.: C4.5 Programs for Machine Learning. Morgan Kaufman Publishers, San Mateo, California (1992)
8. Witten, I.H., Frank, E.: Data Mining: Practical Machine Learning Tools and Techniques. Morgan Kaufmann, San Francisco (2005)
9. Yager, R.R., Filev, D.P.: Essential of Fuzzy Modelling and Control. John Wiley & Sons, Inc., Chichester (2004)

Forecasting the U.S. Stock Market via Levenberg-Marquardt and Haken Artificial Neural Networks Using ICA&PCA Pre-processing Techniques

Sergey Golovachev

National Research University – Higher School of Economics, Moscow
Department of World Economics and International Affairs

Abstract. Artificial neural networks (ANN) is an approach to solving different tasks. In this paper we forecast U.S. stock market movements using two types of artificial neural networks: a network based on the Levenberg-Marquardt learning mechanism and a synergetic network which was described by German scientist Herman Haken. The Levenberg-Marquardt ANN is widely used for forecasting financial markets, while the Haken ANN is mostly known for the tasks of image recognition. In this paper we apply the Haken ANN for the prediction of the stock market movements. Furthermore, we introduce a novation concerning pre-processing of the input data in order to enhance the predicting power of the abovementioned networks. For this purpose we use Independent Component Analysis (ICA) and Principal Component Analysis (PCA). We also suggest using ANNs to reveal the "mean reversion" phenomenon in the stock returns. The results of the forecasting are compared with the forecasts of the simple auto-regression model and market index dynamics.

Keywords: artificial neural network, back-propagation, independent component analysis, principal component analysis, forecast.

1 The Levenberg-Marquardt Network

Artificial neural networks are a modern approach to various problem-solving tasks. For example, they are used for image recognition and in different bio-physics researches. One of the possible applications of ANNs is forecasting and simulation of financial markets. The idea is the following: a researcher tries to construct such an ANN, so that it can successfully imitate the decision-making process of the "average" stock market participant. This hypothesis results from the fact that ANNs, in turn, try to imitate the design of the biological neural networks, in particular the ones which exist in human brain.

A market participant is an investor whose individual actions have no influence on the price fluctuations, for example a trader operating with insignificant sums of money. Moreover, we argue that the market participant makes his decisions solely on the analysis of the previous dynamics of the stock – thus we assume

S.O. Kuznetsov et al. (Eds.): PReMI 2011, LNCS 6744, pp. 351–357, 2011.

endogenous price-making mechanism. Furthermore, we set the homogeneity of the investors so that they all have the same decision-making algorithms (that is why we call them "average").

While designing the Levenberg-Marquardt ANN it is essential to set some of the key parameters of the network. Firstly, we must set the architecture of the network (number of layers, number of neurons in each, including number of input and output neurons). In our research we use simple three-layer ANN with 2 input neurons, 2 neurons in the hidden layer and 1 output neuron. The results show that such architecture is quite effective while it does not lead to lengthy computational procedure. Secondly, we determine the activation function in the hidden layer which performs a non-linear transformation of the input data. We use a standard logistic function with the range of values $[0;1]$.

The key feature of the Levenberg-Marquardt ANN is using of back-propagation of the errors of the previous iterations as a learning mechanism. The idea of back-propagation rests on the attempt of communicating the error of the network (of the output neuron, in particular) to all other neurons of the network. As a result, after a number of iterations the network optimizes the weights with which neurons in different layers are connected, and the minimum of error is reached. Propagation of the error through the network also requires usage of the Jacobian matrix which contains first derivatives of the elements of the hidden and input layers.

The computational mechanism is as follows (1):

$$w_{new} = w_{old} - (Z^T Z + \lambda I)^{-1} * Z^T * \varepsilon(w_{old}), \qquad (1)$$

where
w_{old}– weight vector of the previous iteration;
w_{new} – weight vector of the current iterations;
Z – Jacobian matrix with the dimensionality m×n; m – is the number of learning examples for each iteration, n – total number of weights in the network;
λ – learning ratio;
I – identical matrix with the dimensionality n×n;
ϵ- vector of n elements, which contains forecast errors for each learning example.

To enhance the predicting power of our model we introduce here pre-processing techniques of the Independent Component Analysis (ICA). This is a method of identifying the key and important signals in the large, noisy data. ICA is often compared with another useful processing tool – Principal Component Analysis (PCA). However, the general difference of ICA from PCA is that we obtain purely independent vectors on which a process can be decomposed, whereas PCA requires only non-correlatedness of such vectors. Moreover, ICA allows non-Gaussian distributions, which is quite useful and realistic assumption, especially for financial data.

The ICA stems from the so-called "cocktail party" problem in acoustics. The problem is the following: assume that we have i number of people(s) talking in the room and j number of microphones(x) which record their voices. For two people and two microphones signals from the microphones are as follows in (2):

$$x_1 = a_{11} * s_1 + a_{12} * s_2$$

$$x_2 = a_{21} * s_1 + a_{22} * s_2 \tag{2}$$

Consequently, we should set mixing matrix A which transforms voices into the recordings, (1):

$$A = \left\{ \begin{array}{cccc} a_{11} & a_{12} & \cdots & a_{li} \\ a_{21} & a_{22} & \cdots & a_{2i} \\ a_{j1} & a_{j2} & \cdots & a_{ji} \end{array} \right\} \tag{3}$$

The task for the researcher consists then in finding a demixing matrix A^{-1} which enables to get the vector of voices s knowing only the vector of the recordings x, (4):

$$s = A^{-1} * x \tag{4}$$

When we apply ICA for the stock market we assume that the empirical stock returns are the "recordings", the noisy signals of the original "voices" which determine the real process of price movements. Consequently, when we obtain a de-mixing matrix A^{-1} then we get a powerful tool for extracting the most important information about the price movements. Furthermore, ICA allows us to reduce the dimensionality of the empirical data without losing significant information. It is very important while using ANNs, because, on the one hand we should present the network as much relevant information as possible, but, on the other hand, too much input information leads to lengthy computational procedures and problems with convergence to a nontrivial solution.

As it was mentioned above, we use two types of inputs in the Levenberg-Marquardt ANN. First input is the logarithmic return of the stock for the day which precedes the day of the forecast. Second input is derived from the processing of ten previous logarithmic returns with ICA algorithm: we get the de-mixing matrix A^{-1} and the subsequent vector of independent components s. Then we transform this vector to the scalar value considering the most influential independent component.

In the section "Results" we show that such pre-processing turns out to be very useful for stock market forecasting. Moreover, it is worth mentioning that ICA can be used as a self-sufficient forecasting tool for various financial markets.

2   The Haken Network

The second ANN which is used for forecasting U.S. stock market is quite different from the Levenberg-Marquardt network. It is the network of Herman Haken, German scientist and the founder of synergetics.

This ANN is self-learning and uses a "library" of pre-set values which by default represent all possible states of the process. Therefore, during a number of iterations the network converges to one of these values. The Haken ANN is widely used for image recognition. For example, when we set a task of recognizing letters of the alphabet we use the whole alphabet as a pre-set "library". It is obvious, because any letter which is presented to the network is essentially a part of the alphabet.

However, we aim to apply the Haken ANN for the stock market forecasting, and the situation here is much more complicated. We must choose the "library" which contains all possible states of the market. To solve this task we resort to two important assumptions. Firstly, we argue that all necessary information which is needed for the forecast is contained in the returns of the stock during ten trading days before the day for which the forecast is calculated. Secondly, we assume that the using of processing techniques of the ICA and PCA, which eventually reduces the information dimensionality, allows us to extract most important and valuable information signals.

Thus, to obtain the "library" of pre-set values we use the eigenvectors of the covariance matrix of the subsequent empirical vectors of stock returns (PCA) or the de-mixing matrix of the empirical vectors obtained from ICA.

The network functions as follows, (5):

$$q^* = q + \sum_{k=1}^{M} \lambda_k v_k^T q v_k + B \sum_{k=1}^{M} (v_k^T q)^2 (v_k^T q) v_k + C(q^T q)q, \tag{5}$$

where

q – vector of M elements which the network tries to optimize. Initially this vector is deliberately made noisy to ignite the process of learning, thus we assume that the real data on the stock market is also noisy in the similar way;

q^*- vector which the network finally reconstructs;

V – matrix which plays a role of the "library" and contains pre-set values which are obtained from PCA or ICA;

λ – learning ratio;

B – computational parameters which calibrating has an influence on the convergence of the network and the speed of learning.

The final forecasting signal is obtained by subtracting the empirical vector from the reconstructed one.

3 Trading Rules

Now we present trading rules which were used while working with the Levenberg-Marquardt and the Haken ANNs.

Firstly, we should specify the data which we forecast. We predict price movements of the 30 liquid stocks of the U.S. index S&P 500[1] in the period from November, 7th, 2008 to May,2nd, 2010.

---

[1] We use closing prices of the following stocks: ExxonMobil, Apple, Microsoft, General Electric, Procter&Gamble, Johnson&Johnson, Bank of America, JPMorgan Chase, Wells Fargo, IBM, Chevron, Sisco Systems, AT&T, Pfizer, Google, Coca Cola, Intel, Hewlett Packard, Wal Mart, Merck, PepsiCo, Oracle, Philip Morris International, ConocoPhillips, Verizon Communications, Schlumberger, Abbott Labs, Goldman Sachs, Mcdonalds, QUALCOMM.

For each trading day t we make forecast via our ANNs for each stock. When the forecasts are made we range them according to their absolute value. The final selection of the stocks in the virtual portfolio is based on two opposing trading rules. According to the Rule A we select from 1 to 5 stocks with the highest forecast value[2] (note that at this step we do not know the real return of day t which makes our forecast truly out-of-sample). According to the Rule B we select from 1 to 5 stocks with the lowest forecast values.

The reason for using Rule B is widely recognized phenomenon of "mean reversion" in the financial data. Thus, if Rule B is successful, then our ANN is capable of detecting this property of the market.

The dynamics of our trade portfolio will be compared to the dynamics of the S&P 500 index and the dynamics of the portfolio if the decision-making was based on the simple auto-regression model (while the trading rules A and B are retained), (6):

$$r_t^* = \alpha_t + \beta_t * r_{t-1}, \tag{6}$$

where
r_t^* - forecast value of the logarithmic return of the stock for the trading day t,
α_t, β_t-auto-regression coefficients,
r_{t-1}- logarithmic return of the stock for the trading day t-1.

4   Results

Now we present some of the results of the forecasting using the Levenberg-Marquardt and the Haken ANNs. Due to the limited space of this paper we demonstrate here only most successful examples.

Figure 1 demonstrates relative dynamics of our virtual portfolio (red line) using the Levenberg-Marquardt ANN and trading Rule B (five stocks with "worst" forecasts). Blue line is a portfolio when the decision-making is based on the auto-regression model. Blue line is the S&P 500 index. The horizontal axis is time and t indicates trading days. The vertical axis displays the value of the portfolio with the initial value of 1.

Figure 2 demonstrates relative dynamics of our virtual portfolio (red line) using the Haken ANN with the PCA pre-processing and trading Rule B (one stock with the "worst" forecast). Blue line is a portfolio when the decision-making is based on the auto-regression model. Green line is the S&P 500 index. The horizontal axis is time and t indicates trading days. The vertical axis displays the value of the portfolio with the initial value of 1.

Figure 3 demonstrates relative dynamics of our virtual portfolio (red line) using the Herman Haken ANN with the ICA pre-processing and trading Rule A (one stock with the "best" forecast). Blue line is a portfolio when the decision-making is based on the auto-regression model. Green line is the S&P 500 index. The horizontal axis is time and t indicates trading days. The vertical axis displays the value of the portfolio with the initial value of 1.

---

[2] Note that in this model we use only long positions, short selling is not allowed.

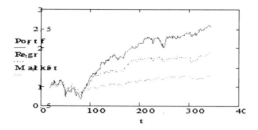

Fig. 1.

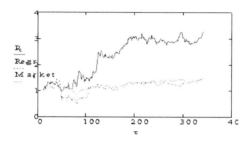

Fig. 2.

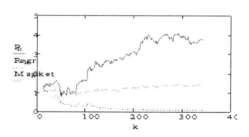

Fig. 3.

5   Conclusions

Using of pre-processing techniques of the ICA and PCA with the ANNs proved to be a reliable decision-support mechanism for trading on the liquid stock market. Dynamics of the subsequent portfolios outperform portfolios which follow simple auto-regression forecast or linked to the stock index. Furthermore, the Levenberg-Marquardt and Haken ANNs displayed the ability to reveal the "mean reversion" phenomenon in the complex market data and use it for future forecasts.

However, despite the success of the Levenberg-Marquardt and the Haken ANNs and proper pre-processing techniques we still face difficulties in making up a strategy which will guarantee robust and stable growth of the portfolio over continuous period of time. Moreover, more theoretical research is needed to justify the argument that it is the neural network decision-making mechanism which is used by traders in real life. It is also obvious that more in-depth study is needed to explain the phenomenon of "mean reversion". Some of these issues will be the topics of the future research.

References

1. Back, A.D., Weigend, A.S.: A First Application of Independent Component Analysis to Extracting Structure from Stock Returns. International Journal of Neural Systems 8(5) (October 1997)
2. Bishop, C.M.: Neural Networks for Pattern Recognition, p. 483. Oxford University Press, Oxford (1995)
3. Bell, J.I., Sejnowsi, T.J.: An information-maximisation approach to blind separation and blind deconvolution. Neural Computation 7(6), 1004–1034 (1995)
4. Górriz, J.M., Puntonet, C.G., Moisés Salmerón, E.W.: Lang Time Series Prediction using ICA Algorithms. In: IEEE International Workshop on Intelligent Data Acquisition and Advanced Computing Systems: Technology and Applications, Lviv, Ukraine, September 8-10 (2003)
5. Hyvärinen, A., Oja, E.: Independent Component Analysis: Algorithms and Applications. Neural Networks 13(4-5), 411–430 (2000)
6. Kröse, B., van der Smagt, P.: An Introduction To Neural Networks, 8th edn. (November 1996)
7. Lu, C.-J., Le, T.-S., Chiu, C.-C.: Financial time series forecasting using independent component analysis and support vector regression. Decision Support Systems 47, 115–125 (2009)

Empirical Study of Matrix Factorization Methods for Collaborative Filtering

Evgeny Kharitonov

Moscow Institute of Physics and Technology
eugene.kharitonov@gmail.com

Abstract. Matrix factorization methods have proved to be very efficient in collaborative filtering tasks. Regularized empirical risk minimization with squared error loss function and L_2-regularization and optimization performed via stochastic gradient descent (SGD) is one of the most widely used approaches.

The aim of the paper is to experimentally compare some modifications of this approach. Namely, we compare Huber's, smooth ϵ-insensitive and squared error loss functions. Moreover, we investigate a possibility to improve the results by applying a more sophisticated optimization technique — stochastic meta-descent (SMD) instead of SGD.

Keywords: collaborative filtering, matrix factorization, loss functions.

1 Introduction

Recommender systems are widely used in online shops and services such as Amazon, Netflix, Google Video and Google News. Collaborative Filtering (CF) is one of successful approaches to build such systems. During the Netflix Prize Challenge the matrix factorization methods attracted a lot of attention and proved to be very efficient.

A considerable portion of practical problems in the field deals with explicit user feedback: users watch movies and explicitly rate them afterwards. Our task is to recommend some new items to the user, which he or she hasn't seen yet.

The general idea behind factor models implies that it is possible to find user- and item-vectors which characterize the user's tastes and items in such a way that their dot product approximates the user's rating of an item. After that, the items with highest predicted user's rating are recommended to him.

Usually these vectors are found via regularized empirical risk minimization with squared error loss and L_2-regularization. The stochastic gradient descent (SGD) has become the most popular technique for this optimization.

The question we address is the following: *Is there a better choice of a loss function and an optimization algorithm, which can result in better recommendation performance?*

In order to answer the question we compare Huber's [1] and smooth ϵ-insensitive [2] loss functions in comparison with squared error loss.

Stochastic meta-descent (SMD) [3] is a more elaborated algorithm which can substitute SGD in this combination.

S.O. Kuznetsov et al. (Eds.): PReMI 2011, LNCS 6744, pp. 358–363, 2011.

2   Model

Let us denote a rating matrix as X $(n \times r)$, with rows and columns corresponding to the users and items, respectively. Elements of X are real numbers or a special sign $*$ which is used if the value of corresponding rating is unknown.

We associate vectors from $\mathbb{R}^k$ with i-th user and j-th item: u_i and m_j, correspondingly.

Our model is based on the idea that it is possible to find such u_i and m_j that the product $u_i \cdot m_j^T$ represents the i-th user rating of the j-th item:

$$\forall i, j : X_{ij} \neq *   \quad X_{ij} \approx u_i \cdot m_j^T$$

It is convenient to formalize the task as a problem of discrepancy minimization between X and its approximation $U \times M^T$ in the cells with known values. In order to do this we introduce a nonnegative loss function L. This function penalizes divergence between predictions and actual values.

More formally, our task is to find U and M, which will minimize divergence for the available data:

$$(U, M) = argmin \frac{1}{T} \sum_{i,j:X_{ij} \neq *} L(X_{ij}, u_i \cdot m_j^T),$$

where T is the number of observed cells in X.

In order to avoid overfitting, a special term is introduced in the target function. Usually it penalizes complex models. We use a L_2 regularization term:

$$(\hat{U}, \hat{M}) = argmin \left(\frac{1}{T} \sum_{i,j:x_{ij} \neq *} L(x_{ij}, u_i \cdot m_j^T) + \lambda_u \sum_i u_i \cdot u_i^T + \lambda_m \sum_j m_j \cdot m_j^T \right)$$

, where $L : \mathbb{R} \times \mathbb{R} \to \mathbb{R}^+$ is the loss function.

3   Loss Functions

We consider the following loss functions (they are described in [4]) $L(x, \hat{x})$:

squared error

$$L(x, \hat{x}) = \frac{1}{2} (x - \hat{x})^2$$

smooth ϵ-insensitive loss [2]

$$L(x, \hat{x}) = log \left(1 + e^{x - \hat{x} - \epsilon} \right) + log \left(1 + e^{\hat{x} - x - \epsilon} \right)$$

Huber's robust loss [1]

$$L(x, \hat{x}) = \begin{cases} \frac{1}{2} (x - \hat{x})^2, & |x - \hat{x}| \leq \sigma \\ \sigma \left(|x - \hat{x}| - \frac{1}{2}\sigma \right), & otherwise \end{cases}$$

Huber's loss function is not as sensitive to outliers as squared error loss function. In addition to robustness to outliers, ϵ-insensitive loss is insensitive to an additive noise with amplitude up to ϵ.

4 Optimization

Both optimization techniques we describe follow the same principle: given rating X_{ij}, they perform gradient descent in factors u_i and m_k. Instead of minimizing previously discussed target function, they minimize its stochastic approximation:

$$F_{ij} = L(x_{ij}, u_i \cdot m_j^T) + \lambda_u u_i \cdot u_i^T + \lambda_m m_j \cdot m_j^T$$

4.1 SGD

SGD was described by Simon Funk[1] and modified in [5].

> **Input:** X, λ_u, λ_m, optimization steps η_u, η_m, number of iterations K
> **Output:** U, M^T
> Initialize U and M^T with small random values;
> $i \leftarrow 0$
> **while** $i < K$ **do**
> > **foreach** $i, j \; : \; x_{ij} \neq *$ **do**
> > > **foreach** $l \in 1 : k$ **do**
> > > > $u_{il} \leftarrow u_{il} - \eta_u \cdot \frac{\partial F_{ij}}{\partial u_{il}}$
> > > > $m_{jl} \leftarrow m_{jl} - \eta_m \cdot \frac{\partial F_{ij}}{\partial m_{jl}}$
> > > **end**
> > **end**
> > $i \leftarrow i + 1$
> **end**

Algorithm 1. SGD scheme

4.2 SMD

Stochastic Meta-Descent (SMD) is an online optimization method described in [3]. It can be considered as an improvement of SGD, since it can be reduced to SGD via proper parameter setting. The main difference is that each optimized coordinate has its own step size which is adjusted simultaneously with regular optimization.

The application of this method requires an ability to perform fast multiplication of Hessian of F_{ij} by an arbitrary vector. This can be achieved in our case since the Hessian can be represented as a sum of a diagonal, a block-diagonal and a rank-1 matrixes.

We omit the description of the method and its adaptation to the optimization problem due to lack of space.

---

[1] Netflix Update: Try This at Home,
http://sifter.org/~simon/journal/20061211.html

4.3   Meta-optimization

Each combination of loss function and optimization technique has several parameters which are to be determined before model training, e.g. optimization rates η_u, η_m, regularization coefficients λ_u, λ_m, parameters of loss functions such as ϵ and σ. However, there is no commonly adopted approach for their selection in literature. In paper [5] a grid search is used to find optimal parameters. Another approach is to use derivative-free optimization to adjust the parameters on a small subset of available data. Similarly to [6] we use Nelder-Mead method for tuning these parameters.

The initial values of parameters in our experiments are presented in Table 1; the number of iterations used for SGD, SMD and Nelder-Mead was equal to 25.

Table 1. Initial parameters

η_u	η_m	λ_u	λ_m	σ	ϵ	μ (SMD)	ν (SMD)
0.01	0.01	0.02	0.02	6.7	0.03	0.08	0.9

5   Evaluation

The authors of [7] thoroughly discuss the main evaluation criteria used in collaborative filtering. We use three of them: RMSE (Rooted Mean Square Error), MAE (Mean Absolute Error) and Precision-N.

The first two criteria characterize how good we approximate X via product of U and M^T:

$$RMSE = \left(\frac{1}{T} \sum_{i,j:x_{ij} \neq *} \left(x_{ij} - u_i \cdot m_j^T \right)^2 \right)^{\frac{1}{2}} \qquad MAE = \frac{1}{T} \sum_{i,j:x_{ij} \neq *} \left| x_{ij} - u_i \cdot m_j^T \right|$$

They have several drawbacks [7]. The main problem is that they evaluate the performance of approximation, not recommendations. For this reason, we also use Precision-N criterion.

A trained model can sort the items recommended to the user in the order of descending *predicted* rating.

For a particular user, Precision-N is a ratio of items with real rating above a predefined threshold t among N items with the highest predicted rating.

$$Precision\text{-}N = \text{Average} \left(\frac{1}{N} |\{\text{items with rating not less than } t \text{ among top-N}\}| \right)$$

In our experiments we used Precision-5 with $t = 4$.

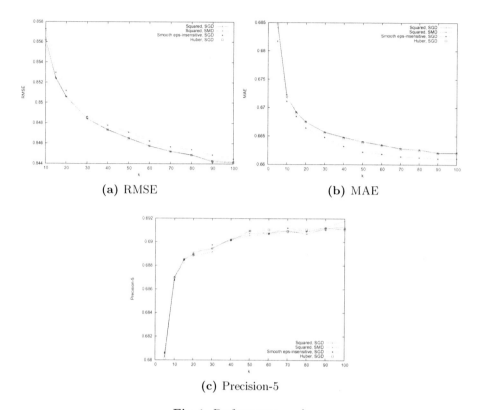

(a) RMSE

(b) MAE

(c) Precision-5

Fig. 1. Performance vs. k

6   Experiments

In the experiments we used an open dataset provided by MovieLens group . It contains about 1 million ratings of 3900 movies obtained from 6040 users.

The dataset was randomly split into 10 approximately equal parts. For each $k \in [1..10]$ the evaluation process consisted of two steps.

First of all, during the meta-optimization step the parameters that optimize target criterion (RMSE, MAE or Precision-5) were calculated for one part of data while learning on eight other parts were chosen. After that, these nine parts were used as training data and the evaluation was performed on the previously unused part.

This process was repeated until all the parts were used as test sets. The results were averaged and are depicted in Figure 1.

We ensured that for every combination tested we used the same learning, validation and test sets, initial approximations for U and M (for fixed k) and the number of meta-optimization and optimization iterations.

The source code is available on http://github.com/n0mad/Demoniac.

7   Discussion

As seen from figures, loss functions that are close to L_2 (Huber's and squared error loss) unsurprisingly result in a better RMSE performance. Similarly, smooth ϵ-insensitive loss (which approximates L_1 loss) achieves a better MAE performance.

More importantly, our experiment has shown that none of the considered modifications did significantly improve Precision-5 in comparison with the standard approach. Thus, taking into consideration simplicity of implementation and lack of additional parameters SGD with L_2 loss and regularization seems to be the best choice.

References

1. Huber, P.J.: Robust statistics. Wiley, New York (1981)
2. Dekel, O., Shalev-Shwartz, S., Singer, Y.: Smooth e-intensive regression by loss symmetrization. In: COLT, pp. 433–447 (2003)
3. Bray, M., Koller-meier, E., Muller, P., Van Gool, L., Schraudolph, N.N.: 3d hand tracking by rapid stochastic gradient descent using a skinning model. In: CVMP, pp. 59–68 (2004)
4. Karatzoglou, A., Smola, A., Weimer, M.: Collaborative filtering on a budget. In: AISTATS, vol. 9, pp. 389–396 (2010)
5. Takács, G., Pilászy, I., Németh, B., Tikk, D.: Scalable collaborative filtering approaches for large recommender systems. Journal of Machine Learning Research 10, 623–656 (2009)
6. Cohen, G., Ruch, P., Hilario, M.: Model selection for support vector classifiers via direct simplex search. In: FLAIRS Conference, pp. 431–435 (2005)
7. Herlocker, J.L., Konstan, J.A., Terveen, L.G., Riedl, J.T.: Evaluating collaborative filtering recommender systems. ACM Transactions on Information Systems 22, 5–53 (2004)

Simultaneous Non-gaussian Data Clustering, Feature Selection and Outliers Rejection

Nizar Bouguila[1], Djemel Ziou[2], and Sabri Boutemedjet[2]

[1] Concordia Institute for Information Systems Engineering, Concordia University, Montreal, Canada, Qc, H3G 2W1
[2] Département d'Informatique, Université de Sherbrooke, Canada, Qc, J1K2R1
bouguila@ciise.concordia.ca,
{djemel.ziou,sabri.boutemedjet}@usherbrooke.ca

Abstract. A method for simultaneous non-Gaussian data clustering, feature selection and outliers rejection is proposed in this paper. The proposed approach is based on finite generalized Dirichlet mixture models learned within a framework including expectation-maximization updates for model parameters estimation and minimum message length criterion for model selection. Through a challenging application involving texture images discrimination, it is demonstrated that the developed procedure performs effectively in avoiding outliers and selecting relevant features.

1 Introduction

Clustering is an important problem in data mining, pattern recognition, computer vision and machine learning applications. It is well-known that this problem becomes more challenging in the presence of outliers and irrelevant features which may compromise the final clustering models [1]. A good clustering model should be sensitive to the extracted features but not to the noise (i.e outliers). A challenging problem in this case is to determine if all the features are necessary and relevant for the clustering task. Over the last few years, there has been a surge of interest in unsupervised feature selection. While the volume of literature on the subject is notably smaller than the literature related to the supervised case, there is nonetheless a steady stream of interesting approaches (see, for instance, [2,3]). All these approaches, however, assume noiseless data that contain only inliers. The approach proposed in [2] was among the earliest, but was based on two main assumptions namely the independency of the features supposed to follow Gaussian distributions. These assumptions have been relaxed then in one of our previous works using generalized Dirichlet mixture models [3].

The current paper sets out to add robustness to the unsupervised feature selection approach that we have proposed in [3] by automatically detecting potential outliers. This is well-known to be a challenging condition for all learning algorithms which may have significant impact on the effectiveness of statistical modeling. The main goal is to accurately identify outliers and remove their effect from the rest of the model fitting. It is worth commenting that the main contribution of the proposed work is that the outliers effects are estimated simultaneously with the features weights and the model's parameters.

S.O. Kuznetsov et al. (Eds.): PReMI 2011, LNCS 6744, pp. 364–369, 2011.

The rest of this paper is organized as follows. After introducing our model and justifying its use and how it can be learned in Section 2, we illustrate the proposed approach on a real application which concerns texture images discrimination in Section 3. Finally, we conclude the paper with a summary of the work in Section 4.

2   Unsupervised Feature Selection and Outliers Rejection

2.1   The Model

Let us consider a data set of N vectors $\mathcal{X} = \{X_1, \ldots, X_N\}$, where each $X_i = (X_{i1}, \ldots, X_{iD})$ is a D-dimensional vector of features representing a given image, for instance. Set of vectors generally contains examples that belong to many clusters and can be modeled by a finite mixture of distributions

$$p(X_i|\Theta) = \sum_{j=1}^{M} p_j p(X_i|\theta_j) \tag{1}$$

where $p_j > 0$, are the mixing proportions, M is the number of mixture components, and $\Theta = \{P = (p_1, \ldots, p_M), \theta = (\theta_1, \ldots, \theta_M)\}$ is the set of parameters in the mixture model. A critical problem in this case is the choice of the probability density function $p(X_i|\theta_j)$ to represent each component. In [3], we have shown that the generalized Dirichlet distribution offers the unusual luxury that by a simple transformation we go from one space to another one where all the variables are independent and follow Beta distributions [4,5]. This allows us to easily formalize the fact that different features may have different weights by approximating a generalized Dirichlet mixture as following [3]

$$p(X_i|\Theta) = \sum_{j=1}^{M} p_j \prod_{d=1}^{D} \left(\rho_d p(X_{id}|\alpha_{jd}, \beta_{jd}) + (1 - \rho_d)p(X_{id}|\alpha_d, \beta_d)\right) \tag{2}$$

where $\Theta = \{P, \{\rho_d\}, \{\alpha_{jd}, \beta_{jd}\}, \{\alpha_d, \beta_d\}\}$ is the set of all the model parameters, ρ_d represents the probability that the dth feature is relevant for clustering, $p(X_{id}|\alpha_{jd}, \beta_{jd})$ is a Beta distribution that represents a feature X_{id} when it is relevant, and $p(X_{id}|\alpha_d, \beta_d)$ is an univariate Beta with parameters α_d, β_d and can be viewed as a common background distribution to explain nonsalient features. It is noteworthy that in the previous model no knowledge is available as to which vector X_i is not representative (i.e. an outlier) and then is not really generated from our assumed statistical model. Model selection, feature selection and parameters estimation are generally dramatically affected by outliers. Thus, it is crucial to extend the model in Eq. 2 to handle outliers. We approach this problem by incorporating an auxiliary outlier component to which we associate a uniform density [1] into the model:

---

[1] Supposing that the outliers follow a uniform distribution is a reasonable common assumption that have been considered in several computer vision and pattern recognition applications (see, for instance, [6,7]).

$$p(\boldsymbol{X}_i|\Theta) = \sum_{j=1}^{M} p_j \prod_{d=1}^{D} \Big(\rho_d p(X_{id}|\alpha_{jd}, \beta_{jd}) + (1-\rho_d)p(X_{id}|\alpha_d, \beta_d)\Big) + p_{M+1}U(\boldsymbol{X}_i)$$

(3)

where $p_{M+1} = 1 - \sum_{j=1}^{M} p_j$ is the probability that $\boldsymbol{X}_i$ was not generated by the central mixture model and $U(\boldsymbol{X}_i)$ is a uniform distribution common for all data to model isolated vectors which are not in any of the M clusters and which show significantly less differentiation among clusters. The previous model can be viewed as a way to robustify unsupervised feature selection to learn the right meaning from the right observations (i.e inliers). Notice that when $p_{M+1} = 0$ the outlier component is removed and the previous equation is reduced to Eq. 2.

2.2   Model Learning

A well-known approach for unknown parameters estimation is the technique of maximum likelihood (ML) which properties have been extensively examined in the past. Using ML the parameters are estimated by maximizing the log-likelihood function as following

$$\hat{\Theta} = \arg\max_{\Theta} \left\{ \log p(\mathcal{X}|\Theta) = \sum_{i=1}^{N} \log \left[\sum_{j=1}^{M} \left(p_j \prod_{d=1}^{D} \Big(\rho_d p_{jd}(X_{id}) + (1-\rho_d)p(X_{id})\Big) \right) \right.\right.$$
$$\left.\left. + p_{M+1}U(\boldsymbol{X}_i) \right] \right\}$$

(4)

where $p_{jd}(X_{id}) = p(X_{id}|\alpha_{jd}, \beta_{jd})$ and $p(X_{id}) = p(X_{id}|\alpha_d, \beta_d)$, which gives us

$$p_j = \frac{\sum_{i=1}^{N} p(j|\boldsymbol{X}_i)}{N} \quad j = 1, \ldots, M+1$$

(5)

where

$$p(j|\boldsymbol{X}_i) = \begin{cases} \dfrac{p_j \prod_{d=1}^{D} \Big(\rho_d p_{jd}(X_{id})+(1-\rho_d)p(X_{id})\Big)}{\sum_{j=1}^{M} \left(p_j \prod_{d=1}^{D} \Big(\rho_d p_{jd}(X_{id})+(1-\rho_d)p(X_{id})\Big) \right)+p_{M+1}U(\boldsymbol{X}_i)} & \text{if } j = 1, \ldots, M \\[3em] \dfrac{p_{M+1}U(\boldsymbol{X}_i)}{\sum_{j=1}^{M} \left(p_j \prod_{d=1}^{D} \Big(\rho_d p_{jd}(X_{id})+(1-\rho_d)p(X_{id})\Big) \right)+p_{M+1}U(\boldsymbol{X}_i)} & \text{if } j = M+1 \end{cases}$$

(6)

is the posterior probability that a vector $\boldsymbol{X}_i$ will be considered as an inlier and then assigned to a cluster $j, j = 1, \ldots, M$ or as an outlier and then affected to cluster $M+1$ which allows to safeguard against erroneous feature selection. Details about the estimation of the other parameters namely α_{jd}, β_{jd}, α_d, β_d and ρ_d can be found in [3]. It is desirable to determine the simplest model that can explain the data accurately. It is noteworthy that the simplicity is measured in our case by the number of mixture components and the number of relevant features. The simplest model can be viewed as the one that maximizes the message length, to reach an acceptable balance between model complexity and goodness of fit. Details and discussions about the computation of the message length can be found in [4,3].

Algorithm

For each candidate value of M:

1. Set $\rho_d \leftarrow 0.5$, $d = 1, \ldots, D$, $j = 1, \ldots, M$ and initialization of the rest of parameters [2].
2. Iterate the two following steps until convergence:
   (a) E-Step: Update $p(j|\boldsymbol{X}_n)$ using Eq. 6.
   (b) M-Step: Update the p_j, ρ_d, β_{jd}, α_{jd}, β_d and α_d as proposed in [3].
3. Calculate the associated message length [3].
4. Select the optimal model that yields the smallest message length.

3   Experimental Results: Texture Discrimination

The problem of texture discrimination has been the subject of several studies in the past (see, for instance, [8,9]). Several texture descriptors have been proposed [10] and applied to several problems such as industrial surface inspection and content-based image retrieval. We shall not elaborate further on the different approaches that have been proposed to model textures which is clearly beyond the scope of this paper. Rather we focus on an important texture feature extraction approach that has received a lot of attention recently. This approach is based on the representation of texture using visual dictionary obtained through the quantization of the appearance of local regions, described by local features, which gives characteristic texture elements generally called *textons* (see, for instance, [11]).

For our experimental evaluation, we use the KTH-TIPS [12] texture data set which is composed of 10 texture classes with 81 images per class (see Fig. 1). We add to this data set 20 different images, taken from different classes of the MIT vistex texture data set, which will be considered as outliers (see Fig. 2). An important step in our application is the extraction of local features to describe the textures. In our case we use the approach proposed in [11] which uses $n \times n$ pixel compact neighborhoods as image descriptors. Using this approach each texture pixel is described by an n^2-dimensional vector which represents the pixel intensities of its $n \times n$ square neighborhood. Following [11], we use $n = 7$, thus

Fig. 1. Examples of images from the 10 different classes in the KTH-TIPS data set

---

[2] The initialization is based on the K-Means algorithm and the method of moments by considering that $M + 1$ clusters are present in the data.

Fig. 2. Sample images from the Vistex data set

each pixel is represented by a 49-dimensional vector. Then, we construct a global *texton* vocabulary via the clustering of the different descriptors. In particular, we extract 10 textons using K-Means (i.e. the textons are actually the K-Means cluster centers) for each texture class and then concatenate the textons of the different classes to form the visual vocabulary. Thus, the vocabulary size is 100. Once the vocabulary of textons is built, each texture image can be represented then by a vector of frequencies which we normalize.

Evaluation results by considering different clustering scenarios and by comparing generalized Dirichlet mixture (GDM) and Gaussian mixture (GM) are summarized in table 1. It is noteworthy that in both cases (GDM or GM), we were able to find the exact number of clusters only when we have rejected the outliers. According to the results in table 1 it is clear that the GDM outperforms the GM which is actually an expected result taking into account the fact that the features vectors are proportional vectors for which the GDM is one of the best choices. It is clear also that feature selection improves the clustering performance especially when combined with outliers rejection.

Table 1. Clustering results for the KTH-TIPS data set by considering different scenarios. Clust denotes clustering without feature selection and outliers rejection, FS denotes feature selection and OR denotes outliers rejection.

	Clust	Clust+FS	Clust+OR	Clust+FS+OR
GDM	72.23%	74.88%	74.31%	76.77%
GM	68.76%	70.13%	70.02%	72.22%

4   Conclusion

The goal of the proposed work is to tackle simultaneously two of the chief obstacles to effective clustering namely the presence of outliers and irrelevant features. Our approach is based on extending the unsupervised feature selection technique that we have previously proposed in [3] to take into account outliers. The merits of the proposed framework have been shown via the clustering of texture images.

Acknowledgment

The completion of this research was made possible thanks to the Natural Sciences and Engineering Research Council of Canada (NSERC).

References

1. Fayyad, U., Piatetsky-Shapiro, G., Smyth, P.: Knowledge Discovery and Data Mining: Towards a Unifying Framework. In: Proc. of the Annual ACM SIGKDD Conference on Knowledge Discovery and Data Mining (KDD), pp. 82–88 (1996)
2. Law, M.H.C., Figueiredo, M.A.T., Jain, A.K.: Simultaneous Feature Selection and Clustering Using Mixture Models. IEEE Transactions on Pattern Analysis and Machine Intelligence 26(9), 1154–1166 (2004)
3. Boutemedjet, S., Bouguila, N., Ziou, D.: A Hybrid Feature Extraction Selection Approach for High-Dimensional Non-Gaussian Data Clustering. IEEE Transactions on Pattern Analysis and Machine Intelligence 31(8), 1429–1443 (2009)
4. Bouguila, N., Ziou, D.: High-Dimensional Unsupervised Selection and Estimation of a Finite Generalized Dirichlet Mixture Model Based on Minimum Message Length. IEEE Transactions on Pattern Analysis and Machine Intelligence 29(10), 1716–1731 (2007)
5. Bouguila, N., Ziou, D.: A New Approach for High-Dimensional Unsupervised Learning: Applications to Image Restoration. In: Pal, S.K., Bandyopadhyay, S., Biswas, S. (eds.) PReMI 2005. LNCS, vol. 3776, pp. 200–205. Springer, Heidelberg (2005)
6. Williams, C.K.I., Titsias, M.K.: Greedy Learning of Multiple Objects in Images using Robust Statistics and Factorial Learning. Neural Computation 16(5), 1039–1062 (2003)
7. Sudderth, E.B., Torralba, A., Freeman, W.T., Wilsky, A.S.: Depth from Familiar Objects: A Hierarchical Model for 3D Scenes. In: Proc. of the IEEE Conference on Computer Vision and Pattern Recognition (CVPR), pp. 2410–2417 (2006)
8. Luettgen, M.R., Willsky, A.S.: Likelihood Calculation for a Class of Multiscale Stochastic Models, with Application to Texture Discrimination. IEEE Transactions on Image Processing 4(2), 194–207 (1995)
9. Ojala, T., Valkealahti, K., Oja, E., Pietikäinen, M.: Texture Discrimination with Multidimensional Distributions of Signed Gray-Level Differences. Pattern Recognition 34, 727–739 (2001)
10. Ojala, T., Mäenpää, T., Viertola, J., Kyllönen, J., Pietikäinen, M.: Empirical Evaluation of MPEG-7 Texture Descriptors with a Large-Scale Experiment. In: Proc. of the 2nd International Workshop on Texture Analysis and Synthesis, pp. 99–102 (2002)
11. Varma, A., Zisserman, A.: Texture classification: are filter banks necessary? In. In: Proc. of the IEEE Conference on Computer Vision and Pattern Recognition (CVPR), pp. 691–698 (2003)
12. Hayman, E., Caputo, B., Fritz, M., Eklundh, J.-O.: On the significance of real-world conditions for material classification. In: Pajdla, T., Matas, J(G.) (eds.) ECCV 2004. LNCS, vol. 3024, pp. 253–266. Springer, Heidelberg (2004)

Simultaneous Clustering: A Survey

Malika Charrad and Mohamed Ben Ahmed

National School of Computer Science
Manouba University, Tunisia
{malika.charrad,mohamed.benahmed}@riadi.rnu.tn
http://www.riadi.rnu.tn/

Abstract. Although most of the clustering literature focuses on one-sided clustering algorithms, simultaneous clustering has recently gained attention as a powerful tool that allows to circumvent some limitations of classical clustering approach. Simultaneous clustering methods perform clustering in the two dimensions simultaneously. In this paper, we introduce a large number of existing simultaneous clustering approaches applied in bioinformatics as well as in text mining, web mining and information retrieval and classify them in accordance with the methods used to perform the clustering and the target applications.

Keywords: Simultaneous clustering, Biclusters, Block clustering.

1 Introduction

Simultaneous clustering, usually designated by biclustering, co-clustering, 2-way clustering or block clustering, is an important technique in two-way data analysis. A number of algorithms that perform simultaneous clustering on rows and columns of a matrix have been proposed to date. The goal of simultaneous clustering is to find sub-matrices, which are subgroups of rows and subgroups of columns that exhibit a high correlation. This type of algorithms has been proposed and used in many fields, such as bioinformatique [23], web mining [8], text mining [3] and social network analysis [18]. A wide range of different articles were published dealing with different kinds of algorithms and methods of simultaneous clustering. Comparisons of several biclustering algorithms can be found, in [23] and [27]. However, these comprehensive surveys focus only on algorithms used to genetic data analysis. In this paper, we give a brief description of a large number of existing approaches to biclustering including approaches based on mixture model, and those based on information theory.

2 Simultaneous Clustering Problem

Clustering is the grouping together of similar subjects. Standard clustering techniques consider the value of each point in all dimensions, in order to form group of similar points. This type of one-way clustering techniques is based on similarity between subjects across all variables.

S.O. Kuznetsov et al. (Eds.): PReMI 2011, LNCS 6744, pp. 370–375, 2011.

Simultaneous clustering algorithms seeks "blocks" of rows and columns that are interrelated. They aim to identify a set of biclusters $B_k(I_k, J_k)$, where I_k is a subset of the rows X and J_k is a subset of the columns Y. I_k rows exhibit similar behavior across J_k columns, or vice versa and every bicluster B_k satisfies some criteria of homogeneity. A biclustering method may assume a specific structure and data type. Madeira and Oliveira introduce in their survey [23] some biclustering structures defined by : single bicluster, exclusive rows biclusters, exclusive columns biclusters, nonoverlapping biclusters with tree structure, and arbitrarily positioned overlapping biclusters. Biclusters can be with constant values, with constant values on rows or columns, with coherent values or with coherent evolution. There are many advantages in a simultaneous rather than one way clustering (table 1). In fact, simultaneous clustering may highlight the association between the row and column clustering that appears from the data analysis as a linked clustering. Furthermore, it allows the researcher to deal with sparse and high dimensional data matrices [2]. Simultaneous clustering is also an interesting paradigm for unsupervised data analysis as it is more informative, has less parameters, is scalable and is able to effectively interwine row and column information.

Table 1. Comparison between Clustering and Simultaneous clustering

Clustering	Simultaneous Clustering
- applied to either the rows or the columns of the data matrix **separately** $\Rightarrow$ **global model**.	- performs clustering in the two dimensions **simultaneously** $\Rightarrow$ **local model**.
- produce **clusters** of rows **or** clusters of columns.	seeks **blocks** of rows **and** columns that are interrelated.
- Each subject in a given subject cluster is defined using **all** the variables. Each variable in a variable cluster characterizes **all** subjects.	- Each subject in a bicluster is selected using **only** a subset of the variables and each variable in a bicluster is selected using **only** a subset of the subjects.
- Clusters are **exhaustive**	- The clusters on rows and columns **should not be exclusive** and/or **exhaustive**

3   Simultaneous Clustering Approaches

A survey of simultaneous clustering algorithms applied on biological data has been given by Madeira and Oliveira in 2004 [23]. These alogorithms are based on five approaches : Iterative Row and Column Clustering Combination (IRCCC), Divide and Conquer (DC), Greedy Iterative Search (GIS), Exhaustive Bicluster Enumeration (EBE) and Distribution Parameter Identification (DPI). The IRCCC approach consists to apply clustering algorithms to the rows and columns of the data matrix, separately, and then to combine results using some sort of iterative procedure. The algorithms based on DC approach begin with the entire data in one block (bicluster) and identifies biclusters at each iteration by splicing a given block into two pieces. GIS approach creates biclusters by adding or removing rows/columns from them, using a criterion that maximizes the local gain. EBE approach identifies biclusters using an exhaustive enumeration of all possible biclusters in the data matrix. DPI approach assumes that the biclusters are generated using a given statistical model and tries to identify the distribution parameters that fit the available data, by minimizing a certain criterion through an iterative approach. All the algorithms presented in this survey analyze biological data from gene expression matrices. Given that there are a number of algorithms based on bipartite graph model ([12] [3]), mixture model [26] and information theory ([13] [30]), which are applied in other fields such as text mining, web mining and information retrieval, we propose to categorize simultaneous clustering methods into five categories : bipartite Graph methods, variance minimization methods, two-way clustering methods, motif and pattern recognition methods and probabilistic and generative methods.

- The bipartite graph methods consists in modeling rows and columns as a weighted bipartite graph and assigning weights to graph edges using similarity measure techniques. The created bipartite graph is then partitioned in a way that minimizes the cut of the partition, i.e. the sum of the weights of the crossing edges between parts of the partition. In [38], the authors created a word-document bipartite graph. The graph was partitioned using a partial singular value decomposition of the associated edge weight matrix of the bipartite graph. Dhillon [12] used the spectral method for partitioning the bipartite graph constructed in the same way as in [38]. [28] proposed an isoperimetric co-clustering algorithm (ICA) for partitioning the word-document matrix. ICA used the same model than spectral partitioning but instead of searching the solutions of the singular word-document system of linear equations, it converts the system to a nonsingular system of equations which is easier to solve. The bipartite graph methods are also used for gene expression analysis. One example is Statistical-Algorithmic Method for Bicluster Analysis (SAMBA) [31].

- The variance minimization methods define clusters as blocks in the matrix with minimal deviation of their elements. This definition has been already considered by Hartigan (1972) [20] and extended by Tibshirani et al. [33]. Some examples are the δ-cluster methods, such as δ-ks clusters [7], δ-pClusters [35] and δ-biclusters [10], which search for blocks of elements having a deviation below δ. FLexible Overlapped biClustering (FLOC) introduced by [36] extend Cheng and Church δ-biclusters by dealing with missing values.

- Two-way clustering methods use one-way clustering such as kmeans [32] [17] [9] [26], Self Organizing Maps [5], Expectation-Minimization algorithm [16] or an hierarchical clustering algorithm [15] to produce clusters on both dimensions of the data matrix separately. One-dimension results are then combined to produce subgroups of rows and columns called biclusters. These methods identify clusters on rows and columns but not directly biclusters.

- Motif and pattern recognition methods define a bicluster as samples sharing a common pattern or motif. To simplify this task, some methods discretize the data such as xMOTIF [25] or binarize the data such as Bimax [27]. Order-Preserving SubMatrices (OPSM) [4] searches for blocks having the same order of values in their columns. Spectral clustering (SPEC) [37] performs a singular value decomposition of the data matrix after normalization. Contiguous column coherent (CCC biclustering) [24] is a method for gene expression time series, which finds patterns in contiguous columns.

Table 2. Simultaneous clustering algorithms

Algorithm	Application	Approach	Data type
Two-way splitting [20]	Other	Variance minimization	Continuous
CROEUC [17]	Other	Two-way clustering	Continuous
CROKI2 [17] [9]	Other	Two-way clustering	Categorical
CROBIN [17]	Other	Two-way clustering	Binary
CTWC [15]	Bioinformatique	Two-way clustering	Continuous
Plaid Models [22]	Bioinformatique	Probabilistic and generative	Continuous
δ-biclusters [10]	Bioinformatique	Variance minimization	Continuous
δ-ks patterns [7]	Bioinformatique	Variance minimization	Continuous
ITWC [32]	Bioinformatique	Two-way clustering	Continuous
DCC [5]	Bioinformatique	Two-way clustering	Continuous
OPSM [4]	Bioinformatique	Motif and pattern recognition	Continuous
SAMBA [31]	Bioinformatique	Probabilistic and generative	Continuous
FLOC [36]	Bioinformatique	Variance minimization	Continuous
Spectral [37]	Bioinformatique	Motif and pattern recognition	Continuous
IT [13]	Text Mining	Probabilistic and generative	Continuous
BSGP [12]	Text Mining	Bi-partite Graph	Categorical
cHawk [1]	Bioinformatique	Bi-partite Graph	Continuous
[30]	Other	Probabilistic and generative	Categorical
Block-EM [16]	Other	Two-way clustering	Continuous binary
Block-CEM [16]	Other	Two-way clustering	Continuous binary
Cemcroki2 [26]	Other	Two-way clustering	Categorical

- Probabilistic and generative methods use model-based techniques to define biclusters [21]. Probabilistic Relational Models (PRMs) [14] and their extension ProBic [34] are fully generative models that combine probabilistic modeling and relational logic. cMonkey [29] is a generative approach which models biclusters by Markov chain processes. Gu and Liu [19] generalized the plaid models proposed in [22] to fully generative models called Bayesian BiClustering model (BBC). The latter models introduced in [6] and [19] are generative models which have the advantage that they select models using well-understood model selection techniques such as maximum likelihood.

Costa et al. [11] introduced a hierarchical model-based co-clustering algorithm. In their method the co-occurrence matrix is characterized in probabilistic terms, by estimating the joint distribution between rows and columns.

The table 2 presents main simultaneous clustering algorithms dealing with continuous, binary or categorical data, the approach they are based on and the domain of application.

4 Conclusion

The survey presented in this work can be used by the interested researcher as a good starting point to learn and apply some of the many techniques proposed in the last few years, and some of the older ones. Many interesting directions for future research have been uncovered by this review work, like the validation of biclustering methods and the statistical significance of biclusters.

References

1. Ahmad, W., Khokhar, A.: cHawk: an efficient biclustering algorithm based on bipartite graph crossing minimization. VLDB. ACM, New York (2007)
2. Balbi, S., Miele, R., Scepi, G.: Clustering of documents from a two-way viewpoint. In: 10th Int. Conf. on Statistical Analysis of Textual Data (2010)
3. Bichot, C.E.: Co-clustering documents and words by minimizing the normalized cut objective function. JMMA 9, 131–147 (2010)
4. Ben-Dor, A., Chor, B., Karp, R.: Discovering local structure in gene expression data: The order–preserving submatrix problem. J. of Comput. Biol. 10, 373–384 (2003)
5. Busygin, S., Jacobsen, G., Kramer, E.: Double conjugated clustering applied to leukemia microarray data. In: 2nd SIAM Int. Conf. on Data Mining (2002)
6. Caldas, J., Kaski, S.: Bayesian biclustering with the plaid model. In: IEEE Intern. Workshop on Machine Learning for Signal Processing, pp. 291–296 (2008)
7. Califano, A., Stolovitzky, G., Tu, Y.: Analysis of gene expression microarays for phenotype classification. In: Int. Conf. on Computational Molecular Biology (2000)
8. Charrad, M., Lechevallier, Y., Ahmed, M.b., Saporta, G.: Block Clustering for Web Pages Categorization. In: Corchado, E., Yin, H. (eds.) IDEAL 2009. LNCS, vol. 5788, pp. 260–267. Springer, Heidelberg (2009)
9. Charrad, M.: une approche generique pour l'analyse croisant usage et contenu de sites Web par des methodes de bipartitionnement. PhD Thesis, Paris (2010)
10. Cheng, Y., Church, G.M.: Biclustering of expression data. In: 8th Int. Conf. on Intelligent Systems for Molecular Biology, pp. 93–103 (2000)
11. Costa, G., Manco, G., Ortale, R.: A hierarchical model-based approach to co-clustering high-dimensional data. In: ACM sym. on App. comput., pp. 886–890 (2008)
12. Dhillon, I.S.: Co-clustering documents and words using bipartite spectral graph partitioning. In: 7th ACM SIGKDD 2001, California, pp. 269–274 (2001)
13. Dhillon, I.S., Mallela, S., Modha, D.S.: Information-theoretic co-clustering. In: ACM SIGKDD, pp. 89–98. ACM, Washington DC (2003)
14. Getoor, L., Friedman, N., Koller, D., Taskar, B.: Learning probabilistic models of link structure. J. Mach. Learn. Res. 3, 679–707 (2002)

15. Getz, G., Levine, E., Domany, E.: Coupled two-way clustering analysis of gene microarray data. Proc. of the Natural Academy of Sciences USA (2000)
16. Govaert, G., Nadif, M.: Clustering with block mixture models. J. of the Pattern Recognition, 463–473 (2003)
17. Govaert, G.: Classification croisee. Th. de doctorat d'Etat, Paris (1983)
18. Grimal, C., Bisson, G.: Classification a partir d'une collection de matrices. CAp2010 (2010)
19. Gu, J.: Bayesian biclustering of gene expression data. BMC Genomics (2008).
20. Hartigan, J.A.: Direct clustering of a data matrix. J. of American Statistical Association 67(337), 123–129 (1972)
21. Hochreiter, S., Bodenhofer, U., Heusel, M., Mayr, A.: FABIA: factor analysis for bicluster acquisition. Bioinformatics journal 26(12), 1520–1527 (2010)
22. Lazzeroni, L., Owen, A.: Plaid models for gene expression data. Technical report, Stanford University (2002)
23. Madeira, S.C., Oliveira, A.L.: Biclustering Algorithms for Biological Data Analysis: A Survey. IEEE/ACM Trans. on Comp. Biol. and Bioinfor., 24–45 (2004)
24. Madeira, S.C., Teixeira, M.C.: Identification of regulatory modules in time series gene expression data using a linear time biclustering algorithm. IEEE ACM (2010)
25. Murali, T.M., Kasif, S.: Extracting conserved gene expression motifs from gene expression data. In: Pacific Sym. on Biocomputing, Hawaii, USA, pp. 77–88 (2003)
26. Nadif, M., Govaert, G.: Block clustering of contingency table and mixture model. In: Famili, A.F., Kok, J.N., Peña, J.M., Siebes, A., Feelders, A. (eds.) IDA 2005. LNCS, vol. 3646, pp. 249–259. Springer, Heidelberg (2005)
27. Prelic, A., Bleuler, S., Zimmermann, P.: A systematic comparison and evaluation of biclustering methods for gene expression data. Bioinformatics, 122–129 (2006)
28. Rege, M., Dong, M.: Co-clustering Documents and Words Using Bipartite Isoperimetric Graph Partitioning. In: 6th IEEE Int. Conf. on Data Mining, pp. 532–541 (2006)
29. Reiss, D.J.: Integrated biclustering of heterogeneous genome-wide datasets for the inference of global regulatory networks. BMC Bioinfor., 280–302 (2006)
30. Robardet, C.: Contribution à la classification non supervisee : proposition d'une methode de bi-partitionnement, PhD Thesis, Claude Bernard University (2002).
31. Tanay, A., Sharan, R., Shamir, R.: Biclustering Algorithms: A Survey. In: Aluru, S. (ed.) Handbook of Comp. Molecular Biology, Chapman, Boca Raton (2004)
32. Tang, C., Zhang, L.A.: Interrelated two-way clustering: an unsupervised approach for gene expression data analysis. In: IEEE Int. Sym. on Bioinfo. and Bioeng. (2001)
33. Tibshirani, R., Hastie, T., Eisen, M.: Clustering methods for the analysis of DNA microarray data. Technical report, Stanford University (1999)
34. Van den, B.T.: Robust Algorithms for Inferring Regulatory Networks Based on Gene Expression Measurements. PhD Thesis (2009)
35. Wang, H., Wang, W., Yang, J., Yu, P.S.: Clustering by pattern similarity in large data sets. In: ACM SIGMOD Int. Conf. on Management of Data, pp. 394–405 (2002)
36. Yang, J., Wang, H., Wang, W., Yu, P.S.: An improved biclustering method for analyzing gene expression profiles. Int. J. on Art. Int. Tools, 771–790 (2005)
37. Klugar, Y., Basri, R., Chang, J.T., Gerstein, M.: Spectral biclustering of microarray data: coclustering genes and conditions. Genome Research 13, 703–716 (2003)
38. Zha, H., He, X., Ding, C., Simon, H., Gu, M.: Bipartite Graph Partitioning and Data Clustering. In: ACM Conf. on Inf. and Knowledge Management, pp. 25–32 (2001)

Analysis of Centrality Measures of Airport Network of India

Manasi Sapre and Nita Parekh

International Institute of Information Technology, Hyderabad 500032, India
isanam5@gmail.com, nita@iiit.ac.in

Abstract. In this paper we analyze the topological properties of airport network of India (ANI) using graph theoretic approach. We show that such an analysis can be useful not only in planning the infrastructure and growth of the air-traffic connectivity, but also in managing the flow of transportation during emergencies such as accidental failure of the airport, close down of the airport due to unexpected climate changes, terrorist attacks, etc. Knowledge of the connectivity pattern and load on various routes can also help in making judicious decisions for reduction of flights to contain the spread of the infectious disease.

Keywords: graph theory, centrality measures, efficiency of a network.

1 Introduction

In recent years, it has been observed that new influenza strains arising in one corner of the world spread rapidly affecting human lives across many countries in a very short span of time. The most recent example is that of swine flu virus, H1N1, which was first reported in April 2009 in Mexico and by August, was declared a pandemic. The main cause of the epidemic turning into pandemic in this case is the densely connected transportation services which have made the world a smaller place and the main "carriers of infectious diseases", i.e. humans can now spread the viral diseases with a much higher rate than ever before. With this view, here we analyze the connection topology of Airport Network of India (ANI) which is a subset of World Airport Network. A number of similar studies on air transportation networks have been reported both at the national level [1,2,3] and at the international level (WAN) [4,5]. In this study we have investigated the topological properties of ANI by representing it as a mathematical graph: each airport corresponds to a *node* in the network and pairs of airports connected by non-stop (direct) passenger flights are linked by *edges*. The role of various graph centrality measures, viz., degree, betweenness, closeness etc. to the stability of the network and the efficient flow of traffic through the whole network has been well studied [5,6]. Here we discuss the impact on the global efficiency of ANI by reducing connections from high-centrality nodes. Such an analysis can help in identifying nodes (airports) whose connectivity needs to be improved to increase revenue from tourism and developing more than one local hubs in different regions for efficient flow of traffic in case of undesirable situations etc.

S.O. Kuznetsov et al. (Eds.): PReMI 2011, LNCS 6744, pp. 376–381, 2011.

2   Method

Construction of ANI: For the construction of the ANI, data was collected for a total of 84 airports in India listed in International Civil Organization Code (ICAO) [7]. Total of 13,909 weekly direct flights from airport i to j from 9 major airlines have been considered (Data updated Dec, 2010) [8]. This connectivity information of flight-routes is represented by the adjacency matrix A of size 84×84, the elements of which have a value "1" or "0" depending on whether there exists an edge (i.e., connectivity) between two nodes or not. The traffic flow on the routes is incorporated by constructing a weighted ANI by assigning weights on edges proportional to the number of flights, N_{ij}, i.e., $w_{ij} = N_{ij}/N$, where N is the total number of flights in the network. We observed that $N_{ij} = N_{ji}$; i.e. the number of incoming and outgoing flights are the same. To analyze the infrastructure capacity of an airport, the strength of node i is defined as $S(i) = \sum_{j=1}^{n} a_{ij} w_{ij}$ where a_{ij} are the elements of the adjacency matrix and w_{ij} are the weights on the edges [9].

Measures Used in the Analysis of ANI:

Efficiency: To analyze the response of the network to external factors, viz., closure of an airport, we compute global efficiency [10] as $E_{glob}(G) = 1/n(n - 1) \sum_{i \neq j \in G} 1/d_{ij}$ where d_{ij} is the shortest path length between nodes i and j.

Degree: Degree of a node i is the number of nodes to which it is directly connected and is given by $k_i = \sum_{j=1}^{n} a_{ij}$ where a_{ij} are the elements of the adjacency matrix.

Betweenness: It is defined as the ratio of number of shortest paths passing through i to the total number shortest paths in the network $B_i = \sum_{i \neq j \neq k} Z_{j-k}(i) / Z_{j-k}$ where Z_{j-k} corresponds to all the shortest paths from node j to node k and $Z_{j-k}(i)$ corresponds to the shortest paths from node j to node k that pass through node i[11].

Closeness: It is defined as the reciprocal of the average shortest path between a node i and all other nodes reachable from it. $Cl_i = 1/\sum_{j \in V} d_{ij}$ where V is the connectivity component which contains all the vertices in the network reachable from vertex i. Nodes having high closeness value are most central in the network, i.e. all other nodes can be reached easily from this node.

The normalized centrality values are obtained by dividing by the maximum value such that all centrality values lie in the range 0 to 1.

3   Results and Discussion

ANI Exhibits Small-world and Scale-free Properties: The clustering coefficient (C) of weighted undirected ANI is **0.645** and its characteristic path length (L) is **2.17**, while the corresponding values of an equivalent randomized ANI network is 0.18 and 2.55 respectively, i.e., $C_{ANI} \gg C_{rand}$ and $L_{ANI} \sim L_{rand}$, suggesting that ANI is a small-world network [12]. To analyze the distribution of flights in ANI, we considered cumulative strength distribution, $P(> S)$ as a function of strength S, since ANI is small network. Double Pareto law is observed for the distributions of the strength, $P(> S)$ as seen in Fig. 1 (a) with exponent $\gamma^1_{cum} = 0.36$ and $\gamma^2_{cum} = 0.71$ and for betweenness measure, $\gamma^1_{cum} = 0.21$ and $\gamma^2_{cum} = 0.54$ (Fig. 1 (b)). This indicates the scale-free nature of ANI, i.e., a few nodes has very large number of connections/flights while majority of nodes have very few connections. The properties of scale-free networks have been extensively studied and these networks have been shown to be robust against random removal of nodes but break down on targeted attacks [13]. Below we analyze the effect of targeted removal of high centrality nodes on the overall efficiency of the network.

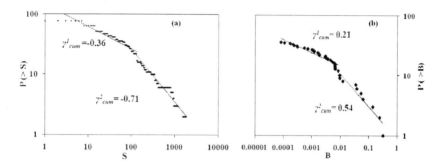

Fig. 1. (a) Cumulative strength disribution and (b) cumulative betweenness exhibit double Pareto law

The Role of High Centrality Nodes in ANI: In the event of disease spread it would be most desirous to identify crucial airports and routes to restrict transmission of disease and avoid a pandemic situation. However, complete close down of important airports or important routes is not economically viable. This led us to analyze the effect of fractional reduction of flights from an "important" airport on the overall efficiency of the network. Such an analysis would not only be useful in containing/delaying the spread of disease during an eventuality but also to assess the loss of connectivity during closure of certain airports/routes in unavoidable weather conditions, accidental failures etc. Preliminary analysis of our results has been presented in our earlier work [14].

Analysis of High Degree Nodes: In Table 1 is shown the comparison of top 10 airports listed based on their centrality values. It is clear from the table that Delhi, Mumbai and Kolkata top the list, these three being local hubs for northern, western, and eastern regions of India, respectively. The fall in connectivity in top 10 high-degree airports is $\sim 80.5\%$, while the drop in its strength (i.e. total number of flights from it) is $\sim 89.5\%$, clearly bringing out the effect of large number of flights on certain routes. In Fig. 2 the global efficiency of ANI is computed as a function of reduction of edges (routes) from six airports selected based on their strength. It has been shown that centrality of an airport and the socio-eonomic factors of that city are highly correlated [15]. Delhi being the

Table 1. Top 10 airports with high centrality values

Strength	S_i	Degree	k_i	Closeness	Cl_i	Betweenness	B_i	City	Cases
New Delhi	352	New Delhi	51	New Delhi	0.75	New Delhi	0.472	New Delhi	3703
Mumbai	314	Mumbai	48	Mumbai	0.70	Mumbai	0.400	Mumbai	3000
Bengaluru	167	Kolkata	33	Kolkata	0.63	Kolkata	0.220	Chennai	1935
Kolkata	141	Bengaluru	25	Bengaluru	0.62	Bengaluru	0.130	Bengaluru	1643
Chennai	138	Chennai	23	Hyderabad	0.58	Chennai	0.100	Trichy	1317
Hyderabad	95	Hyderabad	21	Chennai	0.57	Hyderabad	0.080	Chandigarh	1300
Ahmedabad	62	Ahmedabad	17	Ahmedabad	0.57	Guwahati	0.050	Jaipur	1008
Guwahati	53	Goa	13	Goa	0.56	Kochi	0.030	Hyderabad	773
Kochi	44	Kochi	11	Guwahati	0.55	Ahmedabad	0.010	Lucknow	673
Goa	37	Guwahati	10	Kochi	0.51	Goa	0.006	Ahmedabad	275

capital and well connected to all the parts of the country, we observe that on reducing flights from Delhi has maximum effect on the global efficiency of ANI, followed by Mumbai which is the financial capital of the country. On completely removing flights from either of these two airports, the overall efficiency of the network falls by $\sim 35\%$ as seen in Fig. 2 resulting in disconnected clusters of airports. However, in the southern part of India, the traffic flow seems to be well distributed among the three local hubs, viz., Hyderabad, Chennai and Bengaluru (sharing about 30-50% direct flights). Removal of any one of these airports does not have any signifiant reduction in the efficiency of ANI. Though their centrality values are high, their importance in the network is reduced beause of the presence of other two local hubs in southern region which provide alternate flight-routes. Developing more than one local hub would not only ease the traffic flow but also develop healthy competition among airports resulting in improved infrastructure, reduced fares etc. as suggested by Malighetti *et al* [5].

The spread of infectious diseases through transportation network has become quite evident over the years. It may be noted from Table 1 that all the cities reported having high number of swine flu have either direct international flights or are directly connected to one having international flights, suggesting multiple entry points in the country. A strong correlation between cases and flights (Fig. 3), indicates the role of air transportation in the spread of disease. Thus, appropriately choosing airports/routes for reducing flights can result in reducing the impact. For example, on removing flights to Kolkata, the whole eastern region can be excluded.

Analysis of High Betweenness Nodes: From Table 1 it is clear that most high-degree nodes also have high betweenness values. It would be interesting to identify nodes having high betweenness value and low degree, e.g. Guwahati ($k = 10$, $B = 0.05$) as it connects to remote places in eastern India. In Table 2 is summarized the effect of cutting off flights from Delhi to airports having top four ranking betweeness values. On removing flights from Delhi to Kolkata, out of 9 airports in eastern India, hop-count increases for 8 of them to reach Delhi. Similarly, on removing the Delhi-Mumbai route, 5 airports out of 18 in the western part of India are affected. Thus by restricting flights on certain routes, delay in the spread of disease can be obtained. However, no such pattern

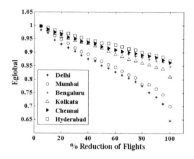

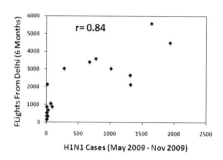

Fig. 2. The impact on E_{global} of ANI as a function of reduction of flights-routes from six major hubs in ANI: Delhi, Mumbai, Bengaluru, Kolkata, Chennai and Hyderabad.

Fig. 3. Correlation between no. of flights from Delhi and no. of reported swine-flu cases (obtained from Ministry of Health of India [16]), r = 0.84

is observed in the case of removing flights from Delhi to either Hyderabad, Chennai, or Bengaluru. If similar local hubs are developed in western/northern regions, connectivity can be improved which would also help in the economic development of those regions.

Analysis of High Closeness Nodes: The closeness values indicate the accessibility of an airport to any other airport in the country. For ANI we observe that majority of airports have average closeness value ($\sim$ 0.45), suggesting a good inter-connectivity between cities. This measure can have important implication in developing tourism to hill stations (e.g., Kullu Manali, Darjeeling), wild-life sanctuaries (e.g., Corbett National Park.), historical places (e.g., Agra, Hampi) and religious places (e.g., Puri, Tirupati) apart from improving connectivity to major industrial cities (e.g., Jamshedpur). These airports, in general, do not have high-degree or high-betweenness values and in some cases are not connected by air. Their closeness values can be increased by connecting them to the nearest local hubs. Our analysis of closeness values of various tourist spots show that the most popular tourist spot, Goa (0.55), indeed has high closeness value but hill-stations, e.g., Kullu-Manali (0.37) or Agatti Island (0.33) do not, suggesting the improvement of their connectivity to improve revenue through tourism.

Table 2. The increased "hops" for airports when flights from Delhi to four high-betweenness airports are cut-off is shown.(No. given in bracket)

Kolkata	Silchar(3) Lilabari(2)	Tezpur (3) Shillong(2)	Jorhat(3) Gaya(2)	Aizwal(2)	Dimapur(2)
Mumbai	Latur(3)	Solapur(3)	Kandla(3)	Bhavnagar(2)	Nasik(2)
Chennai	Madurai(2)	Trichy (1)			
Bengaluru	Agatti(3)	Mangaluru(2)			

4   Conclusion

Graph theoretic analysis of weighted ANI helps in identifying "critical" nodes, not necessarily the ones with high connections but also the ones lying on high traffic-routes (high betweenness) or geographically well distant nodes (high closeness). Analysis of these high-centrality nodes can help in improving efficiency of ANI, tourism in the country and containing the spread of disease.

References

1. Li, W., Chai, X.: Statistical analysis of airport network of China. Phys. Rev.E. 69, 46106 (2004)
2. Guida, M., Funaro, M.: Topology of Italian airport network. Chaos Solitons and Fractals 31, 527–536 (2007)
3. Bagler, G.: Analysis of airport network of India as a complex weighted network. Physica A 387, 2972–2980 (2008)
4. Guimera, R., Mossa, S., Turtschi, A., Amaral, L.A.N.: The worldwide air transportation network: Anomalous centrality, community structure and cities' global roles. PNAS 2, 7794–7799 (2005)
5. Malighetti, G., Martini, G., Paleari, S., Redondi, R.: The Impacts of Airport Centrality in the EU Network and Inter-Airport Competition on Airport Efficiency. MPRA (2009)
6. Berger, A., Müller-Hannemann, M., Rechner, S., Zock, A.: Efficient computation of time-dependent centralities in air transportation networks. In: Katoh, N., Kumar, A. (eds.) WALCOM 2011. LNCS, vol. 6552, pp. 77–88. Springer, Heidelberg (2011)
7. http://www.icao.int
8. The data from the sites of major airlines (2010)
9. Barrat, A., Barthélemy, M., Pastor-Satorras, R., Vespignani, A.: The architecture of complex weighted network. Proc. Natl. Acad. Sci (USA) 101(11), 3747–3752 (2004)
10. Latora, V., Marchiori, M.: Efficient Behavior of Small World Networks. Phys. Rev. Lett. 87, 198701 (2001)
11. Newman, M.E.J.: The structure of scientific collaboration network. Proc. Natl. Aca. Sci. 98, 404–409 (2001)
12. Watts, D.J., Strogatz, S.H.: Collective dynamics of 'small-world' networks. Nature 393, 440–442 (1998)
13. Barabási, A.-L., Albert, R.: Emergence of scaling in random networks. Science 286, 509–512 (1999)
14. Sapre, M., Parekh, N.: Analysis of Airport Network of India. In: Poster presentation at Grace Hopper Coneference in Computer Science, Bangalore (2010)
15. Wang, J., Mo, H., Wang, F., Jin, F.: Exploring the network struture and nodal centrality of China's air transport network: A complex network approach. Journal of Transport Geography (in press) (2010)
16. http://www.mohfw.nic.in/

Clusters of Multivariate Stationary Time Series by Differential Evolution and Autoregressive Distance

Roberto Baragona

Sapienza University of Rome, Dept. of Communication and Social Research
Via Salaria 113, Rome, Italy
roberto.baragona@uniroma1.it
http://w3.uniroma1.it/statstsmeh

Abstract. Clustering MTS is a difficult task that has to be performed in several application fields. We propose a method based on the coefficients of vector autoregressive (VAR) models and differential evolution (DE) that may be applied to sets of stationary MTS. Results from a simulation experiment that includes both linear and non linear MTS are displayed for comparison with genetic algorithms (GAs), principal component analysis (PCA) and the k-means algorithm. Part of the Australian Sign Language (Auslan) data are examined to show the comparative performance of our procedure on a real world data set.

Keywords: Autoregressive distance, Cluster analysis, Differential evolution, Multivariate time series.

1 Introduction

MTS are of chief interest in a large set of application fields, e.g. econometrics, environmental sciences, seismology, medicine, data mining, speech recognition, video image analysis. Surveys are for example [7] and [8,9]. Often data are collected by automatic devices (sensors, electronic transaction documents, the Internet) and a large amount of information is available. The standard organization for MTS is a rectangular array with m rows (series components, variables, locations) and n columns (observations taken at regular time intervals). Clustering is a common device which is used to reduce a large set of MTS to a smaller set of MTS representative of homogeneous groups. We assume that data are unlabeled, so that we have to check the existence and find the groups using only the available data. We examine in this paper the features that may be computed from the popular VAR model estimated matrices of coefficients. We observe for motivating such a choice that such features are simple and effective for clustering stationary MTS and may be easily and quickly computed by least squares. Many other features have been suggested. PCA of similarity matrices has been proposed for developing procedures for MTS classification [17,14,1]. Extensions of spectral measures for MTS have been discussed by [5]. The approach introduced by [9] splits the clustering procedure into two steps. In the first step each

S.O. Kuznetsov et al. (Eds.): PReMI 2011, LNCS 6744, pp. 382–387, 2011.

MTS is converted into a sequence of discrete values. In the second step either the dynamic time warping or a symmetric version of the Kullback-Leibler distance is computed from the discrete data. Many algorithms are available to cluster a set of features, in general a set of unlabeled data (see, e.g., [6]). Most efficient specially for complicated large data set have been found the meta heuristic methods (see, e.g., [16]) which solve the clustering problems put in terms of an optimization problems with respect to some cluster internal validity index (see, e.g., [3,11]). In particular the most used meta heuristic for clustering maybe are the GAs often in the presence of multiple objective functions (see, e.g., [2]). However DE ([15]) seems more suited to deal with real valued potential solutions, and we suggest using this method for clustering MTS. The paper is organized as follows. In Sect. 2 the features that we use for clustering are introduced. The DE method is illustrated in Sect. 3. In Sect. 4 a simulation study is reported that support the use of the AR weights and DE for clustering MTS. An application to a well-known set of real world data is presented in Sect. 5. Sect. 6 concludes.

2   The Autoregressive Weights for Multivariate Time Series

Let $x_t = (x_{1,t}, x_{2,t}, \ldots, x_{m,t})'$, where t is a discrete valued time index, be a real valued m-dimensional MTS which admits the VAR infinite representation

$$x_t = \sum_{i=1}^{\infty} \Pi_i x_{t-i} + a_t, \tag{1}$$

where the Π_i are $m \times m$ matrices of coefficients and a_t is a m-dimensional white noise with zero mean and variance covariance matrix Σ_a. Examples of such MTS are the popular finite order stationary VAR, the invertible vector moving-average (VMA) and the finite order stationary and invertible vector AR and MA (VARMA) models. Given a MTS data set $\{x_1, x_2, \ldots, x_n\}$ a finite order L VAR may be fitted to x_t with L large enough to obtain a good approximation of Eqn. (1). [10] suggested a test of hypothesis for every pair of MTS in a given set based on the VAR parameter coefficient matrices estimates $\hat{\Pi}_i$, $i = 1, \ldots, L$. Let $\hat{\pi}_i$ be the column vector obtained by stacking the columns of $\hat{\Pi}_i$, $i = 1, \ldots, L$. A set of measurements that may be used to characterize the MTS is the vector $\hat{\pi} = (\hat{\pi}'_1, \hat{\pi}'_2, \ldots, \hat{\pi}'_L)'$. These measurements may be viewed as an extension to the multivariate framework of the AR distance index introduced by [12] for univariate time series. We call these measurements as the features of interest that may capture the characteristic behavior of each MTS in a given set. A distance measure, e.g. the Euclidean metric, between two feature vectors may be assumed as the distance between the respective MTS.

3   Differential Evolution Based Clustering

Most clustering algorithms which include centers evolution use GAs. The contribution of the present paper aims at showing that DE is a better choice than GAs if, as it is the case with the AR distance here, chromosomes with real valued genes are employed. DE is a population based method that evolves a population of potential solutions through a sequence of generations. Each solution is a vector $x = (x_1, x_2, \ldots, x_m)' \in R^m$ which at each generation undergoes the DE process. A vector v_0 (called the base vector) different from x is selected randomly in the population. Then two other vectors v_1 and v_2 are randomly selected and their difference is scaled by the scale factor $F \in (0,1)$. A new potential solution u called mutant is computed $u = v_0 + F(v_1 - v_2)$ and recombined with the initial individual vector x to produce an offspring vector y by means of uniform crossover. This means that each element of y is assumed equal to the corresponding element of the mutant u with a fixed probability p_c or equal to the original element of the vector x with probability $(1 - p_c)$. Finally y replaces x in the population if a better value of the objective function is obtained. Basically the population size remains the same during the whole DE process. More details and variants may be found in [13]. For implementing the examples in the following Sect. 4 and 5 we used the Matlab code from [13] modified for the purpose of clustering MTS. The population consists in a set of vectors with length $g \times m^2 L$, where g is the number of cluster and $m^2 L$ the total number of the VAR coefficients. Each vector encodes a sequence of g centers that represent clusters of the sequences of AR weights computed from the MTS data set. We implemented the fuzzy clustering method with objective function the FCM index J_m for which GAs have been proposed ([3]). The centers evolution includes the update that takes place in the FCM algorithm as soon as the new clusters have been defined and produces an improvement of the rate of convergence to the optimal solution. The same device has been included in the GAs clustering that we use for performance comparison.

4   Experiments on Artificial Data Sets

In the following simulation experiments the AR weights are computed by fitting a VAR(L) to each artificial MTS in a given set. Then we compare the procedure based on DE, GAs, PCA and the k-means algorithm. Comparison is made in terms of the misclassification error rate (MSCR) and the modified Rand index (MRI) ([4]). As a first experiment, a set of 2-dimensional artificial time series data of length 100 has been generated as in [9] from the bivariate VARMA models

$$x_t - \mu = \Phi(x_{t-1} - \mu) + a_t - \Theta a_{t-1}, \tag{2}$$

where $\mu = (10, 20)'$,

$$\Phi = \begin{pmatrix} 1.2 & -0.5 \\ 0.6 & 0.3 \end{pmatrix}, \qquad \Theta = \begin{pmatrix} -0.6 & 0.3 \\ 0.3 & 0.6 \end{pmatrix},$$

and $\{a_t\}$ is a sequence of independent identically normally distributed vector random variables with mean zero and variance covariance matrix

$$\Sigma = \begin{pmatrix} 1.0 & 0.5 \\ 0.5 & 1.25 \end{pmatrix}.$$

Three clusters were produced, the first one by the VAR(1) obtained by setting in Eqn. (2) $\Theta = 0$, the second one by the VMA(1) with $\Phi = 0$, and the third one by the full VARMA(1,1) model (2). The procedure suggested in Liao (2007) is reported to produce, in 9 runs, some misclassification that arises from confusion between the VAR(1) model and the VARMA(1,1) model. We generated 300 artificial MTS, 100 for each cluster. We run our procedure for 1000 replications using the features computed as the AR weights obtained by fitting a VAR(2) model to each MTS. On such features the DE, GA, PCA and k-means clustering algorithms have been applied. The three clusters have been recovered almost exactly by the first two algorithms. PCA and k-means produce inferior results, with MSCR about 1% and MRI slightly less than 0.9. We run a similar but more difficult simulation experiment by generating 3-dimensional time series and using in Eqn. (2) a stronger AR structure and a weaker MA structure, so as to make more likely a possible confusion between MTS in clusters 1 and 3. We obtained the results displayed in Table 1. According to both cluster external validity indexes the DE gives better results than GA in terms of both average and standard error. The 3 clusters are recovered satisfactorily with MSCR about 3%, and MRI greater than 0.9. Both PCA and k-means give inferior results in all respects. Then the proposed procedure has been checked on a set of non linear MTS generated by 2 two-regime bivariate threshold models (VTAR). The VAR features have been computed of order 5 and DE performance is quite satisfactory as the cluster structure is exactly recovered while other algorithms show higher MSCR and lower MRI. This experiment shows that our method is able to deal with non linear as well with linear MTS. For all simulation experiments we may explain the better performance of DE based clustering of MTS VAR coefficients as in DE the feasible solutions are put in terms of real valued alleles. DE has been developed since its beginning to deal with real valued solutions while theory and practice of GAs mainly rely on binary encoding of the solutions. On the other hand, clustering MTS by using PCA reduces the size of the data set and saves computation time but it seems unable to distinguish between underlying models with an accuracy comparable to GAs or DE.

Table 1. Clustering results for 3-dimensional MTS data set

Algorithm	MSCR	MRI
DE	0.0272	0.9227
	(0.0181)	(0.0383)
GA	0.0332	0.9169
	(0.0527)	(0.0654)
PCA	0.1005	0.8698
	(0.1848)	(0.2082)
k-means	0.1563	0.7880
	(0.2063)	(0.2201)

The standard errors of the estimates are reported in parentheses.

5   The Australian Sign Language Data

This data consists of sample of Auslan signs. 27 examples of each of 95 Auslan signs were captured from a native signer using high-quality position trackers. Each vector time series has 15 components series while the length varies from 45 to 60 data points. The data have been downloaded from the UCI Machine Learning Repository (http://archive.ics.uci.edu/ml). As in [9] only 5 samples of each of the words 'alive', 'all', 'boy', 'cold' from the directory 'john4' have been used for illustration purpose and only the first 11 numeric variables are used. However we considered only the variables 1-4 to avoid singularity of the variance covariance matrices, as variables 5 and 6 have constant values equal to -1 and variables $7 - 11$ have values that are very similar each other. The DE, GA, PCA and k-means algorithms have been applied on the feature set which included the VAR weights computed as the estimates of the matrix coefficients of a VAR(2) model fitted to each one of the 20 4-dimensional MTS. On Table 2 results are evaluated according to the MSCR and the MRI. DE outperforms the remaining algorithms. The word 'cold' is correctly recovered by both DE and GA for all the 5 samples. The words 'alive' and 'all' are recognized for 4 out of 5 samples and the word 'boy' for 3 out of 5 samples by DE. The GA, on the other hand, displays some confusion between the words 'alive' and 'boy'. The procedure suggested by [9] too makes a specific error in mistaking one of the 'boy' signs as an 'all' sign.

Table 2. Clustering algorithms applied to 20 samples from the Auslan data set

Algorithm	MSCR	MRI
DE	0.2000	0.5136
GA	0.4500	0.2344
PCA	0.5000	0.2073
k-means	0.5500	0.1979

6   Conclusions

A method based on AR distance and DE has been proposed for clustering stationary MTS. Results from a simulation experiment seem quite satisfactory in comparison with GAs and PCA based clustering and the k-means algorithm and support the use of our procedure for clustering linear and non linear MTS. The execution time for a set of 300 MTS with 100 observations each is on the average 0.359 sec for feature extraction while, for the clustering procedure, 1.578 sec for DE, 3.094 sec for GA, 0.871 sec for PCA and 0.015 sec for k-means. So DE seems to attain a fair trade-off between speed and performance. An application to some data from the Auslan data set confirms the better performance of our procedure with respect to competing alternatives.

Acknowledgments. Research financially supported by 'Ministero dell'Istruzione, Universitá e Ricerca Scientifica', Italy, through grant 'Progetto di Interesse Nazionale 2007' PRIN2007.

References

1. Allefeld, C., Bialonski, S.: Detecting syncronization clusters in multivariate time series via coarse-graining of Markov chains. Tech. rep., arXiv:0707.2479v1 [physics.data-an] (July 17, 2007)
2. Bandyopadhyay, S., Baragona, R., Maulik, U.: Clustering multivariate time series by genetic multiobjective optimization. Metron 68, 161–183 (2010)
3. Bezdek, J.C., Pal, N.R.: Some new indexes of cluster validity. IEEE T. Sist. Man Cyb. – Part B: Cybernetics 28, 301–315 (1998)
4. Hubert, L., Arabie, P.: Comparing partitions. J. Classif. 2, 193–218 (1985)
5. Kakizawa, Y., Shumway, R.H., Taniguchi, M.: Discrimination and clustering for multivariate time series. J. Am. Stat. Assoc. 93, 328–340 (1998)
6. Kaufman, L., Rousseeuw, P.J.: Finding Groups in Data. Wiley, New York (2005)
7. Keogh, E., Kasetty, S.: On the need for time series data mining benchmarks: A survey and empirical demonstration. Data Min. Knowl. Disc. 7, 349–371 (2003)
8. Liao, T.W.: Clustering of time series data - a survey. Pattern Recogn. 38, 1857–1874 (2005)
9. Liao, T.W.: A clustering procedure for exploratory mining of vector time series. Pattern Recogn. 40, 2550–2562 (2007)
10. Maharaj, E.A.: Comparison and classification of stationary multivariate time series. Pattern Recogn. 32, 1129–1138 (1999)
11. Pakhira, M.K., Bandyopadhyay, S., Maulik, U.: Validity index for crisp and fuzzy clusters. Pattern Recogn. 37, 487–501 (2004)
12. Piccolo, D.: A distance measure for classifying ARIMA models. J. Time Ser. Anal. 11, 153–164 (1990)
13. Price, K.V., Storn, R., Lampinen, J.: Differential evolution, a practical approach to global optimization. Springer, Berlin (2005)
14. Singhal, A., Seborg, D.E.: Clustering multivariate time-series data. J. Chemometr. 19, 427–438 (2005)
15. Storn, R., Price, K.: Differential evolution - a simple and efficient heuristic for global optimization over continuous spaces. J. Global Optim. 11, 341–359 (1997)
16. Winker, P.: Optimization heuristics in econometrics: applications of threshold accepting. Wiley, Chichester (2001)
17. Yang, K., Shahabi, C.: A PCA-based similarity measure for multivariate time series. In: MMDB 2004: Proceedings of the 2nd ACM international workshop on Multimedia databases, pp. 65–74. ACM, New York (2004)

Neuro-fuzzy Methodology for Selecting Genes Mediating Lung Cancer

Rajat K. De[1] and Anupam Ghosh[2]

[1] Department of Machine Intelligence Unit,
Indian Statistical Institute, Kolkata, India
rajat@isical.ac.in
[2] Department of Computer Science and Engineering,
Netaji Subhash Engineering College, Kolkata, India
anupam.ghosh@rediffmail.com

Abstract. In this article, we describe neuro-fuzzy models under supervised and unsupervised learning for selecting a few possible genes mediating a disease. The methodology involves grouping of genes based on correlation coefficient using microarray gene expression patterns. The most important group is selected using existing neuro-fuzzy systems [1,2,3,4,5]. Finally, a few possible genes are selected from the most important group using the aforesaid neuro-fuzzy systems. The effectiveness of the methodology has been demonstrated on lung cancer gene expression data sets. The superiority of the methodology has been established with four existing gene selection methods like SAM, SNR, NA and BR. The enrichment of each gene ontology category of the resulting genes was calculated by its P-value. The genes output the low P-value, and indicate that they are biologically significant. According to the methodology, we have found more true positive genes than the other existing algorithms.

1 Introduction

Gene selection refers to the task of selecting some informative genes. The goal of gene selection algorithms is to filter out a small set of informative genes that best explains experimental variations. It is much cheaper to focus on a small number of informative genes, from the whole genome, that can differentially express in various diseases. Therefore, using effective gene selection methods, a small list of highly informative genes can be discovered from whole gene set [6], which have direct/indirect role in causing diseases. Thus, these genes can be utilized to construct the classifier for discriminating disease patterns. From data mining point of view, the task of gene selection can be viewed as that of feature selection that is widely used in data preprocessing stage [7,8]. However, gene selection, unlike feature selection in the area of machine learning literature, is characterized by the great difference between a huge number of genes and very small number of samples.

Several attempts have been made during the past several years for developing methodologies or using feature selection algorithms that select informative

S.O. Kuznetsov et al. (Eds.): PReMI 2011, LNCS 6744, pp. 388–393, 2011.

genes from microarray gene expression data. These genes improve the efficiency of the system in terms of disease prediction accuracy. The attempts include Noise sampling method [9], Bayesian regularization model (BR) [10,11], Significance Analysis of Microarray (SAM) [12], Signal-to-Noise Ratio (SNR) [13], Neighborhood analysis (NA) [9]. Most of the above methods are claimed to be capable of extracting a set of highly informative genes [6].

The present article is an attempt in this regard and provides neuro-fuzzy methodology for gene selection. The methodology involves grouping of genes using correlation coefficient, followed by selecting the most important group using the neuro-fuzzy models. Then the most informative genes are selected using neuro-fuzzy methods again. It is to be mentioned here that neuro-fuzzy methods have been developed in [1,2,3,4,5] for the purposed of feature selection. Neuro-fuzzy methodologies are applicable in data rich environment, i.e., if the number of samples is quite large compared to the number of features. However, in the present problem, the number of microarray measurements (samples) is quite low compared to the number of genes (features). In order to tackle this situation, we have proposed a way of generating more data so that neuro-fuzzy systems can be effectively used.

Incorporation of fuzzy set theory enables one to deal with uncertainties in different tasks of a pattern recognition system, arising from deficiency (e.g., vagueness,incompleteness, etc.) in information, in an efficient manner. Artificial Neural Networks, having the capability of fault tolerance, adaptivity, and generalization, and scope for massive parallelism, are widely used in dealing with learning and optimization tasks. In the area of pattern recognition, neuro-fuzzy approaches have been attempted mostly for designing classification/clustering/feature selection or extraction methodologies; the problem of gene selection has not been addressed.

The effectiveness of the proposed methodology, along with its superior performance over several of other methods, is demonstrated using one microarray gene expression data set dealing with human lung. The performance comparison is made using t-test and P-value (in terms of the number of enriched attributes).

2   Methodology

Here we describe the proposed methodology for gene selection. The task of gene selection has been considered as the task of feature selection in pattern recognition literature. Since the number of genes is very large compared to the number of measurements (samples), we have grouped the genes based on the correlation coefficient. Then the groups are evaluated using neuro-fuzzy systems under supervised (NFS) [2,3,4,5] and unsupervised (NFU) [1,3,4,5] learning, and the most important group is selected. Finally, important genes are selected from the most important group using NFS and NFU. For details of NFS and NFU, one may refer to [1,2,3,4,5].

Let us consider a set $\mathbf{X} = (\mathbf{x}_1, \mathbf{x}_2, \ldots, \mathbf{x}_n)$ of n genes for each of which p expression values in normal samples and q expression values in diseased samples are given. We now compute the correlation coefficient among these genes based on their expression values in normal samples. Thus the correlation coefficient r_{ij} between ith and jth genes is given by

$$r_{ij} = \frac{\sum_{k=1}^{p}(x_{i_k} - m_i) \times (x_{j_k} - m_j)}{(\sum_{i=1}^{p}(x_{i_k} - m_i)^2)^{1/2} \times (\sum_{i=1}^{p}(x_{j_k} - m_j)^2)^{1/2}} \tag{1}$$

Here m_i and m_j are the mean of expression values of ith and jth genes, respectively, over normal samples. The term x_{i_k} denotes kth expression value of ith gene. The correlation coefficient assumes values in the interval $[-1, 1]$. When $r_{ij} = -1 (+1)$, there is a strong negative (positive) correlation between ith and jth genes. Genes with high positive correlation are placed into the same group. The main idea of grouping is as follows. If a gene is strongly correlated with another gene, then the expression value of one of them is linearly dependent on that of the other. In that case, we may consider one of them as a representative gene and ignore the other.

We now find out the groups of genes in such a way that the genes in the same groups are strongly correlated. In order to do this, we have computed r_{ij} (Equation (1)) for each pair of genes. If $r_{ij} \geq 0.75$, then we place these genes in the same group. In this way, the first group of genes is created. Then we continue in the same way on the remaining genes, and the second group is created. We proceed in this way till all the genes are placed in one of the groups. Note that some singleton groups may also be formed by this process. Thus we have a few groups containing the genes. This process reduces the number of genes and hence reduces the curse of dimensionality. It is to be mentioned here that one may choose other high value (< 1) instead of 0.75 as the threshold.

We now use NFS or NFU [1,2,3,4,5], in the next step, for selecting the most important group. Since the number of measurements (samples) is quite low, we need to generate more data. This will be helpful to create a data rich environment where artificial neural networks are more effective. We proceed as follows.

After grouping, let us assume that we have K groups, viz., $G_1, G_2, \ldots, G_k, \ldots,$ G_K such that $|G_k| = n_k, \forall k$. Let us also assume that a member of G_k is represented by $\mathbf{g}_k = [g_{k1}, g_{k2}, \ldots, g_{kl}, \ldots, g_{kp}]^T$ such that and $\mathbf{g}_k = \mathbf{x}_j$, for some value of j. Then we choose one gene for each group and form a vector $\mathbf{v} = [v_1, v_2, \ldots, v_k, \ldots, v_K]^T$, where $v_k = g_{kl}$, lth sample value. That is, the components of vector $\mathbf{v}$ is the lth normal sample value of K genes that are drawn from each group G_k. Similarly, other $\mathbf{v}$s are formed by the other normal sample values and we have a total of p such vectors for each draw of K genes, one from each group. We thus create a set S of all such vectors from normal samples $\mathbf{v}$ so that the numbers of such vectors in S is

$$s = |S| = p \times \prod_{k=1}^{K} n_k \tag{2}$$

Similarly, another set S' of vectors $\mathbf{v}'$ is created from the diseased samples such that

$$s' = |S'| = q \times \prod_{k=1}^{K} n_k \qquad (3)$$

Now we have two sets, S and S' of vectors $\mathbf{v}$ and $\mathbf{v}'$ respectively. For NFS, we consider that normal and diseased samples form two classes, viz., *normal* and *diseased*. We take the number of input nodes as K, and the other nodes along which the architecture of the system is decided automatically [2,3,4,5]. In the case of NFU, the number of input nodes is $2K$, and the other nodes along which its architecture is decided automatically [1,3,4,5]. The first K nodes receive the vectors $\mathbf{v}$ as their inputs and second K nodes receive $\mathbf{v}'$. Thus the number of such presentations is $s \times s'$. After learning in both the systems, we get weight values representing importance of each group. Thus the most important group is selected for which the weight value is the highest.

Once the most important group is selected, only the genes in this group are considered. If the number of genes in the most important group is N ($N \ll n$), the numbers of input nodes in NFS and NFU are N and $2N$, respectively. The remaining parts of the architecture of both the systems are determined automatically. As in the case of selection of groups, the number of classes for NFS is 2. For NFU, the first N input nodes receive expression values of genes (in the most important group) of normal samples and the next N nodes receive that of diseased samples. Thus the number of presentations in NFU is $p \times q$. After learning, we get weight values corresponding to each gene representing its importance. Then we select a few important genes based on the connection weights of NFS or NFU.

3   Results

In this section, the effectiveness of the proposed methodology is demonstrated on human lung expression data [14]. A comparative analysis with SAM, SNR, BR, NA is also included.

We have found 6 groups, containing 1659, 1247, 1290, 741, 666, and 1526 genes respectively. The group containing 1659 genes has been selected as the most important group by both NFS and NFU. Applying NFS and NFU, we have found 30 and 32 genes respectively. Among these genes, we have found 22 genes that are present in both the results. Finally, we have selected 20 most important genes based on the connection weights of NFS and NFU. These selected genes are then evaluated for their role in causing lung cancer through computing the number of functional enrichments. We have performed t-test for the genes identified by other gene selection algorithms like SAM, SNR, NA and BR. But highly significant (99.9% significance level) genes like PFKP, TYMS, IARS, and HLA-B are not present in the first twenty selected genes by these methods. This result suggests that NFS and NFU are able to find more significant genes than the existing methods.

Table 1. Comparative results on number of attributes of various sets of genes

Dataset	Gene set	NFS	NFU	SAM	SNR	NA	BR
Lung	First 5	62	80	14	21	26	27
expression	First 10	75	76	13	9	15	21
Data	First 15	80	82	30	14	16	16
	First 20	82	75	28	13	15	16

In order to validate the results statistically, we have applied t-test on the genes identified by NFS, NFU, SAM, SNR, NA and BR. Here we have identified some important genes like CALCA (4.02), PFKP (5.78), TYMS (3.98), IGFBP3 (6.98), IARS (5.98), HBB (7.08), HLA-B (5.42), SFTPA2 (6.89), and TNF (4.23). The number in the bracket indicates t-value corresponding to the gene. The t-value of these set of genes exceeds the value for $p = 0.001$. It indicates that these set of genes are highly significant (99.9% level of significance). Similarly, genes like IGHG3 (2.67), PRKACA (2.89), SORT1 (2.76), MEN1 (3.15), SFTPA1 (2.92) and IGHM (3.25) exceeds the t-value for $p = 0.01$. This means that these genes are significant at the level of 99%. Likewise, RPLP0 (2.12), SMCIL1 (2.07), MGP (2.31), RNASE1 (2.43), SFTPC (2.37), and HLA-DRA (2.27) genes are important at the level of 95% significance.

In our study, the enrichment of each GO category [15] for each of the genes has been calculated by its P-value. A low P-value indicates that the genes belonging to the enriched functional categories are biologically significant. Here only functional categories with $P - value < 5.0 \times 10^{-5}$ are considered. We have made comparative study, with other methods, viz., SAM, SNR, NA, BR in terms of their ability to identify functionally enriched genes. Table 1 shows the number of functionally enriched attributes corresponding to these methods for different sets of genes. It is found that NFS and NFU performed the best. These results show that the proposed methodology has been able to select more important genes responsible for mediating a disease than the other methods considered here.

4   Conclusions

In this article, we have provided a methodology based on neuro-fuzzy models for the selection of genes whose over/under expression may cause diseases. The methodology, first of all, finds various groups of genes based on correlation values. This is followed by determining the most important group. The genes in this groups are evaluated using NFS and NFU. This results in important genes is mediating development of a particular disease. The effectiveness of the methodology is demonstrated on various gene expression data sets where each gene is treated as a feature. The most important genes obtained by the methodology are also verified using their P-values [15]. The superior performance of the methodology compared to some existing ones have been shown. The results are verified using t-test, some existing results.

References

1. Pal, S.K., De, R.K., Basak, J.: Unsupervised feature evaluation: A neuro-fuzzy approach. IEEE Trans. Neural Networks 11, 366–376 (2000)
2. De, R.K., Basak, J., Pal, S.K.: Neuro-fuzzy feature evaluation with theoretical analysis. Neural Networks 12, 1429–1455 (1999)
3. Basak, J., De, R.K., Pal, S.K.: Fuzzy feature evaluation index and connectionist realization-ii: Theoretical analysis. Information Sciences 111, 1–17 (1998)
4. Basak, J., De, R.K., Pal, S.K.: Unsupervised feature selection using neuro-fuzzy approach. Pattern Recognition Letters 19, 997–1006 (1998)
5. Pal, S.K., Basak, J., De, R.K.: Fuzzy feature evaluation index and connectionist realization. Information Sciences 105, 173–188 (1998)
6. Bezdek, J., Pal, S.K.: Fuzzy models for pattern recognition. IEEE Press, New York (1992)
7. Kraaijveld, M.A., Mao, J., Jain, A.K.: A nonlinear projection method based on kohonen topology preserving maps. IEEE Trans. Neural Networks 6, 548–559 (1995)
8. Rubner, J., Tavan, P.: A self-organizing network for principal component analysis. Europhys. Lett 10, 693–698 (1989)
9. Golub, T.R., Slonim, T.K., Tamayo, P., Huard, C., Gaasenbeek, M., Mesirov, J.P., Coller, H., Downing, J.R., Caliguri, M.A., Bloomeld, C.D., Lander, E.S.: Molecular classification of cancer: class discovery and class prediction by gene expression monitoring. Science 286, 531–537 (1999)
10. Shevade, S.K., Keerthi, S.S.: A simple and efficient algorithm for gene selection using sparse logistic regression. Bioinformatics 19, 2246–2253 (2003)
11. Cawley, G.C., Talbot, N.L.C.: Gene selection in cancer classification using sparse logistic regression with bayesian regularization. Bioinformatics 22, 2348–2355 (2006)
12. Goh, L., Song, Q., Kasabov, N.: A novel feature selection method to improve classification of gene expression data. In: APBC (2004)
13. Tusher, V.G., Tibshirani, R., Chu, G.: Significance analysis of microarrays applied to the ionizing radiation response. Proc. Natl. Acad. Sci. USA 98 (2001)
14. Beer, G.D., et al.: Gene-expression profilespredict survival of patients with lung adenocarcinoma. Nature Medicine 8, 816–823 (2002)
15. Kim, D.W., Lee, K.H., Lee, D.: Detecting clusters of different geometrical shapes in microarray gene expression data. Bioinformatics 21, 1927–1934 (2005)

A Methodology for Handling a New Kind of Outliers Present in Gene Expression Patterns

Anindya Bhattacharya[1] and Rajat K. De[2,*]

[1] Department of Computer Science and Engineering,
Netaji Subhash Engineering College, Kolkata 700152, India
[2] Machine Intelligence Unit, Indian Statistical Institute, Kolkata 700108, India

Abstract. Performance of clustering algorithms is largely dependent on selected similarity measure. Efficiency in handling outliers is a major contributor to the effectiveness of a similarity measure. In the present work, we discuss the problem of handling outliers with different existing similarity measures, and introduce the concepts of a new kind of outliers present in gene expression patterns. We formulate a new similarity, incorporated in Euclidean distance and Pearson correlation coefficient, and then use them in various clustering algorithms to group different gene expression profiles. Assessment of the results are done by using functional annotation. Different existing similarity measures in their traditional form are also used with clustering algorithms for performance comparisons. The results suggest that the new similarity improves performance, in terms of finding biologically relevant groups of genes, of all the considered clustering algorithms.

1 Introduction

Clustering algorithm involves measuring similarity between a pair of objects. Some standard similarity measures used in various clustering algorithms include Euclidean distance, various correlation coefficients, Mahalanabis distance. Choice of a similarity measure plays an important role in the performance of a clustering algorithm.

If the objects in a dataset are evenly distributed over the space, the aforesaid similarity measures would be effective. On the other hand, if some of objects due to noise or other factors, called outliers, are included in a dataset, these similarity measures may not lead to good performance of the clustering algorithms. They may be biased towards these outliers. There exist various methods for handling such outliers. They include, among others, statistical approach [1]-[3], distance-based approach, clustering-based approach [4]-[6], density-based local outlier detection approach [7,5] and deviation-based approach [8].

If the expression value(s) of a single (both) gene(s) corresponding to a sample differ much from its (their) mean expression value(s) of the other samples, then the expression value(s) for this(ese) sample(s) differ drastically for the pair of

---

* Corresponding author.

S.O. Kuznetsov et al. (Eds.): PReMI 2011, LNCS 6744, pp. 394–399, 2011.

genes. This gives rise to the notion of a different kind of outlier which is introduced here. That is, the sample is an outlier with respect to the gene pair. Distance/similarity measures used by different clustering algorithms are unable to treat an outlier sample and a normal sample differently. All the samples contribute equally during the measurement of distance/similarity.

In order to improve performance of the various similarity measures (including Euclidean distance and Pearson correlation coefficient), with respect to better ability of handling outliers, we introduce the concept of assigning weight values to samples. Instead of using a sample value for the similarity measure, we multiply a weight value with expression value of a sample and then use the resulting value. Weight values are determined in such a way that possible outliers are assigned smaller weight values (*i.e.*, nearly equal to zero). Weight values for non outliers are large, and are nearly equal to 'one'. With this new similarity, Euclidean distance or Pearson correlation coefficient involves low contribution of outlier samples and high contribution of non outlier samples.

In order to incorporate this varying contribution, we assign a weight value to gene expression samples. Any similarity measure that computes pair wise distance similarity, can use the weight assignment technique for better handling the outliers. For comparison, Euclidean distance with weight (WD) and without weight (D), Pearson correlation coefficient with weight ($WCorr$) and without weight ($Corr$), Spearman rank-order correlation coefficient ($RankCorr$) and Jackknife correlation coefficient ($JackCorr$) are used with clustering algorithms K-means [9,8,10], DCCA [11] and ACCA [12]. All the instances of these algorithms are applied to different gene expression datasets and performances are assessed.

2   A New Kind of Outlier

Due to error or other factors in microarray measurements, the expression profiles for a pair of genes may be similar over all the samples except for a few. For these few samples, expression values of the same pair of genes may differ drastically from the other samples. In other words, the expression value(s) of a single (both) gene(s) corresponding to the sample differ much from its (their) mean expression value(s) over the other samples. The sample(s) for which the expression values differ drastically for the pair of genes, give rise to the notion of a different kind of outlier. That is, the sample is an outlier with respect to the gene pair. It may be mentioned here that this outlier is different from the notion of outliers already available in literature [8]. In the later case, the gene as a whole needs to be treated as an outlier with respect to a group of genes, in contrary to the former one where a sample is considered as an outlier corresponding to a gene pair. This situation affects clustering if we consider similarity computation based on expression values only. We introduce a novel methodology to take care of the effect of such outliers.

3   A Methodology for Handling a New Kind of Outliers

Let us consider a set of n genes $X = \{g_1, g_2, \ldots, g_n\}$, for each of which m expression values are given. Let us also consider a set of m microarray experiments/samples (measurements) $Y = \{e_1, e_2, \ldots, e_m\}$. For each experiment, we have n expression values corresponding to n genes in X. That is, for each gene g_i, there is an m-dimensional vector $\mathbf{x}_i$, where x_{il} is the expression value of g_i in l^{th} experiment e_l. Similarity between gene pair (g_i, g_j) may be computed using Euclidean distance $D(\mathbf{x}_i, \mathbf{x}_j)$ or Pearson correlation coefficient $Corr(\mathbf{x}_i, \mathbf{x}_j)$, and are defined, respectively, as

$$D(\mathbf{x}_i, \mathbf{x}_j) = \sqrt{\sum_{l=1}^{m} (x_{il} - x_{jl})^2} \tag{1}$$

and

$$Corr(\mathbf{x}_i, \mathbf{x}_j) = \frac{\sum_{l=1}^{m} (x_{il} - \bar{x}_i)(x_{jl} - \bar{x}_j)}{\sqrt{\sum_{l=1}^{m} (x_{il} - \bar{x}_i)^2 \sum_{l=1}^{m} (x_{jl} - \bar{x}_j)^2}}. \tag{2}$$

Here $\bar{x}_i$ and $\bar{x}_j$ are mean values over m expression values of ith and j^{th} genes respectively.

If l^{th} expression values of a co-expressed, co-regulated gene pair (g_i, g_j), corresponding to an experiment e_l, are such that the sample is an outlier with respect to gene pair (g_i, g_j), both Equations 1 and 2 may be biased towards this outlier. That is, if we consider Equation 2 for measuring similarity, the value should ideally be closed to 1 for a pair of co-regulated genes. Due to this outlier, the correlation value will differ much from 1. In order to reduce this type of misleading contribution of outlier, we introduce the notion of weighting coefficient w_{lij} corresponding to l^{th} expression value and gene pair (g_i, g_j), for all l, i, j.

We determine the weight values so as to reduce the effect of such outliers by assigning lower weight values corresponding to the outlier samples of gene pair (g_i, g_j) and a higher weight values to the other samples. In other words, higher the difference in l^{th} expression values of the genes in the pair (g_i, g_j) from their means, lower is the value of the weight w_{lij}. Considering Euclidean distance for computing difference in l^{th} expression values of both the genes g_i and g_j from their means, we have

$$D_{ijl} = \sqrt{(t_{il} - \bar{t}_i)^2 + (t_{jl} - \bar{t}_j)^2}, \tag{3}$$

where t_{il} and t_{jl} are normalized expression values in $[0, 1]$ of x_{il} and x_{jl} respectively. Similarly, $\bar{t}_i$ and $\bar{t}_j$ are mean of normalized expression values, computed over all the samples, of gene g_i and g_j respectively. Here we have considered normalized expression values in Equation 3, for keeping D_{ijl} bounded to

$\sqrt{2}$ ($\sqrt{(1-0)^2 + (0-1)^2} = \sqrt{2}$). For an outlier sample, measured value of D_{ijl} should be high. Weight value w_{lij} for an outlier sample e_l corresponding to a pair of gene (g_i, g_j) should be low. Thus relationship between D_{ijl} and w_{lij} should be such that, increase in D_{ijl} should cause decrease in w_{lij} and vice versa.

In order to reflect such relationship between D_{ijl} and w_{lij}, here we consider exponential function to define weight w_{lij} of a sample e_l corresponding to a pair of gene (g_i, g_j). Thus

$$w_{lij} = e^{-\alpha \times D_{ijl}}, \tag{4}$$

where $\alpha \geq 1$ is a constant. Here the value of α should be such that w_{lij} is nearly equal to zero for $D_{ijl} = \sqrt{2}$. On the other hand, w_{lij} should tend to one for a non-outlier sample. In fact this happens as D_{ijl} tends to zero for a non-outlier sample.

Thus the weight function incorporates w_{lij}, for each lth experiment, in Equations 1 and 2. In these Equations, x_{il} and x_{jl} are replaced by $x_{ijl}^{(w)} = w_{lij} \times x_{il}$ and $x_{jil}^{(w)} = w_{lij} \times x_{jl}$ respectively. Similarly, mean values $\bar{x}_i$ and $\bar{x}_j$, in Equation 2, are replaced by $\bar{x}_{ijl}^{(w)} = \frac{1}{m} \sum_{l=1}^{m} w_{lij} \times x_{il}$ and $\bar{x}_{jil}^{(w)} = \frac{1}{m} \sum_{l=1}^{m} w_{lij} \times x_{jl}$ respectively. It is to be mentioned here that $\bar{x}_{ijl}^{(w)} \neq \bar{x}_{jil}^{(w)}$, although both of them involved the same w_{lij}s. It is further to be noted that the terms $t_{il}, t_{jl}, \bar{t}_i$ and $\bar{t}_j$ in Equation 3 are computed using x_{il}, x_{jl} only. Thus we get distance $WD(\mathbf{x}_i, \mathbf{x}_j)$ and correlation coefficient $WCorr(\mathbf{x}_i, \mathbf{x}_j)$ between a gene pair (g_i, g_j), based on Euclidian distance and Pearson correlation coefficient respectively.

Now the problem remains with the estimation of α-value in Equation 4. This is determined form a plot of WD or $WCorr$ for different pairs of genes with respect to α. From this plot, we have chosen α values at which similarity values (WD or $WCorr$) get saturated.

4   Results

The effectiveness of the weight assignment method along with comparative analysis with the aforesaid similarity measures is demonstrated with K-means [9,8,10], DCCA [11] and ACCA [12] clustering algorithms using five gene expression datasets of Yeast. Datasets are described in Table 1. The performance of all the algorithms is also demonstrated using P-value on functional annotation.

For gene expression data analysis, P-value of GO functional category/ attribute represents the probability of observing at least a given number of genes, in a cluster, from a specific GO functional category/attribute. A specific GO functional category is said to be "enriched" if the corresponding P-value is less than a predefined threshold value. A low P-value indicates that the genes belonging to the enriched functional categories are biologically significant in the corresponding clusters. In the present work, only attributes with P-value $< 1.0 \times 10^{-7}$ are reported as enriched. A clustering solution is considered to be more reliable if the number of enriched functional attributes obtained from a cluster is high. In order to compare the performance of different clustering

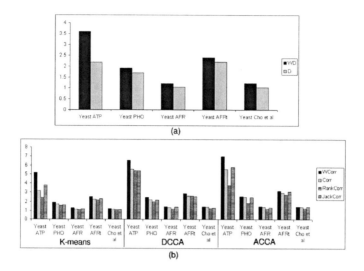

Fig. 1. Average number of functionally enriched attributes per cluster. (a) K-means algorithm with WD and D, (b) K-means, DCCA and ACCA with $WCorr$, $Corr$, $RankCorr$ and $JackCorr$.

algorithms for a microarray gene expression dataset, we can use average number of functionally enriched attributes found per cluster.

Fig. 1 shows that the performance of K-means clustering algorithm with WD (Euclidean distance with weight) is much larger compared to K-means algorithm with D (Euclidean distance but without weight) for all the five datasets. Similarly, Fig. 1 provides the comparative analysis of the clustering algorithms with four similarity measures and shows that $WCorr$ (Pearson correlation coefficient with weight) provides higher number of enriched attributes compared to algorithms with all the other correlation based measures for all the five datasets.

Table 1. Short description of the datasets considered

Name (Organism)	Number of genes	Number of samples
Yeast ATP (Yeast)	6215	3
Yeast PHO (Yeast)	6013	8
Yeast AFR (Yeast)	6184	8
Yeast AFRt (Yeast)	6190	7
Yeast Cho et al. (Yeast)	6457	17

5   Conclusions

Here we have introduced the concepts of a new kind of outlier and a methodology to handle such outliers. New outliers are the samples with respect to a gene pair, for which sample values show large difference from the other samples corresponding to the gene pair. Incorporation of the notion of weight helps in dealing with such outliers while measuring similarity between a pair of gene.

The results suggest that assignment of weight with a similarity measure improves the performance of clustering algorithms in obtaining more biologically significant clusters. The main advantage of weight assignment method is that it is able to deal with outliers without deleting them. Weight assignment method described here is a general framework. Thus it can be used with any distance based similarity measure without changing the basic formulation of that similarity measure.

References

1. Hawkins, D.: Identification of Outliers. Chapman and Hall, London (1980)
2. Rousseeuw, P., Leory, A.: Robust Regression and Outlier Detection. Wiley, New York (1987)
3. Barnett, V., Lewis, T.: Outliers in Statistical Data. Wiley, New York (1994)
4. Kaufman, L., Rousseeuw, P.J.: Finding Groups in Data: An Introduction to Cluster Analysis. Wiley, New York (1990)
5. Shekhar, S., Chawla, S.: A Tour of Spatial Databases. Prentice-Hall, New Jersey (2002)
6. Hu, T., Sung, S.Y.: Detecting pattern-based outliers. Pattern Recognition Letters 24, 3059–3068 (2003)
7. Schiffman, S.S., Reynolds, M.L., Young, F.W.: Introduction to Multidimensional Scaling: Theory, Methods and Applications. Academic Press, New York (1981)
8. Han, J., Kamber, M.: Data Mining: Concepts and Techniques. Morgan Kaufmann, San Francisco (2001)
9. Jain, A.K., Dubes, R.C.: Algorithms for Clustering Data. Prentice-Hall, New Jersey (1988)
10. Tavazoie, S., Hughes, J.D., Campbell, M.J., Cho, R.J., Church, G.M.: Systematic determination of genetic network architecture. Nature Genetics 22, 281–285 (1999)
11. Bhattacharya, A., De, R.K.: Divisive correlation clustering algorithm (DCCA) for grouping of genes: Detecting varying patterns in expression profiles. Bioinformatics 24, 1359–1366 (2008)
12. Bhattacharya, A., De, R.K.: Average correlation clustering algorithm (ACCA) for grouping of co-regulated genes with similar pattern of variation in their expression values. Journal of Biomedical Informatics 43, 560–568 (2010)

Developmental Trend Derived from Modules of Wnt Signaling Pathways

Losiana Nayak and Rajat K. De

Machine Intelligence Unit, Indian Statistical Institute
203 B. T. Road, Kolkata - 700108, India
{losiana_t,rajat}@isical.ac.in
http://www.isical.ac.in/~{losiana_t,rajat}

Abstract. In this paper, we deal with the idea of creating a developmental trend from Wnt signaling pathways of different species. Wnt signaling pathway is involved in many crucial biological processes including from early embryonic development to stem cell management at later stages. The pathway varies in topology and size for each species that gets reflected in its modules. A comparison among species-specific pathways, taking into account the modules and pathway structure (in terms of nodes and edges) will throw light on crucial turning points in the development of Wnt signaling pathway. Hence, 31 species-specific Wnt signaling pathways have been modularized by the Modularization algorithm already developed by the authors. The modules were compared among themselves to find the trend of development. The trend established conserved modules among these pathways.

Keywords: Modularization algorithm, Evolution, Phylogenetic tree construction, Computational Phylogenetics.

1 Introduction

In biological terms, a signal transduction pathway, is a set of established genes and related factors, which operate in synchronous manner to create cascades of reactions, ultimately generating a response to stimuli *in vivo*. From graph theoretical point of view, these genes and related factors can be considered as nodes and the interactions among them as edges of a network. A pathway conceived in such a way is open to all kind of network analysis paradigms. Network comparison (by alignment) to uncover biological functions and phylogeny [1] is one of them. Networks derived from biological pathways (gene regulatory, metabolic, signal transduction, protein-protein interaction networks) can be aligned by size of the network, sequence similarity of the genes/proteins, functional similarity of the enzymes/proteins and presence of common topological structures (graphlets) among others. One or all of these factors are considered while creating a tree from a set of biological networks. In addition to such factors, we add another factor named 'modules' [2]. Modules throw light on operational sophistication of a network. It is dependent on two other parameters, *viz.*, size (nodes) and topology (interactions). A tree generated by taking these three linked parameters can shed enough light on subtle changes of the network among the species,

S.O. Kuznetsov et al. (Eds.): PReMI 2011, LNCS 6744, pp. 400–405, 2011.

if not all. Here, these ideas were implemented for creating a tree from a set of species-specific Wnt signaling pathways.

Table 1. The list of species taken from KEGG/ PATHWAY database. The database uses a unique three letter code, viz., 'hsa' for *H. sapiens* (human) for each species along with their biological and common names (wherever applicable).

Sl. No.	Species Name	Common Name	KEGG Code
01	*H. sapiens*	Human	hsa
02	*M. musculus*	Mouse	mmu
03	*R. norvegicus*	Rat	rno
04	*B. taurus*	Cow	bta
05	*C. familiaris*	Dog	cfa
06	*P. troglodytes*	Chimpanzee	ptr
07	*M. mulatta*	Rhesus Monkey	mcc
08	*M. domestica*	Opossum	mdo
09	*G. gallus*	Chicken	gga
10	*D. rerio*	Zebrafish	dre
11	*X. laevis*	African clawed frog	xla
12	*S. purpuratus*	Purple sea urchin	spu
13	*X. tropicalis*	Western clawed frog	xtr
14	*D. melanogaster*	Fruitfly	dme
15	*E. caballus*	Horse	ecb
16	*N. vectensis*	Sea anemone	nve
17	*A. mellifera*	Honey bee	ame
18	*D. pseudoobscura pseudoobscura*	-	dpo
19	*T. castaneum*	Red flour beetle	tca
20	*A. aegypti*	Yellow fever mosquito	aag
21	*O. anatinus*	Platypus	oaa
22	*C. elegans*	Nematode	cel
23	*A. gambiae*	Mosquito	aga
24	*S. scrofa*	Pig	ssc
25	*B. floridae*	Florida lancelet	bfo
26	*C. intestinalis*	Sea squirt	cin
27	*D. ananassae*	-	dan
28	*B. malayi*	Filaria	bmy
29	*A. pisum*	Pea aphid	api
30	*T. adhaerens*	-	tad
31	*C. briggsae*	-	cbr

Wnt molecules are secreted cysteine-rich, lipid-modified glycoproteins. They bind to Frizzled seven-transmembrane-span receptors (FZDs) along with co-receptor LRPs (Lipoprotein Receptor-related Proteins) and initiate the downstream steps. These protein-protein and protein-DNA interactions altogether are known as Wnt signaling pathway [3]. Wnt signaling pathway is involved in regulation of cell fate determination, proliferation, differentiation, migration and apoptosis [4]. It enables cells to influence behavior of their neighboring cells during development [5]. In matured organisms, Wnts are implicated in maintaining stem cell-like fates in the intestinal epithelium [6], skin [7] and hematopoietic cells [8].

In this article, we have created modules from Wnt signaling pathways of 31 different species. By comparing these modules, a distance score is established between each pair of species and such scores were utilized in creating a tree. The tree reflects the course of development of Wnt signaling pathway among the taken set of species along with detection of conserved modules.

2 Methodology

Species-specific Wnt signaling pathways of KEGG/ Pathway database [9] were taken as data. The database is maintained by the Kanehisa Laboratories, Bioinformatics Center, Kyoto University and the Human Genome Center, University of Tokyo. It is a collection of manually drawn pathway maps, whose XML data files along with KGML and PNG diagrams are publicly accessible. Detail information of these species is given in Table 1. The database uses a unique three letter code for each species along with their biological and common names (wherever applicable), *viz.*, 'hsa' for *H. sapiens* (human). These three letter codes are used extensively in this manuscript.

The species-specific pathways were modularized by the algorithm developed by Nayak et al., 2007 [2]. The algorithm creates a set of modules, for each value of the user defined parameter c. The parameter decides whether a node belongs to a particular module or not. A node gets excluded from a module, if it has more than c relations that lie outside the module boundary. In general, a range of c-value is fixed for running the modularization algorithm. The lowest possible c-value is the lowest total degree of a node, while the upper limit of c-value is the highest total degree of a node found in a considered network. The task is to choose the ideal c-value that can create best partitions. *Modus operandi* of the algorithm can be followed by going through the pseudocode (Algorithm 1). Implementation of the algorithm is done in C. Wnt signaling pathways of the above-mentioned species were subjected to modularization for $c=3$ (as meaningful modules have been found from Wnt signaling pathway of hsa for the same c-value). We are getting 2 to 8 modules for each species that vary in their size (number of nodes present in the module) as shown in Table 2. It gives module details (number of connected nodes, relations and modules) of all the considered pathways.

Algorithm 1. [Pseudocode for Modularization Algorithm]

Ensure: Node Pool (universal set of connected nodes) is not empty
  FOR Creating modules from a network DO
  repeat
    FOR Building a complete module DO
    Find start/central node (the node with maximum total degree); exclude it from the node pool
    Include the central node's neighbors in the module
    repeat
      FOR Extending the module DO
      Check the total relation of added nodes
      IF all the relations are lying in the modules THEN
      The node is a permanent member of the module; exclude it from the node pool
      IF Number of relations lying outside the module is $>c$ THEN
      Exclude it from the module; decrease its associated nodes' total degree by one
      IF Number of relations lying outside the module is $<=c$ THEN
      Include further neighbors of the added nodes in the module
    until All the relations of each node present in the module are accounted for
  until Node pool is Empty

The tree of development was created by taking into account distance between three factors, *i.e.*, the number of connected nodes, the number of relations and the number of modules. For example, distance between hsa and spu is $(|60 - 39|) + (|70 - 45|) + (|8 - 6|)/3 = 16$. Average distance (if the mod value is found to be non-zero) between these three parameters of different species were used to create a distance matrix. A tree (Figure 1) was constructed using this matrix by Phylip package (Version 3.6) [10].

3   Results and Discussion

In this section, we have compared modules of 31 different species (aag, aga, ame, api, bfo, bmy, bta, cbr, cel, cin, cfa, dan, dme, dpo, dre, ecb, gga, hsa, mcc, mdo, mmu, nve, oaa, ptr, rno, ssc, spu, tad, tca, xla and xtr). Module details are given in Table 2.

Table 2. Module information of species-specific Wnt signaling pathways. [sp.: three lettered species code, n: number of connected nodes in a species-specific pathway; r: number of relations present the connected component of a species-specific pathway; t: total number of modules created from a species-specific pathway]. The modules have been created for $c=3$. Each module's size in terms of nodes is given with it in parentheses. The table throws light on the developmental trend of Wnt signaling pathways among the taken set of species.

sp.	n	r	t	WNT	(DVL)1	Axin	β-catenin	TCF	p53	(DVL)2	PLC
hsa	60	70	8	WNT [8]	(DVL)1 [7]	Axin [4]	β-catenin [8]	TCF [14]	p53 [2]	(DVL)2 [10]	PLC [7]
mmu	60	70	8	WNT [8]	(DVL)1 [7]	Axin [4]	β-catenin [8]	TCF [14]	p53 [2]	(DVL)2 [10]	PLC [7]
rno	59	69	8	WNT [7]	(DVL)1 [7]	Axin [4]	β-catenin [8]	TCF [14]	p53 [2]	(DVL)2 [10]	PLC [7]
bta	58	68	8	WNT [7]	(DVL)1 [6]	Axin [4]	β-catenin [8]	TCF [14]	P53 [2]	(DVL)2 [10]	PLC [7]
cfa	58	68	8	WNT [8]	(DVL)1 [7]	Axin [4]	β-catenin [7]	TCF [13]	p53 [2]	(DVL)2 [10]	PLC [7]
ptr	58	67	8	WNT [8]	(DVL)1 [7]	Axin [4]	β-catenin [8]	TCF [13]	p53 [2]	(DVL)2 [10]	PLC [6]
mcc	55	63	8	WNT [7]	(DVL)1 [6]	Axin [4]	β-catenin [8]	TCF [13]	p53 [2]	(DVL)2 [8]	PLC [7]
mdo	54	64	7	WNT [8]	(DVL)1 [7]	Axin[2]	β-catenin [9]	TCF [11]	-	(DVL)2 [10]	PLC [7]
gga	54	63	8	WNT [7]	(DVL)1 [6]	Axin [3]	β-catenin [8]	TCF [11]	p53 [2]	(DVL)2 [10]	PLC [7]
dre	52	60	7	WNT [8]	-	Axin [4]	β-catenin [7]	TCF [13]	p53 [2]	(DVL)2 [11]	PLC [7]
xla	43	45	6	WNT [7]	-	-	β-catenin [8]	TCF [11]	p53 [2]	(DVL)2 [8]	PLC [7]
spu	39	45	6	-	(DVL)1 [7]	Axin [2]	β-catenin [5]	TCF [10]	-	(DVL)2 [9]	PLC [6]
xtr	37	36	6	WNT [3]	-	-	β-catenin [7]	TCF [6]	p53 [2]	(DVL)2 [12]	PLC [7]
dme	36	42	7	WNT [6]	(DVL)1 [5]	Axin [2]	β-catenin [6]	TAK1 [2]	-	(DVL)2 [9]	PLC [6]
ecb	36	38	7	(Frizzled)1 [5]	(DVL)1 [3]	-	β-catenin [9]	TAK1 [2]	p53 [2]	(DVL)2 [8]	PLC [7]
nve	32	33	6	(Frizzled)1 [5]	-	Axin [5]	β-catenin [6]	TAK1 [2]	-	(DVL)2 [7]	PLC [7]
ame	30	32	5	-	(DVL)1 [4]	-	β-catenin [9]	TAK1 [2]	-	(DVL)2 [8]	PLC [7]
dpo	28	30	4	(Frizzled)1 [8]	-	-	β-catenin [7]	-	-	(DVL)2 [8]	PLC [5]
tca	26	27	4	(Frizzled)1 [7]	-	-	β-catenin [7]	-	-	(DVL)2 [6]	PLC [6]
aag	24	22	4	(Frizzled)1 [4]	-	-	β-catenin [4]	-	-	(DVL)2 [10]	PLC [6]
oaa	22	22	4	WNT [2]	-	-	β-catenin [7]	-	-	(DVL)2 [8]	PLC [5]
cel	22	20	3	-	-	-	β-catenin [10]	-	-	RhoA [6]	PLC [6]
aga	20	18	3	(Frizzled)1 [11]	-	-	β-catenin [4]	-	-	-	PLC [5]
ssc	19	16	4	FRP [2]	-	-	β-catenin [5]	TCF [7]	-	-	PLC [5]
bfo	18	16	3	-	-	-	β-catenin [9]	-	-	(DVL)2 [5]	PLC [4]
cin	17	14	3	-	(DVL)1 [7]	-	-	-	-	(DVL)2 [5]	PLC [5]
dan	16	12	4	-	(DVL)1 [2]	-	β-catenin [4]	-	-	(DVL)2 [5]	PLC [5]
bmy	13	11	3	-	(DVL)1 [4]	-	-	-	-	(DVL)2 [5]	PLC [4]
api	13	10	3	-	(DVL)1 [4]	-	-	-	-	(DVL)2 [5]	PLC [4]
tad	6	4	2	-	-	-	-	-	-	Rac [2]	PLC [4]
cbr	4	3	1	-	(DVL)1 [4]	-	-	-	-	-	-

Comparison of the modules brought forward their functional conservation among the taken species. Modules Wnt and $\beta-catenin$ were found to be conserved in 9 species (hsa, mmu, rno, bta, cfa, ptr, mcc, mdo and gga). Module TCF was found to be conserved in 5 species (hsa, mmu, rno, bta and cfa). Module $Tp53$ was observed in altogether 12 species (hsa, mmu, rno, bta, cfa, ptr, mcc, gga, dre, xla, xtr and ecb) and it was conserved by size and topology in all these species. Module $(DVL)2$ was conserved in 11 species (hsa, mmu, rno, bta, cfa, ptr, mdo, gga, dre, spu and dme) and module PLC turned out to be the most conserved module, found in a maximum number of 17 species (hsa, mmu, rno, bta, cfa, ptr, mcc, mdo, gga, dre, xla, spu, xtr, dme, ecb, nve and ame).

Figure 1 provides an incidental peek of Wnt signaling pathway development in different species. The tree is analyzed by considering taxonomy of the taken

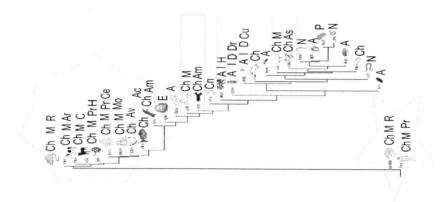

Fig. 1. Tree created from 31 species-specific Wnt signaling pathways. The species, belonging to the same Phylum, Class, Order and Family, which show proximity among them, are marked separately. [A: Phylum Arthropoda, Ch: Phylum Chordata, Cn: Phylum Cnidaria, E: Phylum Echinodermata, N: Phylum Nematoda, P: Phylum Placozoa, Ac: Class Actinopterygii, Am: Class Amphibia, As: Class Ascidiacea, Av: Class Aves, I: Class Insecta, M: Class Mammalia, Ar: Order Artiodactyla, C: Order Carnivora, D: Order Diptera, H: Order Hymenoptera, Mo: Order Monotremata, Pr: Order Primates, R: Order Rodentia, Ce: Family Cercopithecidae, Cu: Family Culicidae, Dr: Family Drosophilidae, H: Family Hominidae].

species. Many species of Phylum Chordata [(hsa, mmu, rno, bta cfa, ptr, mcc, mdo, gga, dre and xla), (ecb and xtr) and (ssc and cin)] and some species of Phylum Arthropoda (amc, dpo and aag) are found to be placed closer to each other. Further closeness among the Chordates is found as we proceed towards Class specifications. All of them belong to Class Mammalia with exception of five species [gga: Class Aves, dre: Class Actinopterygii, (xla and xtr): Class Amphibia and cin: Class Ascidiacea]. These species show gradual divergence. All the three Arthropods belong to Class Insecta. Among the closely placed Mammalians, three species (hsa, ptr and mcc) belong to Order Primates and two species (mmu and rno) to Order Rodentia. Two species of Class Insecta (dpo and aag) belong to Order Diptera. These species are found in proximity of each other in the tree, indicating towards a further level of conservation in development. Further specification in terms of Family throws some light on variation in development among these species. The species, belonging to the same Phylum, Class, Order and Family, which show proximity in the tree, are marked separately (Figure 1).

4   Conclusions

This article emphasizes on deriving the developmental trend from modules of species-specific Wnt signaling pathways. Here, we have done a comparative study among 31 species-specific set of modules. Module PLC is the most conserved module, found in a maximum number of 17 species. A developmental trend was established among the modules (created by the modularization algorithm) of these 31 species. This study established that hsa and mmu have the most developed Wnt signaling pathway, followed by several species like rno, bta, mcc among others. The species having the least developed Wnt signaling pathway is cbr. It possesses a single rudimentary module $(DVL)1$. The developmental tree displays conservation at Class level and gradual divergence as we proceed towards the lower ranks, in accordance to basic principle of evolution. But, quite a number of discrepancies were also found that defy the general notion of evolution. They may turn out to be environmental influence on development of the pathway, if prodded further. In short, this work displays conservation of Wnt signaling pathway at Phylum level that gradually decreases as the Phyla diversify into various Classes, Orders and Families, with some exceptions that possibly reflect effect of other factors on pathway development.

Acknowledgement. Losiana Nayak is grateful to the CSIR, India, for providing her a Senior Research Fellowship [No. 9/93(102)08].

References

1. Kuchaiev, O., Milenkovic, T., Memisevic, V., Hayes, W., Przulj, N.: Topological network alignment uncovers biological function and phylogeny. J. R. Soc. Interface 7, 1341–1354 (2010)
2. Nayak, L., De, R.K.: An algorithm for modularization of MAPK and calcium signaling pathways: Comparative analysis among different species. J. Biomed. Inform. 40, 726–749 (2007)
3. Cadigan, K.M., Liu, Y.I.: Wnt signaling: complexity at the surface. J. Cell Sci. 119, 395–402 (2006)
4. Willert, K., Brown, J.D., Danenberg, E., Duncan, A.W., Weissman, I.L., et al.: Wnt proteins are lipid-modified and can act as stem cell growth factors. Nature 423, 448–452 (2003)
5. Logan, C.Y., Nusse, R.: The Wnt signaling pathway in development and disease. Annu. Rev. Cell Dev. Biol. 20, 781–810 (2004)
6. Pinto, D., Clevers, H.: Wnt, stem cells and cancer in the intestine. Biol. Cell 97, 185–196 (2005)
7. Lowry, W.E., Blanpain, C., Nowak, J.A., Guasch, G., Lewis, L., et al.: Defining the impact of β-catenin/tcf transactivation on epithelial stem cells. Genes and Dev. 19, 1596–1611 (2005)
8. Reya, T., Duncan, A.W., Ailles, L., Domen, J., Scherer, D.C.: A role for Wnt signalling in self-renewal of haematopoietic stem cells. Nature 423, 409–414 (2003)
9. Kanehisa, M., Goto, S.: KEGG: Kyoto Encyclopedia of Genes and Genomes. Nucleic Acids Res. 28, 27–30 (2000)
10. Felsenstein, J.: PHYLIP - Phylogeny Inference Package (Version 3.2). Cladistics 5, 164–166 (1989)

Evaluation of Semantic Term and Gene Similarity Measures

Michal Kozielski and Aleksandra Gruca

Silesian University of Technology, Akademicka 16, 44-100 Gliwice, Poland
{michal.kozielski,aleksandra.gruca}@polsl.pl

Abstract. In this paper we present the results of the research verifying how the functional description of genes contained in Gene Ontology database is related to genes expression values recorded during biological experiments. We compare several different gene similarity measures and semantic term similarity measures, and evaluate how the similarity of genes based on Gene Ontology terms is correlated with similarity of genes based on expression profiles. The analysis are preformed on three different datasets and we show that there is no single term similarity measure that always gives the best correlation results. The choice of the best term similarity measure depends on dataset characteristic.

Keywords: genes similarity, semantic term similarity, Gene Ontology database, experssion analysis.

1 Introduction

Gene Ontology (GO) is a database created throughout the years where the scientists introduced the knowledge resulting from the biological experiments in the form of gene-term annotations. Gene Ontology is also often used in the gene analysis where it can be regarded as an expert knowledge that helps to interpret results of the biological or medical experiments. In that way Gene Ontology can be also utilised in revealing the information hidden in gene expression data [7]. It is therefore needed to verify how the information contained in Gene Ontology is related to the experiments performed and which methods of the Gene Ontology analysis are best fitted to the gene expression analysis.

The semantic gene similarity evaluation consists of two steps: (1) term similarity calculation, (2) gene similarity based on term similarity calculation.

Several studies of Gene Ontology analysis were performed [5]. These studies, among others, analysed different similarity measures that can be applied to GO analysis and analysed how the Gene Ontology similarity is correlated with the similarity of different biological domains, e.g. protein sequence [5].

However, there are few approaches to analysis of the correlation of Gene Ontology based and gene expression based similarity. The work [8] presented interesting dependencies between both similarities but no conclusions on the quality of the similarity measures were drawn. The work [6] pointed Resnik similarity measure as giving the best correlation with the similarity of gene expression values.

S.O. Kuznetsov et al. (Eds.): PReMI 2011, LNCS 6744, pp. 406–411, 2011.

There are however two issues that are left ambiguous in this work: which method was used in order to calculate gene similarity in case of Lin and Jiang-Conrath term similarity methods; how was the gene expression similarity aggregated in order to improve the GO-expression correlation.

In our opinion additional research and discussion on the topic presented is needed. The contribution of our work covers analysis and comparison of three semantic term similarity measures and three pairwise, term based gene similarity measures. The analysis was performed on three datasets having different characteristics.

The paper is organised as follows. Sections 2 and 3 present semantic term similarity measures and term based gene similarity measures respectively. In section 4 the datasets, experiments and their results are presented. The final conclusions are drawn in section 5.

2   Semantic Term Similarity Measures

Semantic similarity of the Gene Ontology terms can be calculated applying the concept of *Information Content* $\tau(a)$ of an ontology term $a \in A$ defined as $\tau(a) = -ln(P(a))$, where $P(a)$ is a ratio of a number of annotations to a term a, to a number of analysed genes.

The simplest similarity measure proposed by Resnik [5,6] takes under consideration only the *Information Content* of the common ancestor $\tau_{ca}(a_i, a_j)$ of the compared terms a_i and a_j:

$$s_A^{(R)}(a_i, a_j) = \tau_{ca}(a_i, a_j). \tag{1}$$

More complex approach was proposed by Jiang-Conrath [5,6], where term similarity is defined as:

$$s_A^{(JC)}(a_i, a_j) = (d_A^{(JC)}(a_i, a_j) + 1)^{-1}, \tag{2}$$

where $d_A^{(JC)}(a_i, a_j)$ is a term distance defined as:

$$d_A^{(JC)}(a_i, a_j) = \tau(a_i) + \tau(a_j) - 2\tau_{ca}(a_i, a_j). \tag{3}$$

Another approach was presented by Lin [5,6]:

$$s_A^{(L)}(a_i, a_j) = \frac{2\tau_{ca}(a_i, a_j)}{\tau(a_i) + \tau(a_j)}. \tag{4}$$

3   Gene Similarity Measures

When the term similarity is known it is possible to calculate gene similarity based on the similarity of terms describing the genes. The similarity $s_G(g_k, g_p)$ between genes g_k and g_p can be calculated according to one of the approaches presented in literature.

The very simple approach ([6]) may be to take the maximal similarity value of the terms annotated to the analysed genes

$$s_G(g_k, g_p) = max(s_A(a_i, a_j)), \tag{5}$$

where a_i and a_j belong to the term sets describing genes g_k and g_p respectively. This approach is referred further as Max method.

The more complex approach, which will be further referred to as Avg-max, may be found in [1]:

$$s_G(g_k, g_p) = (m_k + m_p)^{-1}(\sum_i \max_j(s_A(a_i, a_j)) + \sum_j \max_i(s_A(a_i, a_j))), \tag{6}$$

where m_k and m_p are the number of annotations of genes g_k and g_p respectively, a_i and a_j belong to the term sets describing genes g_k and g_p respectively.

Another method, which is further referred to as Avg-sum, was applied in [8]:

$$s_G(g_k, g_p) = (m_k m_p)^{-1} \sum (s_A(a_i, a_j)), \tag{7}$$

where m_k and m_p are the number of annotations of genes g_k and g_p respectively, a_i and a_j belong to the term sets describing genes g_k and g_p respectively.

4   Analysis

4.1   Datasets

Three datasets of different characteristics were used in the experiments performed. Yeast1 dataset [3] consists of 274 genes, 79 expression attributes, 645 GO terms. Human dataset [4] consists of 296 genes, 18 expression attributes, 1711 GO terms. Yeast2 dataset [2] consists of 1099 genes, 17 expression attributes, and 1552 GO terms.

To annotate genes we used GO terms from Biological Process ontology only. In all cases we included into analysis only genes that were described by at least one GO term. Analysing correlation of GO based similarity and gene expression based similarity it is needed to present the values and distribution of gene expression similarity within each dataset. As it was shown in the work [8] there is a nonlinear relation between the GO and gene expression based similarity. This observation can influence the results of the analysis in the present work because if the similarity of genes in a gene expression domain is little then there will be

Table 1. Average value of gene expression similarity

Yeast1	Human	Yeast2
0.257	0.045	0.057

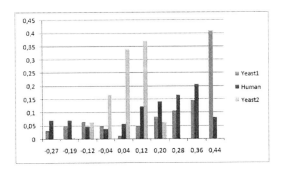

Fig. 1. Histogram showing the distribution of the similarity values in gene expression domain

little correlation of this similarity with the GO based one. It may be noticed in Table 1 that the average value of gene expression similarity, calculated as a Pearson correlation coefficient, is smaller for Human dataset then for Yeast2 dataset, which should result in its worse correlation with Gene Ontology based similarity. However, the distributions presented in Fig. 1 show that for the Human dataset the gene expression similarity has greater variance (the histogram is spread along the whole x axis) comparing to Yeast2 dataset. Thus, the differences in average values can be compensated and it is Human dataset which can give better results.

4.2   Experiments and Results

The following methods were applied in the experiments. Gene expression based similarity was calculated as Pearson correlation of the expression values.

Gene Ontology annotations were introduced to the analysis by means of binary array where "1" represented annotation of a gene to a term. The annotation table was constructed in such way that annotation of a gene to a term resulted in annotation of that gene to all the parents of a given term.

GO term similarity was calculated by means of Jiang-Conrath (2), Lin (4) and Resnik (1) methods. Gene similarity was calculated on the basis of term similarity by means of Max (5), Avg-max (6) and Avg-sum (7) methods.

The results of the experiments (correlation between gene expression based and GO based similarity matrices) are presented in the Table 2.

The Max gene similarity is not applicable to Jiang-Conrath and Lin similarity measures since it produces in these cases the similarity matrix containing only a value 1. It results from the fact that if two genes are annotated to the terms having common ancestor, then that ancestor annotates both genes in the calculated annotation table. Calculating gene similarity as a pairwise term similarity we have to calculate also self-similarity of such common ancestor. The self-similarity of a term in case of both Jiang-Conrath and Lin similarity measures equals 1 and this is maximal similarity value that can be calculated. In

Table 2. Correlation of gene expression based and GO based similarity

		Yeast1	Human	Yeast2
Max	Resnik	0.257	0.006	-0.013
Avg-max	Jiang-Conrath	0.420	0.089	0.015
	Lin	0.368	0.075	0.005
	Resnik	0.180	-0.024	0.001
Avg-sum	Jiang-Conrath	0.383	0.117	0.028
	Lin	0.352	0.089	0.011
	Resnik	0.039	-0.068	-0.038

case of Resnik measure the self-similarity of a term is equal to its information content and therefore it is possible to apply the Max method jointly only with Resnik measure.

The results show that the method Avg-sum gave the highest absolute correlation values in case of two out of three datasets analysed. Considering term similarity measures it is Jiang-Conrath that gives the best results in most cases.

The second experiment performed stems from the following two facts mentioned above: (1) the dependency between gene similarity matrices based on expression values and on Gene Ontology is not linear, (2) the best correlation between such similarity matrices is received when the genes that are highly similar in expression domain are taken under consideration.

Knowing these two facts we compared the correlation of the full similarity matrices with the correlation calculated for the matrices indexed by the values of expression based similarity s_e fulfilling the condition $s_e > \varepsilon$. The values of $\varepsilon = 0.5$ and $\varepsilon = 0.6$ were taken under consideration. The results of the experiment, when gene similarity was calculated by means of Avg-sum, are presented in Table 3.

Table 3. Correlation of gene expression based similarity and GO based similarity for the matrices reduced by ε condition (Avg-sum method); A - full data, B - data reduced for $\varepsilon = 0.5$, C - data reduced for $\varepsilon = 0.6$

	Yeast1			Human			Yeast2		
	A	B	C	A	B	C	A	B	C
Jiang-Conrath	0.383	0.402	0.334	0.117	0.232	0.304	0.028	0.176	0.298
Lin	0.352	0.392	0.323	0.089	0.133	0.192	0.011	0.149	0.256
Resnik	0.039	-0.181	-0.224	-0.068	-0.285	-0.355	-0.038	-0.250	-0.385

The results presented in Table 3 show that the dataset reduction applied improves in most cases the correlation between the similarity matrices compared. It can be also noticed that the results for the Resnik similarity measure gain the greater improvement (when absolute value of a correlation coefficient is taken under consideration) and become better then the results for Jiang-Conrath measure. It can be however disputable if the negatively correlated similarity matrices can be applied successfully in all types of analysis.

5   Conclusions

The work presented analysis and comparison of three semantic term similarity measures and three pairwise, term based gene similarity measures. The analysis was performed on three datasets having different characteristics.

The results of the experiments showed that Jiang-Conrath and Resnik term similarity measures can give the best results of gene expression based similarity and GO based similarity. Jiang-Conrath term similarity measure however, performs better on raw data, gives always positively correlated results and seems to be more suitable for further applications. Considering gene similarity measures that were analysed it is Avg-sum method that gives the best results.

References

1. Azuaje, F., Wang, H., Bodenreider, O.: Ontology-driven similarity approaches to supporting gene functional assessment. In: Proceedings Of The Eighth Annual Bio-Ontologies Meeting, Michigan (2005)
2. Cho, R.J., Campbell, M.J., Winzeler, E.A., Steinmetz, L., Conway, A., Wodicka, L., Wolfsberg, T.G., Gabrielian, A.E., Landsman, D., Lockhart, D.J., Davis, R.W.: A genome-wide transcriptional analysis of the mitotic cell cycle. Mol. Cell 2, 65–73 (1998)
3. Eisen, M.B., Spellman, P.T., Brown, P.O., Botstein, D.: Cluster analysis and display of genome-wide expression patterns. Proc. Natl. Acad. Sci. USA 95, 14863–14868 (1998)
4. Iyer, V.R., Eisen, M.B., Ross, D.T., Schuler, G., Moore, T., Lee, J.C., Trent, J.M., Staudt, L.M., Hudson, J., Boguski, M.S., Lashkari, D., Shalon, D., Botstein, D., Brown, P.O.: The transcriptional program in the response of human fibroblasts to serum. Science 283, 83–87 (1999)
5. Pesquita, C., Faria, D., Falcao, A.O., Lord, P., Couto, F.M.: Semantic Similarity in Biomedical Ontologies. PLoS Comput. Biol. 5(7), 1–12 (2009)
6. Sevilla, J.L., Segura, V., Podhorski, A., Guruceaga, E., Mato, J.M., Martinez-Cruz, L.A., Corrales, F.J., Rubio, A.: Correlation between gene expression and GO semantic similarity. IEEE/ACM Transactions on Computational Biology and Bioinformaticsm 2(4), 330–338 (2005)
7. Sikora, M., Gruca, A.: Induction and selection of the most interesting Gene Ontology based multiattribute rules for descriptions of gene groups. Pattern Recogn. Letters 32, 258–269 (2011)
8. Wang, H., Azuaje, F., Bodenreider, O., Dopazo, J.: Gene expression correlation and gene ontology-based similarity: an assessment of quantitative relationships. In: Proceedings of the 2004 IEEE Symposium on Computational Intelligence in Bioinformatics and Computational Biology, CIBCB 2004, pp. 25–31 (2004)

Finding Bicliques in Digraphs: Application into Viral-Host Protein Interactome

Malay Bhattacharyya[1], Sanghamitra Bandyopadhyay[1], and Ujjwal Maulik[2]

[1] Machine Intelligence Unit, Indian Statistical Institute
203 B. T. Road, Kolkata - 700108, India
{malay_r,sanghami}@isical.ac.in
[2] Department of Computer Science and Engineering, Jadavpur University
Kolkata - 700032, India
umaulik@cse.jdvu.ac.in

Abstract. We provide the first formalization true to the best of our knowledge to the problem of finding bicliques in a directed graph. The problem is addressed employing a two-stage approach based on an existing biclustering algorithm. This novel problem is useful in several biological applications of which we focus only on analyzing the viral-host protein interaction graphs. Strong and significant bicliques of HIV-1 and human proteins are derived using the proposed methodology, which provides insights into some novel regulatory functionalities in case of the acute immunodeficiency syndrome in human.

1 Introduction

The problem of finding bicliques, i.e. complete subgraphs in an undirected bipartite graph, is a well-known NP-complete problem [4]. Bipartite graphs are recognized as a triplet (V_1, V_2, E) in general, where V_1, V_2 denote two distinct sets of vertices and $E \subseteq V_1 \times V_2$ is a set of edges. For many real-life applications, directions are also included in graphs depicting regulatory information and they are formalized as a directed graph (digraph) G, where we distinguish between the edges (i, j) and (j, i). In several emerging applications, we are interested in exploring biclique-like compact structures in digraphs. In this paper, we formalize the problem of finding bicliques in digraphs. We show that there is a correspondence between the problem of finding bicliques in digraphs and a special type of biclustering. Based on this observation, we propose a method for exploring bicliques in digraphs.

Various studies on gene expression datasets have contributed a lot in the development of different biclustering algorithms. A quality review of majority of the existing biclustering approaches like Cheng and Church's algorithm (CCA) [3], SAMBA [9], co-clustering, etc. can be found in [8] and [7]. Broadly speaking, biclusters are of four types – fixed value, fixed row/column, additive coherent value, and coherent evolution [6]. While SAMBA and co-clustering are designed to find constant value biclusters, CCA can simultaneously find constant value and constant row/column biclusters. On the other side, SAMBA is able to uncover overlapping biclusters, while co-clustering (which is designed to only look

S.O. Kuznetsov et al. (Eds.): PReMI 2011, LNCS 6744, pp. 412–417, 2011.

for disjoint patterns) and Cheng and Church's method (which masks the identified bicluster with random values in each iteration) can't find such biclusters. Another divide-and-conquer based biclustering algorithm has recently been proposed that pursues inclusion-maximal procedure to prune out all-0 submatrices recursively from the input binary adjacency matrix to obtain overlapping biclusters [8]. This exact algorithm is applicable only to binary data and thus more suitable to finding bicliques. As can be seen reviewing the literature, only the heuristic algorithm SAMBA has considered the directional changes in expression values while finding statistically significant biclusters. But unfortunately, none of these methods are applicable to directed graphs where directions are also considered in the graph structure.

In this paper, we revise the methodology proposed in [8] to find out bicliques in digraphs where all the directions involved in the substructure are mono-directional. We define this as directed bicliques. The problem of finding directed bicliques is formalized in the following section. Sections 4 and 5 describe the proposed methodology and empirical results on the HIV-1-human protein interactome (the comprehensive set of interactions) forming a graph structure, respectively. Finally, Section 5 concludes the paper.

2   Problem Definition

A directed bipartite graph, in a generalized form, can be represented as a triplet $G = (V_1, V_2, E)$, where $V_1 \cap V_2 = \phi$ and $E \subseteq \{V_1 \times V_2\} \cup \{V_2 \times V_1\}$. We define a directed biclique, hereafter referred as DBClique, as a complete subgraph of a directed bipartite graph as per the following.

Definition 1 (DBClique). *A DBClique is a fully connected subgraph $G' = (V_1', V_2', E') \subseteq G$ of a directed bipartite graph G such that either $i \in V_1', j \in V_2', \forall (i, j) \in E'$ or $i \in V_2', j \in V_1', \forall (i, j) \in E'$.*

A directed bipartite graph is shown in Fig. 1(a) in which the sets of vertices {II, III} and {2, 3, 4} form a DBClique. Notably, this corresponds to a special kind of constant value biclusters. If we construct an interaction matrix (as shown in Fig. 1(b)) from the directed bipartite graph in Fig. 1(a), it somehow corresponds to an all-1 submatrix, but not an exact one. We provide a lemma to highlight a correspondence between the problem of finding DBCliques and a variant of biclustering. For this, let us first define the matrix representation of a directed bipartite graph as follows.

Definition 2 (Interaction matrix of a directed bipartite graph). *The interaction matrix of a directed bipartite graph $G = (V_1, V_2, E)$ is defined as a $|V_1| \times |V_2|$ matrix $\mathcal{I}$ such that*

$$\mathcal{I}_{ij} = \begin{cases} 0, & \text{if } (i, j) \notin E \text{ and } (j, i) \notin E \\ 1, & \text{if } (i, j) \in E \text{ and } (j, i) \notin E \\ -1, & \text{if } (i, j) \notin E \text{ and } (j, i) \in E \\ X, & \text{if } (i, j) \in E \text{ and } (j, i) \in E \end{cases},$$

$\forall i \in V_1, j \in V_2.$

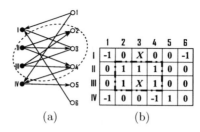

	1	2	3	4	5	6
I	-1	0	X	0	0	-1
II	0	1	1	1	0	0
III	0	1	X	1	0	0
IV	-1	0	0	-1	1	0

(a)   (b)

Fig. 1. The one-to-one correspondence between a single (a) DBClique in a directed bipartite graph and (b) a special kind of bicluster in its representative interaction matrix reflected as a submatrix

An example interaction matrix is shown in Fig. 1(b). The character 'X' in the matrix $\mathcal{I}$ defined beforehand is behaviorally a *don't care* entry. Based on this representation, we can equate a DBClique to a bicluster through the following lemma.

Lemma 1. *Given a directed bipartite graph $G = (V_1, V_2, E)$, a DBClique $G' = (V_1', V_2', E') \subseteq G$ corresponds to a bicluster in the interaction matrix of G such that all the elements in the submatrix are either '1' or '-1', with the entries of 'X' additionally allowed.*

Proof. Certainly, an entry 'X' in any submatrix of a bicluster represents both '1' and '-1'. Thus, a bicluster with all the entries either '1' or 'X' will correspond to an edge (i, j) directed from V_1 to V_2. Equivalently, a bicluster with all '-1' or 'X' will correspond to an edge (i, j) directed from V_2 to V_1. Thus the lemma.   □

Our motivation is to find out the set of maximal DBCliques from a given directed bipartite graph.

3   Proposed Method

We describe the two-stage algorithm to find out DBCliques in digraphs using the previous lemma. The methodology is based on the Bimax algorithm [8]. The approach for finding out maximal overlapping DBCliques (all '1' and all '-1' biclusters) is described in detail in Algorithm 1. The key step in this algorithm is pursuing separate phases (steps 2-5 and steps 6-9) for finding out the regulating (all '1') and regulated (all '-1') DBCliques. After this, we apply a divide-and-conquer process (adopted in [9]) to find out the maximal DBCliques from the given directed bipartite graph.

4   Experimental Results

To demonstrate the effectiveness of the methodology, we collect the interaction information (5134 interactions in total) between 19 HIV-1 and 1448 human proteins as reported in a recently published dataset [5]. It consists of two types

Algorithm 1. An Algorithm for Finding out Bicliques in Digraphs

Input: A directed bipartite graph $G = (V_1, V_2, E)$.
Output: The set of maximal DBCliques.
Steps of the algorithm:
1: Obtain the correspondent interaction matrix $\mathcal{I}$ from G
2: Replace the entries 'X' with '1' and '-1' with '0' in $\mathcal{I}$ // Finding the all '1' biclusters
3: Partition $\mathcal{I} = \mathcal{I}_0 \cup \mathcal{I}_1 \cup \mathcal{I}_2$ such that the size of $\mathcal{I}_0$ maximizes and it contains only 0's.
4: Go to the previous step and apply the same individually on $\mathcal{I}_1$ and $\mathcal{I}_2$ until no further partitioning is possible.
5: Return the DBCliques corresponding to the biclusters
6: Replace the entries 'X' with '-1' and '1' with '0' in $\mathcal{I}$ // Finding the all '-1' biclusters
7: Partition $\mathcal{I} = \mathcal{I}_0 \cup \mathcal{I}_1 \cup \mathcal{I}_2$ such that the size of $\mathcal{I}_0$ maximizes and it contains only 0's.
8: Go to the previous step and apply the same individually on $\mathcal{I}_1$ and $\mathcal{I}_2$ until no further partitioning is possible.
9: Return the DBCliques corresponding to the biclusters

of interactions, viz., direct physical interactions and indirect interactions, categorized into 65 more specific types. The corresponding bipartite graph thus contains 19 vertices representing HIV-1 proteins and 1448 vertices representing human proteins, and 5134 edges representing the viral-host interactions. The interaction matrix of size 19×1448 corresponding to the bipartite graph is constructed. All the 65 interaction types are biologically classified into three types – regulating, regulated by and two-way (where the regulation is bidirectional). As per this, an entry '0' in the matrix denotes the absence of interaction between the corresponding pair of HIV-1 and human proteins, an entry of '1' represents the regulation of the HIV-1 protein on the human protein, an entry of '-1' denotes that the HIV-1 protein is regulated by the human protein and 'X' represents a two-way interaction. Now, to find out the all '1' and all '-1' biclusters from this, we applied the element-replacement strategies (steps 2 and 6) given in Algorithm 1 and the resulting binary matrices are processed further.

The available codes of Bimax biclustering method, as implemented in the BicAT toolbox [1], is employed to iteratively find out the matrix partitions of the binary data matrices. The lower bound of HIV-1 and human protein sizes are both set to 3 for obtaining a bicluster, i.e., we aim to find only those DBCliques which contain at least 3 HIV-1 proteins and 3 human proteins. With this restriction, the numbers of all '1' and all '-1' DBCliques are found to be 113 and 25, respectively. Further neglecting *don't care* entries in these matrices, we ended up with 54 and 7 strong DBCliques, respectively for the all '1' and all '-1' cases. Several of these bicliques forms a strong (with high *clustering co-efficient*) bipartite subgraph which contains the HIV-1 proteins like env_gp120, pol_RT, tat, etc. On the other side, many of the human proteins like CD4, LCK, MAPK1 etc. and also several kinase proteins are obtained within this module. There are several literature evidences where CD4 has been reported as an important cell membrane protein that act as the receptor and co-receptor for the viral entry, respectively [2]. The details of the DBCliques obtained are listed in Table 1.

The all '1' and all '-1' submatrices obtained are nothing but the representatives of strong modulated regulation between two sets of proteins. It becomes evident from the maximum sizes of the DBCliques that the immunodeficiency signal passing in either directions between HIV-1 and human proteins are equally

Table 1. The DBCliques obtained from the HIV-1-human protein interaction network containing at least three HIV-1 and human proteins each. The size of a DBClique is defined based on the number of edges it contains.

Bicluster type	*Don't care* allowed	# DBCliques obtained	Maximum size (HIV-1, Human)
All '1'	Yes	113	(6, 5)
All '-1'	Yes	25	(3, 13)
All '1'	No	54	(4, 5)
All '-1'	No	7	(3, 8)

significant. Further analysis from the Gene Ontology (GO) also shows the significant p-values ($< 1.0\text{E}-3$) for several of the DBCliques obtained representing highly coherent groups of regulatory functional proteins. As for example, consider the largest-sized and strong DBClique corresponding to the all '-1' bicluster. It consists of three HIV-1 proteins tat, env_gp120 and matrix, and eight heat shock 70kDa proteins (1A, 1B, 2, 4, 5, 6, 8 isoform 1 and 9 precursor) of human. These proteins are generally expressed when cells are exposed to elevated temperatures or other stresses likewise the entry of viral proteins. In fact, the env_gp120 protein is associated with the insertion of viral proteins in the host body in case of AIDS. Thus, this substructure is a biologically significant regulatory module in passing the immunodeficiency signal in human.

We have further carried out relative studies between the proposed method and several other algorithms to show the enhanced biological significance of the DBCliques in comparison with the conventional bicliques. All these algorithms are applied on the binary data matrix obtained from the interaction network ignoring directions. The comparative results are shown in Table 2. Notably, every biclique is a DBClique but not the vice versa, and therefore DBCliques include additional information in their substructures. This is reflected from the better p-values obtained representing more biological coherence for DBCliques as compared to the bicliques. In fact, some of these results appear to be very insignificant producing poor p-values ($> 1.0\text{E}-2$). Thus, it appears that the DBCliques are significant substructures in a regulatory biological network.

Table 2. Comparison of the largest bicliques (consisting of at least three HIV-1 and human proteins) derived by various algorithms from the HIV-1-human protein interaction network. The proposed method exclude the *Don't care* conditions and returns DBCliques. Crossed cells in the third column represent insignificant p-values.

Analytical details	Bimax	CC	ISA	Proposed
# Bicliques obtained	197	60	10	61
Largest biclique found	(4, 9)	(19, 392)	(5, 76)	(3, 8)
Best p-value from GO	1.9E-6	×	×	2.3E-12
Best annotation (GO Term)	Regulation of cytokinesis (GO:0032465)	Not applicable	Not applicable	Response to protein stimulus (GO:0051789)

5   Concluding Remarks

The problem of finding bicliques in directed bipartite graphs is addressed in this paper based on an optimal biclustering algorithm. We provide exact solutions to this problem and it is demonstrated that the problem reduces to a special class of biclustering problem. The analysis on the interaction network of HIV-1 and human proteins demonstrates the effectiveness of the proposed methodology and its usefulness.

Acknowledgments

A part of the work was carried out when S. Bandyopadhyay visited the Max Planck Institute for Informatics, Saarbrücken, Germany, and U. Maulik visited the German Cancer Research Center, Heidelberg, Germany, with Humboldt Fellowship for Experienced Researchers in 2010.

References

1. Barkow, S., Bleuler, S., Prelić, A., Zimmermann, P., Zitzler, E.: BicAT: a Biclustering Analysis Toolbox. Bioinformatics 22(10), 1282–1283 (2006)
2. Brass, A.L., Dykxhoorn, D.M., Benita, Y., Yan, N., Engelman, A., Xavier, R.J., Lieberman, J., Elledge, S.J.: Identification of Host Proteins Required for HIV Infection Through a Functional Genomic Screen. Science 319(5865), 921–926 (2008)
3. Cheng, Y., Church, G.: Biclustering of Expression Data. In: Proceedings of the 8th ISMB Conference, AAAI Press, pp. 93–103. AAAI Press, Menlo Park (2000)
4. Ding, C., Zhang, Y., Li, T.: Biclustering Protein Complex Interactions with a Biclique Finding Algorithm. In: Proceedings of the Sixth International Conference on Data Mining, Hong Kong, pp. 178–187 (2006)
5. Fu, W., Sanders-Beer, B.E., Katz, K.S., Maglott, D.R., Pruitt, K.D., Ptak, R.G.: Human immunodeficiency virus type 1, human protein interaction database at NCBI. Nucleic Acids Research 37(Database Issue), D417–D422 (2009)
6. Madeira, S.C., Oliveira, A.L.: Biclustering algorithms for biological data analysis: a survey. IEEE/ACM Transactions on Computational Biology and Bioinformatics 1, 24–45 (2004)
7. Pandey, G., Atluri, G., Steinbach, M., Myers, C.L., Kumar, V.: An Association Analysis Approach to Biclustering. In: Proceedings of the 15th ACM SIGKDD Conference on Knowledge Discovery and Data Mining, Paris, France (2009)
8. Prelić, A., Bleuler, S., Zimmermann, P., Wille, A., Bühlmann, P., Gruissem, P., Hennig, L., Thiele, L., Zitzler, E.: A systematic comparison and evaluation of biclustering methods for gene expression data. Bioinformatics 22(9), 1122–1129 (2006)
9. Tanay, A., Sharan, R., Shamir, R.: Discovering statistically significant biclusters in gene expression data. Bioinformatics 18, S136–S144 (2002)

Advantages of the Extended Water Flow Algorithm for Handwritten Text Segmentation

Darko Brodić

University of Belgrade, Technical Faculty Bor,
V. J. 12, 19210 Bor, Serbia
dbrodic@tf.bor.ac.rs

Abstract. This paper identifies the advantages of the specific approach to water flow algorithm for multi-skewed handwritten text line segmentation. Original water flow algorithm assumes that hypothetical water flows, from both left and right sides of the document image frame, face obstruction from part of character, character, and group of characters in text lines. The stripes of areas left unwetted on the document image frame are finally labeled for the extraction of text lines. However, the method defines parameter water flow angle for flooding which depends on the text line slopes of each specific document. The estimation of the appropriate parameter value is difficult and limited as well. The limitation is manifested by possible election of only 4 values for this parameter. Extended approach has introduced enlargement of the parameter range. Consequently, decision making and the selection of the small values of the parameter below the minimum given by the original method shows improvement in the handwritten text line segmentation process. It is confirmed by the measurement on different types of letters.

Keywords: Image processing; Document image processing; Text line segmentation; Handwritten text; Water flow algorithm.

1 Introduction

Text line segmentation of handwritten text is a key element of the optical character recognition [1]. It implies a labeling process that assign the same label to spatially aligned units, connected components or characteristic points [1]. Further, based on the obtained labels, text is divided into different regions each one representing text line. After text line segmentation is finished, it provides the essential information for the consecutive documents image steps such as baseline detection, skew identification and correction, other text feature extraction and character recognition.

Related work on text line segmentation can be categorized in few directions [1,2]: projection based methods, Hough transform methods, grouping methods, methods for processing overlapping and touching components, stochastic methods, smearing methods, and others method.

In smearing methods the consecutive black pixels along the horizontal direction are smeared [3]. Consequently, the white space between black pixels is filled

S.O. Kuznetsov et al. (Eds.): PReMI 2011, LNCS 6744, pp. 418–423, 2011.

with black pixels. It is valid only if their distance is within a predefined threshold. This way, enlarged area of black pixels around text is formed. It is so-called boundary growing area. Hence, the smeared image encloses text lines.

As mentioned many methods can be employed for text line segmentation, but smearing algorithms have the benefits. They are efficient and computationally inexpensive. Algorithm proposed in [4] is classified as smearing method. It assumed a hypothetical flow of water in a particular direction across image frame in a way that it faces obstruction from the characters of the text lines. As a result of algorithm, unwetted image frames are extracted. These areas are of major importance for text line segmentation. In our paper, this algorithm is extended as well as in [5,6] and further investigated, improved and adapted.

The rest of the paper is organized as follows: Section 2 describes basic water flow algorithm and introduces extended approach to water flow algorithm. Section 3 defines testing process and shows measurement results including comparative analysis. Section 4 makes conclusions.

2   Water Flow Algorithm

Document text image is obtained as result of scanning process. It is grayscale text image described by intensity matrix $D(i,j) \in \{0,\ldots,255\}$, where $i \in \{1, M\}$ and $j \in \{1, N\}$ [7]. After applying intensity segmentation with binarization, it is converted into binary image $X(i,j)$. Hence, where $D(i,j) \geq D_{th}$, then $X(i,j)$ is 1, elsewhere $X(i,j)$ is 0. Consequently, D_{th} represents the threshold sensitivity decision value. It is obtained by global [8] or local binarization method [9,10,11].

Basic water flow algorithm [4] assumes hypothetical water flows under few angles of the document image frame from left to right and vice versa. In this hypothetically assumed situation, water is flowing across the image frame. Areas that are not wetted form unwetted ones. The stripes of unwetted areas are labeled for the extraction of text lines. Further, this hypothetical water flow is expected to fill up the gaps between text elements in the same text lines. Hence, unwetted areas left on the image frame lies under the text lines. Once the labeling is completed, the image is divided into two different types of stripes. First one contains text lines. The other one contains space between text lines. Furthermore, water flow angle α, as shown in Fig.1, is introduced as a referent parameter in [4]. This angle is measured between two lines which intersect each other at the endpoint of an obstacle. However, it is formed by labeling original document image using spatial filter mask. These masks for the water flows from left to right are shown in Fig.1.

Accordingly, algorithm creates unwetted areas under fixed water flow angles from the set $\{14°, 18°, 26.6°, 45°\}$ [4]. Using of the spatial filter masks is defined by the position of the text black pixels. They represent prospective seed points. If the pixel represents corner one, then the spatial filter mask will be exploited. Thus, it activates the algorithm process. As the result, unwetted stripes bounded text. This circumstance for $\alpha = 26.6°$ is shown in Fig.2.

In the extended approach, originally extraction of the rectangular bounding box over the text objects is prerequisite. Further, they represent control areas

0	1
0	0
0	1

0	1	1
0	0	0
0	1	1

0	1	1	1
0	0	0	0
0	1	1	1

0	1	1	1	1
0	0	0	0	0
0	1	1	1	1

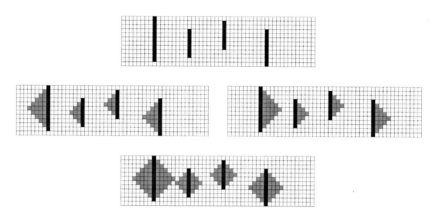

Fig. 1. Spatial filter mask defined by water flow angle: $\alpha = 45°$ (left), $\alpha = 26.6°$ (middle left), $\alpha = 18°$ (middle right), and $\alpha = 14°$ (right)

Fig. 2. Water flow algorithm with water flow angle $\alpha = 26.6°$: Initial sample text containing four I letters (top), unwetted areas made by water flow from left to right (middle left), unwetted areas made by water flow from right to left (middle right), and united unwetted areas (bottom).

authorized for the extended water flow algorithm criteria activation. Bounding box is a rectangular region whose edges are parallel to the coordinate axes. It is defined by its endpoints: x_{min}, y_{min}, x_{max}, and y_{max}. Hence, each pixel $X(i,j)$ that belongs to the bounding box is given by [12]:

$$X(i,j) \mid (x_{min} \leq i \leq x_{max}) \wedge (y_{min} \leq j \leq y_{max}). \tag{1}$$

Inclusion of the point $X(i,j)$ in the bounding box is tested by verifying these four inequalities. If any one of them fails, then the point is not inside [13]. All text objects like letters, part of words or words are surrounded by bounding boxes [14]. It should be noted that from this point all actions are referred only to text in each independent bounding box.

Apart from original algorithm procedure, unwetted areas could be determined by lines. Each line is defined as:

$$y = ax + b, \tag{2}$$

where slope $a = \tan(\alpha)$. Two lines defined by angle α make connection in specific pixel creating closed unwetted area [5,6].

Modification made on water flow algorithm is in its definition. Consequently, it forms the water flow function which determines the water flow angle α. Still, making straight lines from boundary pixel type and connecting each others in specified point makes unwetted region as well. Currently, modified water flow algorithm is open to choose different water flow angle from 0° to 90°. In addition, different decision-making process on boundary text pixels is made. Fig.3 illustrates these circumstances [5,6].

	i	i+1			i	i+1			i	i+1
j-1	1	1		j-1	0	1		j-1	1	1
j	0	1		j	0	1		j	0	1
j+1	0	1		j+1	1	1		j+1	1	1

Fig. 3. Pixel type determination: upper boundary pixel (left), lower boundary pixel (middle), and boundary pixel for additional investigation (right)

Due to pixel type, the slope is $-\alpha$ or $+\alpha$. However, pixel without complete location has been additionally investigated. It depends on neighbor area of pixels. Apart from [5], enlarged window composed of R x S pixels, defined as a basis. In [6] $R = 5$ and $S = 7$ is proposed for complete investigation.

The main achievement of unwetted area is text line segmentation. However, the problem originates in broken words of text lines. Algorithm should contribute to join those words by unwetted areas. Those areas can be lengthen by using smaller angle α. This is represented in Fig.4.

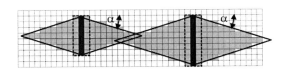

Fig. 4. Extended water flow algorithm involving water flow function $y = ax + b$ defining and bounding boxes surrounding text (box with dotted lines)

3   Testing, Results and Comparative Analysis

The proposed approach was tested using a group of binary handwritten documents images. These documents were written in English as well as in Serbian Latin and Cyrillic letters. The total number of analyzed handwritten text lines was 220. For the sake of conformity, documents body is the only considered in the analysis of the line segmentation.

Table 1 presents the number of correctly segmented text lines as well as different types of segmented errors. Errors are divided in 3 groups: split lines error, joined lines error, and lines including outlier words [15].

Split lines error represents the text lines which are wrongly divided by algorithm in two or more components [15]. Joined lines error corresponds to the situation where the sequence of n consecutive lines is considered by the algorithm as a unique line. In this situation n - 1 line represent the group of the erroneous [15]. Lines including outlier words correspond to lines containing words that are incorrectly assigned to two adjacent lines [15].

Table 1. Text lines segmentation results produced by original method with α = 14° [4] and extended method with from the set {8°, 10°, 12°}.

Table 1. Text lines segmentation results produced by original method with $\alpha = 14°$ [4] and extended method with α from the set {8°, 10°, 12°}

Water flow angle	14°		12°		10°		8°	
	#	%	#	%	#	%	#	%
Correctly segmented	88	40.00%	96	43.64%	144	65.45%	180	81.82%
Split lines error	132	60.00%	124	56.36%	76	34.55%	40	18.18%
Joined line error	0	0%	0	0%	0	0%	0	0%
Lines including outlier words	0	0%	0	0%	0	0%	0	0%
Sum	220	100%	220	100%	220	100%	220	100%

One of the representative results from test samples is given in Fig. 5.

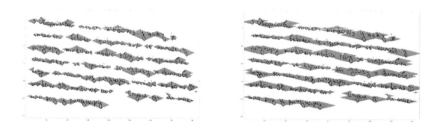

Fig. 5. Application of the algorithm to the handwritten sample text: $\alpha = 14°$ (left), and $\alpha = 8°$ (right)

From the above results the use of smaller water flow angle contributes to the better text segmentation results. Especially, water flow angles below 10° give segmentation results improvement. Hence, obtained results confirmed advantage of the extended over basic approach for the water flow algorithm.

4   Conclusions

In this paper, an extended approach to water flow algorithm for text line segmentation is presented. Water flow algorithm assumes the flow of the hypothetical water under few specified angles to the image frame from left to right and vice versa. Instead of using limited choices of parameter called water flow angle, new approach introduced approach to freely choose this parameter. Furthermore, choosing smaller water flow angles contributes to the enlarged unwetted area which leads to better text line segmentation results. It is upheld by testing with the group of handwritten documents in Serbian and English language. Hence, the extended approach of the water flow algorithm confirms better text line segmentation ability.

References

1. Likforman-Sulem, L., Zahour, A., Taconet, B.: Text Line Segmentation of Historical Documents: A Survey. IJDAR 9(2-4), 123–138 (2007)
2. Amin, A., Wu, S.: Robust Skew Detection in Mixed Text/Graphics Documents. In: 8th ICDAR, Seoul, Korea, pp. 247–251 (2005)
3. Shi, Z., Govindaraju, V.: Line Separation for Complex Document Images using Fuzzy Runlength. In: Int. Workshop on Document Image Analysis for Libraries, Palo Alto, USA, pp. 306–312 (2004)
4. Basu, S., et al.: Text Line Extraction from Multi-skewed Handwritten Documents. Pattern Recognition 40(6), 1825–1839 (2007)
5. Brodic, D., Milivojevic, Z.: An Approach to Modification of Water Flow Algorithm for Segmentation and Text Parameters Extraction. In: Camarinha-Matos, L.M., Pereira, P., Ribeiro, L. (eds.) IFIP AICT, vol. 314, pp. 323–331. Springer, Heidelberg (2010)
6. Brodic, D., Milivojevic, Z.: Text Line Segmentation by Adapted Water Flow Algorithm. In: 10th Symposium NEUREL, Belgrade, Serbia, pp. 225–229 (2010)
7. Gonzalez, R.C., Woods, R.E.: Digital Image Processing, 2nd edn. Prentice-Hall, Englewood Cliffs (2002)
8. Otsu, N.: A Threshold Selection Method from Gray-level Histograms. IEEE Tran. on Systems, Man, and Cybernetics 9(1), 62–66 (1979)
9. Sauvola, L., Pietikainen, M.: Adaptive Document Image Binarization. Pattern Recognition 33(2), 225–236 (2000)
10. Bukhari, S.S., Shafait, F., Bruesl, T.M.: Adaptive Binarization of Unconstrained Hand-held Camera-captured Document Images. J. of Universal Computer Science 15(18), 3343–3363 (2009)
11. Khashman, A., Sekeroglu, B.: Document Image Binarisation Using a Supervised Neural Network. Int. J. of Neural Systems 18(5), 405–418 (2008)
12. Preparata, F.P., Shamos, M.I.: Computational Geometry: An Introduction. Springer, Berlin (1985)
13. Chang, C.M.: Detecting Ellipses via Bounding Boxes. Asian Journal of Health and Information Sciences 1(1), 73–84 (2006)
14. Wang, J., Leung, M.K.H., Hui, S.C.: Cursive Word Reference Line Detection. Pattern Recognition 30(3), 503–511 (1997)
15. Sanchez, A., et al.: Text Line Segmentation in Images of Handwritten Historical Documents. In: 1st IPTA, Sousse, Brasil, pp. 1–6 (2008)

Construction of Model of Structured Documents Based on Machine Learning

Sergey Golubev[1,2]

[1] Moscow Institute of Physics and Technology, Dolgoprudny, Russia
[2] ABBYY Software, Moscow, Russia
Gergey_G@abbyy.com

Abstract. In this paper we consider the problem of structured document recognition. The document recognition system is proposed. This system incorporates a recognition module based on methods of structured image recognition, a graph document model and a method of document model generalization. The machine learning component makes the process of document model construction easier and less time-consuming.

Keywords: document recognition, machine learning, graph document model.

1 Introduction

The extensive development of information technologies and electronic document management systems poses the problem of converting paper documents into digital form. While modern OCR systems can recognize symbols with high precision, simple character recognition is often insufficient. To capture the data correctly, a recognition of logical document structure is needed. The most precise and flexible methods of recognition of document structure are those based on structured pattern recognition [1,2]. These methods use the model of document structure which is compared to the document image during recognition.

The most widespread document model is the graph model where text blocks and separator lines form graph vertices, whereas graph edges correspond to relations between them [3]. The recognition problem in this case is the problem of matching of two graphs: the model graph and the document graph which is formed from the document image prior to recognition process. Systems based on graph models often allows automatic construction of document model based on methods of machine learning.

Another document recognition system based on the methods of structured pattern recognition is the ABBYY FlexiLayout system [4]. This system uses more complex special-purpose document model (structural description). In comparison with graph based methods the FlexiLayout system can reach higher recognition quality especially for documents with complex structure. The main drawback of the ABBYY FlexiLayout system is that the document description is designed to be created manually which is difficult and time-consuming. It

S.O. Kuznetsov et al. (Eds.): PReMI 2011, LNCS 6744, pp. 424–431, 2011.

seems reasonable to combine the FlexiLayout document recognition system with the methods of machine learning. This allows us to take advantage of both the precision of the FlexiLayout system and the easy constructing of graph based document model. We propose a trainable system for document recognition which incorporates the FlexiLayuot recognition module and a training module. The training module uses an intermediate graph document model on the training stage. The graph model is then converted into the FlexiLayout document description. In this paper we will discuss the graph document model and the process of its construction.

2   Problem Setting

In this work a special class of documents, so called forms, is discussed. The distinctive feature of this document class is that the document structure consists of the static part (which is presented by headings, separator lines etc.) and data elements. The examples of forms are various questionaries, financial documents like invoices, payment orders, etc.

All forms can be divided in four classes in terms of structure complexity: fixed forms, semi-fixed forms, flex-forms and free forms. A fixed form is a document that maintains all characteristics of its layout (except for scanning distortions such as stretching, skew etc.). The recognition of fixed-forms is a relatively simple task and does not require structure recognition. Semi-fixed forms are created from fixed-forms by relaxing some restrictions on the document layout. An example of semi-fixed form is an electronic template which allows to move succeeding data fields, if more space is needed for the given field or section. The recognition of semi-fixed forms can be performed using table or graph based document models. In a flex-form (also called context-form) each data element has an identifiable local context associated with it. The data element and the related context may be located in varying places on the document image. However, the relative position of the data element to its context is relatively constant. Free forms include documents which are not fixed, semi-fixed or flex-forms, extraction of data from this documents may require advanced natural language processing. In current paper we will consider the first three types of forms: fixed, semi-fixed and flex-forms.

The problem of form recognition is the following: given a document image the system must detect the localization of data elements so as to recognize the required data (using OCR technologies) and input it into the database. The system uses certain number of document images with marked locations of data elements as training set. After the training process the system must be able to locate the data elements on any other document image of the same document type.

The recognition problem is solved in two stages. On the first stage a model is generated on the base of training examples, on the second stage this model is used to solve recognition (prediction, classification) problem. In our work we use the ABBYY FlexiLayout system as a recognition module. Thereby the model is the FlexiLayout structural description (for more information on structural descriptions see [4]). The FlexiLayout document model contains the descriptions of the document structural elements. The description of each structural element defines its attributes, allowing to detect the structural element on the document image. Unlike the graph based methods the FlexiLayout system does not use *a priori* extraction of structural elements. Instead, structural elements are detected directly during the recognition process according to the document description and taking into account the particular features of a document type. Particularly important feature of the system is the ability to calculate attributes of structural elements and relations between them "on the fly". For example the distance between two elements may be calculated using the size of detected rectangle of one of the elements. The relative positions of structural elements are described in the model in terms of metrical and ordering relations. In this respect the FlexiLayout model is similar to graph models. In fact a graph model with metrical relations may be converted into the FlexiLayout description if the labels of graph vertices have the appropriate format. The FlexiLayuot model also supports fuzzy relations between elements.

The document description uses a specialized language to describe attributes of structural elements and relations between them. Therefore it is not convenient for machine learning and it was designed mainly to be created manually by system operator. Therefore, it is preferable to use a simpler graph model on the stage of model generation. When the intermediate graph model is generated in the learning process it is then converted into FlexiLayout structural description. FlexiLayout description in then used for document recognition. In the following section we will discuss the intermediate graph document model and the method of its generalization.

3   Document Model

In structural pattern recognition methods it is convenient to represent the document image as a set of image objects. The input document image is a raster image obtained by scanning the paper document. This image is subjected to segmentation process which extracts connected pixel components. Connected components are the images of separate letters, punctuation symbols, parts of separator lines and pictures. Each connected component is classified and recognized (if it represents letter). We use classified and recognized connected components as elementary image objects. The elementary image object is described by its type, surrounding rectangle and Unicode code of recognized symbol (for letters, diacritics and punctuation symbols). The image object is either an elementary object or a combination of elementary objects.The complex image object is described by its constituents. The following hierarchy of image objects is used:

1. Letter → Word → Text line → Text fragment
2. Separator fragment → Separator line
3. Picture fragment → Picture

The intermediate representation of the document structure uses a graph model, which allows us to take advantage of well-known methods of graph data processing [5,6,8]. Document model in our case should be able to represent both single document image and generalized document structure. In the first case it is called a *document graph* and in the second case, a *template graph*.

The vertices of the graph correspond to image objects in the case of document graph or to elements of logical structure in the case of generalized description. Graph edges correspond to metric relations between objects. Thereby the document model is an oriented labeled graph with labels on vertices and edges: $G_D = (V, E, L_V, L_E, f_V, f_E)$, where V is the set of vertices, E is the set of edges, L_V, L_E are sets of vertex and edge labels respectively, f_V, f_E are mappings taking vertices and edges to their labels.

Vertex labels have the following form: $l_V = (id, description)$, where:

id is an image object or structural element identifier, describing its logical role in document structure, which can possess values from the set $R, S, F_1, F_2, , F_N$, where:

   F_i are identifiers of data elements. Since data elements set is known for particular document type and positions of data elements are marked on images from training set, the objects which correspond to data elements have unique identifiers.

   R is an identifier of static text object.

   S is an identifier of separator line .

description is a description of the set of image objects, which can represent the element of logical structure on the image. This set can be defined in several ways: the set consisting of single image object, the set of phrases consisting of given keywords, the set of text strings consisting of characters from a given alphabet, etc.

Edge labels have the following form: $l_E = (xDistamce, yDistance)$, where $xDistance$, $yDistance$ — distance between rectangles measured horizontally and vertically, respectively and represented as intervals. This distance may be positive or negative depending on vertex order so the edges of document graph are directional.

4   Document Model Generalization

Consider the following definition. A template graph G_T *describes* a document graph G_D if there exists a mapping $X : V(G_T) \rightarrow V'(G_D)$, where $V'(G_D) \subseteq V(G_D)$, and for vertices $v, u \in V(G_T)$ and their images $v', u' \in V'(G_D)$ the following conditions are fulfilled:

1. $id(v) = id(v')$, i.e. vertices have the same identifiers.
2. Object described by the label of vertex v', is a member of the objects set described by the label of vertex v.

3. The label l of vertex $e = (v, u)$ is the generalization of the label l' of vertex $e' = (v', u')$, in the sense that *distance* intervals of the label l are comprised in *distance* intervals of the label l'.

We will perform construction of template graph by generalizing it successively with document graphs from the training image set. Let G_T be a template graph constructed on some document set and G_D be a document graph of the next document in the training set. A template graph can be generalized from the graph G_D in the following way. One need to build the mapping of template graph vertex subset to document graph vertex subset: $Y : V'(G_T) \rightarrow V'(G_D)$, where $V'(G_T) \subseteq V(G_T)$, $V'(G_D) \subseteq V(G_D)$, so that identifiers of image vertices and counter image vertices match. After that the labels of vertices from set $V'(G_T)$ should be generalized with the labels of vertices from set $V'(G_D)$ so that object sets described by vertex labels comprise new objects described by vertex labels from $V'(G_D)$. Similarly the intervals of edge labels of graph G_T should be generalized with the intervals of corresponding edge labels of graph G_D.

Obviously there is a large number of such mappings and corresponding template graphs. We must define some measure to choose the most appropriate template graph. It should be noted that discussed vertex mapping corresponds to an edit path between graphs [5]. In general a probabilistic measure can be used for edit path [7], however in our case it is reasonable to use specific measure which is more relevant to our problem setting.

Assume the following measure for vertex mapping and the corresponding template graph G_T':

$$Q = \left(\prod Q_V(v_i \rightarrow u_j) \right) * Q_U(V(G_T) \setminus V'(G_T)) * Q_U(V(G_D) \setminus V'(G_D)), \quad (1)$$

where Q_V is the measure of pair of vertices from mapping Y, Q_U is the measure of sets $V(G_T) \setminus V'(G_T)$ and $V(G_D) \setminus V'(G_D)$, i.e. sets of vertices without image or counter image. The measure Q_U depends on the number of elements in the corresponding set and has the following form: $Q_U(V(G)\backslash V'(G)) = U^{|V(G)\backslash V'(G)|}$, i.e. for every missed vertex a constant penalty U is given. Since vertex identifiers are the same for image and counter image vertices, correspondence between document data elements is unambiguous and we should consider only static objects in template graph measure.

$$Q_V(v \rightarrow u) = Q_V(v') = (1 - \alpha) * \max Q_E(e_i) + \alpha * \sum Q_E(e_i)/N_F), \quad (2)$$

where $Q_E(e_i)$ is the measure if i-th edge, coming from vertex v' of graph G_T', which is the result of matching vertex v of graph G_T to vertex u of graph G_D, $i \in [1, N_F]$; N_F is data elements count in current document type; α is an empirical factor.

Edge measure has the following form:

$$Q_E(e_i) = \max \left(0; 1 - \left(\frac{\Delta x + \Delta y + 4 - \sqrt{(\Delta x - \Delta y)^2 + 16}}{2} \right)^2 \right), \quad (3)$$

where $\Delta x = Width(xDistance)/W$, $Width(xDistance)$ is the width of the interval $xDistance$ if edge e_i, W is the characteristic interval width which is about page size; the same is for Δy. This empirical measure is chosen from the following considerations. First, the function isolines must be concave, i.e. the measure of edge with intervals (for example) $\Delta x = 1$, $\Delta y = 0$ should be higher than measure of edge with intervals $\Delta x = 1/2$, $\Delta y = 1/2$. Second, the measure must be close to 1 for edges resulting from correct object matching (Δx and Δy are sufficiently less than 1), and decline substantially while Δx and Δy get closer to 1. In our case the isolines are hyperbolas $y = \frac{4}{x+a} - a$, $a \in [1,2]$. The edge measure function plot in area $\Delta x \in [0,1]$, $\Delta y \in [0,1]$ is a surface obtained by "sliding" hyperbola $y = \frac{4}{x+1} - 1$, $z = 0$ along parabola $z = 1 - x^2$, $x = y$.

With template measure being defined, the problem is to find a vertex mapping between graphs with the best measure. This can be done in the following way:

– We will sequentially choose corresponding pairs for vertices of template graph using search tree. Search tree node corresponds to decision of matching vertex v_i to vertex u_j or leaving vertex v_i without match.
– For each nonterminal node and the corresponding tree path we will define partial measure Q_P, which in contrast to Q does not take into account unmatched vertices, i.e. $Q_U(V(G_T) \setminus V'(G_T))$ depends only on examined vertices of template graph, and $Q_U(V(G_D) \setminus V'(G_D))$ is omitted.
– The tree search is performed in the order of descending of path measure. Since the path measure cannot increase with adding new nodes to the path, then the measure of current path is an upper estimate of all extensions if this path. Thus, the search method may be based on the Dijkstra's algorithm for trees.

5   Experimental Evaluation

Efficiency of suggested recognition method was tested using cross-validation technique with increasing size of the training set. Testing document set was sorted randomly. On each iteration the first n documents were used as the training set and the $(n+1)$-th document was used to test recognition quality. The percentage of recognition errors was calculated. The test was performed several times with different sorting of document set, then the average error percentage for n-th iteration was calculated. This allows us to estimate the required size of the training set and the minimum error percentage the system can reach. Fig. 1 shows the dependence of error percentage on the size of the training set.

It can be seen that for semi-fixed forms with moderate structure variations the system needs 5-10 training samples to achieve sufficient precision of about 95% (5% of errors). For more complex forms with grater structure variations (so called flex-forms) larger training set is needed (at least 20 document samples). The recognition precision in this case is only 75-80%. This in insufficient for using the system in the automatic mode. However, since the result of training process is the FlexiLayout document description, the document model may still be adjusted manually. This allows one to increase recognition quality to appropriate level.

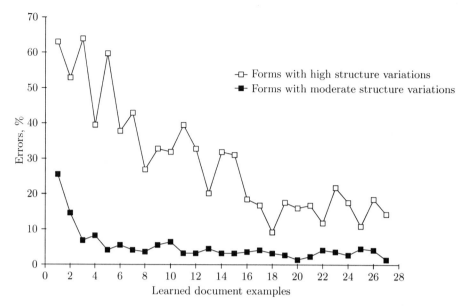

Fig. 1. Dependence of recognition errors percentage on training set size

6   Conclusion

A graph document model and structured documents recognition framework was proposed. We showed that the application of machine learning techniques in FlexiLayout document recognition system allows one to significantly reduce time costs for creating document model while maintaining sufficient recognition quality. Experiments showed that automatically generated document model allows the FlexiLayout system to recognize semi-structured documents with high precision. In case of flex-forms with significant structure variations the document description must be adjusted manually after being generated. However, even in this case the usage of automatic construction of document model results in considerable time saving. The further study will be aimed at increasing the recognition quality for complex documents with high structure variations.

References

1. Farrow, G.S.D., et al.: Model Matching in Intelligent Document Understanding. In: Proc. of ICDAR 1995 (1995)
2. Hirayama, Y.: Analyzing Form Images by Using Line-Shared-Adjacent Cell Relations. In: Proc. of IAPR 1996 (1996)
3. Yuan, J., Tang, Y.Y., Suen, C.Y.: Four Directional Adjacency Graphs (FDAG) and Their Application in Locating Fields in Forms. In: Proc. of ICDAR 1995 (1995)
4. Zuyev, K.A.: System for Identification of Structure of Printed Documents, Candidate of Science Dissertation, MGUL (in Russian) (1999)

5. Cook, D., Holder, L.: Mining Graph Data. Wiley Interscience, Hoboken (2006)
6. Kuramochi, M., Karypis, G.: An efficient algorithm for discovering frequent subgraphs, Tech. Rep. 02-026 Minneapolis, University of Minnesota (2002)
7. Neuhaus, M., Bunke, H.: A probabilistic approach to learning costs for graph edit distance. In: Proceedings 17th International Conference on Pattern Recognition, vol. 3 (2004)
8. Yan, X., Han, J.: gSpan: Graph-Based Substructure Pattern Mining. In: Proc. IEEE International Conference on Data Mining (ICDM 2002), Los Alamitos (2002)

Segmental K-Means Learning with Mixture Distribution for HMM Based Handwriting Recognition

Tapan Kumar Bhowmik, Jean-Paul van Oosten, and Lambert Schomaker

Faculty of Mathematics and Natural Sciences, University of Groningen, Netherlands
tkbhowmik@ai.rug.nl, J.P.van.Oosten@ai.rug.nl, L.Schomaker@ai.rug.nl

Abstract. This paper investigates the performance of hidden Markov models (HMMs) for handwriting recognition. The Segmental K-Means algorithm is used for updating the transition and observation probabilities, instead of the Baum-Welch algorithm. Observation probabilities are modelled as multi-variate Gaussian mixture distributions. A deterministic clustering technique is used to estimate the initial parameters of an HMM. Bayesian information criterion (BIC) is used to select the topology of the model. The wavelet transform is used to extract features from a grey-scale image, and avoids binarization of the image.

1 Introduction

Hidden Markov models (HMMs) are a common classification technique for time series and sequences in areas such as speech recognition, bio-informatics and handwriting recognition. HMMs are used to model processes which behave according to the Markov property: The next state is only influenced by the current state, not by the past.

Using mixture models as the observation probabilities has been proven to be very successful in handwriting recognition. Baum-Welch and Segmental K-means are algorithms for training HMMs [1,2]. Baum-Welch, although proven [3] to converge is not ideal: the convergence claim is proven theoretically, but empirically, there are still conditions where convergence does not occur, or computation restarts are otherwise needed. These restarts can greatly increase the, already lengthy, duration of training. As a first improvement, Segmental K-means are used with single Gaussian observation distributions. However, a simple example of a character image illustrates that distributions are multivariate. This paper proposes to use Segmental K-means with multi-variate Gaussian mixture observation distributions. Segmental K-means has the advantage over Baum-Welch that not every possible path is updated, only the most likely (Viterbi) path [2], which has a positive effect on computation time.

Because of its great importance, the initialisation of model parameters is investigated in this paper as well and a deterministic method is introduced to address this problem. Ideally, all segmentation is avoided, in the x-y space, but in luminance space as well. Therefore, algorithms are needed which can handle

S.O. Kuznetsov et al. (Eds.): PReMI 2011, LNCS 6744, pp. 432–439, 2011.

grey-scale. This is important in situations with low-quality images, such as in the Monk system [4] for historical manuscript retrieval.

The primary goal of this paper is not getting the best performance, but rather to see whether the combination of segmental K-means, the solution to the initialisation problem and grey-scale features is feasible for use in handwriting recognition.

2   Features

2.1   Feature Extraction with Wavelet Transform

The wavelet transform is a tool that finds application in many areas including image processing. Due to the multi-resolution property, it decomposes the signal at different scales. For a given image, the wavelet transform produces one low frequency subband image reflecting an approximation of the original image and three high frequency components of the image reflecting the detail. The approximation component is used here as a normalization image in the present recognition problem. In our experiment, we have considered Daubechies wavelet lowpass filter with four coefficients $[0.4830, 0.8365, 0.2241, -0.1294]$ [5]. For a raw input image we first calculate as much as possible the smallest rectangle object region of the image, then normalize it to a square image of size 64×64 with an interpolation technique. The wavelet decomposition algorithm with the above lowpass filter is applied to this normalized image to get 32×32 image. To make the pixel values with range $[0, 255]$, a scaling factor is used. The 32×32 scaled image is again divided into 16 blocks each of size 8×8. The 64 pixel values of each block are considered as the initial feature vector. This pipeline is shown in Fig. 1 for the digit "0" (zero).

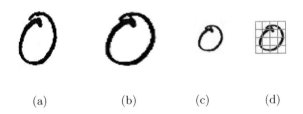

(a)   (b)   (c)   (d)

Fig. 1. (a) Original image of digit "0" (b) 64×64 normalized pixel image (c) 32×32 wavelet-decomposed image and (d) corresponding image 4×4 grid of 8×8 wavelet-values

In this paper, the goal is to exploit the good character representation with the wavelet feature within a hidden Markov scheme. Therefore, a virtual time axis needs to be constructed. An observation sequence is obtained by moving through the image from top to bottom, from left to right. This order is arbitrary, but a good first approach with regards to making segments.

2.2   Feature Reduction with PCA

In mathematical terms, feature reduction problem can be stated as: given the
p-dimensional random variable $\mathbf{x} = (x_1, x_2, ...x_p)^T$, find a lower dimensional
representation of it, $\mathbf{y} = (y_1, y_2, ...y_d)^T$ with $d \leq p$, that captures content
in the original data, according to some criteria. Let us assume that we have
n observations, each being a realization of the p-dimensional random variable
$\mathbf{x} = (x_1, x_2, ...x_p)^T$ with mean $\mu = \mathbf{E}(\mathbf{x}) = (\mu_1, \mu_2, ...\mu_p)^T$, $\mu_i = \frac{1}{n}\sum x_i$ and
covariance matrix $\Sigma_{p \times p} = E(\mathbf{x} - \mu)(\mathbf{x} - \mu)^T = \frac{1}{n}\sum(x_i - \mu_i)(x_i - \mu_i)^T$ where
$i = 1, 2, ..., p$. Let $\mathbf{\Phi_i} = (\Phi_{i1}, \Phi_{i2}, ...\Phi_{ip})^T$ be the eigen vector corresponding to
eigen value λ_i of $\Sigma_{p \times p}$, where $i = 1, 2, ..., p$, $\lambda_i \geq \lambda_j$ for all $i < j$ and all the
eigen vectors are mutually orthogonal for different λ_i. The Karhunen-Loeve lin-
ear transform on the basis of new coordinate system whose axis along $\{\mathbf{\Phi_i}\}$ is
defined as $y_i = \Phi_{i1}x_1 + \Phi_{i2}x_2 + ... + \Phi_{ip}x_p$, $i = 1, 2, ..., d(d \leq p)$, where y_i is
the ith principal component. Since a lower component is less significant than a
higher one, depending upon the value of λ_i, lower components $y_i(i > d)$ can be
removed to reduce the dimension of features.

In this experiment for each block out of $8 \times 8 = 64$ features, the 16 most
significant components are chosen for the actual feature vector. Since number of
blocks is 16 (4×4), the total number of feature vectors is 16, each with a size
of 16 features. In our HMM framework each feature vector is considered as an
observation symbol (O_i). So for an input image we get an observation sequence
$\mathbf{O} = O_1, O_2, ..., O_{16}$ with each observation having 16 dimensions.

3   HMM Parameter Estimation

An HMM consists of three sets of parameters $\lambda = (\pi, A, B)$, where π is the initial
state probability distribution, A is the state transition probability distribution
matrix and B is the observation symbol probability distribution. The modeling
of handwritten characters with HMMs can be regarded as the estimation of
model parameters λ_c for each character class c which represents almost the
characteristic of input sequence of data of that particular class. The estimation
of model parameters involves mainly three steps: selection of topology, estimation
of initial parameters of model λ, based on topology and finally re-estimate λ in
such a way that it maximizes the probability $P(O|\lambda)$ i.e., $P(O|\hat{\lambda}) \geq P(O|\lambda)$,
where $\hat{\lambda}$ is the re-estimated model.

3.1   Topology Selection and Initial Parameter Estimation

Before going to estimate the model parameters we need to define the topology
of the model which means the number of states, the number of mixture component per state (if observation probability is realized from Gaussian mixture
distributions) and the transition between states for the model. Here we always
consider ergodic (fully connected states transition) topology for transition between states. The number of states and the number of mixture component per

state are chosen randomly from a range of possible values of number of state and number of mixture component. Let N be the number of states and M the number of mixture components per state. Also assume that Q_t is a random variable with N possible values $\{1, 2, ...N\}$, representing a discrete state. Then we can define $A = \{a_{ij}\} = \{P(Q_t = j/Q_{t-1} = i)\}$, a hidden and time independent stochastic transition matrix and $\pi = \{\pi_i\} = \{P(Q_{t=1} = i)\}$, the probability of being in state i at time $t = 1$. Let a particular observation sequence be described as $O = (O_1 = o_1, ..., O_T = o_T)$. The probability of a particular observation at a particular time t for state j be described by: $b_j(o_t) = P(O_t = o_t/Q_t = j)$. The complete collection of parameters for all observation distributions is represented by $B = \{b_j(.)\}$. Let us assume that probability of observation for a particular state is emitted from a Gaussian mixture distribution. So we can write $b_j(o_t) = \sum_{k=1}^{M} c_{jk}\mathcal{N}(o_t|\mu_{jk}, \Sigma_{jk}) = \sum_{k=1}^{M} c_{jk}b_{jk}(o_t)$, where M is the number of components in the mixture.

Initialization of Mixtures through PCA based K-means Clustering[6]:
Let $X = \{\mathbf{x_1}, \mathbf{x_2}, ..., \mathbf{x_n}\}$ be the set of n observations, each of dimension d. For initializing N mixtures with each having M components, the data X has been partitioned into $K(= NM)$ clusters $\{C_{11}, C_{12}, ..., C_{1M}, C_{21}, ..., C_{NM}\}$. The goal of the K-means clustering is to find an exclusive partition in such a way that the criterion value $SSE = \sum_{j=1}^{N} \sum_{k=1}^{M} \sum_{\mathbf{x_i} \in C_{jk}} \|\mathbf{x_i} - \mu_{jk}\|$ (where $\mu_{jk} = \frac{1}{n_{jk}} \sum_{\mathbf{x_i} \in C_{jk}} \mathbf{x_i}$ denotes the mean of cluster C_{jk} and n_{jk} denotes the number of instances in C_{jk}) is minimized. Since the first principal direction (the eigen vector corresponding to the largest eigen value of the covariance matrix $\Sigma_{d \times d}$) is the direction which contributes the most to the SSE, it is a good candidate direction for splitting the cluster. Starting from a single cluster, divide it into two sub-clusters, choose the sub-cluster with the largest within-cluster SSE_{jk} as the next cluster to partition, repeat the process until K clusters are produced. At each split stage, for the selected cluster C_{jk}, we divide it into two sub-clusters $C_{jk}^{(1)}$ and $C_{jk}^{(2)}$ according to the following rule: for any $\mathbf{x_i} \in C_{jk}$, if y_i (the projected value of $\mathbf{x_i}$ in first principle direction of $\mathbf{x_i} \in C_{jk}$) $\leq \bar{y}_i$ (mean of y_i), assign $\mathbf{x_i}$ to $C_{jk}^{(1)}$, otherwise, assign $\mathbf{x_i}$ to $C_{jk}^{(2)}$. The mean value of each cluster is considered as the initial cluster center. Once we get the initial cluster centers, run K-means clustering to get the final clusters. For each cluster C_{jk} we then calculate mean μ_{jk} and covariance matrix Σ_{jk}. And c_{jk} has been calculated by $c_{jk} = \frac{n_{jk}}{\sum_k n_{jk}}$. These are the initial parameters for the mixtures.

Initialization of initial state probability and state transition probability: Initial state probabilities and state transition probabilities have been chosen randomly in such a way that they satisfy the following criteria: $\sum_i \pi_i = 1$ and $\sum_j a_{ij} = 1$.

3.2   Re-estimation of Model Parameter through Segmental K-Means

We now define the following variables before describing the Segmental K-Means algorithm:

$$\alpha_t(i) = P(O_1 = o_1, ..., O_t = o_t, Q_t = i|\lambda), \tag{1}$$

is the probability of seeing the partial observation sequence, $o_1, o_2, ..., o_t$, (until time t) and ending up in state i at time t, given the model λ.

$$\beta_t(i) = P(O_{t+1} = o_{t+1}, ..., O_T = o_T|Q_t = i, \lambda), \tag{2}$$

is the probability of the ending partial observation sequence, $o_{t+1}, o_{t+2}, ..., o_T$ given that we started at state i at time t and the model λ.

$$\xi_t(i,j) = \frac{P(Q_t = i, Q_{t+1} = j|O, \lambda)}{P(O|\lambda)} = \frac{\alpha_t(i)a_{ij}b_j(o_{t+1})\beta_{t+1}(j)}{\sum_i^N \sum_j^N \alpha_t(i)a_{ij}b_j(o_{t+1})\beta_{t+1}(j)}, \tag{3}$$

is the probability of being in state i at time t and being state j at time $t+1$, given the model λ and observation sequence O.

$$\gamma_t(i) = P(Q_t = i|O, \lambda) = \frac{\alpha_t(i)\beta_t(i)}{\sum_{j=1}^N \alpha_t(j)\beta_t(j)} = \sum_{j=1}^N \xi_t(i,j), \tag{4}$$

is the probability of being in state i at time t, given the observation sequence O, and the model λ.

Segmental K-Means Algorithm:

The Baum-Welch algorithm defines $\xi_t(i,j)$ for all states i and j. In contrast, the segmental k-means algorithm finds the most likely state sequence using the Viterbi algorithm and calculates $\xi_t(i,j)$ only over the states found in the most likely state sequence. The algorithm works as follows:
For an input observation sequence $\mathbf{o} = (o_1, o_2, ..., o_T)$

1. Calculate $\alpha_t(i)$ and $\beta_t(i)$ through the Forward-Backward algorithm, which is described explicitly in [1]. To prevent rounding errors in implementations, $\alpha_t(i)$ and $\beta_t(i)$ need to be scaled, as discussed in [7].
2. Estimate $\xi_t(i,j)$
   Find the optimal state sequence for the input sequence $\mathbf{o}$ with the Viterbi algorithm [1] and then assign each observation o_t to a particular state according to the Viterbi state sequence. Then,

$$\xi_t(i,j) = \begin{cases} 1 \text{ if observation } o_t \text{ assigned to state } i \text{ and } o_{t+1} \text{ assigned to state } j \\ 0 \text{ otherwise} \end{cases}$$

3. Estimate $\gamma_t(i)$ (the probability of being in state i at time t) from $\xi_t(i,j)$ (the probability of being in state i at time t and state j at time $t+1$), according to equation (4) and in particular, $\gamma_T(i) = \sum_{j=1}^N \xi_{T-1}(i,j)$.

4. Update the model parameters

$$\bar{\pi}_i = \gamma_1(i), \tag{5}$$

the expected relative frequency spent in state i at time $t = 1$.

$$\bar{a}_{ij} = \frac{\sum_{t=1}^{T-1} \xi_t(i,j)}{\sum_{t=1}^{T-1} \gamma_t(i)}, \tag{6}$$

the expected number of transitions from state i to state j relative to the expected total number of transitions away from state i. We now define the probability that the kth component of the ith mixture generated observation o_t as $\gamma_t(i,k) = \gamma_t(i)\frac{c_{ik}b_{ik}(o_t)}{b_i(o_t)}$, then

$$\bar{c}_{ik} = \frac{\sum_{t=1}^{T} \gamma_t(i,k)}{\sum_{t=1}^{T} \gamma_t(i)} \tag{7}$$

$$\bar{\mu}_{ik} = \frac{\sum_{t=1}^{T} \gamma_t(i,k)o_t}{\sum_{t=1}^{T} \gamma_t(i,k)} \tag{8}$$

$$\bar{\Sigma}_{ik} = \frac{\sum_{t=1}^{T} \gamma_t(i,k)(o_t - \bar{\mu}_{ik})(o_t - \bar{\mu}_{ik})^T}{\sum_{t=1}^{T} \gamma_t(i,k)} \tag{9}$$

In case of multiple observation sequences, let us assume that if L be the number of sequences with T_l be the length of the sequence l, then the equations above become:

$$\bar{\pi}_i = \frac{\sum_{l=1}^{L} \gamma_1^l(i)}{L}$$

$$\bar{a}_{ij} = \frac{\sum_{l=1}^{L} \sum_{t=1}^{T_l-1} \xi_t^l(i,j)}{\sum_{l=1}^{L} \sum_{t=1}^{T_l-1} \gamma_t^l(i)}$$

$$\bar{c}_{ik} = \frac{\sum_{l=1}^{L} \sum_{t=1}^{T_l} \gamma_t^l(i,k)}{\sum_{l=1}^{L} \sum_{t=1}^{T_l} \gamma_t^l(i)}$$

$$\bar{\mu}_{ik} = \frac{\sum_{l=1}^{L} \sum_{t=1}^{T_l} \gamma_t^l(i,k)o_t^l}{\sum_{l=1}^{L} \sum_{t=1}^{T_l} \gamma_t^l(i,k)}$$

$$\bar{\Sigma}_{ik} = \frac{\sum_{l=1}^{L} \sum_{t=1}^{T_l} \gamma_t^l(i,k)(o_t^l - \bar{\mu}_{ik})(o_t^l - \bar{\mu}_{ik})^T}{\sum_{l=1}^{L} \sum_{t=1}^{T_l} \gamma_t^l(i,k)}$$

From Step-1 to Step-4 is repeated until any observation o_t is reassigned a new state in Step-2. Step 1 to step 4 is repeated as long as any observation is reassigned to a new state in step 2.

4   Experimental Results

The following experiments are performed on three datasets. The first two are handwritten Bangla numerals and basic characters, the third is a MNIST dataset of 70 000 handwritten arabic numerals. The Bangla numerals dataset consists of 10 000 training instances and 2 000 instances for testing. The Bangla basic characters dataset has 45 classes and the number of training instances are 500 per class, and 100 for testing. Finally, the MNIST dataset is used as well, with 60 000 training instances and 10 000 testing instances. The following accuracies can be reported on the previously mentioned test sets, using the selected models as described in the Model Selection section: 96.25% for Bangla numerals, 80.00% for Bangla basic characters and 97.19% for MNIST dataset. The accuracy on same dataset of basic characters is relatively better than the accuracy is found previously on single stage classification with SVM classifiers [5].

4.1   Model Selection

An important but difficult task is to choose a relevant number of components or a number of hidden states in the HMM when observation probabilities are emitted from a finite mixture distribution. Many criteria (BIC, ICL, PML, etc.) or procedures [8] have been proposed to answer this open question. But there is no guarantee that any particular criterion will work satisfactory on a particular dataset. In this study we have used BIC criterion[9] for selecting the number of states and the number of mixture per state in HMM. If the number of state in the model is N and the number of components in the mixture is M, then according to BIC criterion $BIC(\lambda) = logP(X|\hat{\lambda}) - \frac{1}{2}\nu(\hat{\lambda})log(n)$, where $\nu(\hat{\lambda})$ is the number of free parameters in the model and n is the size of the observation set X generating model $\{\lambda\}$ and $\hat{\lambda}$ is the Maximum Likelihood estimate of the model λ. Here $\nu(\hat{\lambda}) = N(M\frac{d(d+1)}{2} + Md + (M-1)) + (N^2 - 1)$, d is the dimension of the observation. The first term $M\frac{d(d+1)}{2}$ is the number of free parameters for covariance matrix of a mixture, the second term Md is for mean, the third term $(M-1)$ is for the coefficient of each mixture and the last term $(N^2 - 1)$ is for state probabilities (in the context of ergodic model).

As an example, Fig. 2 shows the BIC values for different numbers of states and mixture components for the model of the Bangla numeral zero and Fig. 3 shows the corresponding model accuracy in the Bangla numerals test set when other competitive models (except zero) are kept constant. From this figure, we can see that the first maximum value of the BIC curve always gives the highest accuracy. In this case, the models $\lambda(4, 8)$, $\lambda(6, 5)$ and $\lambda(8, 4)$ are the models with the highest accuracy, on the basis of the first maxima point of the BIC curve. Since $\lambda(4, 8)$ produces the maximal BIC value with respect to other two models ($\lambda(6, 5)$ and $\lambda(8, 4)$), $\lambda(4, 8)$ has been chosen as the final model for the numeral zero.

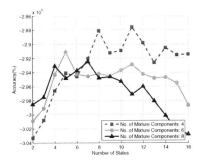

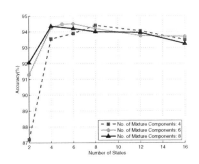

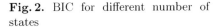

Fig. 2. BIC for different number of states

Fig. 3. Accuracy for different number of states

5 Conclusion

The learning framework of the Segmental K-Means algorithm for HMMs with Gaussian mixture observation densities has been described. A deterministic method to initialize the model parameter has been presented as well. The main advantage of this framework is that it can easily be switched to the Baum-Welch learning algorithm, which is used conventionally to learn the HMM parameters. The only change in the Segmental K-Means algorithm is step 3. A grey-scale feature has been implemented for recognition of isolated handwritten characters. Initial recognition results show that using the segmental k-means learning method for HMMs is quite efficient for handwriting recognition.

References

1. Rabiner, L.: A tutorial on hidden markov models and selected applications in speech recognition. Trans. on. IEEE 77(2), 257–286 (1989)
2. Juang, B.H., Rabiner, L.: The segmental k-means algorithm for estimating parameters of hidden markov models. IEEE Trans. on ASSP 38(9), 1639–1641 (1990)
3. Wu, C.F.J.: On the convergence properties of the EM algorithm. The Annals of Statistics 11(1), 95–103 (1983)
4. van der Zant, T., Schomaker, L., Haak, K.: Handwritten-word spotting using biologically inspired features. IEEE Trans. on PAMI 30(11), 1945–1957 (2008)
5. Bhowmik, T.K., Ghanty, P., Roy, A., Parui, S.K.: Svm-based hierarchical architectures for handwritten bangla character recognition. International Journal on Document Analysis and Recognition(IJDAR) 12(2), 97–108 (2009)
6. Su, T., Dy, J.: A deterministic method for initializing k-means clustering. In: Proc. of The 16th IEEE Int. Conf. on Tools with Artificial Intelligence, pp. 784–786 (2004)
7. Rahimi, A.: An erratum for a tutorial on hidden markov models and selected applications in speech recognition. In: Online article (2000)
8. Celeux, G., Durand, J.B.: Selecting hidden markov model state number with cross-validated likelihood. Computational Statistics 23(4), 541–564 (2008)
9. Biem, A.: A model selection criterion for classification: Application to hmm topology optimization. In: Proceedings of the 7th ICDAR, pp. 104–108 (2003)

Feature Set Selection for On-Line Signatures Using Selection of Regression Variables

Desislava Boyadzieva and Georgi Gluhchev

IICT-BAS, Sofia, Bulgaria
d.n.dimitrova@gmail.com, gluhchev@iinf.bas.bg
http://iict.bas.bg

Abstract. In this paper we approach feature set selection phase in signature verification by applying the method for selection of regression variables based on Mallows Cp criterion for regression. In this way we identify best feature subsets of various sizes for each user of our database on the basis of his/her ten genuine and ten random forgery on-line signatures. Among these subsets we select the best subset that have Cp value closest to p, where p is the number of regression coefficients. Thus, we obtain for each user the best feature subset of a different size. Our aim is to check whether there are common features among best feature subsets for all users which will justify the removal of the rest features from the initial feature set. The results obtained with the database of 140 signatures collected from fourteen users demonstrated that we cannot restrict to common feature set valid for all users but instead of that we have to consider each user best feature set separately in signature verification.

Keywords: Signature verification, feature selection, on-line signatures, selection of regression variables, Mallows Cp criterion.

1 Introduction

Signatures are recognized and accepted modality for authentication. Signature verification is the process of confirming the identity of a user based on the handwritten signature of the user as a form of behavioral biometrics [1]. Different approaches to signature verification are considered in survey paper [3]. Over 100 features used in signature verification are presented in [3].

Since some features demonstrate higher discriminatory capability than others, features selection should be performed after feature extraction. Feature selection is defined as the process of selecting k most discriminatory features out of p available ones ($k \leq p$) and it aims to identify and remove as much irrelevant and redundant information as possible. A review of the work on feature set selection for signatures is performed in [4].

In this paper we investigate the problem of feature set selection for on-line signatures by applying the method for selection of regression variables based on Mallows Cp criterion to identify best feature subsets of various sizes for each of the fourteen users of our database on the basis of his/her ten genuine and ten

S.O. Kuznetsov et al. (Eds.): PReMI 2011, LNCS 6744, pp. 440–445, 2011.

random forgery signatures. Among these subsets we select the best subset that
have Cp value closest to p, where p is the number of regression coefficients. Thus,
we obtain for each user the best feature subset of a different size. Our aim is to
check whether there are common features among best feature subsets for all users
which will justify the removal of the rest features from the initial feature set.
The results obtained demonstrated that we cannot restrict to common feature
set valid for all users but instead of that we have to consider each user best
feature set separately in signature verification.

The paper is structured as follows: Section 2 considers the selection of regression variables; Section 3 presents some experimental results and the last section
draws some conclusion and gives an outlook for feature work.

2   Selection of Regression Variables

Regression analysis is one of the most widely used statistical techniques because
it provides simple methods for establishing a functional relationship among variables. It has extensive applications in many subject areas [2]. Variable selection
in regression analysis is the problem of deciding the variables to be included in
the model such that it provides good forecast.

The formulation of the variable selection problem is as follows. It is assumed
[7] that there are $n \geq k + 1$ observations on a k-vector of input variables $x^t = (x_1, ..., x_k)$, and a scalar response y, such that the jth response $j = 1, ..., n$ is
determined by:

$$y_j = \beta_0 + \sum_{i=1}^{k} \beta_i x_{ij} + e_j. \tag{1}$$

The model (1) is frequently expressed in matrix notation as:

$$Y = X\beta + e. \tag{2}$$

Here Y is the n-vector of observed responses, X is the design matrix of dimension
n x $(k + 1)$, β is the $(k + 1)$-vector of unknown regression coefficients and e is
n-vector of the residuals e_j assumed to be independent $N(0, \sigma^2)$. Regression
parameters or coefficients $\beta_i, i = 0, ..., k$ are unknown constants to be estimated
from the data and their estimates are denoted by b_i. In our experiment we
decided to remove the intercept β_0 from the equation. Then, the vector b of
Least-Squares estimates of the coefficients vector β is given by:

$$b = (X^T X)^{-1} X^T Y. \tag{3}$$

There is no unique technique for selecting best regression equation. If there
are k potential independent variables there are 2^k possible equations to be considered. Variable selection techniques are the following: best subset, backward
elimination, forward selection and stepwise methods [2]. In this paper we consider best subset approach.

A number of criteria have been proposed for selecting the best subset or subsets of independent variables in linear regression analysis. Mallows proposed C_p as a criterion to decide on suitable subset among contending subsets. It is a measure of the standardized total squared error defined as:

$$C_p = \frac{RSS_p}{\hat{\sigma}^2} - (n - 2p). \tag{4}$$

In this equation RSS_p denotes residual sum of squares for the particular regression with p variables including the intercept, if any. $\hat{\sigma}^2$ is an estimate of residual mean square σ^2 for full regression:

$$\hat{\sigma}^2 = \frac{1}{n-k} \sum_{j=1}^{n} (y_j - \sum_{i=1}^{k} \beta_i x_{ij})^2. \tag{5}$$

If a model is adequate, i.e. does not suffer from lack of fit, then $E(RSS_p) = (n - p)\hat{\sigma}^2$ and the following is true for that model:

$$E(C_p) \approx p. \tag{6}$$

This means that we expect C_p value to be about p. A plot of C_p versus p displays the adequate models as points close to the line $C_p = p$. Subsets with small values of C_p and values of C_p close to p are considered good.

Hocking and Leslie [5] further describe a method which allows thus subset to be identified after consideration of only a small fraction of all $\binom{k}{p}$ possible subsets of size p. LaMotte and Hocking [6] modified this algorithm in a way that moderately large problems can be treated with minimum of computation. The algorithm specifies the subset of size r to be deleted. In the following, the terms r-subset and p-subset will always refer, respectively, to subsets being deleted and subsets being retained.

The method for selection of best subset is based on m-variable reductions, i.e. reductions in the regression sum of squares due to eliminating subsets of size m from the k-variable equation. Typically $1 \le m \le 4$ and $m = 1$ in the original method [5]. These m-variable reductions are used to determine the best r-subset to be removed, for $r > m$. The reduction in the regression sum of squares due to removing a set of r variables is given by:

$$Red_r = RSS_p - RSS_k. \tag{7}$$

The set of r variables for which this reduction is minimum specifies the subset of size p $(p = k - r)$ variables in the regression to be retained for which residual sum of squares is minimum. It is suggested in [5] that C_p statistic can also be computed by using this reduction in the following way:

$$C_p = \frac{Red_r}{\hat{\sigma}^2} - (2p - k). \tag{8}$$

The steps of the generalized algorithm are as follows [6]: First, the k-variable equation is fitted with all variables present and the reductions in the regression sum of squares, called univariate reduction, due to deleting each of the k-variables, are calculated. If a single variable, say ith is removed from the regression, its univariate reduction is given by:

$$\Theta_i = \hat{\sigma}^2 t_i^2. \tag{9}$$

$$t_i^2 = \frac{b_i^2}{\hat{\sigma}_{b_i}^2}. \tag{10}$$

The square of t-statistic associated with ith regression coefficient is denoted by t_i^2 and the standard error of the estimated coefficient b_i is denoted by $\hat{\sigma}_{b_i}$. The standard errors of the estimated coefficients are the square roots of the diagonal elements of the coefficient covariance matrix. After this, the variables are relabeled according to the order of these univariate reductions. Having the variables relabeled, the reductions in the regression sum of squares due to all of the $\binom{k}{m}$ subsets of size m are evaluated. These are called m-variable reductions. Each subset of size m is denoted by the subscripts of the variables in that subset in increasing order. That is, a m-subset is described as $(i_1, i_2, ..., i_m)$ where $1 \leq i_j \leq k$ and $i_1 \leq i_2 \leq ... \leq i_m$. Next these m-variable reductions are ordered in increasing order of magnitude and are used to define stages for inspecting the r-subsets. Only those m-subsets whose first index is $(r - m + 1)$ or greater are used to define a stage and hence we evaluate only them. The r-subsets in a stage defined by an m-subset contain r indices consisting of those indices in the defining m-subset and $r - m$ indices which are less than the first index in the m-subset. There are total of $\binom{k-r+m}{m}$ stages defined in this way. The stages are numbered according to the magnitude of the m-variable subset which define them. Thus Stage 1 will consist of r-subsets defined by the m-subset with smallest reduction.

In general, at the qth stage we evaluate the reductions due to all subsets defined in the qth stage and ask if the smallest reduction in the regression sum of squares computed for an r-subset obtained in all Stages before the qth stage $(1, 2, ..., q)$ is less than the reduction due to the m-subset defining Stage $(q+1)$. If so, we terminate having identified the best subset of size p obtained by the corresponding r-subset and if not we proceed to Stage $(q + 1)$.

3   Experiment

The database for our experiment contains 140 signatures collected from fourteen users. All ten signatures of each user are acquired by using a digitizing tablet Wacom Intuos3 A5 PTZ-630 having a resolution of 5080 lines per inch and an acquisition area of the pad of 152.4 x 210.6 mm and sampling rate of 200 points per second. Signature raw data is obtained using the .NET Tablet PC SDK 1.7 in a C# software program. Having raw data, we evaluate all the features listed in Table 1.

Table 1. Signature features

A1	height	A2	height to width ratio	A3	number of points
A4	distance between initial and center point	A5	distance between end and center point	A6	angle of the line between center and initial points
A7	angle of the line between center and end points	A8	angle of the line between initial and end points	A9	distance between leftmost and center points
A10	angle of the line between center and leftmost points	A11	angle of the line between center and rightmost points	A12	distance between leftmost and initial points
A13	distance between rightmost and end points	A14	angle of the line angle of the line between leftmost and initial points	A15	angle of the line between end and rightmost points

The number of features is $k = 15$ and the number of signatures is $n = 20$ (ten genuine and ten random forgeries). For each user we construct a txt file. Each line of that file contains signature features values separated by a semicolon followed by 1 (if genuine, i.e. first class) or -1 (if forgery, i.e. second class). The random forgeries for a given users are just randomly selected signatures of the rest users. Our software program processes each of these fourteen files by performing the method described in Section 2 and finds the best subset of size p $(p = k - r)$ for variable values of r $(3 < r < 13$). Among these subsets we select the subset that have C_p value closest to p. These subsets for each user are listed in Table 2.

Table 2. Best p-subsets for each user

User No	Size of p-subset	Best *p*-subset
1	6	A2;A5;A7;A12;A13;A15
2	9	A3;A5;A6;A7;A8;A9;A10;A11;A12
3	11	A2;A4;A5;A6;A7;A8;A9;A10;A13;A14;A15
4	11	A1;A3;A4;A6;A7;A8;A9;A11;A12;A13;A15
5	5	A1;A2;A5;A9;A15
6	6	A4;A8;A9;A10;A12;A14
7	7	A1;A2;A5;A8;A11;A12;A13
8	9	A1;A2;A3;A4;A5;A8;A9;A10;A15
9	11	A2;A5;A6;A7;A8;A9;A11;A12;A13;A14;A15
10	8	A4;A6;A9;A10;A11;A12;A13;A14
11	9	A1;A3;A4;A5;A6;A7;A9;A11;A13
12	11	A1;A2;A3;A4;A5;A6;A7;A9;A10;A11;A15
13	10	A1;A2;A3;A5;A6;A8;A10;A11;A12;A14
14	10	A1;A2;A3;A4;A5;A7;A8;A9;A10;A11

These results demonstrate that the number of features is significantly reduced for some users but there are not common features among best feature subsets for all users which will justify the removal of the rest features from the initial feature set. That is because all the features have approximately equal number of occurrences in best subsets. The results demonstrated that we cannot restrict to common feature set valid for all users but instead of that we have to consider each user best feature set separately in signature verification.

4   Conclusion

In this paper we present a method for feature set selection based on Mallows Cp criterion for regression and conduct an experiment in order to test it with a database of 140 signatures from fourteen users. The obtained results demonstrate that this approach can be used for feature set reduction for a particular user before his/her signature verification. Probably the small number of features does not allow the presence of common features for all users. Therefore, the focus of our future work will be the application of the method for selection of regression variables for larger feature set. Also, we will experiment with skilled signature forgeries and investigate the problem further.

Acknowledgements

This work is supported by the European Social Fund and Bulgarian Ministry of Education, Youth and Science under Operative Program Human Resources Development, Grant BG051PO001-3.3.04/40.

References

1. Nalwa, V.S., Ekeland, I.: Automatic on-line signature verification. Proceedings of the IEEE 85, 213–239 (1997)
2. Chatterjee, S., Hadi, A.: Regression Analysis by Example, 4th edn. New York (2006)
3. Leclerc, F., Plamondon, R.: Automatic signature verification: the state of the art 1989-1993. International Journal of Pattern Recognition and Artificial Intelligence 8, 643–660 (1994)
4. Richiardi, J., Ketabdar, H., Drygajlo, A.: Local and Global Feature Selection for On-line Signature Verification. In: Eighth International Conference on Document Analysis and Recognition (ICDAR 2005), pp. 625–629 (2005)
5. Hocking, R.R., Leslie, R.n.: Selection of the Best Subset in Regression Analysis. Technometrics 9, 531–540 (1967)
6. LaMotte, L.R., Hocking, R.R.: Computational Efficiency in the Selection of Regression Variables. Technometrics 12, 83–93 (1970)
7. Hocking, R.R.: The Analysis and Selection of Variables in Linear Regression. Biometrics 32, 1–50 (1976)
8. Mallows, C.L.: Some Comments on Cp. Technometrics 15, 661–675 (1973)

Headline Based Text Extraction from Outdoor Images

Ranjit Ghoshal[1], Anandarup Roy[2],
Tapan Kumar Bhowmik[3], and Swapan K. Parui[2]

[1] St. Thomas' Collage of Engineering and Technology
Kolkata- 700023, India
`ranjit.ghoshal@rediffmail.com`
[2] CVPR Unit
Indian Statistical Institute, Kolkata, India
`roy.anandarup@gmail.com,swapan@isical.ac.in`
[3] Faculty of Mathematics and Natural Sciences,
University of Groningen, Netherlands
`tkbhowmik@ai.rug.nl`

Abstract. The goal of this article is to design an effective scheme for extraction of Bangla/Devnagari text from outdoor images. We first segment a color image using fuzzy c-means algorithm. In Bangla/Devnagari script, text may be attached/unattached to the headlines. Hence, after segmentation, headlines are detected from each connected components using morphology. Now, the components attached or close to the detected headlines are separated. Further by applying certain shape and position based purification we could distinguish text and non text. Our experiments on a dataset of 100 outdoor images containing Bangla and/or Devnagari text reveals satisfactory performance.

1 Introduction

With the increasing popularity of digital cameras attached with various handheld devices (mobile phones, PDAs etc), many new computational challenges have gained significance. Extraction and recognition of texts from outdoor images captured by such devices is a challenging problem nowadays due to variations in style, color, background complexity, influence of luminance etc. Automatic detection of text in a natural scene image is useful to blind and foreigners with language barrier. Furthermore, it also has potential applications in robotics, image retrieval and intelligent transport systems.

A survey work of existing methods for detection, localization and extraction of texts embedded in images of natural scenes can be found in [1]. Two broad categories of available methods are connected component (CC) based and texture based algorithms. Earlier, Wu et al. [2] proposed a texture segmentation method to generate candidate text regions. A set of feature components is computed for each pixel and these are clustered using K-means algorithm. More recently, Jung et al. [3] employed a multi-layer perceptron classifier to discriminate between

S.O. Kuznetsov et al. (Eds.): PReMI 2011, LNCS 6744, pp. 446–451, 2011.

text and non-text pixels. Considering Bangla/Devnagari script, Bhattacharya et. al. [4] proposed a scheme based on analysis of CCs for extraction of Devnagari and Bangla texts from camera captured outdoor images. Also a few criteria for robust filtering of text components have been proposed. Bangla and Devnagari are two most popular Indian scripts used by more than 200 and 500 million people respectively in the Indian subcontinent. An unique and common charac-teristic of these two scripts is the existence of certain headlines that act as an interlink among symbols of a word. We here, take an interest into color images embedding text. We first extract a number of color and shape based features from an input color image. The fuzzy c-means clustering is applied on these features, for segmentation (Sect. 2). After color image segmentation, headlines are detected from each CCs using morphology on the skeleton image (Sect. 3). Afterwards, the CCs attached with these headlines are separated. These sepa-rated components may contain both text and non-text. We apply certain shape and position based purification in order to distinguish between text and non text (Sect. 4). However some text portions, that are not connected with headline, will not be separated by the above procedure. To cope this, we increase the area of the bounding box of each CC to a specified limit. The portions that lie inside this modified bounding box are now studied against the previous criteria to obtain text (Sect. 5).

Concerning the dataset, to the best known, no benchmark dataset of outdoor images consisting Bangla and/or Devnagari is available. The present study is based on a set of 100 outdoor images. Initial tests (Sect. 6) show well separation of texts from the images.

2   Color Image Segmentation

Color image segmentation is our first step of text extraction. The fuzzy c-means algorithm is used for color image segmentation. Before applying c-means, we extract some features from the normalized RGB image. Let us consider a pixel p_i of the image. Then p_i can be described by the tuple (r_i, g_i, b_i) i.e. the normalized R, G and B values. Besides, these three color values, we take another shape based feature of p_i. Inside an object (text here), intensity of pixels are assumed to be homogenous. We consider an $n \times n$ window surrounding p_i. Let β_i be the number of pixels having same intensity as p_i inside the $n \times n$ window. Then β_i is our another feature. Combining, the feature vector ($\mathbf{f}_i$) corresponding to the pixel p_i is: $\mathbf{f}_i = (r_i, g_i, b_i, \beta_i)$. These features are sent to the fuzzy c-means clustering procedure.

3   Morphology Based Headline Detection

Most of the Bangla and/or Devnagari characters are connected by the headline. Hence, in order to extract the Bangla and/or Devnagari text portions we should detect the headline that joins them. Here, we apply mathematical morphology operation to obtain the lines inside the image. Further, applying some filtering we are able to detect the headline. The procedure works as follows. At first sufficiently small and large CCs are removed. For each remaining CCs, the skeleton image is constructed by morphological operation. Let us denote the skeleton image by A. With the skeleton image, we perform morphological opening operation to extract straight lines. It is evident that opening of an image A with a linear structuring element B can effectively identify the horizontal line segments present in a CC. However, a suitable choice of the length of this structuring element is crucial for processing at the latter stages and we empirically set this length as 21 pixels for the present dataset. The effect of skeletonisation removes pixels on the boundaries of the image but does not allow components to break apart. After skeletonisation, only the required pixels remain and thus a less number of lines detected. However, if no such lines are detected, we need to apply morphology on the original CC. Also, we may encounter a component small enough that we could not find any horizontal line. Such components remain as it is.

Now we have a set of lines over the image. We next apply some simple criteria to separate out possible headlines. Let a detected line be denoted by L_i. Let H_u and H_l be the heights of the portions of the corresponding CCs lie at the upper and at the lower half of the line L_i. Bangla characters mostly lie at the lower portion of the headline, only a small portion may reside at the upper of the headline. So, for a headline L_i we should have $H_u < H_l$. Thus at the next step we sort out all the lines L_i for which $H_u < H_l$. These lines mostly represent the headlines.

4   Headline Attached Text Portion Separation

After finding the headlines, the components attached with these headlines are separated. These components may include text as well as non-text. However, applying some text specific conditions we are able to separate out text components. These conditions are described below. All the concerned components are subjected to these conditions in the same sequence as given. One important note here, is, the thresholds specified in one condition are found after performing the previous conditions. Thresholds may differ if the sequence is altered.

1. *Removal of boundary attached connected components*: Generally, text like patterns are not attached with boundary of the image. So, we first remove all boundary attached CCs using morphological reconstruction.
2. *Elongatedness ratio*: For elongatedness ratio (ER) we use the measure designed by Roy et. al. [5]. Empirically it is found that a component with ER value greater than 5 is a text part.
3. *Number of holes*: Usually, text like patterns contain less number of holes than non-text patterns. Using the Euler number, we calculate the number of holes inside a component. Found empirically, a text component has less than 9 holes.
4. *Aspect ratio*: The aspect ratio of a non-text component is either very small or very large. We found by experiments, that the aspect ratio of a text component becomes less than 0.3 or greater than 2.0.

5. *Object to background pixels ratio* (r): This measure is computed inside the component bounding box. Due to the elongated nature of Bangla and Devnagari texts, only a few object pixels fall inside bounding box. On the other hand, elongated non-texts are usually straight lines, so, contribute enough object pixels. We observe $0.3 \leq r \leq 3$ could identify text components.

After the above procedure, all the headline attached text components are separated.

5   Identification of Headline Unattached Text

As discussed above, we successfully separate headline attached text portions. However, in Bangla/Devnagari some text components do not meet the headline. Now we consider such components. These components, though not connected, must be close to one/more of already detected text components. Then, if we increase area of the component bounding box enough, the possible text components may lie inside it. With this view, we increase the width of the bounding box by its height and the height by an empirical threshold. Now, the components inside this modified bounding box are subjected to the text identification conditions (Sect. 5).

6   Results and Discussion

In this section we present the results after applying our algorithms to a set of outdoor images from our dataset. Our dataset consists of 100 test images captured by a DSC-W320/P SONY digital still camera (14.1MP). The images contain Bangla and/or Devnagari texts.

Let us first consider the "X-Ray" image (Fig. 1(a)) as an example. Here, besides the arrow and thin boundaries, the text components are in white. The segmented image is shown in Fig. 1(b). Fig. 1(c) presents the headlines detected by morphology. The components that are attached with these headlines are shown in Fig. 1(d). Compering this with Fig. 1(a), we notice, all but three text components are present. These three components are unattached to the headline. Now, we perform the elimination of boundary attached components. As a result (Fig. 1(e)), the big blob at the top of the image is now eliminated. However, the non-text portion present at the bottom of the image is not boundary connected, so remain unchanged. Here, we can filter out this component successfully after testing the elongatedness ratio (Fig. 1(f)). However, the background component present here is elongated enough, so satisfy this criteria. We observe a large number of holes inside this component. Hence, after putting a condition on number of holes we may remove this component as well (Fig. 1(g)). The next two operations i.e. the aspect ratio and the ratio of object and background pixels, do not affect the results. Afterwards, we perform the identification of text components unattached to headlines. Fig. 1(h) gives the result.

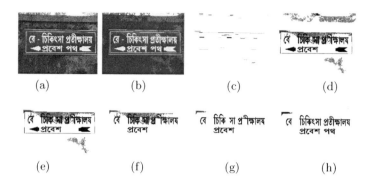

Fig. 1. (a) Input "X-Ray" image, (b) after segmentation, (c) after detecting headlines, (d) all CCs attached with headlines, (e) after removal of boundary attached CCs, (f) after performing elongatedness ratio, (g) after filtering using number of holes, and (h) after retrieving headline unattached text

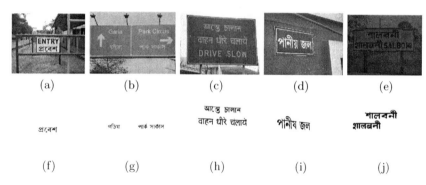

Fig. 2. (a), (b), (c), (d), (e) Sample images and (f), (g), (h), (i), (j) the corresponding segmented text portions

We may notice the components absent in Fig. 1(d) are now identified successfully. In Fig. 2, we present some more results on images from our dataset. As, Fig. 2 suggests, the skew and perspective issue can't affect our procedure to some extent. However, in heavily skewed images the algorithm may fail due to wrong detection of headlines. Also note the successful results of "Salbani" image (Fig. 2(e)) having poor lighting condition.

Fig. 3. Results on images showing degraded performance. (a), (c) The original images and (b), (d) the text portions.

Table 1. The precision and recall computation for our dataset

No. of Images	Status	Total text	Correctly recognized text	Wrongly recognized text	Precision	Recall
62	Perfectly extracted	307	307	27	91.91%	100.00%
32	Partially/extracted with some non text	147	91	29	75.83%	61.90%
06	Poor performance	27	09	31	22.50%	33.33%
100		481	407	87	82.38%	84.61%

The images in Fig. 3 show poor performance. The two images have headline unattached text portions that are not restored. The precision and recall values of our algorithm obtained on the basis of the present set of 100 images are respectively 82.38% and 84.61%. Detailed results are presented in Table 1.

7 Conclusion

This article provides a methodology that aids automatic extraction of visual text entities embedded in complex outdoor images. The proposed method is not very sensitive to image color, text font, skewness and perspective effects. Moreover it analyzes only headline attached CC adding a few CC which are closed to the headline. So, it becomes computationally efficient for real applications. This method can be extended to scanned documents also. The results shown are significant based on a laboratory made dataset. In future, we shall study the use of machine learning tools to improve the performance.

References

1. Liang, J., Doermann, D., Li, H.: Camera based analysis of text and documents: a survey. Int. Journ. on Doc. Anal. and Recog (IJDAR) 7, 84–104 (2005)
2. Wu, V., Manmatha, R., Riseman, E.M.: Textfinder: An automatic system to detect and recognize text in images. IEEE Trans. on Pattern Analysis and Machine Intelligence 21, 1224–1229 (1999)
3. Jung, K., Kim, I.K., Kurata, T., Kourogi, M., Han, H.J.: Text scanner with text detection technology on image sequences. In: Proc. of Int. Conf. on Pattern Recognition, vol. 3, pp. 473–476 (2002)
4. Bhattacharya, U., Parui, S.K., Mondal, S.: Devanagari and bangla text extraction from natural scene images. In: Proc. of the Int. Conf. on Document Analysis and Recognition, pp. 171–175 (2009)
5. Roy, A., Parui, S.K., Paul, A., Roy, U.: A color based image segmentation and its application to text segmentation. In: Proc. of Ind. Conf. on Computer Vision, Graphics & Image Processing, pp. 313–319 (2008)

Incremental Methods in Collaborative Filtering for Ordinal Data

Elena Polezhaeva

Lomonosov Moscow State University, Moscow
lena_polejaeva@mail.ru

Abstract. In modern collaborative filtering applications initial data are typically very large (holding millions of users and items) and come in real time. In this case only incremental algorithms are practically efficient. In this paper a new algorithm based on the symbiosis of Incremental Singular Value Decomposition (ISVD) and Generalized Hebbian Algorithm (GHA) is proposed. The algorithm does not require to store the initial data matrix and effectively updates user/item profiles when a new user or a new item appears or a matrix cell is modified. The results of experiments show how root mean square error (RMSE) depends on the number of algorithm's iterations and data amount.

Keywords: Collaborative filtering, singular value decomposition, Generalized Hebbian algorithm, sparse matrix, large data, ordinal data, incremental data.

1 Introduction

Collaborative Filtering (CF) is used in recommender systems and Customer Relationship Management System (CRM) for personalization. Initial data are represented by a sparse matrix $Y = (y_{ur})_{n \times d}$, in which rows correspond to n users, columns — to d items (documents, films, etc.). Each matrix cell contains information about the usage of an item by a user. So matrix cell may be a rating, a sum paid by user, a mark about visiting site (0 or 1), etc.

The aim is to predict for any user his preferences towards items or, in other words, to fill any empty cell in the initial matrix.

The thin singular value decomposition (SVD) [1] is effective because it uses a compressed representation of the data. Reduced data (profiles) are formed for users and items, then not all data are held. In modern collaborative filtering applications initial data are typically very large (holding millions of users and items), sparse and come in real time. So the requirement of incrementality is very important. It should be possible to update stored data is case of appearing of a new user/item(1) or a new value in a matrix cell(2). Usually it is proposed to solve only one of these incremental problems. In works of Brand [1] new items and ratings are added efficiently. In paper [2] algorithm efficiently incorporates into the model new users or new ratings but doesn't handle the addition of new items.

S.O. Kuznetsov et al. (Eds.): PReMI 2011, LNCS 6744, pp. 452–457, 2011.

In this paper an algorithm is proposed which updates stored data in both cases of incrementality. It is based on incremental singular value decomposition (ISVD) [1] and Generalized Hebbian algorithm (GHA) [3]. The advantage of using GHA is that only known elements of the initial matrix are involved in calculations. As a result it gives data without empty elements for which ISVD may be used. Two situations are considered, when Y contains real data and when Y contains ordinal data (for example, ratings), where $\Omega \subseteq \{1, ..., n\} \times \{1, ..., d\}$ is a set of non-empty elements in Y. Section 2 describes ISVD where data in Y are real. Section 3 outlines a GHA algorithm for ordinal data. Section 4 presents experiments which show how root mean square error (RMSE) [2] depends on the number of the algorithm's iterations, the number of users and the number of known elements in the initial matrix. When the number of users increases the rate of convergence also increases (from 1000 iterations on 600 users to 40 iterations on 940 users). When a data amount increases the number of iterations decreases thus minimizing the working time of the algorithm.

2   Incremental Singular Value Decomposition (ISVD)

SVD is a decomposition of a matrix Y into two orthogonal matrixes U and R and a diagonal matrix S, so that $USR^T = Y$, $U^T Y R = S$. The elements of S are called singular values, the columns of U and R are called left and right singular vectors respectively. Usually all but r largest singular values with respective singular vectors in U and R are rejected which leads to a considerable data compression at the cost of negligible loss of information. This rank r approximation is used for further work.

2.1   Problem Definition

Let $USR^T = Y$ be SVD of the matrix $Y_{n \times d}$ of the rank r where Y is sparse and $U^T U = R^T R = I$. The aim is to modify U, S, R to get new SVD $Y + AB^T$ where A and B have c columns ($A_{n \times c}$, $B_{d \times c}$). In a special case $c = 1$ and A and B are vectors. Deletion and addition of a row or a column may decrease or increase respectively the rank of the matrix Y by 1. Let we have two column vectors a and b and known SVD $USR^T = Y$, where b is a binary vector which indicates which columns should be modified and a vector a is derived from the requirement delete or add new values or modify values in chosen rows and columns. The aim is to find SVD of the matrix $Y + ab^T$ [1].

For example, when a new column is added, the known decomposition may be written with addition of zero column: $US[R^T\ 0] = [Y\ 0]$, then $U'S'R'^T = [Y\ c]$ — desired decomposition, where U', S', R' are to be found, $a = c$, $b = [0, \ldots, 0, 1]^T$.

2.2   New SVD

Let us find the SVD of the following block matrix:

$$Y + AB^T = [U, A] \begin{bmatrix} S & 0 \\ 0 & I \end{bmatrix} [R, B]^T. \tag{1}$$

Let P be an orthogonal basis of column space $\tilde{A} = (I - UU^T)A = A - UU^T A$. Then QR-decomposition is applied to $\tilde{A}$: $\tilde{A} = PR_A$, where P is orthonormal, R_A is upper triangular, $R_A = P^T(I - UU^T)A$. QR-decomposition of matrix $[U, A]$ is:

$$[U, P]\begin{bmatrix} I & U^T A \\ 0 & R_A \end{bmatrix} = [U, A], \tag{2}$$

which can be found from modified Gram–Schmidt orthogonalization [4].

Similarly, let Q be an orthogonal basis of column space $B - RR^T B$, then $QR_B = (I - RR^T)B$ where Q is orthonormal , R_B is upper triangular, $R_B = Q^T(I - RR^T)B$.

Let us represent $Y + AB^T$ as a product of three matrixes:

$$
\begin{aligned}
Y + AB^T &= [U, P]\begin{bmatrix} I & U^T A \\ 0 & R_A \end{bmatrix}\begin{bmatrix} S & 0 \\ 0 & I \end{bmatrix}\begin{bmatrix} I & R^T B \\ 0 & R_B \end{bmatrix}^T [R, Q]^T \\
&= [U, P]\underbrace{\left(\begin{bmatrix} S & 0 \\ 0 & 0 \end{bmatrix} + \begin{bmatrix} U^T A \\ R_A \end{bmatrix}\begin{bmatrix} R^T B \\ R_B \end{bmatrix}^T\right)}_{K}[R, Q]^T;
\end{aligned}
$$

$$K = \begin{bmatrix} S & 0 \\ 0 & 0 \end{bmatrix} + \begin{bmatrix} (U^T A)(B^T R) & (U^T A)R_B^T \\ R_A(B^T R) & R_A R_B^T \end{bmatrix}.$$

Let $U'S'R'^T$ be SVD of matrix K of rank $(r + c)$. Making diagonalization of K: $U'^T K R' = S'$, new matrixes U', S', R' are formed. Then the modification of SVD from rank r to rank $(r + c)$ can be written as:

$$Y + AB^T = ([U\ P]U')S'([R\ Q]R')^T. \tag{3}$$

But instead of making operations with matrixes with big sizes new SVD of $Y + AB^T$ containing five matrixes is used:

$$U_{n \times r}U'_{r \times r}S_{r \times r}R'^T_{r \times r}R^T_{r \times d}, \tag{4}$$

where UU', RR', U, U' are orthonormal.

If only one column or row are added following modifications are done: for new SVD (a — n-dimensional vector, b — d-dimensional vector) modified Gram–Schmidt orthogonalization is used:

$$z = U^T a; \qquad\qquad p = a - Uz;$$
$$w = R^T b; \qquad\qquad q = b - Rw;$$

Then K have simple representation and effective diagonalization may be found:

$$K = \begin{bmatrix} S & 0 \\ 0 & 0 \end{bmatrix} + \begin{bmatrix} zw^T & z\|q\| \\ \|p\|w^T & \|p\|\|q\| \end{bmatrix}.$$

3   Generalized Hebbian Algorithm

Algorithm GHA [3] calculates SVD for sparse data matrix Y. Its advantage is that vectors of SVD are found from $\Omega \subseteq \{1, ..., n\} \times \{1, ..., d\}$ a set of only non-empty elements of Y. This method uses the gradient descent iterations in contrast to classical SVD. As a result it gives data without empty elements for which ISVD defined in previous section may be used.

Matrix factorization is used to estimate missing values [2]:

$$u_i r_j = \sum_{p=1}^{L} u_{ip} r_{pj},$$

where L — number of features for factorization.

Functional is minimized, where Y is given and U, R, β are to be found:

$$\sum_{(i,j)\in\Omega} (\beta_{y_{ij}} - u_i r_j)^2 \rightarrow \min_{u,r,\beta}, \qquad (5)$$

where $\beta_{y_{ij}}$ is a parameter which approximates ordinal ratings in Y; u_i is the i-th row in U; r_j is the j-th column in R; $[y_{ij} = m]$ equals 1 if $y_{ij} = m$ and equals 0 if $y_{ij} \neq m$.

Let us represent:

$$\bar{y}_m = \sum_{(i,j)\in\Omega} [y_{ij} = m].$$

β_m is found analytically:

$$\beta_m = \frac{1}{\bar{y}_m} \sum_{(i,j)\in\Omega} [y_{ij} = m] u_i r_j,$$

Error in a rating calculated by the model is:

$$\varepsilon_{ij} = \beta_{y_{ij}} - u_i r_j.$$

In (5) optimal matrixes U and R minimize the sum of squared errors over non-empty elements of Y. To avoid overfitting regularization is applied by penalizing the square of the Euclidean norm of weights.

The optimization task is:

$$\sum_{(i,j)\in\Omega} (\beta_{y_{ij}} - u_i r_j)^2 + \lambda_1 \sum_{i=1}^{n} \|u_i\|^2 + \lambda_2 \sum_{j=1}^{d} \|r_j\|^2 \rightarrow \min_{u,r,\beta},$$

where $\lambda_1, \lambda_2 \geq 0$ — regularization parameters.

The incremental gradient descent method is used for finding new weights. Such iterations are made:

$$\varepsilon_{ij} = \beta_{y_{ij}} - u_i r_j,$$

$$\tilde{u}_{ip} = (1 - \eta\lambda_1)u_{ip} + \eta \sum_j r_{pj}\varepsilon_{ij}, \tag{6}$$

$$\tilde{r}_{pj} = (1 - \eta\lambda_2)r_{pj} + \eta \sum_i u_{ip}\varepsilon_{ij}, \tag{7}$$

$$\beta_m = \frac{1}{\bar{y}_m} \sum_{(i,j)\in\Omega} [y_{ij} = m]u_i r_j,$$

where η is learning rate.

The aim is to minimize RMSE (root mean square error):

$$RMSE = \sqrt{\frac{1}{|\Omega|} \sum_{(i,j)\in\Omega} \varepsilon_{ij}^2};$$

The result of GHA is data without empty elements for which SVD is used. On the first step of the algorithm matrixes U and R are initialized with small random values. On each step of algorithm we update u_i — i-th row of U and r_j — j-th column of R from (6) and (7). If RMSE doesn't increase on next iterations the algorithm stops.

When a new user is added the matrix R is not updated but the matrix U is initialized with small values. In this case only (6) is updated.

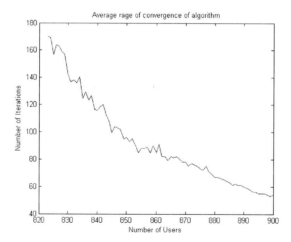

Fig. 1. Graphic shows how the number of iterations of the algorithm depends on the number of users

4   Experiments

Experiments were made on MovieLens data: 943 users, 1682 items, 100000 known ratings. Time factor and data amount have an effect on the rate of convergence of the algorithm. The best results were achieved on rank-15 basis, $\eta = 0.001$ and $\lambda = 0.025$: after 41 iterations $RMSE = 0.923$. Brand in his work [5] achieved $MAE = 0.7910$ using only ISVD and rank-14 basis. It is very interesting that all $\beta \geq 0$ and they increase (even if we don't impose conditions on β): $\beta_1 = 2.52; \beta_2 = 3.03; \beta_3 = 3.28; \beta_4 = 3.63; \beta_5 = 3.96$. When the number of users increases the rate of convergence also increases (from 1000 iterations on 600 users to 40 iterations on 940 users) (Fig.1). When a data amount increases the number of iterations decreases thus minimizing the working time of the algorithm.

5   Results

The proposed method solves two incremental problems in CF and enables to update users' and items' profiles when new rows and columns are added and elements in Y are modified. Two tasks have been solved: when data are real or ordinal. When a new user is added there is no need to retrain the entire model. Addition of a new item is a simple task in which a diagonalizable matrix is calculated.

References

1. Brand, M.: Fast Low-rank modifications of the thin singular value decomposition. Linear Algebra and Its Applications 415(1), 20–30 (2006)
2. Takacs, G., Pilaszy, I., Nemeth, B., Tikk, D.: Scalable Collaborative Filtering Approaches for Large Recommender Systems. The Journal of Machine Learning Research 10, 623–656 (2009)
3. Gorrell, G.: Generalized Hebbian Algorithm for Incremental Singular Value Decomposition in Natural Language Processing. In: Proceedings of EACL (2006)
4. Golub, G.: Matrix Computations, p. 728. Johns Hopkins University Press (1996)
5. Brand, M.: Fast online SVD revisions for lightweight recommender systems. In: SIAM International Conference on Data Mining (SDM) (2003)

A Scheme for Attentional Video Compression

Rupesh Gupta and Santanu Chaudhury

Dept. of EE, Indian Institute of Technology Delhi, New Delhi, India
rupesh.iitdelhi@gmail.com, santanuc@ee.iitd.ac.in

Abstract. In this paper an improved, macroblock (MB) level, visual saliency algorithm, aimed at video compression, is presented. A Relevance Vector Machine (RVM) is trained over 3 dimensional feature vectors, pertaining to global, local and rarity measures of conspicuity, to yield probabalistic values which form the saliency map. These saliency values are used for non-uniform bit-allocation over video frames. A video compression architecture for propagation of saliency values, saving tremendous amount of computation, is also proposed.

1 Introduction

The acuity of the human eye is limited to only 1-2° of visual angle. This means that when viewed from a recommended distance of 1.2 m, the eye can crisply perceive only a 2 cm radial region (computed as $1.2 \times \tan(2°/2)$) on a standard definition 32 inch LCD. Also, a recent eye-tracking study [1] on inter-observer saliency variations in task-free viewing of natural images has concluded that images known to have salient regions generate highly correlated saliency maps for different viewers. However, correctly estimating the points of human eye fixation still remains a challenge. Itti et. al. [2] model visual attention as a combination of low level features pertaining to the degree of dissimilarity between a region and its surroundings. Novel center-surround approaches like [3] model saliency as the fraction of dissimilar pixels in concentric annular regions around each pixel. Hou et. al. [4] take a completely different approach, suppressing the response to frequently occurring features while capturing deviances. Other transform domain approaches like [5,6] follow a similar line of thought. Although these approaches work on psychological patterns with high accuracy, they often fail to detect salient objects in real life images. Some failure cases of these approaches will be shown in our comparison results in Fig. 2.

The failure of these approaches can be attributed to Gestalts grouping principle which concerns the effect produced when the collective presence of a set of elements becomes more meaningful than their presence as separate elements. Thus, we model saliency as a combination of low level, as well as high level features which become important at the higher-level visual cortex. Many authors like [7] resort to a linear combination of features such as contrast, skin color, etc., but do not provide any explanation for the weights chosen. Hence, we propose a learning based feature integration algorithm where we train an RVM with 3 dimensional feature vectors to output probabalistic saliency values.

S.O. Kuznetsov et al. (Eds.): PReMI 2011, LNCS 6744, pp. 458–465, 2011.

One of the earliest automated (as opposed to gaze contingent), visual saliency based, video compression model was proposed by Itti in [8]. In [8] a small number of virtual foveas attempt to track the salient objects, over the video frames; and the non-salient regions are Gaussian blurred to achieve compression. Guo et. al. [5] use their PQFT approach for proto-object detection, and apply a multi-resolution wavelet domain foveation filter suppressing coefficients corresponding to background. Selective blurring can however lead to unpleasing artifacts and generally scores low on subjective evaluation. A novel bit allocation model, achieving compression while preserving visual quality is presented in [9] which we adopt here. In all these compression approaches, the saliency map is computed for each frame which is avoidable considering the inherent temporal redundancy in videos. We propose here a video coding architecture, incorporating visual saliency propagation, to save on a large amount of saliency computation, and hence time. This architecture is most effective for natural video sequences.

The rest of this paper is organized as follows. In Sect. 2, we describe the steps for computing the saliency map. Since all video coding operations are MB based, we learn saliency at MB level to save on unnecessary computation. Section 3 describes a video coding architecture in which various issues relating to saliency propagation/ re-calculation and bit allocation are addressed. We conclude with some conclusions and directions for future research in Sect. 4

2   Generation of Saliency Map

We use color spatial variance, center-surround multi scale ratio of dissimilarity and pulse DCT to construct 3 feature maps. Then, a soft, learning based approach is used to arrive at the final saliency map.

2.1   Global Conspicuity: Color Spatial Variance

The lesser a particular color is globally present in a frame, the more it is likely to catch the viewer's attention. However, a color sparsely distributed over the entire frame need not be conspicuous owing to Gestalt's principles. Hence, spatial variance of colors can be employed as a measure of global conspicuity. We follow the method given in [10], based on representation of color clusters by Gaussian mixture models to calculate their spatial variance, to get this feature map. The feature map is normalized to the range [0,1]

2.2   Local Conspicuity: Multi-scale Ratio of Dissimilarity

The 'pop-out' effect has, since long [2], been attributed to the degree of dissimilarity between a stimulus and its surroundings. A simple method to accurately capture local saliency has been recently proposed in [3]. In this method, a multi-scale filter is designed to simulate the visual field. A summation of the fraction of dissimilar pixels in concentric ring-like regions around each pixel gives a measure of conspicuity. We use this method to construct our second feature map.

However, this approach is slow, since a large number of computations and comparisons are carried out for every pixel. Noting that background pixels generally have very low values of saliency, computation of saliency for these pixels is superfluous. Hence, we first run a SIFT algorithm and locate the keypoints in the image, which are salient not only spatially but also across different scales. We take one keypoint at a time and compute its saliency using [3]. If the saliency of this point is above a threshold (0.4 here, required since a keypoint may lie on a cluttered background), we start growing a region from that point. The saliency value of neighboring pixels is used as region membership criterion and all pixels visited are marked so that they are not re-visited when a different seed point is chosen. We stop when the distance between the new pixel and region mean exceeds a threshold (0.2 here). This feature map is also normalized to [0,1].

2.3 Rarity Conspicuity: Pulse Discrete Cosine Transform

A biologically plausible, real time model simulating lateral inhibition in the receptive field has been proposed in [6]. It has also been shown to outperform other transform domain approaches like [5] both in terms of speed as well as accuracy over psychological patterns. We apply the pulse DCT algorithm to smoothened images to produce our rarity feature map. A Gaussian blurred image simulates the scene viewed from a distance and thus finer edge details in a cluttered background are not noticed, leading to a sparser feature map. We normalize it to the range [0,1].

2.4 Learning to Integrate the Feature Maps

The steps followed for combining the 3 feature maps are as follows. First, we selected 30 images, of size 300×400, encompassing the failure cases of each of the 3 feature maps. 5 viewers were asked to mark each part of the image they considered salient. In accordance with [1], our images (mostly taken from [10]) had well-defined salient regions and hence the markings turned out to be exactly the same for almost all images. Then, an MB level, 3 dimensional training data (total 450×30 points) was prepared taking average values of each of the 3 feature maps over each MB of size 16×16. A target class label '1' was assigned to an MB if more than half of the pixels of that MB were marked salient; else class label '0' was assigned. Next, we trained an RVM over this training data as a binary classification problem. Here we must point out that we are not really interested in a binary label (salient/non-salient) but the relative saliency value of each MB which will later be used for bit allocation. A potential advantage of RVM over SVM, which is desired here, is that it provides posterior probabilities. Also, RVM has better generalization ability and its sparser kernel function leads to faster decisions. The probabilistic outputs of the RVM formed our final saliency map.

To test the machine, we generated a testing data from 120 images (450×120 points) and evaluated the saliency maps obtained against ground truth. Various authors like Bruce et. al. [11] have used area under the ROC curves to quantify the quality of their algorithms. The ROC curve obtained on our own ground truth data is shown in Fig. 1. Also shown in the same figure is a comparison of our result with another leading graph based visual saliency approach [12], which has been shown to outperform various other approaches like [2]. We obtained a 0.90048 (s.e. 0.00136) area under the curve compared to 0.87009 (s.e. 00161) for [12]. In the context of application of saliency to video compression, an FN (actually salient but classified non-salient) is costlier compared to an FP. A very low FN rate, less than 2%, at the cut-off point reflects the potential of our algorithm for such applications. Some results and comparisons with [12] and [11] are shown in Fig. 2. A comparison with [3] and [6] is inherent in these results as our local and rarity feature maps respectively. It is apparent that our approach is better or at least at par with these other high-ranking approaches.

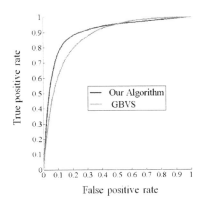

Fig. 1. ROC curves for our approach and [12] obtained by varying thresholds on saliency values

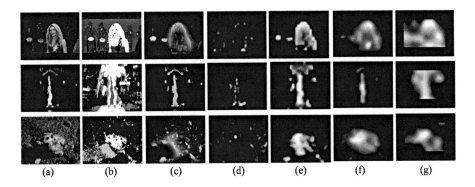

Fig. 2. (a) Input image, (b) global, (c) local [3], (d) rarity [6] feature maps, (e) our resized saliency map, (f) saliency map obtained from [12] and (g) [11]

3   Video Compression Architecture

We wish to employ saliency for the purpose of video compression. However, computation of feature maps for each video frame can prove to be computationally very expensive if we rely on techniques such as those proposed in [5,8,9] as they necessitate calculation of saliency map of each frame. We propose here the use of temporal redundancy inherent in videos to propagate saliency values. Ideally the saliency map should be re-calculated only when there is a large change in saliency. However, to measure this change, we require the saliency for the next frame which is unavailable. Hence, we also propose a workaround to detect the frames for which re-computation of saliency map is indispensable. A block diagram of the architecture is shown in Fig. 3 which is discussed in detail in the following subsections

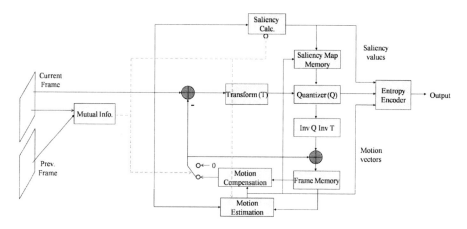

Fig. 3. Our video compression architecture incorporating saliency propagation

3.1   Propagation of Saliency Values

Firstly, we describe the need for the mutual information (MI) computation unit. The idea is that we perform a re-calculation of saliency map on the basis of MI between successive frames. A concise information theoretic shot detection algorithm has been proposed by Cernekova et. al. in [13] and an improved version of the same using motion prediction in [14]. The authors compute the MI between consecutive frames and argue that a small value of MI indicates existence of a cut. We experimented with this method over some video sequences, with saliency map of each frame pre-computed, and plotted the MI distributions for color as well as saliency. MI for an Airtel ad sequence with 9 scene changes is plotted in Fig. 4. It is apparent that not only does this method effectively capture changes in saliency as shown in Fig. 4(a), but also, that the RGB and saliency plots follow a very similar distribution (Fig. 4(b)). Figure 4(b) implies that we can detect the frames requiring re-computation of saliency maps by calculating MI over the color channels. The frame where a large change is detected should be coded as an I frame (or I MBs in H.264) and saliency re-computed for this frame and stored. The method has been found to work best on natural video sequences.

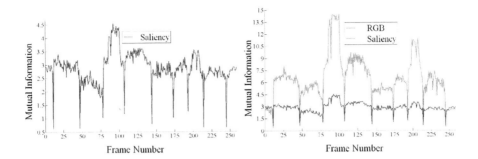

Fig. 4. (a) MI plot for saliency maps, (b) MI plots of RGB and saliency overlaid. An Airtel ad sequence with 9 cuts is used here.

For P frames, we make use of motion vectors to approximate saliency values. We select an MB in the current frame and look for the best match in the reference frame. This best match may or may not exactly overlap an MB in the reference frame, but we have the saliency values for only non overlapping 16×16 MBs. Therefore, we take a weighted average of the saliency values of each of the MBs under the best match region the in reference frame, as the saliency value for the MB in current frame. The weights correspond to the amount of area overlap as shown in Fig. 5

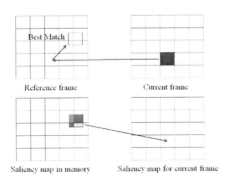

Fig. 5. Image illustrating a weighted averaging of saliency values, the orange, blue, yellow, green colors denote the amount of overlap and hence weights

3.2   Selection of Quantization Parameters

Once the saliency map is obtained, bits may be non-uniformly distributed across a frame. We require a function which can optimally tune the quantization parameters of salient and non-salient MBs to achieve compression, i.e, reduce rate (R), without any significant loss of perceptual quality, i.e, constant distortion (D). In [9], this is posed as a global optimization problem and solved using the method of Lagrange multipliers. The final result for quantization step Q_{istep} for the ith MB having a saliency value w_i is given as:

$$Q_{istep} = \frac{Ws}{w_i S} Q_{step} \ . \tag{1}$$

where W is the sum of saliency values over all MBs, s is the area of MB_i (16×16 here), S is the area of entire frame and Q_{step} is a fixed value depending on the amount of distortion tolerable. This formula implies that the quantization step size should be inversely proportional to the saliency value which is completely justified. We present here a short verification of how this formulation achieves compression without compromising on perceptual quality. Assuming a R-D function [15] for an MB_i is given by:

$$D_i = \sigma_i^2 e^{-\gamma R_i} \ or \ R_i = \frac{1}{\gamma} log \left(\frac{\sigma_i^2}{D_i} \right) \ . \tag{2}$$

where σ_i^2 is variance of encoding signal and γ is a constant coefficient. Ignoring the constant term γ and taking $\sigma_i^2 = 1/\alpha$ we get:

$$R_i = log \left(\frac{1}{\alpha D_i} \right) \ . \tag{3}$$

Now, the average rate R is calculated as $\sum_{i=1}^{N} sR_i/S$, where N is the number of MBs. Noting that $D_i \propto Q_{istep}$, we get after replacing Q_{istep} by (1):

$$R = \frac{Ns}{S} \left[log \left(\frac{1}{\alpha Q_{step}} \right) + log \left(\frac{(w_1.w_2...w_N)^{\frac{1}{N}}}{w_1 + w_2 + ... + w_N} \right) + log \left(\frac{S}{s} \right) \right] \ . \tag{4}$$

From the above equation it is clear that the first term denotes the rate if every MB was quantized with the same parameter Q_{step}, the second term is always ≤ 0 by the AM-GM inequality and the third term is a constant. Thus R is reduced. It can also be readily observed from (1) that overall D ($\sum w_i D_i/W$) remains constant. We limit the Q_{istep} to minimum and maximum values of max(0.5 × Q_{step}, Q_{istep}) and min(1.5 × Q_{step}, Q_{istep}) respectively. Also, we smoothen our saliency map using a Gaussian filter before computing the quantization step. This serves two purposes, firstly, it ensures that the salient object/region is covered completely and secondly, it ensures a smooth transition from salient to non-salient regions.

4   Conclusion

A vast amount of research has gone into modelling of the human visual system with each model having its own merits and shortcomings. The potential which lies in an integration of these models has been demonstrated by the accuracy of our results. A simple and effective learning based approach for such a unification has been presented. Though we make use of only 3 features, this model is easily extendible to more features if desired. We computed saliency at MB level to save computation, however our model is equally applicable at pixel level. The compression framework proposed, to approximate saliency of P frames, can save a lot of computation, speeding-up compression. We plan to integrate our it into the H.264 coding system which remains a challenge owing to the complex mode decision metrics and hybrid coding structures in this standard [16].

References

1. Engelke, U., Maeder, A., Zepernick, H.J.: Analysing Inter-observer Saliency Variations in Task-Free Viewing of Natural Images. In: ICIP, pp. 1085–1088 (2010)
2. Itti, L., Koch, C., Niebur, E.: A Model of Saliency-Based Visual Attention for Rapid Scene Analysis. IEEE Trans. PAMI 20(11), 1254–1259 (1998)
3. Huang, R., Sang, N., Liu, L., Tang, Q.: Saliency Based on Multi-scale Ratio of Dissimilarity. In: ICPR, pp. 13–16 (2010)
4. Hou, X., Zhang, L.: Saliency Detection: A Spectral Residual Approach. In: CVPR, pp. 1–8 (2007)
5. Guo, C., Zhang, L.: A Novel Multiresolution Spatiotemporal Saliency Detection Model and Its Applications in Image and Video Compression. IEEE Trans. Image Proc. 19(1), 185–198 (2010)
6. Yu, Y., Wang, B., Zhang, L.: Pulse Discrete Cosine Transform for Saliency-Based Visual Attention. In: ICDL, pp. 1–6 (2009)
7. Chiang, J., Hsieh, C., Chang, G., Jou, F., Lie, W.: Region-of-Interest Based Rate Control Scheme with Flexible Quality on Demand. In: ICME, pp. 238–242 (2010)
8. Itti, L.: Automatic Foveation for Video Compression Using a Neurobiological Model of Visual Attention. IEEE Trans. Image Proc. 13(10), 1304–1318 (2004)
9. Li, Z., Qin, S., Itti, L.: Visual Attention Guided Bit Allocation in Video Compression. Image and Vision Computing 29(1), 1–14 (2011)
10. Liu, T., Sun, J., Zheng, N.-N., Tang, X., Shum, H.-Y.: Learning to Detect a Salient Object. In: CVPR, pp. 1–8 (2007)
11. Bruce, N.D.B., Tsotsos, J.K.: Saliency Based on Information Maximization. In: NIPS, pp. 155–162 (2006)
12. Harel, J., Koch, C., Perona, P.: Graph-Based Visual Saliency. In: NIPS, pp. 545–552 (2006)
13. Cernekova, Z., Pitas, I., Nikou, C.: Information Theory-Based Shot Cut/Fade Detection and Video Summarization. IEEE Trans. CSVT 16(1), 82–91 (2006)
14. Krulikovska, L., Pavlovic, J., Polec, J., Cernekova, Z.: Abrupt Cut Detection Based on Mutual Information and Motion Prediction. In: ELMAR, pp. 89–92 (2010)
15. Bhaskaran, V., Konstantinides, K.: Image and Video Compression Standards: Algorithms and Architectures. Springer, Heidelberg (1997)
16. Chen, Z., Lin, W., Ngan, K.N.: Perceptual Video Coding: Challenges and Approaches. In: ICME, pp. 784–789 (2010)

Using Conceptual Graphs for Text Mining in Technical Support Services

Michael Bogatyrev and Alexey Kolosoff

Tula State University,
Lenin ave. 92, 300600 Tula, Russia
okkambo@mail.ru, alexey.kolosoff@gmail.com

Abstract. Text mining problems of natural text classification and fact extraction are important in developing information systems for Technical Support Services. An approach which is based on joining acquisition of conceptual graphs and keywords search technique is presented to their solution. Conceptual graphs have been created from e-mail queries sent to Technical Support Service. Correct conceptual graphs acquired from e-mail texts represent facts and situations which become patterns to search in systems resources to resolve users problems. Experimental results of implementing proposed approach are presented.

Keywords: natural language texts classification, conceptual graphs, correctness of conceptual graphs, technical support services.

1 Introduction

Text mining strategies share many techniques such as machine learning, natural language processing, text categorization, clustering, filtering, etc. These techniques can be classified as ones which use texts words and others which use semantic models constructed from text. Two known strategies, Latent Semantic Analysis (LSA) [1] and Formal Concept Analysis (FCA) [2] illustrate that difference. LSA uses term-document matrices which describe the occurrences of terms in textual documents and has been created from documents words. FCA uses conceptual models - conceptual graphs [3] and conceptual structures (formal concept lattices) which are formal models. The mentioned strategies also have different mathematical nature: LSA is founded on geometry and statistics whereas FCA is founded on logic and algebra (the lattice theory).

Traditionally only one approach, based on keywords or formal models, is applied in industrial text mining systems. Nevertheless modern problems of textual analysis may have significant complexity and it becomes necessary to apply hybrid approaches to solve them.

In our work namely that complex problem is investigated. As the result we decided to apply keywords technique and conceptual graphs in our Text Mining system. Although each separate technique does not solve the problem, their combination produces good preliminary results.

S.O. Kuznetsov et al. (Eds.): PReMI 2011, LNCS 6744, pp. 466–471, 2011.

2   Problem Statement

Technical Support Services (TSS) have been intended to help users to solve specific problems with a product - electronics, goods or software. Users send queries to TSS as natural language e-mail texts. It is needed to resolve queries and to find an appropriate decision represented as help topics, useful URLs or e-mail reply. As a rule the system's reply is prepared manually by support team using system's resources as it is shown on Fig.1.

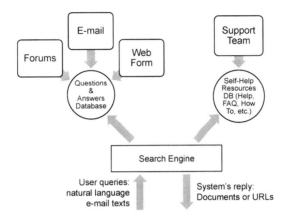

Fig. 1. The structure of a Technical Support Service

When the number of queries significantly grows, automation of creating TSS replies becomes very important. That automation is implemented in the TSS Search Engine shown on Fig.1.

There are two basic text mining problems solved by the Search Engine. The first one is the problem of *natural text classification*. The second is the problem of *fact extraction*. These problems have some peculiarities. The query text must be classified according to various resources of the TSS. TSS database contains documentation, help topics, e-mails of queries and replies. To find an appropriate decision it is needed to refer to all these resources. The decision may exist as an example answer ready to be sent to a user or it can be constructed from separate pieces. Fact extraction problem is to find two kinds of objects in the query texts: *things* which being analyzed text is about and *situations* which took users attention.

3   General Approach to Solution

Considering the problems of natural text classification and fact extraction described in the previous section, we propose the following general approach to their solution:

1. Having a flow of user e-mail queries we nevertheless do not apply classical machine learning technique because the style and contents of queries are very individual. But it is worth to collect queries and corresponding replies in the system's database to apply them in further analysis. So, a kind of self-learning is possible in the system.

2. *Things* and *situations* described in a query are represented by *words* and *phrases*. So we need to find keywords in the query text which correspond to *terms* described in system's database texts. Since learning technique is impossible in the system, another way of keywords extraction is needed. Text filtering is standard and evidently necessary technique for e-mail texts in natural language. We apply *term filtering* to find *direct terms* corresponding to the terms described in systems database texts. For example, the *driver* word in a query in the software TSS has high probability to be the term. So a text containing this word can be classified as referring to the topic "Drivers" in the system's database texts. To implement term filtering a thesaurus as an additional resource must be created in the system.

3. Text filtering is not exhaustive technique for classification. Besides terms, a query text contains many words which can also be useful for analysis. The personal style of an author has certain representation in query text as a set of specific words and language grammar distortions (slang). Nevertheless our analysis of real queries shows that the following heuristic principle is valid: *despite the personal style, every author uses grammatically correct phrases when describes problematic situations.* Therefore semantics of these grammatically correct phrases in a query text may represent useful information about situations we need to extract. We apply conceptual graphs for modelling semantics of sentences or phrases of the text and use their concepts and relations for further analysis.

Conceptual graphs acquisition from natural language texts is the problem which has no closed solution for arbitrary texts. We assume that the following circumstances cause the success of creating conceptual graphs:

1. query texts are not long and all their sentences may be processed for acquisition in appropriate time;

2. grammatically correct phrases in the sentences produce correct conceptual graphs possibly being sub graphs in incorrect conceptual graph of the whole sentence.

The following rough criterion of correctness of conceptual graph is admissible here: *correct conceptual graph has no isolated concepts.* An *isolated concept* is a concept which has no connection to any relation.

4   System Implementation and Experimental Results

The TSS Text Mining system works according to the following stages.

1. **Text documents indexing.** All TSS documents have been indexed according to selected terms. These terms represent topics and main notes presented in system documentation. Terms are either single words or several words phrases (no more than 4 words). Term weights are calculated via the well-known tf-idf formula [4]. The TSS complex index is the only additional modification of TSS information resource realized in standard database technology (MS SQL Server).
2. **Conceptual graphs acquisition and processing.** Conceptual graphs are applied as an instrument of extracting keywords and key phrases according to the principle described below.
3. **Search relevant documents in TSS database.** Keywords and key phrases corresponding to each e-mail text and extracted by conceptual graphs processing have been used as queries for full-text search in TSS indexed database.

Consider the last two stages in some detail.

4.1   Conceptual Graphs Acquisition and Processing

We use our software [5] for conceptual graphs acquisition from natural language texts. The software is based on existing approaches of lexical, morphological and semantic analysis. *Semantic roles labeling* [6] is applied as the main instrument for constructing relations in acquisition algorithm. The acquisition algorithm works with our recently developed *controllable grammatical templates*. Using these templates, it is possible to adapt acquisition algorithm as to certain language grammar (Russian or English in the current version of the system) as to some peculiarities of concrete language. User interface has also tools for recognizing incorrect conceptual graphs.

Conceptual graphs being acquired from all sentences of a query text are applied to detect keywords and key phrases. As a rule, incorrect conceptual graphs indicate that there is no useful information in processed text. For example, conceptual graph acquired from the "Thanks in advance" phrase, G1 = {[advance:"] [thank:"]}[1] is incorrect since it has no relation. TSS user can handle any acquired graph by using interface tools including visualization. That helps finding possibly valid keywords in incorrect conceptual graphs.

All acquired correct conceptual graphs considered as potential source of keywords and key phrases for the next search. Concepts connected with the *agent* relation may represent *terms* and have been picked as keywords. Some term may consist of several words, for example Remote Agent Service. The relation *genitive* in its graph G2 = {[remote*a:"] [service*b:"] [agent*c:"] (genitive?b?c) (attribute?c?a)} indicates that Agent Service is the single whole. All graphs having simple structure with *genitive* and *attribute* relations are considered as sources of keywords and key phrases.

---

[1] Here we use the CGIF format [3] for representing conceptual graphs.

It is known that relations in conceptual graphs have linguistic meaning at first. But some of them can directly indicate *a situation*. That is the *location* relation and it is also considered as key phrases indicator. For example, it is illustrated by the phrase "stop on error" and its conceptual graph G3 = {[error*a:"][stop*b:"](location?b?a)} .

4.2   Search Relevant Documents

All keywords and key phrases extracted by conceptual graphs processing are then treated as queries for full-text search in TSS indexed database. For each e-mail text they constitute a query vector. We devoted special attention to applying LSA search strategy for such queries. We also compared it with other methods which use ranking functions of Okapi BM25 [7], SQL Server iFTS [8] and ranking function of Google. An experiment was conducted on the textual database with more than 7000 help topics belonging to online help systems of three different software products. Employees of the products vendor company were asked to rate (from 1 to 4) the quality of search results (including their ranking) for top 10 most popular queries retrieved from the users queries statistics. A short summary is presented in the table below.

Table 1. Search results ratings for 10 most popular queries

Search Query	LSA	Okapi BM25	SQL Server iFTS	Google
working with grids	3	1	4	4
load testing	4	2	3	3
web testing	4	3	2	3
Remote Agent Service	4	2	2	4
name mapping template	4	3	3	2
stop on error	3	2	4	4
object not found	3	4	4	3
UI Automation Silverlight	4	4	4	3
testing flash applications	4	4	3	4
web service testing	4	4	3	4
Total (max. 40):	37	29	32	34

Here Google refers to Google web search in the online help systems of three different software products (with URLs filtering). As one can see from the table, the LSA search gives the best result. We can explain it by the following informal conclusion: *Latent Semantic Analysis pretends to detect texts which are semantically similar.* Conceptual graphs processing produces a set of keywords which are semantically connected. So, the query produced with conceptual graphs has certain *portion of semantics* which can *resonate* with semantics of TSS documents. It seems that LSA, according to its mathematical nature, is namely that method which can find such peculiar *semantic resonance* of texts.

5   Conclusion and Future Work

Hybrid approach to textual analysis in Technical Support Services is presented. It is based on using conceptual graphs for extracting keywords and key phrases from query text and applying standard full-text search technique. Experimental results show that conceptual graphs represent a valid tool for extracting keywords and key phrases since this tool provides semantic connection between words in key phrases. Conceptual graphs technique usually produces less number of keywords and key phrases than there are in a query text that shortens the time for further search.

Future development of presented technology is planned on the way of creating additional information resource in the TSS system. This resource will be in the form of *conceptual lattice*. Having conceptual lattices as system's information resource, we will apply conceptual graphs as immediate queries in search strategy according to the principles of FCA.

References

1. Landauer, T., Foltz, P.W., Laham, D.: Introduction to Latent Semantic Analysis. Discourse Processes 25, 259–284 (1998)
2. Ganter, B., Wille, R.: Formal Concept Analysis. Mathematical Foundations. Springer, Heidelberg (1999)
3. Sowa, J.F.: Conceptual Structures: Information Processing in Mind and Machine. Addison-Wesley, London (1984)
4. Salton, G., McGill, M.J.: Introduction to modern information retrieval. McGraw-Hill, New York (1983)
5. Bogatyrev, M.Y., Mitrofanova, O.A., Tuhtin, V.V.: Building Conceptual Graphs for Articles Abstracts in Digital Libraries. In: Fourth Conceptual Structures Tool Interoperability Workshop (CS-TIW 2009) at 17th International Conference on Conceptual Structures (ICCS 2009), Moscow, pp. 50–57 (2009)
6. Gildea, D., Jurafsky, D.: Automatic labeling of semantic roles. Computational Linguistics 28, 245–288 (2002)
7. Robertson, S., Walker, S., Jones, S., et al.: Okapi at TREC-3. In: Proceedings of the Third Text Retrieval Conference (TREC 1994), Gaithersburg, USA (1994)
8. Langit, L., Goff, K., Mauri, D., Malik, S.: Smart Business Intelligence Solutions with Microsoft SQL Server 2008. Microsoft Press (2009)

Author Index